# Computer Programs and Software Systems: Theories and Methods

Edited by Alexandro Cyprus

CLANRYE
INTERNATIONAL
www.clanryeinternational.com

Clanrye International,
750 Third Avenue, 9th Floor,
New York, NY 10017, USA



ISBN: 978-1-64726-587-8

**Cataloging-in-publication Data**

Computer programs and software systems : theories and methods / edited by Alexandro Cyprus.
p. cm.
Includes bibliographical references and index.
ISBN 978-1-64726-587-8
1. Computer programs. 2. Computer software. 3. Computer systems. 4. Computer engineering.
I. Cyprus, Alexandro.
QA76.6 .C66 2023
001.642--dc23

For information on all Clanrye International publications
visit our website at www.clanryeinternational.com

CLANRYE INTERNATIONAL

# Contents

# Preface

This book has been a concerted effort by a group of academicians, researchers and scientists, who have contributed their research works for the realization of the book. This book has materialized in the wake of emerging advancements and innovations in this field. Therefore, the need of the hour was to compile all the required researches and disseminate the knowledge to a broad spectrum of people comprising of students, researchers and specialists of the field.

Software is a set of instructions that tells a computer how to operate. This is different from hardware, which is the actual component that does the real work. A software system is a system of interconnected software components that make up a computer system. Major categories of software systems comprise programming software, application software development, and system software. A few examples of software systems include database management systems, computer reservations systems, embedded systems, content management systems, and operating systems. A computer program refers to a set of instructions written in a programming language that a computer can execute or understand. Source code is the human-readable version of a computer program. Compilers are used to convert source code into machine instructions creating an executable file. This book contains some path-breaking studies on the theories and methods related to computer programs and software systems. It will serve as a reference to a broad spectrum of readers.

At the end of the preface, I would like to thank the authors for their brilliant chapters and the publisher for guiding us all-through the making of the book till its final stage. Also, I would like to thank my family for providing the support and encouragement throughout my academic career and research projects.

**Editor**

# 1

# Decomposing Probabilistic Lambda-Calculi

Ugo Dal Lago[1], Giulio Guerrieri[2](✉), and Willem Heijltjes[2]

[1] Dipartimento di Informatica - Scienza e Ingegneria
Università di Bologna, Bologna, Italy
ugo.dallago@unibo.it

[2] Department of Computer Science
University of Bath, Bath, UK
{w.b.heijltjes,g.guerrieri}@bath.ac.uk

**Abstract.** A notion of probabilistic lambda-calculus usually comes with a prescribed reduction strategy, typically call-by-name or call-by-value, as the calculus is non-confluent and these strategies yield different results. This is a break with one of the main advantages of lambda-calculus: confluence, which means that results are independent from the choice of strategy. We present a probabilistic lambda-calculus where the probabilistic operator is decomposed into two syntactic constructs: a generator, which represents a probabilistic event; and a consumer, which acts on the term depending on a given event. The resulting calculus, the Probabilistic Event Lambda-Calculus, is confluent, and interprets the call-by-name and call-by-value strategies through different interpretations of the probabilistic operator into our generator and consumer constructs. We present two notions of reduction, one via fine-grained local rewrite steps, and one by generation and consumption of probabilistic events. Simple types for the calculus are essentially standard, and they convey strong normalization. We demonstrate how we can encode call-by-name and call-by-value probabilistic evaluation.

## 1 Introduction

Probabilistic lambda-calculi [24,22,17,11,18,9,15] extend the standard lambda-calculus with a probabilistic choice operator $N \oplus_p M$, which chooses $N$ with probability $p$ and $M$ with probability $1-p$ (throughout this paper, we let $p$ be $1/2$ and will omit it). Duplication of $N \oplus M$, as is wont to happen in lambda-calculus, raises a fundamental question about its semantics: do the duplicate occurrences represent *the same* probabilistic event, or *different* ones with the same probability? For example, take the term $\top \oplus \bot$ that represents a coin flip between boolean values *true* $\top$ and *false* $\bot$. If we duplicate this term, do the copies represent two distinct coin flips with possibly distinct outcomes, or do these represent a single coin flip that determines the outcome for both copies? Put differently again, when we duplicate $\top \oplus \bot$, do we duplicate the *event*, or only its *outcome*?

In probabilistic lambda-calculus, these two interpretations are captured by the evaluation strategies of call-by-name ($\rightarrow_{\mathsf{cbn}}$), which duplicates events, and call-by-value ($\to_{\mathsf{cbv}}$), which evaluates any probabilistic choice before it is duplicated, and thus only duplicates outcomes. Consider the following example, where $=$ tests equality of boolean values.

$$\top \;\; {}_{\mathsf{cbv}}\!\twoheadleftarrow \;\; (\lambda x.\, x = x)(\top \oplus \bot) \;\; \twoheadrightarrow_{\mathsf{cbn}} \;\; \top \oplus \bot$$

This situation is not ideal, for several, related reasons. Firstly, it demonstrates how probabilistic lambda-calculus is non-confluent, negating one of the central properties of the lambda-calculus, and one of the main reasons why it is the prominent model of computation that it is. Secondly, it means that a probabilistic lambda-calculus must derive its semantics from a prescribed reduction strategy, and its terms only have meaning in the context of that strategy. Thirdly, combining different kinds of probabilities becomes highly involved [15], as it would require specialized reduction strategies. These issues present themselves even in a more general setting, namely that of commutative (algebraic) effects, which in general do not commute with copying.

We address these issues by a decomposition of the probabilistic operator into a *generator* $\boxed{a}$ and a *choice* $\overset{a}{\oplus}$, as follows.

$$N \oplus M \;\; \stackrel{\Delta}{=} \;\; \boxed{a}.\, N \overset{a}{\oplus} M$$

Semantically, $\boxed{a}$ represents a probabilistic event, that generates a boolean value recorded as $a$. The choice $N \overset{a}{\oplus} M$ is simply a conditional on $a$, choosing $N$ if $a$ is false and $M$ if $a$ is true. Syntactically, $a$ is a boolean variable with an occurrence in $\overset{a}{\oplus}$, and $\boxed{a}$ acts as a probabilistic quantifier, binding all occurrences in its scope. (To capture a non-equal chance, one would attach a probability $p$ to a generator, as $\boxed{a}_p$, though we will not do so in this paper.)

The resulting *probabilistic event lambda-calculus* $\Lambda_{\mathsf{PE}}$, which we present in this paper, is confluent. Our decomposition allows us to separate duplicating an *event*, represented by the generator $\boxed{a}$, from duplicating only its *outcome* $a$, through having multiple choice operators $\overset{a}{\oplus}$. In this way our calculus may interpret both original strategies, call-by-name and call-by-value, by different translations of standard probabilistic terms into $\Lambda_{\mathsf{PE}}$: call-by-name by the above decomposition (see also Section 2), and call-by-value by a different one (see Section 7). For our initial example, we get the following translations and reductions.

$$\mathsf{cbn}: \;\; (\lambda x.\, x{=}x)(\boxed{a}.\, \top \overset{a}{\oplus} \bot) \;\; \to_\beta \;\; (\boxed{a}.\, \top \overset{a}{\oplus} \bot){=}(\boxed{b}.\, \top \overset{b}{\oplus} \bot) \;\; \twoheadrightarrow \;\; \top \oplus \bot \qquad (1)$$

$$\mathsf{cbv}: \;\; \boxed{a}.\, (\lambda x.\, x{=}x)(\top \overset{a}{\oplus} \bot) \;\; \to_\beta \;\; \boxed{a}.\, (\top \overset{a}{\oplus} \bot){=}(\top \overset{a}{\oplus} \bot) \;\; \twoheadrightarrow \;\; \top \qquad (2)$$

We present two reduction relations for our probabilistic constructs, both independent of beta-reduction. Our main focus will be on *permutative* reduction (Sections 2, 3), a small-step local rewrite relation which is computationally inefficient but gives a natural and very fine-grained operational semantics. *Projective* reduction (Section 6) is a more standard reduction, following the intuition that $\boxed{a}$ generates a coin flip to evaluate $\overset{a}{\oplus}$, and is coarser but more efficient.

We further prove confluence (Section 4), and we give a system of simple types and prove strong normalization for typed terms by reducibility (Section 5). Omitted proofs can be found in [7], the long version of this paper.

### 1.1 Related Work

Probabilistic $\lambda$-calculi are a topic of study since the pioneering work by Saheb-Djaromi [24], the first to give the syntax and operational semantics of a $\lambda$-calculus with binary probabilistic choice. Giving well-behaved denotational models for probabilistic $\lambda$-calculi has proved to be challenging, as witnessed by the many contributions spanning the last thirty years: from Jones and Plotkin's early study of the probabilistic powerdomain [17], to Jung and Tix's remarkable (and mostly negative) observations [18], to the very recent encouraging results by Goubault-Larrecq [16]. A particularly well-behaved model for probabilistic $\lambda$-calculus can be obtained by taking a probabilistic variation of Girard's coherent spaces [10], this way getting full abstraction [13].

On the operational side, one could mention a study about the various ways the operational semantics of a calculus with binary probabilistic choice can be specified, namely by small-step or big-step semantics, or by inductively or coinductively defined sets of rules [9]. Termination and complexity analysis of higher-order probabilistic programs seen as $\lambda$-terms have been studied by way of type systems in a series of recent results about size [6], intersection [4], and refinement type disciplines [1]. Contextual equivalence on probabilistic $\lambda$-calculi has been studied, and compared with equational theories induced by Böhm Trees [19], applicative bisimilarity [8], or environmental bisimilarity [25].

In all the aforementioned works, probabilistic $\lambda$-calculi have been taken as implicitly endowed with either call-by-name or call-by-value strategies, for the reasons outlined above. There are only a few exceptions, namely some works on Geometry of Interaction [5], Probabilistic Coherent Spaces [14], and Standardization [15], which achieve, in different contexts, a certain degree of independence from the underlying strategy, thus accommodating both call-by-name and call-by-value evaluation. The way this is achieved, however, invariably relies on Linear Logic or related concepts. This is deeply different from what we do here.

Some words of comparison with Faggian and Ronchi Della Rocca's work on confluence and standardization [15] are also in order. The main difference between their approach and the one we pursue here is that the operator ! in their calculus $\Lambda^!_\oplus$ plays *both* the roles of a marker for duplicability and of a checkpoint for any probabilistic choice "flowing out" of the term (*i.e.* being fired). In our calculus, we do not control duplication, but we definitely make use of checkpoints. Saying it another way, Faggian and Ronchi Della Rocca's work is inspired by linear logic, while our approach is inspired by deep inference, even though this is, on purpose, not evident in the design of our calculus.

Probabilistic $\lambda$-calculi can also be seen as vehicles for expressing probabilistic models in the sense of bayesian programming [23,3]. This, however, requires an operator for modeling conditioning, which complicates the metatheory considerably, and that we do not consider here.

Our permutative reduction is a refinement of that for the call-by-name probabilistic $\lambda$-calculus [20], and is an implementation of the equational theory of *(ordered) binary decision trees* via rewriting [27]. Probabilistic decision trees have been proposed with a primitive binary probabilistic operator [22], but not with a decomposition as we explore here.

## 2 The Probabilistic Event $\lambda$-Calculus $\Lambda_{\mathsf{PE}}$

**Definition 1.** The *probabilistic event* $\lambda$*-calculus* ($\Lambda_{\mathsf{PE}}$) is given by the following grammar, with from left to right: a *variable* (denoted by $x, y, z, \ldots$), an *abstraction*, an *application*, a *(labeled) choice*, and a *(probabilistic) generator*.

$$M, N \quad ::= \quad x \mid \lambda x.N \mid NM \mid N \overset{a}{\oplus} M \mid \boxed{a}.N$$

In a term $\lambda x.M$ the abstraction $\lambda x$ binds the free occurrences of the variable $x$ in its scope $M$, and in $\boxed{a}.N$ the generator $\boxed{a}$ binds the *label* $a$ in $N$. The calculus features a decomposition of the usual probabilistic sum $\oplus$, as follows.

$$N \oplus M \quad \triangleq \quad \boxed{a}.N \overset{a}{\oplus} M \tag{3}$$

The generator $\boxed{a}$ represents a probabilistic *event*, whose outcome, a binary value $\{0, 1\}$ represented by the label $a$, is used by the choice operator $\overset{a}{\oplus}$. That is, $\boxed{a}$ flips a coin setting $a$ to 0 (resp. 1), and depending on this $N \overset{a}{\oplus} M$ reduces to $N$ (resp. $M$). We will use the unlabeled choice $\oplus$ as in (3). This convention also gives the translation from a *call-by-name* probabilistic $\lambda$-calculus into $\Lambda_{\mathsf{PE}}$ (the interpretation of a *call-by-value* probabilistic $\lambda$-calculus is in Section 7).

**Reduction.** Reduction in $\Lambda_{\mathsf{PE}}$ will consist of standard $\beta$-reduction $\to_\beta$ plus an evaluation mechanism for generators and choice operators, which implements probabilistic choice. We will present two such mechanisms: *projective* reduction $\to_\pi$ and *permutative* reduction $\to_{\mathsf{p}}$. While projective reduction implements the given intuition for the generator and choice operator, we relegate it to Section 6 and make permutative reduction our main evaluation mechanism, for the reason that it is more fine-grained, and thus more general.

Permutative reduction is based on the idea that any operator distributes over the labeled choice operator (see the reduction steps in Figure 1), even other choice operators, as below.

$$(N \overset{a}{\oplus} M) \overset{b}{\oplus} P \ \sim \ (N \overset{b}{\oplus} P) \overset{a}{\oplus} (M \overset{b}{\oplus} P)$$

To orient this as a rewrite rule, we need to give priority to one label over another. Fortunately, the relative position of the associated generators $\boxed{a}$ and $\boxed{b}$ provides just that. Then to define $\to_{\mathsf{p}}$, we will want every choice to belong to some generator, and make the order of generators explicit.

**Definition 2.** The set $\mathsf{fl}(N)$ of *free labels* of a term $N$ is defined inductively by:

$$\mathsf{fl}(x) = \emptyset \qquad \mathsf{fl}(MN) = \mathsf{fl}(M) \cup \mathsf{fl}(N) \qquad \mathsf{fl}(\lambda x.M) = \mathsf{fl}(M)$$

$$\mathsf{fl}(\boxed{a}.M) = \mathsf{fl}(M) \smallsetminus \{a\} \quad \mathsf{fl}(M \overset{a}{\oplus} N) = \mathsf{fl}(M) \cup \mathsf{fl}(N) \cup \{a\}$$

A term $M$ is *label-closed* if $\mathsf{fl}(M) = \emptyset$.

$$(\lambda x.N)M \rightarrow_\beta N[M/x] \qquad (\beta)$$

$$N \overset{a}{\oplus} N \rightarrow_{\mathsf{p}} N \qquad (\mathsf{i})$$

$$(N \overset{a}{\oplus} M) \overset{a}{\oplus} P \rightarrow_{\mathsf{p}} N \overset{a}{\oplus} P \qquad (\mathsf{c}_1)$$

$$N \overset{a}{\oplus} (M \overset{a}{\oplus} P) \rightarrow_{\mathsf{p}} N \overset{a}{\oplus} P \qquad (\mathsf{c}_2)$$

$$\lambda x.\, (N \overset{a}{\oplus} M) \rightarrow_{\mathsf{p}} (\lambda x.\, N) \overset{a}{\oplus} (\lambda x.\, M) \qquad (\oplus\lambda)$$

$$(N \overset{a}{\oplus} M)P \rightarrow_{\mathsf{p}} (NP) \overset{a}{\oplus} (MP) \qquad (\oplus\mathsf{f})$$

$$N(M \overset{a}{\oplus} P) \rightarrow_{\mathsf{p}} (NM) \overset{a}{\oplus} (NP) \qquad (\oplus\mathsf{a})$$

$$(N \overset{a}{\oplus} M) \overset{b}{\oplus} P \rightarrow_{\mathsf{p}} (N \overset{b}{\oplus} P) \overset{a}{\oplus} (M \overset{b}{\oplus} P) \qquad (\text{if } a < b) \qquad (\oplus\oplus_1)$$

$$N \overset{b}{\oplus} (M \overset{a}{\oplus} P) \rightarrow_{\mathsf{p}} (N \overset{b}{\oplus} M) \overset{a}{\oplus} (N \overset{b}{\oplus} P) \qquad (\text{if } a < b) \qquad (\oplus\oplus_2)$$

$$\boxed{b}.\, (N \overset{a}{\oplus} M) \rightarrow_{\mathsf{p}} (\boxed{b}.\, N) \overset{a}{\oplus} (\boxed{b}.\, M) \qquad (\text{if } a \neq b) \qquad (\oplus\Box)$$

$$\boxed{a}.\, N \rightarrow_{\mathsf{p}} N \qquad (\text{if } a \notin \mathsf{fl}(N)) \qquad (\not\Box)$$

$$\lambda x. \boxed{a}.\, N \rightarrow_{\mathsf{p}} \boxed{a}.\, \lambda x.\, N \qquad (\Box\lambda)$$

$$(\boxed{a}.\, N)M \rightarrow_{\mathsf{p}} \boxed{a}.\, (NM) \qquad (\text{if } a \notin \mathsf{fl}(M)) \qquad (\Box\mathsf{f})$$

**Fig. 1.** Reduction Rules for $\beta$-reduction and p-reduction.

From here on, we consider only label-closed terms (we implicitly assume this, unless otherwise stated). All terms are identified up to renaming of their bound variables and labels. Given some terms $M$ and $N$ and a variable $x$, $M[N/x]$ is the capture-avoiding (for both variables and labels) substitution of $N$ for the free occurrences of $x$ in $M$. We speak of a *representative* $M$ of a term when $M$ is not considered up to such a renaming. A representative $M$ of a term is *well-labeled* if for every occurrence of $\boxed{a}$ in $M$ there is no $\boxed{a}$ occurring in its scope.

**Definition 3 (Order for labels).** Let $M$ be a well-labeled representative of a term. We define an *order* $<_M$ for the labels occurring in $M$ as follows: $a <_M b$ if and only if $\boxed{b}$ occurs in the scope of $\boxed{a}$.

For a well-labeled and label-closed representative $M$, $<_M$ is a finite tree order.

**Definition 4.** *Reduction* $\rightarrow = \rightarrow_\beta \cup \rightarrow_{\mathsf{p}}$ in $\Lambda_{\mathsf{PE}}$ consists of *$\beta$-reduction* $\rightarrow_\beta$ and *permutative* or *p-reduction* $\rightarrow_{\mathsf{p}}$, both defined as the contextual closure of the rules given in Figure 1. We write $\twoheadrightarrow$ for the reflexive–transitive closure of $\rightarrow$, and $\twoheadrightarrow\!\!|$ for reduction to normal form; similarly for $\rightarrow_\beta$ and $\rightarrow_{\mathsf{p}}$. We write $=_{\mathsf{p}}$ for the symmetric and reflexive–transitive closure of $\rightarrow_{\mathsf{p}}$.

$$
\begin{array}{rlr}
\boxed{a}.\,(\lambda x.\,x{=}x)(\top \overset{a}{\oplus} \bot) & \to_{\mathsf{p}} \ \boxed{a}.\,(\lambda x.\,x{=}x)\top \overset{a}{\oplus} (\lambda x.\,x{=}x)\bot & (\oplus\mathsf{a}) \\
& \twoheadrightarrow_{\beta} \ \boxed{a}.\,(\top{=}\top) \overset{a}{\oplus} (\bot{=}\bot) & \\
& = \ \boxed{a}.\,\top \overset{a}{\oplus} \top \ \to_{\mathsf{p}} \ \boxed{a}.\,\top \ \to_{\mathsf{p}} \ \top & (\mathsf{i}, \not\boxed{}) 
\end{array}
$$

**Fig. 2.** Example Reduction of the cbv-translation of the Term on p. 137.

Two example reductions are (1)-(2) on p. 137; a third, complete reduction is in Figure 2. The crucial feature of p-reduction is that a choice $\overset{a}{\oplus}$ *does* permute out of the argument position of an application, but a generator $\boxed{a}$ does *not*, as below. Since the argument of a redex may be duplicated, this is how we characterize the difference between the *outcome* of a probabilistic event, whose duplicates may be identified, and the event itself, whose duplicates may yield different outcomes.

$$
N\,(M \overset{a}{\oplus} P) \to_{\mathsf{p}} (NM) \overset{a}{\oplus} (NP) \qquad\qquad N\,(\boxed{a}.\,M) \not\to_{\mathsf{p}} \boxed{a}.\,N\,M
$$

By inspection of the rewrite rules in Figure 1, we can then characterize the normal forms of $\to_{\mathsf{p}}$ and $\to$ as follows.

**Proposition 5 (Normal forms).** *The normal forms $P_0$ of $\to_{\mathsf{p}}$, respectively $N_0$ of $\to$, are characterized by the following grammars.*

$$
\begin{array}{l}
P_0 ::= P_1 \mid P_0 \oplus P_0' \\
P_1 ::= x \mid \lambda x.P_1 \mid P_1\,P_0
\end{array}
\qquad\qquad
\begin{array}{l}
N_0 ::= N_1 \mid N_0 \oplus N_0' \\
N_1 ::= N_2 \mid \lambda x.N_1 \\
N_2 ::= x \mid N_2\,N_0
\end{array}
$$

## 3 Properties of Permutative Reduction

We will prove strong normalization and confluence of $\to_{\mathsf{p}}$. For strong normalization, the obstacle is the interaction between different choice operators, which may duplicate each other, creating super-exponential growth.[3] Fortunately, Dershowitz's *recursive path orders* [12] seem tailor-made for our situation.

Observe that the set $\Lambda_{\mathsf{PE}}$ endowed with $\to_{\mathsf{p}}$ is a first-order term rewriting system over a countably infinite set of variables and the signature $\Sigma$ given by:

- the binary function symbol $\overset{a}{\oplus}$, for any label $a$;
- the unary function symbol $\boxed{a}$, for any label $a$;
- the unary function symbol $\lambda x$, for any variable $x$;
- the binary function symbol @, letting $@(M, N)$ stand for $MN$.

[3] This was inferred only from a simple simulation; we would be interested to know a rigorous complexity result.

**Definition 6.** Let $M$ be a well-labeled representative of a label-closed term, and let $\Sigma_M$ be the set of signature symbols occurring in $M$. We define $\prec_M$ as the (strict) partial order on $\Sigma_M$ generated by the following rules.

$$\begin{array}{ll} \overset{a}{\oplus} \prec_M \overset{b}{\oplus} & \text{if } a <_M b \\ \overset{a}{\oplus} \prec_M \boxed{b} & \text{for any labels } a, b \\ \boxed{b} \prec_M @, \lambda x & \text{for any label } b \end{array}$$

**Lemma 7.** *The reduction $\rightarrow_{\mathsf{p}}$ is strongly normalizing.*

*Proof.* For the first-order term rewriting system $(\Lambda_{\mathsf{PE}}, \rightarrow_{\mathsf{p}})$ we derive a well-founded recursive path ordering $<$ from $\prec_M$ following [12, p. 289]. Let $f$ and $g$ range over function symbols, let $[N_1, \ldots, N_n]$ denote a multiset and extend $<$ to multisets by the standard multiset ordering, and let $N = f(N_1, \ldots, N_n)$ and $M = g(M_1, \ldots, M_m)$; then

$$N < M \iff \begin{cases} [N_1, \ldots, N_n] < [M_1, \ldots, M_m] & \text{if } f = g \\ [N_1, \ldots, N_n] < [M] & \text{if } f \prec_M g \\ [N] \leq [M_1, \ldots, M_m] & \text{if } f \not\preceq_M g\,. \end{cases}$$

While $\prec_M$ is defined only relative to $\Sigma_M$, reduction may only reduce the signature. Inspection of Figure 1 then shows that $M \rightarrow_{\mathsf{p}} N$ implies $N < M$. □

**Confluence of Permutative Reduction.** With strong normalization, confluence of $\rightarrow_{\mathsf{p}}$ requires only local confluence. We reduce the number of cases to consider, by casting the permutations of $\overset{a}{\oplus}$ as instances of a common shape.

**Definition 8.** We define a *context* $C[\,]$ (with exactly one hole $[\,]$) as follows, and let $C[N]$ represent $C[\,]$ with the hole $[\,]$ replaced by $N$.

$$C[\,] ::= [\,] \mid \lambda x.C[\,] \mid C[\,]M \mid NC[\,] \mid C[\,]\overset{a}{\oplus}M \mid N\overset{a}{\oplus}C[\,] \mid \boxed{a}.C[\,]$$

Observe that the six reduction rules $\oplus\lambda$ through $\oplus\square$ in Figure 1 are all of the following form. We refer to these collectively as $\oplus\star$.

$$C[N\overset{a}{\oplus}M] \rightarrow_{\mathsf{p}} C[N]\overset{a}{\oplus}C[M] \qquad (\oplus\star)$$

**Lemma 9 (Confluence of $\rightarrow_{\mathsf{p}}$).** *Reduction $\rightarrow_{\mathsf{p}}$ is confluent.*

*Proof.* By Newman's lemma and strong normalization of $\rightarrow_{\mathsf{p}}$ (Lemma 7), confluence follows from local confluence. The proof of local confluence consists of joining all critical pairs given by $\rightarrow_{\mathsf{p}}$. Details are in the Appendix of [7]. □

**Definition 10.** We denote the unique $\mathsf{p}$-normal form of a term $N$ by $N_{\mathsf{p}}$.

## 4 Confluence

We aim to prove that $\rightarrow = \rightarrow_\beta \cup \rightarrow_\mathsf{p}$ is confluent. We will use the standard technique of *parallel* $\beta$-reduction [26], a simultaneous reduction step on a number of $\beta$-redexes, which we define via a labeling of the redexes to be reduced. The central point is to find a notion of reduction that is *diamond*, *i.e.* every critical pair can be closed in one (or zero) steps. This will be our *complete* reduction, which consists of parallel $\beta$-reduction followed by p-reduction to normal form.

**Definition 11.** A *labeled* term $P^\bullet$ is a term $P$ with chosen $\beta$-redexes annotated as $(\lambda x.\, N)^\bullet M$. The unique *labeled* $\beta$*-step* $P^\bullet \Rightarrow_\beta P_\bullet$ from $P^\bullet$ to the *labeled reduct* $P_\bullet$ reduces every labeled redex, and is defined inductively as follows.

$$(\lambda x.\, N^\bullet)^\bullet M^\bullet \Rightarrow_\beta N_\bullet[M_\bullet/x] \qquad N^\bullet M^\bullet \Rightarrow_\beta N_\bullet M_\bullet$$
$$x \Rightarrow_\beta x \qquad N^\bullet \overset{a}{\oplus} M^\bullet \Rightarrow_\beta N_\bullet \overset{a}{\oplus} M_\bullet$$
$$\lambda x.\, N^\bullet \Rightarrow_\beta \lambda x.\, N_\bullet \qquad \boxed{a}.\, N^\bullet \Rightarrow_\beta \boxed{a}.\, N_\bullet$$

A *parallel* $\beta$*-step* $P \Rightarrow_\beta P_\bullet$ is a labeled step $P^\bullet \Rightarrow_\beta P_\bullet$ for some labeling $P^\bullet$.

Note that $P_\bullet$ is an unlabeled term, since all labels are removed in the reduction. For the empty labeling, $P^\bullet = P_\bullet = P$, so parallel reduction is reflexive: $P \Rightarrow_\beta P$.

**Lemma 12.** *A parallel* $\beta$*-step* $P \Rightarrow_\beta P_\bullet$ *is a* $\beta$*-reduction* $P \twoheadrightarrow_\beta P_\bullet$.

*Proof.* By induction on the labeled term $P^\bullet$ generating $P \Rightarrow_\beta P_\bullet$. □

**Lemma 13.** *Parallel* $\beta$*-reduction is diamond.*

*Proof.* Let $P^\bullet \Rightarrow_\beta P_\bullet$ and $P^\circ \Rightarrow_\beta P_\circ$ be two labeled reduction steps on a term $P$. We annotate each step with the label of the other, preserved by reduction, to give the span from the doubly labeled term $P^{\bullet\circ} = P^{\circ\bullet}$ below left. Reducing the remaining labels will close the diagram, as below right.

$$P^\circ_\bullet \;{}_\beta\!\Leftarrow\; P^{\bullet\circ} = P^{\circ\bullet} \Rightarrow_\beta P^\bullet_\circ \qquad\qquad P^\circ_\bullet \Rightarrow_\beta P_{\bullet\circ} = P_{\circ\bullet} \;{}_\beta\!\Leftarrow\; P^\bullet_\circ$$

This is proved by induction on $P^{\bullet\circ}$, where only two cases are not immediate: those where a redex carries one but not the other label. One case follows by the below diagram; the other case is symmetric. Below, for the step top right, induction on $N^\bullet$ shows that $N^\bullet[M^\bullet/x] \Rightarrow_\beta N_\bullet[M_\bullet/x]$.

$$\begin{array}{ccccc} (\lambda x.\, N^{\circ\bullet})^\circ M^{\circ\bullet} & \Rightarrow_\beta & N^\bullet_\circ[M^\bullet_\circ/x] & \Rightarrow_\beta & N_{\circ\bullet}[M_{\circ\bullet}/x] \\ = & & & & = \\ (\lambda x.\, N^{\bullet\circ})^\circ M^{\bullet\circ} & \Rightarrow_\beta & (\lambda x.\, N^\circ_\bullet)^\circ M^\circ_\bullet & \Rightarrow_\beta & N_{\bullet\circ}[M_{\bullet\circ}/x] \end{array}$$ □

### 4.1 Parallel Reduction and Permutative Reduction

For the commutation of (parallel) $\beta$-reduction with $\mathsf{p}$-reduction, we run into the minor issue that a permuting generator or choice operator may block a redex: in both cases below, before $\rightarrowtriangle_{\mathsf{p}}$ the term has a redex, but after $\rightarrowtriangle_{\mathsf{p}}$ it is blocked.

$$(\lambda x.\, N \overset{a}{\oplus} M)\, P \rightarrowtriangle_{\mathsf{p}} ((\lambda x.\, N) \overset{a}{\oplus} (\lambda x.\, M))\, P \qquad (\lambda x.\, \boxed{a}.\, N)\, M \rightarrowtriangle_{\mathsf{p}} (\boxed{a}.\, \lambda x.\, N)\, M$$

We address this by an adaptation $\to_{\mathsf{p}}$ of $\mathsf{p}$-reduction on labeled terms, which is a strategy in $\twoheadrightarrow_{\mathsf{p}}$ that permutes past a labeled redex in one step.

**Definition 14.** A *labeled* $\mathsf{p}$-reduction $N^\bullet \to_{\mathsf{p}} M^\bullet$ on labeled terms is a $\mathsf{p}$-reduction of one of the forms

$$(\lambda x.\, N^\bullet \overset{a}{\oplus} M^\bullet)^\bullet P^\bullet \twoheadrightarrow_{\mathsf{p}} (\lambda x.\, N^\bullet)^\bullet P^\bullet \overset{a}{\oplus} (\lambda x.\, M^\bullet)^\bullet P^\bullet$$

$$(\lambda x.\, \boxed{a}.\, N^\bullet)^\bullet M^\bullet \twoheadrightarrow_{\mathsf{p}} \boxed{a}.\, (\lambda x.\, N^\bullet)^\bullet M^\bullet$$

or a single $\mathsf{p}$-step $\rightarrowtriangle_{\mathsf{p}}$ on unlabeled constructors in $N^\bullet$.

**Lemma 15.** *Reduction to normal form in* $\to_{\mathsf{p}}$ *is equal to* $\twoheadrightarrow\!|_{\mathsf{p}}$ *(on labeled terms).*

*Proof.* Observe that $\rightarrowtriangle_{\mathsf{p}}$ and $\to_{\mathsf{p}}$ have the same normal forms. Then in one direction, since $\to_{\mathsf{p}} \subseteq \twoheadrightarrow_{\mathsf{p}}$ we have $\mathrel{\to\!\!\!\to}\!|_{\mathsf{p}} \subseteq \twoheadrightarrow\!|_{\mathsf{p}}$. Conversely, let $N \twoheadrightarrow\!|_{\mathsf{p}} M$. On this reduction, let $P \rightarrowtriangle_{\mathsf{p}} Q$ be the first step such that $P \not\to_{\mathsf{p}} Q$. Then there is an $R$ such that $P \to_{\mathsf{p}} R$ and $Q \rightarrowtriangle_{\mathsf{p}} R$. Note that we have $N \mathrel{\to\!\!\!\to}_{\mathsf{p}} R$. By confluence, $R \twoheadrightarrow\!|_{\mathsf{p}} M$, and by induction on the sum length of paths in $\rightarrowtriangle_{\mathsf{p}}$ from $R$ (smaller than from $N$) we have $R \mathrel{\to\!\!\!\to}\!|_{\mathsf{p}} M$, and hence $N \mathrel{\to\!\!\!\to}\!|_{\mathsf{p}} M$. □

The following lemmata then give the required commutation properties of the relations $\to_{\mathsf{p}}$, $\twoheadrightarrow\!|_{\mathsf{p}}$, and $\Rightarrow_\beta$. Figure 3 illustrates these by commuting diagrams.

**Lemma 16.** *If* $N^\bullet \to_{\mathsf{p}} M^\bullet$ *then* $N_\bullet =_{\mathsf{p}} M_\bullet$.

*Proof.* By induction on the rewrite step $\to_{\mathsf{p}}$. The two interesting cases are:

$$\begin{array}{ccc}
(\lambda x.\, M^\bullet)^\bullet (N^\bullet \overset{a}{\oplus} P^\bullet) & \xrightarrow{\ \mathsf{p}\ } & ((\lambda x.\, M^\bullet)^\bullet N^\bullet) \overset{a}{\oplus} ((\lambda x.\, M^\bullet)^\bullet P^\bullet) \\
\beta \Big\Downarrow & & \Big\Downarrow \beta \\
M_\bullet[(N_\bullet \overset{a}{\oplus} P_\bullet)/x] & \overset{}{\underset{\mathsf{p}}{\twoheadrightarrow}} & M_\bullet[N_\bullet/x] \overset{a}{\oplus} M_\bullet[P_\bullet/x]
\end{array} \qquad (x \in \mathsf{fv}(M))$$

$$\begin{array}{ccc}
(\lambda x.\, M^\bullet)^\bullet (N^\bullet \overset{a}{\oplus} P^\bullet) & \xrightarrow{\ \mathsf{p}\ } & ((\lambda x.\, M^\bullet)^\bullet N^\bullet) \overset{a}{\oplus} ((\lambda x.\, M^\bullet)^\bullet P^\bullet) \\
\beta \Big\Downarrow & & \Big\Downarrow \beta \\
M_\bullet & \underset{\mathsf{p}}{\leftarrowtriangle} & M_\bullet \overset{a}{\oplus} M_\bullet
\end{array} \qquad (x \notin \mathsf{fv}(M))$$

□

How the critical pairs in the above diagrams are joined shows that we cannot use the Hindley-Rosen Lemma [2, Prop. 3.3.5] to prove confluence of $\rightarrow_\beta \cup \rightarrow_{\mathsf{p}}$.

**Lemma 17.** $N_\bullet =_{\mathsf{p}} N_{\mathsf{p}\bullet}$.

*Proof.* Using Lemma 15 we decompose $N^\bullet \twoheadrightarrow\!|_{\mathsf{p}} N^\bullet_{\mathsf{p}}$ as

$$N^\bullet = N^\bullet_1 \rightarrow_{\mathsf{p}} N^\bullet_2 \rightarrow_{\mathsf{p}} \cdots \rightarrow_{\mathsf{p}} N^\bullet_n = N^\bullet_{\mathsf{p}}$$

where $(N_i)_\bullet =_{\mathsf{p}} (N_{i+1})_\bullet$ by Lemma 16. □

### 4.2 Complete Reduction

To obtain a reduction strategy with the diamond property for $\rightarrow$, we combine parallel reduction $\Rightarrow_\beta$ with permutative reduction to normal form $\twoheadrightarrow\!|_{\mathsf{p}}$ into a notion of *complete reduction* $\Rrightarrow$. We will show that it is diamond (Lemma 19), and that any step in $\rightarrow$ maps onto a complete step of $\mathsf{p}$-normal forms (Lemma 20). Confluence of $\rightarrow$ (Theorem 21) then follows: any two paths $\twoheadrightarrow$ map onto complete paths $\Rrightarrow\!\!\!\!\rightarrow$ on $\mathsf{p}$-normal forms, which then converge by the diamond property.

**Definition 18.** A *complete* reduction step $N \Rrightarrow N_{\bullet\mathsf{p}}$ is a parallel $\beta$-step followed by $\mathsf{p}$-reduction to normal form:

$$N \Rrightarrow N_{\bullet\mathsf{p}} \quad := \quad N \Rightarrow_\beta N_\bullet \twoheadrightarrow\!|_{\mathsf{p}} N_{\bullet\mathsf{p}}\ .$$

**Lemma 19 (Complete reduction is diamond).** *If $P \Lleftarrow N \Rrightarrow M$ then for some $Q$, $P \Rrightarrow Q \Lleftarrow M$.*

*Proof.* By the following diagram, where $M = N_{\circ\mathsf{p}}$ and $P = N_{\bullet\mathsf{p}}$, and $Q = N_{\circ\bullet\mathsf{p}}$. The square top left is by Lemma 13, top right and bottom left are by Lemma 17, and bottom right is by confluence and strong normalization of $\mathsf{p}$-reduction.

$$\begin{array}{ccccc}
N^{\circ\bullet} & \xRightarrow{\beta} & N^\bullet_\circ & \xrightarrow{\mathsf{p}}\!\!\!\twoheadrightarrow\!| & N^\bullet_{\circ\mathsf{p}} \\
{\scriptstyle\beta}\Downarrow & & {\scriptstyle\beta}\Downarrow & & {\scriptstyle\beta}\Downarrow \\
N^\circ_\bullet & \xRightarrow{\beta} & N_{\circ\bullet} & =_{\mathsf{p}} & N_{\circ\mathsf{p}\bullet} \\
{\scriptstyle\mathsf{p}}\downarrow\!\!\downarrow & & =_{\mathsf{p}} & & {\scriptstyle\mathsf{p}}\downarrow\!\!\downarrow \\
N^\circ_{\bullet\mathsf{p}} & \xRightarrow{\beta} & N_{\bullet\mathsf{p}\circ} & \xrightarrow{\mathsf{p}}\!\!\!\twoheadrightarrow\!| & N_{\circ\bullet\mathsf{p}}
\end{array}$$

□

**Lemma 20 ($\mathsf{p}$-Normalization maps reduction to complete reduction).** *If $N \rightarrow M$ then $N_{\mathsf{p}} \Rrightarrow M_{\mathsf{p}}$.*

*Proof.* For a $\mathsf{p}$-step $N \rightarrow_{\mathsf{p}} M$ we have $N_{\mathsf{p}} = M_{\mathsf{p}}$ while $\Rightarrow_\beta$ is reflexive. For a $\beta$-step $N \rightarrow_\beta M$ we label the reduced redex in $N$ to get $N^\bullet \Rightarrow_\beta N_\bullet = M$. Then Lemma 17 gives $N_{\mathsf{p}\bullet} =_{\mathsf{p}} M$, and hence $N_{\mathsf{p}} \Rightarrow_\beta N_{\mathsf{p}\bullet} \twoheadrightarrow\!|_{\mathsf{p}} M_{\mathsf{p}}$. □

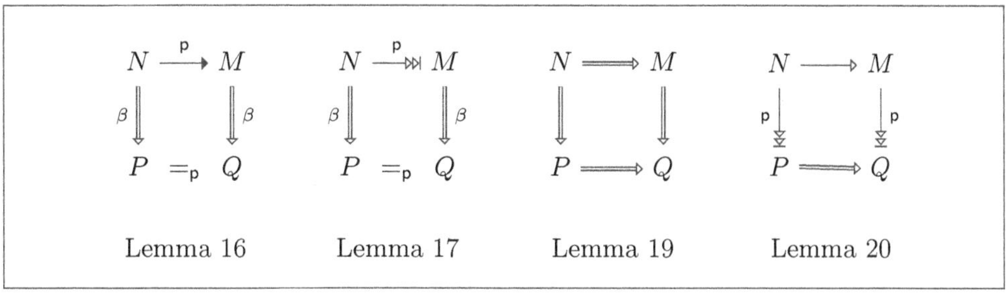


**Fig. 3.** Diagrams for the Lemmata Leading up to Confluence

**Theorem 21.** *Reduction $\rightarrow$ is confluent.*

*Proof.* By the following diagram. For the top and left areas, by Lemma 20 any reduction path $N \twoheadrightarrow M$ maps onto one $N_\mathsf{p} \Rightarrow\!\!\!\!\!\twoheadrightarrow M_\mathsf{p}$. The main square follows by the diamond property of complete reduction, Lemma 19.

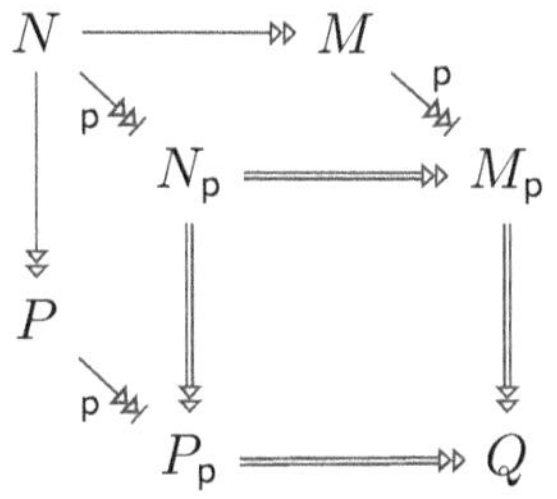

□

# 5 Strong Normalization for Simply-Typed Terms

In this section, we prove that the relation $\rightarrow$ enjoys strong normalization in *simply typed* terms. Our proof of strong normalization is based on the classic reducibility technique, and inherently has to deal with label-open terms. It thus make great sense to turn the order $<_M$ from Definition 3 into something more formal, at the same time allowing terms to be label-*open*. This is in Figure 4. It is easy to realize that, of course modulo label $\alpha$-equivalence, for every term $M$ there is at least one $\theta$ such that $\theta \vdash_L M$. An easy fact to check is that if $\theta \vdash_L M$ and $M \rightarrow N$, then $\theta \vdash_L N$. It thus makes sense to parametrize $\rightarrow$ on a sequence of labels $\theta$, *i.e.*, one can define a family of reduction relations $\rightarrow^\theta$ on pairs in the form $(M, \theta)$. The set of strongly normalizable terms, and the number of steps to normal forms become themselves parametric:

- The set $SN^\theta$ of those terms $M$ such that $\theta \vdash_L M$ and $(M, \theta)$ is strongly normalizing modulo $\rightarrow^\theta$;
- The function $sn^\theta$ assigning to any term in $SN^\theta$ the maximal number of $\rightarrow^\theta$ steps to normal form.

Label Sequences: $\theta \ ::= \ \varepsilon \mid a \cdot \theta$

Label Judgments: $\xi \ ::= \ \theta \vdash_L M$

Label Rules:

$$\frac{}{\theta \vdash_L x} \qquad \frac{\theta \vdash_L M}{\theta \vdash_L \lambda x.M} \qquad \frac{a \cdot \theta \vdash_L M}{\theta \vdash_L \boxed{a}.\,M}$$

$$\frac{\theta \vdash_L M \quad \theta \vdash_L N}{\theta \vdash_L MN} \qquad \frac{\theta \vdash_L M \quad \theta \vdash_L N \quad a \in \theta}{\theta \vdash_L M \overset{a}{\oplus} N}$$

**Fig. 4.** Labeling Terms

Types: $\tau \ ::= \ \alpha \mid \tau \Rightarrow \rho$

Environments: $\Gamma \ ::= \ x_1 : \tau_1, \ldots, x_n : \tau_n$

Judgments: $\pi \ ::= \ \Gamma \vdash M : \tau$

Typing Rules:

$$\frac{}{\Gamma, x : \tau \vdash x : \tau} \qquad \frac{\Gamma, x : \tau \vdash M : \rho}{\Gamma \vdash \lambda x.M : \tau \Rightarrow \rho} \qquad \frac{\Gamma \vdash M : \tau}{\Gamma \vdash \boxed{a}.\,M : \tau}$$

$$\frac{\Gamma \vdash M : \tau \Rightarrow \rho \quad \Gamma \vdash N : \tau}{\Gamma \vdash MN : \rho} \qquad \frac{\Gamma \vdash M : \tau \quad \Gamma \vdash N : \tau}{\Gamma \vdash M \overset{a}{\oplus} N : \tau}$$

**Fig. 5.** Types, Environments, Judgments, and Rules

$$\frac{L_1 \in SN^\theta \quad \cdots \quad L_m \in SN^\theta}{xL_1 \ldots L_m \in SN^\theta} \qquad \frac{ML_1 \ldots L_m \in SN^\theta \quad NL_1 \ldots L_m \in SN^\theta \quad a \in \theta}{M \overset{a}{\oplus} NL_1 \ldots L_m \in SN^\theta}$$

$$\frac{M[L_0/x]L_1 \ldots L_m \in SN^\theta \quad L_0 \in SN^\theta}{(\lambda x.\, M)L_0 \ldots L_m \in SN^\theta} \qquad \frac{ML_1 \ldots L_m \in SN^{a \cdot \theta} \quad \forall i.a \notin L_i}{(\boxed{a}.\, M)L_1 \ldots L_m \in SN^\theta}$$

**Fig. 6.** Closure Rules for Sets $SN^\theta$

We can now define types, environments, judgments, and typing rules in Figure 5.

Please notice that the type structure is precisely the one of the usual, vanilla, simply-typed $\lambda$-calculus (although terms are of course different), and we can thus reuse most of the usual proof of strong normalization, for example in the version given by Ralph Loader's notes [21], page 17.

**Lemma 22.** *The closure rules in Figure 6 are all sound.*

Since the structure of the type system is the one of plain, simple types, the definition of reducibility sets is the classic one:

$$\begin{aligned} Red_\alpha &= \{(\Gamma, \theta, M) \mid M \in SN^\theta \wedge \Gamma \vdash M : \alpha\}; \\ Red_{\tau\Rightarrow\rho} &= \{(\Gamma, \theta, M) \mid (\Gamma \vdash M : \tau \Rightarrow \rho) \wedge (\theta \vdash_L M) \wedge \\ &\qquad \forall(\Gamma\Delta, \theta, N) \in Red_\tau.(\Gamma\Delta, \theta, MN) \in Red_\rho\}. \end{aligned}$$

Before proving that all terms are reducible, we need some auxiliary results.

**Lemma 23.** *1. If $(\Gamma, \theta, M) \in Red_\tau$, then $M \in SN^\theta$.*

2. *If $\Gamma \vdash xL_1 \dots L_m : \tau$ and $L_1, \dots, L_m \in SN^\theta$, then $(\Gamma, \theta, xL_1 \dots L_m) \in Red_\tau$.*
3. *If $(\Gamma, \theta, M[L_0/x]L_1 \dots L_m) \in Red_\tau$ with $\Gamma \vdash L_0 : \rho$ and $L_0 \in SN^\theta$, then $(\Gamma, \theta, (\lambda x. M)L_0 \dots L_m) \in Red_\tau$.*
4. *If $(\Gamma, \theta, ML_1 \dots L_m) \in Red_\tau$ with $(\Gamma, \theta, NL_1 \dots L_m) \in Red_\tau$ and $a \in \theta$, then $(\Gamma, \theta, (M \overset{a}{\oplus} N)L_1 \dots L_m) \in Red_\tau$.*
5. *If $(\Gamma, a \cdot \theta, ML_1 \dots L_m) \in Red_\tau$ and $a \notin L_i$ for all $i$, then $(\Gamma, \theta, (\boxed{a}. M)L_1 \dots L_m) \in Red_\tau$.*

*Proof.* The proof is an induction on $\tau$: If $\tau$ is an atom $\alpha$, then Point 1 follows by definition, while points 2 to 5 come from Lemma 22. If $\tau$ is $\rho \Rightarrow \mu$, Points 2 to 5 come directly from the induction hypothesis, while Point 1 can be proved by observing that $M$ is in $SN^\theta$ if $Mx$ is itself $SN^\theta$, where $x$ is a fresh variable. By induction hypothesis (on Point 2), we can say that $(\Gamma(x : \rho), \theta, x) \in Red_\rho$, and conclude that $(\Gamma(x : \rho), \theta, Mx) \in Red_\mu$. □

The following is the so-called Main Lemma:

**Proposition 24.** *Suppose $y_1 : \tau_1, \dots, y_n : \tau_n \vdash M : \rho$ and $\theta \vdash_L M$, with $(\Gamma, \theta, N_j) \in Red_{\tau_j}$ for all $1 \le j \le n$. Then $(\Gamma, \theta, M[N_1/y_1, \dots, N_n/y_n]) \in Red_\rho$.*

*Proof.* This is an induction on the structure of the term $M$:

- If $M$ is a variable, necessarily one among $y_1, \dots, y_n$, then the result is trivial.
- If $M$ is an application $LP$, then there exists a type $\xi$ such that $y_1 : \tau_1, \dots, y_n : \tau_n \vdash L : \xi \Rightarrow \rho$ and $y_1 : \tau_1, \dots, y_n : \tau_n \vdash P : \xi$. Moreover, $\theta \vdash_L L$ and $\theta \vdash_L P$ we can then safely apply the induction hypothesis and conclude that

$$(\Gamma, \theta, L[\overline{N}/\overline{y}]) \in Red_{\xi\Rightarrow\rho} \qquad (\Gamma, \theta, P[\overline{N}/\overline{y}]) \in Red_\xi\ .$$

  By definition, we get

$$(\Gamma, \theta, (LP)[\overline{N}/\overline{y}]) \in Red_\rho\ .$$

- If $M$ is an abstraction $\lambda x. L$, then $\rho$ is an arrow type $\xi \Rightarrow \mu$ and $y_1 : \tau_1, \dots, y_n : \tau_n, x : \xi \vdash L : \mu$. Now, consider any $(\Gamma\Delta, \theta, P) \in Red_\xi$. Our objective is to prove with this hypothesis that $(\Gamma\Delta, \theta, (\lambda x.L[\overline{N}/\overline{y}])P) \in Red_\mu$. By induction hypothesis, since $(\Gamma\Delta, N_i) \in Red_{\tau_i}$, we get that $(\Gamma\Delta, \theta, L[\overline{N}/\overline{y}, P/x]) \in Red_\mu$. The thesis follows from Lemma 23.

- If $M$ is a sum $L \overset{a}{\oplus} P$, we can make use of Lemma 23 and the induction hypothesis, and conclude.
- If $M$ is a generator $\boxed{a}.\,P$, we can make use of Lemma 23 and the induction hypothesis. We should however observe that $a \cdot \theta \vdash_L P$, since $\theta \vdash_L M$. □

We now have all the ingredients for our proof of strong normalization:

**Theorem 25.** *If $\Gamma \vdash M : \tau$ and $\theta \vdash_L M$, then $M \in SN^\theta$.*

*Proof.* Suppose that $x_1 : \rho_1, \ldots, x_n : \rho_n \vdash M : \tau$. Since $x_1 : \rho_1, \ldots, x_n : \rho_n \vdash x_i : \rho_i$ for all $i$, and clearly $\theta \vdash_L x_i$ for every $i$, we can apply Lemma 24 and obtain that $(\Gamma, \theta, M[\overline{x}/\overline{x}]) \in Red_\tau$ from which, via Lemma 23, one gets the thesis. □

## 6 Projective Reduction

Permutative reduction $\rightarrow_{\mathsf{p}}$ evaluates probabilistic sums purely by rewriting. Here we look at a more standard *projective* notion of reduction, which conforms more closely to the intuition that $\boxed{a}$ generates a probabilistic event to determine the choice $\overset{a}{\oplus}$. Using $+$ for an external probabilistic sum, we expect to reduce $\boxed{a}.\,N$ to $N_0 + N_1$ where each $N_i$ is obtained from $N$ by projecting every subterm $M_0 \overset{a}{\oplus} M_1$ to $M_i$. The question is, in what context should we admit this reduction? We first limit ourselves to reducing in *head* position.

**Definition 26.** The *a-projections* $\pi_0^a(N)$ and $\pi_1^a(N)$ are defined as follows:

$$
\begin{array}{rclrcll}
\pi_0^a(N \overset{a}{\oplus} M) &=& \pi_0^a(N) & \pi_i^a(\lambda x.\,N) &=& \lambda x.\pi_i^a(N) & \\
\pi_1^a(N \overset{a}{\oplus} M) &=& \pi_1^a(M) & \pi_i^a(NM) &=& \pi_i^a(N)\,\pi_i^a(M) & \\
\pi_i^a(\boxed{a}.\,N) &=& \boxed{a}.\,N & \pi_i^a(N \overset{b}{\oplus} M) &=& \pi_i^a(N) \overset{b}{\oplus} \pi_i^a(M) & \text{if } a \neq b \\
\pi_i^a(x) &=& x & \pi_i^a(\boxed{b}.\,N) &=& \boxed{b}.\,\pi_i^a(N) & \text{if } a \neq b.
\end{array}
$$

**Definition 27.** A *head context* $H[\,]$ is given by the following grammar.

$$H[\,] ::= [\,] \mid \lambda x.\,H[\,] \mid H[\,]N$$

**Definition 28.** *Projective head reduction* $\rightarrow_{\pi\mathsf{h}}$ is given by

$$H[\boxed{a}.\,N] \rightarrow_{\pi\mathsf{h}} H[\pi_0^a(N)] + H[\pi_1^a(N)]\ .$$

We can simulate $\rightarrow_{\pi\mathsf{h}}$ by permutative reduction if we interpret the external sum $+$ by an outermost $\oplus$ (taking special care if the label does not occur).

**Proposition 29.** *Permutative reduction simulates projective head reduction:*

$$H[\boxed{a}.\,N] \twoheadrightarrow_{\mathsf{p}} \begin{cases} H[N] & \text{if } a \notin \mathsf{fl}(N) \\ H[\pi_0^a(N)] \oplus H[\pi_1^a(N)] & \text{otherwise.} \end{cases}$$

*Proof.* The case $a \notin \mathsf{fl}(N)$ is immediate by a $\not\boxtimes$ step. For the other case, observe that $H[\boxed{a}.\,N] \twoheadrightarrow_{\mathsf{p}} \boxed{a}.\,H[N]$ by $\square\lambda$ and $\square\mathsf{f}$ steps, and since $a$ does not occur in $H[\,]$, that $H[\pi^a_i(N)] = \pi^a_i(H[N])$. By induction on $N$, if $a$ is minimal in $N$ (*i.e.* $a \in \mathsf{fl}(N)$ and $a \leq b$ for all $b \in \mathsf{fl}(N)$) then $N \twoheadrightarrow_{\mathsf{p}} \pi^a_0(N) \overset{a}{\oplus} \pi^a_1(N)$. As required,

$$H[\boxed{a}.\,N] \twoheadrightarrow_{\mathsf{p}} \boxed{a}.\,H[\pi^a_0(N)] \overset{a}{\oplus} H[\pi^a_1(N)] \quad \text{if } a \in \mathsf{fl}(N)\ . \qquad \square$$

A gap remains between which generators will not be duplicated, which we *should* be able to reduce, and which generators projective head reduction *does* reduce. In particular, to interpret call-by-value probabilistic reduction in Section 7, we would like to reduce under other generators. However, permutative reduction does not permit exchanging generators, and so only simulates reducing in head position. While (independent) probabilistic events are generally considered interchangeable, it is a question whether the below equivalence is desirable.

$$\boxed{a}.\,\boxed{b}.\,N \ \overset{?}{\sim}\ \boxed{b}.\,\boxed{a}.\,N \tag{4}$$

We elide the issue by externalizing probabilistic events, and reducing with reference to a predetermined binary stream $s \in \{0,1\}^{\mathbb{N}}$ representing their outcomes. In this way, we will preserve the intuitions of both permutative and projective reduction: we obtain a qualified version of the equivalence (4) (see (5) below), and will be able to reduce any generator on the *spine* of a term: under (other) generators and choices as well as under abstractions and in function position.

**Definition 30.** The set of *streams* is $\mathbb{S} = \{0,1\}^{\mathbb{N}}$, ranged over by $r, s, t$, and $i \cdot s$ denotes a stream with $i \in \{0,1\}$ as first element and $s$ as the remainder.

**Definition 31.** The *stream labeling* $N^s$ of a term $N$ with a stream $s \in \mathbb{S}$, which annotates generators as $\boxed{a}^i$ with $i \in \{0,1\}$ and variables as $x^s$ with a stream $s$, is given inductively below. We lift $\beta$-reduction to stream-labeled terms by introducing a substitution case for stream-labeled variables: $x^s[M/x] = M^s$.

$$(\lambda x.\,N)^s = \lambda x.\,N^s \qquad\qquad (\boxed{a}.\,N)^{i\cdot s} = \boxed{a}^i.\,N^s$$

$$(N\,M)^s = N^s\,M \qquad\qquad (N \overset{a}{\oplus} M)^s = N^s \overset{a}{\oplus} M^s$$

**Definition 32.** *Projective reduction* $\rightarrow_{\pi}$ on stream-labeled terms is the rewrite relation given by

$$\boxed{a}^i.\,N \rightarrow_{\pi} \pi^a_i(N)\ .$$

Observe that in $N^s$ a generator that occurs under $n$ other generators on the spine of $N$, is labeled with the element of $s$ at position $n+1$. Generators in argument position remain unlabeled, until a $\beta$-step places them on the spine, in which case they become labeled by the new substitution case. We allow to annotate a term with a finite prefix of a stream, *e.g.* $N^i$ with a singleton $i$, so that only part of the spine is labeled. Subsequent labeling of a partly labeled term is then by $(N^r)^s = N^{r\cdot s}$ (abusing notation). To introduce streams via the external probabilistic sum, and to ignore an unused remaining stream after completing a probabilistic computation, we adopt the following equation.

$$N = N^0 + N^1$$

**Proposition 33.** *Projective reduction generalizes projective head reduction:*

$$H[\,\boxed{a}.\,N] \;=\; H[\,\boxed{a}^0.\,N] + H[\,\boxed{a}^1.\,N] \;\longrightarrow_\pi\; H[\pi_0^a(N)] + H[\pi_1^a(N)] \; .$$

Returning to the interchangeability of probabilistic events, we refine (4) by exchanging the corresponding elements of the annotating streams:

$$(\boxed{a}.\,\boxed{b}.\,N)^{i \cdot j \cdot s} \;=\; \boxed{a}^i.\,\boxed{b}^j.\,N^s \xrightarrow{\;\pi\;} \pi_i^a(\pi_j^b(N^s))$$

$$\sim \qquad\qquad\qquad\qquad = \qquad\qquad\qquad\qquad (5)$$

$$(\boxed{b}.\,\boxed{a}.\,N)^{j \cdot i \cdot s} \;=\; \boxed{b}^j.\,\boxed{a}^i.\,N^s \xrightarrow{\;\pi\;} \pi_j^b(\pi_i^a(N^s))$$

Stream-labeling externalizes all probabilities, making reduction deterministic. This is expressed by the following proposition, that stream-labeling commutes with reduction: if a generator remains unlabeled in $M$ and becomes labeled after a reduction step $M \to N$, what label it receives is predetermined. The deep reason is that stream labeling assigns an outcome to each generator in a way that corresponds to a call-by-name strategy for probabilistic reduction.

**Proposition 34.** *If $M \to N$ by a step other than $\not\sqcap$ then $M^s \to N^s$.*

**Remark 35.** The statement is false for the $\not\sqcap$ rule $\boxed{a}.\,N \to_p N$ ($a \notin \mathsf{fl}(N)$), as it removes a generator but not an element from the stream. Arguably, for this reason the rule should be excluded from the calculus. On the other hand, the rule is necessary to implement idempotence of $\oplus$, rather than just $\overset{a}{\oplus}$, as follows.

$$N \oplus N \;=\; \boxed{a}.\,N \overset{a}{\oplus} N \;\to_p\; \boxed{a}.\,N \;\to_p\; N \qquad \text{where } a \notin \mathsf{fl}(N)$$

The below proposition then expresses that projective reduction is an *invariant* for permutative reduction. If $N \to_p M$ by a step (that is not $\not\sqcap$) on a labeled generator $\boxed{a}^i$ or a corresponding choice $\overset{a}{\oplus}$, then $N$ and $M$ reduce to a common term, $N \to_\pi P \,{}_\pi\!\!\leftarrow M$, by the projective steps evaluating $\boxed{a}^i$.

**Proposition 36.** *Projective reduction is an invariant for permutative reduction, as follows (with a case for $\mathsf{c}_2$ symmetric to $\mathsf{c}_1$, and where $D[\,]$ is a context).*

$$\boxed{a}^i.\,C[N \overset{a}{\oplus} N] \xrightarrow{\;\;\mathsf{p}\;\;} \boxed{a}^i.\,C[N] \qquad\qquad \boxed{a}^i.\,C[(N_0 \overset{a}{\oplus} M) \overset{a}{\oplus} N_1] \xrightarrow{\;\;\mathsf{p}\;\;} \boxed{a}^i.\,C[N_0 \overset{a}{\oplus} N_1]$$

$$\searrow_\pi \quad \mathsf{i} \quad \swarrow_\pi \qquad\qquad\qquad\qquad \searrow_\pi \quad \mathsf{c}_1 \quad \swarrow_\pi$$

$$\pi_i^a(C[N]) \qquad\qquad\qquad\qquad\qquad\qquad \pi_i^a(C[N_i])$$

$$\boxed{a}^i.\,C[D[N_0 \overset{a}{\oplus} N_1]] \xrightarrow{\;\;\mathsf{p}\;\;} \boxed{a}^i.\,C[D[N_0] \overset{a}{\oplus} D[N_1]]$$

$$\searrow_\pi \quad \oplus\star \quad \swarrow_\pi$$

$$\pi_i^a(C[D[N_i]])$$

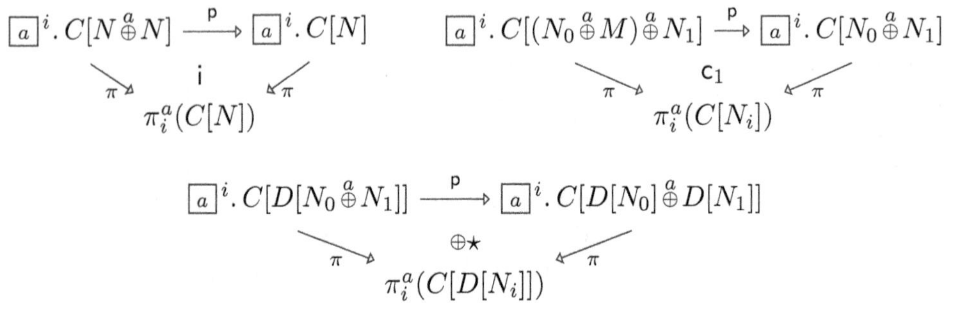

$$\begin{array}{ccc} \lambda x.\,\boxed{a}^{\,i}.\,N & \xrightarrow{\;\mathsf{p}\;} & \boxed{a}^{\,i}.\,\lambda x.\,N \\ \pi\downarrow & \Box\lambda & \downarrow\pi \\ \lambda x.\,\pi_i^a(N) & = & \pi_i^a(\lambda x.\,N) \end{array} \qquad \begin{array}{ccc} (\boxed{a}^{\,i}.\,N)M & \xrightarrow{\;\mathsf{p}\;} & \boxed{a}^{\,i}.\,NM \\ \pi\downarrow & \Box\mathsf{f} & \downarrow\pi \\ \pi_i^a(N)\,M & = & \pi_i^a(N\,M) \end{array}$$

## 7 Call-by-value Interpretation

We consider the interpretation of a call-by-value probabilistic $\lambda$-calculus. For simplicity we will allow duplicating (or deleting) $\beta$-redexes, and only restrict duplicating probabilities; our *values* $V$ are then just deterministic—*i.e.* without choices—terms, possibly applications and not necessarily $\beta$-normal (so that our $\rightarrow_{\beta\mathsf{v}}$ is actually $\beta$-reduction on deterministic terms, unlike [9]). We evaluate the internal probabilistic choice $\oplus_{\mathsf{v}}$ to an external probabilistic choice $+$.

$$N ::= x \mid \lambda x.N \mid MN \mid M \oplus_{\mathsf{v}} N \qquad\qquad (\lambda x.N)V \rightarrow_{\beta\mathsf{v}} N[V/x]$$

$$V, W ::= x \mid \lambda x.V \mid VW \qquad\qquad M \oplus_{\mathsf{v}} N \rightarrow_{\mathsf{v}} M + N$$

The interpretation $[\![N]\!]_{\mathsf{v}}$ of a call-by-value term $N$ into $\Lambda_{\mathsf{PE}}$ is given as follows. First, we translate $N$ to a label-open term $[\![N]\!]_{\mathsf{open}} = \theta \vdash_L P$ by replacing each choice $\oplus_{\mathsf{v}}$ with one $\overset{a}{\oplus}$ with a unique label, where the label-context $\theta$ collects the labels used. Then $[\![N]\!]_{\mathsf{v}}$ is the *label closure* $[\![N]\!]_{\mathsf{v}} = \lfloor \theta \vdash_L P \rfloor$, which prefixes $P$ with a generator $\boxed{a}$ for every $a$ in $\theta$.

**Definition 37.** (Call-by-value interpretation) The *open interpretation* $[\![N]\!]_{\mathsf{open}}$ of a call-by-value term $N$ is as follows, where all labels are fresh, and inductively $[\![N_i]\!]_{\mathsf{open}} = \theta_i \vdash_L P_i$ for $i \in \{1, 2\}$.

$$\begin{array}{rcl} [\![x]\!]_{\mathsf{open}} & = & \vdash_L x \\ [\![\lambda x.N_1]\!]_{\mathsf{open}} & = & \theta_1 \vdash_L \lambda x.P_1 \end{array} \qquad \begin{array}{rcl} [\![N_1 N_2]\!]_{\mathsf{open}} & = & \theta_2 \cdot \theta_1 \vdash_L P_1 P_2 \\ [\![N_1 \oplus_{\mathsf{v}} N_2]\!]_{\mathsf{open}} & = & \theta_2 \cdot \theta_1 \cdot a \vdash_L P_1 \overset{a}{\oplus} P_2 \end{array}$$

The *label closure* $\lfloor \theta \vdash_L P \rfloor$ is given inductively as follows.

$$\lfloor \vdash_L P \rfloor = P \qquad \lfloor a \cdot \theta \vdash_L P \rfloor = \lfloor \theta \vdash_L \boxed{a}.\,P \rfloor$$

The *call-by-value interpretation* of $N$ is $[\![N]\!]_{\mathsf{v}} = \lfloor [\![N]\!]_{\mathsf{open}} \rfloor$.

Our call-by-value reduction may choose an arbitrary order in which to evaluate the choices $\oplus_{\mathsf{v}}$ in a term $N$, but the order of generators in the interpretation $[\![N]\!]_{\mathsf{v}}$ is necessarily fixed. Then to simulate a call-by-value reduction, we cannot choose a fixed context stream a priori; all we can say is that for every reduction, there is some stream that allows us to simulate it. Specifically, a reduction step $C[N_0 \oplus_{\mathsf{v}} N_1] \rightarrow_{\mathsf{v}} C[N_j]$ where $C[\,]$ is a call-by-value term context is simulated by the following projective step.

$$\ldots \boxed{a}^{\,i}.\,\boxed{b}^{\,j}.\,\boxed{c}^{\,k} \ldots D[P_0 \overset{b}{\oplus} P_1] \rightarrow_{\pi} \ldots \boxed{a}^{\,i}.\,\boxed{c}^{\,k} \ldots D[P_j]$$

Here, $[\![C[N_0 \oplus_{\mathsf{v}} N_1]]\!]_{\mathsf{open}} = \theta \vdash_L D[P_0 \overset{b}{\oplus} P_1]$ with $D[\,]$ a $\Lambda_{\mathsf{PE}}$-context, and $\theta$ giving rise to the sequence of generators $\ldots\boxed{a}.\boxed{b}.\boxed{c}\ldots$ in the call-by-value translation. To simulate the reduction step, if $b$ occupies the $n$-th position in $\theta$, then the $n$-th position in the context stream $s$ must be the element $j$. Since $\beta$-reduction survives the translation and labeling process intact, we may simulate call-by-value probabilistic reduction by projective and $\beta$-reduction.

**Theorem 38.** *If* $N \twoheadrightarrow_{\mathsf{v},\beta\mathsf{v}} V$ *then* $[\![N]\!]^s_{\mathsf{v}} \twoheadrightarrow_{\pi,\beta} [\![V]\!]_{\mathsf{v}}$ *for some stream* $s \in \mathbb{S}$.

## 8 Conclusions and Future Work

We believe our decomposition of probabilistic choice in λ-calculus to be an elegant and compelling way of restoring confluence, one of the core properties of the λ-calculus. Our probabilistic event λ-calculus captures traditional call-by-name and call-by-value probabilistic reduction, and offers finer control beyond those strategies. Permutative reduction implements a natural and fine-grained equivalence on probabilistic terms as internal rewriting, while projective reduction provides a complementary and more traditional external perspective.

There are a few immediate areas for future work. Firstly, within probabilistic λ-calculus, it is worth exploring if our decomposition opens up new avenues in semantics. Secondly, our approach might apply to probabilistic reasoning more widely, outside the λ-calculus. Most importantly, we will explore if our approach can be extended to other computational effects. Our use of streams interprets probabilistic choice as a *read* operation from an external source, which means other read operations can be treated similarly. A complementary treatment of *write* operations would allow us to express a considerable range of effects, including input/output and state.

### Acknowledgments

This work was supported by EPSRC Project EP/R029121/1 *Typed Lambda-Calculi with Sharing and Unsharing*. The first author is partially supported by the ANR project 19CE480014 PPS, the ERC Consolidator Grant 818616 DIAPASoN, and the MIUR PRIN 201784YSZ5 ASPRA. We thank the referees for their diligence and their helpful comments. We are grateful to Chris Barrett and—indirectly—Anupam Das for pointing us to Zantema and Van de Pol's work [27].

## References

1. Avanzini, M., Dal Lago, U., Ghyselen, A.: Type-based complexity analysis of probabilistic functional programs. In: 34th Annual ACM/IEEE Symposium on Logic in Computer Science, LICS 2019. pp. 1–13. IEEE Computer Society (2019). https://doi.org/10.1109/LICS.2019.8785725
2. Barendregt, H.P.: The Lambda Calculus – Its Syntax and Semantics, Studies in logic and the foundations of mathematics, vol. 103. North-Holland (1984)

3. Borgström, J., Dal Lago, U., Gordon, A.D., Szymczak, M.: A lambda-calculus foundation for universal probabilistic programming. In: 21st ACM SIGPLAN International Conference on Functional Programming, ICFP 2016. pp. 33–46. ACM (2016). https://doi.org/10.1145/2951913.2951942
4. Breuvart, F., Dal Lago, U.: On intersection types and probabilistic lambda calculi. In: roceedings of the 20th International Symposium on Principles and Practice of Declarative Programming, PPDP 2018. pp. 8:1–8:13. ACM (2018). https://doi.org/10.1145/3236950.3236968
5. Dal Lago, U., Faggian, C., Valiron, B., Yoshimizu, A.: The geometry of parallelism: classical, probabilistic, and quantum effects. In: Proceedings of the 44th ACM SIGPLAN Symposium on Principles of Programming Languages, POPL 2017. pp. 833–845. ACM (2017). https://doi.org/10.1145/3009837
6. Dal Lago, U., Grellois, C.: Probabilistic termination by monadic affine sized typing. ACM Transactions on Programming Languages and Systems **41**(2), 10:1–10:65 (2019). https://doi.org/10.1145/3293605
7. Dal Lago, U., Guerrieri, G., Heijltjes, W.: Decomposing probabilistic lambda-calculi (long version) (2020), https://arxiv.org/abs/2002.08392
8. Dal Lago, U., Sangiorgi, D., Alberti, M.: On coinductive equivalences for higher-order probabilistic functional programs. In: The 41st Annual ACM SIGPLAN-SIGACT Symposium on Principles of Programming Languages, POPL '14. pp. 297–308. ACM (2014). https://doi.org/10.1145/2535838.2535872
9. Dal Lago, U., Zorzi, M.: Probabilistic operational semantics for the lambda calculus. RAIRO - Theoretical Informatics and Applications **46**(3), 413–450 (2012). https://doi.org/10.1051/ita/2012012
10. Danos, V., Ehrhard, T.: Probabilistic coherence spaces as a model of higher-order probabilistic computation. Information and Compututation **209**(6), 966–991 (2011). https://doi.org/10.1016/j.ic.2011.02.001
11. de'Liguoro, U., Piperno, A.: Non deterministic extensions of untyped lambda-calculus. Information and Computation **122**(2), 149–177 (1995). https://doi.org/10.1006/inco.1995.1145
12. Dershowitz, N.: Orderings for term-rewriting systems. Theoretical Computer Science **17**, 279–301 (1982). https://doi.org/10.1016/0304-3975(82)90026-3
13. Ehrhard, T., Pagani, M., Tasson, C.: Full abstraction for probabilistic PCF. Journal of the ACM **65**(4), 23:1–23:44 (2018). https://doi.org/10.1145/3164540
14. Ehrhard, T., Tasson, C.: Probabilistic call by push value. Logical Methods in Computer Science **15**(1) (2019). https://doi.org/10.23638/LMCS-15(1:3)2019
15. Faggian, C., Ronchi Della Rocca, S.: Lambda calculus and probabilistic computation. In: 34th Annual ACM/IEEE Symposium on Logic in Computer Science, LICS 2019. pp. 1–13. IEEE Computer Society (2019). https://doi.org/10.1109/LICS.2019.8785699
16. Goubault-Larrecq, J.: A probabilistic and non-deterministic call-by-push-value language. In: 34th Annual ACM/IEEE Symposium on Logic in Computer Science, LICS 2019. pp. 1–13. IEEE Computer Society (2019). https://doi.org/10.1109/LICS.2019.8785809
17. Jones, C., Plotkin, G.D.: A probabilistic powerdomain of evaluations. In: Proceedings of the Fourth Annual Symposium on Logic in Computer Science (LICS '89). pp. 186–195. IEEE Computer Society (1989). https://doi.org/10.1109/LICS.1989.39173
18. Jung, A., Tix, R.: The troublesome probabilistic powerdomain. Electronic Notes in Theoretical Computer Science **13**, 70–91 (1998). https://doi.org/10.1016/S1571-0661(05)80216-6

19. Leventis, T.: Probabilistic Böhm trees and probabilistic separation. In: Proceedings of the 33rd Annual ACM/IEEE Symposium on Logic in Computer Science, LICS 2018. pp. 649–658. IEEE Computer Society (2018). https://doi.org/10.1145/3209108.3209126
20. Leventis, T.: A deterministic rewrite system for the probabilistic $\lambda$-calculus. Mathematical Structures in Computer Science **29**(10), 1479–1512 (2019). https://doi.org/10.1017/S0960129519000045
21. Loader, R.: Notes on simply typed lambda calculus. Reports of the laboratory for foundations of computer science ECS-LFCS-98-381, University of Edinburgh, Edinburgh (1998), http://www.lfcs.inf.ed.ac.uk/reports/98/ECS-LFCS-98-381/
22. Manber, U., Tompa, M.: Probabilistic, nondeterministic, and alternating decision trees. In: 14th Annual ACM Symposium on Theory of Computing. pp. 234–244 (1982). https://doi.org/10.1145/800070.802197
23. Ramsey, N., Pfeffer, A.: Stochastic lambda calculus and monads of probability distributions. In: Conference Record of POPL 2002: The 29th SIGPLAN-SIGACT Symposium on Principles of Programming Languages. pp. 154–165. POPL '02 (2002). https://doi.org/10.1145/503272.503288
24. Saheb-Djahromi, N.: Probabilistic LCF. In: Mathematical Foundations of Computer Science 1978, Proceedings, 7th Symposium. Lecture Notes in Computer Science, vol. 64, pp. 442–451. Springer (1978). https://doi.org/10.1007/3-540-08921-7_92
25. Sangiorgi, D., Vignudelli, V.: Environmental bisimulations for probabilistic higher-order languages. In: Proceedings of the 43rd Annual ACM SIGPLAN-SIGACT Symposium on Principles of Programming Languages, POPL 2016. pp. 595–607 (2016). https://doi.org/10.1145/2837614.2837651
26. Takahashi, M.: Parallel reductions in lambda-calculus. Information and Computation **118**(1), 120–127 (1995). https://doi.org/10.1006/inco.1995.1057
27. Zantema, H., van de Pol, J.: A rewriting approach to binary decision diagrams. The Journal of Logic and Algebraic Programming **49**(1-2), 61–86 (2001). https://doi.org/10.1016/S1567-8326(01)00013-3

# 2

# Non-Idempotent Intersection Types in Logical Form*

Thomas Ehrhard [✉]

Université de Paris, IRIF, CNRS, F-75013 Paris, France
ehrhard@irif.fr

**Abstract.** Intersection types are an essential tool in the analysis of operational and denotational properties of lambda-terms and functional programs. Among them, non-idempotent intersection types provide precise quantitative information about the evaluation of terms and programs. However, unlike simple or second-order types, intersection types cannot be considered as a logical system because the application rule (or the intersection rule, depending on the presentation of the system) involves a condition stipulating that the proofs of premises must have the same structure. Using earlier work introducing an indexed version of Linear Logic, we show that non-idempotent typing can be given a logical form in a system where formulas represent hereditarily indexed families of intersection types.

**Keywords:** Lambda Calculus · Denotational Semantics · Intersection Types · Linear Logic

## Introduction

Intersection types, introduced in the work of Coppo and Dezani [4,5] and developed since then by many authors, are still a very active research topic. As quite clearly explained in [13], the Coppo and Dezani intersection type system $D\Omega$ can be understood as a syntactic presentation of the denotational interpretation of $\lambda$-terms in the Engeler's model, which is a model of the pure $\lambda$-calculus in the cartesian closed category of prime-algebraic complete lattices and Scott continuous functions.

Intersection types can be considered as formulas of the propositional calculus with implication $\Rightarrow$ and conjunction $\wedge$ as connectives. However, as pointed out by Hindley [12], intersection types deduction rules depart drastically from the standard logical rules of intuitionistic logic (and of any standard logical system) by the fact that, in the $\wedge$-introduction rule, it is assumed that the proofs of the two premises are typings of the *same* $\lambda$-term, which means that, in some sense made precise by the typing system itself, they have the same structure. Such requirements on *proofs* premises, and not only on formulas proven in premises, are absent from standard (intuitionistic or classical) logical systems where the proofs of premises are completely independent from each other. Many authors have addressed this issue, we refer to [14] for a discussion on several solutions which mainly focus on the design of *à la Church* presentations of intersection typing systems, thus enriching $\lambda$-terms with additional structures. Among the most recent and convincing contributions to this line of research we should certainly mention [15].

In our "new" approach to this problem — not so new actually since it dates back to [3] —, we change formulas instead of changing terms. It is based on a specific model of Linear Logic (and thus of the $\lambda$-calculus): the *relational model.* It is fair to credit Girard for the introduction of this model since it appears at least implicitly in [11]. It was probably known by many people in the Linear Logic community as a piece of folklore since the early 1990's and is presented formally in [3]. In this quite simple and canonical denotational model, types are interpreted as sets (without any additional structure) and a closed term of type $\sigma$ is interpreted as a subset of the interpretation of $\sigma$. It is quite easy to define, in this semantic framework, analogues of the usual models of the pure $\lambda$-calculus such as Scott's $D_\infty$ or Engeler's model, which in some sense are simpler than the original ones since the sets interpreting types need not to be pre-ordered. As explained in the work of De Carvalho [6,7], the intersection type counterpart of this semantics is a typing system where "intersection" is non-idempotent (in sharp contrast with the original systems introduced by Coppo and Dezani), sometimes called *system R*. Notice that the precise connection between the idempotent and non-idempotent approaches is analyzed in [8], in a quite general Linear Logic setting by means of an extensional collapse.

In order to explain our approach, we restrict first to simple types, interpreted as follows in the relational model: a basic type $\alpha$ is interpreted as a given set $[\![\alpha]\!]$ and the type $\sigma \Rightarrow \tau$ is interpreted as the set $\mathcal{M}_{\mathrm{fin}}([\![\sigma]\!]) \times [\![\tau]\!]$ (where $\mathcal{M}_{\mathrm{fin}}(E)$ is the set of finite multisets of elements of $E$). Remember indeed that intersection types can be considered as a syntactic presentation of denotational semantics, so it makes sense to define intersection types relative to simple types (in the spirit of [10]) as we do in Section 3: an intersection type relative to the base type $\alpha$ is an element of $[\![\alpha]\!]$ and an intersection type relative to $\sigma \Rightarrow \tau$ is a pair $([\,a_1, \dots, a_n\,], b)$ where the $a_i$s are intersection types relative to $\sigma$ and $b$ is an intersection type relative to $\tau$; with more usual notations[1] $([\,a_1, \dots, a_n\,], b)$ would be written $(a_1 \wedge \dots \wedge a_n) \to b$. Then, given a type $\sigma$, the main idea consists in representing an indexed family of elements of $[\![\sigma]\!]$ as a formula of a new logical system. If $\sigma = (\varphi \Rightarrow \psi)$ then the family can be written[2] $([\,a_k \mid k \in K \text{ and } u(k) = j\,], b_j)_{j \in J}$ where $J$ and $K$ are indexing sets, $u : K \to J$ is a function such that $f^{-1}(\{j\})$ is finite for all $j \in J$, $(b_j)_{j \in J}$ is a family of elements of $[\![\psi]\!]$ (represented by a formula $B$) and $(a_k)_{k \in K}$ is a family of elements of $[\![\varphi]\!]$ (represented by a formula $A$): in that case we introduce the implicative formula $(A \Rightarrow_u B)$ to represent the family

[1] That we prefer not to use for avoiding confusions between these two levels of typing.

[2] We use $[\cdots]$ for denoting multisets much as one uses $\{\cdots\}$ for denoting sets, the only difference is that multiplicities are taken into account.

$([\,a_k \mid k \in K \text{ and } u(k) = j\,], b_j)_{j \in J}$. It is clear that a family of simple types has generally infinitely many representations as such formulas; this huge redundancy makes it possible to establish a tight link between inhabitation of intersection types with provability of formulas representing them (in an indexed version $\mathsf{LJ}(I)$ of intuitionistic logic). Such a correspondence is exhibited in Section 3 in the simply typed setting and the idea is quite simple:

> given a type $\sigma$, a family $(a_j)_{j \in J}$ of elements of $[\![\sigma]\!]$, and a closed $\lambda$-term of type $\sigma$, it is equivalent to say that $\vdash M : a_j$ holds for all $j$ and to say that some (and actually any) formula $A$ representing $(a_j)_{j \in J}$ has an $\mathsf{LJ}(I)$ proof[3] whose underlying $\lambda$-term is $M$.

In Section 4 we extend this approach to the untyped $\lambda$-calculus taking as underlying model of the pure $\lambda$-calculus our relational version $\mathsf{R}_\infty$ of Scott's $D_\infty$. We define an adapted version of $\mathsf{LJ}(I)$ and establish a similar correspondence, with some slight modifications due to the specificities of $\mathsf{R}_\infty$.

## 1 Notations and preliminary definitions

If $E$ is a set, a *finite multiset of elements of* $E$ is a function $m : E \to \mathbb{N}$ such that the set $\{a \in E \mid m(a) \neq 0\}$ (called the *domain* of $m$) is finite. The cardinal of such a multiset $m$ is $\#m = \sum_{a \in E} m(a)$. We use $+$ for the obvious addition operation on multisets, and if $a_1, \dots, a_n$ are elements of $E$, we use $[\,a_1, \dots, a_n\,]$ for the corresponding multiset (taking multiplicities into account); for instance $[\,0, 1, 0, 2, 1\,]$ is the multiset $m$ of elements of $\mathbb{N}$ such that $m(0) = 2$, $m(1) = 2$, $m(2) = 1$ and $m(i) = 0$ for $i > 2$. If $(a_i)_{i \in I}$ is a family of elements of $E$ and if $J$ is a finite subset of $I$, we use $[\,a_i \mid i \in J\,]$ for the multiset of elements of $E$ which maps $a \in E$ to the number of elements $i \in J$ such that $a_i = a$ (which is finite since $J$ is). We use $\mathcal{M}_{\mathrm{fin}}(E)$ for the set of finite multisets of elements of $E$.

We use $+$ to denote set union when we we want to stress the fact that the involved sets are disjoint. A function $u : J \to K$ is *almost injective* if $\#u^{-1}\{k\}$ is finite for each $k \in K$ (equivalently, the inverse image of any finite subset of $K$ under $u$ is finite). If $s = (a_1, \dots, a_n)$ is a sequence of elements of $E$ and $i \in \{1, \dots, n\}$, we use $(s) \setminus i$ for the sequence $(a_1, \dots, a_{i-1}, a_{i+1}, \dots, a_n)$. Given sets $E$ and $F$, we use $F^E$ for the set of function from $E$ to $F$. The elements of $F^E$ are sometimes considered as functions $u$ (with a functional notation $u(e)$ for application) and sometimes as indexed families $a$ (with index notations $a_e$ for application) especially when $E$ is countable.

If $i \in \{1, \dots, n\}$ and $j \in \{1, \dots, n-1\}$, we define $\mathsf{s}(j, i) \in \{1, \dots, n\}$ as follows: $\mathsf{s}(j, i) = j$ if $j < i$ and $\mathsf{s}(j, i) = j + 1$ if $j \geq i$.

[3] Any such proof can be stripped from its indexing data giving rise to a proof of $\sigma$ in intuitionistic logic.

## 2 The relational model of the λ-calculus

Let $\mathbf{Rel}_!$ the category whose objects are sets[4] and $\mathbf{Rel}_!(X, Y) = \mathcal{P}(\mathcal{M}_{\mathrm{fin}}(X) \times Y)$ with $\mathsf{Id}_X = \{([a], a) \mid a \in X\}$ and composition of $s \in \mathbf{Rel}_!(X, Y)$ and $t \in \mathbf{Rel}_!(Y, Z)$ given by

$$t \circ s = \{(m_1 + \cdots + m_k, c) \mid \\ \exists b_1, \ldots, b_k \in Y \ ([b_1, \ldots, b_k], c) \in t \text{ and } \forall j \, (m_j, b_j) \in s\}.$$

It is easily checked that this composition law is associative and that $\mathsf{Id}$ is neutral for composition[5]. This category has all countable products: let $(X_j)_{j \in J}$ be a countable family of sets, their product is $X = \&_{j \in J} X_j = \bigcup_{j \in J} \{j\} \times X_j$ and projections $(\mathsf{pr}_j)_{j \in J}$ given by $\mathsf{pr}_j = \{([(j, a)], a) \mid a \in X_j\} \in \mathbf{Rel}_!(X, X_j)$ and if $(s_j)_{j \in J}$ is a family of morphisms $s_j \in \mathbf{Rel}_!(Y, X_j)$ then their tupling is $\langle s_j \rangle_{j \in J} = \{([a], (j, b))) \mid j \in J \text{ and } ([a], b) \in s_j\} \in \mathbf{Rel}_!(Y, X)$.

The category $\mathbf{Rel}_!$ is cartesian closed with object of morphisms from $X$ to $Y$ the set $(X \Rightarrow Y) = \mathcal{M}_{\mathrm{fin}}(X) \times Y$ and evaluation morphism $\mathsf{Ev} \in \mathbf{Rel}_!((X \Rightarrow Y) \ \& \ X, Y)$ is given by $\mathsf{Ev} = \{([(1, [a_1, \ldots, a_k], b), (2, a_1), \ldots, (2, a_k)], b) \mid a_1, \ldots, a_k \in X \text{ and } b \in Y\}$. The transpose (or curryfication) of $s \in \mathbf{Rel}_!(Z \ \& \ X, Y)$ is $\mathsf{Cur}(s) \in \mathbf{Rel}_!(Z, X \Rightarrow Y)$ given by $\mathsf{Cur}(s) = \{([c_1, \ldots, c_n], ([a_1, \ldots, a_k], b)) \mid ([(1, c_1), \ldots, (1, c_n), (2, a_1), \ldots, (2, a_k)], c) \in s\}$.

**Relational $D_\infty$.** Let $\mathsf{R}_\infty$ be the least set such that $(m_0, m_1, \ldots) \in \mathsf{R}_\infty$ as soon as $m_0, m_1 \ldots$ are finite multisets of elements of $\mathsf{R}_\infty$ which are almost all equal to $[\,]$. Notice in particular that $\mathsf{e} = ([\,], [\,], \ldots) \in \mathsf{R}_\infty$ and satisfies $\mathsf{e} = ([\,], \mathsf{e})$. By construction we have $\mathsf{R}_\infty = \mathcal{M}_{\mathrm{fin}}(\mathsf{R}_\infty) \times \mathsf{R}_\infty$, that is $\mathsf{R}_\infty = (\mathsf{R}_\infty \Rightarrow \mathsf{R}_\infty)$ and hence $\mathsf{R}_\infty$ is a model of the pure λ-calculus in $\mathbf{Rel}_!$ which also satisfies the η-rule. See [1] for general facts on this kind of model.

## 3 The simply typed case

We assume to be given a set of type atoms $\alpha, \beta, \ldots$ and of variables $x, y, \ldots$; types and terms are given as usual by $\sigma, \tau, \ldots := \alpha \mid \sigma \Rightarrow \tau$ and $M, N, \ldots := x \mid (M)\, N \mid \lambda x^\sigma\, N$.

With any type atom we associate a set $[\![\alpha]\!]$. This interpretation is extended to all types by $[\![\sigma \Rightarrow \tau]\!] = [\![\sigma]\!] \Rightarrow [\![\tau]\!] = \mathcal{M}_{\mathrm{fin}}([\![\sigma]\!]) \times [\![\tau]\!]$. The relational semantics of this λ-calculus can be described as a non-idempotent intersection type system, with judgments of shape $x_1 : m_1 : \sigma_1, \ldots, x_n : m_n : \sigma_n \vdash M : a : \sigma$ where the $x_i$'s are pairwise distinct variables, $M$ is a term, $a \in [\![\sigma]\!]$ and $m_i \in \mathcal{M}_{\mathrm{fin}}([\![\sigma_i]\!])$ for each $i$. Here are the typing rules:

$$\frac{j \neq i \Rightarrow m_j = [\,] \text{ and } m_i = [a]}{(x_i : m_i : \sigma_i)_{i=1}^{n} \vdash x_i : a : \sigma} \qquad \frac{\Phi, x : m : \sigma \vdash M : b : \tau}{\Phi \vdash \lambda x^\sigma\, M : (m, b) : \sigma \Rightarrow \tau}$$

[4] We can restrict to countable sets.

[5] This results from the fact that $\mathbf{Rel}_!$ arises as the Kleisli category of the $\mathsf{LL}$ model of sets and relations, see [3] for instance.

$$\frac{\Phi \vdash M : ([a_1, \ldots, a_k], b) : \sigma \Rightarrow \tau \qquad (\Phi_l \vdash N : a_l : \sigma)_{l=1}^{k}}{\Psi \vdash (M)\, N : b : \tau}$$

where $\Phi = (x_i : m_i : \sigma_i)_{i=1}^n$, $\Phi_l = (x_i : m_i^l : \sigma_i)_{i=1}^n$ for $l = 1, \ldots, k$ and $\Psi = (x_i : m_i + \sum_{l=1}^k m_i^l : \sigma_i)_{i=1}^n$.

### 3.1 Why do we need another system?

The trouble with this deduction system is that it cannot be considered as the term decorated version of an underlying "logical system for intersection types" allowing to prove sequents of shape $m_1 : \sigma_1, \ldots, m_n : \sigma_n \vdash a : \sigma$ (where non-idempotent intersection types $m_i$ and $a$ are considered as logical formulas, the ordinary types $\sigma_i$ playing the role of "kinds") because, in the application rule above, it is required that all the proofs of the $k$ right hand side premises have the same shape given by the $\lambda$-term $N$. We propose now a "logical system" derived from [3] which, in some sense, solves this issue. The main idea is quite simple and relies on three principles: (1) replace *hereditarily* multisets with indexed families in intersection types, (2) instead of proving single types, prove indexed families of hereditarily indexed types and (3) represent syntactically such families (of hereditarily indexed types) as formulas of a new system of *indexed logic*.

### 3.2 Minimal $\mathsf{LJ}(I)$

We define now the syntax of indexed formulas. Assume to be given an infinite countable set $I$ of indices. Then we define indexed types $A$; with each such type we associate an underlying type $\underline{A}$, a set $\mathsf{d}(A)$ and a family $\langle A \rangle \in [\![\underline{A}]\!]^{\mathsf{d}(A)}$. These formulas are given by the following inductive definition:

- if $J \subseteq I$ and $f : J \to [\![\alpha]\!]$ is a function then $\alpha[f]$ is a formula with $\underline{\alpha[f]} = \alpha$, $\mathsf{d}(\alpha[f]) = J$ and $\langle \alpha[f] \rangle = f$
- and if $A$ and $B$ are formulas and $u : \mathsf{d}(A) \to \mathsf{d}(B)$ is almost injective then $A \Rightarrow_u B$ is a formula with $\underline{A \Rightarrow_u B} = \underline{A} \Rightarrow \underline{B}$, $\mathsf{d}(A \Rightarrow_u B) = \mathsf{d}(B)$ and, for $k \in \mathsf{d}(B)$, $\langle A \Rightarrow_u B \rangle_k = ([\, \langle A \rangle_j \mid j \in \mathsf{d}(A) \text{ and } u(j) = k \,], \langle B \rangle_k)$.

**Proposition 1.** *Let $\sigma$ be a type, $J$ be a subset of $I$ and $f \in [\![\sigma]\!]^J$. There is a formula $A$ such that $\underline{A} = \sigma$, $\mathsf{d}(A) = J$ and $\langle A \rangle = f$ (actually, there are infinitely many such $A$'s as soon as $\sigma$ is not an atom and $J \neq \emptyset$).*

*Proof.* The proof is by induction on $\sigma$. If $\sigma$ is an atom $\alpha$ then we take $A = \alpha[f]$. Assume that $\sigma = (\rho \Rightarrow \tau)$ so that $f(j) = (m_j, b_j)$ with $m_j \in \mathcal{M}_{\text{fin}}([\![\rho]\!])$ and $b_j \in [\![\tau]\!]$. Since each $m_j$ is finite and $I$ is infinite, we can find a family $(K_j)_{j \in J}$ of pairwise disjoint finite subsets of $I$ such that $\#K_j = \#m_j$. Let $K = \bigcup_{j \in J} K_j$, there is a function $g : K \to [\![\rho]\!]$ such that $m_j = [\, g(k) \mid k \in K_j \,]$ for each $j \in J$ (choose first an enumeration $g_j : K_j \to [\![\rho]\!]$ of $m_j$ for each $j$ and then define $g(k) = g_j(k)$ where $j$ is the unique element of $J$ such that $k \in K_j$). Let $u : K \to J$ be the unique function such that $k \in K_{u(k)}$ for all $k \in K$; since each $K_j$ is finite, this function $u$ is almost injective. By inductive hypothesis there is a formula $A$ such that $\underline{A} = \rho$, $\mathsf{d}(A) = K$ and $\langle A \rangle = g$, and there is a formula $B$ such that $\underline{B} = \tau$, $\mathsf{d}(B) = J$ and $\langle B \rangle = (b_j)_{j \in J}$. Then the formula $A \Rightarrow_u B$ is well formed (since $u$ is an almost injective function $\mathsf{d}(A) = K \to \mathsf{d}(B) = J$) and satisfies $\underline{A \Rightarrow_u B} = \sigma$, $\mathsf{d}(A \Rightarrow_u B) = J$ and $\langle A \Rightarrow_u B \rangle = f$ as contended. □

As a consequence, for any type $\sigma$ and any element $a$ of $[\![\sigma]\!]$ (so $a$ is a non-idempotent intersection type of kind $\sigma$), one can find a formula $A$ such that $\underline{A} = \sigma$, $\mathsf{d}(A) = \{j\}$ (where $j$ is an arbitrary element of $I$) and $\langle A \rangle_j = a$. In other word, any intersection type can be represented as a formula (in infinitely many different ways in general of course, but up to renaming of indices, that is, up to "hereditary $\alpha$-equivalence", this representation is unique).

For any formula $A$ and $J \subseteq I$, we define a formula $A\lceil_J$ such that $\underline{A\lceil_J} = \underline{A}$, $\mathsf{d}(A\lceil_J) = \mathsf{d}(A) \cap J$ and $\langle A\lceil_J \rangle = \langle A \rangle \lceil_J$. The definition is by induction on $A$.

- $\alpha[f]\lceil_J = \alpha[f \lceil_J]$
- $(A \Rightarrow_u B)\lceil_J = (A\lceil_K \Rightarrow_v B\lceil_J)$ where $K = u^{-1}(\mathsf{d}(B) \cap J)$ and $v = u \lceil_K$.

Let $u : \mathsf{d}(A) \to J$ be a *bijection* (so that $u(\mathsf{d}(A)) = J$), we define a formula $u_*(A)$ such that $\underline{u_*(A)} = \underline{A}$, $\mathsf{d}(u_*(A)) = u(\mathsf{d}(A))$ and $\langle u_*(A) \rangle_j = \langle A \rangle_{u^{-1}(j)}$. The definition is by induction on $A$:

- $u_*(\alpha[f]) = \alpha[f \circ u^{-1}]$
- $u_*(A \Rightarrow_v B) = (A \Rightarrow_{u \circ v} u_*(B))$.

Using these two auxiliary notions, we can give a set of three deduction rules for a minimal natural deduction allowing to prove formulas in this indexed intuitionistic logic. This logical system allows to derive sequents which are of shape

$$A_1^{u_1}, \ldots, A_n^{u_n} \vdash B \tag{1}$$

where for each $i = 1, \ldots, n$, the function $u_i : \mathsf{d}(A_i) \to \mathsf{d}(B)$ is almost injective (it is not required that $\mathsf{d}(B) = \bigcup_{i=1}^{n} u_i(\mathsf{d}(A_i))$). Notice that the expressions $A_i^{u_i}$ are not formulas; this construction $A^u$ is part of the syntax of sequents, just as the "," separating these pseudo-formulas. Given a formula $A$ and $u : \mathsf{d}(A) \to J$ almost injective, it is nevertheless convenient to define $\langle A^u \rangle \in \mathcal{M}_{\mathrm{fin}}([\![\underline{A}]\!])^J$ by $\langle A^u \rangle_j = [\,\langle A \rangle_k \mid u(k) = j\,]$. In particular, when $u$ is a bijection, $\langle A^u \rangle_j = [\,\langle A \rangle_{u^{-1}(j)}\,]$.

The crucial point here is that such a sequent (1) involves no $\lambda$-term.

The main difference between the original system $\mathsf{LL}(I)$ of [3] and the present system is the way axioms are dealt with. In $\mathsf{LL}(I)$ there is no explicit identity axiom and only "atomic axioms" restricted to the basic constants of $\mathsf{LL}$; indeed it is well-known that in $\mathsf{LL}$ all identity axioms can be $\eta$-expanded, leading to proofs using only such atomic axioms. In the $\lambda$-calculus, and especially in the untyped $\lambda$-calculus we want to deal with in next sections, such $\eta$-expansions are hard to handle so we prefer to use explicit identity axioms.

The axiom is

$$\frac{j \neq i \Rightarrow \mathsf{d}(A_j) = \emptyset \text{ and } u_i \text{ is a bijection}}{A_1^{u_1}, \ldots, A_n^{u_n} \vdash u_{i*}(A_i)}$$

so that for $j \neq i$, the function $u_j$ is empty. A special case is

$$\frac{j \neq i \Rightarrow \mathsf{d}(A_j) = \emptyset \text{ and } u_i \text{ is the identity function}}{A_1^{u_1}, \dots, A_n^{u_n} \vdash A_i}$$

which may look more familiar, but the general axiom rule, allowing to "delocalize" the proven formula $A_i$ by an arbitrary bijection $u_i$, is required as we shall see. The $\Rightarrow$ introduction rule is quite simple

$$\frac{A_1^{u_1}, \dots, A_n^{u_n}, A^u \vdash B}{A_1^{u_1}, \dots, A_n^{u_n} \vdash A \Rightarrow_u B}$$

Last the $\Rightarrow$ elimination rule is more complicated (from a Linear Logic point of view, this is due to the fact that it combines 3 LL logical rules: $\multimap$ elimination, contraction and promotion). We have the deduction

$$\frac{C_1^{u_1}, \dots, C_n^{u_n} \vdash A \Rightarrow_u B \qquad D_1^{v_1}, \dots, D_n^{v_n} \vdash A}{E_1^{w_1}, \dots, E_n^{w_n} \vdash B}$$

under the following conditions, to be satisfied by the involved formulas and functions: for each $i = 1, \dots, n$ one has $\mathsf{d}(C_i) \cap \mathsf{d}(D_i) = \emptyset$, $\mathsf{d}(E_i) = \mathsf{d}(C_i) + \mathsf{d}(D_i)$, $C_i = E_i \restriction_{\mathsf{d}(C_i)}$, $D_i = E_i \restriction_{\mathsf{d}(D_i)}$, $w_i \restriction_{\mathsf{d}(C_i)} = u_i$, and $w_i \restriction_{\mathsf{d}(D_i)} = u \circ v_i$.

Let $\pi$ be a deduction tree of the sequent $A_1^{u_1}, \dots, A_n^{u_n} \vdash B$ in this system. By dropping all index information we obtain a derivation tree $\underline{\pi}$ of $\underline{A_1}, \dots, \underline{A_n} \vdash \underline{B}$, and, upon choosing a sequence $\vec{x}$ of $n$ pairwise distinct variables, we can associate with this derivation tree a simply typed $\lambda$-term $\underline{\pi}_{\vec{x}}$ which satisfies $x_1 : \underline{A_1}, \dots, x_n : \underline{A_n} \vdash \underline{\pi}_{\vec{x}} : \underline{B}$.

### 3.3 Basic properties of $\mathsf{LJ}(I)$

We prove some basic properties of this logical system. This is also the opportunity to get some acquaintance with it. Notice that in many places we drop the type annotations of variables in $\lambda$-terms, first because they are easy to recover, and second because the very same results and proofs are also valid in the untyped setting of Section 4.

**Lemma 1 (Weakening).** *Assume that $\Phi \vdash A$ is provable by a proof $\pi$ and let $B$ be a formula such that $\mathsf{d}(B) = \emptyset$. Then $\Phi' \vdash A$ is provable by a proof $\pi'$, where $\Phi'$ is obtained by inserting $B^{0_{\mathsf{d}(A)}}$ at any place in $\Phi$. Moreover $\underline{\pi}_{\vec{x}} = \underline{\pi'}_{\vec{x'}}$ (where $\vec{x'}$ is obtained from $\vec{x}$ by inserting a dummy variable at the same place).*

The proof is an easy induction on the proof of $\Phi \vdash A$.

**Lemma 2 (Relocation).** *Let $\pi$ be a proof of $(A_i^{u_i})_{i=1}^n \vdash A$ let $u : \mathsf{d}(A) \to J$ be a bijection, there is a proof $\pi'$ of $(A_i^{u \circ u_i})_{i=1}^n \vdash u_*(A)$ such that $\underline{\pi'}_{\vec{x}} = \underline{\pi}_{\vec{x}}$.*

The proof is a straightforward induction on $\pi$.

**Lemma 3 (Restriction).** *Let $\pi$ be a proof of $(A_i^{u_i})_{i=1}^n \vdash A$ and let $J \subseteq \mathsf{d}(A)$. For $i = 1, \dots, n$, let $K_i = {u_i}^{-1}(J) \subseteq \mathsf{d}(A_i)$ and $u'_i = u_i \restriction_{K_i} : K_i \to J$. Then the sequent $((A_i \restriction_{K_i})^{u'_i})_{i=1}^n \vdash A \restriction_J$ has a proof $\pi'$ such that $\underline{\pi'}_{\vec{x}} = \underline{\pi}_{\vec{x}}$.*

*Proof.* By induction on $\pi$. Assume that $\pi$ consists of an axiom $(A_j^{u_j})_{j=1}^n \vdash u_{i*}(A_i)$ with $\mathsf{d}(A_j) = \emptyset$ if $j \neq i$, and $u_i$ a bijection. With the notations of the lemma, $K_j = \emptyset$ for $j \neq i$ and $u'_i$ is a bijection $K_i \to J$. Moreover $u'_{i*}(A_i \restriction_{K_i}) = u_{i*}(A_i) \restriction_J$ so that $((A_i \restriction_{K_i})^{u'_i})_{i=1}^n \vdash A \restriction_J$ is obtained by an axiom $\pi'$ with $\underline{\pi'}_{\vec{x}} = x_i = \underline{\pi}_{\vec{x}}$.

Assume that $\pi$ ends with a $\Rightarrow$-introduction rule:

$$\frac{\begin{array}{c}\rho \\ (A_i^{u_i})_{i=1}^{n+1} \vdash B\end{array}}{(A_i^{u_i})_{i=1}^n \vdash A_{n+1} \Rightarrow_{u_{n+1}} B}$$

with $A = (A_{n+1} \Rightarrow_{u_{n+1}} B)$, and we have $\underline{\pi}_{\vec{x}} = \lambda x_{n+1}\, \underline{\rho}_{\vec{x}, x_{n+1}}$. With the notations of the lemma we have $A \restriction_J = (A_{n+1} \restriction_{K_{n+1}} \Rightarrow_{u'_{n+1}} B \restriction_J)$. By inductive hypothesis there is a proof $\rho'$ of $(A_i \restriction_{K_i}^{u'_i})_{i=1}^{n+1} \vdash B \restriction_J$ such that $\underline{\rho'}_{\vec{x}, x_{n+1}} = \underline{\rho}_{\vec{x}, x_{n+1}}$ and hence we have a proof $\pi'$ of $(A_i \restriction_{K_i}^{u'_i})_{i=1}^n \vdash A \restriction_J$ with $\underline{\pi'}_{\vec{x}} = \lambda x_{n+1}\, \underline{\rho'}_{\vec{x}, x_{n+1}} = \underline{\pi}_{\vec{x}}$ as contended.

Assume last that $\pi$ ends with a $\Rightarrow$-elimination rule:

$$\frac{\begin{array}{c}\mu \\ (B_i^{v_i})_{i=1}^n \vdash B \Rightarrow_v A\end{array} \qquad \begin{array}{c}\rho \\ (C_i^{w_i})_{i=1}^n \vdash B\end{array}}{(A_i^{u_i})_{i=1}^n \vdash A}$$

with $\mathsf{d}(A_i) = \mathsf{d}(B_i) + \mathsf{d}(C_i)$, $B_i = A_i \restriction_{\mathsf{d}(B_i)}$ and $C_i = A_i \restriction_{\mathsf{d}(C_i)}$, $u_i \restriction_{\mathsf{d}(B_i)} = v_i$ and $u_i \restriction_{\mathsf{d}(C_i)} = v \circ w_i$ for $i = 1, \ldots, n$, and of course $\underline{\pi}_{\vec{x}} = \left(\underline{\mu}_{\vec{x}}\right) \underline{\rho}_{\vec{x}}$. Let $L = v^{-1}(J) \subseteq \mathsf{d}(B)$. Let $L_i = {v_i}^{-1}(J)$ and $R_i = {w_i}^{-1}(L)$ for $i = 1, \ldots, n$ (we also set $v'_i = v_i \restriction_{L_i}$, $w'_i = w_i \restriction_{R_i}$ and $v' = v \restriction_L$). By inductive hypothesis, we have a proof $\mu'$ of $(B_i \restriction_{L_i}^{v'_i})_{i=1}^n \vdash B \restriction_L \Rightarrow_{v'} A \restriction_J$ such that $\underline{\mu'}_{\vec{x}} = \underline{\mu}_{\vec{x}}$ and a proof $\rho'$ of $(C_i \restriction_{R_i}^{w'_i})_{i=1}^n \vdash B \restriction_L$ such that $\underline{\rho'}_{\vec{x}} = \underline{\rho}_{\vec{x}}$. Now, setting $K_i = {u_i}^{-1}(K)$, observe that

- $\mathsf{d}(B_i) \cap K_i = L_i = \mathsf{d}(B_i \restriction_{L_i})$ and $u_i \restriction_{L_i} = v'_i$ since $u_i \restriction_{\mathsf{d}(B_i)} = v_i$
- $\mathsf{d}(C_i) \cap K_i = R_i = \mathsf{d}(C_i) \cap {w_i}^{-1}(L)$ since $u_i \restriction_{\mathsf{d}(C_i)} = v \circ w_i$ and $L = v^{-1}(J)$, hence $\mathsf{d}(C_i) \cap K_i = \mathsf{d}(C_i \restriction_{R_i})$, and also $u_i \restriction_{L_i} = v' \circ w'_i$.

It follows that $\mathsf{d}(A_i \restriction_{K_i}) = L_i + R_i$, and, setting $u'_i = u_i \restriction_{K_i}$, we have $u'_i \restriction_{L_i} = v'_i$ and $u'_i \restriction_{R_i} = v' \circ w'_i$. Hence we have a proof $\pi'$ of $(A_i \restriction_{K_i}^{u'_i})_{i=1}^n \vdash A \restriction_J$ such that $\underline{\pi'}_{\vec{x}} = \left(\underline{\mu'}_{\vec{x}}\right) \underline{\rho'}_{\vec{x}} = \left(\underline{\mu}_{\vec{x}}\right) \underline{\rho}_{\vec{x}} = \underline{\pi}_{\vec{x}}$ as contended. □

Though substitution lemmas are usually trivial, the $\mathsf{LJ}(I)$ substitution lemma requires some care in its statement and proof[6].

**Lemma 4 (Substitution).** *Assume that* $(A_j^{u_j})_{j=1}^n \vdash A$ *with a proof* $\mu$ *and that, for some* $i \in \{1, \ldots, n\}$, $(B_j^{v_j})_{j=1}^{n-1} \vdash A_i$ *with a proof* $\rho$. *Then there is a proof* $\pi$ *of* $(C_j^{w_j})_{j=1}^{n-1} \vdash A$ *such that* $\underline{\pi}_{(\vec{x})\setminus i} = \underline{\mu}_{\vec{x}} \left[\underline{\rho}_{(\vec{x})\setminus i}/x_i\right]$ *as soon as for each* $j = 1, \ldots, n-1$, $\mathsf{d}(C_j) = \mathsf{d}(A_{\mathsf{s}(j,i)}) + \mathsf{d}(B_j)$ *for each* $j = 1, \ldots, n-1$ *(remember that this requires also that* $\mathsf{d}(A_{\mathsf{s}(j,i)}) \cap \mathsf{d}(B_j) = \emptyset$*) with:*

[6] We use notations introduced in Section 1, especially for $\mathsf{s}(j,i)$.

– $C_j \restriction_{\mathsf{d}(A_{\mathsf{s}(j,i)})} = A_{\mathsf{s}(j,i)}$ *and* $w_j \restriction_{\mathsf{d}(A_{\mathsf{s}(j,i)})} = u_{\mathsf{s}(j,i)}$
– $C_j \restriction_{\mathsf{d}(B_j)} = B_j$ *and* $w_j \restriction_{\mathsf{d}(B_j)} = u_i \circ v_j$.

*Proof.* By induction on the proof $\mu$. Assume that $\mu$ is an axiom, so that there is a $k \in \{1, \ldots, n\}$ such that $A = u_{k*}(A_k)$, $u_k$ is a bijection and $\mathsf{d}(A_j) = \emptyset$ for all $j \neq k$. In that case we have $\underline{\mu}_{\vec{x}} = x_k$. There are two subcases to consider. Assume first that $k = i$. By Lemma 2 there is a proof $\rho'$ of $(B_j^{u_i \circ v_j})_{j=1}^{n-1} \vdash u_{i*}(A_i)$ such that $\underline{\rho'}_{(\vec{x})\setminus i} = \underline{\rho}_{(\vec{x})\setminus i}$. We have $C_j = B_j$ and $w_j = u_i \circ v_j$ for $j = 1, \ldots, n-1$, so that $\rho'$ is a proof of $(C_j^{w_j})_{j=1}^{n-1} \vdash A$, so we take $\pi = \rho'$ and equation $\underline{\pi}_{(\vec{x})\setminus i} = \underline{\mu}_{\vec{x}} \left[\underline{\rho}_{(\vec{x})\setminus i}/x_i\right]$ holds since $\underline{\mu}_{\vec{x}} = x_i$. Assume next that $k \neq i$, then $\mathsf{d}(A_i) = \emptyset$ and hence $\mathsf{d}(B_j) = \emptyset$ (and $v_j = 0_\emptyset$) for $j = 1, \ldots, n-1$. Therefore $C_j = A_{\mathsf{s}(j,i)}$ and $w_j = v_{\mathsf{s}(j,i)}$ for $j = 1, \ldots, n-1$. So our target sequent $(C_j^{w_j})_{j=1}^{n-1} \vdash A$ can also be written $(A_{\mathsf{s}(j,i)}^{u_{\mathsf{s}(j,i)}})_{j=1}^{n-1} \vdash u_{k*}(A_k)$ and is provable by a proof $\pi$ such that $\underline{\pi}_{(\vec{x})\setminus i} = x_k$ as contended.

Assume now that $\mu$ is a $\Rightarrow$-intro, that is $A = (A_{n+1} \Rightarrow_{u_{n+1}} A')$ and $\mu$ is

$$\frac{\begin{array}{c}\theta \\ (A_j^{u_j})_{j=1}^{n+1} \vdash A'\end{array}}{(A_j^{u_j})_{j=1}^{n} \vdash A}$$

We set $B_n = A_{n+1} \restriction_\emptyset$ and of course $v_{n+1} = 0_{\mathsf{d}(A)}$. Then we have a proof $\rho'$ of $(B_j^{v_j})_{j=1}^{n} \vdash A_i$ such that $\underline{\rho'}_{(\vec{x})\setminus i, x_{n+1}} = \underline{\rho}_{(\vec{x})\setminus i}$ by Lemma 1. We set $C_n = A_{n+1}$ and $w_n = u_{n+1}$. Then by inductive hypothesis applied to $\theta$ we have a proof $\pi^0$ of $(C_j^{w_j})_{j=1}^{n} \vdash A'$ which satisfies $\underline{\pi^0}_{(\vec{x})\setminus i, x_{n+1}} = \underline{\theta}_{\vec{x}, x_{n+1}} \left[\underline{\rho}_{(\vec{x})\setminus i}/x_i\right]$ and applying a $\Rightarrow$-introduction rule we get a proof $\pi$ of $(C_j^{w_j})_{j=1}^{n-1} \vdash A$ such that $\underline{\pi}_{(\vec{x})\setminus i} = \lambda x_{n+1} \left(\underline{\theta}_{\vec{x}, x_{n+1}} \left[\underline{\rho}_{(\vec{x})\setminus i}/x_i\right]\right) = \underline{\mu}_{\vec{x}} \left[\underline{\rho}_{(\vec{x})\setminus i}/x_i\right]$ as expected.

Assume last that the proof $\mu$ ends with

$$\frac{\begin{array}{c}\varphi \\ (E_j^{s_j})_{j=1}^{n} \vdash E \Rightarrow_s A\end{array} \qquad \begin{array}{c}\psi \\ (F_j^{t_j})_{j=1}^{n} \vdash E\end{array}}{(A_j^{u_j})_{j=1}^{n} \vdash A}$$

with $\mathsf{d}(A_j) = \mathsf{d}(E_j) + \mathsf{d}(F_j)$, $A_j \restriction_{\mathsf{d}(E_j)} = E_j$, $A_j \restriction_{\mathsf{d}(F_j)} = F_j$, $u_j \restriction_{\mathsf{d}(E_j)} = s_j$ and $u_j \restriction_{\mathsf{d}(F_j)} = s \circ t_j$, for $j = 1, \ldots, n$. And we have $\underline{\mu}_{\vec{x}} = \left(\underline{\varphi}_{\vec{x}}\right) \underline{\psi}_{\vec{x}}$. The idea is to "share" the substituting proof $\rho$ of $(B_j^{v_j})_{j=1}^{n} \vdash A_i$ among $\varphi$ and $\psi$ according to what they need, as specified by the formulas $E_i$ and $F_i$. So we write $\mathsf{d}(B_j) = L_j + R_j$ where $L_j = {v_j}^{-1}(\mathsf{d}(E_i))$ and $R_j = {v_j}^{-1}(\mathsf{d}(F_i))$ and by Lemma 3 we have two proofs $\rho^L$ of $(B_j \restriction_{L_j}^{v_j^L})_{j=1}^{n-1} \vdash E_i$ and $(B_j \restriction_{R_j}^{v_j^R})_{j=1}^{n-1} \vdash F_i$ where we set $v_j^L = v_j \restriction_{L_j}$ and $v_j^R = v_j \restriction_{R_j}$, obtained from $\rho$ by restriction. These proofs satisfy $\underline{\rho^L}_{(\vec{x})\setminus i} = \underline{\rho^R}_{(\vec{x})\setminus i} = \underline{\rho}_{(\vec{x})\setminus i}$.

Now we want to apply the inductive hypothesis to $\varphi$ and $\rho^L$, in order to get a proof of the sequent $(G_j^{w_j^L})_{j=1}^{n-1} \vdash E \Rightarrow_s A$ where $G_j = C_j\upharpoonright_{\mathsf{d}(E_{\mathsf{s}(j,i)})+L_j}$ (observe indeed that $\mathsf{d}(E_{\mathsf{s}(j,i)}) \subseteq \mathsf{d}(A_{\mathsf{s}(j,i)})$ and $L_j \subseteq \mathsf{d}(B_j)$ and hence are disjoint by our assumption that $\mathsf{d}(C_j) = \mathsf{d}(A_{\mathsf{s}(j,i)}) + \mathsf{d}(B_j)$) and $w_j^L = w_j\upharpoonright_{\mathsf{d}(E_{\mathsf{s}(j,i)})+L_j}$. With these definitions, and by our assumptions about $C_j$ and $w_j$, we have for all $j = 1, \dots, n-1$

$$
\begin{aligned}
G_j\upharpoonright_{\mathsf{d}(E_{\mathsf{s}(j,i)})} &= C_j\upharpoonright_{\mathsf{d}(A_{\mathsf{s}(j,i)})}\upharpoonright_{\mathsf{d}(E_{\mathsf{s}(j,i)})} = A_{\mathsf{s}(j,i)}\upharpoonright_{\mathsf{d}(E_{\mathsf{s}(j,i)})} = E_{\mathsf{s}(j,i)} \\
w_j^L\upharpoonright_{\mathsf{d}(E_{\mathsf{s}(j,i)})} &= w_j\upharpoonright_{\mathsf{d}(A_{\mathsf{s}(j,i)})}\upharpoonright_{\mathsf{d}(E_{\mathsf{s}(j,i)})} = u_{\mathsf{s}(j,i)}\upharpoonright_{\mathsf{d}(E_{\mathsf{s}(j,i)})} = s_{\mathsf{s}(j,i)} \\
G_j\upharpoonright_{L_j} &= C_j\upharpoonright_{\mathsf{d}(B_j)}\upharpoonright_{L_j} = B_j\upharpoonright_{L_j} \\
w_j^L\upharpoonright_{L_j} &= w_j\upharpoonright_{\mathsf{d}(B_j)}\upharpoonright_{L_j} = (u_i \circ v_j)\upharpoonright_{L_j} = u_i\upharpoonright_{\mathsf{d}(E_i)} \circ v_j^L = s_i \circ v_j^L\,.
\end{aligned}
$$

Therefore the inductive hypothesis applies yielding a proof $\varphi'$ of $(G_j^{w_j^L})_{j=1}^{n-1} \vdash E \Rightarrow_s A$ such that $\underline{\varphi'}_{(\vec{x})\setminus i} = \underline{\varphi}_{\vec{x}}\left[\underline{\rho^L}_{(\vec{x})\setminus i}/x_i\right] = \underline{\varphi}_{\vec{x}}\left[\underline{\rho}_{(\vec{x})\setminus i}/x_i\right]$.

Next we want to apply the inductive hypothesis to $\psi$ and $\rho^R$, in order to get a proof of the sequent $(H_j^{r_j})_{j=1}^{n-1} \vdash E$ where, for $j = 1, \dots, n-1$, $H_j = C_j\upharpoonright_{\mathsf{d}(F_{\mathsf{s}(j,i)})+R_j}$ (again $\mathsf{d}(F_{\mathsf{s}(j,i)}) \subseteq \mathsf{d}(A_{\mathsf{s}(j,i)})$ and $R_j \subseteq \mathsf{d}(B_j)$ are disjoint by our assumption that $\mathsf{d}(C_j) = \mathsf{d}(A_{\mathsf{s}(j,i)}) + \mathsf{d}(B_j)$) and $r_j$ is defined by $r_j\upharpoonright_{\mathsf{d}(F_{\mathsf{s}(j,i)})} = t_{\mathsf{s}(j,i)}$ and $r_j\upharpoonright_{R_j} = t_i \circ v_j^R$. Remember indeed that $v_j^R : R_j \to \mathsf{d}(F_i)$ and $t_i : \mathsf{d}(F_i) \to \mathsf{d}(E)$. We have

$$
\begin{aligned}
H_j\upharpoonright_{\mathsf{d}(F_{\mathsf{s}(j,i)})} &= C_j\upharpoonright_{\mathsf{d}(A_{\mathsf{s}(j,i)})}\upharpoonright_{\mathsf{d}(F_{\mathsf{s}(j,i)})} = A_{\mathsf{s}(j,i)}\upharpoonright_{\mathsf{d}(F_{\mathsf{s}(j,i)})} = F_{\mathsf{s}(j,i)} \\
H_j\upharpoonright_{R_j} &= C_j\upharpoonright_{\mathsf{d}(B_j)}\upharpoonright_{R_j} = B_j\upharpoonright_{R_j}
\end{aligned}
$$

and hence by inductive hypothesis there is a proof $\psi'$ of $(H_j^{r_j})_{j=1}^{n-1} \vdash E$ such that $\underline{\psi'}_{(\vec{x})\setminus i} = \underline{\psi}_{\vec{x}}\left[\underline{\rho^R}_{(\vec{x})\setminus i}/x_i\right] = \underline{\psi}_{\vec{x}}\left[\underline{\rho}_{(\vec{x})\setminus i}/x_i\right]$.

To end the proof of the lemma, it will be sufficient to prove that we can apply a $\Rightarrow$-elimination rule to the sequents $(G_j^{w_j^L})_{j=1}^{n-1} \vdash E \Rightarrow_s A$ and $(H_j^{r_j})_{j=1}^{n-1} \vdash E$ in order to get a proof $\pi$ of the sequent $(C_j^{w_j})_{j=1}^{n-1} \vdash A$. Indeed, the proof $\pi$ obtained in that way will satisfy $\underline{\pi}_{(\vec{x})\setminus i} = \left(\underline{\varphi'}_{(\vec{x})\setminus i}\right)\underline{\psi'}_{(\vec{x})\setminus i} = \underline{\mu}_{\vec{x}}\left[\underline{\rho}_{(\vec{x})\setminus i}/x_i\right]$.

Let $j \in \{1, \dots, n-1\}$. We have $C_j\upharpoonright_{\mathsf{d}(G_j)} = G_j$ and $C_j\upharpoonright_{\mathsf{d}(H_j)} = H_j$ simply because $G_j$ and $H_j$ are defined by restricting $C_j$. Moreover $\mathsf{d}(G_j) = \mathsf{d}(E_{\mathsf{s}(j,i)}) + L_j$ and $\mathsf{d}(H_j) = \mathsf{d}(F_{\mathsf{s}(j,i)}) + R_j$. Therefore $\mathsf{d}(G_j) \cap \mathsf{d}(H_j) = \emptyset$ and

$$
\mathsf{d}(C_j) = \mathsf{d}(A_{\mathsf{s}(j,i)}) + \mathsf{d}(B_j) = \mathsf{d}(E_{\mathsf{s}(j,i)}) + \mathsf{d}(F_{\mathsf{s}(j,i)}) + L_j + R_j = \mathsf{d}(G_j) + \mathsf{d}(H_j)\,.
$$

We have $w_j\upharpoonright_{\mathsf{d}(G_j)} = w_j^L$ by definition of $w_j^L$ as $w_j\upharpoonright_{\mathsf{d}(E_{\mathsf{s}(j,i)})+L_j}$. We have

$$
\begin{aligned}
w_j\upharpoonright_{\mathsf{d}(H_j)}\upharpoonright_{\mathsf{d}(F_{\mathsf{s}(j,i)})} &= w_j\upharpoonright_{\mathsf{d}(A_{\mathsf{s}(j,i)})}\upharpoonright_{\mathsf{d}(F_{\mathsf{s}(j,i)})} = u_{\mathsf{s}(j,i)}\upharpoonright_{\mathsf{d}(F_{\mathsf{s}(j,i)})} \\
&= s \circ t_{\mathsf{s}(j,i)} = (s \circ r_j)\upharpoonright_{\mathsf{d}(F_{\mathsf{s}(j,i)})} \\
w_j\upharpoonright_{\mathsf{d}(H_j)}\upharpoonright_{R_j} &= w_j\upharpoonright_{\mathsf{d}(B_j)}\upharpoonright_{R_j} = (u_i \circ v_j)\upharpoonright_{R_j} \\
&= u_i\upharpoonright_{\mathsf{d}(F_i)} \circ v_j^R = s \circ t_i \circ v_j^R = s \circ r_j\upharpoonright_{R_j} = (s \circ r_j)\upharpoonright_{R_j}
\end{aligned}
$$

and therefore $w_j\restriction_{\mathsf{d}(H_j)} = s \circ r_j$ as required. □

We shall often use the two following consequences of the Substitution Lemma.

**Lemma 5.** *Given a proof $\mu$ of $(A_j^{u_j})_{j=1}^n \vdash A$ and a proof $\rho$ of $B^v \vdash A_i$ (for some $i \in \{1, \ldots, n\}$), there is a proof $\pi$ of $(A_j^{u_j})_{j=1}^{i-1}, B^{u_i \circ v}, (A_j^{u_j})_{j=i+1}^n \vdash A$ such that $\underline{\pi}_{\vec{x}} = \underline{\mu}_{\vec{x}}\left[\underline{\rho}_{x_i}/x_i\right]$*

*Proof.* By weakening we have a proof $\mu'$ of $(A_j^{u_j})_{j=1}^i, B\restriction_\emptyset^{0_{\mathsf{d}(A)}}, (A_j^{u_j})_{j=i+1}^n \vdash A$ such that $\underline{\mu'}_{\vec{x}} = \underline{\mu}_{(\vec{x})\setminus i+1}$ (where $\vec{x}$ is a list of pairwise distinct variables of length $n+1$), as well as a proof $\rho'$ of $(A_j\restriction_\emptyset^{0_{\mathsf{d}(A_i)}})_{j=1}^i, B^v, (A_j\restriction_\emptyset^{0_{\mathsf{d}(A_i)}})_{j=i+1}^n \vdash A_i$ such that $\underline{\rho'}_{\vec{x}} = \underline{\rho}_{x_{i+1}}$. By Lemma 4, we have a proof $\pi'$ of $(A_j^{u_j})_{j=1}^{i-1}, B^{u_i \circ v}, (A_j^{u_j})_{j=i+1}^n \vdash A$ which satisfies $\underline{\pi'}_{(\vec{x})\setminus i} = \underline{\mu'}_{\vec{x}}\left[\underline{\rho'}_{(\vec{x})\setminus i}/x_i\right] = \underline{\mu}_{\vec{x}}\left[\underline{\rho}_{x_i}/x_i\right]$. □

**Lemma 6.** *Given a proof $\mu$ of $A^v \vdash B$ and a proof $\rho$ of $(A_j^{u_j})_{j=1}^n \vdash A$, there is a proof $\pi$ of $(A_j^{v \circ u_j})_{j=1}^n \vdash B$ such that $\underline{\pi}_{\vec{x}} = \underline{\mu}_x\left[\underline{\rho}_{\vec{x}}/x\right]$.*

The proof is similar to the previous one.

If $A$ and $B$ are formulas such that $\underline{A} = \underline{B}$, $\mathsf{d}(A) = \mathsf{d}(B)$ and $\langle A \rangle = \langle B \rangle$, we say that $A$ and $B$ are similar and we write $A \sim B$. One fundamental property of our deduction system is that two formulas which represent the same family of intersection types are logically equivalent.

**Theorem 1.** *If $A \sim B$ then $A^{\mathsf{Id}} \vdash B$ with a proof $\pi$ such that $\underline{\pi}_x \sim_\eta x$.*

*Proof.* Assume that $A = \alpha[f]$, then we have $B = A$ and $A^{\mathsf{Id}} \vdash B$ is an axiom.

Assume that $A = (C \Rightarrow_u D)$ and $B = (E \Rightarrow_v F)$. We have $D \sim F$ and hence $D^{\mathsf{Id}} \vdash F$ with a proof $\rho$ such that $\underline{\rho}_x \sim_\eta x$. And there is a bijection $w : \mathsf{d}(E) \to \mathsf{d}(C)$ such that $w_*(E) \sim C$ and $u \circ w = v$. By inductive hypothesis we have a proof $\mu$ of $w_*(E)^{\mathsf{Id}} \vdash C$ such that $\underline{\mu}_y \sim_\eta y$, and hence using the axiom $E^w \vdash w_*(E)$ and Lemma 5 we have a proof $\mu'$ of $E^w \vdash C$ such that $\underline{\mu'}_x = \underline{\mu}_x$.

There is a proof $\pi^1$ of $(C \Rightarrow_u D)^{\mathsf{Id}}, C^u \vdash D$ such that $\underline{\pi^1}_{x,y} = (x)\,y$ (consider the two axioms $(C \Rightarrow_u D)^{\mathsf{Id}}, C\restriction_\emptyset^{0_{\mathsf{d}(D)}} \vdash C \Rightarrow_u D$ and $(C \Rightarrow_u D)\restriction_\emptyset^{0_{\mathsf{d}(C)}}, C^{\mathsf{Id}} \vdash C$ and use a $\Rightarrow$-elimination rule). So by Lemma 5 there is a proof $\pi^2$ of $(C \Rightarrow_u D)^{\mathsf{Id}}, E^{u \circ w} \vdash D$, that is of $(C \Rightarrow_u D)^{\mathsf{Id}}, E^v \vdash D$, such that $\underline{\pi^2}_{x,y} = (x)\,\underline{\mu}_y$. Applying Lemma 6 we get a proof $\pi^3$ of $(C \Rightarrow_u D)^{\mathsf{Id}}, E^v \vdash F$ such that $\underline{\pi^3}_{x,y} = \underline{\rho}_z\left[(x)\,\underline{\mu}_y/z\right]$. We get the expected proof $\pi$ by a $\Rightarrow$-introduction rule so that $\underline{\pi}_x = \lambda y\,\underline{\rho}_z\left[(x)\,\underline{\mu}_y/z\right]$. By inductive hypothesis $\underline{\pi}_x \sim_\eta x$. □

### 3.4 Relation between intersection types and $\mathsf{LJ}(I)$

Now we explain the precise connection between non-idempotent intersection types and our logical system $\mathsf{LJ}(I)$. This connection consists of two statements:

- the first one means that any proof of $\mathsf{LJ}(I)$ can be seen as a typing derivation in non-idempotent intersection types (soundness)
- and the second one means that any non-idempotent intersection typing can be seen as a derivation in $\mathsf{LJ}(I)$ (completeness).

**Theorem 2 (Soundness).** *Let $\pi$ be a deduction tree of the sequent $(A_i^{u_i})_{i=1}^n \vdash B$ and $\overrightarrow{x}$ a sequence of $n$ pairwise distinct variables. Then the $\lambda$-term $\underline{\pi}_{\overrightarrow{x}}$ satisfies $(x_i : \langle A_i^{u_i}\rangle_j : \underline{A_i})_{i=1}^n \vdash \underline{\pi}_{\overrightarrow{x}} : \langle B\rangle_j : \underline{B}$ in the intersection type system, for each $j \in \mathsf{d}(B)$.*

*Proof.* We prove the first part by induction on $\pi$ (in the course of this induction, we recall the precise definition of $\underline{\pi}_{\overrightarrow{x}}$). If $\pi$ is the proof

$$\frac{q \neq i \Rightarrow \mathsf{d}(A_q) = \emptyset \text{ and } u_i \text{ is a bijection}}{(A_q^{u_q})_{q=1}^n \vdash u_{i*}(A_i)}$$

(so that $B = u_{i*}(A_i)$) then $\underline{\pi}_{\overrightarrow{x}} = x_i$. We have $\langle A_q^{u_q}\rangle_j = [\,]$ if $q \neq i$, $\langle A_i^{u_i}\rangle_j = [\,\langle A_i\rangle_{u_i^{-1}(j)}\,]$ and $\langle u_{i*}(A_i)\rangle_j = \langle A_i\rangle_{u_i^{-1}(j)}$. It follows that $(x_q : \langle A_q^{u_q}\rangle_j : \underline{A_q})_{q=1}^n \vdash x_i : \langle B\rangle_j : \underline{B}$ is a valid axiom in the intersection type system.

Assume that $\pi$ is the proof

$$\frac{\begin{array}{c}\pi^0 \\ A_1^{u_1}, \ldots, A_n^{u_n}, A^u \vdash B\end{array}}{A_1^{u_1}, \ldots, A_n^{u_n} \vdash A \Rightarrow_u B}$$

where $\pi^0$ is the proof of the premise of the last rule of $\pi$. By inductive hypothesis the $\lambda$-term $\underline{\pi^0}_{\overrightarrow{x},x}$ satisfies $(x_i : \langle A_i^{u_i}\rangle_j : \underline{A_i})_{i=1}^n, x : \langle A^u\rangle_j : \underline{A} \vdash \underline{\pi^0}_{\overrightarrow{x},x} : \langle B\rangle_j : \underline{B}$ from which we deduce $(x_i : \langle A_i^{u_i}\rangle_j : \underline{A_i})_{i=1}^n \vdash \lambda x^{\underline{A}}\, \underline{\pi^0}_{\overrightarrow{x},x} : (\langle A^u\rangle_j, \langle B\rangle_j) : \underline{A} \Rightarrow \underline{B}$ which is the required judgment since $\underline{\pi}_{\overrightarrow{x}} = \lambda x^{\underline{A}}\, \underline{\pi^0}_{\overrightarrow{x},x}$ and $(\langle A_i^{u_i}\rangle_j, \langle B\rangle_j) = \langle A \Rightarrow_u B\rangle_j$ as easily checked.

Assume last that $\pi$ ends with

$$\frac{\begin{array}{c}\pi^1 \\ C_1^{u_1}, \ldots, C_n^{u_n} \vdash A \Rightarrow_u B\end{array} \qquad \begin{array}{c}\pi^2 \\ D_1^{v_1}, \ldots, D_n^{v_n} \vdash A\end{array}}{E_1^{w_1}, \ldots, E_n^{w_n} \vdash B}$$

with: for each $i = 1, \ldots, n$ there are two disjoint sets $L_i$ and $R_i$ such that $\mathsf{d}(E_i) = L_i + R_i$, $C_i = E_i \lceil_{L_i}$, $D_i = E_i \lceil_{R_i}$, $w_i \lceil_{L_i} = u_i$, and $w_i \lceil_{R_i} = u \circ v_i$.

Let $j \in \mathsf{d}(B)$. By inductive hypothesis, the judgment $(x_i : \langle C_i^{u_i}\rangle_j : \underline{C_i})_{i=1}^n \vdash \underline{\pi^1}_{\overrightarrow{x}} : \langle A \Rightarrow_u B\rangle_j : \underline{A} \Rightarrow \underline{B}$ is derivable in the intersection type system. Let $K_j = u^{-1}(\{j\})$, which is a finite subset of $\mathsf{d}(A)$. By inductive hypothesis again, for each $k \in K_j$ we have $(x_i : \langle D_i^{u_i} \rangle_k : \underline{D_i})_{i=1}^n \vdash \underline{\pi^2}_{\vec{x}} : \langle A \rangle_k : \underline{A}$. Now observe that $\langle A \Rightarrow_u B \rangle_j = ([\, \langle A \rangle_k \mid k \in K_j \,], \langle B \rangle_j)$ so that

$$(x_i : \langle C_i^{u_i} \rangle_j + \sum_{k \in K_j} \langle D_i^{u_i} \rangle_k : \underline{E_i})_{i=1}^n \vdash (\underline{\pi^1}_{\vec{x}})\, \underline{\pi^2}_{\vec{x}} : \langle B \rangle_j : \underline{B}$$

is derivable in intersection types (remember that $\underline{C_i} = \underline{D_i} = \underline{E_i}$). Since $\underline{\pi}_{\vec{x}} = (\underline{\pi^1}_{\vec{x}})\, \underline{\pi^2}_{\vec{x}}$ it will be sufficient to prove that

$$\langle E_i^{w_i} \rangle_j = \langle C_i^{u_i} \rangle_j + \sum_{k \in K_j} \langle D_i^{v_i} \rangle_k \,. \tag{2}$$

For this, since $\langle E_i^{w_i} \rangle_j = [\, \langle E_i \rangle_l \mid w_i(l) = j \,]$, consider an element $l$ of $\mathsf{d}(E_i)$ such that $w_i(l) = j$. There are two possibilities: (1) either $l \in L_i$ and in that case we know that $\langle E_i \rangle_l = \langle C_i \rangle_l$ since $E_i \!\upharpoonright_{L_i} = C_i$ and moreover we have $u_i(l) = w_i(l) = j$ (2) or $l \in R_i$. In that case we have $\langle E_i \rangle_l = \langle D_i \rangle_l$ since $E_i \!\upharpoonright_{R_i} = D_i$. Moreover $u(v_i(l)) = w_i(l) = j$ and hence $v_i(l) \in K_j$. Therefore

$$[\, \langle E_i \rangle_l \mid l \in L_i \text{ and } w_i(l) = j \,] = [\, \langle C_i \rangle_l \mid u_i(l) = j \,] = \langle C_i^{u_i} \rangle_j$$
$$[\, \langle E_i \rangle_l \mid l \in R_i \text{ and } w_i(l) = j \,] = [\, \langle D_i \rangle_l \mid v_i(l) \in K_j \,] = \sum_{k \in K_j} \langle D_i^{v_i} \rangle_k$$

and (2) follows. □

**Theorem 3 (Completeness).** *Let $J \subseteq I$. Let $M$ be a $\lambda$-term and $x_1, \ldots, x_n$ be pairwise distinct variables, such that $(x_i : m_i^j : \sigma_i)_{i=1}^n \vdash M : b_j : \tau$ in the intersection type system for all $j \in J$. Let $A_1, \ldots, A_n$ and $B$ be formulas and let $u_1, \ldots, u_n$ be almost injective functions such that $u_i : \mathsf{d}(A_i) \to J = \mathsf{d}(B)$. Assume also that $\underline{A_i} = \sigma_i$ for each $i = 1, \ldots, n$ and that $\underline{B} = \tau$. Last assume that, for all $j \in J$, one has $\langle B \rangle_j = b_j$ and $\langle A_i^{u_i} \rangle_j = m_i^j$ for $i = 1, \ldots, n$. Then the judgment $(A_i^{u_i})_{i=1}^n \vdash B$ has a proof $\pi$ such that $\underline{\pi}_{\vec{x}} \sim_\eta M$.*

*Proof.* By induction on $M$. Assume first that $M = x_i$ for some $i \in \{1, \ldots, n\}$. Then we must have $\tau = \sigma_i$, $m_q^j = [\,]$ for $q \neq i$ and $m_i^j = [\, b_j \,]$ for all $j \in J$. Therefore $\mathsf{d}(A_q) = \emptyset$ and $u_q$ is the empty function for $q \neq i$, $u_i$ is a bijection $\mathsf{d}(A_i) \to J$ and $\forall k \in \mathsf{d}(A_i)\ \langle A_i \rangle_k = b_{u_i(k)}$, in other words $u_{i*}(A_i) \sim B$. By Theorem 1 we know that the judgment $(u_{i*}(A_i))^{\mathsf{Id}} \vdash B$ is provable in $\mathsf{LJ}(I)$ with a proof $\rho$ such that $\underline{\rho}_x \sim_\eta x$. We have a proof $\theta$ of $(A_i^{u_i})_{i=1}^n \vdash u_{i*}(A_i)$ which consists of an axiom so that $\underline{\theta}_{\vec{x}} = x_i$ and hence by Lemma 6 we have a proof $\pi$ of $(A_i^{u_i})_{i=1}^n \vdash B$ such that $\underline{\pi}_{\vec{x}} = \underline{\rho}_x\, [\underline{\theta}_{\vec{x}}/x] \sim_\eta x_i$.

Assume that $M = \lambda x^\sigma\, N$, that $\tau = (\sigma \Rightarrow \varphi)$ and that we have a family of deductions (for $j \in J$) of $(x_i : m_i^j : \sigma_i)_{i=1}^n \vdash M : (m^j, c_j) : \sigma \Rightarrow \varphi$ with $b_j = (m^j, c_j)$ and the premise of this conclusion in each of these deductions is $(x_i : m_i^j : \sigma_i)_{i=1}^n, x : m^j : \sigma \vdash N : c_j : \varphi$. We must have $B = (C \Rightarrow_u D)$ with $\underline{D} = \varphi$, $\underline{C} = \sigma$, $\mathsf{d}(D) = J$, $u : \mathsf{d}(C) \to \mathsf{d}(D)$ almost injective, $\langle D \rangle_j = c_j$ and

$[\langle C\rangle_k \mid k \in \mathsf{d}(C) \text{ and } u(k)=j] = m^j$, that is $\langle C^u\rangle_j = m^j$, for each $j \in J$. By inductive hypothesis we have a proof $\rho$ of $(A_i^{u_i})_{i=1}^n, C^u \vdash D$ such that $\underline{\rho_{\vec{x},x}} \sim_\eta N$ from which we obtain a proof $\pi$ of $(A_i^{u_i})_{i=1}^n \vdash C \Rightarrow_u D$ such that $\underline{\pi_{\vec{x}}} = \lambda x^\sigma\, \underline{\rho_{\vec{x},x}} \sim_\eta M$ as expected.

Assume last that $M = (N)\,P$ and that we have a $J$-indexed family of deductions $(x_i : m_i^j : \sigma_i)_{i=1}^n \vdash M : b_j : \tau$. Let $A_1,\dots,A_n$, $u_1,\dots,u_n$ and $B$ be $\mathsf{LJ}(I)$ formulas and almost injective functions as in the statement of the theorem.

Let $j \in J$. There is a finite set $L_j \subseteq I$ and multisets $m_i^{j,0}$, $(m_i^{j,l})_{l\in L_j}$ such that we have deductions[7] of $(x_i : m_i^{j,0} : \sigma_i)_{i=1}^n \vdash N : ([\,a_l^j \mid l \in L_j\,], b_j) : \sigma \Rightarrow \tau$ and, for each $l \in L_j$, of $(x_i : m_i^{j,l} : \sigma_i)_{i=1}^n \vdash P : a_l^j : \sigma$ with

$$m_i^j = m_i^{j,0} + \sum_{l\in L_j} m_i^{j,l}\,. \tag{3}$$

We assume the finite sets $L_j$ to be pairwise disjoint (this is possible because $I$ is infinite) and we use $L$ for their union. Let $u : L \to J$ be the function which maps $l \in L$ to the unique $j$ such that $l \in L_j$, this function is almost injective. Let $A$ be an $\mathsf{LL}(J)$ formula such that $\underline{A} = \sigma$, $\mathsf{d}(A) = L$ and $\langle A\rangle_l = a_l^{u(l)}$; such a formula exists by Proposition 1.

Let $i \in \{1,\dots,n\}$. For each $j \in J$ we know that

$$[\,\langle A_i\rangle_r \mid r \in \mathsf{d}(A_i) \text{ and } u_i(r) = j\,] = m_i^j = m_i^{j,0} + \sum_{l\in L_j} m_i^{j,l}$$

and hence we can split the set $\mathsf{d}(A_i) \cap {u_i}^{-1}(\{j\})$ into disjoint subsets $R_i^{j,0}$ and $(R_i^{j,l})_{l\in L_j}$ in such a way that

$$[\,\langle A_i\rangle_r \mid r \in R_i^{j,0}\,] = m_i^{j,0} \quad \text{and} \quad \forall l \in L_j\ [\,\langle A_i\rangle_r \mid r \in R_i^{j,l}\,] = m_i^{j,l}\,.$$

We set $R_i^0 = \bigcup_{j\in J} R_i^{j,0}$; observe that this is a disjoint union because $R_i^{j,0} \subseteq {u_i}^{-1}(\{j\})$. Similarly we define $R_i^1 = \bigcup_{l\in L} R_i^{u(l),l}$ which is a disjoint union for the following reason: if $l, l' \in L$ satisfy $u(l) = u(l') = j$ then $R_i^{j,l}$ and $R_i^{j,l'}$ have been chosen disjoint and if $u(l) = j$ and $u(l') = j'$ with $j \neq j'$ we have $R_i^{j,l} \subseteq {u_i}^{-1}\{j\}$ and $R_i^{j',l'} \subseteq {u_i}^{-1}(\{j'\})$. Let $v_i : R_i^1 \to L$ be defined by: $v_i(r)$ is the unique $l \in L$ such that $r \in R_i^{u(l),l}$. Since each $R_i^{j,l}$ is finite the function $v_i$ is almost injective. Moreover $u \circ v_i = u_i\lceil_{R_i^1}$.

We use $u_i'$ for the restriction of $u_i$ to $R_i^0$ so that $u_i' : R_i^0 \to J$. By inductive hypothesis we have $((A_i\lceil_{R_i^0})^{u_i'})_{i=1}^n \vdash A \Rightarrow_u B$ with a proof $\mu$ such that $\underline{\mu_{\vec{x}}} \sim_\eta N$. Indeed $[\,\langle A_i\lceil_{R_i^0}\rangle_r \mid r \in R_i^0 \text{ and } u_i'(r) = j\,] = m_i^{j,0}$ and $\langle A \Rightarrow_u B\rangle_j = ([\,a_l^j \mid u(l) = j\,], b_j)$ for each $j \in J$. For the same reason we have $((A_i\lceil_{R_i^1})^{v_i})_{i=1}^n \vdash A$ with a proof $\rho$ such that $\underline{\rho_{\vec{x}}} \sim_\eta P$. Indeed for each $l \in L = \mathsf{d}(A)$ we have

[7] Notice that our $\lambda$-calculus is in *Church style* and hence the type $\sigma$ is uniquely determined by the sub-term $N$ of $M$.

$[\langle A_i \upharpoonright_{R_i^1} \rangle_r \mid v_i(r) = l] = m_i^{j,l}$ and $\langle A \rangle_l = a_l^j$ where $j = u(l)$. By an application rule we get a proof $\pi$ of $(A_i^{u_i})_{i=1}^n \vdash B$ such that $\underline{\pi}_{\vec{x}} = \left(\underline{\mu}_{\vec{x}}\right) \underline{\rho}_{\vec{x}} \sim_\eta (N) P = M$ as contended. □

# 4 The untyped Scott case

Since intersection types usually apply to the pure $\lambda$-calculus, we move now to this setting by choosing in $\mathbf{Rel}_!$ the set $\mathsf{R}_\infty$ as model of the pure $\lambda$-calculus. The $\mathsf{R}_\infty$ intersection typing system has the elements of $\mathsf{R}_\infty$ as types, and the typing rules involve sequents of shape $(x_i : m_i)_{i=1}^n \vdash M : a$ where $m_i \in \mathcal{M}_{\mathrm{fin}}(\mathsf{R}_\infty)$ and $a \in \mathsf{R}_\infty$.

We use $\Lambda$ for the set of terms of the pure $\lambda$-calculus, and $\Lambda_\Omega$ as the pure $\lambda$-calculus extended with a constant $\Omega$ subject to the two following $\rightsquigarrow_\omega$ reduction rules: $\lambda x\, \Omega \rightsquigarrow_\omega \Omega$ and $(\Omega)\, M \rightsquigarrow_\omega \Omega$. We use $\sim_{\eta\omega}$ for the least congruence on $\Lambda_\Omega$ which contains $\rightsquigarrow_\eta$ and $\rightsquigarrow_\omega$ and similarly for $\sim_{\beta\eta\omega}$. We define a family $(\mathcal{H}(x))_{x \in \mathcal{V}}$ of subsets of $\Lambda_\Omega$ minimal such that, for any sequence $\vec{x} = (x_1, \dots, x_n)$ and $\vec{y} = (y_1, \dots, y_k)$ such that $\vec{x}, \vec{y}$ is repetition-free, and for any terms $M_i \in \mathcal{H}(x_i)$ (for $i = 1, \dots, n$), one has $\lambda\vec{x}\, \lambda\vec{y}\, (x)\, M_1 \cdots M_n\, O_1 \cdots O_l \in \mathcal{H}(x)$ where $O_j \sim_\omega \Omega$ for $j = 1, \dots, l$. Notice that $x \in \mathcal{H}(x)$.

The typing rules of $\mathsf{R}_\infty$ are

$$\frac{}{x_1 : [\,], \dots, x_i : [\,a\,], \dots, x_n : [\,] \vdash x_i : a} \qquad \frac{\Phi, x : m \vdash M : a}{\Phi \vdash \lambda x\, M : (m, a)}$$

$$\frac{\Phi \vdash M : ([\,a_1, \dots, a_k\,], b) \qquad (\Phi_j \vdash N : a_j)_{j=1}^k}{\Phi + \sum_{j=1}^k \Phi_j \vdash (M)\, N : b}$$

where we use the following convention: when we write $\Phi + \Psi$ it is assumed that $\Phi$ is of shape $(x_i : m_i)_{i=1}^n$ and $\Psi$ is of shape $(x_i : p_i)_{i=1}^n$, and then $\Phi + \Psi$ is $(x_i : m_i + p_i)_{i=1}^n$. This typing system is just a "proof-theoretic" rephrasing of the denotational semantics of the terms of $\Lambda_\Omega$ in $\mathsf{R}_\infty$.

**Proposition 2.** *Let $M, M' \in \Lambda_\Omega$ and $\vec{x} = (x_1, \dots, x_n)$ be a list of pairwise distinct variables containing all the free variables of $M$ and $M'$. Let $m_i \in \mathcal{M}_{\mathrm{fin}}(\mathsf{R}_\infty)$ for $i = 1, \dots, n$ and $b \in \mathsf{R}_\infty$. If $M \sim_{\beta\eta\omega} M'$ then $(x_i : m_i)_{i=1}^n \vdash M : b$ iff $(x_i : m_i)_{i=1}^n \vdash M' : b$.*

## 4.1 Formulas

We define the associated formulas as follows, each formula $A$ being given together with $\mathsf{d}(A) \subseteq I$ and $\langle A \rangle \in \mathsf{R}_\infty^{\mathsf{d}(A)}$.

- If $J \subseteq I$ then $\varepsilon_J$ is a formula with $\mathsf{d}(\varepsilon_J) = J$ and $\langle \varepsilon_J \rangle_j = \mathsf{e}$ for $j \in J$
- and if $A$ and $B$ are formulas and $u : \mathsf{d}(A) \to \mathsf{d}(B)$ is almost injective then $A \Rightarrow_u B$ is a formula with $\mathsf{d}(A \Rightarrow_u B) = \mathsf{d}(B)$ and $\langle A \Rightarrow_u B \rangle_j = ([\,\langle A \rangle_k \mid u(k) = j\,], \langle B \rangle_j) \in \mathsf{R}_\infty$.

We can consider that there is a type $\mathsf{o}$ of pure $\lambda$-terms interpreted as $\mathsf{R}_\infty$ in **Rel**$_!$, such that $(\mathsf{o} \Rightarrow \mathsf{o}) = \mathsf{o}$, and then for any formula $A$ we have $\underline{A} = \mathsf{o}$.

Operations of restriction and relocation of formulas are the same as in Section 3 (setting $\varepsilon_J \upharpoonright_K = \varepsilon_{J \cap K}$) and satisfy the same properties, for instance $\langle A \upharpoonright_K \rangle = \langle A \rangle \upharpoonright_K$ and one sets $u_*(\varepsilon_J) = \varepsilon_K$ if $u : J \to K$ is a bijection.

The deduction rules are exactly the same as those of Section 3, plus the axiom $\vdash \varepsilon_\emptyset$. With any deduction $\pi$ of $(A_i^{u_i})_{i=1}^n \vdash B$ and sequence $\overrightarrow{x} = (x_1, \ldots, x_n)$ of pairwise distinct variables, we can associate a *pure* $\underline{\pi}_{\overrightarrow{x}} \in \Lambda_\Omega$ defined exactly as in Section 3 (just drop the types associated with variables in abstractions). If $\pi$ consists of an instance of the additional axiom, we set $\underline{\pi}_{\overrightarrow{x}} = \Omega$.

**Lemma 7.** *Let $A, A_1, \ldots, A_n$ be a formula such that $\mathsf{d}(A) = \mathsf{d}(A_i) = \emptyset$. Then $(A_i^{0_\emptyset})_{i=1}^n \vdash A$ is provable by a proof $\pi$ which satisfies $\underline{\pi}_{x_1,\ldots,x_k} \sim_\omega \Omega$.*

The proof is a straightforward induction on $A$ using the additional axiom, Lemma 1 and the observations that if $\mathsf{d}(B \Rightarrow_u C) = \emptyset$ then $u = 0_\emptyset$.

One can easily define a size function $\mathsf{sz} : \mathsf{R}_\infty \to \mathbb{N}$ such that $\mathsf{sz}(\mathsf{e}) = 0$ and $\mathsf{sz}([\, a_1, \ldots, a_k \,], a) = \mathsf{sz}(a) + \sum_{i=1}^k (1 + \mathsf{sz}(a_i))$. First we have to prove an adapted version of Proposition 1; here it will be restricted to finite sets.

**Proposition 3.** *Let $J$ be a finite subset of $I$ and $f \in \mathsf{R}_\infty^J$. There is a formula $A$ such that $\mathsf{d}(A) = J$ and $\langle A \rangle = f$.*

*Proof.* Observe that, since $J$ is finite, there is an $N \in \mathbb{N}$ such that $\forall j \in J\ \forall q \in \mathbb{N}\ q \geq N \Rightarrow f(j)_q = [\,]$ (remember that $f(j) \in \mathcal{M}_{\mathrm{fin}}(\mathsf{R}_\infty)^{\mathbb{N}}$). Let $N(f)$ be the least such $N$. We set $\mathsf{sz}(f) = \sum_{j \in J} \mathsf{sz}(f(j))$ and the proof is by induction on $(\mathsf{sz}(f), N(f))$ lexicographically.

If $\mathsf{sz}(f) = 0$ this means that $f(j) = \mathsf{e}$ for all $j \in J$ and hence we can take $A = \varepsilon_J$. Assume that $\mathsf{sz}(f) > 0$, one can write[8] $f(j) = (m_j, a_j)$ with $m_j \in \mathcal{M}_{\mathrm{fin}}(\mathsf{R}_\infty)$ and $a_j \in \mathsf{R}_\infty$ for each $j \in J$. Just as in the proof of Proposition 1 we choose a set $K$, a function $g : K \to \mathsf{R}_\infty$ and an almost injective function $u : K \to J$ such that $m_j = [\, g(k) \mid u(k) = j \,]$. The set $K$ is finite since $J$ is and we have $\mathsf{sz}(g) < \mathsf{sz}(f)$ because $\mathsf{sz}(f) > 0$. Therefore by inductive hypothesis there is a formula $B$ such that $\mathsf{d}(B) = K$ and $\langle B \rangle = g$. Let $f' : J \to \mathsf{R}_\infty$ defined by $f'(j) = a_j$, we have $\mathsf{sz}(f') \leq \mathsf{sz}(f)$ and $N(f') < N(f)$ and hence by inductive hypothesis there is a formula $C$ such that $\langle C \rangle = f$. We set $A = (B \Rightarrow_u C)$ which satisfies $\langle A \rangle = f$ as required. □

Theorem 1 still holds up to some mild adaptation. First notice that $A \sim B$ simply means now that $\mathsf{d}(A) = \mathsf{d}(B)$ and $\langle A \rangle = \langle B \rangle$.

**Theorem 4.** *If $A$ and $B$ are such that $A \sim B$ then $A^{\mathsf{Id}} \vdash B$ with a proof $\pi$ which satisfies $\underline{\pi}_x \in \mathcal{H}(x)$.*

[8] This is also possible if $\mathsf{sz}(f) = 0$ actually.

*Proof.* By induction on the sum of the sizes of $A$ and $B$. Assume that $A = \varepsilon_J$ so that $\mathsf{d}(B) = J$ and $\forall j \in J\ \langle B\rangle_j = \mathsf{e}$. There are two cases as to $B$. In the first case $B$ is of shape $\varepsilon_K$ but then we must have $K = J$ and we can take for $\pi$ an axiom so that $\underline{\pi}_x = x \in \mathcal{H}(x)$. Otherwise we have $B = (C \Rightarrow_u D)$ with $\mathsf{d}(D) = J$, $\forall j \in J\ \langle D\rangle_j = \mathsf{e}$ and $\mathsf{d}(C) = \emptyset$, so that $u = 0_J$. We have $A \sim D$ and hence by inductive hypothesis we have a proof $\rho$ of $A^{\mathsf{Id}} \vdash D$ such that $\underline{\rho}_x \in \mathcal{H}(x)$. By weakening and $\Rightarrow$-introduction we get a proof $\pi$ of $A^{\mathsf{Id}} \vdash B$ which satisfies $\underline{\pi}_x = \lambda y\, \underline{\rho}_x \in \mathcal{H}(x)$.

Assume that $A = (C \Rightarrow_u D)$. If $B = \varepsilon_J$ then we must have $\mathsf{d}(C) = \emptyset$, $u = 0_J$ and $D \sim B$ and hence by inductive hypothesis we have a proof $\rho$ of $D^{\mathsf{Id}} \vdash B$ such that $\underline{\rho}_x \in \mathcal{H}(x)$. By Lemma 7 there is a proof $\theta$ of $\vdash C$ such that $\underline{\theta} \sim_\omega \Omega$. Hence there is a proof $\pi$ of $A^{\mathsf{Id}} \vdash B$ such that $\underline{\pi}_x = \underline{\rho}_y\, [(x)\, \underline{\theta}/y] \in \mathcal{H}(x)$.

Assume last that $B = (E \Rightarrow_v F)$, then we must have $D \sim F$ and there must be a bijection $w : \mathsf{d}(E) \to \mathsf{d}(C)$ such that $u \circ w = v$ and $w_*(E) \sim C$. We reason as in the proof of Lemma 1: by inductive hypothesis we have a proof $\rho$ of $D^{\mathsf{Id}} \vdash F$ and a proof $\mu$ of $w_*(E)^{\mathsf{Id}} \vdash C$ from which we build a proof $\pi$ of $A^{\mathsf{Id}} \vdash B$ such that $\underline{\pi}_x = \lambda y\, \underline{\rho}_z \left[(x)\, \underline{\mu}_y/z\right] \in \mathcal{H}(x)$ by inductive hypothesis. □

**Theorem 5 (Soundness).** *Let $\pi$ be a deduction tree of $A_1^{u_1}, \dots, A_n^{u_n} \vdash B$ and $\overrightarrow{x}$ a sequence of $n$ pairwise distinct variables. Then the $\lambda$-term $\underline{\pi}_{\overrightarrow{x}} \in \Lambda_\Omega$ satisfies $(x_i : \langle A_i^{u_i}\rangle_j)_{i=1}^n \vdash \underline{\pi}_{\overrightarrow{x}} : \langle B\rangle_j$ in the $\mathsf{R}_\infty$ intersection type system, for each $j \in \mathsf{d}(B)$.*

The proof is exactly the same as that of Theorem 2, dropping all simple types.

For all $\lambda$-term $M \in \Lambda$, we define $\mathcal{H}_\Omega(M)$ as the least subset of element of $\Lambda_\Omega$ such that:

- if $O \in \Lambda_\Omega$ and $O \sim_\omega \Omega$ then $O \in \mathcal{H}_\Omega(M)$ for all $M \in \Lambda$
- if $M = x$ then $\mathcal{H}(x) \subseteq \mathcal{H}_\Omega(M)$
- if $M = \lambda y\, N$ and $N' \in \mathcal{H}_\Omega(N)$ then $\lambda y\, N' \in \mathcal{H}_\Omega(M)$
- if $M = (N)\, P$, $N' \in \mathcal{H}_\Omega(N)$ and $P' \in \mathcal{H}_\Omega(P)$ then $(N')\, P' \in \mathcal{H}_\Omega(M)$.

The elements of $\mathcal{H}_\Omega(M)$ can probably be seen as approximates of $M$.

**Theorem 6 (Completeness).** *Let $J \subseteq I$ be finite. Let $M \in \Lambda_\Omega$ and $x_1, \dots, x_n$ be pairwise distinct variables, such that $(x_i : m_i^j)_{i=1}^n \vdash M : b_j$ in the $\mathsf{R}_\infty$ intersection type system for all $j \in J$. Let $A_1, \dots, A_n$ and $B$ be formulas and let $u_1, \dots, u_n$ be almost injective functions such that $u_i : \mathsf{d}(A_i) \to J = \mathsf{d}(B)$. Assume also that, for all $j \in J$, one has $\langle B\rangle_j = b_j$ and $\langle A_i^{u_i}\rangle_j = m_i^j$ for $i = 1, \dots, n$. Then the judgment $A_1^{u_1}, \dots, A_n^{u_n} \vdash B$ has a proof $\pi$ such that $\underline{\pi}_{\overrightarrow{x}} \in \mathcal{H}_\Omega(M)$.*

The proof is very similar to that of Theorem 3.

## 5 Concluding remarks and acknowledgments

The results presented in this paper show that, at least in non-idempotent intersection types, the problem of knowing whether all elements of a given family of intersection types $(a_j)_{j\in J}$ are inhabited by a common $\lambda$-term can be reformulated logically: is it true that one (or equivalently, any) of the indexed formulas $A$ such that $\mathsf{d}(A) = J$ and $\forall j \in \langle A\rangle_j = a_j$ is provable in $\mathsf{LJ}(I)$? Such a strong connection between intersection and Indexed Linear Logic was already mentioned in the introduction of [2], but we never made it more explicit until now.

To conclude we propose a typed $\lambda$-calculus *à la Church* to denote proofs of the $\mathsf{LJ}(I)$ system of Section 4. The syntax of *pre-terms* is given by $s, t \ldots :=$ $x[J] \mid \lambda x : A^u\, s \mid (s)\, t$ where in $x[J]$, $x$ is a variable and $J \subseteq I$ and, in $\lambda x : A^u\, s$, $u$ is an almost injective function from $\mathsf{d}(A)$ to a set $J \subseteq I$. Given a pre-term $s$ and a variable $x$, the *domain of $x$ in $s$* is the subset $\mathsf{dom}(x, s)$ of $I$ given by $\mathsf{dom}(x, x[J]) = J$, $\mathsf{dom}(x, y[J]) = \emptyset$ if $y \neq x$, $\mathsf{dom}(x, \lambda y : A^u\, s) = \mathsf{dom}(x, s)$ (assuming of course $y \neq x$) and $\mathsf{dom}(x, (s)\, t) = \mathsf{dom}(x, s) \cup \mathsf{dom}(x, t)$. Then a pre-term $s$ is a term if any subterm of $t$ which is of shape $(s_1)\, s_2$ satisfies $\mathsf{dom}(x, s_1) \cap \mathsf{dom}(x, s_2) = \emptyset$ for all variable $x$. A typing judgment is an expression $(x_i : A_i^{u_i})_{i=1}^n \vdash s : B$ where the $x_i$'s are pairwise distinct variables, $s$ is a term and each $u_i$ is an almost injective function $\mathsf{d}(A_i) \to \mathsf{d}(B)$. The following typing rules exactly mimic the logical rules of $\mathsf{LJ}(I)$:

$$\frac{\mathsf{d}(A) = \emptyset}{((x_i : A_i^{0_\emptyset})_{i=1}^n) \vdash \Omega : A}$$

$$\frac{q \neq i \Rightarrow \mathsf{d}(A_i) = \emptyset \text{ and } u_i \text{ bijection}}{(x_q : A_q^{u_q})_{q=1}^n \vdash x_i[\mathsf{d}(A_i)] : u_{i*}(A_i)} \qquad \frac{(x_i : A_i^{u_i})_{i=1}^n, x : A^u \vdash s : B}{(x_i : A_i^{u_i})_{i=1}^n \vdash \lambda x : A^u\, s : A \Rightarrow_u B}$$

$$\frac{(x_i : A_i\lceil^{v_i}_{\mathsf{dom}(x_i,s)})_{i=1}^n \vdash s : A \Rightarrow_u B \qquad (x_i : A_i\lceil^{w_i}_{\mathsf{dom}(x_i,t)})_{i=1}^n \vdash t : A}{(x_i : A_i^{v_i + (u \circ w_i)})_{i=1}^n \vdash (s)\, t : B}$$

The properties of this calculus, and more specifically of its $\beta$-reduction, and its connections with the resource calculus of [9] will be explored in further work.

Another major objective will be to better understand the meaning of $\mathsf{LJ}(I)$ formulas, using ideas developed in [3] where a *phase semantics* is introduced and related to (non-uniform) coherence space semantics. In the intuitionistic present setting, it is tempting to look for Kripke-like interpretations with the hope of generalizing indexed logic beyond the (perhaps too) specific relational setting we started from.

Last, we would like to thank Luigi Liquori and Claude Stolze for many helpful discussions on intersection types and the referees for their careful reading and insightful comments and suggestions.

## References

1. F. Breuvart, G. Manzonetto, and D. Ruoppolo. Relational graph models at work. *Logical Methods in Computer Science*, 14(3), 2018.
2. A. Bucciarelli and T. Ehrhard. On phase semantics and denotational semantics in multiplicative-additive linear logic. *Annals of Pure and Applied Logic*, 102(3):247–282, 2000.

3. A. Bucciarelli and T. Ehrhard. On phase semantics and denotational semantics: the exponentials. *Annals of Pure and Applied Logic*, 109(3):205–241, 2001.
4. M. Coppo and M. Dezani-Ciancaglini. An extension of the basic functionality theory for the λ-calculus. *Notre Dame Journal of Formal Logic*, 21(4):685–693, 1980.
5. M. Coppo, M. Dezani-Ciancaglini, and B. Venneri. Functional characters of solvable terms. *Mathematical Logic Quarterly*, 27(2-6):45–58, 1981.
6. D. de Carvalho. Execution time of lambda-terms via denotational semantics and intersection types. *CoRR*, abs/0905.4251, 2009.
7. D. de Carvalho. Execution time of λ-terms via denotational semantics and intersection types. *MSCS*, 28(7):1169–1203, 2018.
8. T. Ehrhard. The Scott model of linear logic is the extensional collapse of its relational model. *Theoretical Computer Science*, 424:20–45, 2012.
9. T. Ehrhard and L. Regnier. Uniformity and the Taylor expansion of ordinary lambda-terms. *Theoretical Computer Science*, 403(2-3):347–372, 2008.
10. T. S. Freeman and F. Pfenning. Refinement Types for ML. In D. S. Wise, editor, *Proceedings of the ACM SIGPLAN'91 Conference on Programming Language Design and Implementation (PLDI), Toronto, Ontario, Canada, June 26-28, 1991*, pages 268–277. ACM, 1991.
11. J.-Y. Girard. Normal functors, power series and the λ-calculus. *Annals of Pure and Applied Logic*, 37:129–177, 1988.
12. J. R. Hindley. Coppo-dezani types do not correspond to propositional logic. *Theoretical Computer Science*, 28:235–236, 1984.
13. J.-L. Krivine. *Lambda-Calculus, Types and Models*. Ellis Horwood Series in Computers and Their Applications. Ellis Horwood, 1993. Translation by René Cori from French 1990 edition (Masson).
14. L. Liquori and S. R. D. Rocca. Intersection-types à la Church. *Information and Computation*, 205(9):1371–1386, 2007.
15. L. Liquori and C. Stolze. The Delta-calculus: Syntax and Types. In H. Geuvers, editor, *4th International Conference on Formal Structures for Computation and Deduction, FSCD 2019, June 24-30, 2019, Dortmund, Germany.*, volume 131 of *LIPIcs*, pages 28:1–28:20. Schloss Dagstuhl - Leibniz-Zentrum fuer Informatik, 2019.

# 3

# Constructing Infinitary Quotient-Inductive Types

Marcelo P. Fiore, Andrew M. Pitts, and S. C. Steenkamp(✉)

Department of Computer Science and Technology
University of Cambridge, Cambridge CB3 0FD, UK
s.c.steenkamp@cl.cam.ac.uk

**Abstract** This paper introduces an expressive class of quotient-inductive types, called QW-types. We show that in dependent type theory with uniqueness of identity proofs, even the infinitary case of QW-types can be encoded using the combination of inductive-inductive definitions involving strictly positive occurrences of Hofmann-style quotient types, and Abel's size types. The latter, which provide a convenient constructive abstraction of what classically would be accomplished with transfinite ordinals, are used to prove termination of the recursive definitions of the elimination and computation properties of our encoding of QW-types. The development is formalized using the Agda theorem prover.

**Keywords:** dependent type theory · higher inductive types · inductive-inductive definitions · quotient types · sized types · category theory

## 1 Introduction

One of the key features of proof assistants based on dependent type theory such as Agda, Coq and Lean is their support for inductive definitions of families of types. Homotopy Type Theory [29] introduces a potentially very useful extension of the notion of inductive definition, the *higher inductive types* (HITs). To define an ordinary inductive type one declares how its elements are constructed. To define a HIT one not only declares element constructors, but also declares equality constructors in identity types (possibly iterated ones), specifying how the constructed elements and identities are to be equated. In this paper we work in a dependent type theory satisfying uniqueness of identity proofs (UIP), so that identity types are trivial in dimensions higher than one. Nevertheless, as Altenkirch and Kaposi [5] point out, HITs are still useful in such a one-dimensional setting. They introduce the term *quotient inductive type* (QIT) for this truncated form of HIT.

Figure 1 gives two examples of QITs, using Agda-style notation for dependent type theory; in particular, $\mathsf{Set}$ denotes a universe of types and $\equiv$ denotes the identity type. The first example specifies the element and equality constructors for the type $\mathsf{Bag}\,X$ of finite multisets of elements from a type $X$. The second example, adapted from [5], specifies the element and equality constructors for the type $\omega\mathsf{Tree}\,X$ of trees whose nodes are labelled with elements of $X$ and that have unordered countably infinite branching. Both examples illustrate the nice feature

Finite multisets:

$$
\begin{aligned}
&\mathsf{data}\ \mathsf{Bag}(X:\mathsf{Set}):\mathsf{Set}\ \mathsf{where}\\
&\quad [] : \mathsf{Bag}\,X\\
&\quad \_{::}\_ : X \to \mathsf{Bag}\,X \to \mathsf{Bag}\,X\\
&\quad \mathsf{swap} : (x\ y : X)(ys : \mathsf{Bag}\,X) \to x :: y :: ys \equiv y :: x :: ys
\end{aligned}
$$

Unordered countably branching trees (elements of $\mathsf{isIso}\,f$ witness that $f$ is a bijection):

$$
\begin{aligned}
&\mathsf{data}\ \omega\mathsf{Tree}(X:\mathsf{Set}):\mathsf{Set}\ \mathsf{where}\\
&\quad \mathsf{leaf} : \omega\mathsf{Tree}\,X\\
&\quad \mathsf{node} : X \to (\mathbb{N} \to \omega\mathsf{Tree}\,X) \to \omega\mathsf{Tree}\,X\\
&\quad \mathsf{perm} : (x : X)(f : \mathbb{N} \to \mathbb{N})(\_ : \mathsf{isIso}\,f)(g : \mathbb{N} \to \omega\mathsf{Tree}\,X) \to\\
&\qquad\qquad\qquad\qquad \mathsf{node}\,x\,g \equiv \mathsf{node}\,x\,(g \circ f)
\end{aligned}
$$

**Figure 1.** Two examples of QITs

of QITs that users only have to specify the particular identifications between data needed for their applications. Thus the standard property of equality that it is an equivalence relation respecting the constructors is inherited by construction from the usual properties of identity types, without the need to say so in the declaration of the QIT.

The second example also illustrates a more technical aspect of QITs, that they enable constructive versions of structures that classically use non-constructive choice principles. The first example in Figure 1 only involves element constructors of finite arity ([] is nullary and $x :: \_$ is unary) and consequently $\mathsf{Bag}\,X$ is isomorphic to the type obtained from the ordinary inductive type of finite lists over $X$ by quotienting by the congruence generated by swap. Of course this assumes, as we do in this paper, that the type theory comes with Hofmann-style *quotient types* [18, Section 3.2.6.1]. By contrast, the second example in the figure involves an element constructor with countably infinite arity. So if one first forms the ordinary inductive type of *ordered* countably branching trees (by dropping the equality constructor perm from the declaration) and then quotients by a suitable relation to get the equalities specified by perm, one needs the axiom of countable choice to be able to lift the node element constructor to the quotient; see [5, Section 2.2] for a detailed discussion. The construction of the Cauchy reals as a higher inductive-inductive type [29, Section 11.3] provides a similar, but more complicated example where use of countable choice is avoided. Such examples have led to the folklore that as far as constructive type theories go, infinitary QITs are more expressive than the combination of ordinary inductive (or inductive-recursive, or inductive-inductive) types with quotient types. In this paper we use Abel's *sized types* [2] to show that, for a wide class of QITs, this view is not justified. Thus we make two main contributions:

First we define a family of QITs called *QW-types* and give elimination and computation rules for them (Section 2). The usual W-types of Martin-Löf [22] are inductive types giving the algebraic terms over a possibly infinitary signature.

One specifies a QW-type by giving a family of equations between such terms. So such QITs give initial algebras for possibly infinitary algebraic theories. As we indicate in Section 3, they can encode a very wide range of examples of possibly infinitary quotient-inductive types, namely those that do not involve constructors taking previously constructed equalities as arguments (so do not cover the infinitary extension of the very general scheme considered by Dybjer and Moeneclaey [12]). In set theory with the Axiom of Choice (AC), QW-types can be constructed simply as Quotients of the underlying W-type—hence the name.

Secondly, we prove that contrary to expectation, without AC it is still possible to construct QW-types using quotients, but not simply by quotienting a W-type. Instead, the type to be quotiented and the relation by which to quotient are given simultaneously by definitions that refer to each other. Thus our construction (in Section 4) involves *inductive-inductive* definitions [15]. The elimination and computation functions which witness that the quotiented type correctly represents the required QW-type are defined recursively. In order to prove that our recursive definitions terminate we combine the use of inductive definitions involving strictly positive occurrences of quotient types with sized types (currently, we do not know whether it is possible to avoid sizing in favour of, say, a suitable well-founded termination ordering). Sized types provide a convenient constructive abstraction of what classically would be accomplished with sequences of transfinite ordinal length.

### The type theory in which we work

To present our results we need a version of Martin-Löf Type Theory with (1) uniqueness of identity proofs, (2) quotient types and hence also function extensionality, (3) inductive-inductive datatypes (with strictly positive occurrences of quotient types) and (4) sized types. Lean 3 provides (1) and (2) out of the box, but also the Axiom of Choice, unfortunately. Neither it, nor Coq provide (3) and (4). Agda provides (1) via unrestricted dependent pattern-matching, (2) via a combination of postulates and the rewriting mechanism of Cockx and Abel [8], (3) via its very liberal mechanism for mutual definitions and (4) thanks to the work of Abel [2]. Therefore we make use of the type theory implemented by Agda (version 2.6.0.1) to give formal proofs of our results. The Agda code can be found at DOI: 10.17863/CAM.48187. In this paper we describe the results informally, using Agda-style notation for dependent type theory. In particular we use Set to denote the universe at the lowest level of a countable hierarchy of (Russell-style) universes. We also use Agda's convention that an implicit argument of an operation can be made explicit by enclosing it in {braces}.

*Acknowledgement* We would like to acknowledge the contribution Ian Orton made to the initial development of the work described here. He and the first author supervised the third author's Master's dissertation *Quotient Inductive Types: A Schema, Encoding and Interpretation*, in which the notion of QW-type (there called a $W^+$-type) was introduced.

## 2 QW-types

We begin by recalling some facts about types of well-founded trees, the W-types of Martin-Löf [22]. We take *signatures* to be elements of the dependent product

$$\mathsf{Sig} = \textstyle\sum A : \mathsf{Set}, (A \to \mathsf{Set}) \tag{1}$$

So a signature is given by a pair $\Sigma = (A, B)$ consisting of a type $A : \mathsf{Set}$ and a family of types $B : A \to \mathsf{Set}$. Each such signature determines a polynomial endofunctor [1, 16] $\mathsf{S}\{\Sigma\} : \mathsf{Set} \to \mathsf{Set}$ whose value at $X : \mathsf{Set}$ is the following dependent product

$$\mathsf{S}\{\Sigma\}X = \textstyle\sum a : A, (B\,a \to X) \tag{2}$$

An $\mathsf{S}$-*algebra* is by definition an element of the dependent product

$$\mathsf{Alg}\{\Sigma\} = \textstyle\sum X : \mathsf{Set}, (\mathsf{S}\,X \to X) \tag{3}$$

S-algebra morphisms $(X, s) \to (X', s')$ are given by functions $h : X \to X'$ together with an element of the type

$$\mathsf{isHom}\,h = (a : A)(b : B\,a \to X) \to s'(a, h \circ b) \equiv h(s(a, b)) \tag{4}$$

Then the W-type $\mathsf{W}\{\Sigma\}$ determined by $\Sigma$ is the underlying type of an initial S-algebra. More generally, Dybjer [11] shows that the initial algebra of any non-nested, strictly positive endofunctor on $\mathsf{Set}$ is given by a W-type; and Abbott, Altenkirch, and Ghani [1] extend this to the case with nested uses of W-types as part of their work on containers. (These proofs take place in extensional type theory [22], but work just as well in the intensional type theory with uniqueness of identity proofs and function extensionality that we are using here.)

More concretely, given a signature $\Sigma = (A, B)$, if one thinks of elements $a : A$ as names of operation symbols whose (not necessarily finite) arity is given by the type $B\,a : \mathsf{Set}$, then the elements of $\mathsf{W}\{\Sigma\}$ represent the closed algebraic terms (i.e. well-founded trees) over the signature. From this point of view it is natural to consider not only closed terms solely built up from operations, but also open terms additionally built up with variables drawn from some type $X$. As well as allowing operators of possibly infinite arity, we also allow terms involving possibly infinitely many variables (the second example in Figure 1 involves such terms). Categorically, the type $\mathsf{T}\{\Sigma\}X$ of such open terms is the free S-algebra on $X$ and is another W-type, for the signature obtained from $\Sigma$ by adding the elements of $X$ as nullary operations. Nevertheless, it is convenient to give a direct inductive definition:

$$\begin{aligned} &\mathsf{data} : \mathsf{T}\{\Sigma : \mathsf{Sig}\}(X : \mathsf{Set}) : \mathsf{Set}\ \mathsf{where} \\ &\eta : X \to \mathsf{T}\,X \\ &\sigma : \mathsf{S}(\mathsf{T}\,X) \to \mathsf{T}\,X \end{aligned} \tag{5}$$

Given an S-algebra $(Y, s) : \mathsf{Alg}\{\Sigma\}$ and a function $f : X \to Y$, the unique morphism of S-algebras from the free S-algebra $(\mathsf{T}\,X, \sigma)$ on $X$ to $(Y, s)$ has underlying function $\mathsf{T}\,X \to Y$ mapping each $t : \mathsf{T}\,X$ to the element $t \gg\!= f$ in $Y$ defined[1] by recursion on the structure of $t$:

$$\begin{aligned} \eta\, x \gg\!= f &= f\, x \\ \sigma(a, b) \gg\!= f &= s(a, \lambda x \to b\, x \gg\!= f) \end{aligned} \tag{6}$$

As the notation suggests, $\gg\!=$ is the Kleisli lifting operation ("bind") for a monad structure on $\mathsf{T}$; indeed, it is the free monad on the endofunctor $\mathsf{S}$.

The notion of "QW-type" that we introduce in this section is obtained from that of W-type by considering not only the algebraic terms over a given signature, but also equations between terms. To code equations we use a type-theoretic rendering of a categorical notion of equational system introduced by Fiore and Hur, referred to as *term equational system* [14, Section 2] and as *monadic equational system* [13, Section 5], here instantiated to free monads on signatures.

**Definition 1.** *A* system of equations *over a signature* $\Sigma : \mathsf{Sig}$ *is specified by*

- *a type* $E : \mathsf{Set}$ *(whose elements* $e : E$ *name the equations)*
- *a family of types* $V : E \to \mathsf{Set}$ *(*$V\, e : \mathsf{Set}$ *contains the variables used in the equation named* $e : E$*)*
- *for each* $e : E$*, elements* $l\, e$ *and* $r\, e$ *of type* $\mathsf{T}(V\, e)$*, the free* $\mathsf{S}$*-algebra on* $V\, e$ *(the terms with variables from* $V\, e$ *that are equated by the equation named* $e$*).*

*Thus a system of equations over* $\Sigma$ *is an element of the dependent product*

$$\begin{aligned} \mathsf{Syseq}\{\Sigma\} = \textstyle\sum E : \mathsf{Set}, \textstyle\sum V : (E \to \mathsf{Set}), \\ ((e : E) \to \mathsf{T}(V\, e)) \times ((e : E) \to \mathsf{T}(V\, e)) \end{aligned} \tag{7}$$

*An* $\mathsf{S}\{\Sigma\}$*-algebra* $\mathsf{S}\,X \to X$ satisfies *the system of equations* $\varepsilon = (E, V, l, r) : \mathsf{Syseq}\{\Sigma\}$ *if there is an element of type*

$$\mathsf{Sat}\{\varepsilon\}X = (e : E)(\rho : V\, e \to X) \to ((l\, e) \gg\!= \rho) \equiv ((r\, e) \gg\!= \rho) \tag{8}$$

The category-theoretic view of QW-types is that they are simply $\mathsf{S}$-algebras that are initial among those satisfying a given system of equations:

**Definition 2.** *A* QW-type *for a signature* $\Sigma = (A, B) : \mathsf{Sig}$ *and system of equations* $\varepsilon = (E, V, l, r) : \mathsf{Syseq}\{\Sigma\}$ *is given by a type* $\mathsf{QW}\{\Sigma\}\{\varepsilon\} : \mathsf{Set}$ *equipped with an* $\mathsf{S}$*-algebra structure and a proof that it satisfies the equations*

$$\mathsf{qwintro} : \mathsf{S}(\mathsf{QW}) \to \mathsf{QW} \tag{9}$$

$$\mathsf{qwequ} : \mathsf{Sat}\{\varepsilon\}(\mathsf{QW}) \tag{10}$$

*together with functions that witness that it is the initial such algebra:*

$$\mathsf{qwrec} : (X : \mathsf{Set})(s : \mathsf{S}\,X \to X) \to \mathsf{Sat}\,X \to \mathsf{QW} \to X \tag{11}$$

$$\mathsf{qwrechom} : (X : \mathsf{Set})(s : \mathsf{S}\,X \to X)(p : \mathsf{Sat}\,X) \to \mathsf{isHom}(\mathsf{qwrec}\,X\, s\, p) \tag{12}$$

$$\begin{aligned} \mathsf{qwuniq} : (X : \mathsf{Set})(s : \mathsf{S}\,X \to X)(p : \mathsf{Sat}\,X)(f : \mathsf{QW} \to X) \to \\ \mathsf{isHom}\, f \to \mathsf{qwrec}\,X\, s\, p \equiv f \end{aligned} \tag{13}$$

[1] Note that the definition of $\gg\!=$ depends on the $\mathsf{S}$-algebra structure $s$; in Agda we use *instance arguments* to hide this dependence.

Given the definitions of $\mathsf{S}\{\Sigma\}$ in (2) and $\mathsf{Sat}\{\varepsilon\}$ in (8), properties (9) and (10) suggest that a QW-type is an instance of the notion of quotient-inductive type [5] with element constructor qwintro and equality constructor qwequ. For this to be so, $\mathsf{QW}\{\Sigma\}\{\varepsilon\}$ needs to have the requisite dependently-typed elimination and computation[2] properties for these element and equality constructors. As Proposition 1 below shows, these follow from (11)–(13), because we are working in a type theory with function extensionality (by virtue of assuming quotient types). To state the proposition we need a dependent version of (6). For each

$$\begin{aligned}&P : \mathsf{QW} \to \mathsf{Set}\\&p : (a : A)(b : B\,a \to \mathsf{QW}) \to ((x : B\,a) \to P(b\,x)) \to P(\mathsf{qwintro}(a, b))\end{aligned} \tag{14}$$

type $X$ : Set, function $f : X \to \sum x : \mathsf{QW}, P\,x$ and term $t : \mathsf{T}(X)$, we get an element $\mathsf{lift}\,P\,p\,f\,t : P(t \gg\!= \mathsf{fst} \circ f)$ defined by recursion on the structure of $t$:

$$\begin{aligned}\mathsf{lift}\,P\,p\,f\,(\eta\,x) &= \mathsf{snd}(f\,x)\\\mathsf{lift}\,P\,p\,f\,(\sigma(a, b)) &= p\,a\,(\lambda x \to b\,x \gg\!= (\mathsf{fst} \circ f))(\mathsf{lift}\,P\,p\,f \circ b)\end{aligned} \tag{15}$$

**Proposition 1.** *For a QW-type as in the above definition, given $P$ and $p$ as in* (14) *and a term of type*

$$(e : E)(f : V\,e \to \textstyle\sum x : \mathsf{QW}, P\,x) \to \mathsf{lift}\,P\,p\,f\,(l\,e) \equiv\equiv \mathsf{lift}\,P\,p\,f\,(r\,e) \tag{16}$$

*there are elimination and computation terms:*

$$\begin{aligned}&\mathsf{qwelim} : (x : \mathsf{QW}) \to P\,x\\&\mathsf{qwcomp} : (a : A)(b : B\,a \to \mathsf{QW}) \to \mathsf{qwelim}(\mathsf{qwintro}(a, b)) \equiv p\,a\,b\,(\mathsf{qwelim} \circ b)\end{aligned}$$

*(Note that* (16) *uses McBride's* heterogeneous *equality type [23], which we denote by $\equiv\equiv$, because* $\mathsf{lift}\,P\,p\,f\,(l\,e)$ *and* $\mathsf{lift}\,P\,p\,f\,(r\,e)$ *inhabit different types, namely* $P(l\,e \gg\!= \mathsf{fst} \circ f)$ *and* $P(r\,e \gg\!= \mathsf{fst} \circ f)$ *respectively.)* □

The proof of the proposition can be found in the accompanying Agda code (DOI: 10.17863/CAM.48187).

So QW-types are in particular quotient-inductive types (QITs). Conversely, in the next section we show that a wide range of QITs can be encoded as QW-types. Then in Section 4 we prove:

**Theorem 1.** *In constructive dependent type theory with uniqueness of identity proofs (or equivalently the Axiom K of Streicher [27]) and universes with inductive-inductive datatypes [15] permitting strictly positive occurrences of quotient types [18] and sized types [2], for every signature and system of equations (Definition 1) there is a QW-type as in Definition 2.*

---

[2] We only establish the computation property up to propositional rather than definitional equality; so, using the terminology of Shulman [25], these are *typal* quotient-inductive types.

*Remark 1 (Free algebras).* Definition 2 defines QW-types as *initial* algebras. A corollary of Theorem 1 is that *free-algebras* also exist. In other words, given a signature $\Sigma$ and a type $X$ : Set, there is an S-algebra

$$(\mathsf{F}\{\Sigma\}\{\varepsilon\}X\,,\ \mathsf{S}\{\Sigma\}(\mathsf{F}\{\Sigma\}\{\varepsilon\}X) \to \mathsf{F}\{\Sigma\}\{\varepsilon\}X)$$

satisfying a system of equations $\varepsilon$ and equipped with a function $X \to \mathsf{F}\{\Sigma\}\{\varepsilon\}X$, and which is universal among such S-algebras. Thus $\mathsf{QW}\{\Sigma\}\{\varepsilon\}$ is isomorphic to $\mathsf{F}\{\Sigma\}\{\varepsilon\}\varnothing$, where $\varnothing$ is the empty datatype.

To see that such free algebras can be constructed as QW-types, given a signature $\Sigma = (A, B)$, let $\Sigma_X$ be the signature $(X \uplus A, B')$, where $X \uplus A$ is the coproduct datatype (with constructors $\mathsf{inl} : X \to X \uplus A$ and $\mathsf{inr} : A \to X \uplus A$) and where $B' : X \uplus A \to \mathsf{Set}$ maps each $\mathsf{inl}\,x$ to $\varnothing$ and each $\mathsf{inr}\,a$ to $B\,a$. Given a system of equations $\varepsilon = (E, V, l, r)$, let $\varepsilon_X$ be the system $(E, V, l_X, r_X)$ where for each $e : E$, $l_X\,e = l\,e \ggg\!= \eta$ and $r_X\,e = r\,e \ggg\!= \eta$ (using $\eta : V\,e \to \mathsf{T}\{\Sigma_X\}(V\,e)$ as in (5) and the $\mathsf{S}\{\Sigma\}$-algebra structure $s$ on $\mathsf{T}\{\Sigma_X\}(V\,e)$ given by $s(a, b) = \sigma(\mathsf{inr}\,a, b)$). Then one can show that the QW-type $\mathsf{QW}\{\Sigma_X\}\{\varepsilon_X\}$ is the free algebra $\mathsf{F}\{\Sigma\}\{\varepsilon\}X$, with the function $X \to \mathsf{F}\{\Sigma\}\{\varepsilon\}X$ sending each $x : X$ to $\mathsf{qwintro}(\mathsf{inl}\,x, \_) : \mathsf{QW}\{\Sigma_X\}\{\varepsilon_X\}$, and the $\mathsf{S}\{\Sigma\}$-algebra structure on $\mathsf{F}\{\Sigma\}\{\varepsilon\}X$ being given by the function sending $(a, b) : \mathsf{S}(\mathsf{QW}\{\Sigma_X\}\{\varepsilon_X\})$ to $\mathsf{qwintro}(\mathsf{inr}\,a, b)$.

*Remark 2 (Strictly positive equational systems).* A very general, categorical notion of equational system was introduced by Fiore and Hur [14, Section 3]. They regard any endofunctor $S$ : Set $\to$ Set as a *functorial signature.* A *functorial term* over such a signature, $S \rhd G \vdash L$, is specified by another functorial signature $G$ : Set $\to$ Set (the term's context) together with a functor $L$ from $S$-algebras to $G$-algebras that commutes with the forgetful functors to Set. Then an *equational system* is given by a pair of such terms in the same context, $S \rhd G \vdash L$ and $S \rhd G \vdash R$ say. An $S$-algebra $s : S\,X \to X$ satisfies the equational system if $L(X, s)$ and $R(X, s)$ are equal $G$-algebras.

Taking the *strictly positive* endofunctors Set $\to$ Set to be the smallest collection containing the identity and constant endofunctors and closed under forming dependent products and dependent functions over fixed types then, as in [11] (and also in the type theory in which we work), up to isomorphism every such endofunctor is of the form $\mathsf{S}\{\Sigma\}$ for some signature $\Sigma$ : Sig. If we restrict attention to equational systems $S \rhd G \vdash L, R$ with $S$ and $G$ strictly positive, then it turns out that such equational systems are in bijection with the systems of equations from Definition 1, and the two notions of satisfaction for an algebra coincide in that case. (See our Agda development for a proof of this.) So Dybjer's characterisation of W-types as initial algebras for strictly positive endofunctors generalises to the fact that *QW-types are initial among the algebras satisfying strictly positive equational systems in the sense of Fiore and Hur.*

## 3 Quotient-inductive types

Higher inductive types (HITs) are originally motivated by their use in homotopy type theory to construct homotopical cell complexes, such as spheres, tori, and so on [29]. Intuitively, a higher inductive type is an inductive type with point constructors also allowing for path constructors, surface constructors, etc., which are represented as elements of (iterated) identity types. For example, the sphere is given by the HIT[3]:

$$\begin{aligned}&\mathsf{data}\ \mathsf{S}^2 : \mathsf{Set}\ \mathsf{where}\\ &\quad \mathsf{base} : \mathsf{S}^2\\ &\quad \mathsf{surf} : \mathsf{refl} \equiv_{\mathsf{base} \equiv_{\mathsf{S}^2} \mathsf{base}} \mathsf{refl}\end{aligned} \tag{17}$$

In the presence of the UIP axiom we will refer to HITs as *quotient inductive types* (QITs) [5], since all paths beyond the first level are trivial and any HIT is truncated to an h-set. We use the terms *element constructor* and *equality constructor* to refer to the point constructors and the only non-trivial level of path constructors.

We believe that QW-types can be used to encode a wide range of QITs: see Conjecture 1 below. As evidence, we give several examples of QITs encoded as QW-types, beginning with the two examples of QITs in Figure 1, giving the corresponding signature $(A, B)$ and system of equations $(E, V, l, r)$ as in Definition 2.

*Example 1 (Finite multisets).* The element constructors for finite multisets are encoded exactly as with a W-type: the constructors are [] and $x :: \_$ for each $x : X$. So we take $A$ to be $\mathbb{1} \uplus X$, the coproduct of the unit type $\mathbb{1}$ (whose single constructor is denoted tt) with $X$. The arity of [] is zero, and the arity of each $x :: \_$ is one, represented by the empty type $\varnothing$ and unit type $\mathbb{1}$ respectively; so we take $B : A \to \mathsf{Set}$ to be the function $[\lambda\_ \to \mathbb{0} \mid \lambda\_ \to \mathbb{1}] : \mathbb{1} \uplus X \to \mathsf{Set}$ mapping $\mathsf{inl}\,\mathsf{tt}$ to $\varnothing$ and each $\mathsf{inr}\, x$ to $\mathbb{1}$.

The swap equality constructor is parameterised by elements of $E = X \times X$. For each $(x, y) : E$, $\mathsf{swap}\, x\, y$ yields an equation involving a single free variable (called $ys : \mathsf{Bag}\, X$ in Figure 1); so we take $V : E \to \mathsf{Set}$ to be $\lambda\_ \to \mathbb{1}$. Each side of the equation named by $\mathsf{swap}\, x\, y$ is coded by an element of $\mathsf{T}\{\Sigma\}(V(x, y)) = \mathsf{T}\{\Sigma\}(\mathbb{1})$. Recalling the definition of $\mathsf{T}$ from (5), the single free variable corresponds to $\eta\,\mathsf{tt} : \mathsf{T}\{\Sigma\}(\mathbb{1})$ and then the left-hand side of the equation is $\sigma(\mathsf{inr}\, x, (\lambda\_ \to \sigma(\mathsf{inr}\, y, (\lambda\_ \to \eta\,\mathsf{tt}))))$ and the right-hand side is $\sigma(\mathsf{inr}\, y, (\lambda\_ \to \sigma(\mathsf{inr}\, x, (\lambda\_ \to \eta\,\mathsf{tt}))))$.

So, altogether, the signature and system of equations for the QW-type corresponding to the first example in Figure 1 is:

$$\begin{aligned}&A = \mathbb{1} \uplus X && E = X \times X\\ &B = [\lambda\_ \to \varnothing \mid \lambda\_ \to \mathbb{1}] && V = \lambda\_ \to \mathbb{1}\\ &l = \lambda\,(x, y) \to \sigma(\mathsf{inr}\, x, (\lambda\_ \to \sigma(\mathsf{inr}\, y, (\lambda\_ \to \eta\,\mathsf{tt}))))\\ &r = \lambda\,(x, y) \to \sigma(\mathsf{inr}\, y, (\lambda\_ \to \sigma(\mathsf{inr}\, x, (\lambda\_ \to \eta\,\mathsf{tt}))))\end{aligned}$$

[3] The subscript on $\equiv$ will be treated as an implicit argument and omitted when clear.

*Example 2 (Unordered countably-branching trees).* Here the element constructors are $\mathsf{leaf}$ of arity zero and, for each $x : X$, $\mathsf{node}\, x$ of arity $\mathbb{N}$. So we use the signature with $A = \mathbb{1} \uplus X$ and $B = [\lambda\_ \to \varnothing \mid \lambda\_ \to \mathbb{N}]$.

The $\mathsf{perm}$ equality constructor is parameterised by elements of

$$E = X \times \sum f : (\mathbb{N} \to \mathbb{N}),\ \mathsf{isIso}\, f$$

For each element $(x, f, i)$ of that type, $\mathsf{perm}\, x\, f\, i$ yields an equation involving an $\mathbb{N}$-indexed family of variables (called $g : \mathbb{N} \to \omega\mathsf{Tree}\, X$ in Figure 1); so we take $V : E \to \mathsf{Set}$ to be $\lambda\_ \to \mathbb{N}$. Each side of the equation named by $\mathsf{perm}\, x\, f\, i$ is coded by an element of $\mathsf{T}\{\Sigma\}(V(x, f, i)) = \mathsf{T}\{\Sigma\}(\mathbb{N})$. The $\mathbb{N}$-indexed family of variables is represented by the function $\eta : \mathbb{N} \to \mathsf{T}\{\Sigma\}(\mathbb{N})$ and its permuted version by $\eta \circ f$. Thus the left- and right-hand sides of the equation named by $\mathsf{perm}\, x\, f\, i$ are coded respectively by the elements $\sigma(\mathsf{inr}\, x, \eta)$ and $\sigma(\mathsf{inr}\, x, \eta \circ f)$ of $\mathsf{T}\{\Sigma\}(\mathbb{N})$.

So, altogether, the signature and system of equations for the QW-type corresponding to the second example in Figure 1 is:

$$\begin{aligned} A &= \mathbb{1} \uplus X & E &= X \times \textstyle\sum f : (\mathbb{N} \to \mathbb{N}),\ \mathsf{isIso}\, f \\ B &= [\lambda\_ \to \varnothing \mid \lambda\_ \to \mathbb{N}] & V &= \lambda\_ \to \mathbb{N} \\ l &= \lambda\,(x, \_, \_) \to \sigma(\mathsf{inr}\, x, \eta) \\ r &= \lambda\,(x, f, \_) \to \sigma(\mathsf{inr}\, x, \eta \circ f) \end{aligned}$$

That unordered countably-branching trees are a QW-type is significant since no previous work on various subclasses of QITs (or indeed QIITs [19, 10]) supports infinitary QITs [6, 26, 28, 12, 19, 10]. See Example 5 for another, more substantial infinitary QW-type. So this extension represents one of our main contributions. QW-types generalise prior developments; the internal encodings for particular subclasses of 1-HITs given by Sojakova [26] and Swan [28] are direct instances of QW-types, as the next two examples show.

*Example 3.* *W-suspensions* [26] are an instance of QW-types. The data for a W-suspension is: $A', C' : \mathsf{Set}$, a type family $B' : A' \to \mathsf{Set}$ and functions $l', r' : C' \to A'$. The equivalent QW-type is:

$$\begin{aligned} A &= A' & E &= C' & l &= \lambda\, c \to \sigma((l'\, c), \eta) \\ B &= B' & V &= \lambda\, c \to (B'\,(l'\, c)) \times (B'\,(r'\, c)) & r &= \lambda\, c \to \sigma((r'\, c), \eta) \end{aligned}$$

*Example 4.* The non-indexed case of *W-types with reductions* [28] are QW-types. The data of such a type is: $Y : \mathsf{Set}$, $X : Y \to \mathsf{Set}$ and a reindexing map $R : (y : Y) \to Xy$. The reindexing map identifies a term $\sigma\ (y, \alpha)$ with some $\alpha\ (R\, y)$ used to construct it. The equivalent QW-type is given by:

$$\begin{aligned} A &= Y & E &= Y & l &= \lambda y \to \sigma\ (y, \eta) \\ B &= X & V &= X & r &= \lambda y \to \eta\ (R\, i) \end{aligned}$$

*Example 5.* Lumsdaine and Shulman [21, Section 9] give an example of a HIT not constructible in type theory from only pushouts and $\mathbb{N}$. Their HIT $F$ can be thought of as a set of notations for countable ordinals. It consists of three point constructors: $0 : F$, $S : F \to F$, and $\mathsf{sup} : (\mathbb{N} \to F) \to F$, and five path constructors which are omitted here for brevity. It is inspired by the infinitary algebraic theory of Blass [7, Section 9] and hence it is not surprising that it can be encoded by a QW-type; the details can be found in our Agda code.

### 3.1 General QIT schemas

Basold, Geuvers, and van der Weide [6] present a schema (though not a model) for infinitary QITs that do not support conditional path equations. Constructors are defined by arbitrary polynomial endofunctors built up using (non-dependent) products and sums, which means in particular that parameters and arguments can occur in any order. They require constructors to be in uncurried form.

Dybjer and Moeneclaey [12, Sections 3.1 and 3.2] present a schema for finitary QITs that supports *conditional* path equations, where constructors are allowed to take inductive arguments not just of the datatype being declared, but also of its identity type. This schema can be generalised to infinitary QITs with conditional path equations. We believe this extension of their schema to be the most general schema for QITs. The schema requires all parameters to appear before all arguments, whereas the schema for regular inductive types in Agda is more flexible, allowing parameters and arguments in any order.

We wish to combine the schema for infinitary QITs of Basold, Geuvers, and van der Weide [6] with the schema for QITs with conditional path equations of Dybjer and Moeneclaey [12] to provide a general schema. Moreover, we would like to combine the arbitrarily ordered parameters and arguments of the former with the curried constructors of the latter in order to support flexible pattern matching.

For consistency with the definition of inductive types in Agda [9, equation (25) and figure 1] we will define strictly positive (i.e. polynomial) endofunctors in terms of strictly positive telescopes.

A telescope is given by the grammar:

$$\begin{aligned} \Delta ::= {} & \epsilon && \text{empty telescope} \\ \mid {} & (x : A)\Delta \quad (x \notin \mathrm{dom}(\Delta)) && \text{non-empty telescope} \end{aligned} \tag{18}$$

A telescope extension $(x : A)\Delta$ binds (free) occurrences of $x$ inside the tail $\Delta$. The type $A$ may contain free variables that are later bound by further telescope extensions on the left. A telescope can also exist in a context which binds any free variables not already bound in the telescope. Such a context is implicit in the following definitions. A function type $\Delta \to C$ from a telescope $\Delta$ to a type $C$ is defined as an iterated dependent function type by:

$$\begin{aligned} \epsilon \to C &\stackrel{\text{def}}{=} C \\ (x : A)\Delta \to C &\stackrel{\text{def}}{=} (x : A) \to (\Delta \to C) \end{aligned} \tag{19}$$

A *strictly positive* endofunctor on a variable $Y$ is presented by a strictly positive telescope

$$\Delta = (x_1 : \Phi_1(Y))(x_2 : \Phi_2(Y)) \cdots (x_n : \Phi_n(Y))\epsilon \tag{20}$$

where each type scheme $\Phi_i$ is described by a expression on $Y$ made up of Π-types, Σ-types, and any (previously defined "constant") types $A$ not containing $Y$, according to the grammar:

$$\Phi(Y), \Psi(Y) ::= \quad (y : A) \to \Phi(Y) \quad | \quad \Sigma p : \Phi(Y), \Psi(Y) \quad | \quad A \quad | \quad Y \tag{21}$$

For example, $\Delta \stackrel{\text{def}}{=} (x : X)(f : \mathbb{N} \to Y)\epsilon$ is the strictly positive telescope for the $\mathsf{node}$ constructor in Figure 1. In this instance, reordering $x$ and $f$ is permitted by exchange. Note that the variable $Y$ can never appear in the argument position of a Π-type.

Now it is possible to define the form of the endpoints of an equality (within the context of a strictly positive telescope), corresponding to the notion of an abstract syntax tree with free variables. With this intuition in mind, we can take the definition in Dybjer and Moeneclaey's presentation [12] of endpoints given by *point constructor patterns*:

$$l, r, p ::= \quad c_i\ k \quad | \quad y \tag{22}$$

Where $y : Y$ is in the context of the telescope for the equality constructor, and $k$ is a term built without any rule for $Y$, but which may use other point constructor patterns $p : Y$. (That is, any sub-term of type $Y$ must either be a variable $y : Y$ found in the telescope, or a constructor for $Y$ applied to further point constructor patterns and earlier defined constants. It could not, for instance, use the function application rule for $Y$ with some function $g : M \to Y$, not least since such functions cannot be defined before defining $Y$.) Note that this exactly matches the type $\mathsf{T}$ in (5).

Basold, Geuvers, and van der Weide's presentation has a sightly more general notion of *constructor term* [6, Definition 6] (Dybjer and Moeneclaey's presentation [12] has more restricted telescopes). It is defined by rules which operate in the context of a strictly positive (polynomial) telescope and permit use of its bound variables, and the use of constructors $c_i$, but not any other rules for $Y$. We take the dependent form of their rules for products and functions. Note that these rules do not allow the use of terms of type $\equiv_Y$ in the endpoints.

As with inductive types, the element constructors of QITs are specified by strictly positive telescopes. The equality constructors also permit *conditions* to appear in strictly positive positions, where $l$ and $r$ are constructor terms according to grammar (22):

$$\Phi(Y), \Psi(Y) ::= (\textit{same grammar as in } (21)) \mid l \equiv_Y r \tag{23}$$

**Definition 3.** *A* QIT *is defined by a list of named element constructors and equality constructors:*

$$
\begin{aligned}
&\mathsf{data}\ \mathsf{Y} : \mathsf{Set}\ \mathsf{where}\\
&\quad \mathsf{c}_1 : \Delta_1 \to \mathsf{Y}\\
&\quad \vdots\\
&\quad \mathsf{c}_n : \Delta_n \to \mathsf{Y}\\
&\quad \mathsf{p}_1 : \Theta_1 \to l_1 \equiv_{\mathsf{Y}} r_1\\
&\quad \vdots\\
&\quad \mathsf{p}_m : \Theta_m \to l_m \equiv_{\mathsf{Y}} r_m
\end{aligned}
$$

*where $\Delta_i$ are strictly positive telescopes on* Y *according to* (21), *and $\Theta_j$ are strictly positive telescopes on* Y *and $\equiv_{\mathsf{Y}}$ in which conditions may also occur in strictly positive positions according to* (23).

QITs without equality constructors are inductive types. If none of the equality constructors contain $Y$ in an argument position then it is called *non-recursive*, otherwise it is called *recursive* [6]. If none of the equality constructors contain an equality in $Y$ then we call it a *non-conditional*, or *equational*, QIT, otherwise it is called a *conditional* [12], or *quasi-equational*, QIT. If all of the constant types $A$ in any of the constructors are finite (isomorphic to $\mathsf{Fin}\ n$ for $n : \mathbb{N}$) then it is called a *finitary* QIT [12]. Otherwise, it is called a *generalised* [12], or *infinitary*, QIT. We are not aware of any existing examples in the literature of HITs which allow the point constructors to be conditional (though it is not difficult to imagine), nor any schemes for HITs that allow such definitions. However, we do believe this is worth investigating further.

*Conjecture 1.* Any equational QIT can be encoded as a QW-type.

We believe this can be proved analogously to the approach of Dybjer [11] for inductive types, though the endpoints still need to be considered and we have not yet translated the schema in definition 3 into Agda.

*Remark 3.* Assuming Conjecture 1, Basold, Geuvers, and van der Weide's schema [6], being an equational (non-conditional) instance of Definition 3, can be encoded as a QW-type.

## 4 Construction of QW-types

In Section 2 we defined a QW-type to be initial among algebras over a given (possibly infinitary) signature satisfying a given systems of equations (Definition 2). If one interprets these notions in classical Zermelo-Fraenkel set theory with the axiom of Choice (ZFC), one regains the usual notion from universal algebra of initial algebras for infinitary equational theories. Since in the set-theoretic interpretation there is an upper bound on the cardinality of arities of operators in a given signature $\Sigma$, the ordinal-indexed sequence $\mathsf{S}^{\alpha}(\varnothing)$ of iterations of the functor in (2) starting from the empty set eventually becomes stationary; and so the sequence has a small colimit, namely the set $\mathsf{W}\{\Sigma\}$ of well-founded trees over $\Sigma$. A system of equations $\varepsilon$ (Definition 1) over $\Sigma$ generates a $\Sigma$-congruence relation $\sim$ on $\mathsf{W}\{\Sigma\}$. The quotient set $\mathsf{W}\{\Sigma\}/\sim$ yields the desired initial algebra for $(\Sigma, \varepsilon)$ provided the $\mathsf{S}$-algebra structure on $\mathsf{W}\{\Sigma\}$ induces one on the quotient set. It does so, because for each operator, using AC one can pick representatives of the (possibly infinitely many) equivalence classes that are the arguments of the operator, apply the interpretation of the operator in $\mathsf{W}\{\Sigma\}$ and then take the equivalence class of that. So the set-theoretic model of type theory in ZFC models QW-types.

Is this use of choice really necessary? Blass [7, Section 9] shows that if one drops AC and just works in ZF, then provided a certain large cardinal axiom is consistent with ZFC, it is consistent with ZF that there is an infinitary equational theory with no initial algebra. He shows this by first exhibiting a countably presented equational theory whose initial algebra has to be an uncountable regular cardinal; and secondly appealing to the construction of Gitik [17] of a model of ZF with no uncountable regular cardinals (assuming a certain large cardinal axiom). Lumsdaine and Shulman [21] turn the infinitary equational theory of Blass into a higher-inductive type that cannot be proved to exist in ZF (and hence cannot be constructed in type theory just using pushouts and the natural numbers). We noted in Example 5 that this higher inductive type can be presented as a QW-type.

So one cannot hope to construct QW-types using a type theory which is interpretable in just ZF. However, the type theory in which we work, with its universes closed under inductive-inductive definitions, already requires going beyond ZF to be able to give it a naive, classical set-theoretic interpretation (by assuming the existence of enough strongly inaccessible cardinals, for example). So the above considerations about initial algebras for infinitary equational theories in classical set theory do not rule out the construction of QW-types in the type theory in which we work. However, something more than just quotienting a W-type is needed in order to prove Theorem 1.

Figure 2 gives a first attempt to do this (which later we will modify using sized types to get around a termination problem). The definition is relative to a given signature $\Sigma : \mathsf{Sig}$ and system of equations $\varepsilon = (E, V, l, r) : \mathsf{Syseq}\,\Sigma$. It makes use of quotient types, which we add to Agda via postulates, as shown in Figure 3.[4] The REWRITE pragma makes $\mathsf{elim}\, R\, B\, f\, e\, (\mathsf{mk}\, R\, x)$ definitionally equal to $f\, x$ and is not merely a computational convenience—this is what allows function extensionality to be proved from these postulated quotient types. The POLARITY pragmas enable the postulated quotients to be used in datatype declarations at positions that Adga deems to be strictly positive; a case in point being the definitions of $\mathsf{Q}_0$ and $\mathsf{Q}_1$ in Figure 2. Agda's test for strict positivity is sound with respect to a set-theoretic semantics of inductively defined datatypes that are built up using strictly positive uses of dependent functions; the semantics of such datatypes uses initial algebras for endofunctors possessing a rank. Here we

[4] The actual implementation is polymorphic in universe levels, but for simplicity here we just give the level-zero version.

```
mutual
  data Q₀ : Set where
    sq : T Q → Q₀

  data Q₁ : Q₀ → Q₀ → Set where
    sqeq : (e : E)(ρ : V e → Q) → Q₁ (sq(T'ρ (l e))) (sq(T'ρ (r e)))
    sqη : (x : Q₀) → Q₁ (sq(η(qu x))) x
    sqσ : (s : S(T Q)) → Q₁ (sq(σ s)) (sq(ι(S'(qu ∘ sq) s)))

  Q : Set
  Q = Q₀/Q₁

  qu : Q₀ → Q
  qu = quot.mk Q₁

QW{Σ}{ε} = Q
```

**Figure 2.** First attempt at constructing QW-types

are allowing the inductively defined datatypes to be built up using quotients as well, but this is semantically unproblematic, since quotienting does not increase rank. (Later we need to combine the use of POLARITY with sized types; the semantics of this has been studied for System $\mathrm{F}_\omega$ [3], but needs to be explored further for Agda.)

We build up the underlying inductive type $\mathsf{Q}_0$ to be quotiented using a constructor sq that takes well-founded trees $\mathsf{T}(\mathsf{Q}_0/\mathsf{Q}_1)$ of whole equivalence classes with respect to a relation $\mathsf{Q}_1$ that is mutually inductively defined with $\mathsf{Q}_0$—an instance of an inductive-inductive definition [15]. The definition of $\mathsf{Q}_1$ makes use of the actions on functions of the signature endofunctor S and its associated free monad T (Section 2); those actions are defined as follows:

$$\begin{aligned}&\mathsf{S}' : \{X\ Y : \mathsf{Set}\} \to (X \to Y) \to \mathsf{S}\,X \to \mathsf{S}\,Y\\&\mathsf{S}'\,f\,(a,b) = (a, f \circ b)\end{aligned} \tag{24}$$

$$\begin{aligned}&\mathsf{T}' : \{X\ Y : \mathsf{Set}\} \to (X \to Y) \to \mathsf{T}\,X \to \mathsf{T}\,Y\\&\mathsf{T}'\,f\,t = t \gg= (\eta \circ f)\end{aligned} \tag{25}$$

The definition of $\mathsf{Q}_1$ also uses the natural transformation $\iota : \{X : \mathsf{Set}\} \to \mathsf{S}\,X \to \mathsf{T}\,X$ defined by $\iota = \sigma \circ \mathsf{S}'\,\eta$.

Turning to the proof of Theorem 1 using the definitions in Figure 2, the S-algebra structure (9) is easy to define without using any form of choice, because of the type of $\mathsf{Q}_0$'s constructor sq. Indeed, we can just take qwintro to be $\mathsf{qu} \circ \mathsf{sq} \circ \iota : \mathsf{S(QW)} \to \mathsf{QW}$.[5] The first constructor sqeq of the data type $\mathsf{Q}_1$ ensures that the quotient $\mathsf{Q}_0/\mathsf{Q}_1$ satisfies the equations in $\varepsilon$, so that we get qwequ as in (10); and the other two constructors, sq$\eta$ and sq$\sigma$ make identifications that

[5] The use of the free monad $\mathsf{T}\{\Sigma\}$ in the domain of sq, rather than just $\mathsf{S}\{\Sigma\}$, seems necessary in order to define $\mathsf{Q}_1$ with the properties needed for (10)–(13).

```
module quot where
  postulate
    ty : {A : Set}(R : A → A → Set) → Set
    mk : {A : Set}(R : A → A → Set) → A → ty R
    eq : {A : Set}(R : A → A → Set){x y : A} → R x y → mk R x ≡ mk R y
    elim : {A : Set}(R : A → A → Set)(B : ty R → Set)(f : (x : A) → B(mk R x))
           (e : {x y : A} → R x y → f x ≡≡ f y)(z : ty R) → B z
    comp : {A : Set}(R : A → A → Set)(B : ty R → Set)(f : (x : A) → B(mk R x))
             (e : {x y : A} → R x y → f x ≡≡ f y)(x : A) → elim R B f e (mk R x) ≡ f x
{-# REWRITE comp -#}
{-# POLARITY ty ++ ++ -#}
{-# POLARITY mk _ _ * -#}

_/_ : (A : Set)(R : A → A → Set) → Set
A/R = quot.ty R
```

**Figure 3.** Quotient types

enable the construction of functions qwrec, qwrechom and qwuniq as in (11)–(13). However, there is a problem. Given $X$ : Set, $s : \mathsf{S}\,X \to X$ and $e : \mathsf{Sat}\,X$, for $\mathsf{qwrec}\,X\,s\,e$ we have to construct a function $\mathsf{r} : \mathsf{Q} \to X$. Since $\mathsf{Q} = \mathsf{Q}_0/\mathsf{Q}_1$ is a quotient, we will have to use the eliminator quot.elim from Figure 3 to define r. The following is an obvious candidate definition

$$
\begin{aligned}
&\mathsf{mutual}\\
&\quad \mathsf{r} : \mathsf{Q} \to X\\
&\quad \mathsf{r} = \mathsf{quot.elim}\,\mathsf{Q}_1\,(\lambda\_ \to X)\,\mathsf{r}_0\,\mathsf{r}_1\\[4pt]
&\quad \mathsf{r}_0 : \mathsf{Q}_0 \to X\\
&\quad \mathsf{r}_0(\mathsf{sq}\,t) = t \ggg\!= \mathsf{r}\\[4pt]
&\quad \mathsf{r}_1 : \{x\;y : \mathsf{Q}_0\} \to \mathsf{Q}_1\,x\,y \to \mathsf{r}_0\,x \equiv \mathsf{r}_0\,y\\
&\quad \mathsf{r}_1 = \cdots
\end{aligned}
\tag{26}
$$

(where we have elided the details of the invariance proof $\mathsf{r}_1$). The problem with this mutually recursive definition is that it is not clear to us (and certainly not to Agda) whether it gives totally defined functions: although the value of $\mathsf{r}_0$ at a typical element $\mathsf{sq}\,t$ is explained in terms of the structurally smaller element $t$, the explanation involves r, whose definition uses the whole function $\mathsf{r}_0$ rather than some application of it at a structurally smaller argument. Agda's termination checker rejects the definition.

We get around this problem by using a type-based termination method, namely Agda's implementation of sized types [2]. Intuitively, this provides a type Size of "sizes" which give a constructive abstraction of features of ordinals in ZF when they are used to index sequences of sets that eventually become stationary, such as in various transfinite constructions of free algebras [20, 14]. In Agda, the type Size comes equipped with various relations and functions: given sizes

$$
\begin{array}{l}
\mathsf{mutual}\\
\quad \mathsf{data}\ \mathsf{Q}_0(i : \mathsf{Size}) : \mathsf{Set}\ \mathsf{where}\\
\quad\quad \mathsf{sq} : \{j : \mathsf{Size}{<}\, i\} \to \mathsf{T}(\mathsf{Q}\, j) \to \mathsf{Q}_0\, i\\[1ex]
\quad \mathsf{data}\ \mathsf{Q}_1(i : \mathsf{Size}) : \mathsf{Q}_0\, i \to \mathsf{Q}_0\, i \to \mathsf{Set}\ \mathsf{where}\\
\quad\quad \mathsf{sqeq} : \{j : \mathsf{Size}{<}\, i\}(e : E)(\rho : V\ e \to \mathsf{Q}\, j) \to \mathsf{Q}_1\, i\ (\mathsf{sq}(\mathsf{T'}\rho\,(l\, e)))\ (\mathsf{sq}(\mathsf{T'}\rho\,(r\, e)))\\
\quad\quad \mathsf{sq}\eta : \{j : \mathsf{Size}{<}\, i\}(x : \mathsf{Q}_0\, j) \to \mathsf{Q}_1\, i\ (\mathsf{sq}(\eta(\mathsf{qu}\, j\, x)))\ (\phi_0\, i\, x)\\
\quad\quad \mathsf{sq}\sigma : \{j : \mathsf{Size}{<}\, i\}\{k : \mathsf{Size}{<}\, j\}(s : \mathsf{S}(\mathsf{T}(\mathsf{Q}\, k))) \to\\
\quad\quad\quad\quad\quad\quad \mathsf{Q}_1\, i\ (\mathsf{sq}(\sigma\, s))\ (\mathsf{sq}(\iota(\mathsf{S'}(\mathsf{qu}\, j \circ \mathsf{sq})\, s)))\\
\quad \mathsf{Q} : \mathsf{Size} \to \mathsf{Set}\\
\quad \mathsf{Q}\, i = (\mathsf{Q}_0\, i)/\mathsf{Q}_1\, i\\[1ex]
\quad \mathsf{qu} : (i : \mathsf{Size}) \to \mathsf{Q}_0\, i \to \mathsf{Q}\, i\\
\quad \mathsf{qu}\, i = \mathsf{quot.mk}\,(\mathsf{Q}_1\, i)\\[1ex]
\quad \phi_0 : (i : \mathsf{Size})\{j : \mathsf{Size}{<}\, i\} \to \mathsf{Q}_0\, j \to \mathsf{Q}_0\, i\\
\quad \phi_0\, i\,(\mathsf{sq}\, z) = \mathsf{sq}\, z\\[1ex]
\mathsf{QW}\{\Sigma\}\{\varepsilon\} = \mathsf{Q}\, \infty
\end{array}
$$

**Figure 4.** Construction of QW-types using sized types

$i, j$ : Size, there is a relation $i$ : Size< $j$ to indicate strictly increasing size (so the type Size< $j$ is treated as a subtype of Size); there is a successor operation $\uparrow$ : Size → Size (and also a join operation $\_\sqcup^s\_$ : Size → Size → Size, but we do not need it here); and a size $\infty$ : Size to indicate where a sequence becomes stationary. Thus we construct the QW-type QW{Σ}{ε} as Q $\infty$ for a suitable size-indexed sequence of types Q : Size → Set, shown in Figure 4.

For each size $i$ : Size, the type Q $i$ is a quotient $\mathsf{Q}_0\, i/\mathsf{Q}_1\, i$, where the constructors of the data types $\mathsf{Q}_0\, i$ and $\mathsf{Q}_1\, i$ take arguments of smaller sizes $j$ : Size< $i$. Consequently in the following sized version of (26)

$$
\begin{array}{l}
\mathsf{mutual}\\
\quad \mathsf{r} : \{i : \mathsf{Size}\} \to \mathsf{Q}\, i \to X\\
\quad \mathsf{r}\{i\} = \mathsf{quot.elim}\,(\mathsf{Q}_1\, i)\,(\lambda\_ \to X)\,(\mathsf{r}_0\,\{i\})\,(\mathsf{r}_1\,\{i\})\\[1ex]
\quad \mathsf{r}_0 : \{i : \mathsf{Size}\} \to \mathsf{Q}_0\, i \to X\\
\quad \mathsf{r}_0\{i\}(\mathsf{sq}\,\{j\}\, t) = t \gg\!= \mathsf{r}\,\{j\}\\[1ex]
\quad \mathsf{r}_1 : \{i : \mathsf{Size}\}\{x\ y : \mathsf{Q}_0\, i\} \to \mathsf{Q}_1\, i\, x\, y \to \mathsf{r}_0\, x \equiv \mathsf{r}_0\, y\\
\quad \mathsf{r}_1 = \cdots
\end{array}
\tag{27}
$$

the definition of $\mathsf{r}_0\{i\}$ involves a recursive call via r to the whole function $\mathsf{r}_0$, but at a size $j$ which is smaller than $i$. So now Agda accepts that the definition of qwrec $X\ s\ e$ as r $\infty$, with r as in (27), is terminating.

Thus we get a function qwrec for (11). We still have (9), but now with qwintro = qu $\infty \circ$ sq $\{\infty\} \circ \iota$; and as before, the constructor sqeq of $\mathsf{Q}_1$ in Figure 4 ensures that QW = $(\mathsf{Q}_0\, \infty)/\mathsf{Q}_1\, \infty$ satisfies the equations $\varepsilon$. With these definitions it turns out that each qwrec $X\ s\ e$ is an S-algebra morphism up to definitional equality, so that the function qwrechom needed for (12) is straightforward to define. Finally, the function qwuniq needed for (13) can be constructed via a sequence of lemmas making use of the other two constructors of the data type $\mathsf{Q}_1$, namely $\mathsf{sq}\eta$, which makes use of an auxiliary function for coercing between different size instances of $\mathsf{Q}_0$, and $\mathsf{sq}\sigma$. We refer the reader to the accompanying Agda code (DOI: 10.17863/CAM.48187) for the details of the construction of qwuniq. Altogether, the sized definitions in Figure 4 allow us to complete a proof of Theorem 1.

## 5 Conclusion

QW-types are a general form of QIT that capture many examples, including simple 1-cell complexes and non-recursive QITs [6], non-structural QITs [26], W-types with reductions [28], and also infinitary QITs (e.g. unordered infinitely branching trees [5], and ordinals [21]). They also capture the notion of initial (and free) algebras for strictly positive equational systems [14], analogously to how W-types capture the notion of initial (and free) algebras for strictly positive endofunctors (see Remark 2). Using Agda to formalise our results, we have shown that it is possible to construct any QW-type, even infinitary ones, in intensional type theory satisfying UIP, using inductive-inductive definitions permitting strictly positive occurrences of quotients and sized types (see Theorem 1 and Section 4). We conclude by mentioning related work and some possible directions for future work.

*Quotients of monads.* In view of Remark 2, Section 4 gives a construction of initial algebras for equational systems [14] on the *free* monad $\mathsf{T}\{\Sigma\}$ generated by a signature $\Sigma$. By a suitable change of signature (see Remark 1) this extends to a construction of free algebras, rather than just initial ones. We can show that the construction works for an arbitrary strictly positive monad and not just for free ones. Given such a construction one gets a quotient monad morphism from the base monad to the quotient monad. This contravariantly induces a forgetful functor from the algebras of the latter to that of the former. Using the adjoint triangle theorem, one should be able to construct a left adjoint. This would then cover examples such as the free group over a monoid, free ring over a group, etc.

*Quotient inductive-inductive types.* The notion of QW-type generalises to *indexed* QW-types, analogously to the generalisation of W-types to Petersson-Synek trees for inductively defined indexed families of types [24, Chapter 16], and we will consider it in subsequent work. More generally, we wonder whether our analysis of QITs using quotients, inductive-inductive and sized types can be extended to cover the notion of *quotient inductive-inductive* type (QIIT) [4, 19]. Dijkstra [10] studies such types in depth and in Chapter 6 of his thesis gives a construction for finitary ones in terms of countable colimits, and hence in terms of countable coproducts and quotients. One could hope to pass to the infinitary case by using sized types as we have done, provided an analogue for QIITs can be found of the monadic construction in Section 4 for our class of QITs, the QW-types. Kaposi, Kovács, and Altenkirch [19] give a specification of finitary QIITs using a domain-specific type theory called the *theory of signatures* and prove existence of QIITs matching this specification. It might be possible to encode their theory of signatures using QW-types (it can already be encoded as a QIIT), or to extend QW-types making this possible. This would allow infinitary QIITs.

*Schemas for QITs.* We have shown by example that QW-types can encode a wide range of QITs. However, we have yet to extend this to a proof of Conjecture 1 that every instance of the schema for QITs considered in Section 3 can be so encoded.

*Conditional path equations.* In Section 3 we mentioned the fact that Dybjer and Moeneclaey [12] give a model for finitary 1-HITs and 2-HITs in which constructors are allowed to take arguments involving the identity type of the datatype being declared. On the face of it, QW-types are not able to encode such *conditional* QITs. We plan to consider whether it is possible to extend the notion of QW-type to allow encoding of infinitary QITs with such conditional equations.

*Homotopy Type Theory (HoTT).* Our development makes use of UIP (and heterogeneous equality), which is well-known to be incompatible with the Univalence Axiom [29, Example 3.1.9]. Given the interest in HoTT, it is certainly worth investigating whether a result like Theorem 1 holds in univalent foundations for a suitably coherent version of QW-types. We are currently investigating this using set-truncation.

*Pattern matching for QITs and HITs.* Our reduction of QITs to induction-induction, strictly positive quotients and sized types is of theoretical interest, but in practice one could wish for more direct support in systems like Agda, Lean and Coq for the very useful notion of quotient inductive types (or more generally, for higher inductive types). Even having better support for the special case of quotient types would be welcome. It is not hard to envisage the addition of a general schema for declaring QITs; but when it comes to defining functions on them, having to do that with eliminator forms rapidly becomes cumbersome (for example, for functions of several QIT arguments). Some extension of dependently typed pattern matching to cover equality constructors as well as element constructors is needed and the third author has begun work on that based on the approach of Cockx and Abel [9].[6]

[6] In this context it is worth mentioning that the `cubical` features of recent versions of Agda give access to cubical type theory [30]. This allows for easy declaration of HITs and hence in particular QITs (and quotients avoiding the need for POLARITY pragmas) and a certain amount of pattern matching when it comes to defining functions on them: the value of a function on a path constructor can be specified by using generic elements of the interval type in point-level patterns; but currently the user is given little mechanised assistance to solve the definitional equality constraints on end-points of paths that are generated by this method.

## References


1. Abbott, M., Altenkirch, T., Ghani, N.: Containers: Constructing strictly positive types. Theoretical Computer Science *vol. 342*(1), 3–27 (2005). DOI: 10.1016/j.tcs.2005.06.002.
2. Abel, A.: Type-Based Termination, Inflationary Fixed-Points, and Mixed Inductive-Coinductive Types. Electronic Proceedings in Theoretical Computer Science *vol. 77*, 1–11 (2012). DOI: 10.4204/EPTCS.77.1.
3. Abel, A., Pientka, B.: Well-Founded Recursion with Copatterns and Sized Types. J. Funct. Prog. *vol. 26*, e2 (2016). DOI: 10.1017/S0956796816000022.
4. Altenkirch, T., Capriotti, P., Dijkstra, G., Kraus, N., Nordvall Forsberg, F.: Quotient Inductive-Inductive Types. In: Baier, C., Dal Lago, U. (eds.) Foundations of Software Science and Computation Structures, FoSSaCS 2018, LNCS, vol. 10803, pp. 293–310. Springer, Heidelberg (2018).
5. Altenkirch, T., Kaposi, A.: Type Theory in Type Theory Using Quotient Inductive Types. In: Proceedings of the 43rd Annual ACM SIGPLAN-SIGACT Symposium on Principles of Programming Languages - POPL 2016, pp. 18–29. ACM Press, St. Petersburg, FL, USA (2016). DOI: 10.1145/2837614.2837638.
6. Basold, H., Geuvers, H., van der Weide, N.: Higher Inductive Types in Programming. Journal of Universal Computer Science *vol. 23*(1), 27 (2017). DOI: 10.3217/jucs-023-01-0063.
7. Blass, A.: Words, Free Algebras, and Coequalizers. Fundamenta Mathematicae *vol. 117*(2), 117–160 (1983).
8. Cockx, J., Abel, A.: "Sprinkles of Extensionality for Your Vanilla Type Theory". Abstract for the 22nd International Conference on Types for Proofs and Programs (TYPES 2016), Novi Sad, Serbia.
9. Cockx, J., Abel, A.: Elaborating Dependent (Co)Pattern Matching. Proceedings of the ACM on Programming Languages *vol. 2*, 1–30 (2018). DOI: 10.1145/3236770.
10. Dijkstra, G.: Quotient Inductive-Inductive Definitions. PhD thesis, University of Nottingham (2017), URL: http://eprints.nottingham.ac.uk/42317/1/thesis.pdf.
11. Dybjer, P.: Representing Inductively Defined Sets by Wellorderings in Martin-Löf's Type Theory. Theoretical Computer Science *vol. 176*(1-2), 329–335 (1997). DOI: 10.1016/S0304-3975(96)00145-4.
12. Dybjer, P., Moeneclaey, H.: Finitary Higher Inductive Types in the Groupoid Model. Electronic Notes in Theoretical Computer Science *vol. 336*, 119–134 (2018). DOI: 10.1016/j.entcs.2018.03.019.
13. Fiore, M.: An Equational Metalogic for Monadic Equational Systems. Theory and Applications of Categories *vol. 27*(18), 464–492 (2013). URL: https://emis.de/journals/TAC/volumes/27/18/27-18.pdf.
14. Fiore, M., Hur, C.-K.: On the Construction of Free Algebras for Equational Systems. Theoretical Computer Science *vol. 410*(18), 1704–1729 (2009). DOI: 10.1016/j.tcs.2008.12.052.
15. Forsberg, F.N., Setzer, A.: A Finite Axiomatisation of Inductive-Inductive Definitions. In: Berger, U., Diener, H., Schuster, P., Seisenberger, M. (eds.) Logic, Construction, Computation, Ontos mathematical logic, pp. 259–287. De Gruyter (2012). DOI: 10.1515/9783110324921.259.
16. Gambino, N., Kock, J.: Polynomial Functors and Polynomial Monads. Math. Proc. Camb. Phil. Soc. *vol. 154*(1), 153–192 (2013). DOI: 10.1017/S0305004112000394.
17. Gitik, M.: All Uncountable Cardinals Can Be Singular. Israel J. Math. *vol. 35*(1–2), 61–88 (1980).

18. Hofmann, M.: Extensional Concepts in Intensional Type Theory. PhD thesis, University of Edinburgh (1995).
19. Kaposi, A., Kovács, A., Altenkirch, T.: Constructing Quotient Inductive-Inductive Types. Proc. ACM Program. Lang. *vol. 3*, 1–24 (2019). DOI: 10.1145/3290315.
20. Kelly, M.: A Unified Treatment of Transfinite Constructions for Free Algebras, Free Monoids, Colimits, Associated Sheaves, and so on. Bull. Austral. Math. Soc. *vol. 22*, 1–83 (1980).
21. Lumsdaine, P.L., Shulman, M.: Semantics of Higher Inductive Types. Math. Proc. Camb. Phil. Soc. (2019). DOI: 10.1017/S030500411900015X.
22. Martin-Löf, P.: Constructive Mathematics and Computer Programming. In: Cohen, L.J., Łoś, J., Pfeiffer, H., Podewski, K.-P. (eds.) Studies in Logic and the Foundations of Mathematics, pp. 153–175. Elsevier (1982). DOI: 10.1016/S0049-237X(09)70189-2.
23. McBride, C.: Dependently Typed Functional Programs and their Proofs. PhD thesis, University of Edinburgh (1999).
24. Nordström, B., Petersson, K., Smith, J.M.: *Programming in Martin-Löf's Type Theory*. Oxford University Press (1990).
25. Shulman, M.: Brouwer's Fixed-Point Theorem in Real-Cohesive Homotopy Type Theory. Mathematical Structures in Computer Science *vol. 28*, 856–941 (2018).
26. Sojakova, K.: Higher Inductive Types as Homotopy-Initial Algebras. In: Proceedings of the 42nd Annual ACM SIGPLAN-SIGACT Symposium on Principles of Programming Languages - POPL '15, pp. 31–42. ACM Press, Mumbai, India (2015). DOI: 10.1145/2676726.2676983.
27. Streicher, T.: Investigations into Intensional Type Theory. Habilitation Thesis, Ludwig Maximilian University (1993).
28. Swan, A.: W-Types with Reductions and the Small Object Argument. (2018). arXiv:1802.07588 [math].
29. The Univalent Foundations Program, *Homotopy Type Theory: Univalent Foundations for Mathematics*. http://homotopytypetheory.org/book, Institute for Advanced Study (2013).
30. Vezzosi, A., Mörtberg, A., Abel, A.: Cubical Agda: A Dependently Typed Programming Language with Univalence and Higher Inductive Types. Proc. ACM Program. Lang. *vol. 3*(ICFP), 87:1–87:29 (2019). DOI: 10.1145/3341691.

# 4

# Contextual Equivalence for Signal Flow Graphs

Filippo Bonchi[1], Robin Piedeleu[2⋆], Paweł Sobociński[3⋆⋆], and Fabio Zanasi[2⋆](✉)

[1] Università di Pisa, Italy
[2] University College London, UK, {r.piedeleu, f.zanasi}@ucl.ac.uk
[3] Tallinn University of Technology, Estonia

**Abstract.** We extend the signal flow calculus—a compositional account of the classical signal flow graph model of computation—to encompass affine behaviour, and furnish it with a novel operational semantics. The increased expressive power allows us to define a canonical notion of contextual equivalence, which we show to coincide with denotational equality. Finally, we characterise the realisable fragment of the calculus: those terms that express the computations of (affine) signal flow graphs.

**Keywords:** signal flow graphs · affine relations · full abstraction · contextual equivalence · string diagrams

## 1 Introduction

Compositional accounts of models of computation often lead one to consider *relational* models because a decomposition of an input-output system might consist of internal parts where flow and causality are not always easy to assign. These insights led Willems [33] to introduce a new current of control theory, called *behavioural* control: roughly speaking, behaviours and observations are of prime concern, notions such as state, inputs or outputs are secondary. Independently, programming language theory converged on similar ideas, with *contextual equivalence* [25,28] often considered as *the* equivalence: programs are judged to be different if we can find some context in which one behaves differently from the other, and what is observed about "behaviour" is often something quite canonical and simple, such as termination. Hoare [17] and Milner [23] discovered that these programming language theory innovations also bore fruit in the non-deterministic context of concurrency. Here again, research converged on studying simple and canonical contextual equivalences [24,18].

This paper brings together all of the above threads. The model of computation of interest for us is that of signal flow graphs [32,21], which are feedback systems well known in control theory [21] and widely used in the modelling of linear dynamical systems (in continuous time) and signal processing circuits (in discrete time). The *signal flow calculus* [10,9] is a syntactic presentation with an underlying compositional denotational semantics in terms of linear relations. Armed with *string diagrams* [31] as a syntax, the tools and concepts of programming language theory and concurrency theory can be put to work and the calculus can be equipped with a structural operational semantics. However, while in previous work [9] a connection was made between operational equivalence (essentially trace equivalence) and denotational equality, the signal flow calculus was not quite expressive enough for contextual equivalence to be a useful notion.

The crucial step turns out to be moving from *linear* relations to *affine* relations, i.e. linear subspaces translated by a vector. In recent work [6], we showed that they can be used to study important physical phenomena, such as current and voltage sources in electrical engineering, as well as fundamental synchronisation primitives in concurrency, such as mutual exclusion. Here we show that, in addition to yielding compelling mathematical domains, affinity proves to be the magic ingredient that ties the different components of the story of signal flow graphs together: it provides us with a canonical and simple notion of observation to use for the *definition* of contextual equivalence, and gives us the expressive power to prove a bona fide full abstraction result that relates contextual equivalence with denotational equality.

To obtain the above result, we extend the signal flow calculus to handle affine behaviour. While the denotational semantics and axiomatic theory appeared in [6], the operational account appears here for the first time and requires some technical innovations: instead of traces, we consider *trajectories*, which are infinite traces that may start in the past. To record the time, states of our transition system have a runtime environment that keeps track of the global clock.

Because the affine signal flow calculus is oblivious to flow directionality, some terms exhibit pathological operational behaviour. We illustrate these phenomena with several examples. Nevertheless, for the linear sub-calculus, it is known [9] that every term is denotationally equal to an executable realisation: one that is in a form where a consistent flow can be identified, like the classical notion of signal flow graph. We show that the question has a more subtle answer in the affine extension: not all terms are realisable as (affine) signal flow graphs. However, we are able to characterise the class of diagrams for which this is true.

*Related work.* Several authors studied signal flow graphs by exploiting concepts and techniques of programming language semantics, see e.g. [4,22,29,2]. The most relevant for this paper is [2], which, independently from [10], proposed the same syntax and axiomatisation for the ordinary signal flow calculus and shares with our contribution the same methodology: the use of *string diagrams* as a mathematical playground for the compositional study of different sorts of systems. The idea is common to diverse, cross-disciplinary research programmes, including Categorical Quantum Mechanics [1,11,12], Categorical Network Theory [3], Monoidal Computer [26,27] and the analysis of (a)synchronous circuits [14,15].

*Outline* In Section 2 we recall the affine signal flow calculus. Section 3 introduces the operational semantics for the calculus. Section 4 defines contextual equivalence and proves full abstraction. Section 5 introduces a well-behaved class of circuits, that denotes functional input-output systems, laying the groundwork for Section 6, in which the concept of realisability is introduced before a characterisation of which circuit diagrams are realisable. Missing proofs can be found in the extended version of this paper [7].

## 2    Background: the Affine Signal Flow Calculus

The *Affine Signal Flow Calculus* extends the signal flow calculus [9] with an extra generator $\vdash$ that allows to express affine relations. In this section, we first recall its syntax and denotational semantics from [6] and then we highlight two key properties for proving full abstraction that are enabled by the affine extension. The operational semantics is delayed to the next section.

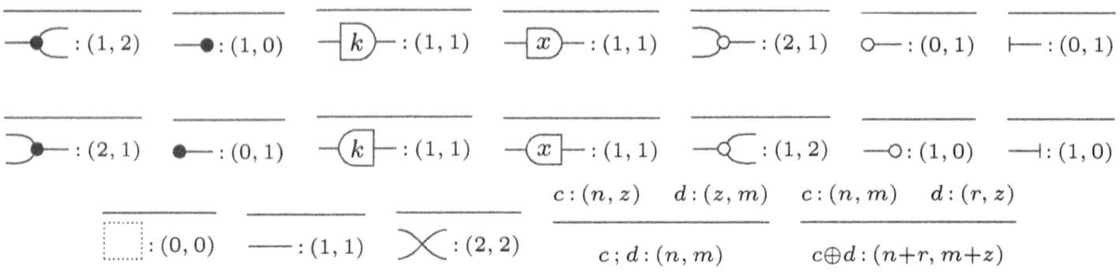

**Fig. 1.** Sort inference rules.

### 2.1   Syntax

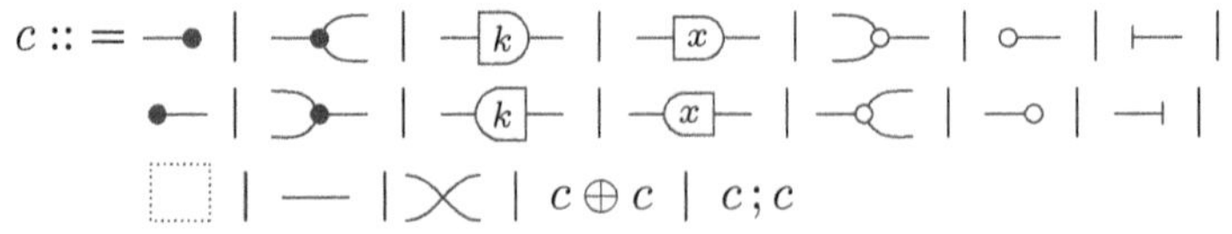

$$c ::= \; \text{—}\bullet \; | \; \text{—}\mathord{<} \; | \; \text{—}\boxed{k}\text{—} \; | \; \text{—}\boxed{x}\text{—} \; | \; \mathord{>}\text{—} \; | \; \circ\text{—} \; | \; \vdash \; | \qquad (1)$$

$$\bullet\text{—} \; | \; \mathord{>}\text{—} \; | \; \text{—}\boxed{k}\text{—} \; | \; \text{—}\boxed{x}\text{—} \; | \; \mathord{>}\mathord{<} \; | \; \text{—}\circ \; | \; \dashv \; | \qquad (2)$$

$$\boxed{\phantom{x}} \; | \; \text{—} \; | \; \times \; | \; c \oplus c \; | \; c\,;c \qquad\qquad (3)$$

The syntax of the calculus, generated by the grammar above, is parametrised over a given field k, with $k$ ranging over k. We refer to the constants in rows (1)-(2) as *generators*. Terms are constructed from generators, $\boxed{\phantom{x}}$, $\text{—}$, $\times$, and the two binary operations in (3). We will only consider those terms that are *sortable*, i.e. they can be associated with a pair $(n, m)$, with $n, m \in \mathbb{N}$. Sortable terms are called *circuits*: intuitively, a circuit with sort $(n, m)$ has $n$ ports on the left and $m$ on the right. The sorting discipline is given in Fig. 1. We delay discussion of computational intuitions to Section 3 but, for the time being, we observe that the generators of row (2) are those of row (1) "reflected about the $y$-axis".

### 2.2   String Diagrams

It is convenient to consider circuits as the arrows of a symmetric monoidal category ACirc (for Affine Circuits). Objects of ACirc are natural numbers (thus

ACirc is a *prop* [19]) and morphisms $n \to m$ are the circuits of sort $(n, m)$, quotiented by the laws of symmetric monoidal categories [20,31][4]. The circuit grammar yields the symmetric monoidal structure of ACirc: sequential composition is given by $c\,;d$, the monoidal product is given by $c \oplus d$, and identities and symmetries are built by pasting together — and $\times$ in the obvious way. We will adopt the usual convention of writing morphisms of ACirc as *string diagrams*,

meaning that $c\,;c'$ is drawn $\boxed{c}\boxed{c'}$ and $c \oplus c'$ is drawn $\frac{\boxed{c}}{\boxed{c'}}$ . More suc-

cinctly, ACirc is the free prop on generators (1)-(2). The free prop on (1)-(2) sans ⊢ and ⊣, hereafter called Circ, is the signal flow calculus from [9].

*Example 1.* The diagram  represents the circuit

$$((\bullet\!\!-\,;\,-\!\!\blacktriangleleft\bigcirc)\oplus\!-)\,;\,(-\!\!\oplus\!(\bigcirc\!\!-\,;\,-\!\!\blacktriangleleft\bigcirc))\,;\,(((-\!\!\oplus\!-\boxed{x}\!-)\oplus\!-)\,;\,((\bigcirc\!\!-\,;\,-\!\bullet)\oplus\!-)).$$

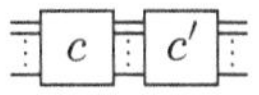

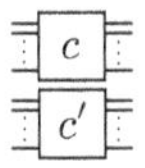

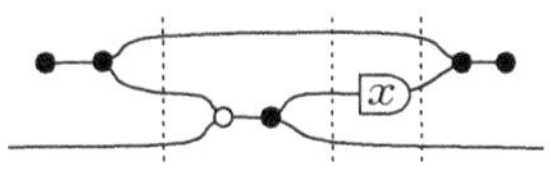

## 2.3 Denotational Semantics and Axiomatisation

The semantics of circuits can be given denotationally by means of affine relations.

**Definition 1.** *Let* k *be a field. An affine subspace of* $\mathsf{k}^d$ *is a subset* $V \subseteq \mathsf{k}^d$ *that is either empty or for which there exists a vector* $a \in \mathsf{k}^d$ *and a linear subspace* $L$ *of* $\mathsf{k}^d$ *such that* $V = \{a + v \mid v \in L\}$. *A* k-affine relation *of type* $n \to m$ *is an affine subspace of* $\mathsf{k}^n \times \mathsf{k}^m$, *considered as a* k-vector space.

Note that every linear subspace is affine, taking $a$ above to be the zero vector. Affine relations can be organised into a prop:

**Definition 2.** *Let* k *be a field. Let* $\mathsf{ARel}_\mathsf{k}$ *be the following prop:*

- *arrows* $n \to m$ *are* k-*affine relations.*
- *composition is relational: given* $G = \{(u, v) \mid u \in \mathsf{k}^n, v \in \mathsf{k}^m\}$ *and* $H = \{(v, w) \mid v \in \mathsf{k}^m, w \in \mathsf{k}^l\}$, *their composition is* $G\,;H := \{(u, w) \mid \exists v.(u, v) \in G \wedge (v, w) \in H\}$.
- *monoidal product given by* $G \oplus H = \left\{ \left( \begin{pmatrix} u \\ u' \end{pmatrix}, \begin{pmatrix} v \\ v' \end{pmatrix} \right) \mid (u, v) \in G, (u', v') \in H \right\}$.

In order to give semantics to ACirc, we use the prop of affine relations over the field $\mathsf{k}(x)$ of fractions of polynomials in $x$ with coefficients from k. Elements $q \in \mathsf{k}(x)$ are a fractions $\frac{k_0 + k_1 \cdot x^1 + k_2 \cdot x^2 + \cdots + k_n \cdot x^n}{l_0 + l_1 \cdot x^1 + l_2 \cdot x^2 + \cdots + l_m \cdot l^m}$ for some $n, m \in \mathbb{N}$ and $k_i, l_i \in \mathsf{k}$. Sum, product, 0 and 1 in $\mathsf{k}(x)$ are defined as usual.

---

[4] This quotient is harmless: both the denotational semantics from [6] and the operational semantics we introduce in this paper satisfy those axioms on the nose.

**Definition 3.** *The prop morphism* $[\![\cdot]\!]\colon \mathsf{ACirc} \to \mathsf{ARel}_{\mathsf{k}(x)}$ *is inductively defined on circuits as follows. For the generators in* (1)

 $\longmapsto \left\{\left(p, \begin{pmatrix} p \\ p \end{pmatrix}\right) \mid p \in \mathsf{k}(x)\right\}$ 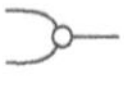 $\longmapsto \left\{\left(\begin{pmatrix} p \\ q \end{pmatrix}, p+q\right) \mid p, q \in \mathsf{k}(x)\right\}$

 $\longmapsto \{(p, \bullet) \mid p \in \mathsf{k}(x)\}$  $\longmapsto \{(\bullet, 0)\}$  $\longmapsto \{(\bullet, 1)\}$

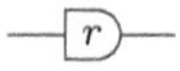 $\longmapsto \{(p, p \cdot r) \mid p \in \mathsf{k}(x)\}$ 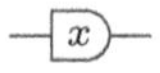 $\longmapsto \{(p, p \cdot x) \mid p \in \mathsf{k}(x)\}$

*where* $\bullet$ *is the only element of* $\mathsf{k}(x)^0$. *The semantics of components in* (2) *is symmetric, e.g.* •— *is mapped to* $\{(p, \bullet) \mid p \in \mathsf{k}(x)\}$. *For* (3)

— $\longmapsto \{(p, p) \mid p \in \mathsf{k}(x)\}$  $\longmapsto \left\{\left(\begin{pmatrix} p \\ q \end{pmatrix}, \begin{pmatrix} q \\ p \end{pmatrix}\right) \mid p, q \in \mathsf{k}(x)\right\}$

 $\longmapsto \{(\bullet, \bullet)\}$ $\quad c_1 \oplus c_2 \longmapsto [\![c_1]\!] \oplus [\![c_2]\!]$ $\quad c_1 \mathbin{;} c_2 \longmapsto [\![c_1]\!] \mathbin{;} [\![c_2]\!]$

The reader can easily check that the pair of 1-dimensional vectors $\left(1, \frac{1}{1-x}\right) \in \mathsf{k}(x)^1 \times \mathsf{k}(x)^1$ belongs to the denotation of the circuit in Example 1.

The denotational semantics enjoys a sound and complete axiomatisation. The axioms involve only basic interactions between the generators (1)-(2). The resulting theory is that of *Affine Interacting Hopf Algebras* ($\mathbb{aIH}$).The generators in (1) form a Hopf algebra, those in (2) form another Hopf algebra, and the interaction of the two give rise to two Frobenius algebras. We refer the reader to [6] for the full set of equations and all further details.

**Proposition 1.** *For all* $c, d$ *in* $\mathsf{ACirc}$, $[\![c]\!] = [\![d]\!]$ *if and only if* $c \stackrel{\mathbb{aIH}}{=} d$.

## 2.4 Affine vs Linear Circuits

It is important to highlight the differences between $\mathsf{ACirc}$ and $\mathsf{Circ}$. The latter is the purely linear fragment: circuit diagrams of $\mathsf{Circ}$ denote exactly the *linear* relations over $\mathsf{k}(x)$ [8], while those of $\mathsf{ACirc}$ denote the *affine* relations over $\mathsf{k}(x)$.

The additional expressivity afforded by affine circuits is essential for our development. One crucial property is that every polynomial fraction can be expressed as an affine circuit of sort (0, 1).

**Lemma 1.** *For all* $p \in \mathsf{k}(x)$, *there is* $c_p \in \mathsf{ACirc}[0, 1]$ *with* $[\![c_p]\!] = \{(\bullet, p)\}$.

*Proof.* For each $p \in \mathsf{k}(x)$, let $P$ be the linear subspace generated by the pair of 1-dimensional vectors $(1, p)$. By fullness of the denotational semantics of $\mathsf{Circ}$ [8], there exists a circuit $c$ in $\mathsf{Circ}$ such that $[\![c]\!] = P$. Then, $[\![$⊢— $; c]\!] = \{(\bullet, p)\}$. □

The above observation yields the following:

**Proposition 2.** *Let* $(u, v) \in \mathsf{k}(x)^n \times \mathsf{k}(x)^m$. *There exist circuits* $c_u \in \mathsf{ACirc}[0, n]$ *and* $c_v \in \mathsf{ACirc}[m, 0]$ *such that* $[\![c_u]\!] = \{(\bullet, u)\}$ *and* $[\![c_v]\!] = \{(v, \bullet)\}$.

*Proof.* Let $u = \begin{pmatrix} p_1 \\ \vdots \\ p_n \end{pmatrix}$ and $v = \begin{pmatrix} q_1 \\ \vdots \\ q_m \end{pmatrix}$. By Lemma 1, for each $p_i$, there exists a circuit $c_{p_i}$ such that $[\![c_{p_i}]\!] = \{(\bullet, p_i)\}$. Let $c_u = c_{p_1} \oplus \ldots \oplus c_{p_n}$. Then $[\![c_u]\!] = \{(\bullet, u)\}$. For $c_v$, it is enough to see that Proposition 1 also holds with 0 and 1 switched, then use the argument above. □

Proposition 2 asserts that any behaviour $(u, v)$ occurring in the denotation of some circuit $c$, i.e., such that $(u, v) \in [\![c]\!]$, can be expressed by a pair of circuits $(c_u, c_v)$. We will, in due course, think of such a pair as a *context*, namely an environment with which a circuit can interact. Observe that this is not possible with the linear fragment $\mathsf{Circ}$, since the only singleton linear subspace is 0.

Another difference between linear and affine concerns circuits of sort $(0, 0)$. Indeed $\mathsf{k}(x)^0 = \{\bullet\}$, and the only linear relation over $\mathsf{k}(x)^0 \times \mathsf{k}(x)^0$ is the singleton $\{(\bullet, \bullet)\}$, which is $id_0$ in $\mathsf{ARel}_{\mathsf{k}(x)}$. But there is another affine relation, namely the *empty relation* $\emptyset \in \mathsf{k}(x)^0 \times \mathsf{k}(x)^0$. This can be represented by $\vdash\!\!\circ$, for instance, since $[\![\vdash\!\!\circ]\!] = \{(\bullet, 1)\} \,;\, \{(0, \bullet)\} = \emptyset$.

**Proposition 3.** *Let* $c \in \mathsf{ACirc}[0, 0]$. *Then* $[\![c]\!]$ *is either* $id_0$ *or* $\emptyset$.

## 3 Operational Semantics for Affine Circuits

Here we give the structural operational semantics of affine circuits, building on previous work [9] that considered only the core linear fragment, $\mathsf{Circ}$. We consider circuits to be *programs* that have an observable behaviour. Observations are possible interactions at the circuit's interface. Since there are two interfaces: a left and a right, each transition has two labels.

In a transition $t \triangleright c \xrightarrow[w]{v} t' \triangleright c'$, $c$ and $c'$ are *states*, that is, circuits augmented with information about which values $k \in \mathsf{k}$ are stored in each register ($-\!\boxed{x}\!\!\rangle\!-$ and $-\!\langle\!\!\boxed{x}\!-$) at that instant of the computation. When transitioning to $c'$, the $v$ above the arrow is a vector of values with which $c$ synchronises on the left, and the $w$ below the arrow accounts for the synchronisation on the right. States are decorated with runtime contexts: $t$ and $t'$ are (possibly negative) integers that—intuitively—indicate the time when the transition happens. Indeed, in Fig. 2, every rule advances time by 1 unit. "Negative time" is important: as we shall see in Example 3, some executions must start in the past.

The rules in the top section of Fig. 2 provide the semantics for the generators in (1): $-\!\!\bullet\!\!\!<$ is a *copier*, duplicating the signal arriving on the left; $-\!\!\bullet$ accepts any signal on the left and discards it, producing nothing on the right; $>\!\!\circ\!-$ is an *adder* that takes two signals on the left and emits their sum on the right, $\circ\!-$ emits the constant 0 signal on the right; $-\!\boxed{k}\!\!\rangle\!-$ is an *amplifier*, multiplying the signal on the left by the scalar $k \in \mathsf{k}$. All the generators described so far are stateless. State is provided by $-\!\overset{l}{\boxed{x}}\!\!\rangle\!-$ which is a *register*; a synchronous one place buffer with the value $l$ stored. When it receives some value $k$ on the left, it emits $l$ on the right and stores $k$. The behaviour of the affine generator $\vdash$

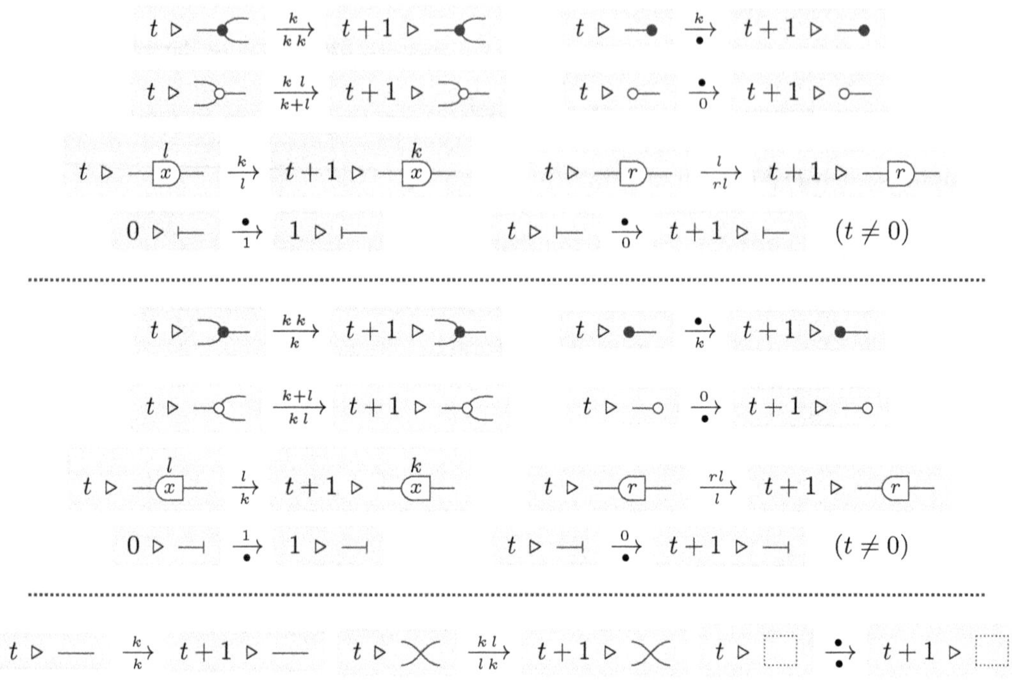

$$\frac{t \rhd c \xrightarrow[v]{u} t+1 \rhd c' \qquad t \rhd d \xrightarrow[w]{v} t+1 \rhd d'}{t \rhd c\,;d \xrightarrow[w]{u} t+1 \rhd c'\,;d'}$$

$$\frac{t \rhd c \xrightarrow[v_1]{u_1} t+1 \rhd c' \qquad t \rhd d \xrightarrow[v_2]{u_2} t+1 \rhd d'}{t \rhd c \oplus d \xrightarrow[v_1\, v_2]{u_1\, u_2} t+1 \rhd c' \oplus d'}$$

**Fig. 2.** Structural rules for operational semantics, with $p \in \mathbb{Z}$, $k, l$ ranging over $\mathsf{k}$ and $u, v, w$ vectors of elements of $\mathsf{k}$ of the appropriate size. The only vector of $\mathsf{k}^0$ is written as $\bullet$ (as in Definition 3), while a vector $(k_1 \ \ldots \ k_n)^T \in \mathsf{k}^n$ as $k_1 \ldots k_n$.

depends on the time: when $t = 0$, it emits 1, otherwise it emits 0. Observe that the behaviour of all other generators is time-independent.

So far, we described the behaviour of the components in (1) using the intuition that signal flows from left to right: in a transition $\xrightarrow[w]{v}$, the signal $v$ on the left is thought as trigger and $w$ as effect. For the generators in (2), whose behaviour is defined by the rules in the second section of Fig. 2, the behaviour is symmetric—indeed, here it is helpful to think of signals as flowing from right to left. The next section of Fig. 2 specifies the behaviours of the structural connectors of (3): $\times$ is a *twist*, swapping two signals, $\square$ is the empty circuit and — is the *identity* wire: the signals on the left and on the right ports are equal. Finally, the rule for sequential ; composition forces the two components to have the same value $v$ on the shared interface, while for parallel $\oplus$ composition, components can proceed independently. Observe that both forms of composition require component transitions to happen at the same time.

**Definition 4.** *Let $c \in$ ACirc. The* initial state $c_0$ *of $c$ is the one where all the registers store $0$. A* computation *of $c$ starting at time $t \leq 0$ is a (possibly infinite) sequence of transitions*

$$t \triangleright c_0 \xrightarrow[w_t]{v_t} t+1 \triangleright c_1 \xrightarrow[w_{t+1}]{v_{t+1}} t+2 \triangleright c_2 \xrightarrow[w_{t+2}]{v_{t+2}} \dots \tag{4}$$

Since all transitions increment the time by 1, it suffices to record the time at which a computation starts. As a result, to simplify notation, we will omit the runtime context after the first transition and, instead of (4), write

$$t \triangleright \ c_0 \xrightarrow[w_t]{v_t} c_1 \xrightarrow[w_{t+1}]{v_{t+1}} c_2 \xrightarrow[w_{t+2}]{v_{t+2}} \dots$$

*Example 2.* The circuit in Example 1 can perform the following computation.

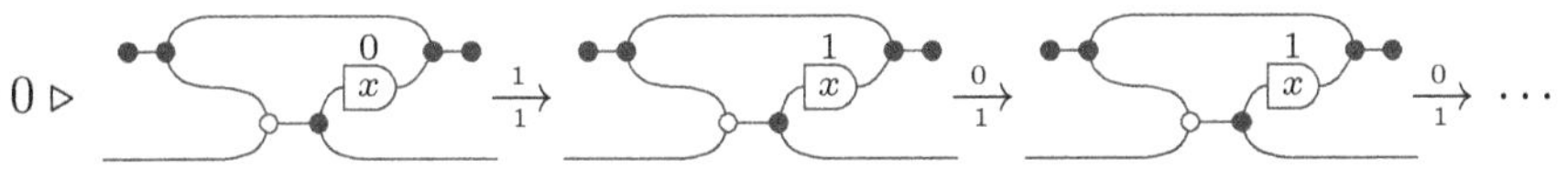

In the example above, the flow has a clear left-to-right orientation, albeit with a feedback loop. For arbitrary circuits of ACirc this is not always the case, which sometimes results in unexpected operational behaviour.

*Example 3.* In $\vdash\!\boxed{x}\!\dashv$ is not possible to identify a consistent flow: $\vdash$ goes from left to right, while $\boxed{x}\!\dashv$ from right to left. Observe that there is no computation starting at $t = 0$, since in the initial state the register contains $0$ while $\vdash$ must emit 1. There is, however, a (unique!) computation starting at time $t = -1$, that loads the register with 1 before $\vdash$ can also emit 1 at time $t = 0$.

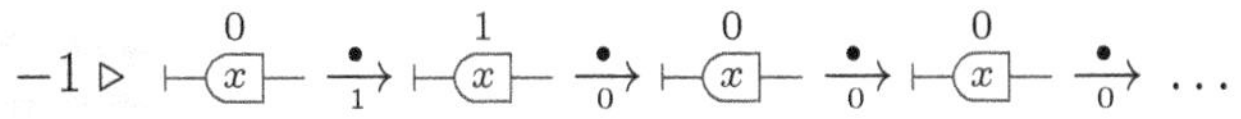

$$-1 \triangleright \ \vdash\!\boxed{x}\!\dashv \xrightarrow[1]{\bullet} \vdash\!\boxed{x}\!\dashv \xrightarrow[0]{\bullet} \vdash\!\boxed{x}\!\dashv \xrightarrow[0]{\bullet} \vdash\!\boxed{x}\!\dashv \xrightarrow[0]{\bullet} \dots$$

Similarly, $\vdash\!\boxed{x}\!\boxed{x}\!\dashv$ features a unique computation starting at time $t = -2$.

$$-2 \triangleright \ \vdash\!\boxed{x}\!\boxed{x}\!\dashv \xrightarrow[1]{\bullet} \vdash\!\boxed{x}\!\boxed{x}\!\dashv \xrightarrow[0]{\bullet} \vdash\!\boxed{x}\!\boxed{x}\!\dashv \xrightarrow[0]{\bullet} \vdash\!\boxed{x}\!\boxed{x}\!\dashv \xrightarrow[0]{\bullet} \dots$$

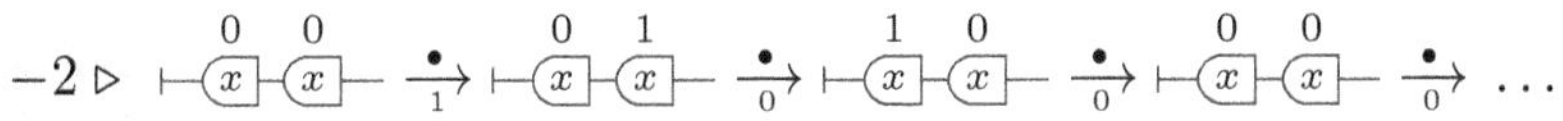

It is worthwhile clarifying the reason why, in the affine calculus, some computations start in the past. As we have already mentioned, in the linear fragment the semantics of all generators is time-independent. It follows easily that time-independence is a property enjoyed by all purely linear circuits. The behaviour of $\vdash$, however, enforces a particular action to occur at time 0. Considering this in conjunction with a right-to-left register results in $\vdash\!\boxed{x}\!\dashv$, and the effect is to anticipate that action by one step to time -1, as shown in Example 3. It is obvious that this construction can be iterated, and it follows that the presence of a single time-dependent generator results in a calculus in which the computation of some terms must start at a finite, but unbounded time in the past.

*Example 4.* Another circuit with conflicting flow is ⊢○. Here there is no possible transition at $t = 0$, since at that time ⊢ must emit a 1 and ─○ can only synchronise on a 0. Instead, the circuit ☐ can always perform an infinite computation $t \triangleright$ ☐ $\xrightarrow{\cdot}{\cdot}$ ☐ $\xrightarrow{\cdot}{\cdot}$ …, for any $t \leq 0$. Roughly speaking, the computations of these two $(0, 0)$ circuits are operational mirror images of the two possible denotations of Proposition 3. This intuition will be made formal in Section 4. For now, it is worth observing that for all $c$, ☐ $\oplus c$ can perform the same computations of $c$, while ⊢○ $\oplus c$ cannot ever make a transition at time 0.

*Example 5.* Consider the circuit ─⟨x⟩─⟨x⟩─, which again features conflicting flow. Our equational theory equates it with ──, but the computations involved are subtly different. Indeed, for any sequence $a_i \in \mathsf{k}$, it is obvious that ── admits the computation

$$0 \triangleright \quad \text{──} \quad \xrightarrow{a_0}{a_0} \quad \text{──} \quad \xrightarrow{a_1}{a_1} \quad \text{──} \quad \xrightarrow{a_2}{a_2} \quad \text{…} \tag{5}$$

The circuit ─⟨x⟩─⟨x⟩─ admits a similar computation, but we must begin at time $t = -1$ in order to first "load" the registers with $a_0$:

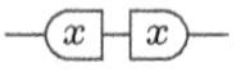

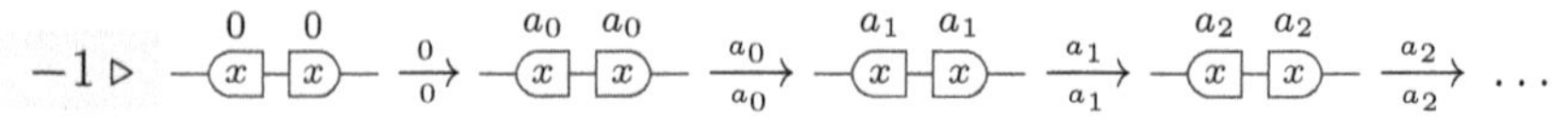

$$-1 \triangleright \quad \overset{0 \quad 0}{─⟨x⟩─⟨x⟩─} \quad \xrightarrow{0}{0} \quad \overset{a_0 \quad a_0}{─⟨x⟩─⟨x⟩─} \quad \xrightarrow{a_0}{a_0} \quad \overset{a_1 \quad a_1}{─⟨x⟩─⟨x⟩─} \quad \xrightarrow{a_1}{a_1} \quad \overset{a_2 \quad a_2}{─⟨x⟩─⟨x⟩─} \quad \xrightarrow{a_2}{a_2} \quad \text{…} \tag{6}$$

The circuit ─⟨x⟩─⟨x⟩─, which again is equated with ── by the equational theory, is more tricky. Although every computation of ── can be reproduced, ─⟨x⟩─⟨x⟩─ admits additional, problematic computations. Indeed, consider

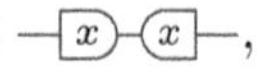

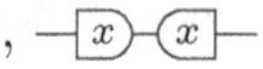

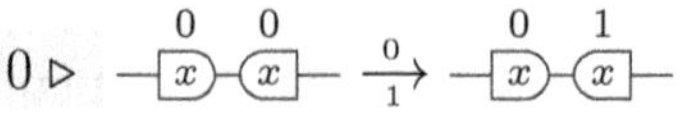

$$0 \triangleright \quad \overset{0 \quad 0}{─⟨x⟩─⟨x⟩─} \quad \xrightarrow{0}{1} \quad \overset{0 \quad 1}{─⟨x⟩─⟨x⟩─} \tag{7}$$

at which point no further transition is possible—the circuit can deadlock.

The following lemma is an easy consequence of the rules of Fig. 2 and follows by structural induction. It states that all circuits can stay idle *in the past.*

**Lemma 2.** *Let $c \in \mathsf{ACirc}[n, m]$ with initial state $c_0$. Then $t \triangleright c_0 \xrightarrow{0}{0} c_0$ if $t < 0$.*

## 3.1   Trajectories

For the non-affine version of the signal flow calculus, we studied in [9] *traces* arising from computations. For the affine extension, this is not possible since, as explained above, we must also consider computations that start in the past. In this paper, rather than traces we adopt a common control theoretic notion.

**Definition 5.** *An $(n, m)$-trajectory $\sigma$ is a $\mathbb{Z}$-indexed sequence $\sigma : \mathbb{Z} \to \mathsf{k}^n \times \mathsf{k}^m$ that is finite in the past, i.e., for which $\exists j \in \mathbb{Z}$ such that $\sigma(i) = (0,0)$ for $i \leq j$.*

By the universal property of the product we can identify $\sigma : \mathbb{Z} \to \mathsf{k}^n \times \mathsf{k}^m$ with the pairing $\langle \sigma_l, \sigma_r \rangle$ of $\sigma_l : \mathbb{Z} \to \mathsf{k}^n$ and $\sigma_r : \mathbb{Z} \to \mathsf{k}^m$. A $(k, m)$-trajectory $\sigma$ and $(m, n)$-trajectory $\tau$ are *compatible* if $\sigma_r = \tau_l$. In this case, we can define their composite, a $(k, n)$-trajectory $\sigma \,;\tau$ by $\sigma\,;\tau := \langle \sigma_l, \tau_r \rangle$. Given an $(n_1, m_1)$-trajectory $\sigma_1$, and an $(n_2, m_2)$-trajectory $\sigma_2$, their product, an $(n_1+n_2, m_1+m_2)$-trajectory $\sigma_1 \oplus \sigma_2$, is defined $(\sigma_1 \oplus \sigma_2)(i) := \begin{pmatrix} \sigma(i) \\ \tau(i) \end{pmatrix}$. Using these two operations we can organise *sets* of trajectories into a prop.

**Definition 6.** *The composition of two sets of trajectories is defined as* $S\,;T := \{\sigma\,;\tau \mid \sigma \in S, \tau \in T$ *are compatible*$\}$. *The product of sets of trajectories is defined as* $S_1 \oplus S_2 := \{\sigma_1 \oplus \sigma_2 \mid \sigma_1 \in S_1, \sigma_2 \in S_2\}$.

Clearly both operations are strictly associative. The unit for $\oplus$ is the singleton with the unique $(0,0)$-trajectory. Also ; has a two sided identity, given by sets of "copycat" $(n, n)$-trajectories. Indeed, we have that:

**Proposition 4.** *Sets of $(n, m)$-trajectories are the arrows $n \to m$ of a prop* Traj *with composition and monoidal product given as in Definition 6.*

Traj serves for us as the domain for operational semantics: given a circuit $c$ and an *infinite* computation

$$t \rhd c_0 \xrightarrow[v_t]{u_t} c_1 \xrightarrow[v_{t+1}]{u_{t+1}} c_2 \xrightarrow[v_{t+2}]{u_{t+2}} \cdots$$

its associated trajectory $\sigma$ is

$$\sigma(i) = \begin{cases} (u_i, v_i) & \text{if } i \geq t, \\ (0,0) & \text{otherwise.} \end{cases} \tag{8}$$

**Definition 7.** *For a circuit $c$, $\langle c \rangle$ is the set of trajectories given by its infinite computations, following the translation* (8) *above.*

The assignment $c \mapsto \langle c \rangle$ is compositional, that is:

**Theorem 1.** $\langle \cdot \rangle \colon$ ACirc $\to$ Traj *is a morphism of props.*

*Example 6.* Consider the computations (5) and (6) from Example 5. According to (8) both are translated into the trajectory $\sigma$ mapping $i \geq 0$ into $(a_i, a_i)$ and $i < 0$ into $(0, 0)$. The reader can easily verify that, more generally, it holds that $\langle$—$\rangle = \langle$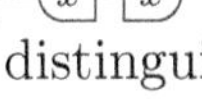$\rangle$. At this point it is worth to remark that the two circuits would be distinguished when looking at their traces: the trace of computation (5) is different from the trace of (6). Indeed, the full abstraction result in [9] does not hold for all circuits, but only for those of a certain kind. The affine extension obliges us to consider computations that starts in the past and, in turn, this drives us toward a stronger full abstraction result, shown in the next section.

Before concluding, it is important to emphasise that $\langle$—$\rangle = \langle$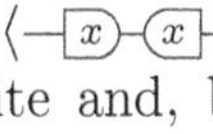$\rangle$ also holds. Indeed, problematic computations, like (7), are all finite and, by definition, do not give rise to any trajectory. The reader should note that the use of trajectories is not a semantic device to get rid of problematic computations. In fact, trajectories do not appear in the statement of our full abstraction result; they are merely a convenient tool to prove it. Another result (Proposition 9) independently takes care of ruling out problematic computations.

# 4 Contextual Equivalence and Full Abstraction

This section contains the main contribution of the paper: a traditional full abstraction result asserting that contextual equivalence agrees with denotational equivalence. It is not a coincidence that we prove this result in the affine setting: affinity plays a crucial role, both in its statement and proof. In particular, Proposition 3 gives us two possibilities for the denotation of (0, 0) circuits: *(i)* $\emptyset$—which, roughly speaking, means that there is a problem (see e.g. Example 4) and no infinite computation is possible—or *(ii)* $id_0$, in which case infinite computations are possible. This provides us with a basic notion of observation, akin to observing termination vs non-termination in the λ-calculus.

**Definition 8.** *For a circuit* $c \in \mathsf{ACirc}[0,0]$ *we write* $c \uparrow$ *if* $c$ *can perform an infinite computation and* $c \not\uparrow$ *otherwise. For instance* ⬚ $\uparrow$, *while* ⊢○ $\not\uparrow$.

To be able to make observations about arbitrary circuits we need to introduce an appropriate notion of context. Roughly speaking, contexts for us are (0, 0)-circuits with a hole into which we can plug another circuit. Since ours is a variable-free presentation, "dangling wires" assume the role of free variables [16]: restricting to (0, 0) contexts is therefore analogous to considering *ground* contexts—i.e. contexts with no free variables—a standard concept of programming language theory.

To define contexts formally, we extend the syntax of Section 2.1 with an extra generator "$-$" of sort $(n, m)$. A (0, 0)-circuit of this extended syntax is a *context* when "$-$" occurs exactly once. Given an $(n, m)$-circuit $c$ and a context $C[-]$, we write $C[c]$ for the circuit obtained by replacing the unique occurrence of "$-$" by $c$.

With this setup, given an $(n, m)$-circuit $c$, we can insert it into a context $C[-]$ and observe the possible outcome: either $C[c] \uparrow$ or $C[c] \not\uparrow$. This naturally leads us to contextual equivalence and the statement of our main result.

**Definition 9.** *Given* $c, d \in \mathsf{ACirc}[n,m]$, *we say that they are* contextually equivalent, *written* $c \equiv d$, *if for all contexts* $C[-]$,

$$C[c] \uparrow \text{ iff } C[d] \uparrow .$$

*Example 7.* Recall from Example 5, the circuits —— and —[x]-(x]—. Take the context $C[-] = c_\sigma \,;\; - \;; c_\tau$ for $c_\sigma \in \mathsf{ACirc}[0,1]$ and $c_\tau \in \mathsf{ACirc}[1,0]$. Assume that $c_\sigma$ and $c_\tau$ have a single infinite computation. Call $\sigma$ and $\tau$ the corresponding trajectories. If $\sigma = \tau$, both $C[$——$]$ and $C[$—[x]-(x]—$]$ would be able to perform an infinite computation. Instead if $\sigma \neq \tau$, none of them would perform any infinite computation: —— would stop at time $t$, for $t$ the first moment such that $\sigma(t) \neq \tau(t)$, while $C[$—[x]-(x]—$]$ would stop at time $t+1$.

Now take as context $C[-] =$ ●—$\,;\; - \;;$—●. In contrast to $c_\sigma$ and $c_\tau$, ●— and —● can perform more than one single computation: at any time they can nondeterministically emit any value. Thus every computation of $C[$——$] =$ ●—●

can *always* be extended to an infinite one, forcing synchronisation of $\bullet\!-$ and $-\!\bullet$ at each step. For $C[-\![x\rangle\!\langle x]\!-] = \bullet\!-\![x\rangle\!\langle x]\!-\!\bullet$, $\bullet\!-$ and $-\!\bullet$ may emit different values at time $t$, but the computation will get stuck at $t+1$. However, our definition of $\uparrow$ only cares about whether $C[-\![x\rangle\!\langle x]\!-]$ *can* perform an infinite computation. Indeed it can, as long as $\bullet\!-$ and $-\!\bullet$ consistently emit the same value at each time step.

If we think of contexts as tests, and say that a circuit $c$ passes test $C[-]$ if $C[c]$ perform an infinite computation, then our notion of contextual equivalence is *may-testing* equivalence [13]. From this perspective, $-$ and $-\![x\rangle\!\langle x]\!-$ are not *must equivalent*, since the former must pass the test $\bullet\!-\,;\,-\,;\,-\!\bullet$ while $-\![x\rangle\!\langle x]\!-$ may not. It is worth to remark here that the distinction between may and must testing will cease to make sense in Section 5 where we identify a certain class of circuits equipped with a proper flow directionality and thus a deterministic, input-output, behaviour.

**Theorem 2 (Full abstraction).** *$c \equiv d$ iff $c \stackrel{\mathbb{IH}}{=} d$*

The remainder of this section is devoted to the proof of Theorem 2. We will start by clarifying the relationship between fractions of polynomials (the denotational domain) and trajectories (the operational domain).

## 4.1 From Polynomial Fractions to Trajectories

The missing link between polynomial fractions and trajectories are *(formal) Laurent series*: we now recall this notion. Formally, a Laurent series is a function $\sigma\colon \mathbb{Z} \to \mathsf{k}$ for which there exists $j \in \mathbb{Z}$ such that $\sigma(i) = 0$ for all $i < j$. We write $\sigma$ as $\dots, \sigma(-1), \underline{\sigma(0)}, \sigma(1), \dots$ with position 0 underlined, or as formal sum $\sum_{i=d}^{\infty} \sigma(i)x^i$. Each Laurent series $\sigma$ has then a *degree* $d \in \mathbb{Z}$, which is the first non-zero element. Laurent series form a field $\mathsf{k}((x))$: sum is pointwise, product is by convolution, and the inverse $\sigma^{-1}$ of $\sigma$ with degree $d$ is defined as:

$$\sigma^{-1}(i) = \begin{cases} 0 & \text{if } i < -d \\ \sigma(d)^{-1} & \text{if } i = -d \\ \frac{\sum_{i=1}^{n}\left(\sigma(d+i)\cdot\sigma^{-1}(-d+n-i)\right)}{-\sigma(d)} & \text{if } i{=}{-d}{+}n \text{ for } n{>}0 \end{cases} \tag{9}$$

Note (formal) power series, which form 'just' a ring $\mathsf{k}[[x]]$, are a particular case of Laurent series, namely those $\sigma$s for which $d \geq 0$. What is most interesting for our purposes is how polynomials and fractions of polynomials relate to $\mathsf{k}((x))$ and $\mathsf{k}[[x]]$. First, the ring $\mathsf{k}[x]$ of polynomials embeds into $\mathsf{k}[[x]]$, and thus into $\mathsf{k}((x))$: a polynomial $p_0 + p_1x + \cdots + p_nx^n$ can also be regarded as the power series $\sum_{i=0}^{\infty} p_ix^i$ with $p_i = 0$ for all $i > n$. Because Laurent series are closed under division, this immediately gives also an embedding of the field of polynomial fractions $\mathsf{k}(x)$ into $\mathsf{k}((x))$. Note that the full expressiveness of $\mathsf{k}((x))$ is required: for instance, the fraction $\frac{1}{x}$ is represented as the Laurent series $\dots, 0, 1, \underline{0}, 0, \dots,$

which is not a power series, because a non-zero value appears before position 0. In fact, fractions that are expressible as power series are precisely the *rational* fractions, i.e. of the form $\frac{k_0+k_1x+k_2x^2\cdots+k_nx^n}{l_0+l_1x+l_2x^2\cdots+l_nx^n}$ where $l_0 \neq 0$.

Rational fractions form a ring $\mathsf{k}\langle x\rangle$ which, differently from the full field $\mathsf{k}(x)$, embeds into $\mathsf{k}[[x]]$. Indeed, whenever $l_0 \neq 0$, the inverse of $l_0 + l_1x + l_2x^2 \cdots + l_nx^n$ is, by (9), a *bona fide* power series. The commutative diagram on the right is a summary.

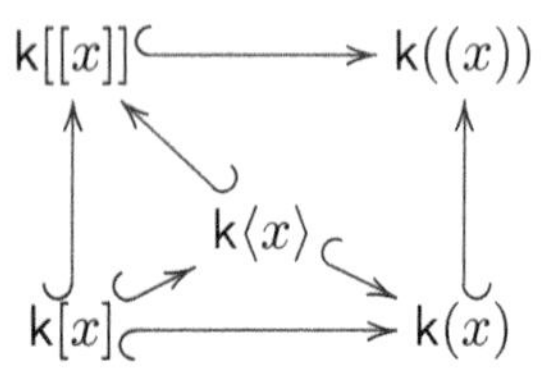


Relations between $\mathsf{k}((x))$-vectors organise themselves into a prop $\mathsf{ARel}_{\mathsf{k}((x))}$ (see Definition 2). There is an evident prop morphism $\iota\colon \mathsf{ARel}_{\mathsf{k}(x)} \to \mathsf{ARel}_{\mathsf{k}((x))}$: it maps the empty affine relation on $\mathsf{k}(x)$ to the one on $\mathsf{k}((x))$, and otherwise applies pointwise the embedding of $\mathsf{k}(x)$ into $\mathsf{k}((x))$. For the next step, observe that trajectories are in fact rearrangements of Laurent series: each pair of vectors $(u, v) \in \mathsf{k}((x))^n \times \mathsf{k}((x))^m$, as on the left below, yields the trajectory $\kappa(u, v)$ defined for all $i \in \mathbb{Z}$ as on the right below.

$$(u,v) = \left( \begin{pmatrix} \alpha^1 \\ \vdots \\ \alpha^n \end{pmatrix}, \begin{pmatrix} \beta^1 \\ \vdots \\ \beta^m \end{pmatrix} \right) \qquad \kappa(u,v)(i) = \left( \begin{pmatrix} \alpha^1(i) \\ \vdots \\ \alpha^n(i) \end{pmatrix}, \begin{pmatrix} \beta^1(i) \\ \vdots \\ \beta^m(i) \end{pmatrix} \right)$$

Similarly to $\iota$, the assignment $\kappa$ extends to sets of vectors, and also to a prop morphism from $\mathsf{ARel}_{\mathsf{k}((x))}$ to $\mathsf{Traj}$. Together, $\kappa$ and $\iota$ provide the desired link between operational and denotational semantics.

**Theorem 3.** $\langle\cdot\rangle = \kappa \circ \iota \circ [\![\cdot]\!]$

*Proof.* Since both are symmetric monoidal functors from a free prop, it is enough to check the statement for the generators of $\mathsf{ACirc}$. We show, as an example, the case of $-\!\!\bullet\!\!\subset$. By Definition 3, $[\![-\!\!\bullet\!\!\subset]\!] = \left\{ \left( p, \begin{pmatrix} p \\ p \end{pmatrix} \right) \mid p \in \mathsf{k}(x) \right\}$. This is mapped by $\iota$ to $\left\{ \left( \alpha, \begin{pmatrix} \alpha \\ \alpha \end{pmatrix} \right) \mid \alpha \in \mathsf{k}((x)) \right\}$. Now, to see that $\kappa(\iota([\![-\!\!\bullet\!\!\subset]\!])) = \langle -\!\!\bullet\!\!\subset \rangle$, it is enough to observe that a trajectory $\sigma$ is in $\kappa(\iota([\![-\!\!\bullet\!\!\subset]\!]))$ precisely when, for all $i$, there exists some $k_i \in \mathsf{k}$ such that $\sigma(i) = \left( k_i, \begin{pmatrix} k_i \\ k_i \end{pmatrix} \right)$. □

### 4.2 Proof of Full Abstraction

We now have the ingredients to prove Theorem 2. First, we prove an adequacy result for (0, 0) circuits.

**Proposition 5.** *Let* $c \in \mathsf{ACirc}[0,0]$. *Then* $[\![c]\!] = id_0$ *if and only if* $c\uparrow$.

*Proof.* By Proposition 3, either $[\![c]\!] = id_0$ or $[\![c]\!] = \emptyset$, which, combined with Theorem 3, means that $\langle c\rangle = \kappa \circ \iota(id_0)$ or $\langle c\rangle = \kappa \circ \iota(\emptyset)$. By definition of $\iota$ this implies that either $\langle c\rangle$ contains a trajectory or not. In the first case $c\uparrow$; in the second $c\not\uparrow$. □

Next we obtain a result that relates denotational equality in all contexts to equality in $\mathsf{a}\mathbb{IH}$. Note that it is not trivial: since we consider ground contexts it does not make sense to merely consider "identity" contexts. Instead, it is at this point that we make another crucial use of affinity, taking advantage of the increased expressivity of affine circuits, as showcased by Proposition 2.

**Proposition 6.** *If* $[\![C[c]]\!] = [\![C[d]]\!]$ *for all contexts* $C[-]$*, then* $c \overset{\mathsf{a}\mathbb{IH}}{=} d$.

*Proof.* Suppose that $c \overset{\mathsf{a}\mathbb{IH}}{\neq} d$. Then $[\![c]\!] \neq [\![d]\!]$. Since both $[\![c]\!]$ and $[\![d]\!]$ are affine relations over $\mathsf{k}(x)$, there exists a pair of vectors $(u, v) \in \mathsf{k}(x)^n \times \mathsf{k}(x)^m$ that is in one of $[\![c]\!]$ and $[\![d]\!]$, but not both. Assume wlog that $(u, v) \in [\![c]\!]$ and $(u, v) \notin [\![d]\!]$. By Proposition 2, there exists $c_u$ and $c_v$ such that $[\![c_u\,; c\,; c_v]\!] = [\![c_u]\!]\,; [\![c]\!]\,; [\![c_v]\!] = \{(\bullet, u)\}\,; [\![c]\!]\,; \{(v, \bullet)\}$. Since $(u, v) \in [\![c]\!]$, then $[\![c_u\,; c\,; c_v]\!] = \{(\bullet, \bullet)\}$. Instead, since $(u, v) \notin [\![d]\!]$, we have that $[\![c_u\,; d\,; c_v]\!] = \emptyset$. Therefore, for the context $C[-] = c_u\,;\, -\,; c_v$, we have that $[\![C[c]]\!] \neq [\![C[d]]\!]$. □

The proof of our main result is now straightforward.

*Proof of Theorem 2.* Let us first suppose that $c \overset{\mathsf{a}\mathbb{IH}}{=} d$. Then $[\![C[c]]\!] = [\![C[d]]\!]$ for all contexts $C[-]$, since $[\![\cdot]\!]$ is a morphism of props. By Corollary 5, it follows immediately that $C[c] \uparrow$ if and only if $C[d] \uparrow$, namely $c \equiv d$.

Conversely, suppose that, for all $C[-]$, $C[c] \uparrow$ iff $C[d] \uparrow$. Again by Corollary 5, we have that $[\![C[c]]\!] = [\![C[d]]\!]$. We conclude by invoking Proposition 6. □

## 5 Functional Behaviour and Signal Flow Graphs

There is a sub-prop $\mathsf{SF}$ of $\mathsf{Circ}$ of classical *signal flow graphs* (see *e.g.* [21]). Here signal flows left-to-right, possibly featuring *feedback loops*, provided that these go through at least one register. Feedback can be captured algebraically via an operation $\mathsf{Tr}(\cdot)\colon \mathsf{Circ}[n+1, m+1] \to \mathsf{Circ}[n, m]$ taking $c\colon n+1 \to m+1$ to:

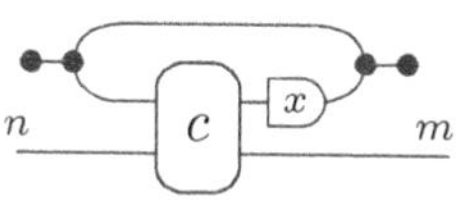


Following [9], let us call $\overrightarrow{\mathsf{Circ}}$ the free sub-prop of $\mathsf{Circ}$ of circuits built from (3) and the generators of (1), without ⊢—. Then $\mathsf{SF}$ is defined as the closure of $\overrightarrow{\mathsf{Circ}}$ under $\mathsf{Tr}(\cdot)$. For instance, the circuit of Example 2 is in $\mathsf{SF}$.

Signal flow graphs are intimately connected to the executability of circuits. In general, the rules of Figure 2 do not assume a fixed flow orientation. As a result, some circuits in $\mathsf{Circ}$ are not executable as *functional input-output* systems, as we have demonstrated with ⊢(x)—, ⊢○ and —[x]-(x)— of Examples 3-5. Notice that none of these are signal flow graphs. In fact, the circuits of $\mathsf{SF}$ do not have pathological behaviour, as we shall state more precisely in Proposition 9.

At the denotational level, signal flow graphs correspond precisely to *rational* functional behaviours, that is, matrices whose coefficients are in the ring $\mathsf{k}\langle x\rangle$

of *rational fractions* (see Section 4.1). We call such matrices, rational matrices. One may check that the semantics of a signal flow graph $c\colon (n, m)$ is always of the form $[\![c]\!] = \{(v, A \cdot v) \mid v \in \mathsf{k}(x)^n\}$, for some $m \times n$ rational matrix $A$. Conversely, all relations that are the graph of rational matrices can be expressed as signal flow graphs.

**Proposition 7.** *Given $c\colon (n, m)$, we have $[\![c]\!] = \{(p, A \cdot p) \mid p \in \mathsf{k}(x)^n\}$ for some rational $m \times n$ matrix $A$ iff there exists a signal flow graph $f$, i.e., a circuit $f\colon (n, m)$ of* SF, *such that $[\![f]\!] = [\![c]\!]$.*

*Proof.* This is a folklore result in control theory which can be found in [30]. The details of the translation between rational matrices and circuits of SF can be found in [10, Section 7]. □

The following gives an alternative characterisation of rational matrices—and therefore, by Proposition 7, of the behaviour of signal flow graphs—that clarifies their role as realisations of circuits.

**Proposition 8.** *An $m \times n$ matrix is rational iff $A \cdot r \in \mathsf{k}\langle x \rangle^m$ for all $r \in \mathsf{k}\langle x \rangle^n$.*

Proposition 8 is another guarantee of good behaviour—it justifies the name of inputs (resp. outputs) for the left (resp. right) ports of signal flow graphs. Recall from Section 4.1 that rational fractions can be mapped to Laurent series of nonnegative degree, i.e., to plain power series. Operationally, these correspond to trajectories that start after $t = 0$. Proposition 8 guarantees that any trajectory of a signal flow graph whose first nonzero value on the left appears at time $t = 0$, will not have nonzero values on the right starting before time $t = 0$. In other words, signal flow graphs can be seen as processing a stream of values from left to right. As a result, their ports can be clearly partitioned into inputs and outputs.

But the circuits of SF are too restrictive for our purposes. For example, 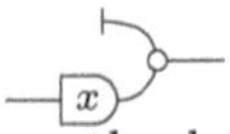 can also be seen to realise a functional behaviour transforming inputs on the left into outputs on the right yet it is not in SF. Its behaviour is no longer linear, but affine. Hence, we need to extend signal flow graphs to include functional affine behaviour. The following definition does just that.

**Definition 10.** *Let* ASF *be the sub-prop of* ACirc *obtained from* all *the generators in* (1), *closed under* Tr(·). *Its circuits are called* affine signal flow graphs.

As before, none of 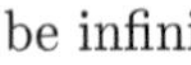, 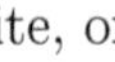 and 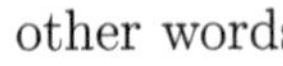 from Examples 3-5 are affine signal flow graphs. In fact, ASF rules out pathological behaviour: all computations can be extended to be infinite, or in other words, do not get stuck.

**Proposition 9.** *Given an affine signal flow graph $f$, for every computation*

$$t \triangleright f_0 \xrightarrow[v_t]{u_t} f_1 \xrightarrow[v_{p+1}]{u_{t+1}} \dots f_n$$

*there exists a trajectory $\sigma \in \langle c \rangle$ such that $\sigma(i) = (u_i, v_i)$ for $t \le i \le t + n$.*

*Proof.* By induction on the structure of affine signal flow graphs. □

If $\mathsf{SF}$ circuits correspond precisely to $\mathsf{k}\langle x\rangle$-matrices, those of $\mathsf{ASF}$ correspond precisely to $\mathsf{k}\langle x\rangle$-affine transformations.

**Definition 11.** *A map* $f\colon \mathsf{k}(x)^n \to \mathsf{k}(x)^m$ *is an* affine map *if there exists an* $m \times n$ *matrix* $A$ *and* $b \in \mathsf{k}(x)^m$ *such that* $f(p) = A \cdot p + b$ *for all* $p \in \mathsf{k}(x)^n$. *We call the pair* $(A, b)$ *the representation of* $f$.

The notion of rational affine map is a straightforward extension of the linear case and so is the characterisation in terms of rational input-output behaviour.

**Definition 12.** *An affine map* $f\colon p \mapsto A \cdot p + b$ *is* rational *if* $A$ *and* $b$ *have coefficients in* $\mathsf{k}\langle x\rangle$.

**Proposition 10.** *An affine map* $f\colon \mathsf{k}(x)^n \to \mathsf{k}(x)^m$ *is rational iff* $f(r) \in \mathsf{k}\langle x\rangle^m$ *for all* $r \in \mathsf{k}\langle x\rangle^n$.

The following extends the correspondence of Proposition 7, showing that $\mathsf{ASF}$ is the rightful affine heir of $\mathsf{SF}$.

**Proposition 11.** *Given* $c\colon (n, m)$, *we have* $[\![c]\!] = \{(p, f(p)) \mid p \in \mathsf{k}(x)^n\}$ *for some rational affine map* $f$ *iff there exists an affine signal flow graph* $g$, *i.e., a circuit* $g\colon (n, m)$ *of* $\mathsf{ASF}$, *such that* $[\![g]\!] = [\![c]\!]$.

*Proof.* Let $f$ be given by $p \mapsto Ap + b$ for some rational $m \times n$ matrix $A$ and vector $b \in \mathsf{k}\langle x\rangle^m$. By Proposition 7, we can find a circuit $c_A$ of $\mathsf{SF}$ such that $[\![c_A]\!] = \{(p, A \cdot p) \mid p \in \mathsf{k}(x)\}$. Similarly, we can represent $b$ as a signal flow graph $c_b$ of sort $(1, m)$. Then, the circuit on the right is clearly in $\mathsf{ASF}$ and verifies $[\![c]\!] = \{(p, Ap + b) \mid p \in \mathsf{k}(x)\}$ as required.

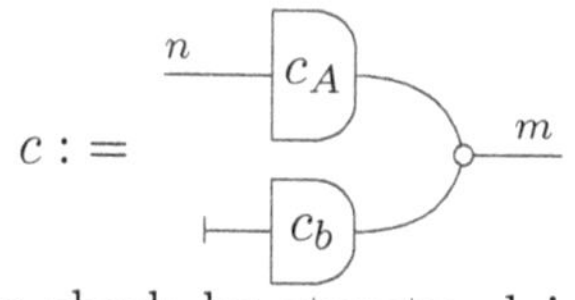


For the converse direction it is straightforward to check by structural induction that the denotation of affine signal flow graphs is the graph (in the set-theoretic sense of pairs of values) of some rational affine map. □

## 6 Realisability

In the previous section we gave a restricted class of morphisms with good behavioural properties. We may wonder how much of $\mathsf{ACirc}$ we can capture with this restricted class. The answer is, in a precise sense: most of it.

Surprisingly, the behaviours realisable in $\mathsf{Circ}$—the purely linear fragment—are not more expressive. In fact, from an operational (or denotational, by full abstraction) point of view, $\mathsf{Circ}$ is nothing more than jumbled up version of $\mathsf{SF}$. Indeed, it turns out that $\mathsf{Circ}$ enjoys a *realisability* theorem: any circuit $c$ of $\mathsf{Circ}$ can be associated with one of $\mathsf{SF}$, that implements or realises the behaviour of $c$ into an executable form.

But the corresponding realisation may not flow neatly from left to right like signal flow graphs do—its inputs and outputs may have been moved from one side to the other. Consider for example, the circuit on the right

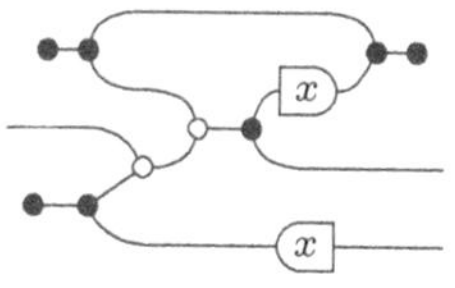

It does not belong to SF but it can be read as a signal flow graph with an input that has been bent and moved to the bottom right. The behaviour it realises can therefore executed by rewiring this port to obtain a signal flow graph:

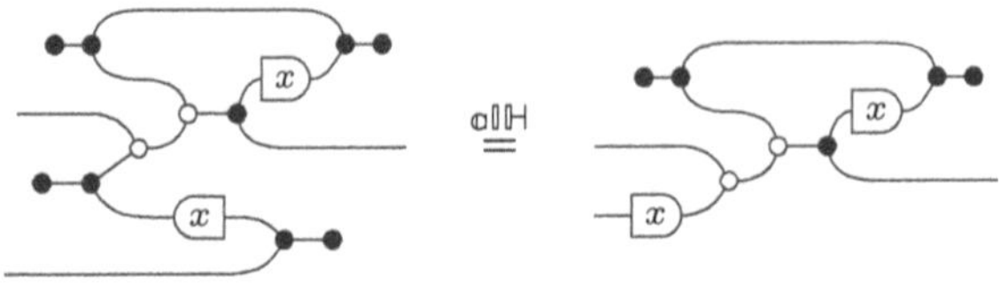

We will not make this notion of rewiring precise here but refer the reader to [9] for the details. The intuition is simply that a rewiring partitions the ports of a circuit into two sets—that we call inputs and outputs—and uses ●◖ or ◗● to bend input ports to the left and and output ports to the right. The realisability theorem then states that we can always recover a (not necessarily unique) signal flow graph from any circuit by performing these operations.

**Theorem 4.** *[9, Theorem 5] Every circuit in* Circ *is equivalent to the rewiring of a signal flow graph, called its* realisation.

This theorem allows us to extend the notion of inputs and outputs to all circuits of Circ.

**Definition 13.** *A port of a circuit c of* Circ *is an* input *(resp.* output*) port, if there exists a realisation for which it is an input (resp. output).*

Note that, since realisations are not necessarily unique, the same port can be both an input and an output. Then, the realisability theorem (Theorem 4) says that every port is always an input, an output or both (but never neither).

An output-only port is an output port that is not an input port. Similarly an input-only port in an input port that is not an output port.

*Example 8.* The left port of the register —[$x$⟩— is input-only whereas its right port is output-only. In the identity wire, both ports are input and output ports. The single port of ○— is output-only ; that of —● is input-only.

While in the purely linear case, all behaviours are realisable, the general case of ACirc is a bit more subtle. To make this precise, we can extend our definition of realisability to include affine signal flow graphs.

**Definition 14.** *A circuit of* ACirc *is* realisable *if its ports can be rewired so that it is equivalent to a circuit of* ASF.

*Example 9.* ⊢— is realisable; ⊢⟨$x$]— is not.

Notice that Proposition 11, gives the following equivalent semantic criterion for realisability. Realisable behaviours are precisely those that map rationals to rationals.

**Theorem 5.** *A circuit c is realisable iff its ports can be partitioned into two sets, that we call inputs and outputs, such that the corresponding rewiring of c is an affine rational map from inputs to outputs.*

We offer another perspective on realisability below: realisable behaviours correspond precisely to those for which the ⊢— constants are connected to inputs of the underlying Circ-circuit. First, notice that, since

in $\mathbb{aIH}$, we can assume without loss of generality that each circuit contains exactly one ⊢— .

**Proposition 12.** *Every circuit c of* ACirc *is equivalent to one with precisely one* ⊢— *and no* —⊣.

For $c\colon (n, m)$ a circuit of ACirc, we will call $\hat{c}$ the circuit of Circ of sort $(n+1, m)$ that one obtains by first transforming $c$ into an equivalent circuit with a single ⊢— and no —⊣ as above, then removing this ⊢—, and replacing it by an identity wire that extends to the left boundary.

**Theorem 6.** *A circuit c is realisable iff* ⊢— *is connected to an input port of* $\hat{c}$.

## 7 Conclusion and Future Work

We introduced the operational semantics of the *affine* extension of the signal flow calculus and proved that contextual equivalence coincides with denotational equality, previously introduced and axiomatised in [6]. We have observed that, at the denotational level, affinity provides two key properties (Propositions 2 and 3) for the proof of full abstraction. However, at the operational level, affinity forces us to consider computations starting in the *past* (Example 3) as the syntax allows terms lacking a proper flow directionality. This leads to circuits that might deadlock (⊢○ in Example 4) or perform some problematic computations (—[x]—⟨x]— in Example 5). We have identified a proper subclass of circuits, called affine signal flow graphs (Definition 10), that possess an inherent flow directionality: in these circuits, the same pathological behaviours do not arise (Proposition 9). This class is not too restrictive as it captures all desirable behaviours: a realisability result (Theorem 5) states that all and only the circuits that do not need computations to start in the past are equivalent to (the rewiring of) an affine signal flow graph.

The reader may be wondering why we do not restrict the syntax to affine signal flow graphs. The reason is that, like in the behavioural approach to control theory [33], the lack of flow direction is what allows the (affine) signal flow calculus to achieve a strong form of compositionality and a complete axiomatisation (see [9] for a deeper discussion).

We expect that similar methods and results can be extended to other models of computation. Our next step is to tackle Petri nets, which, as shown in [5], can be regarded as terms of the signal flow calculus, but over $\mathbb{N}$ rather than a field.

## References

1. Abramsky, S., Coecke, B.: A categorical semantics of quantum protocols. In: Proceedings of the 19th Annual IEEE Symposium on Logic in Computer Science (LICS), 2004. pp. 415–425. IEEE (2004)
2. Baez, J., Erbele, J.: Categories in control. Theory and Applications of Categories **30**, 836–881 (2015)
3. Baez, J.C.: Network theory (2014), `http://math.ucr.edu/home/baez/networks/`, website (retrieved 15/04/2014)
4. Basold, H., Bonsangue, M., Hansen, H., Rutten, J.: (Co)Algebraic characterizations of signal flow graphs. In: van Breugel, F., Kashefi, E., Palamidessi, C., Rutten, J. (eds.) Horizons of the Mind. A Tribute to Prakash Panangaden, Lecture Notes in Computer Science, vol. 8464, pp. 124–145. Springer International Publishing (2014)
5. Bonchi, F., Holland, J., Piedeleu, R., Sobociński, P., Zanasi, F.: Diagrammatic algebra: from linear to concurrent systems. Proceedings of the 46th ACM SIGPLAN Symposium on Principles of Programming Languages (POPL) **3**, 1–28 (2019)
6. Bonchi, F., Piedeleu, R., Sobociński, P., Zanasi, F.: Graphical affine algebra. In: Proceedings of the 34th Annual ACM/IEEE Symposium on Logic in Computer Science (LICS). pp. 1–12 (2019)
7. Bonchi, F., Piedeleu, R., Sobociński, P., Zanasi, F.: Contextual equivalence for signal flow graphs (2020), `https://arxiv.org/abs/2002.08874`
8. Bonchi, F., Sobociński, P., Zanasi, F.: A categorical semantics of signal flow graphs. In: Proceedings of the 25th International Conference on Concurrency Theory (CONCUR). pp. 435–450. Springer (2014)
9. Bonchi, F., Sobocinski, P., Zanasi, F.: Full abstraction for signal flow graphs. In: Proceedings of the 42nd Annual ACM SIGPLAN Symposium on Principles of Programming Languages (POPL). pp. 515–526 (2015)
10. Bonchi, F., Sobocinski, P., Zanasi, F.: The calculus of signal flow diagrams I: linear relations on streams. Information and Computation **252**, 2–29 (2017)
11. Coecke, B., Duncan, R.: Interacting quantum observables. In: Proceedings of the 35th international colloquium on Automata, Languages and Programming (ICALP), Part II. pp. 298–310 (2008)
12. Coecke, B., Kissinger, A.: Picturing Quantum Processes - A first course in Quantum Theory and Diagrammatic Reasoning. Cambridge University Press (2017)
13. De Nicola, R., Hennessy, M.C.: Testing equivalences for processes. Theoretical Computer Science **34**(1-2), 83–133 (1984)
14. Ghica, D.R.: Diagrammatic reasoning for delay-insensitive asynchronous circuits. In: Computation, Logic, Games, and Quantum Foundations. The Many Facets of Samson Abramsky, pp. 52–68. Springer (2013)
15. Ghica, D.R., Jung, A.: Categorical semantics of digital circuits. In: Proceedings of the 16th Conference on Formal Methods in Computer-Aided Design (FMCAD). pp. 41–48 (2016)
16. Ghica, D.R., Lopez, A.: A structural and nominal syntax for diagrams. In: Proceedings 14th International Conference on Quantum Physics and Logic (QPL). pp. 71–83 (2017)
17. Hoare, C.A.R.: Communicating Sequential Processes. Prentice Hall (1985)
18. Honda, K., Yoshida, N.: On reduction-based process semantics. Theoretical Computer Science **152**(2), 437–486 (1995)

19. Mac Lane, S.: Categorical algebra. Bulletin of the American Mathematical Society **71**, 40–106 (1965)
20. Mac Lane, S.: Categories for the Working Mathematician. Springer (1998)
21. Mason, S.J.: Feedback Theory: I. Some Properties of Signal Flow Graphs. MIT Research Laboratory of Electronics (1953)
22. Milius, S.: A sound and complete calculus for finite stream circuits. In: Proceedings of the 2010 25th Annual IEEE Symposium on Logic in Computer Science (LICS). pp. 421–430 (2010)
23. Milner, R.: A Calculus of Communicating Systems, Lecture Notes in Computer Science, vol. 92. Springer (1980)
24. Milner, R., Sangiorgi, D.: Barbed bisimulation. In: Proceedings of the 19th International Colloquium on Automata, Languages and Programming (ICALP). pp. 685–695 (1992)
25. Morris Jr, J.H.: Lambda-calculus models of programming languages. Ph.D. thesis, Massachusetts Institute of Technology (1969)
26. Pavlovic, D.: Monoidal computer I: Basic computability by string diagrams. Information and Computation **226**, 94–116 (2013)
27. Pavlovic, D.: Monoidal computer II: Normal complexity by string diagrams. arXiv:1402.5687 (2014)
28. Plotkin, G.D.: Call-by-name, call-by-value and the $\lambda$-calculus. Theoretical Computer Science **1**(2), 125–159 (1975)
29. Rutten, J.J.M.M.: A tutorial on coinductive stream calculus and signal flow graphs. Theoretical Computer Science **343**(3), 443–481 (2005)
30. Rutten, J.J.M.M.: Rational streams coalgebraically. Logical Methods in Computer Science **4**(3) (2008)
31. Selinger, P.: A survey of graphical languages for monoidal categories. Springer Lecture Notes in Physics **13**(813), 289–355 (2011)
32. Shannon, C.E.: The theory and design of linear differential equation machines. Tech. rep., National Defence Research Council (1942)
33. Willems, J.C.: The behavioural approach to open and interconnected systems. IEEE Control Systems Magazine **27**, 46–99 (2007)

# 5

# A Duality Theoretic View on Limits of Finite Structures*

Mai Gehrke[1], Tomáš Jakl[1], and Luca Reggio[2](✉)

[1] CNRS and Université Côte d'Azur, Nice, France
{mgehrke,tomas.jakl}@unice.fr
[2] Institute of Computer Science of the Czech Academy of Sciences, Prague, Czech Republic and Mathematical Institute, University of Bern, Switzerland
luca.reggio@math.unibe.ch

**Abstract.** A systematic theory of *structural limits* for finite models has been developed by Nešetřil and Ossona de Mendez. It is based on the insight that the collection of finite structures can be embedded, via a map they call the *Stone pairing*, in a space of measures, where the desired limits can be computed. We show that a closely related but finer grained space of measures arises — via Stone-Priestley duality and the notion of types from model theory — by enriching the expressive power of first-order logic with certain "probabilistic operators". We provide a sound and complete calculus for this extended logic and expose the functorial nature of this construction.
The consequences are two-fold. On the one hand, we identify the logical gist of the theory of structural limits. On the other hand, our construction shows that the duality-theoretic variant of the Stone pairing captures the adding of a layer of quantifiers, thus making a strong link to recent work on semiring quantifiers in logic on words. In the process, we identify the model theoretic notion of *types* as the unifying concept behind this link. These results contribute to bridging the strands of logic in computer science which focus on semantics and on more algorithmic and complexity related areas, respectively.

**Keywords:** Stone duality · finitely additive measures · structural limits · finite model theory · formal languages · logic on words

## 1 Introduction

While topology plays an important role, via Stone duality, in many parts of semantics, topological methods in more algorithmic and complexity oriented areas of theoretical computer science are not so common. One of the few examples, the one we want to consider here, is the study of limits of finite relational structures. We will focus on the *structural limits* introduced by Nešetřil and Ossona de Mendez [15,17]. These provide a common generalisation of various notions of limits of finite structures studied in probability theory, random graphs, structural graph theory, and finite model theory. The basic construction in this work is the so-called *Stone pairing*. Given a relational signature $\sigma$ and a first-order formula $\varphi$ in the signature $\sigma$ with free variables $v_1, \ldots, v_n$, define

$$\langle \varphi, A \rangle = \frac{|\{\overline{a} \in A^n \mid A \models \varphi(\overline{a})\}|}{|A|^n} \qquad \textit{(the probability that a random assignment in } A \textit{ satisfies } \varphi\textit{).} \tag{1}$$

Nešetřil and Ossona de Mendez view the map $A \mapsto \langle \text{-}, A \rangle$ as an embedding of the finite $\sigma$-structures into the space of probability measures over the Stone space dual to the Lindenbaum-Tarski algebra of all first-order formulas in the signature $\sigma$. This space is complete and thus provides the desired limit objects for all sequences of finite structures which embed as Cauchy sequences.

Another example of topological methods in an algorithmically oriented area of computer science is the use of profinite monoids in automata theory. In this setting, profinite monoids are the subject of the extensive theory, based on theorems by Eilenberg and Reiterman, and used, among others, to settle decidability questions [18]. In [4], it was shown that this theory may be understood as an application of Stone duality, thus making a bridge between semantics and more algorithmically oriented work. Bridging this semantics-versus-algorithmics gap in theoretical computer science has since gained quite some momentum, notably with the recent strand of research by Abramsky, Dawar and co-workers [2,3]. In this spirit, a natural question is whether the structural limits of Nešetřil and Ossona de Mendez also can be understood semantically, and in particular whether the topological component may be seen as an application of Stone duality.

More precisely, recent work on understanding quantifiers in the setting of logic on finite words [5] has shown that adding a layer of certain quantifiers (such as classical and modular quantifiers) corresponds dually to measure space constructions. The measures involved are not classical but only finitely additive and they take values in finite semirings rather than in the unit interval. Nevertheless, this appearance of *measures as duals of quantifiers* begs the further question whether the measure spaces in the theory of structural limits may be obtained via Stone duality from a semantic addition of certain quantifiers to classical first-order logic.

The purpose of this paper is to address this question. Our main result is that the Stone pairing of Nešetřil and Ossona de Mendez is related by a retraction to a Stone space of measures, which is dual to the Lindenbaum-Tarski algebra of a logic fragment obtained from first-order logic by adding one layer of probabilistic quantifiers, and which arises in exactly the same way as the spaces of semiring-valued measures in logic on words. That is, the Stone pairing, although originating from other considerations, may be seen as arising by duality from a semantic construction.

A foreseeable hurdle is that spaces of classical measures are valued in the unit interval $[0,1]$ which is not zero-dimensional and hence outside the scope of Stone duality. This is well-known to cause problems e.g. in attempts to combine non-determinism and probability in domain theory [12]. However, in the structural limits of Nešetřil and Ossona de Mendez, at the base, one only needs to talk about finite models equipped with normal distributions and thus only the finite intervals $I_n = \{0, \frac{1}{n}, \frac{2}{n}, \dots, 1\}$ are involved. A careful duality-theoretic analysis identifies a codirected diagram (i.e. an inverse limit system) based on these intervals compatible with the Stone pairing. The resulting inverse limit, which we denote $\mathbf{\Gamma}$, is a Priestley space. It comes equipped with an algebra-like structure, which allows us to reformulate many aspects of the theory of structural limits in terms of $\mathbf{\Gamma}$-valued measures as opposed to $[0,1]$-valued measures.

The analysis justifying the structure of $\mathbf{\Gamma}$ is based on duality theory for double quasi-operator algebras [7,8]. In the presentation, we have tried to compromise between giving interesting topo-relational insights into why $\mathbf{\Gamma}$ is as it is, and not overburdening the reader with technical details. Some interesting features of $\mathbf{\Gamma}$, dictated by the nature of the Stone pairing and the ensuing codirected diagram, are that

- $\mathbf{\Gamma}$ is based on a version of $[0,1]$ in which the rationals are doubled;
- $\mathbf{\Gamma}$ comes with section-retraction maps $[0,1] \xhookrightarrow{\iota} \mathbf{\Gamma} \xrightarrow{\gamma} [0,1]$;
- the map $\iota$ is lower semicontinuous while the map $\gamma$ is continuous.

These features are a consequence of general theory and precisely allow us to witness continuous phenomena relative to $[0,1]$ in the setting of $\mathbf{\Gamma}$.

## Our contribution

We show that the ambient measure space for the structural limits of Nešetřil and Ossona de Mendez can be obtained via *"adding a layer of quantifiers"* in a suitable enrichment of first-order logic. The conceptual framework for seeing this is that of *types* from classical model theory. More precisely, we will see that a variant of the Stone pairing is a map into a space of measures with values in a Priestley space $\mathbf{\Gamma}$. Further, we show that this map is in fact the embedding of the finite structures into the space of (0-)types of an extension of first-order logic, which we axiomatise. On the other hand, $\mathbf{\Gamma}$-valued measures and $[0,1]$-valued measures are tightly related by a retraction-section pair which allows the transfer of properties. These results identify the logical gist of the theory of structural limits and provide a new interesting connection between logic on words and the theory of structural limits in finite model theory.

*Outline of the paper.* In section 2 we briefly recall Stone-Priestley duality, its application in logic via spaces of types, and the particular instance of logic on words (needed only to show the similarity of the constructions). In Section 3 we introduce the Priestley space $\mathbf{\Gamma}$ with its additional operations, and show that it admits $[0,1]$ as a retract. The spaces of $\mathbf{\Gamma}$-valued measures are introduced in

Section 4, and the retraction of $\mathbf{\Gamma}$ onto $[0,1]$ is lifted to the appropriate spaces of measures. In Section 5 we introduce the $\mathbf{\Gamma}$-valued Stone pairing and make the link with logic on words. Further, we compare convergence in the space of $\mathbf{\Gamma}$-valued measures with the one considered by Nešetřil and Ossona de Mendez. Finally, in Section 6 we show that constructing the space of $\mathbf{\Gamma}$-valued measures dually corresponds to enriching the logic with probabilistic operators.

# 2 Preliminaries

*Notation.* Throughout this paper, if $X \xrightarrow{f} Y \xrightarrow{g} Z$ are functions, their composition is denoted $g \cdot f$. For a subset $S \subseteq X$, $f_{\restriction S} \colon S \to Y$ is the obvious restriction. Given any set $T$, $\wp(T)$ denotes its power-set. Further, for a poset $P$, $P^{\partial}$ is the poset obtained by turning the order of $P$ upside down.

## 2.1 Stone-Priestley duality

In this paper, we will need Stone duality for bounded distributive lattices in the order topological form due to Priestley [19]. It is a powerful and well established tool in the study of propositional logic and semantics of programming languages, see e.g. [9,1] for major landmarks. We briefly recall how this duality works.

A *compact ordered space* is a pair $(X, \leq)$ where $X$ is a compact space and $\leq$ is a partial order on $X$ which is closed in the product topology of $X \times X$. (Note that such a space is automatically Hausdorff). A compact ordered space is a *Priestley space* provided it is *totally order-disconnected.* That is, for all $x, y \in X$ such that $x \not\leq y$, there is a *clopen* (i.e. simultaneously closed and open) $C \subseteq X$ which is an up-set for $\leq$, and satisfies $x \in C$ but $y \notin C$. We recall the construction of the Priestley space of a distributive lattice $D$.[3]

A non-empty proper subset $F \subset D$ is a *prime filter* if it is *(i)* upward closed (in the natural order of $D$), *(ii)* closed under finite meets, and *(iii)* if $a \vee b \in F$, either $a \in F$ or $b \in F$. Denote by $X_D$ the set of all prime filters of $D$. By Stone's Prime Filter Theorem, the map

$$[\![\text{-}]\!] \colon D \to \wp(X_D), \quad a \mapsto [\![a]\!] = \{F \in X_D \mid a \in F\}$$

is an embedding. Priestley's insight was that $D$ can be recovered from $X_D$, if the latter is equipped with the inclusion order and the topology generated by the sets of the form $[\![a]\!]$ and their complements. This makes $X_D$ into a Priestley space — the *dual space* of $D$ — and the map $[\![\text{-}]\!]$ is an isomorphism between $D$ and the lattice of clopen up-sets of $X_D$. Conversely, any Priestley space $X$ is the dual space of the lattice of its clopen up-sets. We call the latter the *dual lattice* of $X$. This correspondence extends to morphisms. In fact, Priestley duality states that the category of distributive lattices with homomorphisms is dually equivalent to the category of Priestley spaces and continuous monotone maps.

[3] We assume all distributive lattices are bounded, with the bottom and top denoted by 0 and 1, respectively. The bounds need to be preserved by homomorphisms.

When restricting to Boolean algebras, we recover the celebrated Stone duality restricted to Boolean algebras and *Boolean spaces*, i.e. compact Hausdorff spaces in which the clopen subsets form a basis.

### 2.2 Stone duality and logic: type spaces

The *theory of types* is an important tool for first-order logic. We briefly recall the concept as it is closely related to, and provides the link between, two otherwise unrelated occurrences of topological methods in theoretical computer science.

Consider a signature $\sigma$ and a first-order theory $T$ in this signature. For each $n \in \mathbb{N}$, let $\mathrm{Fm}_n$ denote the set of first-order formulas whose free variables are among $\overline{v} = \{v_1, \ldots, v_n\}$, and let $\mathrm{Mod}_n(T)$ denote the class of all pairs $(A, \alpha)$ where $A$ is a model of $T$ and $\alpha$ is an interpretation of $\overline{v}$ in $A$. Then the satisfaction relation, $(A, \alpha) \models \varphi$, is a binary relation from $\mathrm{Mod}_n$ to $\mathrm{Fm}_n$. It induces the equivalence relations of elementary equivalence $\equiv$ and logical equivalence $\approx$ on these sets, respectively. The quotient $\mathrm{FO}_n(T) = \mathrm{Fm}_n/{\approx}$ carries a natural Boolean algebra structure and is known as the *n-th Lindenbaum-Tarski algebra* of $T$. Its dual space is $\mathrm{Typ}_n(T)$, the *space of n-types* of $T$, whose points can be identified with elements of $\mathrm{Mod}_n(T)/{\equiv}$. The Boolean algebra $\mathrm{FO}(T)$ of *all* first-order formulas modulo logical equivalence over $T$ is the directed colimit of the $\mathrm{FO}_n(T)$ for $n \in \mathbb{N}$ while its dual space, $\mathrm{Typ}(T)$, is the codirected limit of the $\mathrm{Typ}_n(T)$ for $n \in \mathbb{N}$ and consists of models equipped with interpretations of the full set of variables.

If we want to study finite models, there are two equivalent approaches: e.g. at the level of sentences, we can either consider the theory $T_{\mathit{fin}}$ of finite $T$-models, or the closure of the collection of all finite $T$-models in the space $\mathrm{Typ}_0(T)$. This closure yields a space, which should tell us about finite $T$-structures. Indeed, it is equal to $\mathrm{Typ}_0(T_{\mathit{fin}})$, the space of pseudofinite $T$-structures. For an application of this, see [10]. Below, we will see an application in finite model theory of the case $T = \emptyset$ (in this case we write $\mathrm{FO}(\sigma)$ and $\mathrm{Typ}(\sigma)$ instead of $\mathrm{FO}(\emptyset)$ and $\mathrm{Typ}(\emptyset)$).

In light of the theory of types as exposed above, the Stone pairing of Nešetřil and Ossona de Mendez (see equation (1)) can be regarded as an embedding of finite structures into the space of probability measures on $\mathrm{Typ}(\sigma)$, which set-theoretically are finitely additive functions $\mathrm{FO}(\sigma) \to [0, 1]$.

### 2.3 Duality and logic on words

As mentioned in the introduction, spaces of measures arise via duality in *logic on words* [5]. Logic on words, as introduced by Büchi, see e.g. [14] for a recent survey, is a variation and specialisation of finite model theory where only models based on words are considered. I.e., a word $w \in A^*$ is seen as a relational structure on $\{1, \ldots, |w|\}$, where $|w|$ is the length of $w$, equipped with a unary relation $P_a$, for each $a \in A$, singling out the positions in the word where the letter $a$ appears. Each sentence $\varphi$ in a language interpretable over these structures yields a language $L_\varphi \subseteq A^*$ consisting of the words satisfying $\varphi$. Thus, logic fragments are considered modulo the theory of finite words and the Lindenbaum-Tarski algebras are subalgebras of $\wp(A^*)$ consisting of the appropriate $L_\varphi$'s, cf. [10] for a treatment of first-order logic on words.

For lack of logical completeness, the duals of the Lindenbaum-Tarski algebras have more points than those given by models. Nevertheless, the dual spaces of types, which act as compactifications and completions of the collections of models, provide a powerful tool for studying logic fragments by topological means. The central notion is that of *recognition*, in which, a Boolean subalgebra $\mathcal{B} \subseteq \wp(A^*)$ is studied by means of the dual map $\eta\colon \beta(A^*) \to X_{\mathcal{B}}$. Here $\beta(A^*)$ is the Stone dual of $\wp(A^*)$, also known in topology as the Čech-Stone compactification of the discrete space $A^*$, and $X_{\mathcal{B}}$ is the Stone dual of $\mathcal{B}$. The set $A^*$ embeds in $\beta(A^*)$, and $\eta$ is uniquely determined by its restriction $\eta_0\colon A^* \to X_{\mathcal{B}}$. Now, Stone duality implies that $L \subseteq A^*$ is in $\mathcal{B}$ iff there is a clopen subset $V \subseteq X_{\mathcal{B}}$ so that $\eta_0^{-1}(V) = L$. Anytime the latter is true for a map $\eta$ and a language $L$ as above, one says that $\eta$ *recognises* $L$.[4]

When studying logic fragments via recognition, the following inductive step is central: given a notion of quantifier and a recogniser for a Boolean algebra of formulas with a free variable, construct a recogniser for the Boolean algebra generated by the formulas obtained by applying the quantifier. This problem was solved in [5], using duality theory, in a general setting of *semiring quantifiers*. The latter are defined as follows: let $(S, +, \cdot, 0_S, 1_S)$ be a semiring, and $k \in S$. Given a formula $\psi(v)$, the formula $\exists_{S,k} v.\psi(v)$ is true of a word $w \in A^*$ iff $k = 1_S + \cdots + 1_S$, $m$ times, where $m$ is the number of assignments of the variable $v$ in $w$ satisfying $\psi(v)$. If $S = \mathbb{Z}/q\mathbb{Z}$, we obtain the so-called *modular quantifiers*, and for $S$ the two-element lattice we recover the existential quantifier $\exists$.

To deal with formulas with a free variable, one considers maps of the form $f\colon \beta((A \times 2)^*) \to X$ (the extra bit in $A \times 2$ is used to mark the interpretation of the free variable). In [5] (see also [6]), it was shown that $L_{\psi(v)}$ is recognised by $f$ iff for every $k \in S$ the language $L_{\exists_{S,k} v.\psi(v)}$ is recognised by the composite

$$\xi\colon A^* \xrightarrow{\ R\ } \widehat{\mathbf{S}}(\beta((A \times 2)^*)) \xrightarrow{\ \widehat{\mathbf{S}}(f)\ } \widehat{\mathbf{S}}(X), \tag{2}$$

where $\widehat{\mathbf{S}}(X)$ is the space of finitely additive $S$-valued measures on $X$, and $R$ maps $w \in A^*$ to the measure $\mu_w\colon \wp((A \times 2)^*) \to S$ sending $K \subseteq (A \times 2)^*$ to the sum $1_S + \cdots + 1_S$, $n_{w,K}$ times. Here, $n_{w,K}$ is the number of interpretations $\alpha$ of the free variable $v$ in $w$ such that the pair $(w, \alpha)$, seen as an element of $(A \times 2)^*$, belongs to $K$. Finally, $\widehat{\mathbf{S}}(f)$ sends a measure to its pushforward along $f$.

## 3 The space $\mathbf{\Gamma}$

Central to our results is a Priestley space $\mathbf{\Gamma}$ closely related to $[0, 1]$, in which our measures will take values. Its construction comes from the insight that the range

---

[4] Here, being beyond the scope of this paper, we are ignoring the important role of the monoid structure available on the spaces (in the form of profinite monoids or BiMs, cf. [10,5]).

of the Stone pairing $\langle \text{-}, A\rangle$, for a finite structure $A$ and formulas restricted to a fixed number of free variables, can be confined to a chain $I_n = \{0, \frac{1}{n}, \frac{2}{n}, \ldots, 1\}$. Moreover, the floor functions $f_{mn,n} \colon I_{mn} \twoheadrightarrow I_n$ are monotone surjections. The ensuing system $\{f_{mn,n} \colon I_{mn} \twoheadrightarrow I_n \mid m, n \in \mathbb{N}\}$ can thus be seen as a codirected diagram of finite discrete posets and monotone maps. Let us define $\mathbf{\Gamma}$ to be the limit of this diagram. Then, $\mathbf{\Gamma}$ is naturally equipped with a structure of Priestley space, see e.g. [11, Corollary VI.3.3], and can be represented as based on the set

$$\{r^- \mid r \in (0,1]\} \cup \{q^\circ \mid q \in \mathbb{Q} \cap [0,1]\}.$$

The order of $\mathbf{\Gamma}$ is the unique total order which has $0^\circ$ as bottom element, satisfies $r^* < s^*$ if and only if $r < s$ for $* \in \{-, \circ\}$, and such that $q^\circ$ is a cover of $q^-$ for every rational $q \in (0,1]$ (i.e. $q^- < q^\circ$, and there is no element strictly in between). In a sense, the values $q^-$ represent approximations of the values of the form $q^\circ$. Cf. Figure 1. The topology of $\mathbf{\Gamma}$ is generated by the sets of the form

$$\uparrow p^\circ = \{x \in \mathbf{\Gamma} \mid p^\circ \leq x\} \quad \text{and} \quad \downarrow q^- = \{x \in \mathbf{\Gamma} \mid x \leq q^-\}$$

for $p, q \in \mathbb{Q} \cap [0,1]$ such that $q \neq 0$. The distributive lattice dual to $\mathbf{\Gamma}$, denoted by $\mathbf{L}$, is given by

$$\mathbf{L} = \{\bot\} \cup (\mathbb{Q} \cap [0,1])^\partial, \text{ with } \bot <_{\mathbf{L}} q \text{ and } q \leq_{\mathbf{L}} p \text{ for every } p \leq q \text{ in } \mathbb{Q} \cap [0,1].$$

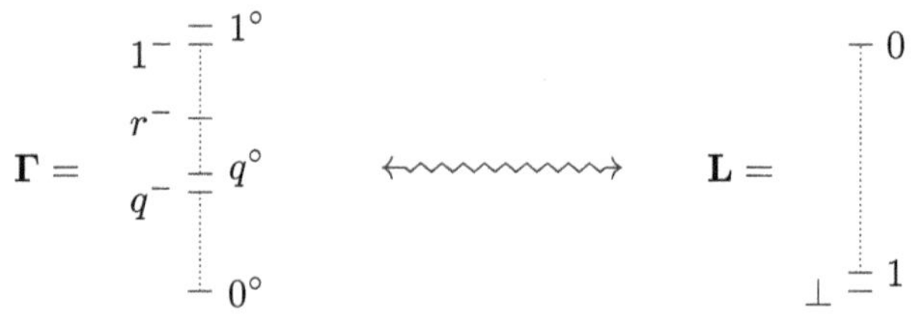


**Fig. 1.** The Priestley space $\mathbf{\Gamma}$ and its dual lattice $\mathbf{L}$

### 3.1 The algebraic structure on $\mathbf{\Gamma}$

When defining measures we need an algebraic structure available on the space of values. The space $\mathbf{\Gamma}$ fulfils this requirement as it comes equipped with a partial operation $- \colon \mathrm{dom}(-) \to \mathbf{\Gamma}$, where $\mathrm{dom}(-) = \{(x,y) \in \mathbf{\Gamma} \times \mathbf{\Gamma} \mid y \leq x\}$ and

$$\begin{aligned} r^\circ - s^\circ &= (r-s)^\circ \\ r^- - s^\circ &= (r-s)^- \end{aligned} \qquad \left.\begin{aligned} r^\circ - s^- \\ r^- - s^- \end{aligned}\right\} = \begin{cases} (r-s)^\circ & \text{if } r - s \in \mathbb{Q} \\ (r-s)^- & \text{otherwise.} \end{cases}$$

In fact, this (partial) operation is dual to the truncated addition on the lattice $\mathbf{L}$. However, explaining this would require us to delve into extended Priestley duality for lattices with operations, which is beyond the scope of this paper. See [9] and also [7,8] for details. It also follows from the general theory that there exists another partial operation definable from $-$, namely:

$$\sim \colon \mathrm{dom}(-) \to \mathbf{\Gamma}, \quad x \sim y = \bigvee \{x - q^\circ \mid y < q^\circ \leq x\}.$$

Next, we collect some basic properties of $-$ and $\sim$, needed in Section 4, which follow from the general theory of [7,8]. First, recall that a map into an ordered topological space is *lower* (resp. *upper*) *semicontinuous* provided the preimage of any open down-set (resp. open up-set) is open.

**Lemma 1.** *If* $\mathrm{dom}(-)$ *is seen as a subspace of* $\mathbf{\Gamma} \times \mathbf{\Gamma}^{\partial}$*, the following hold:*

1. $\mathrm{dom}(-)$ *is a closed up-set in* $\mathbf{\Gamma} \times \mathbf{\Gamma}^{\partial}$*;*
2. *both* $-\colon \mathrm{dom}(-) \to \mathbf{\Gamma}$ *and* $\sim\colon \mathrm{dom}(-) \to \mathbf{\Gamma}$ *are monotone in the first coordinate, and antitone in the second;*
3. $-\colon \mathrm{dom}(-) \to \mathbf{\Gamma}$ *is lower semicontinuous;*
4. $\sim\colon \mathrm{dom}(-) \to \mathbf{\Gamma}$ *is upper semicontinuous.*

### 3.2 The retraction $\mathbf{\Gamma} \twoheadrightarrow [0,1]$

In this section we show that, with respect to appropriate topologies, the unit interval $[0,1]$ can be obtained as a topological retract of $\mathbf{\Gamma}$, in a way which is compatible with the operation $-$. This will be important in Sections 4 and 5, where we need to move between [0,1]-valued and $\mathbf{\Gamma}$-valued measures. Let us define the monotone surjection given by collapsing the doubled elements:

$$\gamma\colon \mathbf{\Gamma} \to [0,1],\ r^-, r^\circ \mapsto r. \tag{3}$$

The map $\gamma$ has a right adjoint, given by

$$\iota\colon [0,1] \to \mathbf{\Gamma},\ r \mapsto \begin{cases} r^\circ & \text{if } r \in \mathbb{Q} \\ r^- & \text{otherwise.} \end{cases} \tag{4}$$

Indeed, it is readily seen that $\gamma(y) \leq x$ iff $y \leq \iota(x)$, for all $y \in \mathbf{\Gamma}$ and $x \in [0,1]$. The composition $\gamma \cdot \iota$ coincides with the identity on $[0,1]$, i.e. $\iota$ is a section of $\gamma$. Moreover, this retraction lifts to a topological retract provided we equip $\mathbf{\Gamma}$ and $[0,1]$ with the topologies consisting of the open down-sets:

**Lemma 2.** *The map* $\gamma\colon \mathbf{\Gamma} \to [0,1]$ *is continuous and the map* $\iota\colon [0,1] \to \mathbf{\Gamma}$ *is lower semicontinuous.*

*Proof.* To check continuity of $\gamma$ observe that, for a rational $q \in (0,1)$, $\gamma^{-1}(q,1]$ and $\gamma^{-1}[0,q)$ coincide, respectively, with the open sets

$$\bigcup\{\uparrow p^\circ \mid p \in \mathbb{Q} \cap [0,1] \text{ and } q < p\} \text{ and } \bigcup\{\downarrow p^- \mid p \in \mathbb{Q} \cap (0,1] \text{ and } p < q\}.$$

Also, $\iota$ is lower semicontinuous, for $\iota^{-1}(\downarrow q^-) = [0,q)$ whenever $q \in \mathbb{Q} \cap (0,1]$. □

It is easy to see that both $\gamma$ and $\iota$ preserve the minus structure available on $\mathbf{\Gamma}$ and [0,1] (the unit interval is equipped with the usual minus operation $x - y$ defined whenever $y \leq x$), that is,

- $\gamma(x - y) = \gamma(x \sim y) = \gamma(x) - \gamma(y)$ whenever $y \leq x$ in $\mathbf{\Gamma}$, and
- $\iota(x - y) = \iota(x) - \iota(y)$ whenever $y \leq x$ in [0,1].

**Remark.** $\iota\colon [0,1] \to \mathbf{\Gamma}$ is not upper semicontinuous because, for every $q \in \mathbb{Q} \cap [0,1]$, $\iota^{-1}(\uparrow q^\circ) = \{x \in [0,1] \mid q^\circ \leq \iota(x)\} = \{x \in [0,1] \mid \gamma(q^\circ) \leq x\} = [q,1]$.

## 4 Spaces of measures valued in $\mathbf{\Gamma}$ and in $[0, 1]$

The aim of this section is to replace $[0, 1]$-valued measures by $\mathbf{\Gamma}$-valued measures. The reason for doing this is two-fold. First, the space of $\mathbf{\Gamma}$-valued measures is Priestley (Proposition 4), and thus amenable to a duality theoretic treatment and a dual logic interpretation (cf. Section 6). Second, it retains more topological information than the space of $[0, 1]$-valued measures. Indeed, the former retracts onto the latter (Theorem 10).

Let $D$ be a distributive lattice. Recall that, classically, a monotone function $m\colon D \to [0, 1]$ is a (finitely additive, probability) measure provided $m(0) = 0$, $m(1) = 1$, and $m(a) + m(b) = m(a \vee b) + m(a \wedge b)$ for every $a, b \in D$. The latter property is equivalently expressed as

$$\forall a, b \in D,\ m(a) - m(a \wedge b) = m(a \vee b) - m(b). \tag{5}$$

We write $\mathcal{M}_{\mathrm{I}}(D)$ for the set of all measures $D \to [0, 1]$, and regard it as an ordered topological space, with the structure induced by the product order and product topology of $[0, 1]^D$. The notion of (finitely additive, probability) $\mathbf{\Gamma}$-valued measure is analogous to the classical one, except that the finite additivity property (5) splits into two conditions, involving $-$ and $\sim$.

**Definition 3.** *Let $D$ be a distributive lattice. A* $\mathbf{\Gamma}$-valued measure *(or simply a* measure*) on $D$ is a function $\mu\colon D \to \mathbf{\Gamma}$ such that*

1. *$\mu(0) = 0^\circ$ and $\mu(1) = 1^\circ$,*
2. *$\mu$ is monotone, and*
3. *for all $a, b \in D$,*

$$\mu(a) \sim \mu(a \wedge b) \leq \mu(a \vee b) - \mu(b) \quad \text{and} \quad \mu(a) - \mu(a \wedge b) \geq \mu(a \vee b) \sim \mu(b).$$

*We denote by $\mathcal{M}_{\Gamma}(D)$ the subspace of $\mathbf{\Gamma}^D$ consisting of the measures $\mu\colon D \to \mathbf{\Gamma}$.*

Since $\mathbf{\Gamma}$ is a Priestley space, so is $\mathbf{\Gamma}^D$ equipped with the product order and topology. Hence, we regard $\mathcal{M}_{\Gamma}(D)$ as an ordered topological space, whose topology and order are induced by those of $\mathbf{\Gamma}^D$. In fact $\mathcal{M}_{\Gamma}(D)$ is a Priestley space:

**Proposition 4.** *For any distributive lattice $D$, $\mathcal{M}_{\Gamma}(D)$ is a Priestley space.*

*Proof.* It suffices to show that $\mathcal{M}_{\Gamma}(D)$ is a closed subspace of $\mathbf{\Gamma}^D$. Let

$$C_{1,2} = \{f \in \mathbf{\Gamma}^D \mid f(0) = 0^\circ\} \cap \{f \in \mathbf{\Gamma}^D \mid f(1) = 1^\circ\} \cap \bigcap_{a \leq b} \{f \in \mathbf{\Gamma}^D \mid f(a) \leq f(b)\}.$$

Note that the evaluation maps $\mathrm{ev}_a\colon \mathbf{\Gamma}^D \to \mathbf{\Gamma}$, $f \mapsto f(a)$, are continuous for every $a \in D$. Thus, the first set in the intersection defining $C_{1,2}$ is closed because it is the equaliser of the evaluation map $\mathrm{ev}_0$ and the constant map of value $0^\circ$. Similarly, for the set $\{f \in \mathbf{\Gamma}^D \mid f(1) = 1^\circ\}$. The last one is the intersection of the sets of the form $\langle \mathrm{ev}_a, \mathrm{ev}_b \rangle^{-1}(\leq)$, which are closed because $\leq$ is closed in $\mathbf{\Gamma} \times \mathbf{\Gamma}$. Whence, $C_{1,2}$ is a closed subset of $\mathbf{\Gamma}^D$. Moreover,

$$\mathcal{M}_{\Gamma}(D) = \bigcap_{a, b \in D} \{f \in C_{1,2} \mid f(a) \sim f(a \wedge b) \leq f(a \vee b) - f(b)\}$$

$$\cap \bigcap_{a,b \in D} \{f \in C_{1,2} \mid f(a) - f(a \wedge b) \geq f(a \vee b) \sim f(b)\}.$$

From semicontinuity of $-$ and $\sim$ (Lemma 1) and the following well-known fact in order-topology we conclude that $\mathcal{M}_\Gamma(D)$ is closed in $\mathbf{\Gamma}^D$.

*Fact.* Let $X, Y$ be compact ordered spaces, $f\colon X \to Y$ a lower semicontinuous function and $g\colon X \to Y$ an upper semicontinuous function. If $X'$ is a closed subset of $X$, then so is $E = \{x \in X' \mid g(x) \leq f(x)\}$. □

Next, we prove a property which is very useful when approximating a fragment of a logic by smaller fragments (see, e.g., Section 5.1). Let us denote by **DLat** the category of distributive lattices and homomorphisms, and by **Pries** the category of Priestley spaces and continuous monotone maps.

**Proposition 5.** *The assignment $D \mapsto \mathcal{M}_\Gamma(D)$ yields a contravariant functor $\mathcal{M}_\Gamma\colon$ **DLat** $\to$ **Pries** which sends directed colimits to codirected limits.*

*Proof.* If $h\colon D \to E$ is a lattice homomorphism and $\mu\colon E \to \mathbf{\Gamma}$ is a measure, it is not difficult to see that $\mathcal{M}_\Gamma(h)(\mu) = \mu \cdot h\colon D \to \mathbf{\Gamma}$ is a measure. The mapping $\mathcal{M}_\Gamma(h)\colon \mathcal{M}_\Gamma(E) \to \mathcal{M}_\Gamma(D)$ is clearly monotone. For continuity, recall that the topology of $\mathcal{M}_\Gamma(D)$ is generated by the sets $[\![a < q]\!] = \{\nu\colon D \to \mathbf{\Gamma} \mid \nu(a) < q^\circ\}$ and $[\![a \geq q]\!] = \{\nu\colon D \to \mathbf{\Gamma} \mid \nu(a) \geq q^\circ\}$, with $a \in D$ and $q \in \mathbb{Q} \cap [0,1]$. We have

$$\mathcal{M}_\Gamma(h)^{-1}([\![a < q]\!]) = \{\mu\colon E \to \mathbf{\Gamma} \mid \mu(h(a)) < q^\circ\} = [\![h(a) < q]\!]$$

which is open in $\mathcal{M}_\Gamma(E)$. Similarly, $\mathcal{M}_\Gamma(h)^{-1}([\![a \geq q]\!]) = [\![h(a) \geq q]\!]$, showing that $\mathcal{M}_\Gamma(h)$ is continuous. Thus, $\mathcal{M}_\Gamma$ is a contravariant functor.

The rest of the proof is a routine verification. □

*Remark 6.* We work with the contravariant functor $\mathcal{M}_\Gamma\colon$ **DLat** $\to$ **Pries** because $\mathcal{M}_\Gamma$ is concretely defined on the lattice side. However, by Priestley duality, **DLat** is dually equivalent to **Pries**, so we can think of $\mathcal{M}_\Gamma$ as a covariant functor **Pries** $\to$ **Pries** (this is the perspective traditionally adopted in analysis, and also in the works of Nešetřil and Ossona de Mendez). From this viewpoint, Section 6 provides a description of the endofunctor on **DLat** dual to $\mathcal{M}_\Gamma\colon$ **Pries** $\to$ **Pries**.

Recall the maps $\gamma\colon \mathbf{\Gamma} \to [0,1]$ and $\iota\colon [0,1] \to \mathbf{\Gamma}$ from equations (3)–(4). In Section 3.2 we showed that this is a retraction-section pair. In Theorem 10 this retraction is lifted to the spaces of measures. We start with an easy observation:

**Lemma 7.** *Let $D$ be a distributive lattice. The following statements hold:*

1. *for every $\mu \in \mathcal{M}_\Gamma(D)$, $\gamma \cdot \mu \in \mathcal{M}_\mathrm{I}(D)$,*
2. *for every $m \in \mathcal{M}_\mathrm{I}(D)$, $\iota \cdot m \in \mathcal{M}_\Gamma(D)$.*

*Proof.* 1. The only non-trivial condition to verify is finite additivity. In view of the discussion after Lemma 2, the map $\gamma$ preserves both minus operations on $\mathbf{\Gamma}$. Hence, for every $a, b \in D$, the inequalities $\mu(a) \sim \mu(a \wedge b) \leq \mu(a \vee b) - \mu(b)$ and $\mu(a) - \mu(a \wedge b) \geq \mu(a \vee b) \sim \mu(b)$ imply that $\gamma \cdot \mu(a) - \gamma \cdot \mu(a \wedge b) = \gamma \cdot \mu(a \vee b) - \gamma \cdot \mu(b)$.

2. The first two conditions in Definition 3 are immediate. The third condition follows from the fact that $\iota(r-s) = \iota(r) - \iota(s)$ whenever $s \leq r$ in [0,1], and $x \sim y \leq x - y$ for every $(x, y) \in \text{dom}(-)$. □

In view of the previous lemma, there are well-defined functions

$$\gamma^{\#}\colon \mathcal{M}_{\Gamma}(D) \to \mathcal{M}_{\mathrm{I}}(D),\ \mu \mapsto \gamma \cdot \mu \quad \text{and} \quad \iota^{\#}\colon \mathcal{M}_{\mathrm{I}}(D) \to \mathcal{M}_{\Gamma}(D),\ m \mapsto \iota \cdot m.$$

**Lemma 8.** $\gamma^{\#}\colon \mathcal{M}_{\Gamma}(D) \to \mathcal{M}_{\mathrm{I}}(D)$ *is a continuous and monotone map.*

*Proof.* The topology of $\mathcal{M}_{\mathrm{I}}(D)$ is generated by the sets of the form $\{m \in \mathcal{M}_{\mathrm{I}}(D) \mid m(a) \in O\}$, for $a \in D$ and $O$ an open subset of $[0, 1]$. In turn,

$$(\gamma^{\#})^{-1}\{m \in \mathcal{M}_{\mathrm{I}}(D) \mid m(a) \in O\} = \{\mu \in \mathcal{M}_{\Gamma}(D) \mid \mu(a) \in \gamma^{-1}(O)\}$$

is open in $\mathcal{M}_{\Gamma}(D)$ because $\gamma\colon \mathbf{\Gamma} \to [0, 1]$ is continuous by Lemma 2. This shows that $\gamma^{\#}\colon \mathcal{M}_{\Gamma}(D) \to \mathcal{M}_{\mathrm{I}}(D)$ is continuous. Monotonicity is immediate. □

Note that $\gamma^{\#}\colon \mathcal{M}_{\Gamma}(D) \to \mathcal{M}_{\mathrm{I}}(D)$ is surjective, since it admits $\iota^{\#}$ as a (set-theoretic) section. It follows that $\mathcal{M}_{\mathrm{I}}(D)$ is a compact ordered space:

**Corollary 9.** *For each distributive lattice $D$, $\mathcal{M}_{\mathrm{I}}(D)$ is a compact ordered space.*

*Proof.* The surjection $\gamma^{\#}\colon \mathcal{M}_{\Gamma}(D) \to \mathcal{M}_{\mathrm{I}}(D)$ is continuous (Lemma 8). Since $\mathcal{M}_{\Gamma}(D)$ is compact by Proposition 4, so is $\mathcal{M}_{\mathrm{I}}(D)$. The order of $\mathcal{M}_{\mathrm{I}}(D)$ is clearly closed in the product topology, thus $\mathcal{M}_{\mathrm{I}}(D)$ is a compact ordered space. □

Finally, we see that the set-theoretic retraction of $\mathcal{M}_{\Gamma}(D)$ onto $\mathcal{M}_{\mathrm{I}}(D)$ lifts to the topological setting, provided we restrict to the down-set topologies. If $(X, \leq)$ is a partially ordered topological space, write $X^{\downarrow}$ for the space with the same underlying set as $X$ and whose topology consists of the open down-sets of $X$.

**Theorem 10.** *The maps $\gamma^{\#}\colon \mathcal{M}_{\Gamma}(D)^{\downarrow} \to \mathcal{M}_{\mathrm{I}}(D)^{\downarrow}$ and $\iota^{\#}\colon \mathcal{M}_{\mathrm{I}}(D)^{\downarrow} \to \mathcal{M}_{\Gamma}(D)^{\downarrow}$ are a retraction-section pair of topological spaces.*

*Proof.* It suffices to show that $\gamma^{\#}$ and $\iota^{\#}$ are continuous. It is not difficult to see, using Lemma 8, that $\gamma^{\#}\colon \mathcal{M}_{\Gamma}(D)^{\downarrow} \to \mathcal{M}_{\mathrm{I}}(D)^{\downarrow}$ is continuous. For the continuity of $\iota^{\#}$, note that the topology of $\mathcal{M}_{\Gamma}(D)^{\downarrow}$ is generated by the sets of the form $\{\mu \in \mathcal{M}_{\Gamma}(D) \mid \mu(a) \leq q^{-}\}$, for $a \in D$ and $q \in \mathbb{Q} \cap (0, 1]$. We have

$$\begin{aligned}(\iota^{\#})^{-1}\{\mu \in \mathcal{M}_{\Gamma}(D) \mid \mu(a) \leq q^{-}\} &= \{m \in \mathcal{M}_{\mathrm{I}}(D) \mid m(a) \in \iota^{-1}(\downarrow q^{-})\} \\ &= \{m \in \mathcal{M}_{\mathrm{I}}(D) \mid m(a) < q\},\end{aligned}$$

which is an open set in $\mathcal{M}_{\mathrm{I}}(D)^{\downarrow}$. This concludes the proof. □

## 5 The Γ-valued Stone pairing and limits of finite structures

In the work of Nešetřil and Ossona de Mendez, the Stone pairing $\langle \text{-}, A\rangle$ is $[0, 1]$-valued, i.e. an element of $\mathcal{M}_{\mathrm{I}}(\mathrm{FO}(\sigma))$. In this section, we show that basically the same construction for the recognisers arising from the application of a layer of semiring quantifiers in logic on words (cf. Section 2.3) provides an embedding of finite $\sigma$-structures into the space of $\mathbf{\Gamma}$-valued measures. It turns out that this embedding is a $\mathbf{\Gamma}$-valued version of the Stone pairing. Hereafter we make a notational difference, writing $\langle \text{-}, \text{-} \rangle_{\mathrm{I}}$ for the (classical) [0,1]-valued Stone pairing.

The main ingredient of the construction are the $\mathbf{\Gamma}$-valued finitely supported functions. To start with, we point out that the partial operation $-$ on $\mathbf{\Gamma}$ uniquely determines a partial "plus" operation on $\mathbf{\Gamma}$. Define

$$+ \colon \mathrm{dom}(+) \to \mathbf{\Gamma}, \quad \text{where} \quad \mathrm{dom}(+) = \{(x, y) \mid x \leq 1^\circ - y\},$$

by the following rules (whenever the expressions make sense):

$$r^\circ + s^\circ = (r+s)^\circ, \ r^- + s^\circ = (r+s)^-, \ r^\circ + s^- = (r+s)^-, \ \text{and} \ r^- + s^- = (r+s)^-.$$

Then, for every $y \in \mathbf{\Gamma}$, the function $(\text{-}) + y$ sending $x$ to $x + y$ is left adjoint to the function $(\text{-}) - y$ sending $x$ to $x - y$.

**Definition 11.** *For any set $X$, $\mathcal{F}(X)$ is the set of all functions $f \colon X \to \mathbf{\Gamma}$ s.t.*

1. *the set* $\mathrm{supp}(f) = \{x \in X \mid f(x) \neq 0^\circ\}$ *is finite, and*
2. $f(x_1) + \cdots + f(x_n)$ *is defined and equal to* $1^\circ$, *where* $\mathrm{supp}(f) = \{x_1, \ldots, x_n\}$.

To improve readability, if the sum $y_1 + \cdots + y_m$ exists in $\mathbf{\Gamma}$, we denote it $\sum_{i=1}^m y_i$. Finitely supported functions in the above sense always determine measures over the power-set algebra (the proof is an easy verification and is omitted):

**Lemma 12.** *Let $X$ be any set. There is a well-defined mapping $\int \colon \mathcal{F}(X) \to \mathcal{M}_{\Gamma}(\wp(X))$, assigning to every $f \in \mathcal{F}(X)$ the measure*

$$\textstyle\int f \colon M \mapsto \int_M f = \sum\{f(x) \mid x \in M \cap \mathrm{supp}(f)\}.$$

### 5.1 The $\mathbf{\Gamma}$-valued Stone pairing and logic on words

Fix a countably infinite set of variables $\{v_1, v_2, \ldots\}$. Recall that $\mathrm{FO}_n(\sigma)$ is the Lindenbaum-Tarski algebra of first-order formulas with free variables among $\{v_1, \ldots, v_n\}$. The dual space of $\mathrm{FO}_n(\sigma)$ is the space of $n$-types $\mathrm{Typ}_n(\sigma)$. Its points are the equivalence classes of pairs $(A, \alpha)$, where $A$ is a $\sigma$-structure and $\alpha \colon \{v_1, \ldots, v_n\} \to A$ is an interpretation of the variables. Write $\mathrm{Fin}(\sigma)$ for the set of all finite $\sigma$-structures and define a map $\mathrm{Fin}(\sigma) \to \mathcal{F}(\mathrm{Typ}_n(\sigma))$ as $A \mapsto f_n^A$, where $f_n^A$ is the function which sends an equivalence class $E \in \mathrm{Typ}_n(\sigma)$ to

$$f_n^A(E) = \sum_{(A,\alpha) \in E} \left(\frac{1}{|A|^n}\right)^\circ$$

*(Add $\frac{1}{|A|^n}$ for every interpretation $\alpha$ of the free variables s.t. $(A, \alpha)$ is in the equivalence class).*

By Lemma 12, we get a measure $\int f_n^A \colon \wp(\mathrm{Typ}_n(\sigma)) \to \mathbf{\Gamma}$. Now, for each $\varphi \in \mathrm{FO}_n(\sigma)$, let $[\![\varphi]\!]_n \subseteq \mathrm{Typ}_n(\sigma)$ be the set of (equivalence classes of) $\sigma$-structures with interpretations satisfying $\varphi$. By Stone duality we obtain an embedding $[\![\text{-}]\!]_n \colon \mathrm{FO}_n(\sigma) \hookrightarrow \wp(\mathrm{Typ}_n(\sigma))$. Restricting $\int f_n^A$ to $\mathrm{FO}_n(\sigma)$, we get a measure

$$\mu_n^A \colon \mathrm{FO}_n(\sigma) \to \mathbf{\Gamma}, \quad \varphi \mapsto \textstyle\int_{[\![\varphi]\!]_n} f_n^A.$$

Summing up, we have the composite map

$$\mathrm{Fin}(\sigma) \to \mathcal{M}_\Gamma(\wp(\mathrm{Typ}_n(\sigma))) \to \mathcal{M}_\Gamma(\mathrm{FO}_n(\sigma)), \quad A \mapsto \textstyle\int f_n^A \mapsto \mu_n^A. \tag{6}$$

Essentially the same construction is featured in logic on words, cf. equation (2):

- The set of finite $\sigma$-structures $\mathrm{Fin}(\sigma)$ corresponds to the set of finite words $A^*$.
- The collection $\mathrm{Typ}_n(\sigma)$ of (equivalence classes of) $\sigma$-structures with interpretations corresponds to $(A \times 2)^*$ or, interchangeably, $\beta(A \times 2)^*$ (in the case of one free variable).
- The fragment $\mathrm{FO}_n(\sigma)$ of first-order logic corresponds to the Boolean algebra of languages, defined by formulas with a free variable, dual to the Boolean space $X$ appearing in (2).
- The first map in the composite (6) sends a finite structure $A$ to the measure $\int f_n^A$ which, evaluated on $K \subseteq \mathrm{Typ}_n(\sigma)$, counts the (proportion of) interpretations $\alpha\colon \{v_1, \ldots, v_n\} \to A$ such that $(A, \alpha) \in K$, similarly to $R$ from (2).
- Finally, the second map in (6) sends a measure in $\mathcal{M}_\Gamma(\wp(\mathrm{Typ}_n(\sigma)))$ to its pushforward along $[\![\text{-}]\!]_n\colon \mathrm{FO}_n(\sigma) \hookrightarrow \wp(\mathrm{Typ}_n(\sigma))$. This is the second map in the composition (2).

On the other hand, the assignment $A \mapsto \mu_n^A$ defined in (6) is also closely related to the classical Stone pairing. Indeed, for every formula $\varphi$ in $\mathrm{FO}_n(\sigma)$,

$$\begin{aligned}\mu_n^A(\varphi) &= \sum_{E \in [\![\varphi]\!]_n} f_n^A(E) = \sum_{E \in [\![\varphi]\!]_n} \sum_{(A,\alpha) \in E} \left(\frac{1}{|A|^n}\right)^\circ \\ &= \left(\frac{|\{\overline{a} \in A^n \mid A \models \varphi(\overline{a})\}|}{|A|^n}\right)^\circ = (\langle \varphi, A \rangle_{\mathrm{I}})^\circ. \end{aligned} \tag{7}$$

In this sense, $\mu_n^A$ can be regarded as a $\mathbf{\Gamma}$-valued Stone pairing, relative to the fragment $\mathrm{FO}_n(\sigma)$. Next, we show how to extend this to the full first-order logic $\mathrm{FO}(\sigma)$. First, we observe that the construction is invariant under extensions of the set of free variables (the proof is the same as in the classical case).

**Lemma 13.** *Given $m, n \in \mathbb{N}$ and $A \in \mathrm{Fin}(\sigma)$, if $m \geq n$ then $(\mu_m^A)_{\restriction \mathrm{FO}_n(\sigma)} = \mu_n^A$.*

The Lindenbaum-Tarski algebra of all first-order formulas $\mathrm{FO}(\sigma)$ is the directed colimit of the Boolean subalgebras $\mathrm{FO}_n(\sigma)$, for $n \in \mathbb{N}$. Since the functor $\mathcal{M}_\Gamma$ turns directed colimits into codirected limits (Proposition 5), the Priestley space $\mathcal{M}_\Gamma(\mathrm{FO}(\sigma))$ is the limit of the diagram

$$\left\{\mathcal{M}_\Gamma(\mathrm{FO}_n(\sigma)) \xleftarrow{q_{n,m}} \mathcal{M}_\Gamma(\mathrm{FO}_m(\sigma)) \mid m, n \in \mathbb{N},\ m \geq n\right\}$$

where, for any $\mu\colon \mathrm{FO}_m(\sigma) \to \mathbf{\Gamma}$ in $\mathcal{M}_\Gamma(\mathrm{FO}_m(\sigma))$, the measure $q_{n,m}(\mu)$ is the restriction of $\mu$ to $\mathrm{FO}_n(\sigma)$. In view of Lemma 13, for every $A \in \mathrm{Fin}(\sigma)$, the tuple $(\mu_n^A)_{n \in \mathbb{N}}$ is compatible with the restriction maps. Thus, recalling that limits in the category of Priestley spaces are computed as in sets, by universality of the limit construction, this tuple yields a measure

$$\langle \text{-}, A \rangle_\Gamma : \mathrm{FO}(\sigma) \to \mathbf{\Gamma}$$

in the space $\mathcal{M}_\Gamma(\mathrm{FO}(\sigma))$. This we call the **Γ**-*valued Stone pairing* associated with $A$. As in the classical case, it is not difficult to see that the mapping $A \mapsto \langle \text{-}, A\rangle_\Gamma$ gives an embedding $\langle \text{-}, \text{-}\rangle_\Gamma : \mathrm{Fin}(\sigma) \hookrightarrow \mathcal{M}_\Gamma(\mathrm{FO}(\sigma))$. The following theorem illustrates the relation between the classical Stone pairing $\langle \text{-}, \text{-}\rangle_\mathrm{I} : \mathrm{Fin}(\sigma) \hookrightarrow \mathcal{M}_\mathrm{I}(\mathrm{FO}(\sigma))$, and the **Γ**-valued one.

**Theorem 14.** *The following diagram commutes:*

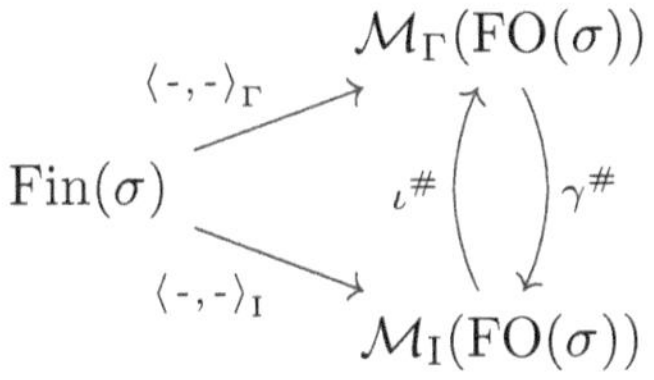


*Proof.* Fix an arbitrary finite structure $A \in \mathrm{Fin}(\sigma)$. Let $\varphi$ be a formula in $\mathrm{FO}(\sigma)$ with free variables among $\{v_1, \ldots, v_n\}$, for some $n \in \mathbb{N}$. By construction, $\langle \varphi, A\rangle_\Gamma = \mu_n^A(\varphi)$. Therefore, by equation (7), $\langle \varphi, A\rangle_\Gamma = (\langle \varphi, A\rangle_\mathrm{I})^\circ$. The statement then follows at once. □

**Remark.** The construction in this section works also for proper fragments, i.e. for sublattices $D \subseteq \mathrm{FO}(\sigma)$. This corresponds to composing the embedding $\mathrm{Fin}(\sigma) \hookrightarrow \mathcal{M}_\Gamma(\mathrm{FO}(\sigma))$ with the restriction map $\mathcal{M}_\Gamma(\mathrm{FO}(\sigma)) \to \mathcal{M}_\Gamma(D)$ sending $\mu\colon \mathrm{FO}(\sigma) \to \mathbf{\Gamma}$ to $\mu_{\restriction D}\colon D \to \mathbf{\Gamma}$. The only difference is that the ensuing map $\mathrm{Fin}(\sigma) \to \mathcal{M}_\Gamma(D)$ need not be injective, in general.

## 5.2 Limits in the spaces of measures

By Theorem 14 the **Γ**-valued Stone pairing $\langle \text{-}, \text{-}\rangle_\Gamma$ and the classical Stone pairing $\langle \text{-}, \text{-}\rangle_\mathrm{I}$ determine each other. However, the notions of convergence associated with the spaces $\mathcal{M}_\Gamma(\mathrm{FO}(\sigma))$ and $\mathcal{M}_\mathrm{I}(\mathrm{FO}(\sigma))$ are different: since the topology of $\mathcal{M}_\Gamma(\mathrm{FO}(\sigma))$ is richer, there are "fewer" convergent sequences. Recall from Lemma 8 that $\gamma^\#\colon \mathcal{M}_\Gamma(\mathrm{FO}(\sigma)) \to \mathcal{M}_\mathrm{I}(\mathrm{FO}(\sigma))$ is continuous. Also, $\gamma^\#(\langle \text{-}, A\rangle_\Gamma) = \langle \text{-}, A\rangle_\mathrm{I}$ by Theorem 14. Thus, for any sequence of finite structures $(A_n)_{n\in\mathbb{N}}$, if

$$\langle \text{-}, A_n\rangle_\Gamma \text{ converges to a measure } \mu \text{ in } \mathcal{M}_\Gamma(\mathrm{FO}(\sigma))$$

then

$$\langle \text{-}, A_n\rangle_\mathrm{I} \text{ converges to the measure } \gamma^\#(\mu) \text{ in } \mathcal{M}_\mathrm{I}(\mathrm{FO}(\sigma)).$$

The converse is not true. For example, consider the signature $\sigma = \{<\}$ consisting of a single binary relation symbol, and let $(A_n)_{n\in\mathbb{N}}$ be the sequence of finite posets displayed in the picture below.

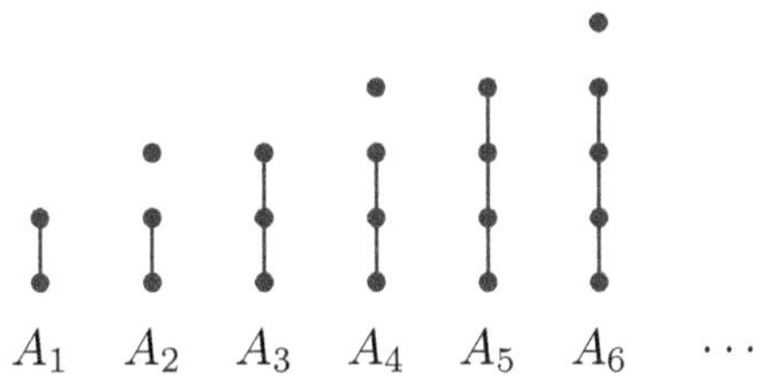

Let $\psi(x) \approx \forall y \neg(x < y) \wedge \exists z \neg(z < x) \wedge \neg(z = x)$ be the formula stating that $x$ is maximal but not the maximum in the order given by $<$. Then, for the sublattice $D = \{\mathbf{f}, \psi, \mathbf{t}\}$ of $\mathrm{FO}(\sigma)$, the sequences $\langle \text{-}, A_n \rangle_\Gamma$ and $\langle \text{-}, A_n \rangle_\mathrm{I}$ converge in $\mathcal{M}_\Gamma(D)$ and $\mathcal{M}_\mathrm{I}(D)$, respectively. However, if we consider the Boolean algebra $B = \{\mathbf{f}, \psi, \neg\psi, \mathbf{t}\}$, then the $\langle \text{-}, A_n \rangle_\mathrm{I}$'s still converge whereas the $\langle \text{-}, A_n \rangle_\Gamma$'s do not. Indeed, the following sequence does not converge in $\mathbf{\Gamma}$:

$$(\langle \neg\psi, A_n \rangle_\Gamma)_n = (1^\circ, (\tfrac{1}{3})^\circ, 1^\circ, (\tfrac{2}{4})^\circ, 1^\circ, (\tfrac{3}{5})^\circ, \ldots),$$

because the odd terms converge to $1^\circ$, while the even terms converge to $1^-$. However, there is a sequence $\langle \text{-}, B_n \rangle_\Gamma$ whose image under $\gamma^\#$ coincides with the limit of the $\langle \text{-}, A_n \rangle_\mathrm{I}$'s (e.g., take the subsequence of even terms of $(A_n)_{n\in\mathbb{N}}$). In the next theorem, we will see that this is a general fact.

Identify $\mathrm{Fin}(\sigma)$ with a subset of $\mathcal{M}_\Gamma(\mathrm{FO}(\sigma))$ (resp. $\mathcal{M}_\mathrm{I}(\mathrm{FO}(\sigma))$) through $\langle \text{-}, \text{-} \rangle_\Gamma$ (resp. $\langle \text{-}, \text{-} \rangle_\mathrm{I}$). A central question in the theory of structural limits, cf. [16], is to determine the closure of $\mathrm{Fin}(\sigma)$ in $\mathcal{M}_\mathrm{I}(\mathrm{FO}(\sigma))$, which consists precisely of the limits of sequences of finite structures. The following theorem gives an answer to this question in terms of the corresponding question for $\mathcal{M}_\Gamma(\mathrm{FO}(\sigma))$.

**Theorem 15.** *Let* $\overline{\mathrm{Fin}(\sigma)}$ *denote the closure of* $\mathrm{Fin}(\sigma)$ *in* $\mathcal{M}_\Gamma(\mathrm{FO}(\sigma))$*. Then the set* $\gamma^\#(\overline{\mathrm{Fin}(\sigma)})$ *coincides with the closure of* $\mathrm{Fin}(\sigma)$ *in* $\mathcal{M}_\mathrm{I}(\mathrm{FO}(\sigma))$*.*

*Proof.* Write $U$ for the image of $\langle \text{-}, \text{-} \rangle_\Gamma : \mathrm{Fin}(\sigma) \hookrightarrow \mathcal{M}_\Gamma(\mathrm{FO}(\sigma))$, and $V$ for the image of $\langle \text{-}, \text{-} \rangle_\mathrm{I} : \mathrm{Fin}(\sigma) \hookrightarrow \mathcal{M}_\mathrm{I}(\mathrm{FO}(\sigma))$. We must prove that $\gamma^\#(\overline{U}) = \overline{V}$. By Theorem 14, $\gamma^\#(U) = V$. The map $\gamma^\#\colon \mathcal{M}_\Gamma(\mathrm{FO}(\sigma)) \to \mathcal{M}_\mathrm{I}(\mathrm{FO}(\sigma))$ is continuous (Lemma 8), and the spaces $\mathcal{M}_\Gamma(\mathrm{FO}(\sigma))$ and $\mathcal{M}_\mathrm{I}(\mathrm{FO}(\sigma))$ are compact Hausdorff (Proposition 4 and Corollary 9). Since continuous maps between compact Hausdorff spaces are closed, $\gamma^\#(\overline{U}) = \overline{\gamma^\#(U)} = \overline{V}$. □

## 6 The logic of measures

Let $D$ be a distributive lattice. We know from Proposition 4 that the space $\mathcal{M}_\Gamma(D)$ of $\mathbf{\Gamma}$-valued measures on $D$ is a Priestley space, whence it has a dual distributive lattice $\mathbf{P}(D)$. In this section we show that $\mathbf{P}(D)$ can be represented as the Lindenbaum-Tarski algebra for a propositional logic $P\mathcal{L}_D$ obtained from $D$ by adding probabilistic quantifiers. Since we adopt a logical perspective, we write $\mathbf{f}$ and $\mathbf{t}$ for the bottom and top elements of $D$, respectively.

The set of propositional variables of $P\mathcal{L}_D$ consists of the symbols $\mathbb{P}_{\geq p}\, a$, for every $a \in D$ and $p \in \mathbb{Q} \cap [0, 1]$. For every measure $\mu \in \mathcal{M}_\Gamma(D)$, we set

$$\mu \models \mathbb{P}_{\geq p}\, a \;\Leftrightarrow\; \mu(a) \geq p^\circ. \tag{8}$$

This satisfaction relation extends in the obvious way to the closure under finite conjunctions and finite disjunctions of the set of propositional variables. Define

$$\varphi \models \psi \quad \text{if,} \quad \forall \mu \in \mathcal{M}_\Gamma(D), \quad \mu \models \varphi \text{ implies } \mu \models \psi.$$

Also, write $\models \varphi$ if $\mu \models \varphi$ for every $\mu \in \mathcal{M}_\Gamma(D)$, and $\varphi \models$ if there is no $\mu \in \mathcal{M}_\Gamma(D)$ with $\mu \models \varphi$.

Consider the following conditions, for any $p, q, r \in \mathbb{Q} \cap [0,1]$ and $a, b \in D$.

(L1) $\mathbb{P}_{\geq q}\, a \models \mathbb{P}_{\geq p}\, a$ whenever $p \leq q$
(L2) $\mathbb{P}_{\geq p}\, \mathbf{f} \models$ whenever $p > 0$, $\models \mathbb{P}_{\geq 0}\, \mathbf{f}$ and $\models \mathbb{P}_{\geq q}\, \mathbf{t}$
(L3) $\mathbb{P}_{\geq q}\, a \models \mathbb{P}_{\geq q}\, b$ whenever $a \leq b$
(L4) $\mathbb{P}_{\geq p}\, a \wedge \mathbb{P}_{\geq q}\, b \models \mathbb{P}_{\geq p+q-r}\, (a \vee b) \vee \mathbb{P}_{\geq r}\, (a \wedge b)$ whenever $0 \leq p+q-r \leq 1$
(L5) $\mathbb{P}_{\geq p+q-r}\, (a \vee b) \wedge \mathbb{P}_{\geq r}\, (a \wedge b) \models \mathbb{P}_{\geq p}\, a \vee \mathbb{P}_{\geq q}\, b$ whenever $0 \leq p+q-r \leq 1$

It is not hard to see that the interpretation in (8) validates these conditions:

**Lemma 16.** *The conditions (L1)–(L5) are satisfied in* $\mathcal{M}_\Gamma(D)$.

Write $\mathbf{P}(D)$ for the quotient of the free distributive lattice on the set

$$\{\mathbb{P}_{\geq p}\, a \mid p \in \mathbb{Q} \cap [0,1],\ a \in D\}$$

with respect to the congruence generated by the conditions (L1)–(L5).

**Proposition 17.** *Let* $F \subseteq \mathbf{P}(D)$ *be a prime filter. The assignment*

$$a \mapsto \bigvee \{q^\circ \mid \mathbb{P}_{\geq q}\, a \in F\} \quad \text{defines a measure } \mu_F \colon D \to \mathbf{\Gamma}.$$

*Proof.* Items (L2) and (L3) take care of the first two conditions defining $\mathbf{\Gamma}$-valued measures (cf. Definition 3). We prove the first half of the third condition, as the other half is proved in a similar fashion. We must show that, for every $a, b \in D$,

$$\mu_F(a) \sim \mu_F(a \wedge b) \leq \mu_F(a \vee b) - \mu_F(b). \tag{9}$$

It is not hard to show that $\mu_F(a) - r^\circ = \bigvee\{p_1^\circ - r^\circ \mid r^\circ \leq p_1^\circ \leq \mu_F(a)\}$, and $x - (\text{-})$ transforms non-empty joins into meets (this follows by Scott continuity of $x - (\text{-})$ seen as a map $[0^\circ, x] \to \mathbf{\Gamma}^\partial$). Hence, equation (9) is equivalent to

$$\bigvee \{p^\circ - r^\circ \mid \mu_F(a \wedge b) < r^\circ \leq p^\circ \leq \mu_F(a)\} \leq \bigwedge \{\mu_F(a \vee b) - q^\circ \mid q^\circ \leq \mu_F(b)\}.$$

To settle this inequality it is enough to show that, provided $\mu_F(a \wedge b) < r^\circ \leq p^\circ \leq \mu_F(a)$ and $q^\circ \leq \mu_F(b)$, we have $(p - r)^\circ \leq \mu_F(a \vee b) - q^\circ$. The latter inequality is equivalent to $(p + q - r)^\circ \leq \mu_F(a \vee b)$. In turn, using (L4) and the fact that $F$ is a prime filter, $\mathbb{P}_{\geq p}\, a, \mathbb{P}_{\geq q}\, b \in F$ and $\mathbb{P}_{\geq r}\, (a \wedge b) \notin F$ entail $\mathbb{P}_{\geq p+q-r}\, (a \vee b) \in F$. Whence,

$$\mu_F(a \vee b) = \bigvee \{s^\circ \mid \mathbb{P}_{\geq s}\, (a \vee b) \in F\} \geq (p + q - r)^\circ.$$ □

We can now describe the dual lattice of $\mathcal{M}_\Gamma(D)$ as the Lindenbaum-Tarski algebra for the logic $P\mathcal{L}_D$, built from the propositional variables $\mathbb{P}_{\geq p}\, a$ by imposing the laws (L1)–(L5).

**Theorem 18.** *Let $D$ be a distributive lattice. Then the lattice $\mathbf{P}(D)$ is isomorphic to the distributive lattice dual to the Priestley space $\mathcal{M}_\Gamma(D)$.*

*Proof.* Let $X_{\mathbf{P}(D)}$ be the space dual to $\mathbf{P}(D)$. By Proposition 17 there is a map $\vartheta \colon X_{\mathbf{P}(D)} \to \mathcal{M}_\Gamma(D)$, $F \mapsto \mu_F$. We claim that $\vartheta$ is an isomorphism of Priestley space. Clearly, $\vartheta$ is monotone. If $\mu_{F_1}(a) \nleq \mu_{F_2}(a)$ for some $a \in D$, we have

$$\bigvee \{q^\circ \mid \mathbb{P}_{\geq q}\, a \in F_1\} = \mu_{F_1}(a) \nleq \mu_{F_2}(a) = \bigwedge \{p^- \mid \mathbb{P}_{\geq p}\, a \notin F_2\}. \tag{10}$$

Equation (10) implies the existence of $p, q$ satisfying $\mathbb{P}_{\geq q}\, a \in F_1$, $\mathbb{P}_{\geq p}\, a \notin F_2$ and $q \geq p$. It follows by (L1) that $\mathbb{P}_{\geq p}\, a \in F_1$. We conclude that $\mathbb{P}_{\geq p}\, a \in F_1 \setminus F_2$, whence $F_1 \not\subseteq F_2$. This shows that $\vartheta$ is an order embedding, whence injective.

We prove that $\vartheta$ is surjective, thus a bijection. Fix a measure $\mu \in \mathcal{M}_\Gamma(D)$. It is not hard to see, using Lemma 16, that the filter $F_\mu \subseteq \mathbf{P}(D)$ generated by

$$\{\mathbb{P}_{\geq q}\, a \mid a \in D,\ q \in \mathbb{Q} \cap [0,1],\ \mu(a) \geq q^\circ\}$$

is prime. Further, $\vartheta(F_\mu)(a) = \bigvee \{q^\circ \mid \mathbb{P}_{\geq q}\, a \in F_\mu\} = \bigvee \{q^\circ \mid \mu(a) \geq q^\circ\} = \mu(a)$ for every $a \in D$. Hence, $\vartheta(F_\mu) = \mu$ and $\vartheta$ is surjective.

To settle the theorem it remains to show that $\vartheta$ is continuous. Note that for a basic clopen of the form $C = \{\mu \in \mathcal{M}_\Gamma(D) \mid \mu(a) \geq p^\circ\}$ where $a \in D$ and $p \in \mathbb{Q} \cap [0,1]$, the preimage $\vartheta^{-1}(C) = \{F \subseteq \mathbf{P}(D) \mid \mu_F(a) \geq p^\circ\}$ is equal to

$$\{F \in X_{\mathbf{P}(D)} \mid \bigvee \{q^\circ \mid \mathbb{P}_{\geq q}\, a \in F\} \geq p^\circ\} = \{F \in X_{\mathbf{P}(D)} \mid \mathbb{P}_{\geq p}\, a \in F\},$$

which is a clopen of $X_{\mathbf{P}(D)}$. Similarly, if $C = \{\mu \in \mathcal{M}_\Gamma(D) \mid \mu(a) \leq q^-\}$ for some $a \in D$ and $q \in \mathbb{Q} \cap (0,1]$, by the claim above $\vartheta^{-1}(C) = \{F \in X_{\mathbf{P}(D)} \mid \mathbb{P}_{\geq q}\, a \notin F\}$, which is again a clopen of $X_{\mathbf{P}(D)}$. □

By Theorem 18, for any distributive lattice $D$, the lattice of clopen up-sets of $\mathcal{M}_\Gamma(D)$ is isomorphic to the Lindenbaum-Tarski algebra $\mathbf{P}(D)$ of our *positive* propositional logic $P\mathcal{L}_D$. Moving from the lattice of clopen up-sets to the Boolean algebra of all clopens logically corresponds to adding negation to the logic. The logic obtained this way can be presented as follows. Introduce a new propositional variable $\mathbb{P}_{<q}\, a$, for each $a \in D$ and $q \in \mathbb{Q} \cap [0,1]$. For a measure $\mu \in \mathcal{M}_\Gamma(D)$, set

$$\mu \models \mathbb{P}_{<q}\, a \;\Leftrightarrow\; \mu(a) < q^\circ.$$

We also add a new rule, stating that $\mathbb{P}_{<q}\, a$ is the negation of $\mathbb{P}_{\geq q}\, a$:

(L6) $\mathbb{P}_{<q}\, a \wedge \mathbb{P}_{\geq q}\, a \models$ and $\models \mathbb{P}_{<q}\, a \vee \mathbb{P}_{\geq q}\, a$

Clearly, (L6) is satisfied in $\mathcal{M}_\Gamma(D)$. Moreover, the Boolean algebra of *all* clopens of $\mathcal{M}_\Gamma(D)$ is isomorphic to the quotient of the free distributive lattice on

$$\{\mathbb{P}_{\geq p}\, a \mid p \in \mathbb{Q} \cap [0,1],\ a \in D\} \cup \{\mathbb{P}_{<q}\, b \mid q \in \mathbb{Q} \cap [0,1],\ b \in D\}$$

with respect to the congruence generated by the conditions (L1)–(L6).

*Specialising to* FO($\sigma$). Let us briefly discuss what happens when we instantiate $D$ with the full first-order logic FO($\sigma$). For a formula $\varphi \in \mathrm{FO}(\sigma)$ with free variables $v_1, \ldots, v_n$ and a $q \in \mathbb{Q} \cap [0,1]$, we have two new sentences $\mathbb{P}_{\geq q}\, \varphi$ and $\mathbb{P}_{<q}\, \varphi$. For a finite $\sigma$-structure $A$ identified with its $\mathbf{\Gamma}$-valued Stone pairing $\langle \text{-}, A \rangle_\Gamma$,

$$A \models \mathbb{P}_{\geq q}\, \varphi \;\; (\text{resp. } A \models \mathbb{P}_{<q}\, \varphi) \quad \text{iff} \quad \langle \varphi, A \rangle_\Gamma \geq q^\circ \;\; (\text{resp. } \langle \varphi, A \rangle_\Gamma < q^\circ).$$

That is, $\mathbb{P}_{\geq q}\, \varphi$ is true in $A$ if a random assignment of the variables $v_1, \ldots, v_n$ in $A$ satisfies $\varphi$ with probability at least $q$. Similarly for $\mathbb{P}_{<q}\, \varphi$. If we regard $\mathbb{P}_{\geq q}$ and $\mathbb{P}_{<q}$ as probabilistic quantifiers that bind all free variables of a given formula, the Stone pairing $\langle \text{-}, \text{-} \rangle_\Gamma : \mathrm{Fin} \to \mathcal{M}_\Gamma(\mathrm{FO}(\sigma))$ can be seen as the embedding of finite structures into the space of types for the logic $P\mathcal{L}_{\mathrm{FO}(\sigma)}$.

## Conclusion

Types are points of the dual space of a logic (viewed as a Boolean algebra). In classical first-order logic, 0-types are just the models modulo elementary equivalence. But when there are not 'enough' models, as in finite model theory, the spaces of types provide completions of the sets of models.

In [5], it was shown that for logic on words and various quantifiers we have that, given a Boolean algebra of formulas with a free variable, the space of types of the Boolean algebra generated by the formulas obtained by quantification is given by a measure space construction. Here we have shown that a suitable enrichment of first-order logic gives rise to a space of measures $\mathcal{M}_\Gamma(\mathrm{FO}(\sigma))$ closely related to the space $\mathcal{M}_\mathrm{I}(\mathrm{FO}(\sigma))$ used in the theory of structural limits. Indeed, Theorem 14 tells us that the ensuing Stone pairings interdetermine each other. Further, the Stone pairing for $\mathcal{M}_\Gamma(\mathrm{FO}(\sigma))$ is just the embedding of the finite models in the completion/compactification provided by the space of types of the enriched logic.

These results identify the logical gist of the theory of structural limits, and provide a new and interesting connection between logic on words and the theory of structural limits in finite model theory. But we also expect that it may prove a useful tool in its own right. Thus, for structural limits, it is an open problem to characterise the closure of the image of the $[0,1]$-valued Stone pairing [16]. Reasoning in the $\mathbf{\Gamma}$-valued setting, native to logic and where we can use duality, one would expect that this is the subspace $\mathcal{M}_\Gamma(\mathrm{Th}(\mathrm{Fin}))$ of $\mathcal{M}_\Gamma(\mathrm{FO}(\sigma))$ given by the quotient $\mathrm{FO}(\sigma) \twoheadrightarrow \mathrm{Th}(\mathrm{Fin})$ onto the theory of pseudofinite structures. The purpose of such a characterisation would be to understand the points of the closure as "generalised models". Another subject that we would like to investigate is that of zero-one laws. The zero-one law for first-order logic states that the sequence of measures for which the $n$th measure, on a sentence $\psi$, yields the proportion of $n$-element structures satisfying $\psi$, converges to a $\{0,1\}$-valued measure. Over $\mathbf{\Gamma}$ this will no longer be true as 1 is split into its 'limiting' and 'achieved' personae. Yet, we expect the above sequence to converge also in this setting and, by Theorem 14, it will converge to a $\{0^\circ, 1^-, 1^\circ\}$-valued measure. Understanding this more fine-grained measure may yield useful information about the zero-one law.

Further, it would be interesting to investigate whether the limits for schema mappings introduced by Kolaitis *et al.* [13] may be seen also as a type-theoretic construction. Finally, we would want to explore the connections with other semantically inspired approaches to finite model theory, such as those recently put forward by Abramsky, Dawar *et al.* [2,3].

## References

1. Abramsky, S.: Domain theory in logical form. Ann. Pure Appl. Logic **51**, 1–77 (1991)
2. Abramsky, S., Dawar, A., Wang, P.: The pebbling comonad in finite model theory. In: 32nd Annual ACM/IEEE Symposium on Logic in Computer Science, LICS. pp. 1–12 (2017)
3. Abramsky, S., Shah, N.: Relating Structure and Power: Comonadic semantics for computational resources. In: 27th EACSL Annual Conference on Computer Science Logic, CSL. pp. 2:1–2:17 (2018)
4. Gehrke, M., Grigorieff, S., Pin, J.-É.: Duality and equational theory of regular languages. In: Automata, languages and programming II, LNCS, vol. 5126, pp. 246–257. Springer, Berlin (2008)
5. Gehrke, M., Petrişan, D., Reggio, L.: Quantifiers on languages and codensity monads. In: 32nd Annual ACM/IEEE Symposium on Logic in Computer Science, LICS. pp. 1–12 (2017)
6. Gehrke, M., Petrişan, D., Reggio, L.: Quantifiers on languages and codensity monads (2019), extended version. Submitted. Preprint available at https://arxiv.org/abs/1702.08841
7. Gehrke, M., Priestley, H.A.: Canonical extensions of double quasioperator algebras: an algebraic perspective on duality for certain algebras with binary operations. J. Pure Appl. Algebra **209**(1), 269–290 (2007)
8. Gehrke, M., Priestley, H.A.: Duality for double quasioperator algebras via their canonical extensions. Studia Logica **86**(1), 31–68 (2007)
9. Goldblatt, R.: Varieties of complex algebras. Ann. Pure Appl. Logic **44**(3), 173–242 (1989)
10. van Gool, S.J., Steinberg, B.: Pro-aperiodic monoids via saturated models. In: 34th Symposium on Theoretical Aspects of Computer Science, STACS. pp. 39:1–39:14 (2017)
11. Johnstone, P.T.: Stone spaces, Cambridge Studies in Advanced Mathematics, vol. 3. Cambridge University Press (1986), reprint of the 1982 edition
12. Jung, A.: Continuous domain theory in logical form. In: Coecke, B., Ong, L., Panangaden, P. (eds.) Computation, Logic, Games, and Quantum Foundations, Lecture Notes in Computer Science, vol. 7860, pp. 166–177. Springer Verlag (2013)
13. Kolaitis, P.G., Pichler, R., Sallinger, E., Savenkov, V.: Limits of schema mappings. Theory of Computing Systems **62**(4), 899–940 (2018)
14. Matz, O., Schweikardt, N.: Expressive power of monadic logics on words, trees, pictures, and graphs. In: Logic and Automata: History and Perspectives. pp. 531–552 (2008)
15. Nešetřil, J., Ossona de Mendez, P.: A model theory approach to structural limits. Commentationes Mathematicae Universitatis Carolinae **53**(4), 581–603 (2012)
16. Nešetřil, J., Ossona de Mendez, P.: First-order limits, an analytical perspective. European Journal of Combinatorics **52**, 368–388 (2016)
17. Nešetřil, J., Ossona de Mendez, P.: A unified approach to structural limits and limits of graphs with bounded tree-depth (2020), to appear in *Memoirs of the American Mathematical Society*
18. Pin, J.-É.: Profinite methods in automata theory. In: 26th Symposium on Theoretical Aspects of Computer Science, STACS. pp. 31–50 (2009)
19. Priestley, H.A.: Representation of distributive lattices by means of ordered Stone spaces. Bull. London Math. Soc. **2**, 186–190 (1970)

# 6

# On Computability of Data Word Functions Defined by Transducers*

Léo Exibard[1,2**(✉)], Emmanuel Filiot[1***], and Pierre-Alain Reynier[2†]

[1] Université Libre de Bruxelles, Brussels, Belgium
leo.exibard@ulb.ac.be
[2] Aix Marseille Univ, Université de Toulon, CNRS, LIS, Marseille, France

**Abstract.** In this paper, we investigate the problem of synthesizing computable functions of infinite words over an infinite alphabet (data $\omega$-words). The notion of computability is defined through Turing machines with infinite inputs which can produce the corresponding infinite outputs in the limit. We use non-deterministic transducers equipped with registers, an extension of register automata with outputs, to specify functions. Such transducers may not define functions but more generally relations of data $\omega$-words, and we show that it is PSPACE-complete to test whether a given transducer defines a function. Then, given a function defined by some register transducer, we show that it is decidable (and again, PSPACE-c) whether such function is computable. As for the known finite alphabet case, we show that computability and continuity coincide for functions defined by register transducers, and show how to decide continuity. We also define a subclass for which those problems are PTIME.

**Keywords:** Data Words · Register Automata · Register Transducers · Functionality · Continuity · Computability.

## 1 Introduction

*Context* Program synthesis aims at deriving, in an automatic way, a program that fulfils a given specification. Such setting is very appealing when for instance the specification describes, in some abstract formalism (an automaton or ideally a logic), important properties that the program must satisfy. The synthesised program is then *correct-by-construction* with regards to those properties. It is particularly important and desirable for the design of safety-critical systems with hard dependability constraints, which are notoriously hard to design correctly.

Program synthesis is hard to realise for general-purpose programming languages but important progress has been made recently in the automatic synthesis of *reactive systems*. In this context, the system continuously receives input signals to which it must react by producing output signals. Such systems are not assumed to terminate and their executions are usually modelled as infinite words over the alphabets of input and output signals. A specification is thus a set of pairs (in,out), where in and out are infinite words, such that out is a legitimate output for in. Most methods for reactive system synthesis only work for *synchronous* systems over *finite* sets of input and output signals $\Sigma$ and $\Gamma$. In this synchronous setting, input and output signals alternate, and thus *implementations* of such a specification are defined by means of *synchronous* transducers, which are Büchi automata with transitions of the form $(q, \sigma, \gamma, q')$, expressing that in state $q$, when getting input $\sigma \in \Sigma$, output $\gamma \in \Gamma$ is produced and the machine moves to state $q'$. We aim at building *deterministic* implementations, in the sense that the output $\gamma$ and state $q'$ uniquely depend on $q$ and $\sigma$. The realisability problem of specifications given as synchronous non-deterministic transducers, by implementations defined by synchronous deterministic transducers is known to be decidable [14,20]. In this paper, we are interested in the *asynchronous* setting, in which transducers can produce none or several outputs at once every time some input is read, i.e., transitions are of the form $(q, \sigma, w, q')$ where $w \in \Gamma^*$. However, such generalisation makes the realisability problem undecidable [2,9].

*Synthesis of Transducers with Registers* In the setting we just described, the set of signals is considered to be finite. This assumption is not realistic in general, as signals may come with unbounded information (e.g. process ids) that we call here *data*. To address this limitation, recent works have considered the synthesis of reactive systems processing *data words* [17,6,16,7]. Data words are infinite words over an alphabet $\Sigma \times \mathcal{D}$, where $\Sigma$ is a finite set and $\mathcal{D}$ is a possibly infinite countable set. To handle data words, just as automata have been extended to *register automata*, transducers have been extended to *register transducers*. Such transducers are equipped with a finite set of registers in which they can store data and with which they can compare data for equality or inequality. While the realisability problem of specifications given as synchronous non-deterministic register transducers ($\mathsf{NRT}_{\mathsf{syn}}$) by implementation defined by synchronous deterministic register transducers ($\mathsf{DRT}_{\mathsf{syn}}$) is undecidable, decidability is recovered for specifications defined by universal register transducers and by giving as input the number of registers the implementation must have [7,17].

*Computable Implementations* In the previously mentioned works, both for finite or infinite alphabets, implementations are considered to be deterministic transducers. Such an implementation is guaranteed to use only a constant amount of memory (assuming data have size $O(1)$). While it makes sense with regards to memory-efficiency, some problems turn out to be undecidable, as already mentioned: realisability of $\mathsf{NRT}_{\mathsf{syn}}$ specifications by $\mathsf{DRT}_{\mathsf{syn}}$, or, in the finite alphabet setting, when both the specification and implementation are asynchronous. In this paper, we propose to study computable implementations, in the sense of (partial) functions $f$ of data $\omega$-words computable by some Turing machine $M$ that has an infinite input $x \in \mathrm{dom}(f)$, and produces longer and longer prefixes of the output

$f(x)$ as it reads longer and longer prefixes of the input $x$. Therefore, such a machine produces the output $f(x)$ in the limit. We denote by TM the class of Turing machines computing functions in this sense. As an example, consider the function $f$ that takes as input any data $\omega$-word $u = (\sigma_1, d_1)(\sigma_2, d_2)\dots$ and outputs $(\sigma_1, d_1)^\omega$ if $d_1$ occurs at least twice in $u$, and otherwise outputs $u$. This function is not computable, as an hypothetic machine could not output anything as long as $d_1$ is not met a second time. However, the following function $g$ is computable. It is defined only on words $(\sigma_1, d_1)(\sigma_2, d_2)\dots$ such that $\sigma_1\sigma_2\dots \in ((a+b)c^*)^\omega$, and transforms any $(\sigma_i, d_i)$ by $(\sigma_i, d_1)$ if the next symbol in $\{a, b\}$ is an $a$, otherwise it keeps $(\sigma_i, d_i)$ unchanged. To compute it, a TM would need to store $d_1$, and then wait until the next symbol in $\{a, b\}$ is met before outputting something. Since the finite input labels are necessarily in $((a + b)c^*)^\omega$, this machine will produce the whole output in the limit. Note that $g$ cannot be defined by any deterministic register transducer, as it needs unbounded memory to be implemented.

However, already in the finite alphabet setting, the problem of deciding if a specification given as some non-deterministic synchronous transducer is realisable by some computable function is open. The particular case of realisability by computable functions of universal domain (the set of all $\omega$-words) is known to be decidable [12]. In the asynchronous setting, the undecidability proof of [2] can be easily adapted to show the undecidability of realisability of specifications given by non-deterministic (asynchronous) transducers by computable functions.

*Functional Specifications* As said before, a specification is in general a relation from inputs to outputs. If this relation is a function, we call it functional. Due to the negative results just mentioned about the synthesis of computable functions from non-functional specifications, we instead here focus on the case of functional specifications and address the following general question: given the specification of a function of data $\omega$-words, is this function "implementable", where we define "implementable" as "being computable by some Turing machine". Moreover, if it is implementable, then we want a procedure to automatically generate an algorithm that computes it. This raises another important question: how to decide whether a specification is functional ? We investigate these questions for asynchronous register transducers, here called register transducers. This asynchrony allows for much more expressive power, but is a source of technical challenge.

*Contributions* In this paper, we solve the questions mentioned before for the class of (asynchronous) non-deterministic register transducers (NRT). We also give fundamental results on this class. In particular, we prove that:

1. deciding whether an NRT defines a function is PSPACE-complete,
2. deciding whether two functions defined by NRT are equal on the intersection of their domains is PSPACE-complete,
3. the class of functions defined by NRT is effectively closed under composition,
4. computability and continuity are equivalent notions for functions defined by NRT, where continuity is defined using the classical Cantor distance,
5. deciding whether a function given as an NRT is computable is PSPACE-c,

6. those problems are in PTIME for a subclass of NRT, called test-free NRT.

Finally, we also mention that considering the class of deterministic register transducers (DRT for short) instead of computable functions as a yardstick for the notion of being "implementable" for a function would yield undecidability. Indeed, given a function defined by some NRT, it is in general undecidable to check whether this function is realisable by some DRT, by a simple reduction from the universality problem of non-deterministic register automata [19].

*Related Work* The notion of continuity with regards to Cantor distance is not new, and for rational functions over finite alphabets, it was already known to be decidable [21]. Its connection with computability for functions of $\omega$-words over a finite alphabet has recently been investigated in [3] for one-way and two-way transducers. Our results lift some of theirs to the setting of data words. The model of test-free NRT can be seen as a one-way non-deterministic version of a model of two-way transducers considered in [5].

## 2 Data Words and Register Transducers

For a (possibly infinite) set $S$, we denote by $S^*$ (resp. $S^\omega$) the set of finite (resp. infinite) words over this alphabet, and we let $S^\infty = S^* \cup S^\omega$. For a word $u = u_1 \dots u_n$, we denote $\|u\| = n$ its length, and, by convention, for $u \in S^\omega$, $\|u\| = \infty$. The empty word is denoted $\varepsilon$. For $1 \leq i \leq j \leq \|u\|$, we let $u[i{:}j] = u_i u_{i+1} \dots u_j$ and $u[i] = u[i{:}i]$ the $i$th letter of $u$. For $u, v \in S^\infty$, we say that $u$ is a prefix of $v$, written $u \preceq v$, if there exists $w \in S^\infty$ such that $v = uw$. In this case, we define $u^{-1}v = w$. For $u, v \in S^\infty$, we say that $u$ and $v$ *mismatch*, written $\mathsf{mismatch}(u, v)$, when there exists a position $i$ such that $1 \leq i \leq \|u\|$, $1 \leq i \leq \|v\|$ and $u[i] \neq v[i]$. Finally, for $u, v \in S^\infty$, we denote by $u \wedge v$ their longest common prefix, i.e. the longest word $w \in S^\infty$ such that $w \preceq u$ and $w \preceq v$.

*Data Words* In this paper, $\Sigma$ and $\Gamma$ are two finite alphabets and $\mathcal{D}$ is a countably infinite set of *data*. We use letter $\sigma$ (resp. $\gamma$, $d$) to denote elements of $\Sigma$ (resp. $\Gamma$, $\mathcal{D}$). We also distinguish an arbitrary data value $\mathsf{d}_0 \in \mathcal{D}$. Given a set $R$, let $\tau_0^R$ be the constant function defined by $\tau_0^R(r) = \mathsf{d}_0$ for all $r \in R$. Given a finite alphabet $A$, a *labelled data* is a pair $x = (a, d) \in A \times \mathcal{D}$, where $a$ is the *label* and $d$ the *data*. We define the projections $\mathsf{lab}(x) = a$ and $\mathsf{dt}(x) = d$. A *data word* over $A$ and $\mathcal{D}$ is an infinite sequence of labelled data, i.e. a word $w \in (A \times \mathcal{D})^\omega$. We extend the projections $\mathsf{lab}$ and $\mathsf{dt}$ to data words naturally, i.e. $\mathsf{lab}(w) \in A^\omega$ and $\mathsf{dt}(w) \in \mathcal{D}^\omega$. A *data word language* is a subset $L \subseteq (A \times \mathcal{D})^\omega$. Note that here, data words are infinite, otherwise they are called *finite data words*.

### 2.1 Register Transducers

Register transducers are transducers recognising data word relations. They are an extension of finite transducers to data word relations, in the same way register automata [15] are an extension of finite automata to data word languages. Here, we define them over infinite data words with a Büchi acceptance condition, and allow multiple registers to contain the same data, with a syntax close to [18]. The current data can be compared for equality with the register contents via tests, which are symbolic and defined via Boolean formulas of the following form. Given $R$ a set of registers, a *test* is a formula $\phi$ satisfying the following syntax:

$$\phi ::= \top \mid \bot \mid r^{=} \mid r^{\neq} \mid \phi \wedge \phi \mid \phi \vee \phi \mid \neg\phi$$

where $r \in R$. Given a valuation $\tau : R \to \mathcal{D}$, a test $\phi$ and a data $d$, we denote by $\tau, d \models \phi$ the satisfiability of $\phi$ by $d$ in valuation $\tau$, defined as $\tau, d \models r^{=}$ if $\tau(r) = d$ and $\tau, d \models r^{\neq}$ if $\tau(r) \neq d$. The Boolean combinators behave as usual. We denote by $\mathsf{Tst}_R$ the set of (symbolic) tests over $R$.

**Definition 1.** *A non-deterministic register transducer (*NRT*) is a tuple* $T = (Q, R, i_0, F, \Delta)$*, where* $Q$ *is a finite set of* states*,* $i_0 \in Q$ *is the* initial *state,* $F \subseteq Q$ *is the set of* accepting *states,* $R$ *is a finite set of* registers *and* $\Delta \subseteq Q \times \Sigma \times \mathsf{Tst}_R \times 2^R \times (\Gamma \times R)^* \times Q$ *is a finite set of* transitions*. We write* $q \xrightarrow[T]{\sigma,\phi|\mathsf{asgn},o} q'$ *for* $(q, \sigma, \phi, \mathsf{asgn}, o, q') \in \Delta$ *(*$T$ *is sometimes omitted).*

The semantics of a register transducer is given by a labelled transition system: we define $L_T = (C, \Lambda, \to)$, where $C = Q \times (R \to \mathcal{D})$ is the set of configurations, $\Lambda = (\Sigma \times \mathcal{D}) \times (\Gamma \times \mathcal{D})^*$ is the set of labels, and we have, for all $(q, \tau), (q', \tau') \in C$ and for all $(l, w) \in \Lambda$, that $(q, \tau) \xrightarrow{(l,w)} (q', \tau')$ whenever there exists a transition $q \xrightarrow[T]{\sigma,\phi|\mathsf{asgn},o} q'$ such that, by writing $l = (\sigma', d)$ and $w = (\gamma'_1, d_1) \dots (\gamma'_n, d_n)$:

- (Matching labels) $\sigma = \sigma'$
- (Compatibility) $d$ satisfies the test $\phi \in \mathsf{Tst}_R$, i.e. $\tau, d \models \phi$.
- (Update) $\tau'$ is the successor register configuration of $\tau$ with regards to $d$ and $\mathsf{asgn}$: $\tau'(r) = d$ if $r \in \mathsf{asgn}$, and $\tau'(r) = \tau(r)$ otherwise
- (Output) By writing $o = (\gamma_1, r_1) \dots (\gamma_m, r_m)$, we have that $m = n$ and for all $1 \le i \le n$, $\gamma_i = \gamma'_i$ and $d_i = \tau'(r_i)$.

Then, a *run* of $T$ is an infinite sequence of configurations and transitions $\rho = (q_0, \tau_0) \xrightarrow[L_T]{(u_1,v_1)} (q_1, \tau_1) \xrightarrow[L_T]{(u_2,v_2)} \cdots$. Its input is $\mathsf{in}(\rho) = u_1 u_2 \dots$, its output is $\mathsf{out}(\rho) = v_1 \cdot v_2 \dots$. We also define its sequence of states $\mathsf{st}(\rho) = q_0 q_1 \dots$, and its *trace* $\mathsf{tr}(\rho) = u_1 \cdot v_1 \cdot u_2 \cdot v_2 \dots$. Such run is *initial* if $(q_0, \tau_0) = (i_0, \tau_0^R)$. It is *final* if it satisfies the Büchi condition, i.e. $\inf(\mathsf{st}) \cap F \neq \varnothing$, where $\inf(\mathsf{st}) = \{q \in Q \mid q = q_i$ for infinitely many $i\}$. Finally, it is *accepting* if it is both initial and final. We then write $(q_0, \tau_0) \xrightarrow[T]{u|v}$ to express that there is a final run $\rho$ of $T$ starting from $(q_0, \tau_0)$ such that $\mathsf{in}(\rho) = u$ and $\mathsf{out}(\rho) = v$. In the whole paper, and unless stated otherwise, we always assume that the output of an accepting run is infinite ($v \in (\Gamma \times \mathcal{D})^\omega$), which can be ensured by a Büchi condition.

A *partial run* is a finite prefix of a run. The notions of input, output and states are extended by taking the corresponding prefixes. We then write $(q_0, \tau_0) \xrightarrow[T]{u|v}$

$(q_n, \tau_n)$ to express that there is a partial run $\rho$ of $T$ starting from configuration $(q_0, \tau_0)$ and ending in configuration $(q_n, \tau_n)$ such that $\mathsf{in}(\rho) = u$ and $\mathsf{out}(\rho) = v$.

Finally, the relation represented by a transducer $T$ is:

$$[\![T]\!] = \big\{(u, v) \in (\Sigma \times \mathcal{D})^\omega \times (\Gamma \times \mathcal{D})^\omega \mid \text{there exists an accepting run } \rho \text{ of } T \text{ such that } \mathsf{in}(\rho) = u \text{ and } \mathsf{out}(\rho) = v\big\}$$

*Example 2.* As an example, consider the register transducer $T_{\mathsf{rename}}$ depicted in Figure 1. It realises the following transformation: consider a setting in which we deal with logs of communications between a set of clients. Such a log is an infinite sequence of pairs consisting of a tag, chosen in some finite alphabet $\Sigma$, and the identifier of the client delivering this tag, chosen in some infinite set of data values. The transformation should modify the log as follows: for a given client that needs to be modified, each of its messages should now be associated with some new identifier. The transformation has to verify that this new identifier is indeed free, *i.e.* never used in the log. Before treating the log, the transformation receives as input the id of the client that needs to be modified (associated with the tag del), and then a sequence of identifiers (associated with the tag ch), ending with #. The transducer is non-deterministic as it has to guess which of these identifiers it can choose to replace the one of the client. In particular, observe that it may associate multiple output words to a same input if two such free identifiers exist.

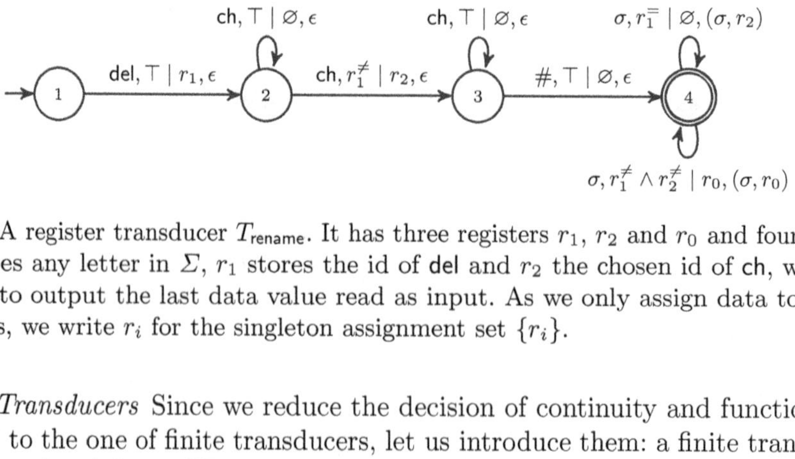


**Fig. 1.** A register transducer $T_{\mathsf{rename}}$. It has three registers $r_1$, $r_2$ and $r_0$ and four states. $\sigma$ denotes any letter in $\Sigma$, $r_1$ stores the id of del and $r_2$ the chosen id of ch, while $r_0$ is used to output the last data value read as input. As we only assign data to single registers, we write $r_i$ for the singleton assignment set $\{r_i\}$.

*Finite Transducers* Since we reduce the decision of continuity and functionality of NRT to the one of finite transducers, let us introduce them: a finite transducer (NFT for short) is an NRT with 0 registers (i.e. $R = \varnothing$). Thus, its transition relation can be represented as $\Delta \subseteq Q \times \Sigma \times \Gamma^* \times Q$. A direct extension of the construction of [15, Proposition 1] allows to show that:

**Proposition 3.** *Let $T$ be an* NRT *with $k$ registers, and let $X \subset_f \mathcal{D}$ be a finite subset of data. Then, $[\![T]\!] \cap (\Sigma \times X)^\omega \times (\Gamma \times X)^\omega$ is recognised by an* NFT *of exponential size, more precisely with $O(|Q| \times |X|^{|R|})$ states.*

### 2.2 Technical Properties of Register Automata

Although automata are simpler machines than transducers, we only use them as tools in our proofs, which is why we define them from transducers, and not the other way around. A non-deterministic register automaton, denoted NRA, is a transducer without outputs: its transition relation is $\Delta \subseteq Q \times \Sigma \times \mathsf{Tst}_R \times 2^R \times \{\varepsilon\} \times Q$ (simply represented as $\Delta \subseteq Q \times \Sigma \times \mathsf{Tst}_R \times 2^R \times Q$). The semantics are the same, except that now we lift the condition that the output $v$ is infinite since there is no output. For $A$ an NRA, we denote $L(A) = \{u \in (\Sigma \times \mathcal{D})^\omega \mid$ there exists an accepting run $\rho$ of $A$ over $u\}$. Necessarily the output of an accepting run is $\varepsilon$. In this section, we establish technical properties about NRA.

Proposition 4, the so-called "indistinguishability property", was shown in the seminal paper by Kaminski and Francez [15, Proposition 1]. Their model differs in that they do not allow distinct registers to contain the same data, and in the corresponding test syntax, but their result easily carries to our setting. It states that if an NRA accepts a data word, then such data word can be relabelled with data from any set containing $\mathsf{d}_0$ and with at least $k+1$ elements. Indeed, at any point of time, the automaton can only store at most $k$ data in its registers, so its notion of "freshness" is a local one, and forgotten data can thus be reused as fresh ones. Moreover, as the automaton only tests data for equality, their actual value does not matter, except for $\mathsf{d}_0$ which is initially contained in the registers.

Such "small-witness" property is fundamental to NRA, and will be paramount in establishing decidability of functionality (Section 3) and computability (Section 4). We use it jointly with Lemma 5, which states that the interleaving of the traces of runs of an NRT can be recognised with an NRA, and Lemma 6, which expresses that an NRA can check whether interleaved words coincide on some bounded prefix, and/or mismatch before some given position.

**Proposition 4 ([15]).** *Let $A$ be an* NRA *with $k$ registers. If $L(A) \neq \varnothing$, then, for any $X \subseteq \mathcal{D}$ of size $|X| \geq k+1$ such that $\mathsf{d}_0 \in X$, $L(A) \cap (\Sigma \times X)^\omega \neq \varnothing$.*

The runs of a register transducer $T$ can be flattened to their traces, so as to be recognised by an NRA. Those traces can then be interleaved, in order to be compared. The proofs of the following properties are straightforward.

Let $\rho_1 = (q_0, \tau_0) \xrightarrow[L_T]{(u_1, u_1')} (q_1, \tau_1) \dots$ and $\rho_2 = (p_0, \mu_0) \xrightarrow[L_T]{(v_1, v_1')} (p_1, \mu_1) \dots$ be two runs of a transducer $T$. Then, we define their *interleaving* $\rho_1 \otimes \rho_2 = u_1 \cdot u_1' \cdot v_1 \cdot v_1' \cdot u_2 \cdot u_2' \cdot v_2 \cdot v_2' \dots$ and $L_\otimes(T) = \{\rho_1 \otimes \rho_2 \mid \rho_1$ and $\rho_2$ are accepting runs of $T\}$.

**Lemma 5.** *If $T$ has $k$ registers, then $L_\otimes(T)$ is recognised by an* NRA *with $2k$ registers.*

**Lemma 6.** *Let $i, j \in \mathbb{N} \cup \{\infty\}$. We define $M_j^i = \{u_1 u_1' v_1 v_1' \cdots \mid \forall k \geq 1, u_k, v_k \in (\Sigma \times \mathcal{D}), u_k', v_k' \in (\Gamma \times \mathcal{D})^*, \forall 1 \leq k \leq j, v_k = u_k$ and $\|u_1' \cdot u_2' \cdots \wedge v_1' \cdot v_2' \dots\| \leq i\}$. Then, $M_j^i$ is recognisable by an* NRA *with 2 registers and with 1 register if $i = \infty$.*

## 3 Functionality, Equivalence and Composition of NRT

In general, since they are non-deterministic, NRT may not define functions but relations, as illustrated by Example 2. In this section, we first show that deciding whether a given NRT defines a function is PSPACE-complete, in which case we call it *functional.* We show, as a consequence, that testing whether two functional NRT define two functions which coincide on their common domain is PSPACE-complete. Finally, we show that functions defined by NRT are closed under composition. This is an appealing property in transducer theory, as it allows to define complex functions by composing simple ones.

*Example 7.* As explained before, the transducer $T_{\mathsf{rename}}$ described in Example 2 is not functional. To gain functionality, one can reinforce the specification by considering that one gets at the beginning a list of $k$ possible identifiers, and that one has to select the first one which is free, for some fixed $k$. This transformation is realised by the register transducer $T_{\mathsf{rename2}}$ depicted in Figure 2 (for $k = 2$).

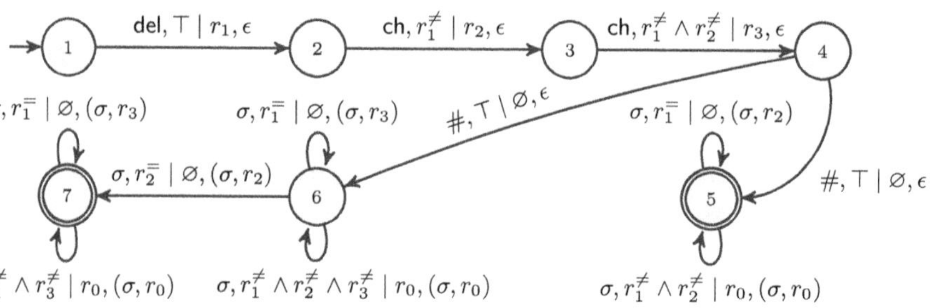


**Fig. 2.** A NRT $T_{\mathsf{rename2}}$, with four registers $r_1, r_2, r_3$ and $r_0$ (the latter being used, as in Figure 1, to output the last read data). After reading the # symbol, it guesses whether the value of register $r_2$ appears in the suffix of the input word. If not, it goes to state 5, and replaces occurrences of $r_1$ by $r_2$. Otherwise, it moves to state 6, waiting for an occurrence of $r_2$, and replaces occurrences of $r_1$ by $r_3$.

Let us start with the functionality problem in the data-free case. It is already known that checking whether an NFT over $\omega$-words is functional is decidable [13,11]. By relying on the pattern logic of [10] designed for transducers of *finite* words, it can be shown that it is decidable in NLOGSPACE.

**Proposition 8.** *Deciding whether an* NFT *is functional is in* NLOGSPACE.

The following theorem shows that a relation between data-words defined by an NRT with $k$ registers is a function iff its restriction to a set of data with at most $2k + 3$ data is a function. As a consequence, functionality is decidable as it reduces to the functionality problem of transducers over a finite alphabet.

**Theorem 9.** *Let $T$ be an* NRT *with $k$ registers. Then, for all $X \subseteq \mathcal{D}$ of size $|X| \geq 2k + 3$ such that $\mathsf{d}_0 \in X$, we have that $T$ is functional if and only if $[\![T]\!] \cap ((\Sigma \times X)^{\omega} \times (\Gamma \times X)^{\omega})$ is functional.*

*Proof.* The left-to-right direction is trivial. Now, assume $T$ is not functional. Let $x \in (\Sigma \times \mathcal{D})^{\omega}$ be such that there exists $y, z \in (\Gamma \times \mathcal{D})^{\omega}$ such that $y \neq z$ and $(x, y), (x, z) \in [\![T]\!]$. Let $i = \|y \wedge z\|$. Then, consider the language $L = \{\rho_1 \otimes \rho_2 \mid \rho_1$ and $\rho_2$ are accepting runs of $T$, $\mathsf{in}(\rho_1) = \mathsf{in}(\rho_2)$ and $\|\mathsf{out}(\rho_1) \wedge \mathsf{out}(\rho_2)\| \leq i\}$. Since, by Lemma 5, $L_\otimes(T)$ is recognised by an NRA with $2k$ registers and, by Lemma 6, $M^i_\infty$ is recognised by an NRA with 2 registers, we get that $L = L_\otimes(T) \cap M^i_\infty$ is recognised by an NRA with $2k+2$ registers.

Now, $L \neq \varnothing$, since, by letting $\rho_1$ and $\rho_2$ be the runs of $T$ both with input $x$ and with respective outputs $y$ and $z$, we have that $w = \rho_1 \otimes \rho_2 \in L$. Let $X \subseteq \mathcal{D}$ such that $|X| \geq 2k+3$ and $\mathsf{d}_0 \in X$. By Proposition 4, we get that $L \cap (\Sigma \times X)^\omega \neq \varnothing$. By letting $w' = \rho'_1 \otimes \rho'_2 \in L \cap (\Sigma \times X)^\omega$, and $x' = \mathsf{in}(\rho'_1) = \mathsf{in}(\rho'_2)$, $y' = \mathsf{out}(\rho'_1)$ and $z' = \mathsf{out}(\rho'_2)$, we have that $(x', y'), (x', z') \in [\![T]\!] \cap ((\Sigma \times X)^\omega \times (\Gamma \times X)^\omega)$ and $\|y' \wedge z'\| \leq i$, so, in particular, $y' \neq z'$ (since both are infinite words). Thus, $[\![T]\!] \cap ((\Sigma \times X)^\omega \times (\Gamma \times X)^\omega)$ is not functional. □

As a consequence of Proposition 8 and Theorem 9, we obtain the following result. The lower bound is obtained by encoding non-emptiness of register automata, which is PSPACE-complete [4].

**Corollary 10.** *Deciding whether an* NRT $T$ *is functional is* PSPACE*-complete.*

Hence, the following problem on the equivalence of NRT is decidable:

**Theorem 11.** *The problem of deciding, given two functions $f, g$ defined by* NRT*, whether for all $x \in \mathrm{dom}(f) \cap \mathrm{dom}(g)$, $f(x) = g(x)$, is* PSPACE*-complete.*

*Proof.* The formula $\forall x \in \mathrm{dom}(f) \cap \mathrm{dom}(g) \cdot f(x) = g(x)$ is true iff the relation $f \cup g = \{(x, y) \mid y = f(x) \vee y = g(x)\}$ is a function. The latter can be decided by testing whether the disjoint union of the transducers defining $f$ and $g$ defines a function, which is in PSPACE by Corollary 10. To show the hardness, we similarly reduce the emptiness problem of NRA $A$ over finite words, just as in the proof of Corollary 10. In particular, the functions $f_1$ and $f_2$ defined in this proof (which have the same domain) are equal iff $L(A) = \varnothing$. □

Note that under the promise that $f$ and $g$ have the same domain, the latter theorem implies that it is decidable to check whether the two functions are equal. However, checking $\mathrm{dom}(f) = \mathrm{dom}(g)$ is undecidable, as the language-equivalence problem for non-deterministic register automata is undecidable, since, in particular, universality is undecidable [19].

Closure under composition is a desirable property for transducers, which holds in the data-free setting [1]. We show that it also holds for functional NRT.

**Theorem 12.** *Let $f, g$ be two functions defined by* NRT*. Then, their composition $f \circ g$ is (effectively) definable by some* NRT*.*

*Proof (Sketch).* By $f \circ g$ we mean $f \circ g : x \mapsto f(g(x))$. Assume $f$ and $g$ are defined by $T_f = (Q_f, R_f, q_0, F_f, \Delta_f)$ and $T_g = (Q_g, R_g, p_0, F_g, \Delta_g)$ respectively. Wlog we assume that the input and output finite alphabets of $T_f$ and $T_g$ are all equal to $\Sigma$, and that $R_f$ and $R_g$ are disjoint. We construct $T$ such that $[\![T]\!] = f \circ g$. The proof is similar to the data-free case where the composition is shown via a product construction which simulates both transducers in parallel, executing the second on the output of the first. Assume $T_g$ has some transition

$p \xrightarrow{\sigma,\phi|\{r\},o} q$ where $o \in (\Sigma \times R_g)^*$. Then $T$ has to be able to execute transitions of $T_f$ while processing $o$, even though $o$ does not contain any concrete data values (it is here the main important difference with the data-free setting). However, if $T$ knows the equality types between $R_f$ and $R_g$, then it is able to trigger the transitions of $T_f$. For example, assume that $o = (a, r_g)$ and assume that the content of $r_g$ is equal to the content of $r_f$, $r_f$ being a register of $T_f$, then if $T_f$ has some transition of the form $p' \xrightarrow{a,r_f^{=}|\{r'_f\},o'} q'$ then $T$ can trigger the transition $(p,q) \xrightarrow{\sigma,\phi|\{r\}\cup\{r'_f:=r_g\},o'} (p',q')$ where the operation $r'_f := r_g$ is a syntactic sugar on top of NRT that intuitively means "put the content of $r_g$ into $r'_f$". □

*Remark 13.* The proof of Theorem 12 does not use the hypothesis that $f$ and $g$ are functions, and actually shows a stronger result, namely that relations defined by NRT are closed under composition.

## 4 Computability and Continuity

We equip the set of (finite or infinite) data words with the usual distance: for $u, v \in (\Sigma \times \mathcal{D})^\omega$, $d(u,v) = 0$ if $u = v$ and $d(u,v) = 2^{-\|u \wedge v\|}$ otherwise. A sequence of (finite or infinite) data words $(x_n)_{n\in\mathbb{N}}$ converges to some infinite data word $x$ if for all $\epsilon > 0$, there exists $N \geq 0$ such that for all $n \geq N$, $d(x_n, x) \leq \epsilon$.

In order to reason with computability, we assume in the sequel that the infinite set of data values $\mathcal{D}$ we are dealing with has an effective representation. For instance, this is the case when $\mathcal{D} = \mathbb{N}$.

We now define how a Turing machine can compute a function of data words. We consider deterministic Turing machines, which three tapes: a read-only one-way input tape (containing the infinite input data word), a two-way working tape, and a write-only one-way output tape (on which it writes the infinite output data word). Consider some input data word $x \in (\Sigma \times \mathcal{D})^\omega$. For any integer $k \in \mathbb{N}$, we let $M(x,k)$ denote the output written by $M$ on its output tape after having read the $k$ first cells of the input tape. Observe that as the output tape is write-only, the sequence of data words $(M(x,k))_{k\geq 0}$ is non-decreasing.

**Definition 14 (Computability).** *A function $f : (\Sigma \times \mathcal{D})^\omega \to (\Gamma \times \mathcal{D})^\omega$ is computable if there exists a deterministic multi-tape machine $M$ such that for all $x \in \mathrm{dom}(f)$, the sequence $(M(x,k))_{k\geq 0}$ converges to $f(x)$.*

**Definition 15 (Continuity).** *A function $f : (\Sigma \times \mathcal{D})^\omega \to (\Gamma \times \mathcal{D})^\omega$ is* continuous *at $x \in \mathrm{dom}(f)$ if (equivalently):*

*(a) for all sequences of data words $(x_n)_{n\in\mathbb{N}}$ converging towards $x$, where for all $i \in \mathbb{N}$, $x_i \in \mathrm{dom}(f)$, we have that $(f(x_n))_{n\in\mathbb{N}}$ converges to $f(x)$.*
*(b) $\forall i \geq 0, \exists j \geq 0, \forall y \in \mathrm{dom}(f), \|x \wedge y\| \geq j \Rightarrow \|f(x) \wedge f(y)\| \geq i$.*

*Then, $f$ is continuous if and only if it is continuous at each $x \in \mathrm{dom}(f)$. Finally, a functional* NRT *$T$ is* continuous *when $[\![T]\!]$ is continuous.*

*Example 16.* We give an example of a non-continuous function $f$. The finite input and output alphabets are unary, and are therefore ignored in the description of $f$. Such function associates with every sequence $s = d_1 d_2 \cdots \in \mathcal{D}^\omega$ the word $f(s) = d_1^\omega$ if $d_1$ occurs infinitely many times in $s$, otherwise $f(s) = s$ itself.

The function $f$ is not continuous. Indeed, by taking $d \neq d'$, the sequence of data words $d(d')^n d^\omega$ converges to $d(d')^\omega$, while $f(d(d')^n d^\omega) = d^\omega$ converges to $d^\omega \neq f(d(d')^\omega) = d(d')^\omega$.

Moreover, $f$ is realisable by some NRT which non-deterministically guesses whether $d_1$ repeats infinitely many times or not. It needs only one register $r$ in which to store $d_1$. In the first case, it checks whether the current data $d$ is equal the content $r$ infinitely often, and in the second case, it checks that this test succeeds finitely many times, using Büchi conditions.

One can show that the register transducer $T_{\mathsf{rename2}}$ considered in Example 7 also realises a function which is not continuous, as the value stored in register $r_2$ may appear arbitrarily far in the input word. One could modify the specification to obtain a continuous function as follows. Instead of considering an infinite log, one considers now an infinite sequence of finite logs, separated by \$ symbols. The register transducer $T_{\mathsf{rename3}}$, depicted in Figure 3, defines such a function.

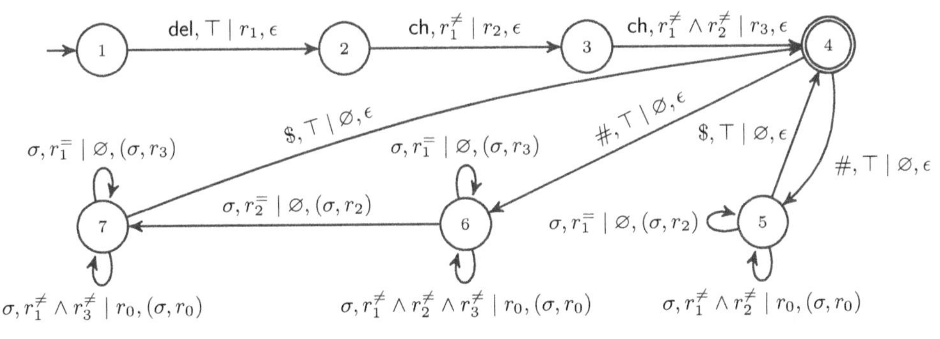


**Fig. 3.** A register transducer $T_{\mathsf{rename3}}$. This transducer is non-deterministic, yet it defines a continuous function.

We now prove the equivalence between continuity and computability for functions defined by NRT. One direction, namely the fact that computability implies continuity, is easy, almost by definition. For the other direction, we rely on the following lemma which states that it is decidable whether a word $v$ can be safely output, only knowing a prefix $u$ of the input. In particular, given a function $f$, we let $\hat{f}$ be the function defined over all finite prefixes $u$ of words in $\mathrm{dom}(f)$ by $\hat{f}(u) = \bigwedge(f(uy) \mid uy \in \mathrm{dom}(f))$, the longest common prefix of all outputs of continuations of $u$ by $f$. Then, we have the following decidability result:

**Lemma 17.** *The following problem is decidable. Given an* NRT $T$ *defining a function* $f$, *two finite data words* $u \in (\Sigma \times \mathcal{D})^*$ *and* $v \in (\Gamma \times \mathcal{D})^*$, *decide whether* $v \preceq \hat{f}(u)$.

**Theorem 18.** *Let $f$ be a function defined by some* NRT $T$*. Then $f$ is continuous iff $f$ is computable.*

*Proof.* $\Leftarrow$ Assuming $f = [\![T]\!]$ is computable by some Turing machine $M$, we show that $f$ is continuous. Indeed, consider some $x \in \text{dom}(f)$, and some $i \geq 0$. As the sequence of finite words $(M(x,k))_{k\in\mathbb{N}}$ converges to $f(x)$ and these words have non-decreasing lengths, there exists $j \geq 0$ such that $|M(x,j)| \geq i$. Hence, for any data word $y \in \text{dom}(f)$ such that $|x \wedge y| \geq j$, the behaviour of $M$ on $y$ is the same during the first $j$ steps, as $M$ is deterministic, and thus $|f(x) \wedge f(y)| \geq i$, showing that $f$ is continuous at $x$.

$\Rightarrow$ Assume that $f$ is continuous. We describe a Turing machine computing $f$; the corresponding algorithm is formalised as Algorithm 1. When reading a finite prefix $x[:j]$ of its input $x \in \text{dom}(f)$, it computes the set $P_j$ of all configurations $(q,\tau)$ reached by $T$ on $x[:j]$. This set is updated along taking increasing values of $j$. It also keeps in memory the finite output word $o_j$ that has been output so far. For any $j$, if $\mathsf{dt}(x[:j])$ denotes the data that appear in $x$, the algorithm then decides, for each input $(\sigma,d) \in \Sigma \times (\mathsf{dt}(x[:j]) \cup \{\mathsf{d}_0\})$ whether $(\sigma,d)$ can safely be output, i.e., whether all accepting runs on words of the form $x[:j]y$, for an infinite word $y$, outputs at least $o_j(\sigma,d)$. The latter can be decided, given $T$, $o_j$ and $x[:j]$, by Lemma 17. Note that it suffices to look at data in $\mathsf{dt}(x[:j]) \cup \{\mathsf{d}_0\}$ only since, by definition of NRT, any data that is output is necessarily stored in some register, and therefore appears in $x[:j]$ or is equal to $\mathsf{d}_0$. Let us show that

**Algorithm 1:** Algorithm describing the machine $M_f$ computing $f$.

**Data:** $x \in \text{dom}(f)$

1 $o := \epsilon$ ;
2 **for** $j = 0$ **to** $\infty$ **do**
3     **for** $(\sigma,d) \in \Sigma \times (dt(x[:j]) \cup \{d_0\})$ **do**
4         **if** $o.(\sigma,d) \preceq \hat{f}(x[:j])$ **then** `// such test is decidable by Lemma 17`
5             $o := o.(\sigma,d)$;
6             output $(\sigma,d)$;
7         **end**
8     **end**
9 **end**

$M_f$ actually computes $f$. Let $x \in \text{dom}(f)$. We have to show that the sequence $(M_f(x,j))_j$ converges to $f(x)$. Let $o_j$ be the content of variable $o$ of $M_f$ when exiting the inner loop at line 8, when the outer loop (line 2) has been executed $j$ times (hence $j$ input symbols have been read). Note that $o_j = M_f(x,j)$. We have $o_1 \preceq o_2 \preceq \dots$ and $o_j \preceq \hat{f}(x[:j])$ for all $j \geq 0$. Hence, $o_j \preceq f(x)$ for all $j \geq 0$. To show that $(o_j)_j$ converges to $f(x)$, it remains to show that $(o_j)_j$ is non-stabilising, i.e. $o_{i_1} \prec o_{i_2} \prec \dots$ for some infinite subsequence $i_1 < i_2 < \dots$. First, note that $f$ being continuous is equivalent to the sequence $(\hat{f}(x[:k]))_k$ converging to $f(x)$. Therefore we have that $f(x) \wedge \hat{f}(x[:k])$ can be arbitrarily long, for sufficiently large $k$. Let $j \geq 0$ and $(\sigma, d) = f(x)[|o_j|+1]$. By the latter property and the fact that $o_j.(\sigma, d) \preceq f(x)$, necessarily, there exists some $k > j$ such that $o_j.(\sigma, d) \preceq \hat{f}(x[:k])$. Moreover, by definition of NRT, $d$ is necessarily a data that appears in some prefix of $x$, therefore there exists $k' \geq k$ such that $d$ appears in $x[:k']$ and $o_j.(\sigma, d) \preceq \hat{f}(x[:k] \preceq \hat{f}(x[:k']$. This entails that $o_j.(\sigma, d) \preceq o_{k'}$. So, we have shown that for all for all $j$, there exists $k' > j$ such that $o_j \prec o_{k'}$, which concludes the proof. □

Now that we have shown that computability is equivalent with continuity for functions defined by NRT, we exhibit a pattern which allows to decide continuity. Such pattern generalises the one of [3] to the setting of data words, the difficulty lying in showing that our pattern can be restricted to a finite number of data.

**Theorem 19.** *Let $T$ be a functional* NRT *with $k$ registers. Then, for all $X \subseteq \mathcal{D}$ such that $|X| \geq 2k+3$ and $\mathsf{d}_0 \in X$, $T$ is not continuous at some $x \in (\Sigma \times \mathcal{D})^\omega$ if and only if $T$ is not continuous at some $z \in (\Sigma \times X)^\omega$.*

*Proof.* The right-to-left direction is trivial. Now, let $T$ be a functional NRT with $k$ registers which is not continuous at some $x \in (\Sigma \times \mathcal{D})^\omega$. Let $f : \mathrm{dom}([\![T]\!]) \to (\Gamma \times \mathcal{D})^\omega$ be the function defined by $T$, as: for all $u \in \mathrm{dom}([\![T]\!])$, $f(u) = v$ where $v \in (\Gamma \times \mathcal{D})^\omega$ is the unique data word such that $(u, v) \in [\![T]\!]$.

Now, let $X \subseteq \mathcal{D}$ be such that $|X| \geq 2k+3$ and $\mathsf{d}_0 \in X$. We need to build two words $u$ and $v$ labelled over $X$ which coincide on a sufficiently long prefix to allow for pumping, hence yielding a converging sequence of input data words whose images do not converge, witnessing non-continuity. To that end, we use a similar proof technique as for Theorem 9: we show that the language of interleaved runs whose inputs coincide on a sufficiently long prefix while their respective outputs mismatch before a given position is recognisable by an NRA, allowing us to use the indistinguishability property. We also ask that one run presents sufficiently many occurrences of a final state $q_f$, so that we can ensure that there exists a pair of configurations containing $q_f$ which repeats in both runs.

On reading such $u$ and $v$, the automaton behaves as a finite automaton, since the number of data is finite ([15, Proposition 1]). By analysing the respective runs, we can, using pumping arguments, bound the position on which the mismatch appears in $u$, then show the existence of a synchronised loop over $u$ and $v$ after such position, allowing us to build the sought witness for non-continuity.

*Relabel over $X$* Thus, assume $T$ is not continuous at some point $x \in (\Sigma \times \mathcal{D})^\omega$. Let $\rho$ be an accepting run of $T$ over $x$, and let $q_f \in \inf(\mathsf{st}(\rho)) \cap F$ be an accepting state repeating infinitely often in $\rho$. Then, let $i \geq 0$ be such that for all $j \geq 0$, there exists $y \in \mathrm{dom}(f)$ such that $\|x \wedge y\| \geq j$ but $\|f(x) \wedge f(y)\| \leq i$. Now, define $K = |Q| \times (2k+3)^{2k}$ and let $m = (2i+3) \times (K+1)$. Finally, pick $j$ such that $\rho[1{:}j]$ contains at least $m$ occurrences of $q_f$. Consider the language:

$$L = \big\{\rho_1 \otimes \rho_2 \big| \|\mathsf{in}(\rho_1) \wedge \mathsf{in}(\rho_2)\| \geq j, \|\mathsf{out}(\rho_1) \wedge \mathsf{out}(\rho_2)\| \leq i \text{ and there are at least } m \text{ occurrences of } q_f \text{ in } \rho_1[1{:}j]\big\}$$

By Lemma 5, $L_\otimes(T)$ is recognised by an NRA with $2k$ registers. Additionnally, by Lemma 6, $M_j^i$ is recognised by an NRA with 2 registers. Thus, $L = L_\otimes(T) \cap O_{m,j}^{q_f} \cap M_j^i$, where $O_{m,j}^{q_f}$ checks there are at least $m$ occurrences of $q_f$ in $\rho_1[1{:}j]$ (this is easily doable from the automaton recognising $L_\otimes(T)$ by adding an $m$-bounded counter), is recognisable by an NRA with $2k+2$ registers.

Choose $y \in \mathrm{dom}(f)$ such that $\|x \wedge y\| \geq j$ but $\|f(x) \wedge f(y)\| \leq i$. By letting $\rho_1$ (resp. $\rho_2$) be an accepting run of $T$ over $x$ (resp. $y$) we have $\rho_1 \otimes \rho_2 \in L$, so $L \neq \varnothing$. By Proposition 4, $L \cap ((\Sigma \times X)^\omega \times (\Gamma \times X)^\omega) \neq \varnothing$. Let $w = \rho_1' \otimes \rho_2' \in L \cap ((\Sigma \times X)^\omega \times (\Gamma \times X)^\omega)$, $u = \mathsf{in}(\rho_1')$ and $v = \mathsf{in}(\rho_2')$. Then, $\|u \wedge v\| \geq j$, $\|f(u) \wedge f(v)\| \leq i$ and there are at least $m$ occurrences of $q_f$ in $\rho_1[1{:}j]$.

Now, we depict $\rho_1'$ and $\rho_2'$ in Figure 4, where we decompose $u$ as $u = u_1 \dots u_m \cdot s$ and $v$ as $v = u_1 \dots u_m \cdot t$; their corresponding images being respectively $u' = u_1' \dots u_m' \cdot s'$ and $u'' = u_1'' \dots u_m'' t''$. We also let $l = (i+1)(K+1)$ and $l' = 2(i+1)(K+1)$. Since the data of $u, v$ and $w$ belong to $X$, we know that $\tau_i, \mu_i : R \to X$.

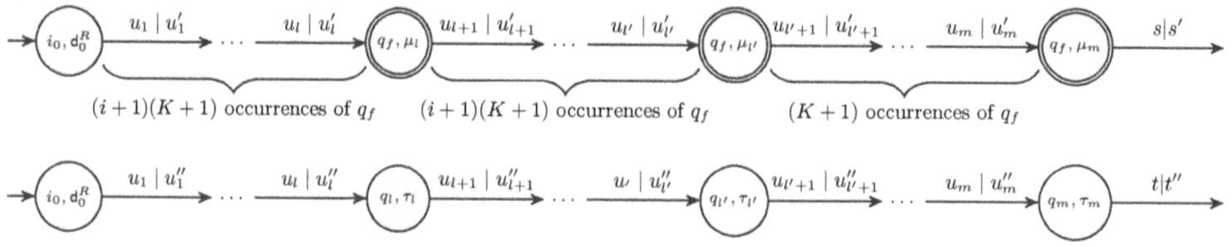


**Fig. 4.** Runs of $f$ over $u = u_1 \dots u_m \cdot s$ and $v = u_1 \dots u_m \cdot t$.

*Repeating configurations* First, let us observe that in a partial run of $\rho_1'$ containing more than $|Q| \times |X|^k$ occurrences of $q_f$, there is at least one productive transition, i.e. a transition whose output is $o \neq \varepsilon$. Otherwise, by the pigeonhole principle, there exists a configuration $\mu : R \to X$ such that $(q_f, \mu)$ occurs at least twice in the partial run. Since all transitions are improductive, it would mean that, by writing $w$ the corresponding part of input, we have $(q_f, \mu) \xrightarrow[T]{w \mid \varepsilon} (q_f, \mu)$. This partial run is part of $\rho_1'$, so, in particular, $(q_f, \mu)$ is accessible, hence by taking $w_0$ such that $(i_0, \tau_0) \xrightarrow[T]{w_0 \mid w_0'} (q_f, \mu)$, we have that $f(w_0 w^\omega) = w_0'$, which is a finite word, contradicting our assumption that all accepting runs produce an infinite output. This implies that, for any $n \geq |Q| \times |X|^k$ (in particular for $n = l$), $\|u_1' \dots u_n'\| \geq i+1$.

*Locate the mismatch* Again, upon reading $u_{l+1} \dots u_{l'}$, there are $(i+1)(K+1)$ occurrences of $q_f$. There are two cases:

(a) There are at least $i+1$ productive transitions in $\rho_2'$. Then, we obtain that $\|u_1'' \dots u_{l'}''\| > i$, so $\mathsf{mismatch}(u_1' \dots u_{l'}', u_1'' \dots u_{l'}'')$, since we know $\|f(u) \wedge f(v)\| \leq i$ and they are respectively prefixes of $f(u)$ and $f(v)$, both of length at least $i+1$. Afterwards, upon reading $u_{l'+1} \dots u_m$, there are $K+1 > |Q| \times |X|^{2k}$ occurrences of $q_f$, so, by the pigeonhole principle, there is a repeating pair: there exist indices $p$ and $p'$ such that $l' \leq p < p' \leq m$ and $(q_f, \mu_p) = (q_f, \mu_{p'})$, $(q_p, \tau_p) = (q_{p'}, \tau_{p'})$. Thus, let $z_P = u_1 \dots u_p$, $z_R = u_{p+1} \dots u_{p'}$ and $z_C = u_{p'+1} \dots u_m \cdot t$ ($P$ stands for *prefix*, $R$ for *repeat* and $C$ for *continuation*; we use capital letters to avoid confusion with indices). By denoting $z'_P = u'_1 \dots u'_p$, $z'_R = u'_{p+1} \dots u'_{p'}$, $z''_P = u''_1 \dots u''_p$, $z''_R = u''_{p+1} \dots u''_{p'}$ and $z''_C = u''_{p'+1} \dots u''_m \cdot t''$ the corresponding images, $z = z_P \cdot {z_R}^\omega$ is a point of discontinuity. Indeed, define $(z_n)_{n \in \mathbb{N}}$ as, for all $n \in \mathbb{N}$, $z_n = z_P \cdot z_R^n \cdot z_C$. Then, $(z_n)_{n \in \mathbb{N}}$ converges towards $z$, but, since for all $n \in \mathbb{N}$, $f(z_n) = z''_P \cdot {z''_L}^n \cdot z''_C$, we have that $f(z_n) \underset{n\infty}{\not\longrightarrow} f(z) = z'_P \cdot {z'_L}^\omega$, since $\mathsf{mismatch}(z'_P, z''_P)$.

(b) Otherwise, by the same reasoning as above, it means there exists a repeating pair with only improductive transitions in between: there exist indices $p$ and $p'$ such that $l \leq p < p' \leq l'$, $(q_f, \mu_p) = (q_f, \mu_{p'})$, $(q_p, \tau_p) = (q_{p'}, \tau_{p'})$, and $(q_f, \mu_p) \xrightarrow{u_{p+1} \dots u_{p'} | \varepsilon} (q_f, \mu_{p'})$, $(q_p, \tau_p) \xrightarrow{u_{p+1} \dots u_{p'} | \varepsilon} (q_{p'}, \tau_{p'})$. Then, by taking $z_P = u_1 \dots u_p$, $z_R = u_{p+1} \dots u_{p'}$ and $z_C = u_{p'+1} \dots u_m \cdot t$, we have, by letting $z'_P = u'_1 \dots u'_p$, $z'_R = u'_{p+1} \dots u'_{p'}$, $z''_P = u''_1 \dots u''_p$, $z''_R = \varepsilon$ and $z''_C = u''_{n'+1} \dots u''_m \cdot t''$, that $z = z_P \cdot {z_R}^\omega$ is a point of discontinuity. Indeed, define $(z_n)_{n \in \mathbb{N}}$ as, for all $n \in \mathbb{N}$, $z_n = z_P \cdot z_R^n \cdot z_C$. Then, $(z_n)_{n \in \mathbb{N}}$ indeed converges towards $z$, but, since for all $n \in \mathbb{N}$, $f(z_n) = z''_P \cdot z''_C$, we have that $f(z_n) \underset{n\infty}{\not\longrightarrow} f(z) = z'_P \cdot {z'_R}^\omega$, since $\mathsf{mismatch}(z'_P, z''_P \cdot z''_C)$ (the mismatch necessarily lies in $z'_P$, since $\|z'_P\| \geq i+1$). □

**Corollary 20.** *Deciding whether an* NRT *defines a continuous function is* PSPACE*-complete.*

*Proof.* Let $X \subseteq \mathcal{D}$ be a set of size $2k+3$ containing $\mathsf{d}_0$. By Theorem 19, $T$ is not continuous iff it is not continuous at some $z \in (\Sigma \times X)^\omega$, iff $[\![T]\!] \cap \big((\Sigma \times X)^\omega \times (\Gamma \times X)^\omega\big)$ is not continuous. By Proposition 3, such relation is recognisable by a finite transducer $T_X$ with $O(|Q| \times |X|^{|R|})$ states, which can be built on-the-fly. By [3], the continuity of functions defined by NFT is decidable in NLOGSPACE, which yields a PSPACE procedure.

For the hardness, we reduce again from the emptiness problem of register automata, which is PSPACE-complete [4]. Let $A$ be a register automaton over some alphabet $\Sigma \times \mathcal{D}$. We construct a transducer $T$ which defines a continuous function iff $L(A) = \varnothing$ iff the domain of $T$ is empty. Let $f$ be a non-continous function realised by some NRT $H$ (it exists by Example 16). Then, let $\# \notin \Sigma$ be a fresh symbol, and define the function $g$ as the function mapping any data word of the form $w(\#, d)w'$ to $w(\#, d)f(w')$ if $w \in L(A)$. The function $g$ is realised by an NRT which simulates $A$ and copies its inputs on the output to implement the identity, until it sees $\#$. If it was in some accepting state of $A$ before seeing $\#$, it branches to some initial state of $H$ and proceeds executing $H$. If there is some $w_0 \in L(A)$, then the subfunction $g_{w_0}$ mapping words of the form $w_0(\#, d)w'$ to $w_0(\#, d)f(w')$ is not continuous, since $f$ is not. Hence $g$ is not continuous. Conversely, if $L(A) = \varnothing$, then $\mathrm{dom}(g) = \varnothing$, so $g$ is continuous. □

In [3], non-continuity is characterised by a specific pattern (Lemma 21, Figure 1), i.e. the existence of some particular sequence of transitions. By applying this characterisation to the finite transducer recognising $[\![T]\!] \cap ((\Sigma \times X)^\omega \times (\Gamma \times X)^\omega)$, as constructed in Proposition 3, we can characterise non-continuity by a similar pattern, which will prove useful to decide (non-)continuity of test-free NRT in NLOGSPACE (cf Section 5):

**Corollary 21 ([3]).** *Let $T$ be an* NRT *with $k$ registers. Then, for all $X \subseteq \mathcal{D}$ such that $|X| \geq 2k+3$ and $\mathsf{d}_0 \in X$, $T$ is not continuous at some $x \in (\Sigma \times \mathcal{D})^\omega$ if and only if it has the pattern of Figure 5.*

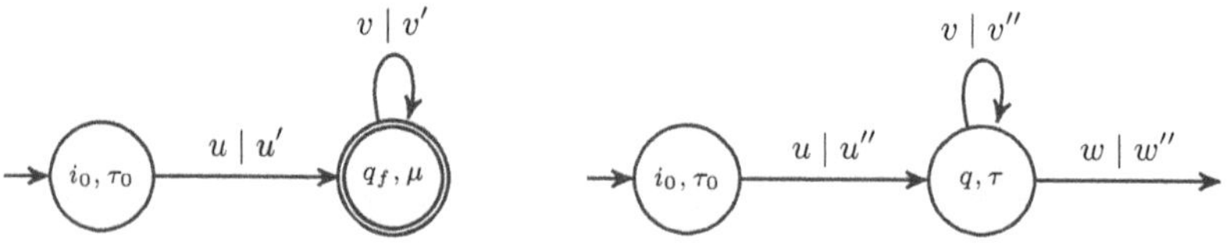


**Fig. 5.** A pattern characterising non-continuity of functions definable by an NRT: we ask that there exist configurations $(q_f, \mu)$ and $(q, \tau)$, where $q_f$ is accepting, as well as finite input data words $u, v$, finite output data words $u', v', u'', v''$, and an infinite input data word $w$ admitting an accepting run from configuration $(q, \tau)$ producing output $w''$, such that $\mathsf{mismatch}(u', u'') \vee (v'' = \varepsilon \wedge \mathsf{mismatch}(u', u''w''))$.

## 5 Test-free Register Transducers

In [7], we introduced a restriction which allows to recover decidability of the bounded synthesis problem for specifications expressed as non-deterministic register automata. Applied to transducers, such restriction also yields polynomial complexities when considering the functionality and computability problems.

An NRT $T$ is *test-free* when its transition function does not depend on the tests conducted over the input data. Formally, we say that $T$ is *test-free* if for all transitions $q \xrightarrow[T]{\sigma,\phi|\mathsf{asgn},o} q'$ we have $\phi = \top$. Thus, we can omit the tests altogether and its transition relation can be represented as $\Delta' \subseteq Q \times \Sigma \times 2^R \times (\Gamma \times R)^* \times Q$.

*Example 22.* Consider the function $f : (\Sigma \times \mathcal{D})^\omega \to (\Gamma \times \mathcal{D})^\omega$ associating, to $x = (\sigma_1, d_1)(\sigma_2, d_2)\ldots$, the value $(\sigma_1, d_1)(\sigma_2, d_1)(\sigma_3, d_1)\ldots$ if there are infinitely many $a$ in $x$, and $(\sigma_1, d_2)(\sigma_2, d_2)(\sigma_3, d_2)\ldots$ otherwise.

$f$ can be implemented using a test-free NRT with one register: it initially guesses whether there are infinitely many $a$ in $x$, if it is the case, it stores $d_1$ in the single register $r$, otherwise it waits for the next input to get $d_2$ and stores it in $r$. Then, it outputs the content of $r$ along with each $\sigma_i$. $f$ is not continuous, as even outputting the first data requires reading an infinite prefix when $d_1 \neq d_2$.

Note that when a transducer is test-free, the existence of an accepting run over a given input $x$ only depends on its finite labels. Hence, the existence of two outputs $y$ and $z$ which mismatch over data can be characterised by a simple pattern (Figure 6), which allows to decide functionality in polynomial time:

**Theorem 23.** *Deciding whether a test-free* NRT *is functional is in* PTIME.

*Proof.* Let $T$ be a test-free NRT such that $T$ is not functional. Then, there exists $x \in (\Sigma \times \mathcal{D})^\omega$, $y, z \in (\Gamma \times \mathcal{D})^\omega$ such that $(x, y), (x, z) \in [\![T]\!]$ and $y \neq z$. Then, let $i$ be such that $y[i] \neq z[i]$. There are two cases. Either $\mathsf{lab}(y[i]) \neq \mathsf{lab}(z[i])$, which means that the finite transducer $T'$ obtained by ignoring the registers of $T$ is not functional. By Proposition 8, such property can be decided in NLOGSPACE, so let us focus on the second case: $\mathsf{dt}(y[i]) \neq \mathsf{dt}(z[i])$.

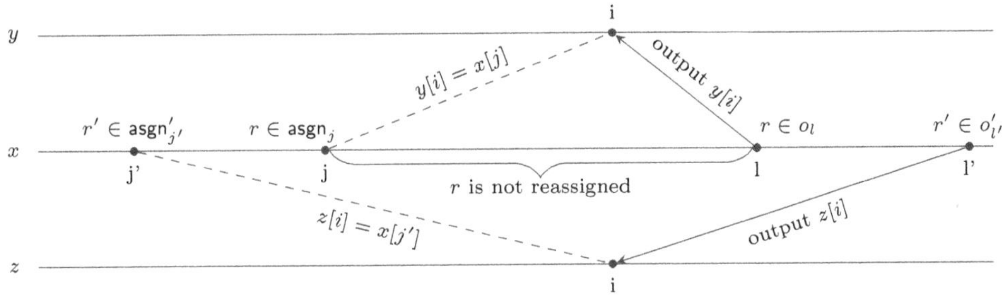


**Fig. 6.** A situation characterising the existence of a mismatch over data. Since acceptance does not depend on data, we can always choose $x$ such that $\mathsf{dt}(x[j]) \neq \mathsf{dt}(x[j'])$. Here, we assume that the labels of $x, y$ and $z$ range over a unary alphabet; in particular $y[i] = x[j]$ iff $\mathsf{dt}(y[i]) = \mathsf{dt}(x[j])$. Finally, for readability, we did not write that $r'$ should not be reassigned between $j'$ and $l'$. Note that the position of $i$ with regards to $j, j', l$ and $l'$ does not matter; nor does the position of $l$ w.r.t. $l'$.

We here give a sketch of the proof: observe that an input $x$ admits two outputs which mismatch over data if and only if it admits two runs which respectively store $x[j]$ and $x[j']$ such that $x[j] \neq x[j']$ and output them later at the same output position $i$; the outputs $y$ and $z$ are then such that $\mathsf{dt}(y[i]) \neq \mathsf{dt}(z[i])$. Since $T$ is test-free, the existence of two runs over the same input $x$ only depends on its finite labels. Then, the registers containing respectively $x[j]$ and $x[j']$ should not be reassigned before being output, and should indeed output their content at the same position $i$ (cf Figure 6). Besides, again because of test-freeness, we can always assume that $x$ is such that $x[j] \neq x[j']$. Overall, such pattern can be checked by a 2-counter Parikh automaton, whose emptiness is decidable in PTIME [8] (under conditions that are satisfied here). □

Now, let us move to the case of continuity. Here again, the fact that test-free NRT conduct no test over the input data allows to focus on the only two registers that are responsible for the mismatch, the existence of an accepting run being only determined by finite labels.

**Theorem 24.** *Deciding whether a test-free* NRT *defines a continuous function is in* PTIME.

*Proof.* Let $T$ be a test-free NRT. First, it can be shown that $T$ is continuous if and only if $T$ has the pattern of Figure 7, where $r$ is coaccessible (since acceptance only depends on finite labels, $T$ can be trimmed[3] in polynomial time).

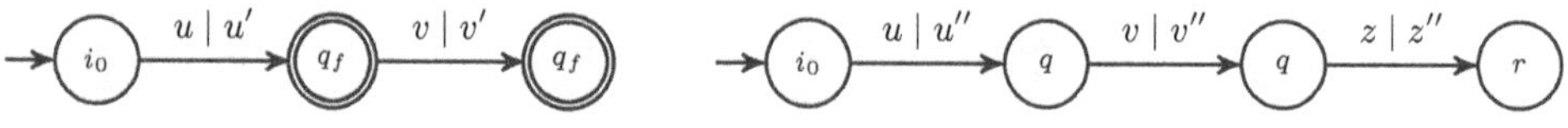


**Fig. 7.** A pattern characterising non-continuity of functions defined by NRT, where we ask that there exist some states $q_f$, $q$ and $r$, where $q_f$ is accepting, as well as finite input data words $u, v, z$ and finite output data words $u', v', u'', v'', z''$ such that $\mathsf{mismatch}(u', u'') \vee (v'' = \varepsilon \wedge \mathsf{mismatch}(u', u''z''))$. Register assignments are not depicted, as there are no conditions on them. We unrolled the loops to highlight the fact that they do not necessarily loop back to the same configuration.

Now, it remains to show that such simpler pattern can be checked in PTIME. We treat each part of the disjunction separately:

(a) there exists $u, u', u'', v, v', v''$ s.t. $i_0 \xrightarrow{u|u'} q_f \xrightarrow{v|v'} q_f$ and $i_0 \xrightarrow{u|u''} q \xrightarrow{v|v''} q$, where $q_f \in F$ and $\mathsf{mismatch}(u', u'')$. Then, as shown in the proof of Theorem 23, there exists a mismatch between some $u'$ and $u''$ produced by the same input $u$ if and only if there exists two runs and two registers $r$ and $r'$ assigned at two distinct positions, and later on output at the same position. Such pattern can similarly be checked by a 2-counter Parikh automaton; the only difference is that here, instead of checking that the two end states are coaccessible with a common $\omega$-word, we only need to check that $q_f \in F$ and that there is a synchronised loop over $q_f$ and $q$, which are regular properties that can be checked by the Parikh automaton with only a polynomial increase.

(b) there exists $u, u', u'', v, v', z, z''$ s.t. $i_0 \xrightarrow{u|u'} q_f \xrightarrow{v|v'} q_f$ and $i_0 \xrightarrow{u|u''} q \xrightarrow{v|\varepsilon} q \xrightarrow{z|z''} r$, where $q_f \in F$ and $\mathsf{mismatch}(u', u''z'')$. By examining again the proof of Theorem 23, it can be shown that to obtain a mismatch, it suffices that the input is the same for both runs only up to position $\max(j, j')$. More precisely, there is a mismatch between $u'$ and $u''z''$ if and only if there exists two registers $r$ and $r'$ and two positions $j, j' \in \{1, \ldots, \|u\|\}$ such that $j \neq j'$, $r$ is stored at position $j$, $r'$ is stored at position $j'$, $r$ and $r'$ are respectively output at input positions $l \in \{1, \ldots, \|u\|\}$ and $l' \in \{1, \ldots, \|uz\|\}$ and they are not reassigned in the meantime. Again, such property, along with the fact that $q_f \in F$ and the existence of a synchronised loop can be checked by a 2-counter Parikh automaton of polynomial size.

Overall, deciding whether a test-free NRT is continuous is in PTIME. □

[3] We say that $T$ is trim when all its states are both accessible and coaccessible.

## References


1. Berstel, J.: Transductions and Context-free Languages. Teubner Verlag (1979), http://www-igm.univ-mlv.fr/~berstel/LivreTransductions/LivreTransductions.html
2. Carayol, A., Löding, C.: Uniformization in Automata Theory. In: Proceedings of the 14th Congress of Logic, Methodology and Philosophy of Science, Nancy, July 19-26, 2011. pp. 153–178. London: College Publications (2014), https://hal.archives-ouvertes.fr/hal-01806575
3. Dave, V., Filiot, E., Krishna, S.N., Lhote, N.: Deciding the computability of regular functions over infinite words. CoRR **abs/1906.04199** (2019), http://arxiv.org/abs/1906.04199
4. Demri, S., Lazic, R.: LTL with the freeze quantifier and register automata. ACM Trans. Comput. Log. **10**(3), 16:1–16:30 (2009). https://doi.org/10.1145/1507244.1507246
5. Durand-Gasselin, A., Habermehl, P.: Regular transformations of data words through origin information. In: Foundations of Software Science and Computation Structures - 19th International Conference, FOSSACS 2016, Held as Part of the European Joint Conferences on Theory and Practice of Software, ETAPS 2016, Eindhoven, The Netherlands, April 2-8, Proceedings. pp. 285–300 (2016). https://doi.org/10.1007/978-3-662-49630-5_17
6. Ehlers, R., Seshia, S.A., Kress-Gazit, H.: Synthesis with identifiers. In: Proceedings of the 15th International Conference on Verification, Model Checking, and Abstract Interpretation - Volume 8318. pp. 415–433. VMCAI 2014 (2014). https://doi.org/10.1007/978-3-642-54013-4_23
7. Exibard, L., Filiot, E., Reynier, P.: Synthesis of data word transducers. In: 30th International Conference on Concurrency Theory, CONCUR 2019, August 27-30, Amsterdam, the Netherlands. pp. 24:1–24:15 (2019). https://doi.org/10.4230/LIPIcs.CONCUR.2019.24
8. Figueira, D., Libkin, L.: Path logics for querying graphs: Combining expressiveness and efficiency. In: 30th Annual ACM/IEEE Symposium on Logic in Computer Science, LICS 2015, Kyoto, Japan, July 6-10. pp. 329–340 (2015). https://doi.org/10.1109/LICS.2015.39
9. Filiot, E., Jecker, I., Löding, C., Winter, S.: On equivalence and uniformisation problems for finite transducers. In: 43rd International Colloquium on Automata, Languages, and Programming, ICALP 2016, July 11-15, Rome, Italy. pp. 125:1–125:14 (2016). https://doi.org/10.4230/LIPIcs.ICALP.2016.125
10. Filiot, E., Mazzocchi, N., Raskin, J.: A pattern logic for automata with outputs. In: Developments in Language Theory - 22nd International Conference, DLT 2018, Tokyo, Japan, September 10-14, Proceedings. pp. 304–317 (2018). https://doi.org/10.1007/978-3-319-98654-8_25
11. Gire, F.: Two decidability problems for infinite words. Inf. Process. Lett. **22**(3), 135–140 (1986). https://doi.org/10.1016/0020-0190(86)90058-X
12. Holtmann, M., Kaiser, L., Thomas, W.: Degrees of lookahead in regular infinite games. Logical Methods in Computer Science **8**(3) (2012). https://doi.org/10.2168/LMCS-8(3:24)2012
13. II, K.C., Pachl, J.K.: Equivalence problems for mappings on infinite strings. Information and Control **49**(1), 52–63 (1981). https://doi.org/10.1016/S0019-9958(81)90444-7
14. J.R. Büchi, L.H. Landweber: Solving sequential conditions finite-state strategies. Transactions of the American Mathematical Society **138**, 295–311 (1969). https://doi.org/10.2307/1994916

15. Kaminski, M., Francez, N.: Finite-memory automata. Theor. Comput. Sci. **134**(2), 329–363 (Nov 1994). https://doi.org/10.1016/0304-3975(94)90242-9
16. Khalimov, A., Kupferman, O.: Register-bounded synthesis. In: 30th International Conference on Concurrency Theory, CONCUR 2019, August 27-30, Amsterdam, the Netherlands. pp. 25:1–25:16 (2019). https://doi.org/10.4230/LIPIcs.CONCUR.2019.25
17. Khalimov, A., Maderbacher, B., Bloem, R.: Bounded synthesis of register transducers. In: Automated Technology for Verification and Analysis, 16th International Symposium, ATVA 2018, Los Angeles, October 7-10. Proceedings (2018). https://doi.org/10.1007/978-3-030-01090-4_29
18. Libkin, L., Tan, T., Vrgoc, D.: Regular expressions for data words. J. Comput. Syst. Sci. **81**(7), 1278–1297 (2015). https://doi.org/10.1016/j.jcss.2015.03.005
19. Neven, F., Schwentick, T., Vianu, V.: Finite state machines for strings over infinite alphabets. ACM Trans. Comput. Logic **5**(3), 403–435 (Jul 2004). https://doi.org/10.1145/1013560.1013562
20. Pnueli, A., Rosner, R.: On the synthesis of a reactive module. In: ACM Symposium on Principles of Programming Languages, POPL. ACM (1989). https://doi.org/10.1145/75277.75293
21. Prieur, C.: How to decide continuity of rational functions on infinite words. Theor. Comput. Sci. **276**(1-2), 445–447 (2002). https://doi.org/10.1016/S0304-3975(01)00307-3

# 7

# Parameterized Synthesis for Fragments of First-Order Logic over Data Words*

Béatrice Bérard[1], Benedikt Bollig[2], Mathieu Lehaut[1](✉), and Nathalie Sznajder[1]

[1] Sorbonne Université, CNRS, LIP6, F-75005 Paris, France
[2] CNRS, LSV & ENS Paris-Saclay, Université Paris-Saclay, Cachan, France

**Abstract.** We study the synthesis problem for systems with a parameterized number of processes. As in the classical case due to Church, the system selects actions depending on the program run so far, with the aim of fulfilling a given specification. The difficulty is that, at the same time, the environment executes actions that the system cannot control. In contrast to the case of fixed, finite alphabets, here we consider the case of parameterized alphabets. An alphabet reflects the number of processes, which is static but unknown. The synthesis problem then asks whether there is a finite number of processes for which the system can satisfy the specification. This variant is already undecidable for very limited logics. Therefore, we consider a first-order logic without the order on word positions. We show that even in this restricted case synthesis is undecidable if both the system and the environment have access to all processes. On the other hand, we prove that the problem is decidable if the environment only has access to a bounded number of processes. In that case, there is even a cutoff meaning that it is enough to examine a bounded number of process architectures to solve the synthesis problem.

## 1 Introduction

Synthesis deals with the problem of automatically generating a program that satisfies a given specification. The problem goes back to Church [9], who formulated it as follows: The environment and the system alternately select an input symbol and an output symbol from a finite alphabet, respectively, and in this way generate an infinite sequence. The question now is whether the system has a *winning strategy*, which guarantees that the resulting infinite run is contained in a given ($\omega$)-regular language representing the specification, no matter how the environment behaves. This problem is decidable and very well understood [8,37], and it has been extended in several different ways (e.g., [24,26,28,36,43]).

In this paper, we consider a variant of the synthesis problem that allows us to model programs with a variable number of processes. As we then deal with an unbounded number of process identifiers, a fixed finite alphabet is not suitable anymore. It is more appropriate to use an infinite alphabet, in which every letter contains a process identifier and a program action. One can distinguish two cases here. In [16], a potentially infinite number of data values are involved in an infinite program run (e.g. by dynamic process generation). In a *parameterized* system [4, 13], on the other hand, one has an unknown but *static* number of processes so that, along each run, the number of processes is finite. In this paper, we are interested in the latter, i.e., parameterized case. Parameterized programs are ubiquitous and occur, e.g., in distributed algorithms, ad-hoc networks, telecommunication protocols, cache-coherence protocols, swarm robotics, and biological systems. The synthesis question asks whether the system has a winning strategy for some number of processes (existential version) or no matter how many processes there are (universal version).

Over infinite alphabets, there are a variety of different specification languages (e.g., [5, 11, 12, 19, 29, 33, 40]). Unlike in the case of finite alphabets, there is no canonical definition of regular languages. In fact, the synthesis problem has been studied for N-memory automata [7], the Logic of Repeating Values [16], and register automata [15,30,31]. Though there is no agreement on a "regular" automata model, first-order (FO) logic over data words can be considered as a canonical logic, and this is the specification language we consider here. In addition to classical FO logic on words over finite alphabets, it provides a predicate $x \sim y$ to express that two events $x$ and $y$ are triggered by the same process. Its two-variable fragment $FO^2$ has a decidable emptiness and universality problem [5] and is, therefore, a promising candidate for the synthesis problem.

Previous generalizations of Church's synthesis problem to infinite alphabets were generally *synchronous* in the sense that the system and the environment perform their actions in strictly alternating order. This assumption was made, e.g., in the above-mentioned recent papers [7, 15, 16, 30, 31]. If there are several processes, however, it is realistic to relax this condition, which leads us to an *asynchronous* setting in which the system has no influence on when the environment acts. Like in [21], where the asynchronous case for a fixed number of processes was considered, we only make the reasonable fairness assumption that the system is not blocked forever.

In summary, the synthesis problem over infinite alphabets can be classified as (*i*) parameterized vs. dynamic, (*ii*) synchronous vs. asynchronous, and (*iii*) according to the specification language (register automata, Logic of Repeating Values, FO logic, etc.). As explained above, we consider here the *parameterized asynchronous case for specifications written in FO logic*. To the best of our knowledge, this combination has not been considered before. For flexible modeling, we also distinguish between three types of processes: those that can only be controlled by the system; those that can only be controlled by the environment; and finally those that can be triggered by both. A partition into system and environment processes is also made in [3, 18], but for a fixed number of processes and in the presence of an arena in terms of a Petri net.

Let us briefly describe our results. We show that the general case of the synthesis problem is undecidable for $FO^2$ logic. This follows from an adaptation of an undecidability result from [16, 17] for a fragment of the Logic of Repeating

Values [11]. We therefore concentrate on an orthogonal logic, namely FO without the order on the word positions. First, we show that this logic can essentially count processes and actions of a given process up to some threshold. Though it has limited expressive power (albeit orthogonal to that of $FO^2$), it leads to intricate behaviors in the presence of an uncontrollable environment. In fact, we show that the synthesis problem is still undecidable. Due to the lack of the order relation, the proof requires a subtle reduction from the reachability problem in 2-counter Minsky machines. However, it turns out that the synthesis problem is decidable if the number of processes that are controllable by the environment is bounded, while the number of system processes remains unbounded. In this case, there is even a cutoff $k$, an important measure for parameterized systems (cf. [4] for an overview): If the system has a winning strategy for $k$ processes, then it has one for any number of processes greater than $k$, and the same applies to the environment. The proofs of both main results rely on a reduction of the synthesis problem to turn-based *parameterized vector games*, in which, similar to Petri nets, tokens corresponding to processes are moved around between states.

The paper is structured as follows. In Section 2, we define FO logic (especially FO without word order), and in Section 3, we present the parameterized synthesis problem. In Section 4, we transform a given formula into a normal form and finally into a parameterized vector game. Based on this reduction, we investigate cutoff properties and show our (un)decidability results in Section 5. We conclude in Section 6. Some proof details can be found in the long version of this paper [2]

## 2 Preliminaries

For a finite or infinite alphabet $\Sigma$, let $\Sigma^*$ and $\Sigma^\omega$ denote the sets of finite and, respectively, infinite words over $\Sigma$. The empty word is $\varepsilon$. Given $w \in \Sigma^* \cup \Sigma^\omega$, let $|w|$ denote the length of $w$ and $Pos(w)$ its set of positions: $|w| = n$ and $Pos(w) = \{1, \ldots, n\}$ if $w = \sigma_1\sigma_2 \ldots \sigma_n \in \Sigma^*$, and $|w| = \omega$ and $Pos(w) = \{1, 2, \ldots\}$ if $w \in \Sigma^\omega$. Let $w[i]$ be the $i$-th letter of $w$ for all $i \in Pos(w)$.

**Executions.** We consider programs involving a finite (but not fixed) number of processes. Processes are controlled by antagonistic protagonists, System and Environment. Accordingly, each process has a *type* among $\mathbb{T} = \{\mathsf{s}, \mathsf{e}, \mathsf{se}\}$, and we let $\mathbb{P}_\mathsf{s}$, $\mathbb{P}_\mathsf{e}$, and $\mathbb{P}_\mathsf{se}$ denote the pairwise disjoint finite sets of processes controlled by System, by Environment, and by both System and Environment, respectively. We let $\mathbb{P}$ denote the triple $(\mathbb{P}_\mathsf{s}, \mathbb{P}_\mathsf{e}, \mathbb{P}_\mathsf{se})$. Abusing notation, we sometimes refer to $\mathbb{P}$ as the disjoint union $\mathbb{P}_\mathsf{s} \cup \mathbb{P}_\mathsf{e} \cup \mathbb{P}_\mathsf{se}$.

Given any set $S$, vectors $s \in S^\mathbb{T}$ are usually referred to as triples $s = (s_\mathsf{s}, s_\mathsf{e}, s_\mathsf{se})$. Moreover, for $s, s' \in \mathbb{N}^\mathbb{T}$, we write $s \leq s'$ if $s_\theta \leq s'_\theta$ for all $\theta \in \mathbb{T}$. Finally, let $s + s' = (s_\mathsf{s} + s'_\mathsf{s},\ s_\mathsf{e} + s'_\mathsf{e},\ s_\mathsf{se} + s'_\mathsf{se})$.

Processes can execute actions from a finite alphabet $A$. Whenever an action is executed, we would like to know whether it was triggered by System or by Environment. Therefore, $A$ is partitioned into $A = A_\mathsf{s} \uplus A_\mathsf{e}$. Let $\Sigma_\mathsf{s} = A_\mathsf{s} \times (\mathbb{P}_\mathsf{s} \cup \mathbb{P}_\mathsf{se})$ and $\Sigma_\mathsf{e} = A_\mathsf{e} \times (\mathbb{P}_\mathsf{e} \cup \mathbb{P}_\mathsf{se})$. Their union $\Sigma = \Sigma_\mathsf{s} \cup \Sigma_\mathsf{e}$ is the set of *events*. A word $w \in \Sigma^* \cup \Sigma^\omega$ is called a $\mathbb{P}$-*execution*.

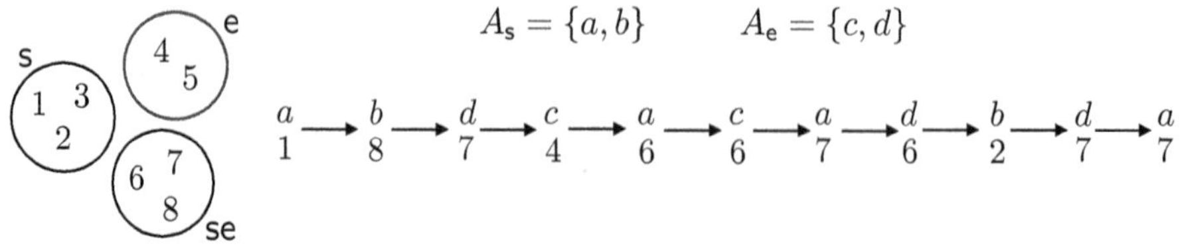


**Fig. 1.** Representation of $\mathbb{P}$-execution as a mathematical structure

**Logic.** Formulas of our logic are evaluated over $\mathbb{P}$-executions. We fix an infinite supply $\mathcal{V} = \{x, y, z, \ldots\}$ of variables, which are interpreted as processes from $\mathbb{P}$ or positions of the execution. The logic $\mathrm{FO}_A[\sim, <, +1]$ is given by the grammar

$$\varphi ::= \theta(x) \mid a(x) \mid x = y \mid x \sim y \mid x < y \mid +1(x, y) \mid \neg\varphi \mid \varphi \vee \varphi \mid \exists x.\varphi$$

where $x, y \in \mathcal{V}$, $\theta \in \mathbb{T}$, and $a \in A$. Conjunction ($\wedge$), universal quantification ($\forall$), implication ($\Longrightarrow$), *true*, and *false* are obtained as abbreviations as usual.

Let $\varphi \in \mathrm{FO}_A[\sim, <, +1]$. By $\mathit{Free}(\varphi) \subseteq \mathcal{V}$, we denote the set of variables that occur free in $\varphi$. If $\mathit{Free}(\varphi) = \emptyset$, then we call $\varphi$ a *sentence*. We sometimes write $\varphi(x_1, \ldots, x_n)$ to emphasize the fact that $\mathit{Free}(\varphi) \subseteq \{x_1, \ldots, x_n\}$.

To evaluate $\varphi$ over a $\mathbb{P}$-execution $w = (a_1, p_1)(a_2, p_2)\ldots$, we consider $(\mathbb{P}, w)$ as a structure $\mathcal{S}_{(\mathbb{P},w)} = (\mathbb{P} \uplus \mathit{Pos}(w), \mathbb{P}_s, \mathbb{P}_e, \mathbb{P}_{se}, (R_a)_{a\in A}, \sim, <, +1)$ where $\mathbb{P} \uplus \mathit{Pos}(w)$ is the universe, $\mathbb{P}_s$ $\mathbb{P}_e$, and $\mathbb{P}_{se}$ are interpreted as unary relations, $R_a$ is the unary relation $\{i \in \mathit{Pos}(w) \mid a_i = a\}$, $< = \{(i, j) \in \mathit{Pos}(w) \times \mathit{Pos}(w) \mid i < j\}$, $+1 = \{(i, i+1) \mid 1 \leq i < |w|\}$, and $\sim$ is the smallest equivalence relation over $\mathbb{P} \uplus \mathit{Pos}(w)$ containing

- $(p, i)$ for all $p \in \mathbb{P}$ and $i \in \mathit{Pos}(w)$ such that $p = p_i$, and
- $(i, j)$ for all $(i, j) \in \mathit{Pos}(w) \times \mathit{Pos}(w)$ such that $p_i = p_j$.

An equivalence class of $\sim$ is often simply referred to as a *class*. Note that it contains exactly one process.

*Example 1.* Suppose $A_s = \{a, b\}$ and $A_e = \{c, d\}$. Let the set of processes $\mathbb{P}$ be given by $\mathbb{P}_s = \{1, 2, 3\}$, $\mathbb{P}_e = \{4, 5\}$, and $\mathbb{P}_{se} = \{6, 7, 8\}$. Moreover, let $w = (a, 1)(b, 8)(d, 7)(c, 4)(a, 6)(c, 6)(a, 7)(d, 6)(b, 2)(d, 7)(a, 7) \in \Sigma^*$. Figure 1 illustrates $\mathcal{S}_{(\mathbb{P},w)}$. The edge relation represents $+1$, its transitive closure is $<$. $\lhd$

An *interpretation* for $(\mathbb{P}, w)$ is a partial mapping $I : \mathcal{V} \to \mathbb{P} \cup \mathit{Pos}(w)$. Suppose $\varphi \in \mathrm{FO}_A[\sim, <, +1]$ such that $\mathit{Free}(\varphi) \subseteq \mathrm{dom}(I)$. The satisfaction relation $(\mathbb{P}, w), I \models \varphi$ is then defined as expected, based on the structure $\mathcal{S}_{(\mathbb{P},w)}$ and interpreting free variables according to $I$. For example, let $w = (a_1, p_1)(a_2, p_2)\ldots$ and $i \in \mathit{Pos}(w)$. Then, for $I(x) = i$, we have $(\mathbb{P}, w), I \models a(x)$ if $a_i = a$.

We identify some fragments of $\mathrm{FO}_A[\sim, <, +1]$. For $R \subseteq \{\sim, <, +1\}$, let $\mathrm{FO}_A[R]$ denote the set of formulas that do not use symbols in $\{\sim, <, +1\} \setminus R$. Moreover, $\mathrm{FO}^2_A[R]$ denotes the fragment of $\mathrm{FO}_A[R]$ that uses only two (reusable) variables.

Let $\varphi(x_1, \ldots, x_n, y) \in \mathrm{FO}_A[\sim, <, +1]$ be a formula and $m \in \mathbb{N}$. We use $\exists^{\geq m} y.\varphi(x_1, \ldots, x_n, y)$ as an abbreviation for

$$\exists y_1 \ldots \exists y_m. \bigwedge_{1 \leq i < j \leq m} \neg(y_i = y_j) \wedge \bigwedge_{1 \leq i \leq m} \varphi(x_1, \ldots, x_n, y_i),$$

if $m > 0$, and $\exists^{\geq 0} y.\varphi(x_1, \ldots, x_n, y) = \mathit{true}$. Thus, $\exists^{\geq m} y.\varphi$ says that there are at least $m$ distinct elements that verify $\varphi$. We also use $\exists^{=m} y.\varphi$ as an abbreviation for $\exists^{\geq m} y.\varphi \wedge \neg\exists^{\geq m+1} y.\varphi$. Note that $\varphi \in \mathrm{FO}_A[R]$ implies that $\exists^{\geq m} y.\varphi \in \mathrm{FO}_A[R]$ and $\exists^{=m} y.\varphi \in \mathrm{FO}_A[R]$.

*Example 2.* Let $A$, $\mathbb{P}$, and $w$ be like in Example 1 and Figure 1.

- $\varphi_1 = \forall x.\big((\mathsf{s}(x) \vee \mathsf{se}(x)) \implies \exists y.(x \sim y \wedge (a(y) \vee b(y)))\big)$ says that each process that System can control executes at least one system action. We have $\varphi_1 \in \mathrm{FO}^2_A[\sim]$ and $(\mathbb{P}, w) \not\models \varphi_1$, as process 3 is idle.
- $\varphi_2 = \forall x.\big(d(x) \implies \exists y.(x \sim y \wedge a(y))\big)$ says that, for every $d$, there is an $a$ on the same process. We have $\varphi_2 \in \mathrm{FO}^2_A[\sim]$ and $(\mathbb{P}, w) \models \varphi_2$.
- $\varphi_3 = \forall x.\big(d(x) \implies \exists y.(x \sim y \wedge x < y \wedge a(y))\big)$ says that every $d$ is *eventually* followed by an $a$ executed by the same process. We have $\varphi_3 \in \mathrm{FO}^2_A[\sim, <]$ and $(\mathbb{P}, w) \not\models \varphi_3$: The event $(d, 6)$ is not followed by some $(a, 6)$.
- $\varphi_4 = \forall x.\big((\exists^{=2} y.(x \sim y \wedge a(y))) \iff (\exists^{=2} y.(x \sim y \wedge d(y)))\big)$ says that each class contains exactly two occurrences of $a$ iff it contains exactly two occurrences of $d$. Moreover, $\varphi_4 \in \mathrm{FO}_A[\sim]$ and $(\mathbb{P}, w) \models \varphi_4$. Note that $\varphi_4 \notin \mathrm{FO}^2_A[\sim]$, as $\exists^{=2} y$ requires the use of three different variable names. ◁

## 3 Parameterized Synthesis Problem

We define an asynchronous synthesis problem. A $\mathbb{P}$-*strategy* (for System) is a mapping $f : \Sigma^* \to \Sigma_{\mathsf{s}} \cup \{\varepsilon\}$. A $\mathbb{P}$-execution $w = \sigma_1\sigma_2 \ldots \in \Sigma^* \cup \Sigma^\omega$ is $f$-*compatible* if, for all $i \in \mathit{Pos}(w)$ such that $\sigma_i \in \Sigma_{\mathsf{s}}$, we have $f(\sigma_1 \ldots \sigma_{i-1}) = \sigma_i$. We call $w$ $f$-*fair* if the following hold: $(i)$ If $w$ is finite, then $f(w) = \varepsilon$, and $(ii)$ if $w$ is infinite and $f(\sigma_1 \ldots \sigma_{i-1}) \neq \varepsilon$ for infinitely many $i \geq 1$, then $\sigma_j \in \Sigma_{\mathsf{s}}$ for infinitely many $j \geq 1$.

Let $\varphi \in \mathrm{FO}_A[\sim, <, +1]$ be a sentence. We say that $f$ is $\mathbb{P}$-*winning* for $\varphi$ if, for every $\mathbb{P}$-execution $w$ that is $f$-compatible and $f$-fair, we have $(\mathbb{P}, w) \models \varphi$.

The existence of a $\mathbb{P}$-strategy that is $\mathbb{P}$-winning for a given formula does not depend on the concrete process identities but only on the cardinality of the sets $\mathbb{P}_{\mathsf{s}}$, $\mathbb{P}_{\mathsf{e}}$, and $\mathbb{P}_{\mathsf{se}}$. This motivates the following definition of winning triples for a formula. Given $\varphi$, let $\mathit{Win}(\varphi)$ be the set of triples $(k_{\mathsf{s}}, k_{\mathsf{e}}, k_{\mathsf{se}}) \in \mathbb{N}^{\mathbb{T}}$ for which there is $\mathbb{P} = (\mathbb{P}_{\mathsf{s}}, \mathbb{P}_{\mathsf{e}}, \mathbb{P}_{\mathsf{se}})$ such that $|\mathbb{P}_\theta| = k_\theta$ for all $\theta \in \mathbb{T}$ and there is a $\mathbb{P}$-strategy that is $\mathbb{P}$-winning for $\varphi$.

Let $\mathbb{0} = \{0\}$ and $k_{\mathsf{e}}, k_{\mathsf{se}} \in \mathbb{N}$. In this paper, we focus on the intersection of $\mathit{Win}(\varphi)$ with the sets $\mathbb{N} \times \mathbb{0} \times \mathbb{0}$ (which corresponds to the usual satisfiability problem); $\mathbb{N} \times \{k_{\mathsf{e}}\} \times \{k_{\mathsf{se}}\}$ (there is a constant number of environment and mixed processes); $\mathbb{N} \times \mathbb{N} \times \{k_{\mathsf{se}}\}$ (there is a constant number of mixed processes); $\mathbb{0} \times \mathbb{0} \times \mathbb{N}$ (each process is controlled by both System and Environment).

**Definition 3 (synthesis problem).** *For fixed* $\mathfrak{F} \in \{\mathrm{FO}, \mathrm{FO}^2\}$*, set of relation symbols* $R \subseteq \{\sim, <, +1\}$*, and* $\mathcal{N}_{\mathsf{s}}, \mathcal{N}_{\mathsf{e}}, \mathcal{N}_{\mathsf{se}} \subseteq \mathbb{N}$*, the (parameterized) synthesis problem is given as follows:*

| $\textsc{Synth}(\mathfrak{F}[R], \mathcal{N}_{\mathsf{s}}, \mathcal{N}_{\mathsf{e}}, \mathcal{N}_{\mathsf{se}})$ |
|---|
| **Input:** $A = A_{\mathsf{s}} \uplus A_{\mathsf{e}}$ *and a sentence* $\varphi \in \mathfrak{F}_A[R]$ |
| **Question:** $Win(\varphi) \cap (\mathcal{N}_{\mathsf{s}} \times \mathcal{N}_{\mathsf{e}} \times \mathcal{N}_{\mathsf{se}}) \neq \emptyset$? |

*The* satisfiability problem *for* $\mathfrak{F}[R]$ *is defined as* $\textsc{Synth}(\mathfrak{F}[R], \mathbb{N}, \mathbb{0}, \mathbb{0})$.

*Example 4.* Suppose $A_{\mathsf{s}} = \{a, b\}$ and $A_{\mathsf{e}} = \{c, d\}$, and consider the formulas $\varphi_1$–$\varphi_4$ from Example 2.

First, we have $Win(\varphi_1) = \mathbb{N}^{\mathbb{T}}$. Given an arbitrary $\mathbb{P}$ and any total order $\sqsubseteq$ over $\mathbb{P}_{\mathsf{s}} \cup \mathbb{P}_{\mathsf{se}}$, a possible $\mathbb{P}$-strategy $f$ that is $\mathbb{P}$-winning for $\varphi_1$ maps $w \in \Sigma^*$ to $(a, p)$ if $p$ is the smallest process from $\mathbb{P}_{\mathsf{s}} \cup \mathbb{P}_{\mathsf{se}}$ wrt. $\sqsubseteq$ that does not occur in $w$, and that returns $\varepsilon$ for $w$ if all processes from $\mathbb{P}_{\mathsf{s}} \cup \mathbb{P}_{\mathsf{se}}$ already occur in $w$.

For the three formulas $\varphi_2$, $\varphi_3$, and $\varphi_4$, observe that, since $d$ is an environment action, if there is at least one process that is exclusively controlled by Environment, then there is no winning strategy. Hence we must have $\mathbb{P}_{\mathsf{e}} = \emptyset$. In fact, this condition is sufficient in the three cases and the strategies described below show that all three sets $Win(\varphi_2)$, $Win(\varphi_3)$, and $Win(\varphi_4)$ are equal to $\mathbb{N} \times \mathbb{0} \times \mathbb{N}$.

- For $\varphi_2$, the very same strategy as for $\varphi_1$ also works in this case, producing an $a$ for every process in $\mathbb{P}_{\mathsf{s}} \cup \mathbb{P}_{\mathsf{se}}$, whether there is a $d$ or not.
- For $\varphi_3$, a winning strategy $f$ will apply the previous mechanism iteratively, performing $(a, p)$ for $p \in \mathbb{P}_{\mathsf{se}} = \{p_0, \ldots, p_{n-1}\}$ over and over again: $f(w) = (a, p_i)$ where $i$ is the number of occurrences of letters from $\Sigma_{\mathsf{s}}$ modulo $n$. By the fairness assumption, this guarantees satisfaction of $\varphi_3$. A more "economical" winning strategy $f'$ may organize pending requests in terms of $d$ in a queue and acknowledge them successively. More precisely, given $u \in \mathbb{P}^*$ and $\sigma \in \Sigma$, we define another word $u \odot \sigma \in \mathbb{P}^*$ by $u \odot (d, p) = u \cdot p$ (inserting $p$ in the queue) and $(p \cdot u) \odot (a, p) = u$ (deleting it). In all other cases, $u \odot \sigma = u$. Let $w = \sigma_1 \ldots \sigma_n \in \Sigma^*$, with queue $((\varepsilon \odot \sigma_1) \odot \sigma_2 \ldots) \odot \sigma_n = p_1 \ldots p_k$. We let $f'(w) = \varepsilon$ if $k = 0$, and $f'(w) = (a, p_1)$ if $k \geq 1$.
- For $\varphi_4$, the strategy $f'$ for $\varphi_3$ ensures that every $d$ has a *corresponding* $a$ so that, in the long run, there are as many $a$'s as $d$'s in every class. $\lhd$

Another interesting question is whether System (or Environment) has a winning strategy as soon as the number of processes is big enough. This leads to the notion of a cutoff (cf. [4] for an overview): Let $\mathcal{N}_{\mathsf{s}}, \mathcal{N}_{\mathsf{e}}, \mathcal{N}_{\mathsf{se}} \subseteq \mathbb{N}$ and $W \subseteq \mathbb{N}^{\mathbb{T}}$. We call $\boldsymbol{k_0} \in \mathbb{N}^{\mathbb{T}}$ a *cutoff* of $W$ wrt. $(\mathcal{N}_{\mathsf{s}}, \mathcal{N}_{\mathsf{e}}, \mathcal{N}_{\mathsf{se}})$ if $\boldsymbol{k_0} \in \mathcal{N}_{\mathsf{s}} \times \mathcal{N}_{\mathsf{e}} \times \mathcal{N}_{\mathsf{se}}$ and either

- for all $\boldsymbol{k} \in \mathcal{N}_{\mathsf{s}} \times \mathcal{N}_{\mathsf{e}} \times \mathcal{N}_{\mathsf{se}}$ such that $\boldsymbol{k} \geq \boldsymbol{k_0}$, we have $\boldsymbol{k} \in W$, or
- for all $\boldsymbol{k} \in \mathcal{N}_{\mathsf{s}} \times \mathcal{N}_{\mathsf{e}} \times \mathcal{N}_{\mathsf{se}}$ such that $\boldsymbol{k} \geq \boldsymbol{k_0}$, we have $\boldsymbol{k} \notin W$.

Let $\mathfrak{F} \in \{\mathrm{FO}, \mathrm{FO}^2\}$ and $R \subseteq \{\sim, <, +1\}$. If, for every alphabet $A = A_{\mathsf{s}} \uplus A_{\mathsf{e}}$ and every sentence $\varphi \in \mathfrak{F}_A[R]$, the set $Win(\varphi)$ has a computable cutoff wrt.

**Table 1.** Summary of results. Our contributions are highlighted in **bold**.

| Synthesis | $(\mathbb{N}, \mathbb{0}, \mathbb{0})$ | $(\mathbb{N}, \{k_e\}, \{k_{se}\})$ | $(\mathbb{N}, \mathbb{N}, \mathbb{0})$ | $(\mathbb{0}, \mathbb{0}, \mathbb{N})$ |
|---|---|---|---|---|
| $FO^2[\sim, <, +1]$ | decidable [5] | ? | ? | **undecidable** |
| $FO^2[\sim, <]$ | NEXPTIME-c. [5] | ? | ? | ? |
| $FO[\sim]$ | **decidable** | **decidable** | ?* | **undecidable** |

*We show, however, that there is no cutoff.

$(\mathcal{N}_s, \mathcal{N}_e, \mathcal{N}_{se})$, then we know that $\text{SYNTH}(\mathfrak{F}[R], \mathcal{N}_s, \mathcal{N}_e, \mathcal{N}_{se})$ is decidable, as it can be reduced to a finite number of simple synthesis problems over a finite alphabet. The latter can be solved, e.g., using attractor-based backward search (cf. [42]). This is how we will show decidability of $\text{SYNTH}(FO[\sim], \mathbb{N}, \{k_e\}, \{k_{se}\})$ for all $k_e, k_{se} \in \mathbb{N}$.

Our contributions are summarized in Table 1. Note that known satisfiability results for data logic apply to our logic, as processes can be simulated by treating every $\theta \in \mathbb{T}$ as an ordinary letter. Let us first state undecidability of the general synthesis problem, which motivates the study of other FO fragments.

**Theorem 5.** *The problem* $\text{SYNTH}(FO^2[\sim, <, +1], \mathbb{0}, \mathbb{0}, \mathbb{N})$ *is undecidable.*

*Proof (sketch).* We adapt the proof from [16, 17] reducing the halting problem for 2-counter machines. We show that their encoding can be expressed in our logic, even if we restrict it to two variables, and can also be adapted to the asynchronous setting. □

# 4 FO[∼] and Parameterized Vector Games

Due to the undecidability result of Theorem 5, one has to switch to other fragments of first-order logic. We will henceforth focus on the logic $FO[\sim]$ and establish some important properties, such as a normal form, that will allow us to deduce a couple of results, both positive and negative.

## 4.1 Satisfiability and Normal Form for FO[∼]

We first show that $FO[\sim]$ logic essentially allows one to count letters in a class up to some threshold, and to count such classes up to some other threshold. Let $B \in \mathbb{N}$ and $\ell \in \{0, \ldots, B\}^A$. Intuitively, $\ell(a)$ imposes a constraint on the number of occurrences of $a$ in a class. We first define an $FO_A[\sim]$-formula $\psi_{B,\ell}(y)$ verifying that, in the class defined by $y$, the number of occurrences of each letter $a \in A$, counted up to $B$, is $\ell(a)$:

$$\psi_{B,\ell}(y) \;=\; \bigwedge_{\substack{a \in A \mid \\ \ell(a) < B}} \exists^{=\ell(a)} z.(y \sim z \wedge a(z)) \wedge \bigwedge_{\substack{a \in A \mid \\ \ell(a) = B}} \exists^{\geq \ell(a)} z.(y \sim z \wedge a(z))$$

**Theorem 6 (normal form for FO[$\sim$]).** *Let* $\varphi \in \mathrm{FO}_A[\sim]$ *be a sentence. There is a computable* $B \in \mathbb{N}$ *such that* $\varphi$ *is effectively equivalent to a disjunction of conjunctions of formulas of the form* $\exists^{\bowtie m} y.(\theta(y) \wedge \psi_{B,\ell}(y))$ *where* $\bowtie \in \{\geq, =\}$, $m \in \mathbb{N}$, $\theta \in \mathbb{T}$, *and* $\ell \in \{0, \ldots, B\}^A$.

The normal form can be obtained using known normal-form constructions [23,41] for general FO logic [2], or using Ehrenfeucht-Fraïssé games [39], or using a direct inductive transformation in the spirit of [23].

*Example 7.* Recall the formula $\varphi_4 = \forall x.((\exists^{=2} y.(x \sim y \wedge a(y))) \iff (\exists^{=2} y.(x \sim y \wedge d(y)))) \in \mathrm{FO}_A[\sim]$ from Example 2, over $A_{\mathsf{s}} = \{a, b\}$ and $A_{\mathsf{e}} = \{c, d\}$. An equivalent formula in normal form is $\varphi_4' = \bigwedge_{\theta \in \mathbb{T},\, \ell \in Z} \exists^{=0} y.(\theta(y) \wedge \psi_{3,\ell}(y))$ where $Z$ is the set of vectors $\ell \in \{0, \ldots, 3\}^A$ such that $\ell(a) = 2 \neq \ell(d)$ or $\ell(d) = 2 \neq \ell(a)$. The formula indeed says that there is no class with $=2$ occurrences of $a$ and $\neq 2$ occurrences of $d$ or vice versa, which is equivalent to $\varphi_4$. $\lhd$

Thanks to the normal form, it is sufficient to test finitely many structures to determine whether a given formula is satisfiable:

**Corollary 8.** *The satisfiability problem for* FO[$\sim$] *over data words is decidable. Moreover, every satisfiable* $\mathrm{FO}_A[\sim]$ *formula has a finite model.*

Note that the satisfiability problem for $\mathrm{FO}^2[\sim]$ is already NEXPTIME-hard, due to NEXPTIME-hardness for two-variable logic with unary relations only [14, 20,22]. In fact, it is NEXPTIME-complete due to the upper bound for $\mathrm{FO}^2[\sim, <]$ [5]. It is worth mentioning that two-variable logic with one equivalence relation on arbitrary structures also has the finite-model property [32].

### 4.2 From Synthesis to Parameterized Vector Games

Exploiting the normal form for $\mathrm{FO}_A[\sim]$, we now present a reduction of the synthesis problem to a strictly turn-based two-player game. This game is conceptually simpler and easier to reason about. The reduction works in both directions, which will allow us to derive both decidability and undecidability results.

Note that, given a formula $\varphi \in \mathrm{FO}_A[\sim]$ (which we suppose to be in normal form with threshold $B$), the order of letters in an execution does not matter. Thus, given some $\mathbb{P}$, a reasonable strategy for Environment would be to just "wait and see". More precisely, it does not put Environment into a worse position if, given the current execution $w \in \Sigma^*$, it lets the System execute as many actions as it wants in terms of a word $u \in \Sigma_{\mathsf{s}}^*$. Due to the fairness assumption, System would be able to execute all the letters from $u$ anyway. Environment can even require System to play a word $u$ such that $(\mathbb{P}, wu) \models \varphi$. If System is not able to produce such a word, Environment can just sit back and do nothing. Conversely, upon $wu$ satisfying $\varphi$, Environment has to be able to come up with a word $v \in \Sigma_{\mathsf{e}}^*$ such that $(\mathbb{P}, wuv) \not\models \varphi$. This leads to a turn-based game in which System and Environment play in strictly alternate order and have to provide a satisfying and, respectively, falsifying execution.

In a second step, we can get rid of process identifiers: According to our normal form, all we are interested in is the *number* of processes that agree on their letters counted up to threshold $B$. That is, a finite execution can be abstracted as a *configuration* $C : L \to \mathbb{N}^{\mathbb{T}}$ where $L = \{0, \dots, B\}^A$. For $\ell \in L$ and $C(\ell) = (n_{\mathsf{s}}, n_{\mathsf{e}}, n_{\mathsf{se}})$, $n_\theta$ is the number of processes of type $\theta$ whose letter count up to threshold $B$ corresponds to $\ell$. We can also say that $\ell$ contains $n_\theta$ tokens of type $\theta$. If it is System's turn, it will pick some pairs $(\ell, \ell')$ and move some tokens of type $\theta \in \{\mathsf{s}, \mathsf{se}\}$ from $\ell$ to $\ell'$, provided $\ell(a) \le \ell'(a)$ for all $a \in A_{\mathsf{s}}$ and $\ell(a) = \ell'(a)$ for all $a \in A_{\mathsf{e}}$. This actually corresponds to adding more system letters in the corresponding processes. The Environment proceeds analogously.

Finally, the formula $\varphi$ naturally translates to an acceptance condition $\mathcal{F} \subseteq \mathfrak{C}^L$ over configurations, where $\mathfrak{C}$ is the set of *local acceptance conditions*, which are of the form $(\bowtie_{\mathsf{s}} n_{\mathsf{s}}\,, \bowtie_{\mathsf{e}} n_{\mathsf{e}}\,, \bowtie_{\mathsf{se}} n_{\mathsf{se}})$ where $\bowtie_{\mathsf{s}}, \bowtie_{\mathsf{e}}, \bowtie_{\mathsf{se}} \in \{=, \geq\}$ and $n_{\mathsf{s}}, n_{\mathsf{e}}, n_{\mathsf{se}} \in \mathbb{N}$.

We end up with a turn-based game in which, similarly to a VASS game [1,6, 10,27,38], System and Environment move tokens along vectors from $L$. Note that, however, our games have a very particular structure so that undecidability for VASS games does not carry over to our setting. Moreover, existing decidability results do not allow us to infer our cutoff results below.

In the following, we will formalize *parameterized vector games*.

**Definition 9.** *A* parameterized vector game *(or simply* game*) is given by a triple* $\mathcal{G} = (A, B, \mathcal{F})$ *where* $A = A_{\mathsf{s}} \uplus A_{\mathsf{e}}$ *is the finite alphabet,* $B \in \mathbb{N}$ *is a bound, and, letting* $L = \{0, \dots, B\}^A$, $\mathcal{F} \subseteq \mathfrak{C}^L$ *is a finite set called* acceptance condition.

*Locations.* Let $\ell_0$ be the location such that $\ell_0(a) = 0$ for all $a \in A$. For $\ell \in L$ and $a \in A$, we define $\ell + a$ by $(\ell + a)(b) = \ell(b)$ for $b \neq a$ and $(\ell + a)(b) = \max\{\ell(a) + 1, B\}$ otherwise. This is extended for all $u \in A^*$ and $a \in A$ by $\ell + \varepsilon = \ell$ and $\ell + ua = (\ell + u) + a$. By $\langle\!\langle w \rangle\!\rangle$, we denote the location $\ell_0 + w$.

*Configurations.* As explained above, a *configuration* of $\mathcal{G}$ is a mapping $C : L \to \mathbb{N}^{\mathbb{T}}$. Suppose that, for $\ell \in L$ and $\theta \in \mathbb{T}$, we have $C(\ell) = (n_{\mathsf{s}}, n_{\mathsf{e}}, n_{\mathsf{se}})$. Then, we let $C(\ell, \theta)$ refer to $n_\theta$. By *Conf*, we denote the set of all configurations.

*Transitions.* A *system transition* (respectively *environment transition*) is a mapping $\tau : L \times L \to (\mathbb{N} \times \{0\} \times \mathbb{N})$ (respectively $\tau : L \times L \to (\{0\} \times \mathbb{N} \times \mathbb{N})$) such that, for all $(\ell, \ell') \in L \times L$ with $\tau(\ell, \ell') \neq (0, 0, 0)$, there is a word $w \in A_{\mathsf{s}}^*$ (respectively $w \in A_{\mathsf{e}}^*$) such that $\ell' = \ell + w$. Let $T_{\mathsf{s}}$ denote the set of system transitions, $T_{\mathsf{e}}$ the set of environment transitions, and $T = T_{\mathsf{s}} \cup T_{\mathsf{e}}$ the set of all transitions.

For $\tau \in T$, let the mappings $out_\tau, in_\tau : L \to \mathbb{N}^{\mathbb{T}}$ be defined by $out_\tau(\ell) = \sum_{\ell' \in L} \tau(\ell, \ell')$ and $in_\tau(\ell) = \sum_{\ell' \in L} \tau(\ell', \ell)$ (recall that sum is component-wise). We say that $\tau \in T$ is *applicable* at $C \in Conf$ if, for all $\ell \in L$, we have $out_\tau(\ell) \le C(\ell)$ (component-wise). Abusing notation, we let $\tau(C)$ denote the configuration $C'$ defined by $C'(\ell) = C(\ell) - out_\tau(\ell) + in_\tau(\ell)$ for all $\ell \in L$. Moreover, for $\tau(\ell, \ell') = (n_{\mathsf{s}}, n_{\mathsf{e}}, n_{\mathsf{se}})$ and $\theta \in \mathbb{T}$, we let $\tau(\ell, \ell', \theta)$ refer to $n_\theta$.

*Plays.* Let $C \in Conf$. We write $C \models \mathcal{F}$ if there is $\kappa \in \mathcal{F}$ such that, for all $\ell \in L$, we have $C(\ell) \models \kappa(\ell)$ (in the expected manner). A *C-play*, or simply *play*, is a finite sequence $\pi = C_0 \tau_1 C_1 \tau_2 C_2 \dots \tau_n C_n$ alternating between configurations and transitions (with $n \geq 0$) such that $C_0 = C$ and, for all $i \in \{1, \ldots, n\}$, $C_i = \tau_i(C_{i-1})$ and

- if $i$ is odd, then $\tau_i \in T_\mathsf{s}$ and $C_i \models \mathcal{F}$ (System's move),
- if $i$ is even, then $\tau_i \in T_\mathsf{e}$ and $C_i \not\models \mathcal{F}$ (Environment's move).

The set of all $C$-plays is denoted by $\mathit{Plays}_C$.

*Strategies.* A *C-strategy* for System is a partial mapping $f : \mathit{Plays}_C \to T_\mathsf{s}$ such that $f(C)$ is defined and, for all $\pi = C_0\tau_1C_1 \ldots \tau_iC_i \in \mathit{Plays}_C$ with $\tau = f(\pi)$ defined, we have that $\tau$ is applicable at $C_i$ and $\tau(C_i) \models \mathcal{F}$. Play $\pi = C_0\tau_1C_1 \ldots \tau_nC_n$ is

- *f-compatible* if, for all odd $i \in \{1, \ldots, n\}$, $\tau_i = f(C_0\tau_1C_1 \ldots \tau_{i-1}C_{i-1})$,
- *f-maximal* if it is not the strict prefix of an $f$-compatible play,
- *winning* if $C_n \models \mathcal{F}$.

We say that $f$ is *winning* for System (from $C$) if all $f$-compatible $f$-maximal $C$-plays are winning. Finally, $C$ is *winning* if there is a $C$-strategy that is winning. Note that, given an initial configuration $C$, we deal with an acyclic finite reachability game so that, if there is a winning $C$-strategy, then there is a positional one, which only depends on the last configuration.

For $\boldsymbol{k} \in \mathbb{N}^\mathbb{T}$, let $C_{\boldsymbol{k}}$ denote the configuration that maps $\ell_0$ to $\boldsymbol{k}$ and all other locations to $(0, 0, 0)$. We set $\mathit{Win}(\mathcal{G}) = \{\boldsymbol{k} \in \mathbb{N}^\mathbb{T} \mid C_{\boldsymbol{k}} \text{ is winning for System}\}$.

**Definition 10 (game problem).** *For sets $\mathcal{N}_\mathsf{s}, \mathcal{N}_\mathsf{e}, \mathcal{N}_\mathsf{se} \subseteq \mathbb{N}$, the game problem is given as follows:*

| GAME($\mathcal{N}_\mathsf{s}, \mathcal{N}_\mathsf{e}, \mathcal{N}_\mathsf{se}$) | |
|---|---|
| **Input:** | *Parameterized vector game* $\mathcal{G}$ |
| **Question:** | $\mathit{Win}(\mathcal{G}) \cap (\mathcal{N}_\mathsf{s} \times \mathcal{N}_\mathsf{e} \times \mathcal{N}_\mathsf{se}) \neq \emptyset$? |

One can show that parameterized vector games are equivalent to the synthesis problem in the following sense:

**Lemma 11.** *For every sentence $\varphi \in \mathrm{FO}_A[\sim]$, there is a parameterized vector game $\mathcal{G} = (A, B, \mathcal{F})$ such that $\mathit{Win}(\varphi) = \mathit{Win}(\mathcal{G})$. Conversely, for every parameterized vector game $\mathcal{G} = (A, B, \mathcal{F})$, there is a sentence $\varphi \in \mathrm{FO}_A[\sim]$ such that $\mathit{Win}(\mathcal{G}) = \mathit{Win}(\varphi)$. Both directions are effective.*

*Example 12.* To illustrate parameterized vector games and the reduction from the synthesis problem, consider the formula $\varphi_4' = \bigwedge_{\theta \in \mathbb{T},\, \ell \in Z} \exists^{=0} y.(\theta(y) \wedge \psi_{3,\ell}(y))$ in normal form from Example 7. For simplicity, we assume that $A_\mathsf{s} = \{a\}$ and $A_\mathsf{e} = \{d\}$. That is, $Z$ is the set of vectors $\langle\!\langle a^i d^j \rangle\!\rangle \in L = \{0, \ldots, 3\}^{\{a,d\}}$ such that $i = 2 \neq j$ or $j = 2 \neq i$. Figure 2 illustrates a couple of configurations $C_0, \ldots, C_5 : L \to \mathbb{N}^\mathbb{T}$. The leftmost location in a configuration is $\ell_0$, the rightmost

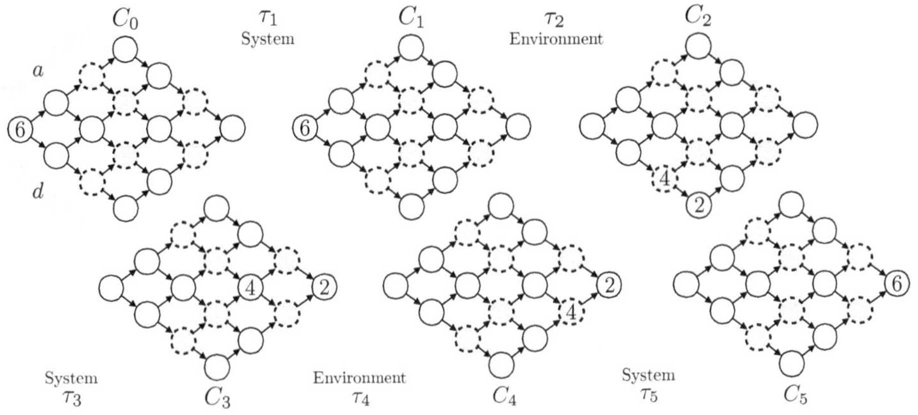


**Fig. 2.** A play of a parameterized vector game

location $\langle\!\langle a^3d^3 \rangle\!\rangle$, the topmost one $\langle\!\langle a^3 \rangle\!\rangle$, and the one at the bottom $\langle\!\langle d^3 \rangle\!\rangle$. Self-loops have been omitted, and locations from $Z$ have gray background and a dashed border.

Towards an equivalent game $\mathcal{G} = (A, 3, \mathcal{F})$, it remains to determine the acceptance condition $\mathcal{F}$. Recall that $\varphi_4'$ says that every class contains two occurrences of $a$ iff it contains two occurrences of $d$. This is reflected by the acceptance condition $\mathcal{F} = \{\kappa\}$ where $\kappa(\ell) = (=0\,, =0\,, =0)$ for all $\ell \in Z$ and $\kappa(\ell) = (\geq 0\,, \geq 0\,, \geq 0)$ for all $\ell \in L \setminus Z$. With this, a configuration is accepting iff no token is on a location from $Z$ (a gray location).

We can verify that $\mathit{Win}(\mathcal{G}) = \mathit{Win}(\varphi_4') = \mathbb{N} \times \mathbb{0} \times \mathbb{N}$. In $\mathcal{G}$, a uniform winning strategy $f$ for System that works for all $\mathbb{P}$ with $\mathbb{P}_{\mathsf{e}} = \emptyset$ proceeds as follows: System first awaits an Environment's move and then moves each token upwards as many locations as Environment has moved it downwards. Figure 2 illustrates an $f$-maximal $C_{(6,0,0)}$-play that is winning for System. We note that $f$ is a "compressed" version of the winning strategy presented in Example 4, as System makes her moves only when really needed. ◁

## 5 Results for FO[$\sim$] via Parameterized Vector Games

In this section, we present our results for the synthesis problem for FO[$\sim$], which we obtain showing corresponding results for parameterized vector games. In particular, we show that (FO[$\sim$], $\mathbb{0}, \mathbb{0}, \mathbb{N}$) and (FO[$\sim$], $\mathbb{N}, \mathbb{N}, \mathbb{0}$) do not have a cutoff, whereas (FO[$\sim$], $\mathbb{N}, \{k_{\mathsf{e}}\}, \{k_{\mathsf{se}}\}$) has a cutoff for all $k_{\mathsf{e}}, k_{\mathsf{se}} \in \mathbb{N}$. Finally, we prove that SYNTH(FO[$\sim$], $\mathbb{0}, \mathbb{0}, \mathbb{N}$) is, in fact, undecidable.

**Lemma 13.** *There is a game* $\mathcal{G} = (A, B, \mathcal{F})$ *such that* $\mathit{Win}(\mathcal{G})$ *does not have a cutoff wrt.* $(\mathbb{0}, \mathbb{0}, \mathbb{N})$.

*Proof.* We let $A_{\mathsf{s}} = \{a\}$ and $A_{\mathsf{e}} = \{b\}$, as well as $B = 2$. For $k \in \{0, 1, 2\}$, define the local acceptance conditions ${}^{=}k = (=0\,, =0\,, =k)$ and ${}^{\geq}k = (=0\,, =0\,, \geq k)$. Set

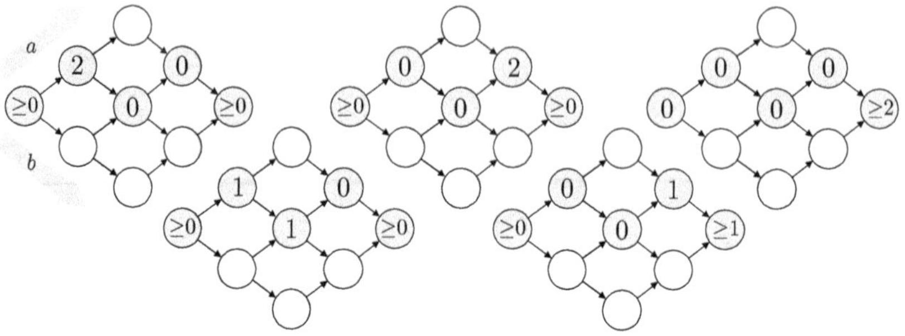


**Fig. 3.** Acceptance conditions for a game with no cutoff wrt. $(\mathbb{0}, \mathbb{0}, \mathbb{N})$

$\ell_1 = \langle\!\langle a \rangle\!\rangle, \ell_2 = \langle\!\langle ab \rangle\!\rangle, \ell_3 = \langle\!\langle a^2 b \rangle\!\rangle$, and $\ell_4 = \langle\!\langle a^2 b^2 \rangle\!\rangle$. For $k_0, \ldots, k_4 \in \{0, 1, 2\}$ and $\bowtie_0, \ldots, \bowtie_4 \in \{=, \geq\}$, let $[^{\bowtie_0} k_0\,, ^{\bowtie_1} k_1\,, ^{\bowtie_2} k_2\,, ^{\bowtie_3} k_3\,, ^{\bowtie_4} k_4]$ denote $\kappa \in \mathfrak{C}^L$ where $\kappa(\ell_i) = (^{\bowtie_i} k_i)$ for all $i \in \{0, \ldots, 4\}$ and $\kappa(\ell') = (^{=}0)$ for $\ell' \notin \{\ell_0, \ldots, \ell_4\}$. Finally,

$$\mathcal{F} = \left\{ \begin{matrix} [^{\geq}0\,, ^{=}2\,, ^{=}0\,, ^{=}0\,, ^{\geq}0] & [^{\geq}0\,, ^{=}0\,, ^{=}0\,, ^{=}2\,, ^{\geq}0] & [^{=}0\,, ^{=}0\,, ^{=}0\,, ^{=}0\,, ^{\geq}2] \\ [^{\geq}0\,, ^{=}1\,, ^{=}1\,, ^{=}0\,, ^{\geq}0] & [^{\geq}0\,, ^{=}0\,, ^{=}0\,, ^{=}1\,, ^{\geq}1] & \end{matrix} \right\} \cup K_{\mathsf{e}}$$

where $K_{\mathsf{e}} = \{\kappa_\ell \mid \ell \in L \text{ such that } \ell(b) > \ell(a)\}$ with $\kappa_\ell(\ell') = (^{\geq}1)$ if $\ell' = \ell$, and $\kappa_\ell(\ell') = (^{\geq}0)$ otherwise. This is illustrated in Figure 3.

There is a winning strategy for System from any initial configuration of size $2n$: Move two tokens from $\ell_0$ to $\ell_1$, wait until Environment sends them both to $\ell_2$, then move them to $\ell_3$, wait until they are moved to $\ell_4$, then repeat with two new tokens from $\ell_0$ until all the tokens are removed from $\ell_0$, and Environment cannot escape $\mathcal{F}$ anymore. However, one can check that there is no winning strategy for initial configurations of odd size. □

**Lemma 14.** *There is a game $\mathcal{G} = (A, B, \mathcal{F})$ such that $Win(\mathcal{G})$ does not have a cutoff wrt.* $(\mathbb{N}, \mathbb{N}, \mathbb{0})$.

*Proof.* We define $\mathcal{G}$ such that System wins only if she has at least as many processes as Environment. Let $A_{\mathsf{s}} = \{a\}$, $A_{\mathsf{e}} = \{b\}$, and $B = 2$. As there are no shared processes, we can safely ignore locations with a letter from both System and Environment. We set $\mathcal{F} = \{\kappa_1, \kappa_2, \kappa_3, \kappa_4\}$ where

$$\begin{matrix} \kappa_1(\langle\!\langle a \rangle\!\rangle) = (=1\,, =0\,, =0) & \kappa_2(\langle\!\langle a \rangle\!\rangle) = (=1\,, =0\,, =0) & \kappa_3(\langle\!\langle a \rangle\!\rangle) = (=0\,, =0\,, =0) \\ \kappa_1(\langle\!\langle b \rangle\!\rangle) = (=0\,, =0\,, =0) & \kappa_2(\langle\!\langle b \rangle\!\rangle) = (=0\,, \geq 2\,, =0) & \kappa_3(\langle\!\langle b \rangle\!\rangle) = (=0\,, \geq 1\,, =0)\,, \end{matrix}$$

$\kappa_4(\ell_0) = (=0\,, =0\,, =0)$, and $\kappa_i(\ell') = (\geq 0\,, \geq 0\,, =0)$ for all other $\ell' \in L$ and $i \in \{1, 2, 3, 4\}$. □

We now turn to the case where the number of processes that can be triggered by Environment is bounded. Note that similar restrictions are imposed in other settings to get decidability, such as limiting the environment to a finite (Boolean) domain [16] or restricting to one environment process [3, 18]. We obtain decidability of the synthesis problem via a cutoff construction:

**Theorem 15.** *Given $k_{\mathsf{e}}, k_{\mathsf{se}} \in \mathbb{N}$, every game $\mathcal{G} = (A, B, \mathcal{F})$ has a cutoff wrt. $(\mathbb{N}, \{k_{\mathsf{e}}\}, \{k_{\mathsf{se}}\})$. More precisely: Let $K$ be the largest constant that occurs in $\mathcal{F}$. Moreover, let $Max = (k_{\mathsf{e}} + k_{\mathsf{se}}) \cdot |A_{\mathsf{e}}| \cdot B$ and $\hat{N} = |L|^{Max+1} \cdot K$. Then, $(\hat{N}, k_{\mathsf{e}}, k_{\mathsf{se}})$ is a cutoff of $Win(\mathcal{G})$ wrt. $(\mathbb{N}, \{k_{\mathsf{e}}\}, \{k_{\mathsf{se}}\})$.*

*Proof.* We will show that, for all $N \geq \hat{N}$,

$$(N, k_{\mathsf{e}}, k_{\mathsf{se}}) \in Win(\mathcal{G}) \iff (N+1, k_{\mathsf{e}}, k_{\mathsf{se}}) \in Win(\mathcal{G}).$$

The main observation is that, when $C$ contains more than $K$ tokens in a given $\ell \in L$, adding more tokens in $\ell$ will not change whether $C \models \mathcal{F}$. Given $C, C' \in Conf$, we write $C <_{\mathsf{e}} C$ if $C \neq C'$ and there is $\tau \in T_{\mathsf{e}}$ such that $\tau(C) = C'$. Note that the length $d$ of a chain $C_0 <_{\mathsf{e}} C_1 <_{\mathsf{e}} \ldots <_{\mathsf{e}} C_d$ is bounded by $Max$. In other words, $Max$ is the maximal number of transitions that Environment can do in a play. For all $d \in \{0, \ldots, Max\}$, let $Conf_d$ be the set of configurations $C \in Conf$ such that the longest chain in $(Conf, <_{\mathsf{e}})$ starting from $C$ has length $d$.

*Claim.* Suppose that $C \in Conf_d$ and $\ell \in L$ such that $C(\ell) = (N, n_{\mathsf{e}}, n_{\mathsf{se}})$ with $N \geq |L|^{d+1} \cdot K$ and $n_{\mathsf{e}}, n_{\mathsf{se}} \in \mathbb{N}$. Set $D = C[\ell \mapsto (N+1, n_{\mathsf{e}}, n_{\mathsf{se}})]$. Then,

$$C \text{ is winning for System} \iff D \text{ is winning for System.}$$

To show the claim, we proceed by induction on $d \in \mathbb{N}$, which is illustrated in Figure 4. In each implication, we distinguish the cases $d = 0$ and $d \geq 1$. For the latter, we assume that equivalence holds for all values strictly smaller than $d$.

For $\tau \in T_{\mathsf{s}}$ and $\ell, \ell' \in L$, we let $\tau[(\ell, \ell', \mathsf{s})\text{++}]$ denote the transition $\eta \in T_{\mathsf{s}}$ given by $\eta(\ell_1, \ell_2, \mathsf{e}) = \tau(\ell_1, \ell_2, \mathsf{e}) = 0$, $\eta(\ell_1, \ell_2, \mathsf{se}) = \tau(\ell_1, \ell_2, \mathsf{se})$, $\eta(\ell_1, \ell_2, \mathsf{s}) = \tau(\ell_1, \ell_2, \mathsf{s}) + 1$ if $(\ell_1, \ell_2) = (\ell, \ell')$, and $\eta(\ell_1, \ell_2, \mathsf{s}) = \tau(\ell_1, \ell_2, \mathsf{s})$ if $(\ell_1, \ell_2) \neq (\ell, \ell')$. We define $\tau[(\ell, \ell', \mathsf{s})\text{--}]$ similarly (provided $\tau(\ell, \ell', \mathsf{s}) \geq 1$).

$\Longrightarrow$: Let $f$ be a winning strategy for System from $C \in Conf_d$. Let $\tau' = f(C)$ and $C' = \tau'(C)$. Note that $C' \models \mathcal{F}$. Since $C(\ell, \mathsf{s}) = N \geq |L|^{d+1} \cdot K$, there is $\ell' \in L$ such that $\ell + w = \ell'$ for some $w \in A_{\mathsf{s}}^*$ and $C'(\ell', \mathsf{s}) = N' \geq |L|^d \cdot K$.

We show that $D = C[\ell \mapsto (N+1, n_{\mathsf{e}}, n_{\mathsf{se}})]$ is winning for System by exhibiting a corresponding winning strategy $g$ from $D$ that will carefully control the position of the additional token. First, set $g(D) = \eta'$ where $\eta' = \tau'[(\ell, \ell', \mathsf{s})\text{++}]$. Let $D' = \eta'(D)$. We obtain $D'(\ell', \mathsf{s}) = N' + 1$. Note that, since $N' \geq K$, the acceptance condition $\mathcal{F}$ cannot distinguish between $C'$ and $D'$. Thus, we have $D' \models \mathcal{F}$.

Case $d = 0$: As, for all transitions $\eta'' \in T_{\mathsf{e}}$, we have $\eta''(D') = D' \models \mathcal{F}$, we reached a maximal play that is winning for System. We deduce that $D$ is winning for System.

Case $d \geq 1$: Take any $\eta'' \in T_{\mathsf{e}}$ and $D''$ such that $D'' = \eta''(D') \not\models \mathcal{F}$. Let $\tau'' = \eta''$ and $C'' = \tau''(C')$. Note that $D'' = C''[(\ell', \mathsf{s}) \mapsto N+1]$, $C'' = D''[(\ell', \mathsf{s}) \mapsto N]$, and $C'', D'' \in Conf_{d^-}$ for some $d^- < d$. As $f$ is a winning strategy for System from $C$, we have that $C''$ is winning for System. By induction hypothesis, $D''$ is winning for System, say by winning strategy $g''$. We let $g(D\,\eta'\,D'\,\eta''\,\pi) = g''(\pi)$ for all $D''$-plays $\pi$. For all unspecified plays, let $g$ return any applicable system transition. Altogether, for any choice of $\eta''$, we have that $g''$ is winning from $D''$. Thus, $g$ is a winning strategy from $D$.

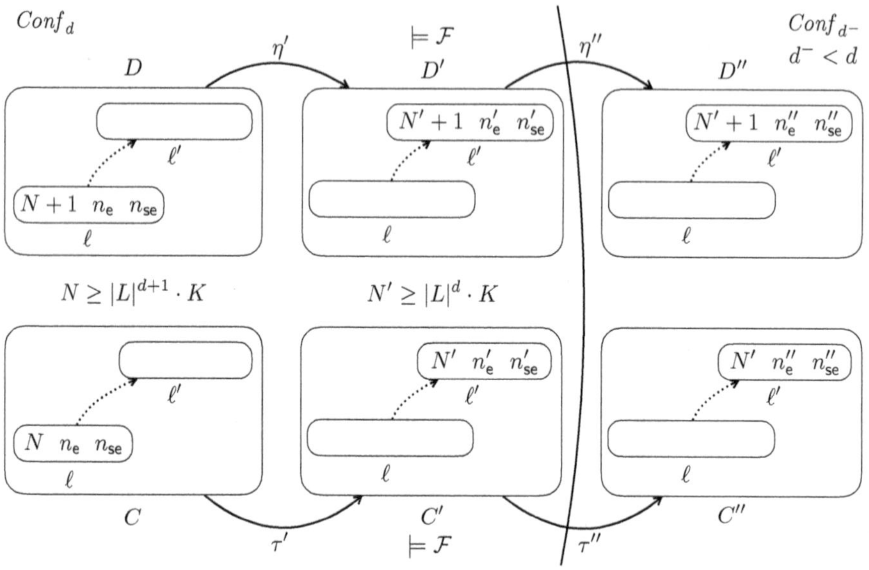


**Fig. 4.** Induction step in the cutoff construction

$\Leftarrow$: Suppose $g$ is a winning strategy for System from $D$. Thus, for $\eta' = g(D)$ and $D' = \eta'(D)$, we have $D' \models \mathcal{F}$. Recall that $D(\ell, \mathsf{s}) \geq (|L|^{d+1} \cdot K) + 1$. We distinguish two cases:

1. Suppose there is $\ell' \in L$ such that $\ell \neq \ell'$, $D'(\ell', \mathsf{s}) = N' + 1$ for some $N' \geq |L|^d \cdot K$, and $\eta'(\ell, \ell', \mathsf{s}) \geq 1$. Then, we set $\tau' = \eta'[(\ell, \ell', \mathsf{s})--]$.
2. Otherwise, we have $D'(\ell, \mathsf{s}) \geq (|L|^d \cdot K) + 1$, and we set $\tau' = \eta'$ (as well as $\ell' = \ell$ and $N' = N$).

Let $C' = \tau'(C)$. Since $D' \models \mathcal{F}$, one obtains $C' \models \mathcal{F}$.

Case $d = 0$: For all transitions $\tau'' \in T_{\mathsf{e}}$, we have $\tau''(C') = C' \models \mathcal{F}$. Thus, we reached a maximal play that is winning for System. We deduce that $C$ is winning for System.

Case $d \geq 1$: Take any $\tau'' \in T_{\mathsf{e}}$ such that $C'' = \tau''(C') \not\models \mathcal{F}$. Let $\eta'' = \tau''$ and $D'' = \eta''(D')$. We have $C'' = D''[(\ell', \mathsf{s}) \mapsto N']$, $D'' = C''[(\ell', \mathsf{s}) \mapsto N' + 1]$, and $C'', D'' \in \mathit{Conf}_{d^-}$ for some $d^- < d$. As $D''$ is winning for System, by induction hypothesis, $C''$ is winning for System, say by winning strategy $f''$. We let $f(C\,\tau'\,C'\,\tau''\,\pi) = f''(\pi)$ for all $C''$-plays $\pi$. For all unspecified plays, let $f$ return an arbitrary applicable system transition. Again, for any choice of $\tau''$, $f''$ is winning from $C''$. Thus, $f$ is a winning strategy from $C$.

This concludes the proof of the claim and, therefore, of Theorem 15. □

**Corollary 16.** *Let $k_{\mathsf{e}}, k_{\mathsf{se}} \in \mathbb{N}$ be the number of environment and the number of mixed processes, respectively. The problems* $\text{Game}(\mathbb{N}, \{k_{\mathsf{e}}\}, \{k_{\mathsf{se}}\})$ *and* $\text{Synth}(\text{FO}[\sim], \mathbb{N}, \{k_{\mathsf{e}}\}, \{k_{\mathsf{se}}\})$ *are decidable.*

In particular, by Theorem 15, the game problem can be reduced to an exponential number of acyclic finite-state games whose size (and hence the time complexity for determining the winner) is exponential in the cutoff and, therefore, doubly exponential in the size of the alphabet, the bound $B$, and the fixed number of processes that are controllable by the environment.

**Theorem 17.** GAME$(\mathbb{0}, \mathbb{0}, \mathbb{N})$ *and* SYNTH$(\mathrm{FO}[\sim], \mathbb{0}, \mathbb{0}, \mathbb{N})$ *are undecidable.*

*Proof.* We provide a reduction from the halting problem for 2-counter machines (2CM) to GAME$(\mathbb{0}, \mathbb{0}, \mathbb{N})$. A 2CM $M = (Q, \Delta, \mathsf{c}_1, \mathsf{c}_2, q_0, q_h)$ has two counters, $\mathsf{c}_1$ and $\mathsf{c}_2$, a finite set of states $Q$, and a set of transitions $\Delta \subseteq Q \times \mathsf{Op} \times Q$ where $\mathsf{Op} = \{\mathsf{c}_i\text{++}, \mathsf{c}_i\text{--}, \mathsf{c}_i\text{==}0 \mid i \in \{1, 2\}\}$. Moreover, we have an initial state $q_0 \in Q$ and a halting state $q_h \in Q$. A configuration of $M$ is a triple $\gamma = (q, \nu_1, \nu_2) \in Q \times \mathbb{N} \times \mathbb{N}$ giving the current state and the current respective counter values. The initial configuration is $\gamma_0 = (q_0, 0, 0)$ and the set of halting configurations is $F = \{q_h\} \times \mathbb{N} \times \mathbb{N}$. For $t \in \Delta$, configuration $(q', \nu_1', \nu_2')$ is a ($t$-)successor of $(q, \nu_1, \nu_2)$, written $(q, \nu_1, \nu_2) \vdash_t (q', \nu_1', \nu_2')$, if there is $i \in \{1, 2\}$ such that $\nu_{3-i}' = \nu_{3-i}$ and one of the following holds: ($i$) $t = (q, \mathsf{c}_i\text{++}, q')$ and $\nu_i' = \nu_i + 1$, or ($ii$) $t = (q, \mathsf{c}_i\text{--}, q')$ and $\nu_i' = \nu_i - 1$, or ($iii$) $t = (q, \mathsf{c}_i\text{==}0, q')$ and $\nu_i = \nu_i' = 0$. A run of $M$ is a (finite or infinite) sequence $\gamma_0 \vdash_{t_1} \gamma_1 \vdash_{t_2} \ldots$. The 2CM halting problem asks whether there is a run reaching a configuration in $F$. It is known to be undecidable [34].

We fix a 2CM $M = (Q, \Delta, \mathsf{c}_1, \mathsf{c}_2, q_0, q_h)$. Let $A_\mathsf{s} = Q \cup \Delta \cup \{a_1, a_2\}$ and $A_\mathsf{e} = \{b\}$ with $a_1$, $a_2$, and $b$ three fresh symbols. We consider the game $\mathcal{G} = (A, B, \mathcal{F})$ with $A = A_\mathsf{s} \uplus A_\mathsf{e}$, $B = 4$, and $\mathcal{F}$ defined below. Let $L = \{0, \ldots, B\}^A$. Since there are only processes shared by System and Environment, we alleviate notation and consider that a configuration is simply a mapping $C : L \to \mathbb{N}$. From now on, to avoid confusion, we refer to configurations of the 2CM $M$ as $M$-configurations, and to configurations of $\mathcal{G}$ as $\mathcal{G}$-configurations.

Intuitively, every valid run of $M$ will be encoded as a play in $\mathcal{G}$, and the acceptance condition will enforce that, if a player in $\mathcal{G}$ deviates from a valid play, then she will lose immediately. At any point in the play, there will be at most one process with only a letter from $Q$ played, which will represent the current state in the simulated 2CM run. Similarly, there will be at most one process with only a letter from $\Delta$ to represent what transition will be taken next. Finally, the value of counter $\mathsf{c}_i$ will be encoded by the number of processes with exactly two occurrences of $a_i$ and two occurrences of $b$ (i.e., $C(\langle\!\langle a_i^2 b^2 \rangle\!\rangle)$).

To increase counter $\mathsf{c}_i$, the players will move a new token to $\langle\!\langle a_i^2 b^2 \rangle\!\rangle$, and to decrease it, they will move, together, a token from $\langle\!\langle a_i^2 b^2 \rangle\!\rangle$ to $\langle\!\langle a_i^4 b^4 \rangle\!\rangle$. Observe that, if $\mathsf{c}_i$ has value 0, then $C(\langle\!\langle a_i^2 b^2 \rangle\!\rangle) = 0$ in the corresponding configuration of the game. As expected, it is then impossible to simulate the decrement of $\mathsf{c}_i$. Environment's only role is to acknowledge System's actions by playing its (only) letter when System simulates a valid run. If System tries to cheat, she loses immediately.

*Encoding an $M$-configuration.* Let us be more formal. Suppose $\gamma = (q, \nu_1, \nu_2)$ is an $M$-configuration and $C$ a $\mathcal{G}$-configuration. We say that $C$ *encodes* $\gamma$ if

- $C(\langle\!\langle q \rangle\!\rangle) = 1$, $C(\langle\!\langle a_1^2 b^2 \rangle\!\rangle) = \nu_1$, $C(\langle\!\langle a_2^2 b^2 \rangle\!\rangle) = \nu_2$,
- $C(\ell) \geq 0$ for all $\ell \in \{\ell_0\} \cup \{\langle\!\langle \hat{q}^2 b^2 \rangle\!\rangle, \langle\!\langle t^2 b^2 \rangle\!\rangle, \langle\!\langle a_i^4 b^4 \rangle\!\rangle \mid \hat{q} \in Q, t \in \Delta, i \in \{1, 2\}\}$,
- $C(\ell) = 0$ for all other $\ell \in L$.

We then write $\gamma = \mathsf{m}(C)$. Let $\mathbb{C}(\gamma)$ be the set of $\mathcal{G}$-configurations $C$ that encode $\gamma$. We say that a $\mathcal{G}$-configuration $C$ is *valid* if $C \in \mathbb{C}(\gamma)$ for some $\gamma$.

*Simulating a transition of $M$.* Let us explain how we go from a $\mathcal{G}$-configuration encoding $\gamma$ to a $\mathcal{G}$-configuration encoding a successor $M$-configuration $\gamma'$. Observe that System cannot change by herself the $M$-configuration encoded. If, for instance, she tries to change the current state $q$, she might move one process from $\ell_0$ to $\langle\!\langle q' \rangle\!\rangle$, but then the $\mathcal{G}$-configuration is not valid anymore. We need to move the process in $\langle\!\langle q \rangle\!\rangle$ into $\langle\!\langle q^2 b^2 \rangle\!\rangle$ and this requires the cooperation of Environment.

Assume that the game is in configuration $C$ encoding $\gamma = (q, \nu_1, \nu_2)$. System will pick a transition $t$ starting in state $q$, say, $t = (q, \mathsf{c}_1{+}{+}, q')$. From configuration $C$, System will go to the configuration $C_1$ defined by $C_1(\langle\!\langle t \rangle\!\rangle) = 1$, $C_1(\langle\!\langle a_1 \rangle\!\rangle) = 1$, and $C_1(\ell) = C(\ell)$ for all other $\ell \in L$.

If the transition $t$ is correctly chosen, Environment will go to a configuration $C_2$ defined by $C_2(\langle\!\langle q \rangle\!\rangle) = 0$, $C_2(\langle\!\langle qb \rangle\!\rangle) = 1$, $C_2(\langle\!\langle t \rangle\!\rangle) = 0$, $C_2(\langle\!\langle tb \rangle\!\rangle) = 1$, $C_2(\langle\!\langle a_1 \rangle\!\rangle) = 0$, $C_2(\langle\!\langle a_1 b \rangle\!\rangle) = 1$ and, for all other $\ell \in L$, $C_2(\ell) = C_1(\ell)$. This means that Environment moves processes in locations $\langle\!\langle t \rangle\!\rangle$, $\langle\!\langle q \rangle\!\rangle$, $\langle\!\langle a_1 \rangle\!\rangle$ to locations $\langle\!\langle tb \rangle\!\rangle$, $\langle\!\langle qb \rangle\!\rangle$, $\langle\!\langle a_1 b \rangle\!\rangle$, respectively.

To finish the transition, System will now move a process to the destination state $q'$ of $t$, and go to configuration $C_3$ defined by $C_3(\langle\!\langle q' \rangle\!\rangle) = 1$, $C_3(\langle\!\langle tb \rangle\!\rangle) = 0$, $C_3(\langle\!\langle t^2 b \rangle\!\rangle) = 1$, $C_3(\langle\!\langle qb \rangle\!\rangle) = 0$, $C_3(\langle\!\langle q^2 b \rangle\!\rangle) = 1$, $C_3(\langle\!\langle a_1 b \rangle\!\rangle) = 0$, $C_3(\langle\!\langle a_1^2 b \rangle\!\rangle) = 1$, and $C_3(\ell) = C_2(\ell)$ for all other $\ell \in L$.

Finally, Environment moves to configuration $C_4$ given by $C_4(\langle\!\langle t^2 b \rangle\!\rangle) = 0$, $C_4(\langle\!\langle t^2 b^2 \rangle\!\rangle) = C_3(\langle\!\langle t^2 b^2 \rangle\!\rangle) + 1$, $C_4(\langle\!\langle q^2 b \rangle\!\rangle) = 0$, $C_4(\langle\!\langle q^2 b^2 \rangle\!\rangle) = C_3(\langle\!\langle q^2 b^2 \rangle\!\rangle) + 1$, $C_4(\langle\!\langle a_1^2 b \rangle\!\rangle) = 0$, $C_4(\langle\!\langle a_1^2 b^2 \rangle\!\rangle) = C_3(\langle\!\langle a_1^2 b^2 \rangle\!\rangle) + 1$, and $C_4(\ell) = C_3(\ell)$ for all other $\ell \in L$. Observe that $C_4 \in \mathbb{C}((q', \nu_1 + 1, \nu_2))$.

Other types of transitions will be simulated similarly. To force System to start the simulation in $\gamma_0$, and not in any $M$-configuration, the configurations $C$ such that $C(\langle\!\langle q_0^2 b^2 \rangle\!\rangle) = 0$ and $C(\langle\!\langle q \rangle\!\rangle) = 1$ for $q \neq q_0$ are not valid, and will be losing for System.

*Acceptance condition.* It remains to define $\mathcal{F}$ in a way that enforces the above sequence of $\mathcal{G}$-configurations. Let $L_{\checkmark} = \{\ell_0\} \cup \{\langle\!\langle a_i^2 b^2 \rangle\!\rangle, \langle\!\langle a_i^4 b^4 \rangle\!\rangle \mid i \in \{1, 2\}\} \cup \{\langle\!\langle q^2 b^2 \rangle\!\rangle \mid q \in Q\} \cup \{\langle\!\langle t^2 b^2 \rangle\!\rangle \mid t \in \Delta\}$ be the set of elements in $L$ whose values do not affect the acceptance of the configuration. By $[\ell_1 \bowtie_1 n_1, \ldots, \ell_k \bowtie_k n_k]$, we denote $\kappa \in \mathfrak{C}^L$ such that $\kappa(\ell_i) = (\bowtie_i n_i)$ for $i \in \{1, \ldots, k\}$ and $\kappa(\ell) = (=0)$ for all $\ell \in L \setminus \{\ell_1, \ldots, \ell_k\}$. Moreover, for a set of locations $\hat{L} \subseteq L$, we let $\hat{L} \geq 0$ stand for "$(\ell \geq 0)$ for all $\ell \in \hat{L}$".

First, we force Environment to play only in response to System by making System win as soon as there is a process where Environment has played more letters than System (see Condition (d) in Table 2).

If $\gamma$ is not halting, the configurations in $\mathbb{C}(\gamma)$ will not be winning for System. Hence, System will have to move to win (Condition (a)).

**Table 2.** Acceptance conditions for the game simulating a 2CM

**Requirements for System**

**(a)** For all $t = (q, \mathsf{op}, q') \in Q$:

$$\mathcal{F}_{(q,t)} = \bigcup_{\hat{q} \in Q} \{[\langle\!\langle q \rangle\!\rangle = 1,\ \langle\!\langle t \rangle\!\rangle = 1,\ \langle\!\langle a_i \rangle\!\rangle = 1,\ \langle\!\langle \hat{q}^2 b^2 \rangle\!\rangle \geq 1,\ (L_{\checkmark} \setminus \{\langle\!\langle \hat{q}^2 b^2 \rangle\!\rangle\}) \geq 0]\} \quad \text{if } \mathsf{op} = \mathsf{c}_i\text{++}$$

$$\mathcal{F}_{(q,t)} = \bigcup_{\hat{q} \in Q} \{[\langle\!\langle q \rangle\!\rangle = 1,\ \langle\!\langle t \rangle\!\rangle = 1,\ \langle\!\langle a_i^3 b^2 \rangle\!\rangle = 1,\ \langle\!\langle \hat{q}^2 b^2 \rangle\!\rangle \geq 1,\ (L_{\checkmark} \setminus \{\langle\!\langle \hat{q}^2 b^2 \rangle\!\rangle\}) \geq 0]\} \quad \text{if } \mathsf{op} = \mathsf{c}_i\text{--}$$

$$\mathcal{F}_{(q,t)} = \bigcup_{\hat{q} \in Q} \{[\langle\!\langle q \rangle\!\rangle = 1,\ \langle\!\langle t \rangle\!\rangle = 1,\ \langle\!\langle a_i^2 b^2 \rangle\!\rangle = 0,\ \langle\!\langle \hat{q}^2 b^2 \rangle\!\rangle \geq 1,\ (L_{\checkmark} \setminus \{\langle\!\langle \hat{q}^2 b^2 \rangle\!\rangle, \langle\!\langle a_i^2 b^2 \rangle\!\rangle\}) \geq 0]\} \quad \text{if } \mathsf{op} = \mathsf{c}_i\text{==}0$$

**(b)** For all $t = (q_0, \mathsf{op}, q') \in Q$ such that $\mathsf{op} \in \{\mathsf{c}_i\text{++}, \mathsf{c}_i\text{==}0\}$:

$$\mathcal{F}_t = \{[\langle\!\langle q_0 \rangle\!\rangle = 1,\ \langle\!\langle t \rangle\!\rangle = 1,\ \langle\!\langle a_i \rangle\!\rangle = 1,\ \ell_0 \geq 0]\} \quad \text{if } \mathsf{op} = \mathsf{c}_i\text{++}$$

$$\mathcal{F}_t = \{[\langle\!\langle q_0 \rangle\!\rangle = 1,\ \langle\!\langle t \rangle\!\rangle = 1,\ \ell_0 \geq 0]\} \quad \text{if } \mathsf{op} = \mathsf{c}_i\text{==}0$$

**(c)** For all $t = (q, \mathsf{op}, q') \in Q$:

$$\mathcal{F}_{(q,t,q')} = \{[\langle\!\langle q^2 b \rangle\!\rangle = 1,\ \langle\!\langle t^2 b \rangle\!\rangle = 1,\ \langle\!\langle a_i^2 b \rangle\!\rangle = 1,\ \langle\!\langle q' \rangle\!\rangle = 1,\ L_{\checkmark} \geq 0]\} \quad \text{if } \mathsf{op} = \mathsf{c}_i\text{++}$$

$$\mathcal{F}_{(q,t,q')} = \{[\langle\!\langle q^2 b \rangle\!\rangle = 1,\ \langle\!\langle t^2 b \rangle\!\rangle = 1,\ \langle\!\langle a_i^4 b^3 \rangle\!\rangle = 1,\ \langle\!\langle q' \rangle\!\rangle = 1,\ L_{\checkmark} \geq 0]\} \quad \text{if } \mathsf{op} = \mathsf{c}_i\text{--}$$

$$\mathcal{F}_{(q,t,q')} = \{[\langle\!\langle q^2 b \rangle\!\rangle = 1,\ \langle\!\langle t^2 b \rangle\!\rangle = 1,\ L_{\checkmark} \geq 0]\} \quad \text{if } \mathsf{op} = \mathsf{c}_i\text{==}0$$

**Requirements for Environment**

**(d)** Let $L_{\mathsf{s<e}} = \{\ell \in L \mid (\sum_{\alpha \in A_{\mathsf{s}}} \ell(\alpha)) < \ell(b)\}$. For all $\ell \in L_{\mathsf{s<e}}$: $\mathcal{F}_\ell = [\ell \geq 1, (L \setminus \{\ell\}) \geq 0]$

**(e)** For all $t = (q, \mathsf{op}, q') \in Q$:

$$\mathcal{F}^{\mathsf{e}}_{(q,t)} = \left\{ \begin{array}{l} [\langle\!\langle qb \rangle\!\rangle = 1,\ \langle\!\langle t \rangle\!\rangle = 1,\ \langle\!\langle a_i \rangle\!\rangle = 1,\ L_{\checkmark} \geq 0],\ [\langle\!\langle q \rangle\!\rangle = 1,\ \langle\!\langle tb \rangle\!\rangle = 1,\ \langle\!\langle a_i \rangle\!\rangle = 1,\ L_{\checkmark} \geq 0], \\ [\langle\!\langle q \rangle\!\rangle = 1,\ \langle\!\langle t \rangle\!\rangle = 1,\ \langle\!\langle a_i b \rangle\!\rangle = 1,\ L_{\checkmark} \geq 0],\ [\langle\!\langle qb \rangle\!\rangle = 1,\ \langle\!\langle tb \rangle\!\rangle = 1,\ \langle\!\langle a_i \rangle\!\rangle = 1,\ L_{\checkmark} \geq 0], \\ [\langle\!\langle qb \rangle\!\rangle = 1,\ \langle\!\langle t \rangle\!\rangle = 1,\ \langle\!\langle a_i b \rangle\!\rangle = 1,\ L_{\checkmark} \geq 0],\ [\langle\!\langle q \rangle\!\rangle = 1,\ \langle\!\langle tb \rangle\!\rangle = 1,\ \langle\!\langle a_i b \rangle\!\rangle = 1,\ L_{\checkmark} \geq 0] \end{array} \right\} \quad \text{if } \mathsf{op} = \mathsf{c}_i\text{++}$$

$$\mathcal{F}^{\mathsf{e}}_{(q,t)} = \left\{ \begin{array}{l} [\langle\!\langle qb \rangle\!\rangle = 1,\ \langle\!\langle t \rangle\!\rangle = 1,\ \langle\!\langle a_i^3 b^2 \rangle\!\rangle = 1,\ L_{\checkmark} \geq 0],\ [\langle\!\langle q \rangle\!\rangle = 1,\ \langle\!\langle tb \rangle\!\rangle = 1,\ \langle\!\langle a_i^3 b^2 \rangle\!\rangle = 1,\ L_{\checkmark} \geq 0], \\ [\langle\!\langle q \rangle\!\rangle = 1,\ \langle\!\langle t \rangle\!\rangle = 1,\ \langle\!\langle a_i^3 b^3 \rangle\!\rangle = 1,\ L_{\checkmark} \geq 0],\ [\langle\!\langle qb \rangle\!\rangle = 1,\ \langle\!\langle tb \rangle\!\rangle = 1,\ \langle\!\langle a_i^3 b^2 \rangle\!\rangle = 1,\ L_{\checkmark} \geq 0], \\ [\langle\!\langle qb \rangle\!\rangle = 1,\ \langle\!\langle t \rangle\!\rangle = 1,\ \langle\!\langle a_i^3 b^3 \rangle\!\rangle = 1,\ L_{\checkmark} \geq 0],\ [\langle\!\langle q \rangle\!\rangle = 1,\ \langle\!\langle tb \rangle\!\rangle = 1,\ \langle\!\langle a_i^3 b^3 \rangle\!\rangle = 1,\ L_{\checkmark} \geq 0] \end{array} \right\} \quad \text{if } \mathsf{op} = \mathsf{c}_i\text{--}$$

$$\mathcal{F}^{\mathsf{e}}_{(q,t)} = \{[\langle\!\langle qb \rangle\!\rangle = 1,\ \langle\!\langle t \rangle\!\rangle = 1,\ L_{\checkmark} \geq 0],\ [\langle\!\langle q \rangle\!\rangle = 1,\ \langle\!\langle tb \rangle\!\rangle = 1,\ L_{\checkmark} \geq 0]\} \quad \text{if } \mathsf{op} = \mathsf{c}_i\text{==}0$$

**(f)** For all $t = (q, \mathsf{op}, q') \in Q$:

$$\mathcal{F}^{\mathsf{e}}_{(q,t,q')} = \left\{ \begin{array}{l} [\langle\!\langle q' \rangle\!\rangle = 1,\ \langle\!\langle q^2 b \rangle\!\rangle = 1,\ \langle\!\langle t^2 b \rangle\!\rangle \geq 0,\ \langle\!\langle a_i^2 b \rangle\!\rangle \geq 0,\ L_{\checkmark} \geq 0], \\ [\langle\!\langle q' \rangle\!\rangle = 1,\ \langle\!\langle q^2 b \rangle\!\rangle \geq 0,\ \langle\!\langle t^2 b \rangle\!\rangle = 1,\ \langle\!\langle a_i^2 b \rangle\!\rangle \geq 0,\ L_{\checkmark} \geq 0], \\ [\langle\!\langle q' \rangle\!\rangle = 1,\ \langle\!\langle q^2 b \rangle\!\rangle \geq 0,\ \langle\!\langle t^2 b \rangle\!\rangle \geq 0,\ \langle\!\langle a_i^2 b \rangle\!\rangle = 1,\ L_{\checkmark} \geq 0], \\ [\langle\!\langle q' b \rangle\!\rangle = 1,\ \langle\!\langle q^2 b \rangle\!\rangle \geq 0,\ \langle\!\langle t^2 b \rangle\!\rangle \geq 0,\ \langle\!\langle a_i^2 b \rangle\!\rangle \geq 0,\ L_{\checkmark} \geq 0] \end{array} \right\} \quad \text{if } \mathsf{op} = \mathsf{c}_i\text{++}$$

$$\mathcal{F}^{\mathsf{e}}_{(q,t,q')} = \left\{ \begin{array}{l} [\langle\!\langle q' \rangle\!\rangle = 1,\ \langle\!\langle q^2 b \rangle\!\rangle = 1,\ \langle\!\langle t^2 b \rangle\!\rangle \geq 0,\ \langle\!\langle a_i^4 b^3 \rangle\!\rangle \geq 0,\ L_{\checkmark} \geq 0], \\ [\langle\!\langle q' \rangle\!\rangle = 1,\ \langle\!\langle q^2 b \rangle\!\rangle \geq 0,\ \langle\!\langle t^2 b \rangle\!\rangle = 1,\ \langle\!\langle a_i^4 b^3 \rangle\!\rangle \geq 0,\ L_{\checkmark} \geq 0], \\ [\langle\!\langle q' \rangle\!\rangle = 1,\ \langle\!\langle q^2 b \rangle\!\rangle \geq 0,\ \langle\!\langle t^2 b \rangle\!\rangle \geq 0,\ \langle\!\langle a_i^4 b^3 \rangle\!\rangle = 1,\ L_{\checkmark} \geq 0], \\ [\langle\!\langle q' b \rangle\!\rangle = 1,\ \langle\!\langle q^2 b \rangle\!\rangle \geq 0,\ \langle\!\langle t^2 b \rangle\!\rangle \geq 0,\ \langle\!\langle a_i^4 b^3 \rangle\!\rangle \geq 0,\ L_{\checkmark} \geq 0] \end{array} \right\} \quad \text{if } \mathsf{op} = \mathsf{c}_i\text{--}$$

$$\mathcal{F}^{\mathsf{e}}_{(q,t,q')} = \left\{ \begin{array}{l} [\langle\!\langle q' \rangle\!\rangle = 1,\ \langle\!\langle q^2 b \rangle\!\rangle = 1,\ \langle\!\langle t^2 b \rangle\!\rangle \geq 0,\ L_{\checkmark} \geq 0], \\ [\langle\!\langle q' \rangle\!\rangle = 1,\ \langle\!\langle q^2 b \rangle\!\rangle \geq 0,\ \langle\!\langle t^2 b \rangle\!\rangle = 1,\ L_{\checkmark} \geq 0], \\ [\langle\!\langle q' b \rangle\!\rangle = 1,\ \langle\!\langle q^2 b \rangle\!\rangle \geq 0,\ \langle\!\langle t^2 b \rangle\!\rangle \geq 0,\ \langle\!\langle a_i^4 b^3 \rangle\!\rangle \geq 0,\ L_{\checkmark} \geq 0] \end{array} \right\} \quad \text{if } \mathsf{op} = \mathsf{c}_i\text{==}0$$

The first transition chosen by System must start from the initial state of $M$. This is enforced by Condition (b).

Once System has moved, Environment will move other processes to leave accepting configurations. The only possible move for her is to add $b$ on a process in locations $\langle\!\langle q \rangle\!\rangle$, $\langle\!\langle t \rangle\!\rangle$, and $\langle\!\langle a_i \rangle\!\rangle$, if $t$ is a transition incrementing counter $\mathsf{c}_i$ (respectively $\langle\!\langle a_i^3 b^2 \rangle\!\rangle$ if $t$ is a transition decrementing counter $\mathsf{c}_i$). All other $\mathcal{G}$-configurations accessible by Environment from already defined accepting configurations are winning for System, as established in Condition (e).

System can now encode the successor configuration of $M$, according to the chosen transition, by moving a process to the destination state of the transition (see Condition (c)).

Finally, Environment makes the necessary transitions for the configuration to be a valid $\mathcal{G}$-configuration. If she deviates, System wins (see Condition (f)).

If Environment reaches a configuration in $\mathbb{C}(\gamma)$ for $\gamma \in F$, System can win by moving the process in $\langle\!\langle q_h \rangle\!\rangle$ to $\langle\!\langle q_h^2 \rangle\!\rangle$. From there, all the configurations reachable by Environment are also winning for System:

$$\mathcal{F}_F = \{[\langle\!\langle q_h^2 \rangle\!\rangle = 1, L_{\checkmark} \geq 0] \ , \ [\langle\!\langle q_h^2 b \rangle\!\rangle = 1, L_{\checkmark} \geq 0] \ , \ [\langle\!\langle q_h^2 b^2 \rangle\!\rangle = 1, L_{\checkmark} \geq 0]\} \, .$$

Finally, the acceptance condition is given by

$$\mathcal{F} = \bigcup_{\ell \in L_{\mathsf{s}<\mathsf{e}}} \mathcal{F}_\ell \cup \bigcup_{t=(q_0,\mathsf{op},q')\in\Delta} \mathcal{F}_t \cup \bigcup_{t=(q,\mathsf{op},q')\in\Delta} (\mathcal{F}_{(q,t)} \cup \mathcal{F}^{\mathsf{e}}_{(q,t)} \cup \mathcal{F}_{(q,t,q')} \cup \mathcal{F}^{\mathsf{e}}_{(q,t,q')}) \cup \mathcal{F}_F \, .$$

Note that a correct play can end in three different ways: either there is a process in $\langle\!\langle q_h \rangle\!\rangle$ and System moves it to $\langle\!\langle q_h^2 \rangle\!\rangle$, or System has no transition to pick, or there are not enough processes in $\ell_0$ for System to simulate a new transition. Only the first kind is winning for System.

We can show that there is an accepting run in $M$ iff there is some $k$ such that System has a winning $C_{(0,0,k)}$-strategy for $\mathcal{G}$. □

## 6 Conclusion

There are several questions that we left open and that are interesting in their own right due to their fundamental character. Moreover, in the decidable cases, it will be worthwhile to provide tight bounds on cutoffs and the algorithmic complexity of the decision problem. Like in [7, 15, 16, 30, 31], our strategies allow the system to have a global view of the whole program run executed so far. However, it is also perfectly natural to consider uniform local strategies where each process only sees its own actions and possibly those that are revealed according to some causal dependencies. This is, e.g., the setting considered in [3, 18] for a fixed number of processes and in [25] for parameterized systems over ring architectures.

Moreover, we would like to study a parameterized version of the control problem [35] where, in addition to a specification, a program in terms of an arena is already given but has to be controlled in a way such that the specification is satisfied. Finally, our synthesis results crucially rely on the fact that the number of processes in each execution is finite. It would be interesting to consider the case with potentially infinitely many processes.

## References


1. P. A. Abdulla, R. Mayr, A. Sangnier, and J. Sproston. Solving parity games on integer vectors. In P. R. D'Argenio and H. C. Melgratti, editors, *CONCUR 2013 - Concurrency Theory - 24th International Conference, CONCUR 2013, Buenos Aires, Argentina, August 27-30, 2013. Proceedings*, volume 8052 of *Lecture Notes in Computer Science*, pages 106–120. Springer, 2013.
2. B. Bérard, B. Bollig, M. Lehaut, and N. Sznajder. Parameterized synthesis for fragments of first-order logic over data words. *CoRR*, abs/1910.14294, 2019.
3. R. Beutner, B. Finkbeiner, and J. Hecking-Harbusch. Translating Asynchronous Games for Distributed Synthesis. In W. Fokkink and R. van Glabbeek, editors, *30th International Conference on Concurrency Theory (CONCUR 2019)*, volume 140 of *Leibniz International Proceedings in Informatics (LIPIcs)*, pages 26:1–26:16, Dagstuhl, Germany, 2019. Schloss Dagstuhl–Leibniz-Zentrum fuer Informatik.
4. R. Bloem, S. Jacobs, A. Khalimov, I. Konnov, S. Rubin, H. Veith, and J. Widder. *Decidability of Parameterized Verification.* Morgan & Claypool Publishers, 2015.
5. M. Bojanczyk, C. David, A. Muscholl, T. Schwentick, and L. Segoufin. Two-variable logic on data words. *ACM Trans. Comput. Log.*, 12(4):27, 2011.
6. T. Brázdil, P. Jancar, and A. Kucera. Reachability games on extended vector addition systems with states. In *ICALP'10, Part II*, volume 6199 of *LNCS*, pages 478–489. Springer, 2010.
7. B. Brütsch and W. Thomas. Playing games in the Baire space. In *Proc. Cassting Workshop on Games for the Synthesis of Complex Systems and 3rd Int. Workshop on Synthesis of Complex Parameters*, volume 220 of *EPTCS*, pages 13–25, 2016.
8. J. R. Büchi and L. H. Landweber. Solving sequential conditions by finite-state strategies. *Transactions of the American Mathematical Society*, 138:295–311, Apr. 1969.
9. A. Church. Applications of recursive arithmetic to the problem of circuit synthesis. In *Summaries of the Summer Institute of Symbolic Logic – Volume 1*, pages 3–50. Institute for Defense Analyses, 1957.
10. J. Courtois and S. Schmitz. Alternating vector addition systems with states. In E. Csuhaj-Varjú, M. Dietzfelbinger, and Z. Ésik, editors, *Mathematical Foundations of Computer Science 2014 - 39th International Symposium, MFCS 2014, Budapest, Hungary, August 25-29, 2014. Proceedings, Part I*, volume 8634 of *Lecture Notes in Computer Science*, pages 220–231. Springer, 2014.
11. S. Demri, D. D'Souza, and R. Gascon. Temporal logics of repeating values. *J. Log. Comput.*, 22(5):1059–1096, 2012.
12. S. Demri and R. Lazić. LTL with the freeze quantifier and register automata. *ACM Transactions on Computational Logic*, 10(3), 2009.
13. J. Esparza. Keeping a crowd safe: On the complexity of parameterized verification. In *STACS'14*, volume 25 of *Leibniz International Proceedings in Informatics*, pages 1–10. Leibniz-Zentrum für Informatik, 2014.
14. K. Etessami, M. Y. Vardi, and T. Wilke. First-order logic with two variables and unary temporal logic. *Inf. Comput.*, 179(2):279–295, 2002.
15. L. Exibard, E. Filiot, and P.-A. Reynier. Synthesis of Data Word Transducers. In W. Fokkink and R. van Glabbeek, editors, *30th International Conference on Concurrency Theory (CONCUR 2019)*, volume 140 of *Leibniz International Proceedings in Informatics (LIPIcs)*, pages 24:1–24:15, Dagstuhl, Germany, 2019. Schloss Dagstuhl–Leibniz-Zentrum fuer Informatik.

16. D. Figueira and M. Praveen. Playing with repetitions in data words using energy games. In A. Dawar and E. Grädel, editors, *Proceedings of the 33rd Annual ACM/IEEE Symposium on Logic in Computer Science, LICS 2018, Oxford, UK, July 09-12, 2018*, pages 404–413. ACM, 2018.
17. D. Figueira and M. Praveen. Playing with repetitions in data words using energy games. *arXiv preprint arXiv:1802.07435*, 2018.
18. B. Finkbeiner and E. Olderog. Petri games: Synthesis of distributed systems with causal memory. *Inf. Comput.*, 253:181–203, 2017.
19. H. Frenkel, O. Grumberg, and S. Sheinvald. An automata-theoretic approach to model-checking systems and specifications over infinite data domains. *J. Autom. Reasoning*, 63(4):1077–1101, 2019.
20. M. Fürer. The computational complexity of the unconstrained limited domino problem (with implications for logical decision problems). In E. Börger, G. Hasenjaeger, and D. Rödding, editors, *Logic and Machines: Decision Problems and Complexity, Proceedings of the Symposium "Rekursive Kombinatorik" held from May 23-28, 1983 at the Institut für Mathematische Logik und Grundlagenforschung der Universität Münster/Westfalen*, volume 171 of *Lecture Notes in Computer Science*, pages 312–319. Springer, 1983.
21. P. Gastin and N. Sznajder. Fair synthesis for asynchronous distributed systems. *ACM Transactions on Computational Logic*, 14(2:9), 2013.
22. E. Grädel, P. G. Kolaitis, and M. Y. Vardi. On the decision problem for two-variable first-order logic. *Bulletin of Symbolic Logic*, 3(1):53–69, 1997.
23. W. Hanf. Model-theoretic methods in the study of elementary logic. In J. W. Addison, L. Henkin, and A. Tarski, editors, *The Theory of Models*. North-Holland, Amsterdam, 1965.
24. F. Horn, W. Thomas, N. Wallmeier, and M. Zimmermann. Optimal strategy synthesis for request-response games. *RAIRO - Theor. Inf. and Applic.*, 49(3):179–203, 2015.
25. S. Jacobs and R. Bloem. Parameterized synthesis. *Logical Methods in Computer Science*, 10(1), 2014.
26. S. Jacobs, L. Tentrup, and M. Zimmermann. Distributed synthesis for parameterized temporal logics. *Inf. Comput.*, 262(Part):311–328, 2018.
27. P. Jancar. On reachability-related games on vector addition systems with states. In *RP'15*, volume 9328 of *LNCS*, pages 50–62. Springer, 2015.
28. M. Jenkins, J. Ouaknine, A. Rabinovich, and J. Worrell. The church synthesis problem with metric. In M. Bezem, editor, *Computer Science Logic, 25th International Workshop / 20th Annual Conference of the EACSL, CSL 2011, September 12-15, 2011, Bergen, Norway, Proceedings*, volume 12 of *LIPIcs*, pages 307–321. Schloss Dagstuhl - Leibniz-Zentrum fuer Informatik, 2011.
29. M. Kaminski and N. Francez. Finite-memory automata. *Theoretical Computer Science*, 134(2):329–363, 1994.
30. A. Khalimov and O. Kupferman. Register-Bounded Synthesis. In W. Fokkink and R. van Glabbeek, editors, *30th International Conference on Concurrency Theory (CONCUR 2019)*, volume 140 of *Leibniz International Proceedings in Informatics (LIPIcs)*, pages 25:1–25:16, Dagstuhl, Germany, 2019. Schloss Dagstuhl–Leibniz-Zentrum fuer Informatik.
31. A. Khalimov, B. Maderbacher, and R. Bloem. Bounded synthesis of register transducers. In S. K. Lahiri and C. Wang, editors, *Automated Technology for Verification and Analysis - 16th International Symposium, ATVA 2018, Los Angeles, CA, USA, October 7-10, 2018, Proceedings*, volume 11138 of *Lecture Notes in Computer Science*, pages 494–510. Springer, 2018.

32. E. Kieronski and M. Otto. Small substructures and decidability issues for first-order logic with two variables. *J. Symb. Log.*, 77(3):729–765, 2012.
33. L. Libkin, T. Tan, and D. Vrgoc. Regular expressions for data words. *J. Comput. Syst. Sci.*, 81(7):1278–1297, 2015.
34. M. L. Minsky. *Computation: Finite and Infinite Machines.* Prentice Hall, Upper Saddle River, NJ, USA, 1967.
35. A. Muscholl. Automated synthesis of distributed controllers. In M. M. Halldórsson, K. Iwama, N. Kobayashi, and B. Speckmann, editors, *Automata, Languages, and Programming - 42nd International Colloquium, ICALP 2015, Kyoto, Japan, July 6-10, 2015, Proceedings, Part II*, volume 9135 of *Lecture Notes in Computer Science*, pages 11–27. Springer, 2015.
36. A. Pnueli and R. Rosner. Distributed reactive systems are hard to synthesize. In *31st Annual Symposium on Foundations of Computer Science, St. Louis, Missouri, USA, October 22-24, 1990, Volume II*, pages 746–757. IEEE Computer Society, 1990.
37. M. O. Rabin. *Automata on infinite objects and Church's problem.* Number 13 in Regional Conference Series in Mathematics. American Mathematical Soc., 1972.
38. J. Raskin, M. Samuelides, and L. V. Begin. Games for counting abstractions. *Electr. Notes Theor. Comput. Sci.*, 128(6):69–85, 2005.
39. A. Sangnier and O. Stietel. Private communication, 2020.
40. L. Schröder, D. Kozen, S. Milius, and T. Wißmann. Nominal automata with name binding. In J. Esparza and A. S. Murawski, editors, *Foundations of Software Science and Computation Structures - 20th International Conference, FOSSACS 2017, Held as Part of the European Joint Conferences on Theory and Practice of Software, ETAPS 2017, Uppsala, Sweden, April 22-29, 2017, Proceedings*, volume 10203 of *Lecture Notes in Computer Science*, pages 124–142, 2017.
41. T. Schwentick and K. Barthelmann. Local normal forms for first-order logic with applications to games and automata. In *Annual Symposium on Theoretical Aspects of Computer Science*, pages 444–454. Springer, 1998.
42. W. Thomas. Church's problem and a tour through automata theory. In *Pillars of Computer Science, Essays Dedicated to Boris (Boaz) Trakhtenbrot on the Occasion of His 85th Birthday*, volume 4800 of *Lecture Notes in Computer Science*, pages 635–655. Springer, 2008.
43. Y. Velner and A. Rabinovich. Church synthesis problem for noisy input. In M. Hofmann, editor, *Foundations of Software Science and Computational Structures - 14th International Conference, FOSSACS 2011, Held as Part of the Joint European Conferences on Theory and Practice of Software, ETAPS 2011, Saarbrücken, Germany, March 26-April 3, 2011. Proceedings*, volume 6604 of *Lecture Notes in Computer Science*, pages 275–289. Springer, 2011.

# 8

# General Supervised Learning as Change Propagation with Delta Lenses

Zinovy Diskin(✉)

McMaster University, Hamilton, Canada
diskinz@mcmaster.ca

**Abstract.** Delta lenses are an established mathematical framework for modelling and designing bidirectional model transformations (Bx). Following the recent observations by Fong et al, the paper extends the delta lens framework with a a new ingredient: learning over a parameterized space of model transformations seen as functors. We will define a notion of an asymmetric learning delta lens with amendment (ala-lens), and show how ala-lenses can be organized into a symmetric monoidal (sm) category. We also show that sequential and parallel composition of well-behaved (wb) ala-lenses are also wb so that wb ala-lenses constitute a full sm-subcategory of ala-lenses.

## 1 Introduction

The goal of the paper is to develop a formal model of *supervised learning* in a very general context of *bidirectional model transformation* or *Bx*, i.e., synchronization of two arbitrary complex structures (called *models*) related by a transformation.[1] Rather than learning parameterized functions between Euclidean spaces as is typical for machine learning (ML), we will consider learning mappings between model spaces and formalize them as parameterized functors between categories, $f\colon P{\times}\mathbf{A} \to \mathbf{B}$, with $P$ being a parameter space. The basic ML-notion of a *training pair* $(A, B') \in \mathbf{A}_0 \times \mathbf{B}_0$ will be considered as an inconsistency between models caused by a change (*delta*) $v\colon B \to B'$ of the target model $B = f(p, A)$, $p \in P$, that was first consistent with $A$ w.r.t. the transformation (functor) $f(p, \_)$. An inconsistency is repaired by an appropriate change of the source structure, $u\colon A \to A'$, changing the parameter $p$ to $p'$, and an *amendment* of the target structure $v^{@}\colon B' \to B^{@}$ so that $f(p', A') = B^{@}$ is a consistent state of the parameterized two-model system.

The setting above without parameterization and learning (i.e., $p' = p$ always holds), and without amendment ($v^{@} = \mathsf{id}_{B'}$ always holds), is well known in the Bx literature under the name of *delta lenses*— mathematical structures, in

[1]Term *Bx* refers to a wide area including file synchronization, data exchange in databases, and model synchronization in Model-Driven software Engineering (MDE), see [7] for a survey. In the present paper, Bx will mainly refer to Bx in the MDE context.

which consistency restoration via change propagation is modelled by functorial-like algebraic operations over categories [12,6]. There are several types of delta lenses tailored for modelling different synchronization tasks and scenarios, particularly, symmetric and asymmetric. In the paper, we only consider asymmetric delta lenses and will often omit explicit mentioning these attributes. Despite their extra-generality, (delta) lenses have been proved useful in the design and implementation of practical model synchronization systems with triple graph grammars (TGG) [5,2]; enriching lenses with amendment is a recent extension of the framework motivated and formalized in [11]. A major advantage of the lens framework for synchronization is its compositionality: a lens satisfying several equational laws specifying basic synchronization requirements is called *well-behaved (wb)*, and basic lens theorems state that sequential and parallel composition of wb lenses is again wb. In practical applications, it allows the designer of a complex synchronizer to avoid integration testing: if elementary synchronizers are tested and proved to be wb, their composition is automatically wb too.

The present paper makes the following contributions to the delta lens framework for Bx. a) We motivate model synchronization enriched with learning and, moreover, with *categorical* learning, in which the parameter space is a category, and introduce the notion of a *wb asymmetric learning (delta) lens* with *amendment* (a *wb ala-lens*) (this is the content of Sect. 3). b) We prove compositionality of wb ala-lenses and show how their universe can be organized into a symmetric monoidal (sm) category (Theorems 1-3 in Sect. 4). All proofs (rather straightforward but notationally laborious) can be found in the long version of the paper [9]. One more compositional result is c) a definition of a *compositional bidirectional transformation language* (Def. 6) that formalizes an important requirement to model synchronization tools, which (surprisingly) is missing from the Bx literature. Background Sect. 2 provides a simple example demonstrating main concepts of Bx and delta lenses in the MDE context. Section 5 briefly surveys related work, and Sect. 6 concludes.

*Notation.* Given a category $\mathbf{A}$, its objects are denoted by capital letters $A$, $A'$, etc. to recall that in MDE applications, objects are complex structures, which themselves have elements $a, a', ....$; the collection of all objects of category $\mathbf{A}$ is denoted by $\mathbf{A}_0$. An arrow with domain $A \in \mathbf{A}_0$ is written as $u\colon A \to \_$ or $u \in \mathbf{A}(A, \_)$; we also write $\mathsf{dom}(u) = A$ (and sometimes $u^{\mathsf{dom}} = A$ to shorten formulas). Similarly, formula $u\colon \_ \to A'$ denotes an arrow with codomain $u.\mathsf{cod} = A'$. Given a functor $f\colon \mathbf{A} \to \mathbf{B}$, its object function is denoted by $f_0\colon \mathbf{A}_0 \to \mathbf{B}_0$.

A subcategory $\mathbf{B} \subset \mathbf{A}$ is called *wide* if it has the same objects. All categories we consider in the paper are small.

## 2 Background: Update propagation and delta lenses

Although Bx ideas work well only in domains conforming to the slogan *any implementation satisfying the specification is good enough* such as code generation (see [10] for discussion), and have limited applications in databases (only so called updatable views can be treated in the Bx-way), we will employ a simple database example: it allows demonstrating the core ideas without any special domain knowledge required by typical Bx-amenable areas. The presentation will be semi-formal as our goal is to motivate the delta lens formalism that abstracts the details away rather than formalize the example as such.

## 2.1 Why deltas.

Bx-lenses first appeared in the work on file synchronization, and if we have two sets of strings, say, $B = \{\text{John}, \text{Mary}\}$ and $B' = \{\text{Jon}, \text{Mary}\}$, we can readily see the difference: John $\neq$ Jon but Mary = Mary. We thus have a structure in-between $B$ and $B'$ (which maybe rather complex if $B$ and $B'$ are big files), but this structure can be recovered by string matching and thus updates can be identified with pairs. The situation dramatically changes if $B$ and $B'$ are object structures, e.g., $B = \{o_1, o_2\}$ with $\mathsf{Name}(o_1) = \text{John}$, $\mathsf{Name}(o_2) = \text{Mary}$ and similarly $B' = \{o'_1, o'_2\}$ with $\mathsf{Name}(o'_1) = \text{Jon}$, $\mathsf{Name}(o'_2) = \text{Mary}$. Now string matching does not say too much: it may happen that $o_1$ and $o'_1$ are the same object (think of a typo in the dataset), while $o_2$ and $o'_2$ are different (although equally named) objects. Of course, for better matching we could use full names or ID numbers or something similar (called, in the database parlance, primary keys), but absolutely reliable keys are rare, and typos and bugs can compromise them anyway. Thus, for object structures that Bx needs to keep in sync, deltas between models need to be independently specified, e.g., by specifying a *sameness relation* $u \subset B \times B'$ between models. For example, $u = \{o_1, o'_1\}$ says that John@$B$ and Jon@$B'$ are the same person while Mary@$B$ and Mary@$B'$ are not. Hence, model spaces in Bx are categories (objects are models and arrows are update/delta specifications) rather than sets (codiscrete categories).

## 2.2 Consistency restoration via update propagation: An Example

Figure 1 presents a simple example of delta propagation for consistency restoration. Models consist of objects (in the sense of OO programming) with attributes (a.k.a. labelled records), e.g., the source model $A$ consists of three objects identified by their oids (object identifiers) #A, #J, #M (think about employees of some company) with attribute values as shown in the table: attribute Expr. refers to Experience measured by a number of years, and Depart. is the column of department names. The schema of the table, i.e., the triple $S_{\mathbf{A}}$ of attributes (Name, Expr., Depart.) with their domains of values ***String***, ***Integer***, ***String*** resp., determines a model space $\mathbf{A}$. A model $X \in \mathbf{A}$ is given by its set of objects $\mathsf{OID}^X$ together with three functions $\mathsf{Name}^X$, $\mathsf{Expr.}^X$, $\mathsf{Depart.}^X$ from the same domain $\mathsf{OID}^X$ to targets ***String***, ***Integer***, ***String*** resp., which are compactly specified by tables as shown for model $A$. The target model space $\mathbf{B}$ is given by a similar schema $S_{\mathbf{B}}$ consisting of two attributes. The $\mathbf{B}$-view $\mathsf{get}(X)$ of an $\mathbf{A}$-model $X$ is computed by selecting those oids $\#O \in \mathsf{OID}^X$ for which $\mathsf{Depart.}^X(\#O)$ is an *IT-department*, i.e., an element of the set $IT \stackrel{\text{def}}{=} \{\text{ML}, \text{DB}\}$. For example, the upper part of the figure shows the IT-view $B$ of model $A$.

We assume that all column names in schemas $S_{\mathbf{A}}$, and $S_{\mathbf{B}}$ are qualified by schema names, e.g., $\mathsf{OID}@S_{\mathbf{A}}$, $\mathsf{OID}@S_{\mathbf{B}}$ etc, so that schemas are disjoint except elementary domains like ***String*** etc. Also disjoint are OID-values, e.g., $\#\mathrm{J}@A$ and $\#\mathrm{J}@B$ are different elements, but constants like John and Mary are elements of set ***String*** shared by both schemas. To shorten long expressions in the diagrams, we will often omit qualifiers and write $\#J = \#J$ meaning $\#J@A = \#J@B$ or $\#J@B = \#J@B'$ depending on the context given by the diagram; often we will also write $\#J$ and $\#J'$ for such OIDs. Also, when we write $\#J = \#J$ inside block arrows denoting updates, we actually mean a pair, e.g., $(\#J@B, \#J@B')$.

Given two models over the same schema, say, $B$ and $B'$ over $S_{\mathbf{B}}$, an update $v\colon B \to B'$ is a relation $v \subset \mathsf{OID}^B \times \mathsf{OID}^{B'}$; if a schema contains several nodes, an update should provide a relation $v_N$ for each node $N$ in the schema.

Note an essential difference between the two parallel updates $v_1, v_2\colon B \to B'$ specified in the figure. Update $v_1$ says that John's name was changed to Jon (think of fixing a typo), and the experience data for Mary were also corrected (either because of a typo or, e.g., because the department started to use a new ML method for which Mary has a longer experience). Update $v_2$ specifies the same story for John but a new story for Mary: it says that Mary $\#M$ left the IT-view and Mary $\#M'$ is a new employee in one of IT-departments.

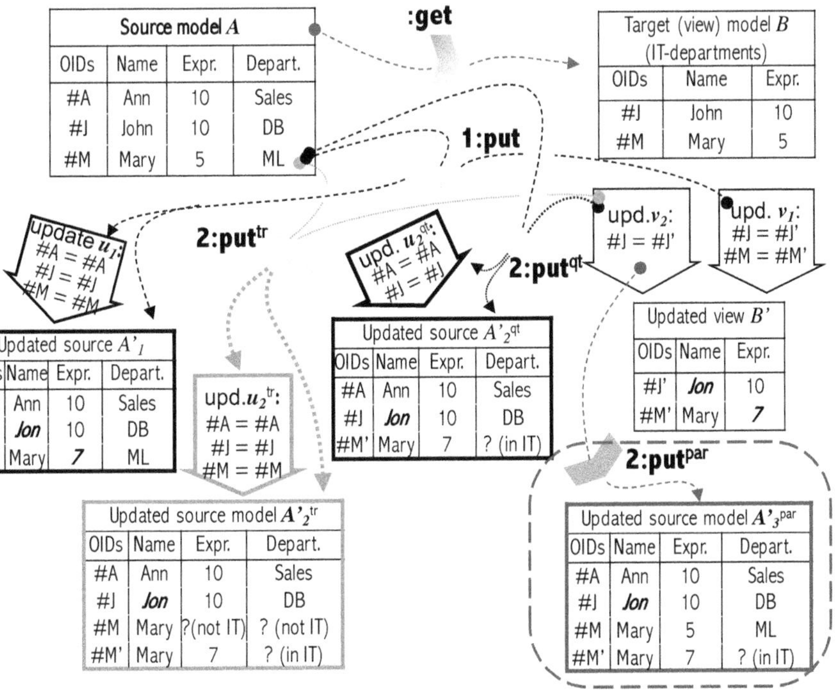


Fig. 1: Example of update propagation

## 2.3 Update propagation and update policies

The updated view $B'$ is inconsistent with the source $A$ and the latter is to be updated accordingly — we say that update $v$ is to be propagated back to $A$. Propagation of $v_1$ is easy: we just update accordingly the values of the attributes as shown in the figure in the block arrow $u_1: A \to A'_1$ (of black colour). Importantly, propagation needs two pieces of data: the view update $v_1$ and the original state $A$ of the source as shown in the figure by two data-flow lines into the chevron 1:put; the latter denotes invocation of the backward propagation operation put (read "put view update back to the source"). The quadruple $1 = (v_1, A, u_1, A')$ can be seen as an *instance* of operation put, hence the notation 1:put (borrowed from the UML).

Propagation of update $v_2$ is more challenging: Mary can disappear from the IT-view because a) she quit the company, b) she transitioned to a non-IT department, and c) the view definition has changed, e.g., the new view must only show employees with experience more than 5 years. Choosing between these possibilities is often called choosing an *(update) policy*. We will consider the case of changing the view in Sect. 3, and in the current section discuss policies a) and b) (ignore for a while the propagation scenario shown in blue in the right lower corner of the figure that shows policy c)).

For policy a), further referred to as *quiting* and briefly denoted by qt, the result of update propagation is shown in the figure with green colour: notice the update (block) arrow $u_2^{\mathsf{qt}}$ and its result, model $A_2'^{\mathsf{qt}}$, produced by invoking operation $\mathsf{put}^{\mathsf{qt}}$. Note that while we know the new employee Mary works in one of IT departments, we do not know in which one. This is specified with a special value '?' (a.k.a. labelled null in the database parlance).

For policy b), further referred to as *transition* and denoted tr, the result of update propagation is shown in the figure with orange colour: notice update arrow $u_2^{\mathsf{tr}}$ and its result, model $A_2'^{\mathsf{tr}}$ produced by $\mathsf{put}^{\mathsf{tr}}$. Mary #M is the old employee who transitioned to a new non-IT department, for which her expertize is unknown. Mary #M' is a new employee in one of IT-departments (we assume that the set of departments is not exhausted by those appearing in a particular state $A \in \mathbf{A}$). There are also updates whose backward propagation is uniquely defined and does not need a policy, e.g., update $v_1$ is such.

An important property of update propagations we have considered is that they restore consistency: the view of the updated source equals to the updated view initiated the update: $\mathsf{get}(A') = B'$; moreover, this equality extends for update arrows: $\mathsf{get}(u_i) = v_i$, $i = 1, 2$. Such extensions can be derived from view definitions if the latter are determined by so called monotonic queries (which encompass a wide class of practically useful queries including the Select-Project-Join class). For views defined by non-monotonic queries, in order to obtain get's action on source updates $u: A \to A'$, a suitable policy is to be added to the view definition (see [1,14,12] for details and discussion). Moreover, normally get preserves identity updates, $\mathsf{get}(\mathsf{id}_A) = \mathsf{id}_{\mathsf{get}(A)}$, and update composition: for any $u: A \to A'$ and $u': A' \to A''$, equality $\mathsf{get}(u; u') = \mathsf{get}(u); \mathsf{get}(u')$ holds.

## 2.4 Delta lenses

Our discussion of the example can be summarized in the following algebraic terms. We have two categories of *models* and *updates*, $\mathbf{A}$ and $\mathbf{B}$, and a functor get: $\mathbf{A} \to \mathbf{B}$ incrementally computing $\mathbf{B}$-views of $\mathbf{A}$-models (we will often write $A$.get for get$(A)$). We also suppose that for a chosen update policy, we have worked out precise procedures for how to propagate any view update backwards. This gives us a family of operations $\mathsf{put}_A : \mathbf{A}(A, \_) \leftarrow \mathbf{B}(A.\mathsf{get}, \_)$ indexed by $\mathbf{A}$-objects, $A \in \mathbf{A}_0$, for which we write $\mathsf{put}_A.v$ or $\mathsf{put}_A(v)$ interchangeably.

**Definition 1 (Delta Lenses ([12]))** Let $\mathbf{A}$, $\mathbf{B}$ be two categories. An *(asymmetric delta) lens* from $\mathbf{A}$ (the source of the lens) to $\mathbf{B}$ (the target) is a pair $\ell = (\mathsf{get}, \mathsf{put})$, where get: $\mathbf{A} \to \mathbf{B}$ is a functor and put is a family of operations $\mathsf{put}_A : \mathbf{A}(A, \_) \leftarrow \mathbf{B}(A.\mathsf{get}, \_)$ indexed by objects of $\mathbf{A}$, $A \in \mathbf{A}_0$. Given $A$, operation $\mathsf{put}_A$ maps any arrow $v$: $A.\mathsf{get} \to B'$ to an arrow $u$: $A \to A'$ such that $A'.\mathsf{get} = B'$. The last condition is called (co)discrete Putget law:

$$(\mathsf{Putget})_0 \quad (\mathsf{put}_A.v).\mathsf{cod}.\mathsf{get}_0 = v.\mathsf{cod} \text{ for all } A \in \mathbf{A}_0 \text{ and } v \in \mathbf{B}(A.\mathsf{get}, \_)$$

where $\mathsf{get}_0$ denotes the object function of functor get. We will write a lens as an arrow $\ell$: $\mathbf{A} \to \mathbf{B}$ going in the direction of get.

Note that family put corresponds to a chosen update policy, e.g., in terms of the example above, for the same view functor get, we have two families of put-operations, $\mathsf{put}^{\mathsf{qt}}$ and $\mathsf{put}^{\mathsf{tr}}$, corresponding to the two updated policies we discussed. These two policies determine two lenses $\ell^{\mathsf{qt}} = (\mathsf{get}, \mathsf{put}^{\mathsf{qt}})$ and $\ell^{\mathsf{tr}} = (\mathsf{get}, \mathsf{put}^{\mathsf{tr}})$ sharing the same get.

**Definition 2 (Well-behavedness)** A *(lens) equational law* is an equation to hold for all values of two variables: $A \in \mathbf{A}_0$ and $v$: $A.\mathsf{get} \to T'$. A lens is called *well-behaved (wb)* if the following two laws hold:

$$(\mathsf{Stability}) \quad \mathsf{id}_A = \mathsf{put}_A.\mathsf{id}_{A.\mathsf{get}} \text{ for all } A \in \mathbf{A}_0$$

$$(\mathsf{Putget}) \quad (\mathsf{put}_A.v).\mathsf{get} = v \text{ for all } A \in \mathbf{A}_0 \text{ and all } v \in \mathbf{B}(A.\mathsf{get}, \_)$$

*Remark 1.* Stability law says that a wb lens does nothing if nothing happens on the target side (no actions without triggers). Putget requires consistency after the backward propagation is finished. Note the distinction between the $\mathrm{Putget}_0$ condition included into the very definition of a lens, and the full Putget law required for the wb lenses. The former is needed to ensure smooth tiling of put-squares (i.e., arrow squares describing application of put to a view update and its result) both horizontally (for sequential composition) and vertically (not considered in the paper). The full Putget assures true consistency as considering a state $B'$ alone does not say much about the real update and elements of $B'$ cannot be properly interpreted. The real story is specified by delta $v$: $B \to B'$, and consistency restoration needs the full (PutGet) law as above. [2]

A more detailed trailer of lenses can be found in the long version [9].

[2]As shown in [6], the $\mathrm{Putget}_0$ condition is needed if we want to define operations put separately from the functor get: then we still need a function $\mathsf{get}_0$: $\mathbf{A}_0 \to \mathbf{B}_0$ and the codiscrete Putget law to ensure a reasonable behaviour of put.

# 3 Asymmetric Learning Lenses with Amendments

We will begin with a brief motivating discussion, and then proceed with formal definitions

## 3.1 Does Bx need categorical learning?

Enriching delta lenses with learning capabilities has a clear practical sense for Bx. Having a lens $(\mathsf{get}, \mathsf{put})$: $\mathbf{A} \to \mathbf{B}$ and inconsistency $A.\mathsf{get} \neq B'$, the idea of learning extends the notion of the search space and allows us to update the transformation itself so that the final consistency is achieved for a new transformation $\mathsf{get}'$: $A.\mathsf{get}' = B'$. For example, in the case shown in Fig. 1, disappearance of Mary #M in the updated view $B'$ can be caused by changing the view definition, which now requires to show only those employees whose experience is more than 5 years and hence Mary #M is to be removed from the view, while Mary #M' is a new IT-employee whose experience satisfies the new definition. Then the update $v_2$ can be propagated as shown in the bottom right corner of Fig. 1, where index par indicates a new update policy allowing for view definition (parameter) change.

To manage the extended search possibilities, we parameterize the space of transformations as a family of mappings $\mathsf{get}_p$: $\mathbf{A} \to \mathbf{B}$ indexed over some parameter space $p \in \mathbf{P}$. For example, we may define the IT-view to be parameterized by the experience of employees shown in the view (including *any* experience as a special parameter value). Then we have two interrelated propagation operations that map an update $B \rightsquigarrow B'$ to a parameter update $p \rightsquigarrow p'$ and a source update $A \rightsquigarrow A'$. Thus, the extended search space allows for new update policies that look for updating the parameter as an update propagation possibility. The possibility to update the transformation appears to be very natural in at least two important Bx scenarios: a) model transformation design and b) model transformation evolution (cf. [21]), which necessitates the enrichment of the delta lens framework with parameterization and learning. Note that all transformations $\mathsf{get}_p$, $p \in \mathbf{P}$ are to be elements of the same lens, and operations put are *not* indexed by $p$, hence, formalization of learning by considering a family of ordinary lenses would *not* do the job.

**Categorical vs. codiscrete learning** Suppose that the parameter $p$ is itself a set, e.g., the set of departments forming a view can vary depending on some context. Then an update from $p$ to $p'$ has a relational structure as discussed above, i.e., $e$: $p \to p'$ is a relation $e \subset p{\times}p'$ specifying which departments disappeared from the view and which are freshly added. This is a general phenomenon: as soon as parameters are structures (sets of objects or graphs of objects and attributes), a parameter change becomes a structured delta and the space of parameters gives rise to a category $\mathbf{P}$. The search/propagation procedure returns an arrow $e$: $p \to p'$ in this category, which updates the parameter value from $p$ to $p'$. Hence, a general model of supervised learning should assume $\mathbf{P}$ to be a category (and we say that learning is *categorical*). The case of the parameter space being a set is captured by considering a codiscrete category $\mathbf{P}$ whose only arrows are pairs of its objects; we call such learning *codiscrete.*

### 3.2 Ala-lenses

The notion of a *parameterized functor (p-functor)* is fundamental for ala-lenses, but is not a lens notion per se and is thus placed into Appendix Sect. A.1. We will work with its exponential (rather than equivalent product-based) formulation but will do uncurrying and currying back if necessary, and often using the same symbol for an arrow $f$ and its uncurried version $\check{f}$.

**Definition 3 (ala-lenses)** Let $\mathbf{A}$ and $\mathbf{B}$ be categories. An *ala-lens* from $\mathbf{A}$ (the *source* of the lens) to $\mathbf{B}$ (the *target*) is a pair $\ell = (\mathsf{get}, \mathsf{put})$ whose first component is a p-functor $\mathsf{get}\colon \mathbf{A} \xrightarrow{\mathbf{P}} \mathbf{B}$ and the second component is a triple of (families of) operations $\mathsf{put} = (\mathsf{put}^{\mathsf{upd}}_{p,A}, \mathsf{put}^{\mathsf{req}}_{p,A}, \mathsf{put}^{\mathsf{self}}_{p,A})$ indexed by pairs $p \in \mathbf{P}_0$, $A \in \mathbf{A}_0$; arities of the operations are specified below after we introduce some notation. Names $\mathsf{req}$ (for 'request') and $\mathsf{upd}$ (for 'update') are chosen to match the terminology in [17].

Categories $\mathbf{A}$, $\mathbf{B}$ are called *model spaces*, their objects are *models* and their arrows are *(model) updates* or *deltas.* Objects of $\mathbf{P}$ are called *parameters* and are denoted by small letters $p, p', ..$ rather than capital ones to avoid confusion with [17], in which capital $P$ is used for the entire parameter set. Arrows of $\mathbf{P}$ are called *parameter deltas.* For a parameter $p \in \mathbf{P}_0$, we write $\mathsf{get}_p$ for the functor $\mathsf{get}(p)\colon \mathbf{A} \to \mathbf{B}$ (read "get $\mathbf{B}$-views of $\mathbf{A}$"), and if $A \in \mathbf{A}_0$ is a source model, its $\mathsf{get}_p$-view is denoted by $\mathsf{get}_p(A)$ or $A.\mathsf{get}_p$ or even $A_p$ (so that $\__p$ becomes yet another notation for functor $\mathsf{get}_p$). Given a parameter delta $e\colon p \to p'$ and a source model $A \in \mathbf{A}_0$, the model delta $\mathsf{get}(e)\colon \mathsf{get}_p(A) \to \mathsf{get}_{p'}(A)$ will be denoted by $\mathsf{get}_e(A)$ or $e_S$ (rather than $A_e$ as we would like to keep capital letters for objects only). In the uncurried version, $\mathsf{get}_e(A)$ is nothing but $\check{\mathsf{get}}(e, \mathsf{id}_S)$

Since $\mathsf{get}_e$ is a natural transformation, for any delta $u\colon A \to A'$ we have a commutative square $e_S; u_{p'} = u_p; e_{A'}$ (whose diagonal is $\check{\mathsf{get}}(e, u)$). We will denote the diagonal of this square by $u.\mathsf{get}_e$ or $u_e\colon A_p \to A'_{p'}$. Thus, we use notation

$$(1)\quad \begin{aligned} A_p &\stackrel{\text{def}}{=} A.\mathsf{get}_p \stackrel{\text{def}}{=} \mathsf{get}_p(A) \stackrel{\text{def}}{=} \mathsf{get}(p)(A) \\ u_e &\stackrel{\text{def}}{=} u.\mathsf{get}_e \stackrel{\text{def}}{=} \mathsf{get}_e(u) \stackrel{\text{def}}{=} \mathsf{get}(e)(u) \stackrel{\text{def}}{=} e_S; u_{p'} \stackrel{\text{nat}}{=} u_p; e_{A'}\colon A_p \to A'_{p'} \end{aligned}$$

Now we describe operations $\mathsf{put}$. They all have the same indexing set $\mathbf{P}_0 \times \mathbf{A}_0$, and the same domain: for any index $p, A$ and any model delta $v\colon A_p \to B'$ in $\mathbf{B}$, the value $\mathsf{put}^{\mathbf{x}}_{p,A}(p, A)$, $\mathbf{x} \in \{\mathsf{req}, \mathsf{upd}, \mathsf{self}\}$ is defined and unique:

$$(2)\quad \begin{aligned} &\mathsf{put}^{\mathsf{upd}}_{p,A}\colon p \to p' && \text{is a parameter delta from } p, \\ &\mathsf{put}^{\mathsf{req}}_{p,A}\colon A \to A' && \text{is a model delta from } A, \\ &\mathsf{put}^{\mathsf{self}}_{p,A}\colon B' \to A'_{p'} && \text{is a model delta from } B' \\ & && \text{called the } \textit{amendment} \text{ and denoted by } v^{@}. \end{aligned}$$

Note that the definition of $\mathsf{put}^{\mathsf{self}}$ involves an equational dependency between all three operations: for all $A \in \mathbf{A}_0$, $v \in \mathbf{B}(A.\mathsf{get}, \_)$, we require

$$(\mathsf{Putget})_0 \quad (\mathsf{put}^{\mathsf{req}}_A.v).\mathsf{cod}.\mathsf{get}_{p'} = (v; \mathsf{put}^{\mathsf{self}}_A).\mathsf{cod} \text{ where } p' = (\mathsf{put}^{\mathsf{upd}}_A.v).\mathsf{cod}$$

We will write an ala-lens as an arrow $\ell = (\mathsf{get}, \mathsf{put})\colon \mathbf{A} \xrightarrow{\mathbf{P}} \mathbf{B}$.

A lens is called *(twice) codiscrete* if categories $\mathbf{A}$, $\mathbf{B}$, $\mathbf{P}$ are codiscrete and thus $\mathsf{get}\colon \mathbf{A} \xrightarrow{\mathbf{P}} \mathbf{B}$ is a parameterized function. If only $\mathbf{P}$ is codiscrete, we call $\ell$ a *codiscretely learning* delta lens, while if only model spaces are codiscrete, we call $\ell$ a *categorically learning* codiscrete lens.

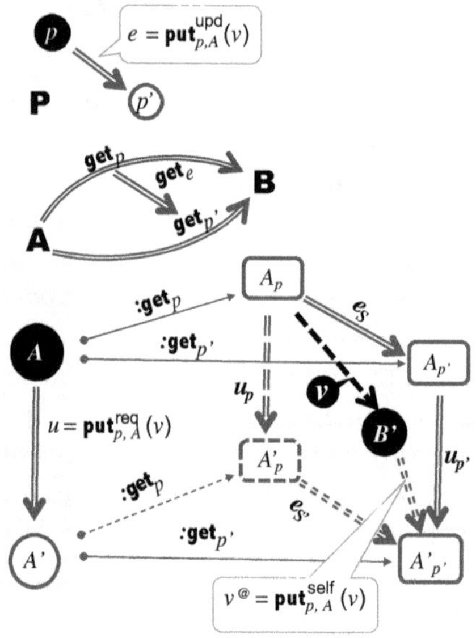


Fig. 2: Ala-lens operations

Diagram in Fig. 2 shows how a lens' operations are interrelated. The upper part shows an arrow $e\colon p \to p'$ in category $\mathbf{P}$ and two corresponding functors from $\mathbf{A}$ to $\mathbf{B}$. The lower part is to be seen as a 3D-prism with visible front face $AA_{p'}A'_{p'}A'$ and visible upper face $AA_pA_{p'}$, the bottom and two back faces are invisible, and the corresponding arrows are dashed. The prism denotes an algebraic term: given elements are shown with black fill and white font while derived elements are blue (recalls being mechanically computed) and blank (double-body arrows are considered as "blank"). The two pairs of arrows originating from $A$ and $A'$ are not blank because they denote pairs of nodes (the UML says *links*) rather than mappings/deltas between nodes. Equational definitions of deltas $e, u, v^@$ are written up in the three callouts near them. The right back face of the prism is formed by the two vertical derived deltas $u_p = u.\mathsf{get}_p$ and $u_{p'} = u.\mathsf{get}_{p'}$, and the two matching them horizontal derived deltas $e_S = \mathsf{get}_e(A)$ and $e_{A'} = \mathsf{get}_e(A')$; together they form a commutative square due to the naturality of $\mathsf{get}(e)$ as explained earlier.

**Definition 4 (Well-behavedness)** An ala-lens is called *well-behaved (wb)* if the following two laws hold for all $p \in \mathbf{P}_0$, $A \in \mathbf{A}_0$ and $v\colon A_p \to B'$:

(Stability) if $v = \mathsf{id}_{A_p}$ then all three propagated updates $e, u, v^@$ are identities:

$$\mathsf{put}^{\mathsf{upd}}_{p,A}(\mathsf{id}_{A_p}) = \mathsf{id}_p, \quad \mathsf{put}^{\mathsf{req}}_{p,A}(\mathsf{id}_{A_p}) = \mathsf{id}_S, \quad \mathsf{put}^{\mathsf{self}}_{p,A}(\mathsf{id}_{A_p}) = \mathsf{id}_{A_p}$$

(Putget) $(\mathsf{put}^{\mathsf{req}}_{p,A}.v).\mathsf{get}_e = v; v^@$ where $e = \mathsf{put}^{\mathsf{upd}}_{p,A}(v)$ and $v^@ = \mathsf{put}^{\mathsf{self}}_{p,A}(v)$

*Remark 2.* Note that Remark 1 about the Putget law is again applicable.

*Example 1 (Identity lenses).* Any category $\mathbf{A}$ gives rise to an ala-lens $id_{\mathbf{A}}$ with the following components. The source and target spaces are equal to $\mathbf{A}$, and the parameter space is $\mathbf{1}$. Functor $\mathsf{get}$ is the identity functor and all $\mathsf{put}$s are identities. Obviously, this lens is wb.

*Example 2 (Iso-lenses).* Let $\iota$: $\mathbf{A} \to \mathbf{B}$ be an isomorphism between model spaces. It gives rise to a wb ala-lens $\ell(\iota)$: $\mathbf{A} \to \mathbf{B}$ with $\mathbf{P}^{\ell(\iota)} = \mathbf{1} = \{*\}$ as follows. Given any $A$ in $\mathbf{A}$ and $v$: $\iota(A) \to B'$ in $\mathbf{B}$, we define $\mathsf{put}_{*,A}^{\ell(\iota).\mathsf{req}}(v) = \iota^{-1}(v)$ while the two other put operations map $v$ to identities.

*Example 3 (Bx lenses).* Examples of wb aa-lenses modelling a Bx can be found in [11]: they all can be considered as ala-lenses with a trivial parameter space $\mathbf{1}$.

*Example 4 (Learners).* Learners defined in [17] are codiscretely learning codiscrete lenses with amendment, and as such satisfy (the amended) Putget (Remark 1). Looking at the opposite direction, ala-lenses are a categorification of learners as detailed in Fig. 8 on p. 194.

# 4 Compositionality of ala-lenses

This section explores the compositional structure of the universe of ala-lenses; especially interesting is their sequential composition. We will begin with a small example demonstrating sequential composition of ordinary lenses and showing that the notion of update policy transcends individual lenses. Then we define sequential and parallel composition of ala-lenses (the former is much more involved than for ordinary lenses) and show that wb ala-lenses can be organized into an sm-category. Finally, we formalize the notion of a compositional update policy via the notion of a compositional bidirectional language.

## 4.1 Compositionality of update policies: An example

Fig. 3 extends the example in Fig. 1 with a new model space $\mathbf{C}$ whose schema consists of the only attribute Name, and a view of the IT-view, in which only employees of the ML department are to be shown. Thus, we now have two functors, get1: $\mathbf{A} \to \mathbf{B}$ and get2: $\mathbf{B} \to \mathbf{C}$, and their composition Get: $\mathbf{A} \to \mathbf{C}$ (referred to as the *long* get). The top part of Fig. 3 shows how it works for model $A$ considered above.

Each of the two policies, policy qt (green) and policy tr (orange), in which person's disappearance from the view are interpreted, resp., as quiting the company and transitioning to a department not included into the view, is applicable to the new view mappings get2 and Get, thus giving us six lenses shown in Fig. 4 with solid arrows; amongst them, lenses, $\mathcal{L}^{\mathsf{qt}}$ and $\mathcal{L}^{\mathsf{tr}}$ are obtained by applying policy *pol* to the (long) functor Get;, and we will refer to them *long* lenses. In addition, we can compose lenses of the same colour as shown in Fig. 4 by dashed arrows (and we can also compose lenses of different colours ($\ell_1^{\mathsf{qt}}$ with $\ell_2^{\mathsf{tr}}$ and $\ell_1^{\mathsf{tr}}$ with $\ell_2^{\mathsf{qt}}$) but we do not need them). Now an important question is how long and composed lenses are related: whether $\mathcal{L}^{pol}$ and $\ell_1^{pol};\ell_2^{pol}$ for $pol \in \{\mathsf{qt},\mathsf{tr}\}$, are equal (perhaps up to some equivalence) or different?

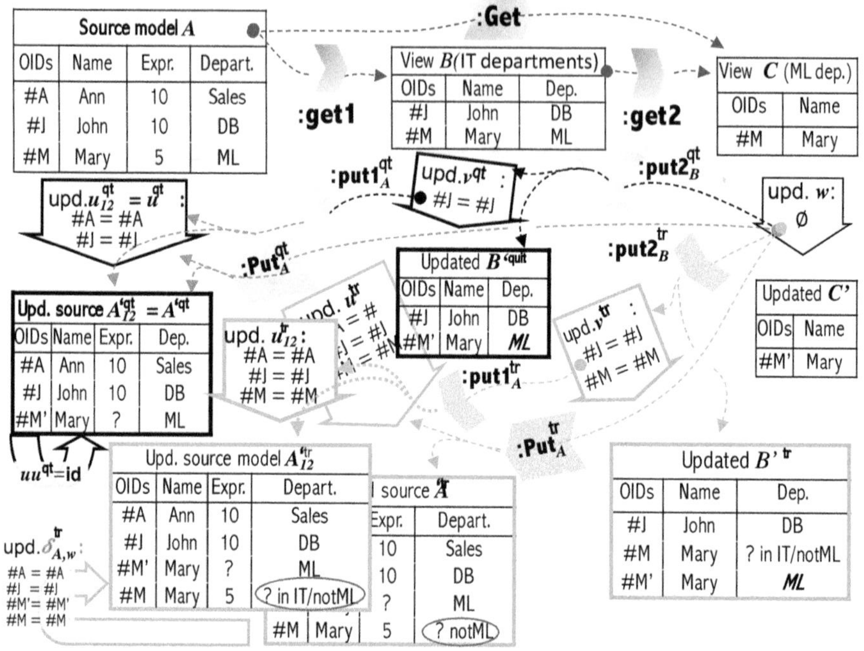

Fig. 3: Example cont'd: functoriality of update policies

Fig. 3 demonstrates how the mechanisms work with a simple example. We begin with an update $w$ of the view $C$ that says that Mary $\#M$ left the ML department, and a new Mary $\#M'$ was hired for ML. Policy qt interprets Mary's disappearance as quiting the company, and hence this Mary doesn't appear in view $B'^{\mathsf{qt}}$ produced by $\mathsf{put2}^{\mathsf{qt}}$ nor in view $A'^{\mathsf{qt}}_{12}$ produced from $B'^{\mathsf{qt}}$ by $\mathsf{put1}^{\mathsf{qt}}$, and updates $v^{\mathsf{qt}}$ and $u^{\mathsf{qt}}_{12}$ are written accordingly. Obviously, Mary also does not appear in view $A'^{\mathsf{qt}}$ produced by the long lens's $\mathsf{Put}^{\mathsf{qt}}$. Thus, $\mathsf{put1}^{\mathsf{qt}}_A(\mathsf{put2}^{\mathsf{qt}}_A(w)) = \mathsf{Put}^{\mathsf{qt}}_A(w)$, and it is easy to understand that such equality will hold for any source model $A$ and any update $w\colon C \to C'$ due to the nature of our two views get1 and get2. Hence, $\mathcal{L}^{\mathsf{qt}} = \ell^{\mathsf{qt}}_1; \ell^{\mathsf{qt}}_2$ where $\mathcal{L}^{\mathsf{qt}} = (\mathsf{Get}, \mathsf{Put}^{\mathsf{qt}})$ and $\ell^{\mathsf{qt}}_i = (\mathsf{get}i, \mathsf{put}i^{\mathsf{qt}})$.

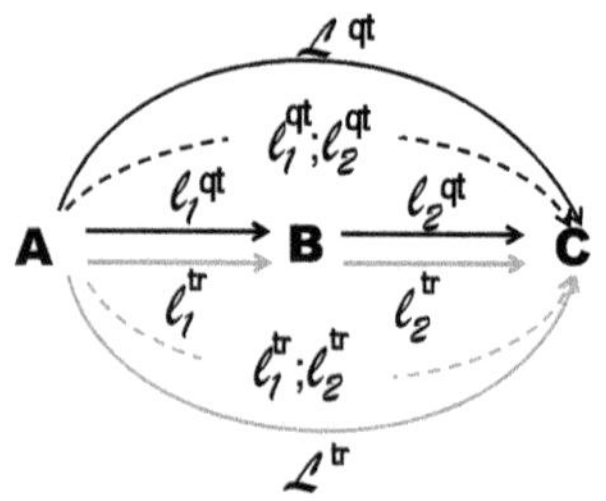

Fig. 4: Lens combination schemas for Fig. 3

The situation with policy tr is more interesting. Model $A'^{\mathsf{tr}}_{12}$ produced by the composed lens $\ell^{\mathsf{tr}}_1; \ell^{\mathsf{tr}}_2$, and model $A'^{\mathsf{tr}}$ produced by the long lens $\mathcal{L}^{\mathsf{tr}} = (\mathsf{Get}, \mathsf{Put}^{\mathsf{tr}})$ are different as shown in the figure (notice the two different values for Mary's department framed with red ovals in the models). Indeed, the composed lens has more information about the old employee Mary—it knows that Mary was in the IT view, and hence can propagate the update more accurately. The comparison update $\delta^{\mathsf{tr}}_{A,w}\colon A'^{\mathsf{tr}} \to A'^{\mathsf{tr}}_{12}$ adds this missing information so that equality $u^{\mathsf{tr}}; \delta^{\mathsf{tr}}_{A,w} = u^{\mathsf{tr}}_{12}$ holds. This is a general phenomenon: functor composition looses information and, in general, functor $\mathsf{Get} = \mathsf{get1}; \mathsf{get2}$ knows less than the pair $(\mathsf{get1}, \mathsf{get2})$. Hence, operation Put back-propagating updates over Get (we will also say *inverting* Get) will, in general, result in less certain models than composition put1 ∘ put2 that inverts the composition get1; get2 (a discussion and examples of this phenomenon in the context of vertical composition of updates can be found in [8]). Hence, comparison updates such as $\delta^{\mathsf{tr}}_{A,w}$ should exist for any $A$ and any $w\colon A.\mathsf{Get} \to C'$, and together they should give rise to something like a natural transformation between lenses, $\delta^{\mathsf{tr}}_{\mathbf{A},\mathbf{B},\mathbf{C}}\colon \mathcal{L}^{\mathsf{tr}} \Rightarrow \ell_1^{\mathsf{tr}}; \ell_2^{\mathsf{tr}}$. To make this notion precise, we need a notion of natural transformation between "functors" put, which we leave for future work. In the present paper, we will consider policies like qt, for which strict equality holds.

## 4.2 Sequential composition of ala-lenses

Let $k\colon \mathbf{A} \to \mathbf{B}$ and $\ell\colon \mathbf{B} \to \mathbf{C}$ be two ala-lenses with parameterized functors $\mathsf{get}^{k}\colon \mathbf{P} \to [\mathbf{A}, \mathbf{B}]$ and $\mathsf{get}^{\ell}\colon \mathbf{Q} \to [\mathbf{B}, \mathbf{C}]$ resp. Their *composition* is the following ala-lens $k;\ell$. Its parameter space is the product $\mathbf{P} \times \mathbf{Q}$, and the get-family is defined as follows. For any pair of parameters $(p, q)$ (we will write $pq$), $\mathsf{get}^{k;\ell}_{pq} = \mathsf{get}^{k}_{p}; \mathsf{get}^{\ell}_{q}\colon \mathbf{A} \to \mathbf{C}$. Given a pair of parameter deltas, $e\colon p \to p'$ in $\mathbf{P}$ and $h\colon q \to q'$ in $\mathbf{Q}$, their $\mathsf{get}^{k;\ell}$-image is the Godement product $*$ of natural transformations, $\mathsf{get}^{k;\ell}(eh) = \mathsf{get}^{k}(e) * \mathsf{get}^{\ell}(h)$ ( we will also write $\mathsf{get}^{k}_{e} \,||\, \mathsf{get}^{\ell}_{h}$)

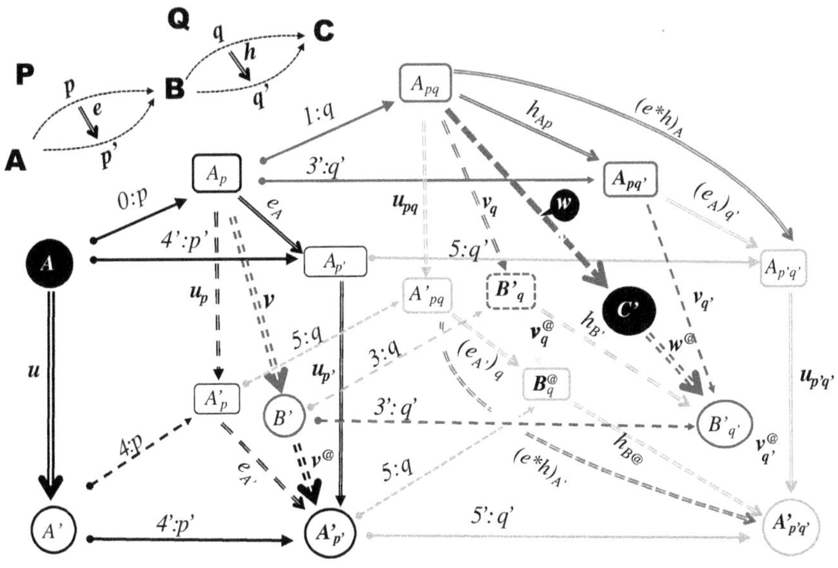

Fig. 5: Sequential composition of apa-lenses

Now we define $k;\ell$'s propagation operations puts. Let $(A, pq, A_{pq})$ with $A \in \mathbf{A}_0$, $pq \in (\mathbf{P}\times\mathbf{Q})_0$, $A.\mathsf{get}^{k}_{p}.\mathsf{get}^{\ell}_{q} = A_{pq} \in \mathbf{C}_0$ be a state of lens $k;\ell$, and $w\colon A_{pq} \to C'$ is a target update as shown in Fig. 3. For the first propagation step, we run lens $\ell$ as shown in Fig. 3 with the blue colour for derived elements: this is just an

instantiation of the pattern of Fig. 2 with the source object being $A_p = A.\mathsf{get}_p$ and parameter $q$. The results are deltas
(3)
$h = \mathsf{put}^{\ell.\mathsf{upd}}_{q,A_p}(w)\colon q \to q', v = \mathsf{put}^{\ell.\mathsf{req}}_{q,A_p}(w)\colon A_p \to B', w^{@} = \mathsf{put}^{\ell.\mathsf{self}}_{q,A_p}(w)\colon C' \to B'_{q'}.$

Next we run lens $k$ at state $(p, A)$ and the target update $v$ produced by lens $\ell$; it is yet another instantiation of pattern in Fig. 2 (this time with the green colour for derived elements), which produces three deltas
(4)
$e = \mathsf{put}^{k.\mathsf{upd}}_{p,A}(v)\colon p \to p', u = \mathsf{put}^{k.\mathsf{req}}_{p,A}(v)\colon A \to A', v^{@} = \mathsf{put}^{k.\mathsf{self}}_{p,A}(v)\colon B' \to A'_{p'}.$

These data specify the green prism adjoint to the blue prism: the edge $v$ of the latter is the "first half" of the right back face diagonal $A_p A'_{p'}$ of the former. In order to make an instance of the pattern in Fig. 2 for lens $k;\ell$, we need to extend the blue-green diagram to a triangle prism by filling-in the corresponding "empty space". These filling-in arrows are provided by functors $\mathsf{get}^{\ell}$ and $\mathsf{get}^{k}$ and shown in orange (where we have chosen one of the two equivalent ways of forming the Godement product – note two curve brown arrows). In this way we obtain yet another instantiation of the pattern in Fig. 2 denoted by $k;\ell$:

(5) $\quad \mathsf{put}^{(k;\ell)\mathsf{upd}}_{A,pq}(w) = (e, h), \quad \mathsf{put}^{(k;\ell)\mathsf{req}}_{A,pq}(w) = u, \quad \mathsf{put}^{(k;\ell)\mathsf{self}}_{A,pq}(w) = w^{@}; v^{@}_{q'}$

where $v^{@}_{q'}$ denotes $v^{@}.\mathsf{get}_{q'}$. Thus, we built an ala-lens $k;\ell$, which satisfies equation $\mathsf{Putget}_0$ by construction.

**Theorem 1 (Sequential composition and lens laws).** *Given ala-lenses $k\colon \mathbf{A} \to \mathbf{B}$ and $\ell\colon \mathbf{B} \to \mathbf{C}$, let lens $k;\ell\colon \mathbf{A} \to \mathbf{C}$ be their sequential composition as defined above. Then the lens $k;\ell$ is wb as soon as lenses $k$ and $\ell$ are such.*

See [9, Appendix A.3] for a proof.

### 4.3 Parallel composition of ala-lenses

Let $\ell_i\colon \mathbf{A}_i \to \mathbf{B}_i$, $i = 1, 2$ be two ala-lenses with parameter spaces $\mathbf{P}_i$. The lens $\ell_1\|\ell_2\colon \mathbf{A}_1 \times \mathbf{A}_2 \to \mathbf{B}_1 \times \mathbf{B}_2$ is defined as follows. Parameter space $\ell_1\|\ell_2.\mathbf{P} = \mathbf{P}_1 \times \mathbf{P}_2$. For any pair $p_1\|p_2 \in (\mathbf{P}_1 \times \mathbf{P}_2)_0$, define $\mathsf{get}^{\ell_1\|\ell_2}_{p_1\|p_2} = \mathsf{get}^{\ell_1}_{p_1} \times \mathsf{get}^{\ell_2}_{p_2}$ (we denote pairs of parameters by $p_1\|p_2$ rather than $p_1 \otimes p_2$ to shorten long formulas going beyond the page width). Further, for any pair of models $A_1\|A_2 \in (\mathbf{A}_1 \times \mathbf{A}_2)_0$ and deltas $v_1\|v_2\colon (A_1\|A_2).\mathsf{get}^{\ell_1\|\ell_2}_{p_1\|p_2} \to B'_1\|B'_2$, we define componentwise

$$e = \mathsf{put}^{(\ell_1\|\ell_2)\mathsf{upd}}_{p_1\|p_2, A_1\|A_2}(v_1\|v_2)\colon p_1\|p_2 \to p'_1\|p'_2$$

by setting $e = e_1\|e_2$ where $e_i = \mathsf{put}^{\ell_i}_{p_i,S_i}(v_i)$, $i = 1, 2$ and similarly for $\mathsf{put}^{(\ell_1\|\ell_2)\mathsf{req}}_{p_1\|p_2,A_1\|A_2}$ and $\mathsf{put}^{(\ell_1\|\ell_2)\mathsf{self}}_{p_1\|p_2,A_1\|A_2}$. The following result is obvious.

**Theorem 2 (Parallel composition and lens laws).** *Lens $\ell_1\|\ell_2$ is wb as soon as lenses $\ell_1$ and $\ell_2$ are such.*

## 4.4 Symmetric monoidal structure over ala-lenses

Our goal is to organize ala-lenses into an sm-category. To make sequential composition of ala-lenses associative, we need to consider them up to some equivalence (indeed, Cartesian product is not strictly associative).

**Definition 5 (Ala-lens Equivalence)** Two parallel ala-lenses $\ell, \hat{\ell}\colon \mathbf{A} \to \mathbf{B}$ are called *equivalent* if their parameter spaces are isomorphic via a functor $\iota\colon \mathbf{P} \to \hat{\mathbf{P}}$ such that for any $A \in \mathbf{A}_0$, $e\colon p \to p' \in \mathbf{P}$ and $v\colon (A.\mathsf{get}_p) \to T'$ the following holds (for $\mathsf{x} \in \{\mathsf{req}, \mathsf{self}\}$):

$$A.\mathsf{get}_e = A.\widehat{\mathsf{get}}_{\iota(e)},\ \iota(\mathsf{put}^{\mathsf{upd}}_{p,A}(v)) = \widehat{\mathsf{put}}_{\iota(p),A}(v), \text{ and } \mathsf{put}^{\mathsf{x}}_{p,A}(v) = \widehat{\mathsf{put}}^{\mathsf{x}}_{\iota(p),A}(v)$$

*Remark 3.* It would be more categorical to require delta isomorphisms (i.e., commutative squares whose horizontal edges are isomorphisms) rather than equalities as above. However, model spaces appearing in Bx-practice are skeletal categories (and even stronger than skeletal in the sense that all isos, including iso loops, are identities), for which isos become equalities so that the generality would degenerate into equality anyway.

It is easy to see that operations of lens' sequential and parallel composition are compatible with lens' equivalence and hence are well-defined for equivalence classes. Below we identify lenses with their equivalence classes by default.

**Theorem 3 (Ala-lenses form an sm-category).** *Operations of sequential and parallel composition of ala-lenses defined above give rise to an sm-category* ***aLaLens****, whose objects are model spaces (= categories) and arrows are (equivalence classes of) ala-lenses.* See [9, p.17 and Appendix A.4] for a proof.

## 4.5 Functoriality of learning in the *delta* lens setting

As example in Sect. 4.1 shows, the notion of update policy transcends individual lenses. Hence, its proper formalization needs considering the entire category of ala-lenses and functoriality of a suitable mapping.

**Definition 6 (Bx-transformation language)** A *compositional bidirectional model transformation language* $\mathcal{L}_{\mathsf{bx}}$ is given by **(i)** an sm-category ***pGet***$(\mathcal{L}_{\mathsf{bx}})$ whose objects are *($\mathcal{L}_{\mathsf{bx}}$-)model spaces* and arrows are *($\mathcal{L}_{\mathsf{bx}}$-)transformations* which is supplied with forgetful functor into ***pCat***, and **(ii)** an sm-functor $L_{\mathcal{L}_{\mathsf{bx}}}$: ***pGet***$(\mathcal{L}_{\mathsf{bx}}) \to$ ***aLaLens*** such that the lower triangle in the inset diagram commutes. (Forgetful functors in this diagram are named "$-X$" with $X$ referring to the structure to be forgotten.)

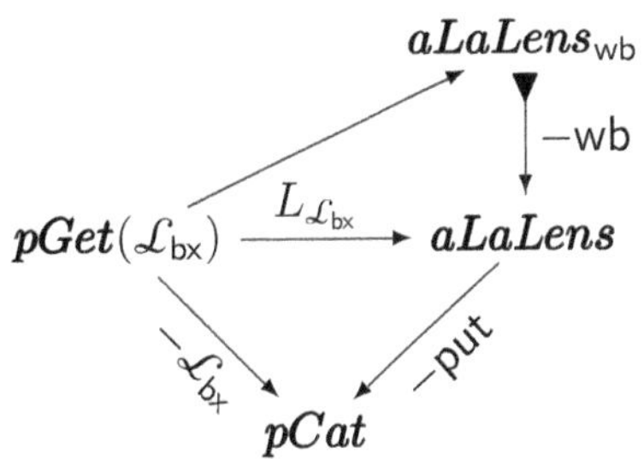


An $\mathcal{L}_{\mathsf{bx}}$-language is *well-behaved (wb)* if functor $L_{\mathcal{L}_{\mathsf{bx}}}$ factorizes as shown by the upper triangle of the diagram.

*Example.* A major compositionality result of Fong *et al* [17] states the existence of an sm-functor from the category of Euclidean spaces and parameterized differentiable functions (pd-functions) ***Para*** into the category ***Learn*** of learning algorithms (*learners*) as shown by the inset commutative diagram. (The functor is itself parameterized by a *step size* $0 < \varepsilon \in \mathbb{R}$ and an *error function* err: $\mathbb{R}\times\mathbb{R} \to \mathbb{R}$ needed to specify the gradient descent procedure.) However, learners are nothing but codiscrete ala-lenses (see Sect. A.2), and thus the inset diagram is a codiscrete specialization of the diagram in Def. 6 above. That is, the category of Euclidean spaces and pd-functions, and the gradient descent method for back propagation, give rise to a (codiscrete) compositional bx-transformation language (over ***pSet*** rather than ***pCat***).

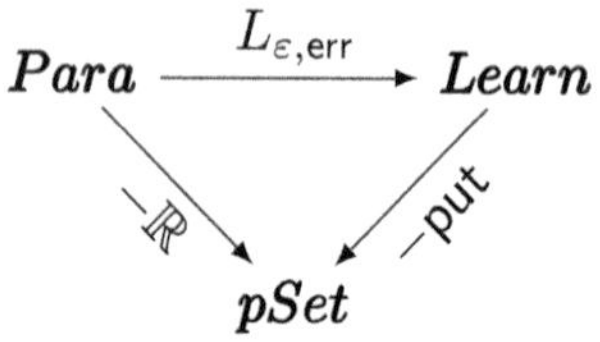


Finding a specifically Bx instance of Def. 6 (e.g., checking whether it holds for concrete languages and tools such as EMOFLON [23] or GROUNDTRAM [22]) is laborious and left for future work.

# 5 Related work

Figure 6 on the right is a simplified version of Fig. 8 on p. 194 convenient for our discussion here: immediate related work should be found in areas located at points (0,1) (codiscrete learning lenses) and (1,0) (delta lenses) of the plane. For the point (0,1), the paper [17] by Fong, Spivak and Tuyéras is fundamental: they defined the notion of a codiscrete learning lens (called a learner), proved a fundamental results about sm-functoriality of the gradient descent approach to ML, and thus laid a foundation for the compositional approach to change propagation with learning. One follow-up of that work is paper [16] by Fong and Johnson, in which they build an sm-functor ***Learn*** $\to$ ***sLens*** which maps learners to so called symmetric lenses. That paper is probably the first one where the terms 'lens' and 'learner' are met, but the initial observation that a learner whose parameter set is a singleton is actually a lens is due to Jules Hedges, see [16].

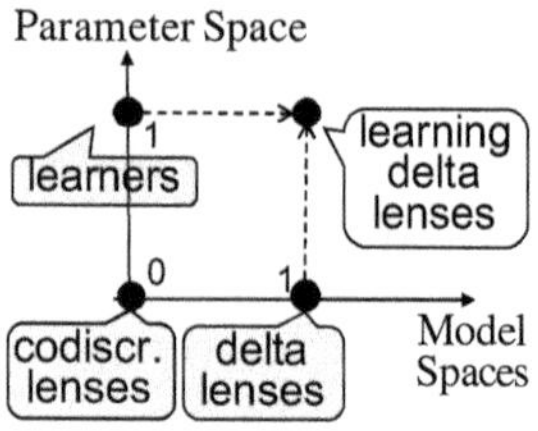


Fig. 6

There are conceptual and technical distinctions between [16] and the present paper. On the conceptual level, by encoding learners as symmetric lenses, they "hide" learning inside the lens framework and make it a technical rather than conceptual idea. In contrast, we consider parameterization and supervised learning as a fundamental idea and a first-class citizen for the lens framework, which grants creation of a new species of lenses. Moreover, while an ordinary lens is a way to invert a functor, a learning lens is a way to invert a parameterized functor so that learning lenses appear as an extension of the parameterization idea from functors to lenses. (This approach can probably be specified formally by treating parameterization as a suitably defined functorial construction.) Besides technical advantages (working with asymmetric lenses is simpler), our asymmetric model seems more adequate to the problem of learning functions rather than relations. On the technical level, the lens framework we develop in the paper is much more general than in [16]: we categorificated both the parameter space and model spaces, and we work with lenses with amendment (which allows us to relax the Putget law if needed).

As for the delta lens roots (the point (1,0) in the figure), delta lenses were motivated and formally defined in [12] (the asymmetric case) and [13] (the symmetric one). Categorical foundations for the delta lens theory were developed by Johnson and Rosebrugh in a series of papers (see [20] for references); this line is continued in Clarke's work [6]. The notion of a delta lens with amendments (in both asymmetric and symmetric variants) was defined in [11], and several composition results were proved. Another extensive body of work within the delta-based area is modelling and implementing model transformations with triple-graph grammars (TGG) [4,23]. TGG provide an implementation framework for delta lenses as is shown and discussed in [5,19,2], and thus inevitably consider change propagation on a much more concrete level than lenses. The author is not aware of any work considering functoriality of update policies developed within the TGG framework.

The present paper is probably the first one at the intersection (1,1) of the plane. The preliminary results have recently been reported at ACT'19 in Oxford to a representative lens community, and no references besides [17], [16] mentioned above were provided.

## 6 Conclusion

The perspective on Bx presented in the paper is an example of a fruitful interaction between two domains—ML and Bx. In order to be ported to Bx, the compositional approach to ML developed in [17] is to be categorificated as shown in Fig. 8 on p. 194. This opens a whole new program for Bx: checking that currently existing Bx languages and tools are compositional (and well-behaved) in the sense of Def. 6 p. 190. The wb compositionality is an important practical requirement as it allows for modular design and testing of bidirectional transformations. Surprisingly, but this important requirement has been missing from the agenda of the Bx community, e.g., the recent endeavour of developing an effective benchmark for Bx-tools [3] does not discuss it.

In a wider context, the main message of the paper is that the learning idea transcends its applications in ML: it is applicable and usable in many domains in which lenses are applicable such as model transformations, data migration, and open games [18]. Moreover, the categorificated learning may perhaps find useful applications in ML itself. In the current ML setting, the object to be learnt is a function $f\colon \mathbb{R}^m \to \mathbb{R}^n$ that, in the OO class modelling perspective, is a very simple structure: it can be seen as one object with a (huge) amount of attributes, or, perhaps, a predefined set of objects, which is not allowed to be changed during the search — only attribute values may be changed. In the delta lens view, such changes constitute a rather narrow class of updates and thus unjustifiably narrow the search space. Learning with the possibility to change dimensions $m, n$ may be an appropriate option in several contexts. On the other hand, while categorification of model spaces extends the search space, categorification of the parameter space would narrow the search space as we are allowed to replace a parameter $p$ by parameter $p'$ only if there is a suitable arrow $e\colon p \to p'$ in category $\mathbf{P}$. This narrowing may, perhaps, improve performance. All in all, the interaction between ML and Bx could be bidirectional!

# A Appendices

## A.1 Category of parameterized functors *pCat*

Category ***pCat*** has all small categories as objects. ***pCat***-arrows $\mathbf{A} \to \mathbf{B}$ are *parameterized* functors (*p-functors*) i.e., functors $f\colon \mathbf{P} \to [\mathbf{A}, \mathbf{B}]$ with $\mathbf{P}$ a small category of *parameters* and $[\mathbf{A}, \mathbf{B}]$ the category of functors from $\mathbf{A}$ to $\mathbf{B}$ and their natural transformations. For an object $p$ and an arrow $e\colon p \to p'$ in $\mathbf{P}$, we write $f_p$ for the functor $f(p)\colon \mathbf{A} \to \mathbf{B}$ and $f_e$ for the natural transformation $f(e)\colon f_p \Rightarrow f_{p'}$. We will write p-functors as labelled arrows $f\colon \mathbf{A} \xrightarrow{\mathbf{P}} \mathbf{B}$. As ***Cat*** is Cartesian closed, we have a natural isomorphism between $\boldsymbol{Cat}(\mathbf{P}, [\mathbf{A}, \mathbf{B}])$ and $\boldsymbol{Cat}(\mathbf{P}{\times}\mathbf{A}, \mathbf{B})$ and can reformulate the above definition in an equivalent way with functors $\mathbf{P}{\times}\mathbf{A} \to \mathbf{B}$. We prefer the former formulation as it corresponds to the notation $f\colon \mathbf{A} \xrightarrow{\mathbf{P}} \mathbf{B}$ visualizing $\mathbf{P}$ as a hidden state of the transformation, which seems adequate to the intuition of parameterized in our context. (If some technicalities may perhaps be easier to see with the product formulation, we will switch to the product view thus doing currying and uncurrying without special mentioning.) Sequential composition of of $f\colon \mathbf{A} \xrightarrow{\mathbf{P}} \mathbf{B}$ and $g\colon \mathbf{B} \xrightarrow{\mathbf{Q}} \mathbf{C}$ is $f.g\colon \mathbf{A} \xrightarrow{\mathbf{P}\times\mathbf{Q}} \mathbf{C}$ given by $(f.g)_{pq} \stackrel{\text{def}}{=} f_p.g_q$ for objects, i.e., pairs $p{\in}\mathbf{P}$, $q{\in}\mathbf{Q}$, and by the Godement product of natural transformations for arrows in $\mathbf{P}{\times}\mathbf{Q}$. That is, given a pair $e\colon p \to p'$ in $\mathbf{P}$ and $h\colon q \to q'$ in $\mathbf{Q}$, we define the transformation $(f.g)_{eh}\colon f_p.g_q \Rightarrow f_{p'}.g_{q'}$ to be the Godement product $f_e * g_h$.

Any category $\mathbf{A}$ gives rise to a p-functor $\mathsf{Id}_{\mathbf{A}}\colon \mathbf{A} \xrightarrow{\mathbf{1}} \mathbf{A}$, whose parameter space is a singleton category $\mathbf{1}$ with the only object $*$, $\mathsf{Id}_{\mathbf{A}}(*) = \mathsf{id}_{\mathbf{A}}$ and $\mathsf{Id}_{A}(\mathsf{id}_*)\colon \mathsf{id}_{\mathbf{A}} \Rightarrow \mathsf{id}_{\mathbf{A}}$ is the identity transformation. It's easy to see that p-functors $\mathsf{Id}\_$ are units of the sequential composition. To ensure associativity we need to consider p-functors up to an equivalence of their parameter spaces. Two parallel p-functors $f\colon \mathbf{A} \xrightarrow{\mathbf{P}} \mathbf{B}$ and $\hat{f}\colon \mathbf{A} \xrightarrow{\hat{\mathbf{P}}} \mathbf{B}$, are *equivalent* if there is an isomorphism $\alpha\colon \mathbf{P} \to \hat{\mathbf{P}}$ such that two parallel functors $f\colon \mathbf{P} \to [\mathbf{A}, \mathbf{B}]$ and $\alpha; \hat{f}\colon \mathbf{P} \to [\mathbf{A}, \mathbf{B}]$ are naturally isomorphic; then we write $f \approx_\alpha \hat{f}$. It's easy to see that if $f \approx_\alpha \hat{f}\colon \mathbf{A} \to \mathbf{B}$ and $g \approx_\beta \hat{g}\colon \mathbf{B} \to \mathbf{C}$, then $f; g \approx_{\alpha\times\beta} \hat{f}; \hat{g}\colon \mathbf{A} \to \mathbf{C}$, i.e., sequential composition is stable under equivalence. Below we will identify p-functors and their equivalence classes. Using a natural isomorphism $(\mathbf{P}{\times}\mathbf{Q}){\times}\mathbf{R} \cong \mathbf{P}{\times}(\mathbf{Q}{\times}\mathbf{R})$, strict associativity of the functor composition and strict associativity of the Godement product, we conclude that sequential composition of (equivalence classes of) p-functors is strictly associative. Hence, ***pCat*** is a category.

Our next goal is to supply it with a monoidal structure. We borrow the latter from the sm-category $(\boldsymbol{Cat},\times)$, whose tensor is given by the product. There is an identical on objects embedding $(\boldsymbol{Cat},\times) \rightarrowtail \boldsymbol{pCat}$ that maps a functor $f\colon \mathbf{A} \to \mathbf{B}$ to a p-functor $\bar{f}\colon \mathbf{A} \xrightarrow{\mathbf{1}} \mathbf{B}$ whose parameter space is the singleton category $\mathbf{1}$. Moreover, as this embedding is a functor, the coherence equations for the associators and unitors that hold in $(\boldsymbol{Cat},\times)$ hold in ***pCat*** as well (this proof idea is borrowed from [17]). In this way, ***pCat*** becomes an sm-category. In a similar way, we define the sm-category ***pSet*** of small sets and parametrized functions between them — the codiscrete version of ***pCat***. The diagram in Fig. 7 shows how these categories are related.

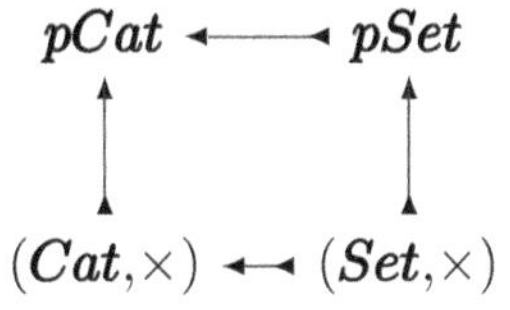


Fig. 7

## A.2 Ala-lenses as categorification of ML-learners

Figure 8 shows a discrete two-dimensional plane with each axis having three points: a space is a singleton, a set, a category encoded by coordinates 0,1,2 resp. Each of the points $x_{ij}$ is then the location of a corresponding sm-category of

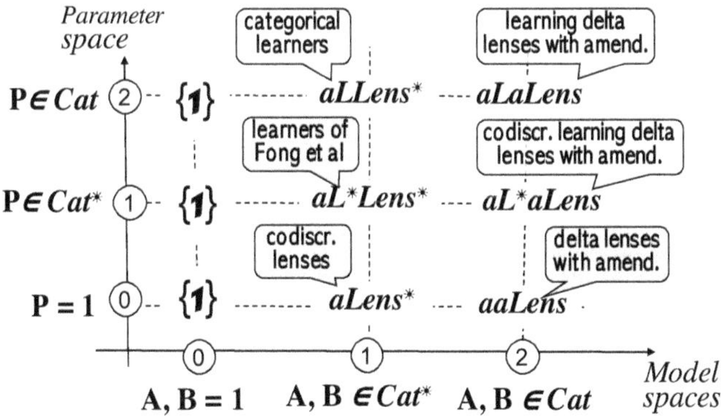


Fig. 8: The universe of categories of learning delta lenses

(asymmetric) learning (delta) lenses. Category $\{\mathit{1}\}$ is a terminal category whose only arrow is the identity lens $\mathit{1} = (\mathsf{id}_{\mathbf{1}}, \mathsf{id}_{\mathbf{1}})\colon \mathbf{1} \to \mathbf{1}$ propagating from a terminal category $\mathbf{1}$ to itself. Label $*$ refers to the codiscrete specialization of the construct being labelled: $\boldsymbol{L}^{*}$ means codiscrete learning (i.e., the parameter space $\mathbf{P}$ is a set considered as a codiscrete category) and $\boldsymbol{aLens}^{*}$ refers to codiscrete model spaces. The category of learners defined in [17] is located at point (1,1), and the category of learning delta lenses with amendments defined in the present paper is located at (2,2). There are also two semi-categorificated species of learning lenses: categorical learners at point (1,2) and codiscretely learning delta lenses at (2,1), which are special cases of ala-lenses.

## References


1. Abiteboul, S., McHugh, J., Rys, M., Vassalos, V., J.Wiener: Incremental Maintenance for Materialized Views over Semistructured Data. In: Gupta, A., Shmueli, O., Widom, J. (eds.) VLDB. Morgan Kaufmann (1998)
2. Anjorin, A.: An introduction to triple graph grammars as an implementation of the delta-lens framework. In: Gibbons, J., Stevens, P. (eds.) Bidirectional Transformations - International Summer School, Oxford, UK, July 25-29, 2016, Tutorial Lectures. Lecture Notes in Computer Science, vol. 9715, pp. 29–72. Springer (2016). https://doi.org/10.1007/978-3-319-79108-1
3. Anjorin, A., Diskin, Z., Jouault, F., Ko, H., Leblebici, E., Westfechtel, B.: Benchmarx reloaded: A practical benchmark framework for bidirectional transformations. In: Eramo and Johnson [15], pp. 15–30, http://ceur-ws.org/Vol-1827/paper6.pdf
4. Anjorin, A., Leblebici, E., Schürr, A.: 20 years of triple graph grammars: A roadmap for future research. ECEASST **73** (2015). https://doi.org/10.14279/tuj.eceasst.73.1031
5. Anjorin, A., Rose, S., Deckwerth, F., Schürr, A.: Efficient model synchronization with view triple graph grammars. In: Modelling Foundations and Applications - 10th European Conference, ECMFA 2014, York, UK, July 21-25, 2014. Proceedings. Lecture Notes in Computer Science, vol. 8569, pp. 1–17. Springer (2014). https://doi.org/10.1007/978-3-319-09195-2_1
6. Clarke, B.: Internal lenses as functors and cofunctors. In: Pre-proceedings of ACT'19, Oxford, 2019. http://www.cs.ox.ac.uk/ACT2019/preproceedings/BryceClarke.pdf
7. Czarnecki, K., Foster, J.N., Hu, Z., Lämmel, R., Schürr, A., Terwilliger, J.F.: Bidirectional transformations: A cross-discipline perspective. In: Theory and Practice of Model Transformations, pp. 260–283. Springer (2009)
8. Diskin, Z.: Compositionality of update propagation: Lax putput. In: Eramo and Johnson [15], pp. 74–89, http://ceur-ws.org/Vol-1827/paper12.pdf
9. Diskin, Z.: General supervised learning as change propagation with delta lenses. CoRR **abs/1911.12904** (2019), http://arxiv.org/abs/1911.12904
10. Diskin, Z., Gholizadeh, H., Wider, A., Czarnecki, K.: A three-dimensional taxonomy for bidirectional model synchronization. Journal of System and Software **111**, 298–322 (2016). https://doi.org/10.1016/j.jss.2015.06.003
11. Diskin, Z., König, H., Lawford, M.: Multiple model synchronization with multiary delta lenses with amendment and K-Putput. Formal Asp. Comput. **31**(5), 611–640 (2019). https://doi.org/10.1007/s00165-019-00493-0, (Sect.7.1 of the paper is unreadable and can be found in http://arxiv.org/abs/1911.11302)
12. Diskin, Z., Xiong, Y., Czarnecki, K.: From State- to Delta-Based Bidirectional Model Transformations: the Asymmetric Case. Journal of Object Technology **10**, 6: 1–25 (2011)
13. Diskin, Z., Xiong, Y., Czarnecki, K., Ehrig, H., Hermann, F., Orejas, F.: From state-to delta-based bidirectional model transformations: the symmetric case. In: MODELS, pp. 304–318. Springer (2011)
14. El-Sayed, M., Rundensteiner, E.A., Mani, M.: Incremental Maintenance of Materialized XQuery Views. In: Liu, L., Reuter, A., Whang, K.Y., Zhang, J. (eds.) ICDE. p. 129. IEEE Computer Society (2006). https://doi.org/10.1109/ICDE.2006.80
15. Eramo, R., Johnson, M. (eds.): Proceedings of the 6th International Workshop on Bidirectional Transformations co-located with The European Joint Conferences

on Theory and Practice of Software, Bx@ETAPS 2017, Uppsala, Sweden, April 29, 2017, CEUR Workshop Proceedings, vol. 1827. CEUR-WS.org (2017), http://ceur-ws.org/Vol-1827
16. Fong, B., Johnson, M.: Lenses and learners. In: Cheney, J., Ko, H. (eds.) Proceedings of the 8th International Workshop on Bidirectional Transformations co-located with the Philadelphia Logic Week, Bx@PLW 2019, Philadelphia, PA, USA, June 4, 2019. CEUR Workshop Proceedings, vol. 2355, pp. 16–29. CEUR-WS.org (2019), http://ceur-ws.org/Vol-2355/paper2.pdf
17. Fong, B., Spivak, D.I., Tuyéras, R.: Backprop as functor: A compositional perspective on supervised learning. In: The 34th Annual ACM/IEEE Symposium on Logic in Computer Science, LICS 2019, Vancouver, BC, Canada, June 24-27, 2019. pp. 1–13. IEEE (2019). https://doi.org/10.1109/LICS.2019.8785665
18. Hedges, J.: From open learners to open games. CoRR **abs/1902.08666** (2019), http://arxiv.org/abs/1902.08666
19. Hermann, F., Ehrig, H., Orejas, F., Czarnecki, K., Diskin, Z., Xiong, Y., Gottmann, S., Engel, T.: Model synchronization based on triple graph grammars: correctness, completeness and invertibility. Software and System Modeling **14**(1), 241–269 (2015). https://doi.org/10.1007/s10270-012-0309-1
20. Johnson, M., Rosebrugh, R.D.: Unifying set-based, delta-based and edit-based lenses. In: The 5th International Workshop on Bidirectional Transformations, Bx 2016. pp. 1–13 (2016), http://ceur-ws.org/Vol-1571/paper_13.pdf
21. Kappel, G., Langer, P., Retschitzegger, W., Schwinger, W., Wimmer, M.: Model transformation by-example: A survey of the first wave. In: Conceptual Modelling and Its Theoretical Foundations - Essays Dedicated to Bernhard Thalheim on the Occasion of His 60th Birthday. pp. 197–215 (2012). https://doi.org/10.1007/978-3-642-28279-9_15
22. Sasano, I., Hu, Z., Hidaka, S., Inaba, K., Kato, H., Nakano, K.: Toward bidirectionalization of ATL with GRoundTram. In: Theory and Practice of Model Transformations - 4th International Conference, ICMT 2011, Zurich, Switzerland, June 27-28, 2011. Proceedings. Lecture Notes in Computer Science, vol. 6707, pp. 138–151. Springer (2011). https://doi.org/10.1007/978-3-642-21732-6_10
23. Weidmann, N., Anjorin, A., Fritsche, L., Varró, G., Schürr, A., Leblebici, E.: Incremental bidirectional model transformation with emoflon: Ibex. In: The 8th International Workshop on Bidirectional Transformations co-located with the Philadelphia Logic Week, Bx@PLW 2019, Philadelphia, PA, USA, June 4, 2019. CEUR Workshop Proceedings, vol. 2355, pp. 45–55. CEUR-WS.org (2019), http://ceur-ws.org/Vol-2355/paper4.pdf

9

# Minimal Coverability Tree Construction Made Complete and Efficient ⋆

Alain Finkel[1,3], Serge Haddad[1,2], and Igor Khmelnitsky[1,2](✉)

[1] LSV, ENS Paris-Saclay, CNRS, Université Paris-Saclay, Cachan, France
{finkel,haddad,khmelnitsky}@lsv.fr
[2] Inria, France
[3] Institut Universitaire de France, France

**Abstract.** Downward closures of Petri net reachability sets can be finitely represented by their set of maximal elements called the minimal coverability set or Clover. Many properties (coverability, boundedness, ...) can be decided using Clover, in a time proportional to the size of Clover. So it is crucial to design algorithms that compute it efficiently. We present a simple modification of the original but incomplete Minimal Coverability Tree algorithm (MCT), computing Clover, which makes it complete: it memorizes accelerations and fires them as ordinary transitions. Contrary to the other alternative algorithms for which no bound on the size of the required additional memory is known, we establish that the additional space of our algorithm is at most doubly exponential. Furthermore we have implemented a prototype `MinCov` which is already very competitive: on benchmarks it uses less space than all the other tools and its execution time is close to the one of the fastest tool.

**Keywords:** Petri nets · Karp-Miller tree algorithm · Coverability · Minimal coverability set · Clover · Minimal coverability tree.

## 1 Introduction

**Coverability and coverability set in Petri nets.** Petri nets are iconic as an infinite-state model used for verifying concurrent systems. Coverability, in Petri nets, is the most studied property for several reasons: (1) many properties like mutual exclusion, safety, control-state reachability reduce to coverability, (2) the coverability problem is EXPSPACE-complete (while reachability is non elementary), and (3) there exist efficient prototypes and numerous case studies. To solve the coverability problem, there are backward and forward algorithms. But these algorithms do not address relevant problems like the repeated coverability problem, the LTL model-checking, the boundedness problem and regularity of the traces.

However these problems are EXPSPACE-complete [4, 1] and are also decidable using the Karp-Miller tree algorithm (KMT) [11] that computes a finite tree labeled by a set of *ω-markings* $C \subseteq \mathbb{N}_\omega^P$ (where $\mathbb{N}_\omega$ is the set of naturals enlarged with an upper bound $\omega$ and $P$ is the set of places) such that the reachability set and the finite set $C$ have the same downward closure in $\mathbb{N}^P$. Thus a marking $\mathbf{m}$ is coverable if there exists some $\mathbf{m}' \geq \mathbf{m}$ with $\mathbf{m}' \in C$. Hence, $C$ can be seen as *one* among all the possible finite representations of the infinite downward closure of the reachability set. This set $C$ allows, for instance, to solve multiple instances of coverability in linear time linear w.r.t. the size of $C$ avoiding to call many times a costly algorithm. Informally the KMT algorithm builds a reachability tree but, in order to ensure termination, substitutes $\omega$ to some finite components of a marking of a vertex when some marking of an ancestor is smaller.

Unfortunately $C$ may contain comparable markings while only the maximal elements are important. The set of maximal elements of $C$ can be defined independently of the KMT algorithm and was called the *minimal coverability set (MCS)* in [6] and abbreviated as the *Clover* in the more general framework of Well Structured Transition Systems (WSTS) [7].

**The minimal coverability tree algorithm.** So in [5, 6] the author computes the minimal coverability set by modifying the KMT algorithm in such a way that at each step of the algorithm, the set of $\omega$-markings labelling vertices is an antichain. But this aggressive strategy, implemented by the so-called Minimal Coverability Tree algorithm (MCT), contains a subtle bug and it may compute a strict under-approximation of Clover as shown in [8, 10].

**Alternative minimal coverability set algorithms.** Since the discovery of this bug, three algorithms (with variants) [10, 14, 13] have been designed for computing the minimal coverability set without building the full Karp-Miller tree. In [10] the authors proposed a minimal coverability set algorithm (called `CovProc`) that is not based on the Karp-Miller tree algorithm but uses a similar but restricted introduction of $\omega$'s. In [14], Reynier and Servais proposed a modification of the MCT, called the Monotone-Pruning algorithm (called `MP`), that keeps but "deactivates" vertices labeled with smaller $\omega$-markings while MCT would have deleted them. Recently in [15], the authors simplified their original proof of correctness. In [16], Valmari and Hansen proposed another algorithm (denoted below as `VH`) for constructing the minimal coverability set without deleting vertices. Their algorithm builds a graph and not a tree as usual. In [13], Piipponen and Valmari improved this algorithm by designing appropriate data structures and heuristics for exploration strategy that may significantly decrease the size of the graph.

**Our contributions.**

1. We introduce the concept of *abstraction* as an $\omega$-transition that mimics the effect of an infinite family of firing sequences of markings w.r.t. coverability. As a consequence adding abstractions to the net does not modify its coverability set. Moreover, the classical Karp-Miller *acceleration* can be formalized as an abstraction whose incidence on places is either $\omega$ or null. The set of accelerations of a net is upward closed and well-ordered. Hence there exists a finite subset of minimal accelerations and we show that the size of all minimal acceleration is bounded by a double exponential.

2. Despite the current opinion that *"The flaw is intricate and we do not see an easy way to get rid of it.... Thus, from our point of view, fixing the bug of the MCT algorithm seems to be a difficult task"* [10], we have found a *simple* modification of MCT which makes it correct. It mainly consists in memorizing discovered accelerations and using them as ordinary transitions.
3. Contrary to *all* existing minimal coverability set algorithms that use an *unknown additional memory* that could be non primitive recursive, we show, by applying a recent result of Leroux [12], that the additional memory required for accelerations, is at most doubly exponential.
4. We have developed a prototype in order to also empirically evaluate the efficiency of our algorithm and the benchmarks (either from the literature or random ones) have confirmed that our algorithm requires significantly less memory than the other algorithms and is close to the fastest tool w.r.t. the execution time.

**Organization.** Section 2 introduces abstractions and accelerations and studies their properties. Section 3 presents our algorithm and establishes its correctness. Section 4 describes our tool and discusses the results of the benchmarks. We conclude and give some perspectives to this work in Section 5. One can find all the missing proofs and an illustration of the behavior of the algorithm in [9].

## 2 Covering abstractions

### 2.1 Petri nets: reachability and covering

Here we define Petri nets differently from the usual way but in an equivalent manner. i.e. based on the backward incidence matrix **Pre** and the incidence matrix **C**. The forward incidence matrix is implicitly defined by $\mathbf{C}+\mathbf{Pre}$. Such a choice is motivated by the introduction of abstractions in section 2.2.

**Definition 1.** *A Petri net (PN) is a tuple* $\mathcal{N} = \langle P, T, \mathbf{Pre}, \mathbf{C}\rangle$ *where:*

- $P$ *is a finite set of* places;
- $T$ *is a finite set of* transitions, *with* $P \cap T = \emptyset$;
- $\mathbf{Pre} \in \mathbb{N}^{P\times T}$ *is the* backward incidence matrix;
- $\mathbf{C} \in \mathbb{Z}^{P\times T}$ *is the* incidence matrix *which fulfills: for all* $p \in P$ *and* $t \in T$, $\mathbf{C}(p,t) + \mathbf{Pre}(p,t) \geq 0$.

*A* marked *Petri net* $(\mathcal{N}, \mathbf{m}_0)$ *is a Petri net* $\mathcal{N}$ *equipped with an initial marking* $\mathbf{m}_0 \in \mathbb{N}^P$.

The column vector of matrix **Pre** (resp. **C**) indexed by $t \in T$ is denoted $\mathbf{Pre}(t)$ (resp. $\mathbf{C}(t)$). A transition $t \in T$ is *fireable* from a marking $\mathbf{m} \in \mathbb{N}^P$ if $\mathbf{m} \geq \mathbf{Pre}(t)$. When $t$ is fireable from $\mathbf{m}$, its *firing* leads to marking $\mathbf{m}' \overset{\text{def}}{=} \mathbf{m} + \mathbf{C}(t)$, denoted by $\mathbf{m} \xrightarrow{t} \mathbf{m}'$. One extends fireability and firing to a sequence $\sigma \in T^*$ by recurrence on its length. The empty sequence $\varepsilon$ is always fireable and let the marking unchanged. Let $\sigma = t\sigma'$ be a sequence with $t \in T$ and $\sigma' \in T^*$. Then $\sigma$

is fireable from $\mathbf{m}$ if $\mathbf{m} \xrightarrow{t} \mathbf{m}'$ and $\sigma'$ is fireable from $\mathbf{m}'$. The firing of $\sigma$ from $\mathbf{m}$ leads to the marking $\mathbf{m}''$ reached by $\sigma'$ from $\mathbf{m}'$. One also denotes this firing by $\mathbf{m} \xrightarrow{\sigma} \mathbf{m}''$.

**Definition 2.** *Let* $(\mathcal{N}, \mathbf{m}_0)$ *be a marked net. The* reachability set $Reach(\mathcal{N}, \mathbf{m}_0)$ *is defined by:*

$$Reach(\mathcal{N}, \mathbf{m}_0) = \{\mathbf{m} \mid \exists \sigma \in T^* \ \mathbf{m}_0 \xrightarrow{\sigma} \mathbf{m}\}$$

In order to introduce the coverability set of a Petri net, let us recall some definitions and results related to ordered sets. Let $(X, \leq)$ be an ordered set. The downward (resp. upward) *closure* of a subset $E \subseteq X$ is denoted by $\downarrow E$ (resp. $\uparrow E$) and defined by:

$$\downarrow E = \{x \in X \mid \exists y \in E \ y \geq x\} \qquad (\text{resp. } \uparrow E = \{x \in X \mid \exists y \in E \ y \leq x\})$$

A subset $E \subseteq X$ is downward (resp. upward) *closed* if $E = \downarrow E$ (resp. $E = \uparrow E$).

An *antichain* $E$ is a set which fulfills: $\forall x \neq y \in E \ \neg(x \leq y \vee y \leq x)$. $X$ is said *FAC* (for Finite AntiChains) if all its antichains are finite. A non empty set $E \subseteq X$ is *directed* if for all $x, y \in E$ there exists $z \in E$ such that $x \leq z$ and $y \leq z$. An *ideal* is a set which is downward closed and directed. There exists an equivalent characterization of FAC sets which provides a finite description of any downward closed set: a set is FAC if and only if every downward closed set admits a finite decomposition in ideals (a proof of this well-known result can be found in [3]).

$X$ is *well founded* if all its (strictly) decreasing sequences are finite. $X$ is *well ordered* if it is FAC and well founded. There are many equivalent characterizations of well order. For instance, a set $X$ is well ordered if and only if for all sequence $(x_n)_{n \in \mathbb{N}}$ in $X$, there exists a non decreasing infinite subsequence. This characterization allows to design algorithms that computes trees whose finiteness is ensured by well order. Let us recall that $(\mathbb{N}, \leq)$ and $(\mathbb{N}^P, \leq)$ are well ordered sets.

We are now ready to introduce the *cover* (also called the coverability set) of a net and to state some of its properties.

**Definition 3.** *Let* $(\mathcal{N}, \mathbf{m}_0)$ *be a marked Petri net.* $Cover(\mathcal{N}, \mathbf{m}_0)$, *its* coverability set, *is defined by:*

$$Cover(\mathcal{N}, \mathbf{m}_0) = \downarrow Reach(\mathcal{N}, \mathbf{m}_0)$$

Since the coverability set is downward closed and $\mathbb{N}^P$ is FAC, it admits a finite decomposition in ideals. The ideals of $\mathbb{N}^P$ can be defined in an elegant way as follows. One first extends the sets of naturals and integers: $\mathbb{N}_\omega = \mathbb{N} \cup \{\omega\}$ et $\mathbb{Z}_\omega = \mathbb{Z} \cup \{\omega\}$. Then one extends the order relation and the addition to $\mathbb{Z}_\omega$: for all $n \in \mathbb{Z}$, $\omega > n$ and for all $n \in \mathbb{Z}_\omega$, $n + \omega = \omega + n = \omega$. $\mathbb{N}_\omega^P$ is also a well ordered set and its members are called $\omega$*-markings*. There is a one-to-one mapping between ideals of $\mathbb{N}^P$ and $\omega$-markings. Let $\mathbf{m} \in \mathbb{N}_\omega^P$. Define $[\![\mathbf{m}]\!]$ by:

$$[\![\mathbf{m}]\!] = \{\mathbf{m}' \in \mathbb{N}^P \mid \mathbf{m}' \leq \mathbf{m}\}$$

$[\![\mathbf{m}]\!]$ is an ideal of $\mathbb{N}^P$ (and all ideal can be defined in such a way). Let $\Omega$ be a set of $\omega$-markings, $[\![\Omega]\!]$ denotes the set $\bigcup_{\mathbf{m}\in\Omega}[\![\mathbf{m}]\!]$. Due to the above properties, there exists a unique finite set with minimal size $Clover(\mathcal{N},\mathbf{m}_0) \subseteq \mathbb{N}^P_\omega$ such that:

$$Cover(\mathcal{N},\mathbf{m}_0) = [\![Clover(\mathcal{N},\mathbf{m}_0)]\!]$$

A more general result can be found in [3] for well structured transition systems.

*Example 1.* The marked net of Figure 1 is unbounded. Its Clover is the following set:

$$\{p_i, p_{bk} + p_m, p_l + p_m + \omega p_{ba}, p_l + p_{bk} + \omega p_{ba} + \omega p_c\}$$

For instance, the marking $p_l+p_{bk}+\alpha p_{ba}+\beta p_c$ is reached thus covered by sequence $t_1 t_5^{\alpha+\beta} t_6^{\beta}$.

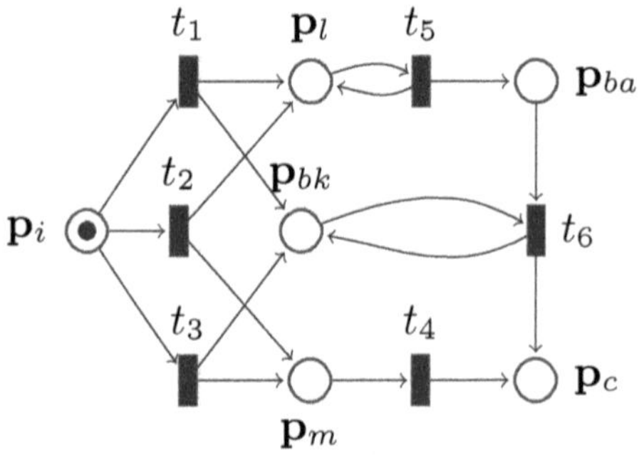


**Fig. 1.** An unbounded Petri net

### 2.2 Abstraction and acceleration

In order to introduce abstractions and accelerations, we generalize the transitions to allow the capability to mark a place with $\omega$ tokens.

**Definition 4.** *Let $P$ be a set of places. An $\omega$-transition* $\mathbf{a}$ *is defined by:*

- $\mathbf{Pre}(\mathbf{a}) \in \mathbb{N}^P_\omega$ *its* backward incidence*;*
- $\mathbf{C}(\mathbf{a}) \in \mathbb{Z}^P_\omega$ *its* incidence *with* $\mathbf{Pre}(\mathbf{a}) + \mathbf{C}(\mathbf{a}) \geq 0$.

For sake of homogeneity, one denotes $\mathbf{Pre}(\mathbf{a})(p)$ (resp. $\mathbf{C}(\mathbf{a})(p)$) by $\mathbf{Pre}(p,\mathbf{a})$ (resp. $\mathbf{C}(p,\mathbf{a})$). An $\omega$-transition $\mathbf{a}$ is fireable from an $\omega$-marking $\mathbf{m} \in \mathbb{N}^P_\omega$ if $\mathbf{m} \geq \mathbf{Pre}(\mathbf{a})$. When $\mathbf{a}$ is fireable from $\mathbf{m}$, its firing leads to the $\omega$-marking $\mathbf{m}' \stackrel{\text{def}}{=} \mathbf{m} + \mathbf{C}(\mathbf{a})$, denoted as previously $\mathbf{m} \xrightarrow{\mathbf{a}} \mathbf{m}'$. One observes that if $\mathbf{Pre}(p,\mathbf{a}) = \omega$ then for all values of $\mathbf{C}(p,\mathbf{a})$, $\mathbf{m}'(\mathbf{a}) = \omega$. So without loss of generality, one assumes that for all $\omega$-transition $\mathbf{a}$, $\mathbf{Pre}(p,\mathbf{a}) = \omega$ implies $\mathbf{C}(p,\mathbf{a}) = \omega$.

In order to define abstractions, we first define the incidences of a sequence $\sigma$ of $\omega$-transitions by recurrence on its length. As previously, we denote $\mathbf{Pre}(p,\sigma) \stackrel{\text{def}}{=}$

$\mathbf{Pre}(\sigma)(p)$ and $\mathbf{C}(p,\sigma) \stackrel{\text{def}}{=} \mathbf{C}(\sigma)(p)$. The base case corresponds to the definition of an $\omega$-transition. Let $\sigma = t\sigma'$, with $t$ an $\omega$-transition and $\sigma'$ a sequence of $\omega$-transitions, then:

- $\mathbf{C}(\sigma) = \mathbf{C}(t) + \mathbf{C}(\sigma')$;
- for all $p \in P$
  - if $\mathbf{C}(p,t) = \omega$ then $\mathbf{Pre}(p,\sigma) = \mathbf{Pre}(p,t)$;
  - else $\mathbf{Pre}(p,\sigma) = \max(\mathbf{Pre}(p,t), \mathbf{Pre}(p,\sigma') - \mathbf{C}(p,t))$.

One checks by recurrence that $\sigma$ is firable from $\mathbf{m}$ if and only if $\mathbf{m} \geq \mathbf{Pre}(\sigma)$ and in this case, $\mathbf{m} \xrightarrow{\sigma} \mathbf{m} + \mathbf{C}(\sigma)$.

An *abstraction* of a net is an $\omega$-transition which concisely expresses the behaviour of the net w.r.t. covering (see Proposition 1). One will observe that a transition $t$ of a net is by construction (with $\sigma_n = t$ for all $n$) an abstraction.

**Definition 5.** *Let $\mathcal{N} = \langle P, T, \mathbf{Pre}, \mathbf{C}\rangle$ be a Petri net and $\mathbf{a}$ be an $\omega$-transition. $\mathbf{a}$ is an* abstraction *if for all $n \geq 0$, there exists $\sigma_n \in T^*$ such that for all $p \in P$ with $\mathbf{Pre}(p, \mathbf{a}) \in \mathbb{N}$:*

1. *$\mathbf{Pre}(p,\sigma_n) \leq \mathbf{Pre}(p,\mathbf{a})$;*
2. *If $\mathbf{C}(p,\mathbf{a}) \in \mathbb{Z}$ then $\mathbf{C}(p,\sigma_n) \geq \mathbf{C}(p,\mathbf{a})$;*
3. *If $\mathbf{C}(p,\mathbf{a}) = \omega$ then $\mathbf{C}(p,\sigma_n) \geq n$.*

The following proposition justifies the interest of abstractions.

**Proposition 1.** *Let $(\mathcal{N}, \mathbf{m}_0)$ be a marked Petri net, $\mathbf{a}$ be an abstraction and $\mathbf{m}$ be an $\omega$-marking such that: $[\![\mathbf{m}]\!] \subseteq Cover(\mathcal{N}, \mathbf{m}_0)$ and $\mathbf{m} \xrightarrow{\mathbf{a}} \mathbf{m}'$. Then $[\![\mathbf{m}']\!] \subseteq Cover(\mathcal{N}, \mathbf{m}_0)$.*

**Proof.** Pick some $\mathbf{m}^* \in [\![\mathbf{m}']\!]$. Denote $n = \max(\mathbf{m}^*(p) \mid \mathbf{m}'(p) = \omega)$ and $\ell = \max(\mathbf{Pre}(p,\sigma_n), n - \mathbf{C}(p,\sigma_n) \mid \mathbf{m}(p) = \omega)$. Let us define $\mathbf{m}^\sharp \in [\![\mathbf{m}]\!]$ by:

- If $\mathbf{m}(p) < \omega$ then $\mathbf{m}^\sharp(p) = \mathbf{m}(p)$;
- Else $\mathbf{m}^\sharp(p) = \ell$.

Let us check that $\sigma_n$ is fireable from $\mathbf{m}^\sharp$. Let $p \in P$,

- If $\mathbf{m}(p) < \omega$ then $\mathbf{m}^\sharp(p) = \mathbf{m}(p) \geq \mathbf{Pre}(p,\mathbf{a}) \geq \mathbf{Pre}(p,\sigma_n)$;
- Else $\mathbf{m}^\sharp(p) = \ell \geq \mathbf{Pre}(p,\sigma_n)$.

Let us show that $\mathbf{m}^\sharp + \mathbf{C}(\sigma_n) \geq \mathbf{m}^*$. Let $p \in P$,

- If $\mathbf{m}(p) < \omega$ and $\mathbf{C}(p,\mathbf{a}) < \omega$ then $\mathbf{m}^\sharp(p) + \mathbf{C}(p,\sigma_n) \geq \mathbf{m}(p) + \mathbf{C}(p,\mathbf{a}) = \mathbf{m}'(p) \geq \mathbf{m}^*(p)$;
- If $\mathbf{m}(p) < \omega$ and $\mathbf{C}(p,\mathbf{a}) = \omega$ then $\mathbf{m}^\sharp(p) + \mathbf{C}(p,\sigma_n) \geq \mathbf{C}(p,\sigma_n) \geq n \geq \mathbf{m}^*(p)$ ;
- If $\mathbf{m}(p) = \omega$ then $\mathbf{m}^\sharp(p) + \mathbf{C}(p,\sigma_n) \geq n - \mathbf{C}(p,\sigma_n) + \mathbf{C}(p,\sigma_n) = n \geq \mathbf{m}^*(p)$.

■

An easy way to build new abstractions consists in concatenating them.

**Proposition 2.** *Let $\mathcal{N} = \langle P, T, \mathbf{Pre}, \mathbf{C} \rangle$ be a Petri net and $\sigma$ be a sequence of abstractions. Then the $\omega$-transition* $\mathbf{a}$ *defined by* $\mathbf{Pre}(\mathbf{a}) = \mathbf{Pre}(\sigma)$ *and* $\mathbf{C}(\mathbf{a}) = \mathbf{C}(\sigma)$ *is an abstraction.*

We now introduce the underlying concept of the Karp and Miller construction.

**Definition 6.** *Let $\mathcal{N} = \langle P, T, \mathbf{Pre}, \mathbf{C} \rangle$ be a Petri net. One says that* $\mathbf{a}$ *is an* acceleration *if* $\mathbf{a}$ *is an abstraction such that* $\mathbf{C}(\mathbf{a}) \in \{0, \omega\}^P$.

The following proposition provides a way to get an acceleration from an arbitrary abstraction.

**Proposition 3.** *Let $\mathcal{N} = \langle P, T, \mathbf{Pre}, \mathbf{C} \rangle$ be a Petri net and* $\mathbf{a}$ *be an abstraction. Define* $\mathbf{a}'$ *an $\omega$-transition as follows. For all $p \in P$:*

- *If* $\mathbf{C}(p, \mathbf{a}) < 0$ *then* $\mathbf{Pre}(p, \mathbf{a}') = \mathbf{C}(p, \mathbf{a}') = \omega$;
- *If* $\mathbf{C}(p, \mathbf{a}) = 0$ *then* $\mathbf{Pre}(p, \mathbf{a}') = \mathbf{Pre}(p, \mathbf{a})$ *and* $\mathbf{C}(p, \mathbf{a}') = 0$;
- *If* $\mathbf{C}(p, \mathbf{a}) > 0$ *then* $\mathbf{Pre}(p, \mathbf{a}') = \mathbf{Pre}(p, \mathbf{a})$ *and* $\mathbf{C}(p, \mathbf{a}') = \omega$.

*Then* $\mathbf{a}'$ *is an acceleration.*

Let us study more deeply the set of accelerations. First we equip the set of $\omega$-transitions with a"natural" order w.r.t. covering.

**Definition 7.** *Let $P$ be a set of places and two $\omega$-transitions* $\mathbf{a}$ *and* $\mathbf{a}'$.

$$\mathbf{a} \leq \mathbf{a}' \text{ if and only if } \mathbf{Pre}(\mathbf{a}) \leq \mathbf{Pre}(\mathbf{a}') \wedge \mathbf{C}(\mathbf{a}) \geq \mathbf{C}(\mathbf{a}')$$

In other words, $\mathbf{a} \leq \mathbf{a}'$ if given any $\omega$-marking $\mathbf{m}$, if $\mathbf{a}'$ is fireable from $\mathbf{m}$ then $\mathbf{a}$ is also fireable and its firing leads to a marking greater or equal that the one reached by the firing of $\mathbf{a}'$.

**Proposition 4.** *Let $\mathcal{N}$ be a Petri net. Then the set of abstractions of $\mathcal{N}$ is upward closed. Similarly, the set of accelerations is upward closed in the set of $\omega$-transitions whose incidence belongs to $\{0, \omega\}^P$.*

**Proposition 5.** *The set of accelerations of a Petri net is well ordered.*

**Proof.** The set of accelerations is a subset of $\mathbb{N}^P \times \{0, \omega\}^P$ (where $P$ is the set of places) with the order obtained by iterating cartesian products of sets $(\mathbb{N}, \leq)$ and $(\{0, \omega\}, \geq)$. These sets are well ordered and the cartesian product preserves this property. So we are done. ■

Since the set of accelerations is well ordered and it is upward closed, it is equal to the upward closure of the finite set of *minimal* accelerations. Let us study the size of a minimal acceleration. Given some Petri net, one denotes $d = |P|$ and $e = \max_{p,t}(\max(\mathbf{Pre}(p, t), \mathbf{Pre}(p, t) + \mathbf{C}(p, t)))$.

We are going to use the following result of Jérôme Leroux (published on HAL in June 2019) which provides a bound for the lengths of shortest sequences between two markings $\mathbf{m}_1$ and $\mathbf{m}_2$ mutually reachable.

**Theorem 1.** *(Theorem 2, [12]) Let $\mathcal{N}$ be a Petri net, $\mathbf{m}_1, \mathbf{m}_2$ be markings, $\sigma_1, \sigma_2$ be sequences of transitions such that $\mathbf{m}_1 \xrightarrow{\sigma_1} \mathbf{m}_2 \xrightarrow{\sigma_2} \mathbf{m}_1$. Then there exist $\sigma'_1, \sigma'_2$ such that $\mathbf{m}_1 \xrightarrow{\sigma'_1} \mathbf{m}_2 \xrightarrow{\sigma'_2} \mathbf{m}_1$ fulfilling:*

$$|\sigma'_1\sigma'_2| \leq ||\mathbf{m}_1 - \mathbf{m}_2||_\infty (3de)^{(d+1)^{2d+4}}$$

One deduces an upper bound on the size of minimal accelerations.
Let $\mathbf{v} \in \mathbb{N}_\omega^P$. One denotes $||\mathbf{v}||_\infty = \max(\mathbf{v}(p) \mid \mathbf{v}(p) \in \mathbb{N})$.

**Proposition 6.** *Let $\mathcal{N}$ be a Petri net and $\mathbf{a}$ be a minimal acceleration. Then $||\mathbf{Pre}(\mathbf{a})||_\infty \leq e(3de)^{(d+1)^{2d+4}}$.*

**Proof.** Let us consider the net $\mathcal{N}' = \langle P', T', \mathbf{Pre}', \mathbf{C}' \rangle$ obtained from $\mathcal{N}$ by deleting the set of places $\{p \mid \mathbf{Pre}(p, \mathbf{a}) = \omega\}$ and adding the set of transitions $T_1 = \{t_p \mid p \in P'\}$ with $\mathbf{Pre}(t_p) = p$ et $\mathbf{C}(t_p) = -p$. Observe that $d' \leq d$ and $e' = e$.
One denotes $P_1 = \{p \mid \mathbf{Pre}(p, \mathbf{a}) < \omega = \mathbf{C}(p, \mathbf{a})\}$. One introduces $\mathbf{m}_1$ the marking obtained by restricting $\mathbf{Pre}(\mathbf{a})$ to $P'$ and $\mathbf{m}_2 = \mathbf{m}_1 + \sum_{p \in P_1} p$.
Let $\{\sigma_n\}_{n \in \mathbb{N}}$ be a family of sequences associated with $\mathbf{a}$. Let $n^* = ||\mathbf{Pre}(\mathbf{a})||_\infty + 1$. Then $\sigma_{n^*}$ is fireable in $\mathcal{N}'$ from $\mathbf{m}_1$ and its firing leads to a marking that covers $\mathbf{m}_2$. By concatenating some occurrences of transitions of $T_1$, one gets a firing sequence in $\mathcal{N}'$ $\mathbf{m}_1 \xrightarrow{\sigma_1} \mathbf{m}_2$. Using the same process, one gets a firing sequence $\mathbf{m}_2 \xrightarrow{\sigma_2} \mathbf{m}_1$.
Let us apply Theorem 1. There exists a sequence $\sigma'_1$ with $\mathbf{m}_1 \xrightarrow{\sigma'_1} \mathbf{m}_2$ and $|\sigma'_1| \leq (3de)^{(d+1)^{2d+4}}$ since $||\mathbf{m}_1 - \mathbf{m}_2||_\infty = 1$. By deleting the transitions of $T_1$ occurring in $\sigma'_1$, one gets a sequence $\sigma''_1 \in T^*$ such that $\mathbf{m}_1 \xrightarrow{\sigma''_1} \mathbf{m}'_2 \geq \mathbf{m}_2$ with $|\sigma''_1| \leq (3de)^{(d+1)^{2d+4}}$.
The $\omega$-transition $\mathbf{a}'$, defined by $\mathbf{Pre}(p, \mathbf{a}') = \mathbf{Pre}(p, \sigma''_1)$ for all $p \in P'$, $\mathbf{Pre}(p, \mathbf{a}') = \omega$ for all $p \in P \setminus P'$ and $\mathbf{C}(\mathbf{a}') = \mathbf{C}(\mathbf{a})$, is an acceleration whose associated family is $\{\sigma''^n_1\}_{n \in \mathbb{N}}$. By definition of $\mathbf{m}_1$, $\mathbf{a}' \leq \mathbf{a}$. Since $\mathbf{a}$ is minimal, $\mathbf{a}' = \mathbf{a}$. Observing that $|\sigma''_1| \leq (3de)^{(d+1)^{2d+4}}$, one gets $||\mathbf{Pre}(\mathbf{a})||_\infty = ||\mathbf{Pre}(\mathbf{a}')||_\infty \leq e(3de)^{(d+1)^{2d+4}}$.

■

Thus given any acceleration, one can easily obtain a smaller acceleration whose (representation) size is exponential.

**Proposition 7.** *Let $\mathcal{N}$ be a Petri net and $\mathbf{a}$ be an acceleration. Then the $\omega$-transition $trunc(\mathbf{a})$ defined by:*

- *$\mathbf{C}(trunc(\mathbf{a})) = \mathbf{C}(\mathbf{a})$;*
- *for all $p$ such that $\mathbf{Pre}(p, \mathbf{a}) \neq \omega$,*
  *$\mathbf{Pre}(p, trunc(\mathbf{a})) = \min(\mathbf{Pre}(p, \mathbf{a}), e(3de)^{(d+1)^{2d+4}})$ ;*
- *for all $p$ such that $\mathbf{Pre}(p, \mathbf{a}) = \omega$, $\mathbf{Pre}(p, trunc(\mathbf{a})) = \omega$.*

*is an acceleration.*

**Proof.** Let $\mathbf{a}' \leq \mathbf{a}$, be a minimal acceleration. For all $p$ such that $\mathbf{Pre}(p, \mathbf{a}) \neq \omega$, $Pre(p, \mathbf{a}') \leq e(3de)^{(d+1)^{2d+4}}$. So $\mathbf{a}' \leq trunc(\mathbf{a})$. Since the set of accelerations is upward closed, one gets that $trunc(\mathbf{a})$ is an acceleration. ■

# 3 A coverability tree algorithm

## 3.1 Specification and illustration

As discussed in the introduction, to compute the clover of a Petri net, most algorithms build coverability trees (or graphs), which are variants of the Karp and Miller tree with the aim of reducing the peak memory during the execution. The seminal algorithm [6] is characterized by a main difference with the KMT construction: when finding that the marking associated with the current vertex strictly covers the marking of another vertex, it deletes the subtree issued from this vertex, and when the current vertex belonged to the removed subtree it substitutes it to the root of the deleted subtree. This operation drastically reduces the peak memory but as shown in [8] entails incompleteness of the algorithm.

Like the previous algorithms that ensure completeness with deletions, our algorithm also needs additional memory. However unlike the other algorithms, it memorizes accelerations instead of $\omega$-markings. This approach has two advantages. First, we are able to exhibit a theoretical upper bound on the additional memory which is doubly exponential, while the other algorithms do not have such a bound. Furthermore, accelerations are reused in the construction and thus may even shorten the execution time and peak space w.r.t. the algorithm in [6].

Before we delve into a high level description of this algorithm, let us present some of the variables, functions, and definitions used by the algorithm. Algorithm 1, denoted from now on as $\mathtt{MinCov}$ takes as an input a marked net $(\mathcal{N}, \mathbf{m}_0)$ and constructs a directed labeled tree $CT = (V, E, \lambda, \delta)$, and a set $\mathsf{Acc}$ of $\omega$-transitions (which by Lemma 2 are accelerations). Each $v \in V$ is labeled by an $\omega$-marking, $\lambda(v) \in \mathbb{N}_\omega^P$. Since $CT$ is a directed tree, every vertex $v \in V$, has a predecessor (except the root $r$) denoted by $prd(v)$ and a set of descendants denoted by $Des(v)$. By convention, $prd(r) = r$. Each edge $e \in E$ is labeled by a firing sequence $\delta(e) \in T_o \cdot \mathsf{Acc}^*$, consisting of an ordinary transition followed by a sequence of accelerations (which by Lemma 1 fulfills $\lambda(prd(v)) \xrightarrow{\delta(prd(v),v)} \lambda(v)$). In addition, again by Lemma 1, $\mathbf{m}_0 \xrightarrow{\delta(r,r)} \lambda(r)$. Let $\gamma = e_1 e_2 \dots e_k \in E^*$ be a path in the tree, we denote by $\delta(\gamma) := \delta(e_1)\delta(e_2)\dots\delta(e_k) \in (T \cup \mathsf{Acc})^*$. The subset $\mathsf{Front} \subset V$ is the set of vertices 'to be processed'.

$\mathtt{MinCov}$ may call function $\mathtt{Delete}(v)$ that removes from $V$ a leaf $v$ of $CT$ and function $\mathtt{Prune}(v)$ that removes from $V$ all descendants of $v \in V$ except $v$ itself as illustrated in the following figure:

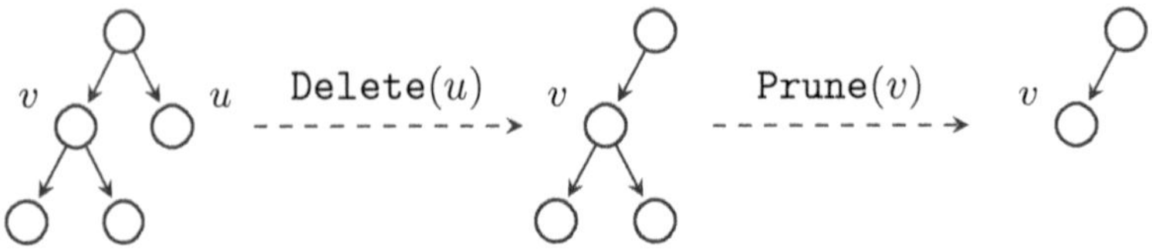


First $\mathtt{MinCov}$ does some initializations, and sets the tree $CT$ to be a single vertex $r$ with marking $\lambda(r) = \mathbf{m}_0$ and $\mathsf{Front} = \{r\}$. Afterwards the main loop builds the tree, where each iteration consists in processing some vertex in Front as follows.

MinCov picks a vertex $u \in \mathsf{Front}$ (line 3). From $\lambda(u)$, MinCov fires a sequence $\sigma \in Acc^*$ reaching some $\mathbf{m}_u$ that maximizes the number of $\omega$ produced, i.e. $|\{p \in P \mid \lambda(u)(p) \neq \omega \wedge \mathbf{m}_u(p) = \omega\}|$. Thus in $\sigma$, no acceleration occurs twice and its length is bounded by $|P|$. Then MinCov updates $\lambda(u)$ with $\mathbf{m}_u$ (line 5) and the label of the edge incoming to $u$ by concatenating $\sigma$. Afterwards it performs one of the following actions according to the marking $\lambda(u)$:

- **Cleaning** (line 7): If there exists $u' \in V \setminus \mathsf{Front}$ with $\lambda(u') \geq \lambda(u)$. The vertex $u$ is redundant and MinCov calls $\texttt{Delete}(u)$
- **Accelerating** (lines 8-16): If there exists $u'$, an ancestor of $u$ with $\lambda(u') < \lambda(u)$ then an acceleration can be computed. The acceleration $\mathbf{a}$ is deduced from the firing sequence labeling the path from $u'$ to $u$. MinCov inserts $\mathbf{a}$ into Acc, calls $\texttt{Prune}(u')$ and pushes back $u'$ in Front.
- **Exploring** (lines 18 - 25): Otherwise MinCov calls $\texttt{Prune}(u')$ followed by $\texttt{Delete}(u')$ for all $u' \in V$ with $\lambda(u') < \lambda(u)$ since they are redundant. Afterwards, it removes $u$ from Front and for all fireable transition $t \in T$ from $\lambda(u)$, it creates a new child for $u$ in $CT$ and inserts it into Front.

For a detailed example of a run of the algorithm see Example 2 in [9].

### 3.2 Correctness Proof

We now establish the correctness of Algorithm 1 by proving the following properties (where for all $W \subseteq V$, $\lambda(W)$ denotes $\bigcup_{v \in W} \lambda(v)$):

- its termination;
- the incomparability of $\omega$-markings associated with vertices in $V$: $\lambda(V)$ is an antichain;
- its consistency: $[\![\lambda(V)]\!] \subseteq Cover(\mathcal{N}, \mathbf{m}_0)$;
- its completeness: $Cover(\mathcal{N}, \mathbf{m}_0) \subseteq [\![\lambda(V)]\!]$.

We get termination by using the well order of $\mathbb{N}_\omega^P$ and Koenig Lemma.

**Proposition 8.** *MinCov terminates.*

**Proof.** Consider the following variation of the algorithm.

Instead of deleting the current vertex when its marking is smaller or equal than the marking of a vertex, one marks it as ‘cut’ and extract it from Front.

Instead of cutting a subtree when the marking of the current vertex $v$ is greater than the marking of a vertex which is not an ancestor of $v$, one marks them as ‘cut’ and extract from Front those who are inside.

Instead of cutting a subtree when the marking of the current vertex $v$ is greater than the marking of a vertex which is an ancestor of $v$, say $v^*$, one marks those on the path from $v^*$ to $v$ (except $v$) as ‘accelerated’, one marks the other vertices

**Algorithm 1:** Computing the minimal coverability set

MinCov($\mathcal{N}, \mathbf{m}_0$)
**Input:** A marked Petri net $(\mathcal{N}, \mathbf{m}_0)$
**Data:** $V$ set of vertices; $E \subseteq V \times V$; $\mathsf{Front} \subseteq V$; $\lambda : V \to \mathbb{N}_\omega^p$; $\delta : E \to T_o\mathsf{Acc}^*$; $CT = (V, E, \lambda, \delta)$ a labeled tree; $\mathsf{Acc}$ a set of $\omega$-transitions;
**Output:** A labeled tree $CT = (V, E, \lambda, \delta)$

$V \leftarrow \{r\}$; $E \leftarrow \emptyset$; $\mathsf{Front} \leftarrow \{r\}$; $\lambda(r) \leftarrow \mathbf{m}_0$; $\mathsf{Acc} \leftarrow \emptyset$; $\delta(r, r) \leftarrow \varepsilon$
**while** $Front \neq \emptyset$ **do**
  Select $u \in \mathsf{Front}$
  Let $\sigma \in \mathsf{Acc}^*$ a maximal fireable sequence of accelerations from $\lambda(u)$
  // Maximal w.r.t. the number of $\omega$'s produced
  $\lambda(u) \leftarrow \lambda(u) + \mathbf{C}(\sigma)$
  $\delta((prd(u), u)) \leftarrow \delta((prd(u), u)) \cdot \sigma$
  **if** $\exists u' \in V \setminus \mathsf{Front}$ *s.t.* $\lambda(u') \geq \lambda(u)$ **then** Delete($u$) // $\lambda(u)$ is covered
  **else if** $\exists u' \in \mathsf{Anc}(V)$ *s.t.* $\lambda(u) > \lambda(u')$ **then**
    // An acceleration was found between $u$ and one of $u$'s ancestors
    Let $\gamma \in E^*$ the path from $u'$ to $u$ in $CT$
    $\mathbf{a} \leftarrow$ NewAcceleration()
    **foreach** $p \in P$ **do**
      **if** $\mathbf{C}(p, \delta(\gamma)) < 0$ **then** $\mathbf{Pre}(p, \mathbf{a}) \leftarrow \omega$; $\mathbf{C}(p, \mathbf{a}) \leftarrow \omega$
      **if** $\mathbf{C}(p, \delta(\gamma)) = 0$ **then** $\mathbf{Pre}(p, \mathbf{a}) \leftarrow \mathbf{Pre}(p, \delta(\gamma))$; $\mathbf{C}(p, \mathbf{a}) \leftarrow 0$
      **if** $\mathbf{C}(p, \delta(\gamma)) > 0$ **then** $\mathbf{Pre}(p, \mathbf{a}) \leftarrow \mathbf{Pre}(p, \delta(\gamma))$; $\mathbf{C}(p, \mathbf{a}) \leftarrow \omega$
    **end**
    $\mathbf{a} \leftarrow trunc(\mathbf{a})$; $\mathsf{Acc} \leftarrow \mathsf{Acc} \cup \{\mathbf{a}\}$; Prune($u'$); $\mathsf{Front} = \mathsf{Front} \cup \{u'\}$ ;
  **else**
    **for** $u' \in V$ **do**
      // Remove vertices labeled by markings covered by $\lambda(u)$
      **if** $\lambda(u') < \lambda(u)$ **then** Prune($u'$); Delete($u'$)
    **end**
    $\mathsf{Front} \leftarrow \mathsf{Front} \setminus \{u\}$
    **foreach** $t \in T \wedge \lambda(u) \geq \mathbf{Pre}(t)$ **do**
      // Add the children of $u$
      $u' \leftarrow$ NewNode(); $V \leftarrow V \cup \{u'\}$; $\mathsf{Front} \leftarrow \mathsf{Front} \cup \{u'\}$); $E \leftarrow E \cup \{(u, u')\}$
      $\lambda(u') \leftarrow \lambda(u) + \mathbf{C}(t)$; $\delta((u, u')) \leftarrow t$
    **end**
  **end**
**end**
**return** $CT$

of the subtree as 'cut' and inserts $v$ again in Front with the marking of $v^*$. All the markings of the subtree in Front are extracted from it.

All the vertices marked as 'cut' or 'accelerated' are ignored for comparisons and discovering accelerations. This alternative algorithm behaves as the original one except that the size of the tree never decreases and so if the algorithm does not terminate the tree is infinite. Since this tree is finitely branching, due to Koenig Lemma it contains an infinite path. On this infinite path, no vertex can be marked as 'cut' since it would belong to a finite subtree. Observe that the marking labelling the vertex following an accelerated subpath has at least one more $\omega$ than the marking of the first vertex of this subpath. So there is an infinite subpath with unmarked vertices in $V$. But $\mathbb{N}_\omega^P$ is well-ordered, so there should be two vertices $v$ and $v'$, where $v'$ is a descendant of $v$ with $\lambda(v') \geq \lambda(v)$, which contradicts the behaviour of the algorithm.

■

Since we are going to use recurrence on the number of iterations of the main loop of Algorithm 1, we introduce the following notations: $CT_n = (V_n, E_n, \lambda_n, \delta_n)$, $\mathsf{Front}_n$, and $\mathsf{Acc}_n$ are the the values of variables $CT$, Front, and Acc at line 2 when $n$ iterations have been executed.

**Proposition 9.** *For all $n \in \mathbb{N}$, $\lambda(V_n \setminus \mathsf{Front}_n)$ is an antichain. Thus on termination, $\lambda(V)$ is an antichain.*

**Proof.** Let us introduce $V' := V \setminus \mathsf{Front}$ and $V'_n := V_n \setminus \mathsf{Front}_n$. We are going to prove by induction on the number $n$ of iterations of the while-loop that $V'_n$ is an antichain. MinCov initializes variables $V$ and Front at line 1. So $V_0 = \{r\}$ and $\mathsf{Front}_0 = \{r\}$, therefore $V'_0 = V_0 \setminus \mathsf{Front}_0 = \emptyset$ is an antichain.
Assume that $V'_n = V_n \setminus \mathsf{Front}_n$ is an antichain. Modifying $V'_n$ can be done by *adding* or *removing* vertices from $V_n$ and *removing* vertices from $\mathsf{Front}_n$ while keeping them in $V_n$. The actions that MinCov may perform in order to modify the sets $V$ and Front are: `Delete` (lines 7 and 19), `Prune` (lines 16 and 19), adding vertices to $V$ (line 23), adding vertices to Front (lines 16 and 23), and removing vertices from Front (line 21).
• Both `Delete` and `Prune` do not add new vertices to $V'$. Thus the antichain feature is preserved.
• MinCov may add vertices to $V$ only at line 23 where it simultaneously adds them to Front and therefore does not add new vertices to $V'$. Thus the antichain feature is preserved.
• Adding vertices to Front may only remove vertices from $V'_n$. Thus the antichain feature is preserved.
• MinCov can only add a vertex to $V'$ when it removes it from Front while keeping it in $V$. This is done only at line 21. There the only vertex MinCov may remove (line 21) is the working vertex $u$. However if (in the iteration) MinCov reaches line 21 then it did not reach line 7 hence, (1) all markings of $\lambda(V'_n) \subseteq \lambda(V_n)$ are either smaller or incomparable to $\lambda_{n+1}(u)$. Moreover, MinCov has also reached line 18-20, where (2) it performs `Delete` on all vertices $u' \in V'_n \subseteq V_n$ with $\lambda_n(u') < \lambda_{n+1}(u)$. Let us denote by $V''_n \subseteq V'_n$ the set $V'$ at the end of line

20. Due to (1) and (2), marking $\lambda_{n+1}(u)$ is incomparable to any marking in $\lambda_{n+1}(V''_n)$. Since $V''_n \subseteq V'_n$, $\lambda_{n+1}(V''_n)$ is an antichain. Combining this fact with the incomparability between $\lambda_{n+1}(u)$ and any marking in $\lambda_{n+1}(V''_n)$, we conclude that the set $\lambda_{n+1}(V'_{n+1}) = \lambda_{n+1}(V''_n) \cup \{\lambda_{n+1}(u)\}$ is an antichain.

■

In order to establish consistency, we prove that the labelling of vertices and edges is compatible with the firing rule and that *Acc* is a set of accelerations.

**Lemma 1.** *For all* $n \in \mathbb{N}$, *for all* $u \in V_n \setminus \{r\}$, $\lambda_n(prd(u)) \xrightarrow{\delta(prd(u),u)} \lambda_n(u)$ *and* $\mathbf{m}_0 \xrightarrow{\delta(r,r)} \lambda_n(r)$.

**Proof.** Let us prove by induction on the number $n$ of iterations of the main loop that for all $v \in V_n$, the assertions of the lemma hold. Initially, $V_0 = \{r\}$ and $\lambda_0(r) = \mathbf{m}_0$. Since $\mathbf{m}_0 \xrightarrow{\varepsilon} \mathbf{m}_0 = \lambda_0(r)$ the base case is established.
Assume that the assertions hold for $CT_n$. Observe that MinCov may change the labeling function $\lambda$ and/or add new vertices in exactly two places: at lines 4-6 and at lines 22-25. Therefore in order to prove the assertion, we show that after each group of lines it still holds.

- After lines 4-6: MinCov computes (1) a maximal fireable sequence $\sigma \in \mathsf{Acc}_n^*$ from $\lambda_n(u)$ (line 4), and updates $u$'s marking to $\mathbf{m}_u = \lambda_n(u) + \mathbf{C}(\sigma)$ (line 5). Since the assertions hold for $CT_n$, (2) if $u \neq r$, $\lambda_n(prd(u)) \xrightarrow{\delta(prd(u),u)} \lambda_n(u)$ else $\mathbf{m}_0 \xrightarrow{\delta(r,r)} \lambda_n(r)$. By concatenation, we get $\lambda_n(prd(u)) \xrightarrow{\delta(prd(u),u)\sigma} \mathbf{m}_u$ if $u \neq r$ and otherwise $\mathbf{m}_0 \xrightarrow{\delta(r,r)\sigma} \mathbf{m}_u$ which establishes that the assertions hold after line 6.
- After lines 22-25: The vertices for which $\lambda$ is updated at these lines are the children of $u$ that are added to the tree. For every fireable transition $t \in T$ from $\lambda(u)$, MinCov creates a child $v_t$ for $u$ (lines 22-23). The marking of any child $v_t$ is set to $\mathbf{m}_{n+1}(v) := \mathbf{m}_{n+1}(u) + \mathbf{C}(t)$ (line 24). Therefore since $\lambda_{n+1}(u) \xrightarrow{t} \lambda_{n+1}(v_t)$, the assertions hold.

■

**Lemma 2.** *At any execution point of MinCov,* Acc *is a set of accelerations.*

**Proof.** At most one acceleration is added per iteration. Let us prove by induction on the number $n$ of iterations of the main loop that $\mathsf{Acc}_n$ is a set of accelerations. Since $\mathsf{Acc}_0 = \emptyset$, the base case is straightforward.
Assume that $\mathsf{Acc}_n$ is a set of accelerations and consider $\mathsf{Acc}_{n+1}$. In an iteration, MinCov may add an $\omega$-transition $\mathbf{a}$ to Acc. Due to the inductive hypothesis, $\delta(\gamma)$ is a sequence of abstractions where $\gamma$ is defined at line 9. Consider $b$, the $\omega$-transition defined by $\mathbf{Pre}(b) = \mathbf{Pre}(\delta(\gamma))$ and $\mathbf{C}(b) = \mathbf{C}(\delta(\gamma))$. Due to Proposition 2, $b$ is an abstraction. Due to Proposition 3, the loop of lines 11-15 transforms $b$ into an acceleration $\mathbf{a}$. Due to Proposition 7, after truncation at line 16, $\mathbf{a}$ is still an acceleration. ■

**Proposition 10.** $[\![\lambda(V)]\!] \subseteq Cover(\mathcal{N}, \mathbf{m}_0)$.

**Proof.** Let $v \in V$. Consider the path $u_0, \ldots, u_k$ of $CT$ from the root $r = u_0$ to $u_k = v$. Let $\sigma \in (T \cup \mathsf{Acc})^*$ denote $\delta(prd(u_0), u_0) \cdots \delta(prd(u_k), u_k)$. Due to Lemma 1, $m_0 \xrightarrow{\sigma} \lambda(v)$. Due to Lemma 2, $\sigma$ is a sequence of abstractions. Due to Proposition 2, the $\omega$-transition $\mathbf{a}$ defined by $\mathbf{Pre}(\mathbf{a}) = \mathbf{Pre}(\sigma)$ and $\mathbf{C}(\mathbf{a}) = \mathbf{C}(\sigma)$ is an abstraction. Due to Proposition 1, $[\![\lambda(v)]\!] \subseteq Cover(\mathcal{N}, \mathbf{m}_0)$. ■

The following definitions are related to an arbitrary execution point of `MinCov` and are introduced to establish its completeness.

**Definition 8.** *Let* $\sigma = \sigma_0 t_1 \sigma_1 \ldots t_k \sigma_k$ *with for all* $i$, $t_i \in T$ *and* $\sigma_i \in \mathsf{Acc}^*$. *Then the firing sequence* $\mathbf{m} \xrightarrow{\sigma} \mathbf{m}'$ *is an* exploring sequence *if:*

- *There exists* $v \in \mathsf{Front}$ *with* $\lambda(v) = \mathbf{m}$
- *For all* $0 \leq i \leq k$, *there does not exist* $v' \in V \setminus \mathsf{Front}$ *with* $\mathbf{m} + \mathbf{C}(\sigma_0 t_1 \sigma_1 \ldots t_i \sigma_i) \leq \lambda(v')$.

**Definition 9.** *Let* $\widehat{\mathbf{m}}$ *be a marking. Then* $\widehat{\mathbf{m}}$ *is* quasi-covered *if:*

- *either there exists* $v \in V \setminus \mathsf{Front}$ *with* $\lambda(v) \geq \widehat{\mathbf{m}}$;
- *or there exists an exploring sequence* $\mathbf{m} \xrightarrow{\sigma} \mathbf{m}' \geq \widehat{\mathbf{m}}$.

In order to prove completeness of the algorithm, we want to prove that at the beginning of every iteration, any $\mathbf{m} \in Cover(\mathcal{N}, \mathbf{m}_0)$ is quasi-covered. To establish this assertion, we introduce several lemmas showing that this assertion is preserved by some actions of the algorithm with some prerequisites. More precisely, Lemma 3 corresponds to the deletion of the current vertex, Lemma 4 to the discovery of an acceleration, Lemma 5 to the deletion of a subtree whose marking of the root is smaller than the marking of the current vertex and Lemma 6 to the creation of the children of the current vertex.

**Lemma 3.** *Let* $CT$, $\mathsf{Front}$ *and* $\mathsf{Acc}$ *be the values of corresponding variables at some execution point of MinCov and* $u \in V$ *be a leaf in* $CT$ *such that the following items hold:*

1. *All* $\mathbf{m} \in Cover(\mathcal{N}, \mathbf{m}_0)$ *are quasi-covered;*
2. $\lambda(V \setminus \mathsf{Front})$ *is an antichain;*
3. *For all* $\mathbf{a} \in \mathsf{Acc}$ *fireable from* $\lambda(u)$, $\lambda(u) = \lambda(u) + \mathbf{C}(\mathbf{a})$;
4. *There exists* $v \in V \setminus \{u\}$ *such that* $\lambda(v) \geq \lambda(u)$.

*Then all* $\mathbf{m} \in Cover(\mathcal{N}, \mathbf{m}_0)$ *are quasi-covered after performing* `Delete`$(u)$.

**Lemma 4.** *Let* $CT$, $\mathsf{Front}$ *and* $\mathsf{Acc}$ *be the values of corresponding variables at some execution point of MinCov. and* $u \in V$ *such that the following items hold:*

1. *All* $\mathbf{m} \in Cover(\mathcal{N}, \mathbf{m}_0)$ *are quasi-covered;*
2. $\lambda(V \setminus \mathsf{Front})$ *is an antichain;*
3. *For all* $v \in V \setminus \{r\}$, $\lambda(prd(v)) \xrightarrow{\delta(prd(v),v)} \lambda(v)$.

*Then all* $\mathbf{m} \in Cover(\mathcal{N}, \mathbf{m}_0)$ *are quasi-covered after performing* `Prune`$(u)$ *and then adding* $u$ *to* $\mathsf{Front}$.

**Lemma 5.** *Let $CT$, Front and Acc be the values of corresponding variables at some execution point of MinCov, $u \in$ Front and $u' \in V$ such that the following items hold:*

1. *All $\mathbf{m} \in Cover(\mathcal{N}, \mathbf{m}_0)$ are quasi-covered;*
2. *$\lambda(V \setminus \mathsf{Front})$ is an antichain;*
3. *For all $v \in V \setminus \{r\}$, $\lambda(prd(v)) \xrightarrow{\delta(prd(v),v)} \lambda(v)$;*
4. *$\lambda(u') < \lambda(u)$ and $u$ is not a descendant of $u'$.*

*Then after performing* `Prune`$(u')$; `Delete`$(u')$,

1. *All $\mathbf{m} \in Cover(\mathcal{N}, \mathbf{m}_0)$ are quasi-covered;*
2. *$\lambda(V \setminus \mathsf{Front})$ is an antichain;*
3. *For all $v \in V \setminus \{r\}$, $\lambda(prd(v)) \xrightarrow{\delta(prd(v),v)} \lambda(v)$.*

**Lemma 6.** *Let $CT$, Front and Acc be the values of corresponding variables at some execution point of MinCov. and $u \in$ Front such that the following items hold:*

1. *All $\mathbf{m} \in Cover(\mathcal{N}, \mathbf{m}_0)$ are quasi-covered;*
2. *$\lambda(V \setminus \mathsf{Front}) \cup \{\lambda(u)\}$ is an antichain;*
3. *For all $\mathbf{a} \in$ Acc fireable from $\lambda(u)$, $\lambda(u) = \lambda(u) + \mathbf{C}(\mathbf{a})$.*

*Then after removing $u$ from Front and for all $t \in T$ fireable from $\lambda(u)$, adding a child $v_t$ to $u$ in Front with marking of $v_t$ defined by $\lambda_u(v_t) = \lambda(u) + \mathbf{C}(t)$, all $\mathbf{m} \in Cover(\mathcal{N}, \mathbf{m}_0)$ are quasi-covered.*

**Proposition 11.** *At the beginning of every iteration, all $\mathbf{m} \in Cover(\mathcal{N}, \mathbf{m}_0)$ are quasi-covered.*

**Proof.** Let us prove by induction on the number of iterations that all $\mathbf{m} \in Cover(\mathcal{N}, \mathbf{m}_0)$ are quasi-covered.
Let us consider the base case. MinCov initializes $V$ and Front to $\{r\}$ and $\lambda(r)$ to $\mathbf{m}_0$. By definition, for all $\mathbf{m} \in Cov(\mathcal{N}, \mathbf{m}_0)$ there exists $\sigma = t_1 t_2 \cdots t_k \in T^*$ such that $\mathbf{m}_0 \xrightarrow{\sigma} \mathbf{m}' \geq \mathbf{m}$. Since $V \setminus \mathsf{Front} = \emptyset$, this firing sequence is an exploring sequence.
Assume that all $\mathbf{m} \in Cover(\mathcal{N}, \mathbf{m}_0)$ are quasi-covered at the beginning of some iteration. Let us examine what may happen during the iteration. In lines 4-6, MinCov computes the maximal fireable sequence $\sigma \in \mathsf{Acc}_n^*$ from $\lambda_n(u)$ (line 4) and sets $u$'s marking to $\mathbf{m}_u := \lambda_n(u) + \mathbf{C}(\sigma)$ (line 5). Afterwards, there are three possible cases: (1) either $\mathbf{m}_u$ is covered by some marking associated with a vertex out of Front, (2) either an acceleration is found, (3) or MinCov computes the successors of $u$ and removes $u$ from Front.

**Line 7.** MinCov calls `Delete`$(u)$. So $CT_{n+1}$ is obtained by deleting $u$. Moreover, $\lambda(u') \geq \mathbf{m}_u$. Let us check the hypotheses of Lemma 3. Assertion 1 follows from induction since (1) the only change in the data is the increasing of $\lambda(u)$ by firing some accelerations and (2) $u$ belongs to Front so cannot cover intermediate markings of exploring sequences. Assertion 2 follows from Proposition 9 since $V \setminus \mathsf{Front}$ is unchanged. Assertion 3 follows immediately from lines 4-6. Assertion 4 follows with $v = u'$. Thus using this lemma the induction is proved in this case.

**Lines 8-16.** Let us check the hypotheses of Lemma 4. Assertions 1 and 2 are established as in the previous case. Assertion 3 holds due to Lemma 1, and the fact that no edge has been added since the beginning of iteration. Thus using this lemma the induction is proved in this case.

**Lines 18-25.** We first show that the hypotheses of Lemma 6 hold before line 21. Let us denote the values of $CT$ and $\mathsf{Front}$ after line 20 by $\widehat{CT}_n$ and $\widehat{\mathsf{Front}}_n$. Observe that for all iteration of Line 19 in the inner loop, the hypotheses of Lemma 5 are satisfied. Therefore, in order to apply Lemma 6 it remains only to check assertions 2 and 3 of this lemma. Assertion 2 holds since (1) $\lambda(V \setminus \mathsf{Front})$ is an antichain, (2) due to Line 7 there is no $w \in V \setminus \mathsf{Front}$ such that $\lambda(w) \geq \lambda(u)$, and (3) by iteration of Line 19 all $w \in V \setminus \mathsf{Front}$ such that $\lambda(w) < \lambda(u)$ have been deleted. Assertion 3 holds due to Line 5 (all useful enabled accelerations have been fired) and Line 8 (no acceleration has been added).

Lines 21-25 correspond to the operations related to Lemma 6. Thus using this lemma, the induction is proved in this case.

∎

The completeness of MinCov is an immediate consequence of the previous proposition.

**Corollary 1.** *When MinCov terminates,* $Cover(\mathcal{N}, \mathbf{m}_0) \subseteq [\![\lambda(V)]\!]$.

**Proof.** By Proposition 11 all $\mathbf{m} \in Cover(\mathcal{N}, \mathbf{m}_0)$ are quasi-covered. Since on termination, $\mathsf{Front}$ is empty for all $\mathbf{m} \in Cover(\mathcal{N}, \mathbf{m}_0)$, there exists $v \in V$ such that $\mathbf{m} \leq \lambda(v)$. ∎

## 4 Tool and benchmarks

In order to empirically evaluate our algorithm, we have implemented a prototype tool which computes the clover and solves the coverability problem. This tool is developed in the programming language Python, using the Numpy library. It can be found on GitHub[3]. All benchmarks were performed on a computer equipped by Intel i5-8250U CPU with 4 cores, 16GB of memory and Ubuntu Linux 18.03.

**Minimal coverability set.** We compare `MinCov` with the tool `MP` [14], the tool `VH` [16], and the tool `CovProc` [10]. We have also implemented the (incomplete) minimal coverability tree algorithm denoted by `AF` in order to measure the additional memory needed for the (complete) tools. Both `MP` and `VH` tools were sent to us by the courtesy of the authors. The tool `MP` has an implementation

[3] https://github.com/IgorKhm/MinCov

in Python and another in C++. For comparison we selected the Python one to avoid biases due to programming language.

We ran two kinds of benchmarks: (1) 123 standard benchmarks from the literature in Table 1, (which were taken from [2]), (2) 100 randomly generated Petri nets also in Table 1, since the benchmarks from the literature do not present all the features that lead to infinite state systems. These random Petri nets have the following properties: (1) $50 < |P|, |T| < 100$, (2) the number of places connected of each transition is bounded by 10, and (3) they are not structurally bounded. The execution time of the tools was limited to 900 seconds.

Table 1 contains a summary of all the instances of the benchmarks. The first column shows the number of instances on which the tool timed out. The time column consists of the total time on instances that did not time out plus 900 seconds for any instance that led to a time out. The #Nodes column consists of the peak number of nodes in instances that did not time out on any of the tools (except `CovProc` which does not provide this number). For `MinCov` we take the peak number of nodes plus accelerations. In the benchmarks from the literature

**Table 1.** Benchmarks for clover

| **123 benchmarks from the literature** | | | | **100 random benchmarks** | | | |
|---|---|---|---|---|---|---|---|
| | T/O | Time | #Nodes | | T/O | Time | #Nodes |
| `MinCov` | 16 | 18127 | **48218** | `MinCov` | **14** | 13989 | **61164** |
| `VH` | **15** | **14873** | 75225 | `VH` | 15 | **13692** | 208134 |
| `MP` | 24 | 23904 | 478681 | `MP` | 21 | 21726 | 755129 |
| `CovProc` | 49 | 47081 | N/A | `CovProc` | 80 | 74767 | N/A |
| `AF` | 19 | 19223 | 45660 | `AF` | 16 | 15888 | 63275 |

we observed that the instances that timed out from `MinCov` are included in those of `AF` and `MP`. However there were instances the timed out on `VH` but did not time out on `MinCov` and vice versa. `MinCov` is the second fastest tool, and compared to `VH` it is 1.2 times slower. A possible explanation would be that `VH` is implemented in C++. As could be expected, w.r.t. memory requirements `MinCov` has the least number of nodes. In the benchmarks from the literature `MinCov` has approximately 10 times less nodes then `MP` and 1.6 times less then `VH`. In the random benchmarks these ratio are significantly higher.

**Coverability.** We compare `MinCov` to the tool `qCover` [2] on the set of benchmarks from the literature in Table 2. In [2], `qCover` is compared to the most competitive tools for coverability and achieves a score of 142 solved instances while the second best tool achieves a score of 122. We split the results into safe instances (not coverable) and unsafe ones (coverable). In both categories we counted the number of instances on which the tools failed (columns T/O) and the total time (columns Time) as in Table 1.

We observed that the tools are complementary, i.e. `qCover` is faster at proving that an instance is safe and `MinCov` is faster at proving that an instance is unsafe.

**Table 2.** Benchmarks for the coverability problem (60 unsafe and 115 safe)

| | Time Unsafe | T/O Unsafe | Time safe | T/O safe | T/O | Time |
|---|---|---|---|---|---|---|
| `MinCov` | **1754** | **1** | 51323 | 53 | 54 | 53077 |
| `qCover` | 26467 | 26 | **11865** | **11** | 37 | 38332 |
| `MinCov` ‖ `qCover` | 1841 | 2 | 13493 | 11 | **13** | **15334** |

Therefore, by splitting the processing time between them we get better results. The third row of Table 2 represents a parallel execution of the tools, where the time for each instance is computed as follows:

$$\mathrm{Time}(\texttt{MinCov} \parallel \texttt{qCover}) = 2\min\left(\mathrm{Time}(\texttt{MinCov}), \mathrm{Time}(\texttt{qCover})\right).$$

Combining both tools is 2.5 times faster than `qCover` and 3.5 times faster than `MinCov`. This confirms the above statement. We could still get better results by dynamically deciding which ratio of CPU to share between the tools depending on some predicted status of the instance.

# 5 Conclusion

We have proposed a simple and efficient modification of the incomplete minimal coverability tree algorithm for building the clover of a net. Our algorithm is based on the introduction of the concepts of covering abstractions and accelerations. Compared to the alternative algorithms previously designed, we have theoretically bounded the size of the additional space. Furthermore we have implemented a prototype which is already very competitive.

From a theoretical point of view, we plan to study how abstractions and accelerations, could be defined in the more general context of well structured transition systems. From an experimental point of view, we will follow three directions in order to increase the performance of our tool. First as in [13], we have to select appropriate data structures to minimize the number of comparisons between $\omega$-markings. Then we want to precompute a set of accelerations using linear programming as the correctness of the algorithm is preserved and the efficiency could be significantly improved. Last we want to take advantage of parallelism in a more general way than simultaneously running several tools.

# References


1. Blockelet, M., Schmitz, S.: Model checking coverability graphs of vector addition systems. In: Proceedings of MFCS 2011. LNCS, vol. 6907, pp. 108–119 (2011)
2. Blondin, M., Finkel, A., Haase, C., Haddad, S.: Approaching the coverability problem continuously. In: Proceedings of TACAS 2016. LNCS, vol. 9636, pp. 480–496. Springer (2016)
3. Blondin, M., Finkel, A., McKenzie, P.: Well behaved transition systems. Logical Methods in Computer Science **13**(3), 1–19 (2017)

4. Demri, S.: On selective unboundedness of VASS. J. Comput. Syst. Sci. **79**(5), 689–713 (2013)
5. Finkel, A.: Reduction and covering of infinite reachability trees. Information and Computation **89**(2), 144–179 (1990)
6. Finkel, A.: The minimal coverability graph for Petri nets. In: Advances in Petri Nets. LNCS, vol. 674, pp. 210–243 (1993)
7. Finkel, A., Goubault-Larrecq, J.: Forward analysis for WSTS, part II: Complete WSTS. Logical Methods in Computer Science **8**(4), 1–35 (2012)
8. Finkel, A., Geeraerts, G., Raskin, J.F., Van Begin, L.: A counter-example to the minimal coverability tree algorithm. Tech. rep., Université Libre de Bruxelles, Belgium (2005), http://www.lsv.fr/Publis/PAPERS/PDF/FGRV-ulb05.pdf
9. Finkel, A., Haddad, S., Khmelnitsky, I.: Minimal coverability tree construction made complete and efficient (2020), https://hal.inria.fr/hal-02479879
10. Geeraerts, G., Raskin, J.F., Van Begin, L.: On the efficient computation of the minimal coverability set of Petri nets. International Journal of Fundamental Computer Science **21**(2), 135–165 (2010)
11. Karp, R.M., Miller, R.E.: Parallel program schemata. J. Comput. Syst. Sci. **3**(2), 147–195 (1969)
12. Leroux, J.: Distance between mutually reachable Petri net configurations (Jun 2019), https://hal.archives-ouvertes.fr/hal-02156549, preprint
13. Piipponen, A., Valmari, A.: Constructing minimal coverability sets. Fundamenta Informaticae **143**(3–4), 393–414 (2016)
14. Reynier, P.A., Servais, F.: Minimal coverability set for Petri nets: Karp and Miller algorithm with pruning. Fundamenta Informaticae **122**(1–2), 1–30 (2013)
15. Reynier, P.A., Servais, F.: On the computation of the minimal coverability set of Petri nets. In: Proceedings of Reachability Problems 2019. LNCS, vol. 11674, pp. 164–177 (2019)
16. Valmari, A., Hansen, H.: Old and new algorithms for minimal coverability sets. Fundamenta Informaticae **131**(1), 1–25 (2014)

# 10

# On the k-synchronizability of Systems

Cinzia Di Giusto (✉), Laetitia Laversa, and Etienne Lozes

Université Côte d'Azur, CNRS, I3S, Sophia Antipolis, France
{cinzia.di-giusto,laetitia.laversa,etienne.lozes}@univ-cotedazur.fr

**Abstract.** We study $k$-synchronizability: a system is $k$-synchronizable if any of its executions, up to reordering causally independent actions, can be divided into a succession of $k$-bounded interaction phases. We show two results (both for mailbox and peer-to-peer automata): first, the reachability problem is decidable for $k$-synchronizable systems; second, the membership problem (whether a given system is $k$-synchronizable) is decidable as well. Our proofs fix several important issues in previous attempts to prove these two results for mailbox automata.

**Keywords:** Verification · Communicating Automata · A/Synchronous communication.

## 1 Introduction

Asynchronous message-passing is ubiquitous in communication-centric systems; these include high-performance computing, distributed memory management, event-driven programming, or web services orchestration. One of the parameters that play an important role in these systems is whether the number of pending sent messages can be bounded in a predictable fashion, or whether the buffering capacity offered by the communication layer should be unlimited. Clearly, when considering implementation, testing, or verification, bounded asynchrony is preferred over unbounded asynchrony. Indeed, for bounded systems, reachability analysis and invariants inference can be solved by regular model-checking [5]. Unfortunately and even if designing a new system in this setting is easier, this is not the case when considering that the buffering capacity is unbounded, or that the bound is not known a priori . Thus, a question that arises naturally is how can we bound the "behaviour" of a system so that it operates as one with unbounded buffers? In a recent work [4], Bouajjani *et al.* introduced the notion of $k$-synchronizable system of finite state machines communicating through mailboxes and showed that the reachability problem is decidable for such systems. Intuitively, a system is $k$-synchronizable if any of its executions, up to reordering causally independent actions, can be chopped into a succession of $k$-bounded interaction phases. Each of these phases starts with at most $k$ send actions that are followed by at most $k$ receptions. Notice that, a system may be $k$-synchronizable even if some of its executions require buffers of unbounded capacity.

As explained in the present paper, this result, although valid, is surprisingly non-trivial, mostly due to complications introduced by the mailbox semantics of communications. Some of these complications were missed by Bouajjani *et al.* and the algorithm for the reachability problem in [4] suffers from false positives. Another problem is the membership problem for the subclass of $k$-synchronizable systems: for a given $k$ and a given system of communicating finite state machines, is this system $k$-synchronizable? The main result in [4] is that this problem is decidable. However, again, the proof of this result contains an important flaw at the very first step that breaks all subsequent developments; as a consequence, the algorithm given in [4] produces both false positives and false negatives.

In this work, we present a new proof of the decidability of the reachability problem together with a new proof of the decidability of the membership problem. Quite surprisingly, the reachability problem is more demanding in terms of causality analysis, whereas the membership problem, although rather intricate, builds on a simpler dependency analysis. We also extend both decidability results to the case of peer-to-peer communication.

**Outline.** Next section recalls the definition of communicating systems and related notions. In Section 3 we introduce $k$-synchronizability and we give a graphical characterisation of this property. This characterisation corrects Theorem 1 in [4] and highlights the flaw in the proof of the membership problem. Next, in Section 4, we establish the decidability of the reachability problem, which is the core of our contribution and departs considerably from [4]. In Section 5, we show the decidability of the membership problem. Section 6 extends previous results to the peer-to-peer setting. Finally Section 7 concludes the paper discussing other related works. Proofs and some additional material are available at https://hal.archives-ouvertes.fr/hal-02272347.

## 2 Preliminaries

A communicating system is a set of finite state machines that exchange messages: automata have transitions labelled with either send or receive actions. The paper mainly considers as communication architecture, mailboxes: i.e., messages await to be received in FIFO buffers that store all messages sent to a same automaton, regardless of their senders. Section 6, instead, treats peer-to-peer systems, their introduction is therefore delayed to that point.

Let $\mathbb{V}$ be a finite set of messages and $\mathbb{P}$ a finite set of processes. A send action, denoted $send(p, q, \mathbf{v})$, designates the sending of message $\mathbf{v}$ from process $p$ to process $q$. Similarly a receive action $rec(p, q, \mathbf{v})$ expresses that process $q$ is receiving message $\mathbf{v}$ from $p$. We write $a$ to denote a send or receive action. Let $S = \{send(p, q, \mathbf{v}) \mid p, q \in \mathbb{P}, \mathbf{v} \in \mathbb{V}\}$ be the set of send actions and $R = \{rec(p, q, \mathbf{v}) \mid p, q \in \mathbb{P}, \mathbf{v} \in \mathbb{V}\}$ the set of receive actions. $S_p$ and $R_p$ stand for the set of sends and receives of process $p$ respectively. Each process is encoded by an automaton and by abuse of notation we say that a *system* is the parallel composition of processes.

**Definition 1 (System).** *A system is a tuple* $\mathfrak{S} = \big((L_p, \delta_p, l_p^0) \mid p \in \mathbb{P}\big)$ *where, for each process p,* $L_p$ *is a finite set of local control states,* $\delta_p \subseteq (L_p \times (S_p \cup R_p) \times L_p)$ *is the transition relation (also denoted* $l \xrightarrow{a}_p l'$*) and* $l_p^0$ *is the initial state.*

**Definition 2 (Configuration).** *Let $\mathfrak{S} = \big((L_p, \delta_p, l_p^0) \mid p \in \mathbb{P}\big)$, a configuration is a pair $(\vec{l}, \texttt{Buf})$ where $\vec{l} = (l_p)_{p\in\mathbb{P}} \in \Pi_{p\in\mathbb{P}} L_p$ is a global control state of $\mathfrak{S}$ (a local control state for each automaton), and $\texttt{Buf} = (b_p)_{p\in\mathbb{P}} \in (\mathbb{V}^*)^{\mathbb{P}}$ is a vector of buffers, each $b_p$ being a word over $\mathbb{V}$.*

We write $\vec{l_0}$ to denote the vector of initial states of all processes $p \in \mathbb{P}$, and $\texttt{Buf}_0$ stands for the vector of empty buffers. The semantics of a system is defined by the two rules below.

[SEND]

$$\frac{l_p \xrightarrow{send(p,q,\mathbf{v})}_p l'_p \quad b'_q = b_q \cdot \mathbf{v}}{(\vec{l}, \texttt{Buf}) \xrightarrow{send(p,q,\mathbf{v})} (\vec{l}[l'_p/l_p], \texttt{Buf}[b'_q/b_q])}$$

[RECEIVE]

$$\frac{l_q \xrightarrow{rec(p,q,\mathbf{v})}_q l'_q \quad b_q = \mathbf{v} \cdot b'_q}{(\vec{l}, \texttt{Buf}) \xrightarrow{rec(p,q,\mathbf{v})} (\vec{l}[l'_q/l_q], \texttt{Buf}[b'_q/b_q])}$$

A send action adds a message in the buffer $b$ of the receiver, and a receive action pops the message from this buffer. An execution $e = a_1 \cdots a_n$ is a sequence of actions in $S \cup R$ such that $(\vec{l_0}, \texttt{Buf}_0) \xrightarrow{a_1} \cdots \xrightarrow{a_n} (\vec{l}, \texttt{Buf})$ for some $\vec{l}$ and $\texttt{Buf}$. As usual $\overset{e}{\Rightarrow}$ stands for $\xrightarrow{a_1} \cdots \xrightarrow{a_n}$. We write $asEx(\mathfrak{S})$ to denote the set of asynchronous executions of a system $\mathfrak{S}$. In a sequence of actions $e = a_1 \cdots a_n$, a send action $a_i = send(p, q, \mathbf{v})$ is *matched* by a reception $a_j = rec(p', q', \mathbf{v}')$ (denoted by $a_i \vdash\!\dashv a_j$) if $i < j$, $p = p'$, $q = q'$, $\mathbf{v} = \mathbf{v}'$, and there is $\ell \geq 1$ such that $a_i$ and $a_j$ are the $\ell$th actions of $e$ with these properties respectively. A send action $a_i$ is *unmatched* if there is no matching reception in $e$. A *message exchange* of a sequence of actions $e$ is a set either of the form $v = \{a_i, a_j\}$ with $a_i \vdash\!\dashv a_j$ or of the form $v = \{a_i\}$ with $a_i$ unmatched. For a message $\mathbf{v}_i$, we will note $v_i$ the corresponding message exchange. When $v$ is either an unmatched $send(p, q, \mathbf{v})$ or a pair of matched actions $\{send(p, q, \mathbf{v}), rec(p, q, \mathbf{v})\}$, we write $\mathsf{proc}_S(v)$ for $p$ and $\mathsf{proc}_R(v)$ for $q$. Note that $\mathsf{proc}_R(v)$ is defined even if $v$ is unmatched. Finally, we write $\mathsf{procs}(v)$ for $\{p\}$ in the case of an unmatched send and $\{p, q\}$ in the case of a matched send.

An execution imposes a total order on the actions. We are interested in stressing the causal dependencies between messages. We thus make use of message sequence charts (MSCs) that only impose an order between matched pairs of actions and between the actions of a same process. Informally, an MSC will be depicted with vertical timelines (one for each process) where time goes from top to bottom, that carry some events (points) representing send and receive actions of this process (see Fig. 1). An arc is drawn between two matched events. We will also draw a dashed arc to depict an unmatched send event. An MSC is, thus, a partially ordered set of events, each corresponding to a send or receive action.

**Definition 3 (MSC).** *A message sequence chart is a tuple $(Ev, \lambda, \prec)$, where*

- *$Ev$ is a finite set of events,*
- *$\lambda : Ev \to S \cup R$ tags each event with an action,*
- *$\prec = (\prec_{po} \cup \prec_{src})^+$ is the transitive closure of $\prec_{po}$ and $\prec_{src}$ where:*
  - *$\prec_{po}$ is a partial order on $Ev$ such that, for all process $p$, $\prec_{po}$ induces a total order on the set of events of process $p$, i.e., on $\lambda^{-1}(S_p \cup R_p)$*

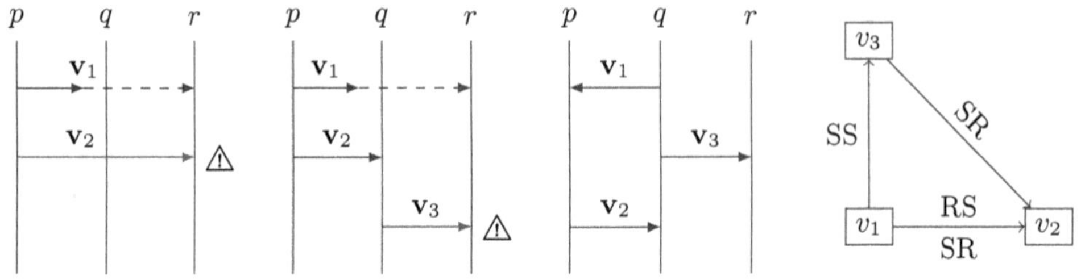


(a) (b) (c) (d)

Fig. 1: (a) and (b): two MSCs that violate causal delivery. (c) and (d): an MSC and its conflict graph

- $\prec_{src}$ *is a binary relation that relates each receive event to its preceding send event :*
  - $*$ *for all events* $r \in \lambda^{-1}(R)$*, there is exactly one events* $s$ *such that* $s \prec_{src} r$
  - $*$ *for all events* $s \in \lambda^{-1}(S)$*, there is at most one event* $r$ *such that* $s \prec_{src} r$
  - $*$ *for any two events* $s, r$ *such that* $s \prec_{src} r$*, there are* $p, q, \mathbf{v}$ *such that* $\lambda(s) = send(p, q, \mathbf{v})$ *and* $\lambda(r) = rec(p, q, \mathbf{v})$.

We identify MSCs up to graph isomorphism (i.e., we view an MSC as a labeled graph). For a given *well-formed* (i.e., each reception is matched) sequence of actions $e = a_1 \dots a_n$, we let $msc(e)$ be the MSC where $Ev = [1..n]$, $\prec_{po}$ is the set of pairs of indices $(i, j)$ such that $i < j$ and $\{a_i, a_j\} \subseteq S_p \cup R_p$ for some $p \in \mathbb{P}$ (i.e., $a_i$ and $a_j$ are actions of a same process), and $\prec_{src}$ is the set of pairs of indices $(i, j)$ such that $a_i \vdash\!\dashv a_j$. We say that $e = a_1 \dots a_n$ is a *linearisation* of $msc(e)$, and we write $asTr(\mathfrak{S})$ to denote $\{msc(e) \mid e \in asEx(\mathfrak{S})\}$ the set of MSCs of system $\mathfrak{S}$.

Mailbox communication imposes a number of constraints on what and when messages can be read. The precise definition is given below, we now discuss some of the possible scenarios. For instance: if two messages are sent to a same process, they will be received in the same order as they have been sent. As another example, unmatched messages also impose some constraints: if a process $p$ sends an unmatched message to $r$, it will not be able to send matched messages to $r$ afterwards (Fig. 1a); or similarly, if a process $p$ sends an unmatched message to $r$, any process $q$ that receives subsequent messages from $p$ will not be able to send matched messages to $r$ afterwards (Fig. 1b). When an MSC satisfies the constraint imposed by mailbox communication, we say that it satisfies causal delivery. Notice that, by construction, all executions satisfy causal delivery.

**Definition 4 (Causal Delivery).** *Let* $(Ev, \lambda, \prec)$ *be an MSC. We say that it satisfies causal delivery if the MSC has a linearisation* $e = a_1 \dots a_n$ *such that for any two events* $i \prec j$ *such that* $a_i = send(p, q, \mathbf{v})$ *and* $a_j = send(p', q, \mathbf{v}')$*, either* $a_j$ *is unmatched, or there are* $i', j'$ *such that* $a_i \vdash\!\dashv a_{i'}$*,* $a_j \vdash\!\dashv a_{j'}$*, and* $i' \prec j'$.

Our definition enforces the following intuitive property.

**Proposition 1.** *An MSC msc satisfies causal delivery if and only if there is a system $\mathfrak{S}$ and an execution $e \in asEx(\mathfrak{S})$ such that $msc = msc(e)$.*

We now recall from [4] the definition of *conflict graph* depicting the causal dependencies between message exchanges. Intuitively, we have a dependency whenever two messages have a process in common. For instance an $\xrightarrow{SS}$ dependency between message exchanges $v$ and $v'$ expresses the fact that $v'$ has been sent after $v$, by the same process.

**Definition 5 (Conflict Graph).** *The conflict graph* $\mathsf{CG}(e)$ *of a sequence of actions* $e = a_1 \cdots a_n$ *is the labeled graph* $(V, \{\xrightarrow{XY}\}_{X,Y \in \{R,S\}})$ *where* $V$ *is the set of message exchanges of* $e$*, and for all* $X, Y \in \{S, R\}$*, for all* $v, v' \in V$*, there is a* $XY$ *dependency edge* $v \xrightarrow{XY} v'$ *between* $v$ *and* $v'$ *if there are* $i < j$ *such that* $\{a_i\} = v \cap X$, $\{a_j\} = v' \cap Y$*, and* $\mathsf{proc}_X(v) = \mathsf{proc}_Y(v')$.

Notice that each linearisation $e$ of an MSC will have the same conflict graph. We can thus talk about an MSC and the associated conflict graph. (As an example see Figs. 1c and 1d.)

We write $v \to v'$ if $v \xrightarrow{XY} v'$ for some $X, Y \in \{R, S\}$, and $v \to^* v'$ if there is a (possibly empty) path from $v$ to $v'$.

## 3 $k$-synchronizable Systems

In this section, we define $k$-synchronizable systems. The main contribution of this part is a new characterisation of $k$-synchronizable executions that corrects the one given in [4].

In the rest of the paper, $k$ denotes a given integer $k \geq 1$. A $k$-exchange denotes a sequence of actions starting with at most $k$ sends and followed by at most $k$ receives matching some of the sends. An MSC is *$k$-synchronous* if there exists a linearisation that is breakable into a sequence of *$k$-exchanges*, such that a message sent during a $k$-exchange cannot be received during a subsequent one: either it is received during the same $k$-exchange, or it remains orphan forever.

**Definition 6 ($k$-synchronous).** *An MSC msc is $k$-synchronous if:*

1. *there exists a linearisation of msc* $e = e_1 \cdot e_2 \cdots e_n$ *where for all* $i \in [1..n]$, $e_i \in S^{\leq k} \cdot R^{\leq k}$,
2. *msc satisfies causal delivery,*
3. *for all* $j, j'$ *such that* $a_j \vdash\!\dashv a_{j'}$ *holds in* $e$, $a_j \vdash\!\dashv a_{j'}$ *holds in some* $e_i$.

*An execution e is $k$-synchronizable if msc(e) is $k$-synchronous.*

We write $sTr_k(\mathfrak{S})$ to denote the set $\{msc(e) \mid e \in asEx(\mathfrak{S})$ and $msc(e)$ is $k$-synchronous$\}$.

*Example 1 ($k$-synchronous MSCs and $k$-synchronizable Executions).*

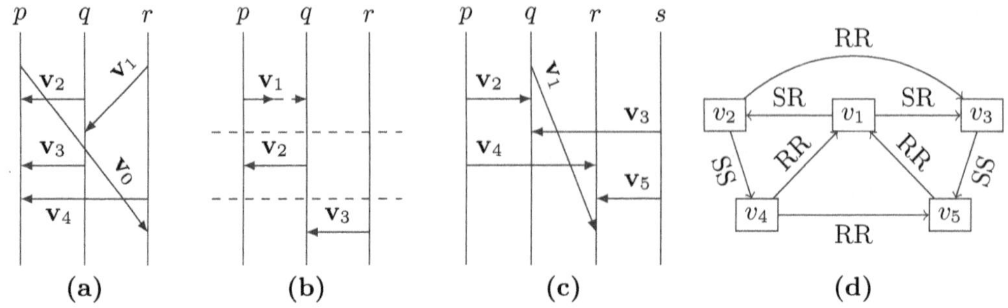


Fig. 2: (a) the MSC of Example 1.1. (b) the MSC of Example 1.2. (c) the MSC of Example 2 and (d) its conflict graph.

1. There is no $k$ such that the MSC in Fig. 2a is $k$-synchronous. All messages must be grouped in the same $k$-exchange, but it is not possible to schedule all the sends first, because the reception of $\mathbf{v}_1$ happens before the sending of $\mathbf{v}_3$. Still, this MSC satisfies causal delivery.
2. Let $e_1 = send(r, q, \mathbf{v}_3) \cdot send(q, p, \mathbf{v}_2) \cdot send(p, q, \mathbf{v}_1) \cdot rec(q, p, \mathbf{v}_2) \cdot rec(r, q, \mathbf{v}_3)$ be an execution. Its MSC, $msc(e_1)$ depicted in Fig. 2b satisfies causal delivery. Notice that $e_1$ can not be divided in 1-exchanges. However, if we consider the alternative linearisation of $msc(e_1)$: $e_2 = send(p, q, \mathbf{v}_1) \cdot send(q, p, \mathbf{v}_2) \cdot rec(q, p, \mathbf{v}_2) \cdot send(r, q, \mathbf{v}_3) \cdot rec(r, q, \mathbf{v}_3)$, we have that $e_2$ is breakable into 1-exchanges in which each matched send is in a 1-exchange with its reception. Therefore, $msc(e_1)$ is 1-synchronous and $e_1$ is 1-synchronizable. Remark that $e_2$ is not an execution and there exists no execution that can be divided into 1-exchanges. A $k$-synchronous MSC highlights dependencies between messages but does not impose an order for the execution.

*Comparison with [4].* In [4], the authors define set $sEx_k(\mathfrak{S})$ as the set of $k$-synchronous executions of system $\mathfrak{S}$ in the $k$-synchronous semantics. Nonetheless as remarked in Example 1.2 not all executions of a system can be divided into $k$-exchanges even if they are $k$-synchronizable. Thus, in order not to lose any executions, we have decided to reason only on MSCs (called traces in [4]).

Following standard terminology, we say that a set $U \subseteq V$ of vertices is a *strongly connected component* (SCC) of a given graph $(V, \rightarrow)$ if between any two vertices $v, v' \in U$, there exist two oriented paths $v \rightarrow^* v'$ and $v' \rightarrow^* v$. The statement below fixes some issues with Theorem 1 in [4].

**Theorem 1 (Graph Characterisation of $k$-synchronous MSCs).** *Let msc be a causal delivery MSC. msc is $k$-synchronous iff every SCC in its conflict graph is of size at most $k$ and if no RS edge occurs on any cyclic path.*

*Example 2 (A 5-synchronous MSC).* Fig. 2c depicts a 5-synchronous MSC, that is not 4-synchronous. Indeed, its conflict graph (Fig. 2d) contains a SCC of size 5 (all vertices are on the same SCC).

*Comparison with [4].* Bouajjani *et al.* give a characterisation of $k$-synchronous executions similar to ours, but they use the word *cycle* instead of SCC, and the subsequent developments of the paper suggest that they intended to say *Hamiltonian cycle* (i.e., a cyclic path that does not go twice through the same vertex). It is not the case that a MSC is $k$-synchronous if and only if every Hamiltonian cycle in its conflict graph is of size at most $k$ and if no RS edge occurs on any cyclic path. Indeed, consider again Example 2. This graph is not Hamiltonian, and the largest Hamiltonian cycle indeed is of size 4 only. But as we already discussed in Example 2, the corresponding MSC is not 4-synchronous.

As a consequence, the algorithm that is presented in [4] for deciding whether a system is $k$-synchronizable is not correct as well: the MSC of Fig. 2c would be considered 4-synchronous according to this algorithm, but it is not.

# 4 Decidability of Reachability for $k$-synchronizable Systems

We show that the reachability problem is decidable for $k$-synchronizable systems. While proving this result, we have to face several non-trivial aspects of causal delivery that were missed in [4] and that require a completely new approach.

**Definition 7 ($k$-synchronizable System).** *A system $\mathfrak{S}$ is* $k$-synchronizable *if all its executions are $k$-synchronizable, i.e., $sTr_k(\mathfrak{S}) = asTr(\mathfrak{S})$.*

In other words, a system $\mathfrak{S}$ is $k$-synchronizable if for every execution $e$ of $\mathfrak{S}$, $msc(e)$ may be divided into $k$-exchanges.

*Remark 1.* In particular, a system may be $k$-synchronizable even if some of its executions fill the buffers with more than $k$ messages. For instance, the only linearisation of the 1-synchronous MSC Fig. 2b that is an execution of the system needs buffers of size 2.

For a $k$-synchronizable system, the reachability problem reduces to the reachability through a $k$-synchronizable execution. To show that $k$-synchronous reachability is decidable, we establish that the set of $k$-synchronous MSCs is regular. More precisely, we want to define a finite state automaton that accepts a sequence $e_1 \cdot e_2 \cdots e_n$ of $k$-exchanges if and only if they satisfy causal delivery.

We start by giving a graph-theoretic characterisation of causal delivery. For this, we define the *extended edges* $v \overset{XY}{\dashrightarrow} v'$ of a given conflict graph. The relation $\overset{XY}{\dashrightarrow}$ is defined in Fig. 3 with $X, Y \in \{S, R\}$. Intuitively, $v \overset{XY}{\dashrightarrow} v'$ expresses that event $X$ of $v$ must happen before event $Y$ of $v'$ due to either their order on the same machine (Rule 1), or the fact that a send happens before its matching receive (Rule 2), or due to the mailbox semantics (Rules 3 and 4), or because of a chain of such dependencies (Rule 5). We observe that in the extended *conflict graph*, obtained applying such rules, a cyclic dependency appears whenever causal delivery is not satisfied.

$$\text{(Rule 1)}\ \frac{v_1 \xrightarrow{XY} v_2}{v_1 \overset{XY}{\dashrightarrow} v_2} \qquad \text{(Rule 2)}\ \frac{v \cap R \neq \emptyset}{v \overset{SR}{\dashrightarrow} v} \qquad \text{(Rule 3)}\ \frac{v_1 \xrightarrow{RR} v_2}{v_1 \overset{SS}{\dashrightarrow} v_2}$$

$$\text{(Rule 4)}\ \frac{v_1 \cap R \neq \emptyset \qquad v_2 \cap R = \emptyset \qquad \mathsf{proc}_R(v_1) = \mathsf{proc}_R(v_2)}{v_1 \overset{SS}{\dashrightarrow} v_2} \qquad \text{(Rule 5)}\ \frac{v_1 \overset{XY}{\dashrightarrow}\overset{YZ}{\dashrightarrow} v_2}{v_1 \overset{XZ}{\dashrightarrow} v_2}$$

Fig. 3: Deduction rules for extended dependency edges of the conflict graph

*Example 3.* Fig. 5a and 5b depict an MSC and its associated conflict graph with some extended edges. This MSC violates causal delivery and there is a cyclic dependency $v_1 \overset{SS}{\dashrightarrow} v_1$.

**Theorem 2 (Graph-theoretic Characterisation of Causal Delivery).** *An MSC satisfies causal delivery iff there is no cyclic causal dependency of the form $v \overset{SS}{\dashrightarrow} v$ for some vertex $v$ of its extended conflict graph.*

Let us now come back to our initial problem: we want to recognise with finite memory the sequences $e_1, e_2 \ldots e_n$ of $k$-exchanges that composed give an MSC that satisfies causal delivery. We proceed by reading each $k$-exchange one by one in sequence. This entails that, at each step, we have only a partial view of the global conflict graph. Still, we want to determine whether the acyclicity condition of Theorem 2 is satisfied in the global conflict graph. The crucial observation is that only the edges generated by Rule 4 may "go back in time". This means that we have to remember enough information from the previously examined $k$-exchanges to determine whether the current $k$-exchange contains a vertex $v$ that shares an edge with some unmatched vertex $v'$ seen in a previous $k$-exchange and whether this could participate in a cycle. This is achieved by computing two sets of processes $C_{S,p}$ and $C_{R,p}$ that collect the following information: a process $q$ is in $C_{S,p}$ if it performs a send action causally after an unmatched send to $p$, or it is the sender of the unmatched send; a process $q$ belongs to $C_{R,p}$ if it receives a message that was sent after some unmatched message directed to $p$. More precisely, we have:

$$C_{S,p} = \{\mathsf{proc}_S(v) \mid v' \overset{SS}{\dashrightarrow} v \ \&\ v' \text{ is unmatched } \&\ \mathsf{proc}_R(v') = p\}$$

$$C_{R,p} = \{\mathsf{proc}_R(v) \mid v' \overset{SS}{\dashrightarrow} v \ \&\ v' \text{ is unmatched } \&\ \mathsf{proc}_R(v') = p \ \&\ v \cap R \neq \emptyset\}$$

These sets abstract and carry from one $k$-exchange to another the necessary information to detect violations of causal delivery. We compute them in any local conflict graph of a $k$-exchange incrementally, i.e., knowing what they were at the end of the previous $k$-exchange, we compute them at the end of the current one. More precisely, let $e = s_1 \cdots s_m \cdot r_1 \cdots r_{m'}$ be a $k$-exchange, $\mathsf{CG}(e) = (V, E)$ its conflict graph and $B : \mathbb{P} \to (2^{\mathbb{P}} \times 2^{\mathbb{P}})$ the function that associates to each $p \in \mathbb{P}$ the two sets $B(p) = (C_{S,p}, C_{R,p})$. Then, the conflict graph $\mathsf{CG}(e, B)$ is the graph $(V', E')$ with $V' = V \cup \{\psi_p \mid p \in \mathbb{P}\}$ and $E' \supseteq E$ as defined below. For each process $p \in \mathbb{P}$, the "summary node" $\psi_p$ shall account for all past unmatched

$$\frac{\begin{array}{c} e = s_1 \cdots s_m \cdot r_1 \cdots r_{m'} \quad s_1 \cdots s_m \in S^* \quad r_1 \cdots r_{m'} \in R^* \quad 0 \le m' \le m \le k \\ (\vec{l}, \mathtt{Buf}_0) \overset{e}{\Rightarrow} (\vec{l'}, \mathtt{Buf}) \text{ for some } \mathtt{Buf} \\ \text{for all } p \in \mathbb{P} \quad B(p) = (C_{S,p}, C_{R,p}) \text{ and } B'(p) = (C'_{S,p}, C'_{R,p}), \\ \mathsf{Unm}_p = \{\psi_p\} \cup \{v \mid v \text{ is unmatched, } \mathsf{proc}_R(v) = p\} \\ C'_{X,p} = C_{X,p} \cup \{p \mid p \in C_{X,q}, v \overset{SS}{\dashrightarrow} \psi_q, (\mathsf{proc}_R(v) = p \text{ or } v = \psi_p)\} \cup \\ \{\mathsf{proc}_X(v) \mid v \in \mathsf{Unm}_p \cap V, X = S\} \cup \{\mathsf{proc}_X(v') \mid v \overset{SS}{\dashrightarrow} v', v \in \mathsf{Unm}_p, v \cap X \ne \emptyset\} \\ \text{for all } p \in \mathbb{P}, p \notin C'_{R,p} \end{array}}{(\vec{l}, B) \xRightarrow[\mathsf{cd}]{e,k} (\vec{l'}, B')}$$

Fig. 4: Definition of the relation $\xRightarrow[\mathsf{cd}]{e,k}$

messages sent to $p$ that occurred in some $k$-exchange before $e$. $E'$ is the set $E$ of edges $\xrightarrow{XY}$ among message exchanges of $e$, as in Definition 5, augmented with the following set of extra edges that takes into account summary nodes.

$$\{\psi_p \xrightarrow{SX} v \mid \mathsf{proc}_X(v) \in C_{S,p} \;\&\; v \cap X \ne \emptyset \text{ for some } X \in \{S, R\}\} \tag{1}$$

$$\cup\ \{\psi_p \xrightarrow{SS} v \mid \mathsf{proc}_X(v) \in C_{R,p} \;\&\; v \cap R \ne \emptyset \text{ for some } X \in \{S, R\}\} \tag{2}$$

$$\cup\ \{\psi_p \xrightarrow{SS} v \mid \mathsf{proc}_R(v) \in C_{R,p} \;\&\; v \text{ is unmatched}\} \tag{3}$$

$$\cup\ \{v \xrightarrow{SS} \psi_p \mid \mathsf{proc}_R(v) = p \;\&\; v \cap R \ne \emptyset\} \ \cup\ \{\psi_q \xrightarrow{SS} \psi_p \mid p \in C_{R,q}\} \tag{4}$$

These extra edges summarise/abstract the connections to and from previous $k$-exchanges. Equation (1) considers connections $\xrightarrow{SS}$ and $\xrightarrow{SR}$ that are due to two sends messages or, respectively, a send and a receive on the same process. Equations (2) and (3) considers connections $\xrightarrow{RR}$ and $\xrightarrow{RS}$ that are due to two received messages or, respectively, a receive and a subsequent send on the same process. Notice how the rules in Fig. 3 would then imply the existence of a connection $\overset{SS}{\dashrightarrow}$, in particular Equation (3) abstract the existence of an edge $\overset{SS}{\dashrightarrow}$ built because of Rule 4. Equations in (4) abstract edges that would connect the current $k$-exchange to previous ones. As before those edges in the global conflict graph would correspond to extended edges added because of Rule 4 in Fig. 3. Once we have this enriched local view of the conflict graph, we take its extended version. Let $\overset{XY}{\dashrightarrow}$ denote the edges of the extended conflict graph as defined from rules in Fig. 3 taking into account the new vertices $\psi_p$ and their edges.

Finally, let $\mathfrak{S}$ be a system and $\xRightarrow[\mathsf{cd}]{e,k}$ be the transition relation given in Fig. 4 among abstract configurations of the form $(\vec{l}, B)$. $\vec{l}$ is a global control state of $\mathfrak{S}$ and $B : \mathbb{P} \to (2^{\mathbb{P}} \times 2^{\mathbb{P}})$ is the function defined above that associates to each process $p$ a pair of sets of processes $B(p) = (C_{S,p}, C_{R,p})$. Transition $\xRightarrow[\mathsf{cd}]{e,k}$ updates these sets with respect to the current $k$-exchange $e$. Causal delivery is verified by checking that for all $p \in \mathbb{P}, p \notin C'_{R,p}$ meaning that there is no cyclic dependency

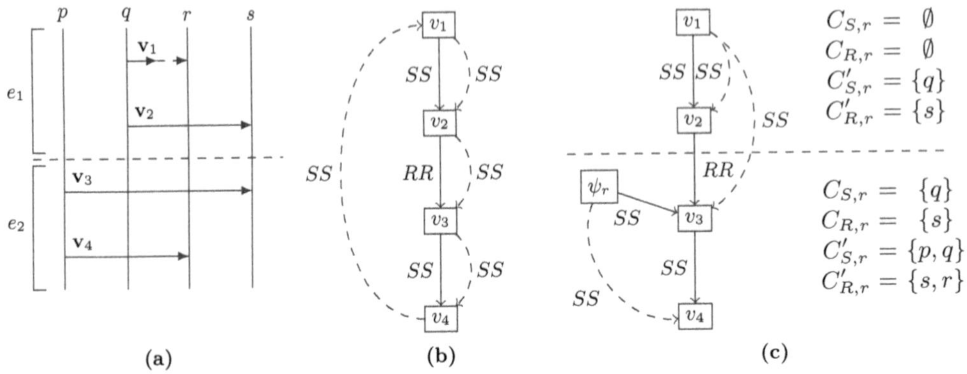


Fig. 5: (a) an MSC (b) its associated global conflict graph, (c) the conflict graphs of its $k$-exchanges

as stated in Theorem 2. The initial state is $(\vec{l_0}, B_0)$, where $B_0 : \mathbb{P} \to (2^{\mathbb{P}} \times 2^{\mathbb{P}})$ denotes the function such that $B_0(p) = (\emptyset, \emptyset)$ for all $p \in \mathbb{P}$.

*Example 4 (An Invalid Execution).* Let $e = e_1 \cdot e_2$ with $e_1$ and $e_2$ the two 2-exchanges of this execution. such that $e_1 = \mathit{send}(q, r, \mathbf{v}_1) \cdot \mathit{send}(q, s, \mathbf{v}_2) \cdot \mathit{rec}(q, s, \mathbf{v}_2)$ and $e_2 = \mathit{send}(p, s, \mathbf{v}_3) \cdot \mathit{rec}(p, s, \mathbf{v}_3) \cdot \mathit{send}(p, r, \mathbf{v}_4) \cdot \mathit{rec}(p, r, \mathbf{v}_4)$. Fig. 5a and 5c show the MSC and corresponding conflict graph of each of the 2-exchanges. Note that two edges of the global graph (in blue) "go across" $k$-exchanges. These edges do not belong to the local conflict graphs and are mimicked by the incoming and outgoing edges of summary nodes. The values of sets $C_{S,r}$ and $C_{R,r}$ at the beginning and at the end of the $k$-exchange are given on the right. All other sets $C_{S,p}$ and $C_{R,p}$ for $p \neq r$ are empty, since there is only one unmatched message to process $r$. Notice how at the end of the second $k$-exchange, $r \in C'_{R,r}$ signalling that message $v_4$ violates causal delivery.

*Comparison with [4].* In [4] the authors define $\overset{e,k}{\underset{\mathsf{cd}}{\Longrightarrow}}$ in a rather different way: they do not explicitly give a graph-theoretic characterisation of causal delivery; instead they compute, for every process $p$, the set $B(p)$ of processes that either sent an unmatched message to $p$ or received a message from a process in $B(p)$. They then make sure that any message sent to $p$ by a process $q \in B(p)$ is unmatched. According to that definition, the MSC of Fig. 5b would satisfy causal delivery and would be 1-synchronous. However, this is not the case (this MSC does not satisfy causal delivery) as we have shown in Example 3. Due to to the above errors, we had to propose a considerably different approach. The extended edges of the conflict graph, and the graph-theoretic characterisation of causal delivery as well as summary nodes, have no equivalent in [4].

Next lemma proves that Fig. 4 properly characterises causal delivery.

**Lemma 1.** *An MSC msc is $k$-synchronous iff there is* $e = e_1 \cdots e_n$ *a linearisation such that* $(\vec{l_0}, B_0) \overset{e_1,k}{\underset{\mathsf{cd}}{\Longrightarrow}} \cdots \overset{e_n,k}{\underset{\mathsf{cd}}{\Longrightarrow}} (\vec{l'}, B')$ *for some global state* $\vec{l'}$ *and some* $B' : \mathbb{P} \to (2^{\mathbb{P}} \times 2^{\mathbb{P}})$.

Note that there are only finitely many abstract configurations of the form $(\vec{l}, B)$ with $\vec{l}$ a tuple of control states and $B : \mathbb{P} \to (2^{\mathbb{P}} \times 2^{\mathbb{P}})$. Moreover, since $\mathbb{V}$ is finite, the alphabet over the possible $k$-exchange for a given $k$ is also finite. Therefore $\overset{e,k}{\underset{\mathsf{cd}}{\Longrightarrow}}$ is a relation on a finite set, and the set $sTr_k(\mathfrak{S})$ of $k$-synchronous MSCs of a system $\mathfrak{S}$ forms a regular language. It follows that it is decidable whether a given abstract configuration of the form $(\vec{l}, B)$ is reachable from the initial configuration following a $k$-synchronizable execution.

**Theorem 3.** *Let $\mathfrak{S}$ be a $k$-synchronizable system and $\vec{l}$ a global control state of $\mathfrak{S}$. The problem whether there exists* $e \in asEx(\mathfrak{S})$ *and* $\mathtt{Buf}$ *such that* $(\vec{l_0}, \mathtt{Buf}_0) \overset{e}{\Rightarrow} (\vec{l}, \mathtt{Buf})$ *is decidable.*

*Remark 2.* Deadlock-freedom, unspecified receptions, and absence of orphan messages are other properties that become decidable for a $k$-synchronizable system because of the regularity of the set of $k$-synchronous MSCs.

## 5 Decidability of *k*-synchronizability for Mailbox Systems

We establish the decidability of $k$-synchronizability; our approach is similar to the one of [4] based on the notion of borderline violation, but we adjust it to adapt to the new characterisation of $k$-synchronizable executions (Theorem 1).

**Definition 8 (Borderline Violation).** *A non $k$-synchronizable execution $e$ is a borderline violation if* $e = e' \cdot r$, *$r$ is a reception and $e'$ is $k$-synchronizable.*

Note that a system $\mathfrak{S}$ that is not $k$-synchronizable always admits at least one borderline violation $e' \cdot r \in asEx(\mathfrak{S})$ with $r \in R$: indeed, there is at least one execution $e \in asEx(\mathfrak{S})$ which contains a unique minimal prefix of the form $e' \cdot r$ that is not $k$-synchronizable; moreover since $e'$ is $k$-synchronizable, $r$ cannot be a $k$-exchange of just one send action, therefore it must be a receive action. In order to find such a borderline violation, Bouajjani *et al.* introduced an instrumented system $\mathfrak{S}'$ that behaves like $\mathfrak{S}$, except that it contains an extra process $\pi$, and such that a non-deterministically chosen message that should have been sent from a process $p$ to a process $q$ may now be sent from $p$ to $\pi$, and later forwarded by $\pi$ to $q$. In $\mathfrak{S}'$, each process $p$ has the possibility, instead of sending a message $\mathbf{v}$ to $q$, to deviate this message to $\pi$; if it does so, $p$ continues its execution as if it really had sent it to $q$. Note also that the message sent to $\pi$ get tagged with the original destination process $q$. Similarly, for each possible reception, a process has the possibility to receive a given message not from the initial sender but from $\pi$. The process $\pi$ has an initial state from which it can receive any messages from the system. Each reception makes it go into a different state. From this state, it is able to send the message back to the original recipient. Once a message is forwarded, $\pi$ reaches its final state and remains idle. The following example illustrates how the instrumented system works.

*Example 5 (A Deviated Message).*
Let $e_1$, $e_2$ be two executions of a system $\mathfrak{S}$ with MSCs respectively $msc(e_1)$ and $msc(e_2)$. $e_1$ is not 1-synchronizable. It is borderline in $\mathfrak{S}$. If we delete the last reception, it becomes indeed 1-synchronizable. $msc(e_2)$ is the MSC obtained from the instrumented system $\mathfrak{S}'$ where the message $\mathbf{v}_1$ is first deviated to $\pi$ and then sent back to $q$ from $\pi$.
Note that $msc(e_2)$ is 1-synchronous. In this case, the instrumented system $\mathfrak{S}'$ in the 1-synchronous semantics "reveals" the existence of a borderline violation of $\mathfrak{S}$.

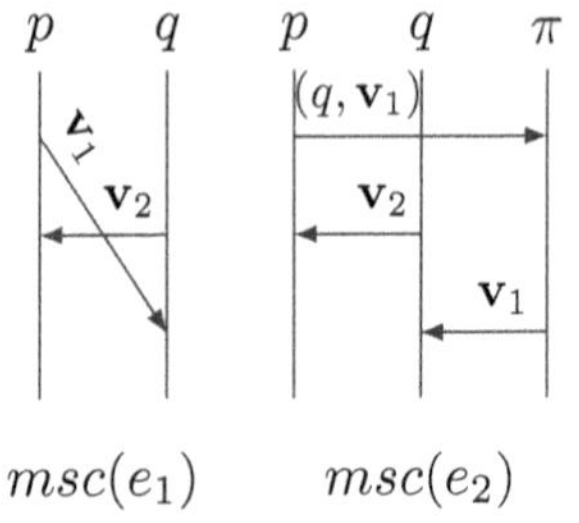


For each execution $e \cdot r \in asEx(\mathfrak{S})$ that ends with a reception, there exists an execution $\mathsf{deviate}(e \cdot r) \in asEx(\mathfrak{S}')$ where the message exchange associated with the reception $r$ has been deviated to $\pi$; formally, if $e \cdot r = e_1 \cdot s \cdot e_2 \cdot r$ with $r = rec(p, q, \mathbf{v})$ and $s \vdash\!\dashv r$, then

$$\mathsf{deviate}(e \cdot r) = e_1 \cdot send(p, \pi, (q, \mathbf{v})) \cdot rec(p, \pi, (q, \mathbf{v})) \cdot e_2 \cdot send(\pi, q, (\mathbf{v})) \cdot rec(\pi, q, \mathbf{v}).$$

**Definition 9 (Feasible Execution, Bad Execution).** *A $k$-synchronizable execution $e'$ of $\mathfrak{S}'$ is* feasible *if there is an execution $e \cdot r \in asEx(\mathfrak{S})$ such that* $\mathsf{deviate}(e \cdot r) = e'$. *A feasible execution $e' =$* $\mathsf{deviate}(e \cdot r)$ *of $\mathfrak{S}'$ is* bad *if execution $e \cdot r$ is not $k$-synchronizable in $\mathfrak{S}$.*

*Example 6 (A Non-feasible Execution).*
Let $e'$ be an execution such that $msc(e')$ is as depicted on the right. Clearly, this MSC satisfies causal delivery and could be the execution of some instrumented system $\mathfrak{S}'$. However, the sequence $e \cdot r$ such that $\mathsf{deviate}(e \cdot r) = e'$ does not satisfy causal delivery, therefore it cannot be an execution of the original system $\mathfrak{S}$. In other words, the execution $e'$ is not feasible.

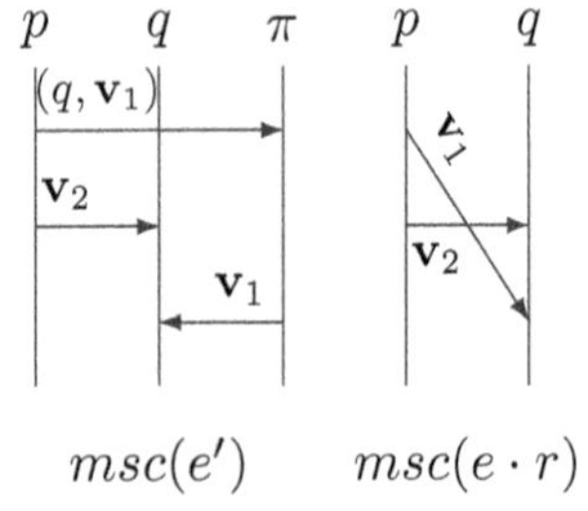


**Lemma 2.** *A system $\mathfrak{S}$ is not $k$-synchronizable iff there is a $k$-synchronizable execution $e'$ of $\mathfrak{S}'$ that is feasible and bad.*

As we have already noted, the set of $k$-synchronous MSCs of $\mathfrak{S}'$ is regular. The decision procedure for $k$-synchronizability follows from the fact that the set of MSCs that have as linearisation a feasible bad execution as we will see, is regular as well, and that it can be recognised by an (effectively computable) non-deterministic finite state automaton. The decidability of $k$-synchronizability follows then from Lemma 2 and the decidability of the emptiness problem for non-deterministic finite state automata.

**Recognition of Feasible Executions.** We start with the automaton that recognises feasible executions; for this, we revisit the construction we just used for recognising sequences of $k$-exchanges that satisfy causal delivery.

In the remainder, we assume an execution $e' \in asEx(\mathfrak{S}')$ that contains exactly one send of the form $send(p, \pi, (q, \mathbf{v}))$ and one reception of the form $rec(\pi, q, \mathbf{v})$, this reception being the last action of $e'$. Let $(V, \{\xrightarrow{XY}\}_{X,Y \in \{R,S\}})$ be the conflict graph of $e'$. There are two uniquely determined vertices $v_{\mathsf{start}}, v_{\mathsf{stop}} \in V$ such that $\mathsf{proc}_R(v_{\mathsf{start}}) = \pi$ and $\mathsf{proc}_S(v_{\mathsf{stop}}) = \pi$ that correspond, respectively, to the first and last message exchanges of the deviation. The conflict graph of $e \cdot r$ is then obtained by merging these two nodes.

**Lemma 3.** *The execution $e'$ is not feasible iff there is a vertex $v$ in the conflict graph of $e'$ such that $v_{\mathsf{start}} \overset{SS}{\dashrightarrow} v \xrightarrow{RR} v_{\mathsf{stop}}$.*

In order to decide whether an execution $e'$ is feasible, we want to forbid that a send action $send(p', q, \mathbf{v}')$ that happens causally after $v_{\mathsf{start}}$ is matched by a receive $rec(p', q, \mathbf{v}')$ that happens causally before the reception $v_{\mathsf{stop}}$. As a matter of fact, this boils down to deal with the deviated send action as an unmatched send. So we will consider sets of processes $C_S^\pi$ and $C_R^\pi$ similar to the ones used for $\xRightarrow[\mathsf{cd}]{e,k}$, but with the goal of computing which actions happen causally after the send to $\pi$. We also introduce a summary node $\psi_{\mathsf{start}}$ and the extra edges following the same principles as in the previous section. Formally, let $B : \mathbb{P} \to (2^{\mathbb{P}} \times 2^{\mathbb{P}})$, $C_S^\pi, C_R^\pi \subseteq \mathbb{P}$ and $e \in S^{\leq k} R^{\leq k}$ be fixed, and let $\mathsf{CG}(e, B) = (V', E')$ be the constraint graph with summary nodes for unmatched sent messages as defined in the previous section. The local constraint graph $\mathsf{CG}(e, B, C_S^\pi, C_R^\pi)$ is defined as the graph $(V'', E'')$ where $V'' = V' \cup \{\psi_{\mathsf{start}}\}$ and $E''$ is $E'$ augmented with

$$\{\psi_{\mathsf{start}} \xrightarrow{SX} v \mid \mathsf{proc}_X(v) \in C_S^\pi \;\&\; v \cap X \neq \emptyset \text{ for some } X \in \{S, R\}\}$$
$$\cup\; \{\psi_{\mathsf{start}} \xrightarrow{SS} v \mid \mathsf{proc}_X(v) \in C_R^\pi \;\&\; v \cap R \neq \emptyset \text{ for some } X \in \{S, R\}\}$$
$$\cup\; \{\psi_{\mathsf{start}} \xrightarrow{SS} v \mid \mathsf{proc}_R(v) \in C_R^\pi \;\&\; v \text{ is unmatched}\} \;\cup\; \{\psi_{\mathsf{start}} \xrightarrow{SS} \psi_p \mid p \in C_R^\pi\}$$

As before, we consider the "closure" $\overset{XY}{\dashrightarrow}$ of these edges by the rules of Fig. 3. The transition relation $\xRightarrow[\mathsf{feas}]{e,k}$ is defined in Fig. 6. It relates abstract configurations of the form $(\vec{l}, B, \vec{C}, \mathtt{dest}_\pi)$ with $\vec{C} = (C_{S,\pi}, C_{R,\pi})$ and $\mathtt{dest}_\pi \in \mathbb{P} \cup \{\perp\}$ storing to whom the message deviated to $\pi$ was supposed to be delivered. Thus, the initial abstract configuration is $(l_0, B_0, (\emptyset, \emptyset), \perp)$, where $\perp$ means that the processus $\mathtt{dest}_\pi$ has not been determined yet. It will be set as soon as the send to process $\pi$ is encountered.

**Lemma 4.** *Let $e'$ be an execution of $\mathfrak{S}'$. Then $e'$ is a $k$-synchronizable feasible execution iff there are $e'' = e_1 \cdots e_n \cdot send(\pi, q, \mathbf{v}) \cdot rec(\pi, q, \mathbf{v})$ with $e_1, \ldots, e_n \in S^{\leq k} R^{\leq k}$, $B' : \mathbb{P} \to 2^{\mathbb{P}}$, $\vec{C'} \in (2^{\mathbb{P}})^2$, and a tuple of control states $\vec{l'}$ such that $msc(e') = msc(e'')$, $\pi \notin C_{R,q}$ (with $B'(q) = (C_{S,q}, C_{R,q})$), and*

$$(\vec{l_0}, B_0, (\emptyset, \emptyset), \perp) \xRightarrow[\mathsf{feas}]{e_1,k} \cdots \xRightarrow[\mathsf{feas}]{e_n,k} (\vec{l'}, B', \vec{C'}, q).$$

$$\frac{\begin{array}{c}(\vec{l},B)\xrightarrow[\text{cd}]{e,k}(\vec{l'},B') \qquad e=a_1\cdots a_n \qquad (\forall v)\ \mathsf{proc}_S(v)\neq\pi \\ (\forall v,v')\ \mathsf{proc}_R(v)=\mathsf{proc}_R(v')=\pi \implies v=v'\wedge \mathtt{dest}_\pi=\bot \\ (\forall v)\ v\ni send(p,\pi,(q,\mathbf{v}))\implies \mathtt{dest}'_\pi=q \quad \mathtt{dest}_\pi\neq\bot\implies \mathtt{dest}'_\pi=\mathtt{dest}_\pi \\ C_X^{\pi}{}'=C_X^\pi\cup\{\mathsf{proc}_X(v')\mid v\overset{SS}{\dashrightarrow}v'\ \&\ v'\cap X\neq\emptyset\ \&\ (\mathsf{proc}_R(v)=\pi \text{ or } v=\psi_{\mathsf{start}})\} \\ \cup\{\mathsf{proc}_S(v)\mid \mathsf{proc}_R(v)=\pi\ \&\ X=S\} \\ \cup\{p\mid p\in C_{X,q}\ \&\ v\overset{SS}{\dashrightarrow}\psi_q\ \&\ (\mathsf{proc}_R(v)=\pi \text{ or } v=\psi_{\mathsf{start}})\} \\ \mathtt{dest}'_\pi\notin C_R^\pi{}'\end{array}}{(\vec{l},B,C_S^\pi,C_R^\pi,\mathtt{dest}_\pi)\xrightarrow[\text{feas}]{e,k}(\vec{l'},B',C_S^\pi{}',C_R^\pi{}',\mathtt{dest}'_\pi)}$$

Fig. 6: Definition of the relation $\xrightarrow[\text{feas}]{e,k}$

*Comparison with [4].* In [4] the authors verify that an execution is feasible with a *monitor* which reviews the actions of the execution and adds processes that no longer are allowed to send a message to the receiver of $\pi$. Unfortunately, we have here a similar problem that the one mentioned in the previous comparison paragraph. According to their monitor, the following execution $e'=\mathsf{deviate}(e\cdot r)$ is feasible, i.e., is runnable in $\mathfrak{S}'$ and $e\cdot r$ is runnable in $\mathfrak{S}$.

$$\begin{aligned} e' = {} & send(q,\pi,(r,\mathbf{v}_1))\cdot rec(q,\pi,(r,\mathbf{v}_1))\cdot send(q,s,\mathbf{v}_2)\cdot rec(q,s,\mathbf{v}_2)\cdot \\ & send(p,s,\mathbf{v}_3)\cdot rec(p,s,\mathbf{v}_3)\cdot send(p,r,\mathbf{v}_4)\cdot rec(p,r,\mathbf{v}_4)\cdot \\ & send(\pi,r,\mathbf{v}_1)\cdot rec(\pi,r,\mathbf{v}_4)\end{aligned}$$

However, this execution is not feasible because there is a causal dependency between $\mathbf{v}_1$ and $\mathbf{v}_3$. In [4] this execution would then be considered as feasible and therefore would belong to set $sTr_k(\mathfrak{S}')$. Yet there is no corresponding execution in $asTr(\mathfrak{S})$, the comparison and therefore the $k$-synchronizability, could be distorted and appear as a false negative.

**Recognition of Bad Executions.** Finally, we define a non-deterministic finite state automaton that recognizes MSCs of bad executions, i.e., feasible executions $e'=\mathsf{deviate}(e\cdot r)$ such that $e\cdot r$ is not $k$-synchronizable. We come back to the "non-extended" conflict graph, without edges of the form $\overset{XY}{\dashrightarrow}$. Let $\mathsf{Post}^*(v)=\{v'\in V\mid v\to^* v'\}$ be the set of vertices reachable from $v$, and let $\mathsf{Pre}^*(v)=\{v'\in V\mid v'\to^* v\}$ be the set of vertices co-reachable from $v$. For a set of vertices $U\subseteq V$, let $\mathsf{Post}^*(U)=\bigcup\{\mathsf{Post}^*(v)\mid v\in U\}$, and $\mathsf{Pre}^*(U)=\bigcup\{\mathsf{Pre}^*(v)\mid v\in U\}$.

**Lemma 5.** *The feasible execution $e'$ is bad iff one of the two holds*

1. $v_{\mathsf{start}}\longrightarrow^*\xrightarrow{RS}\longrightarrow^* v_{\mathsf{stop}}$, *or*
2. *the size of the set* $\mathsf{Post}^*(v_{\mathsf{start}})\cap\mathsf{Pre}^*(v_{\mathsf{stop}})$ *is greater or equal to* $k+2$.

In order to determine whether a given message exchange $v$ of $\mathsf{CG}(e')$ should be counted as reachable (resp. co-reachable), we will compute at the entry and exit of every $k$-exchange of $e'$ which processes are "reachable" or "co-reachable".

*Example 7.* (Reachable and Co-reachable Processes)

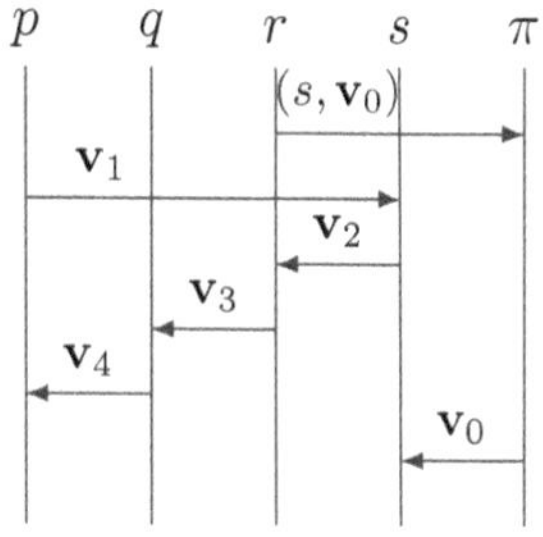


$msc(e)$

Consider the MSC on the right made of five 1-exchanges. While sending message $(s, \mathbf{v}_0)$ that corresponds to $v_{\mathsf{start}}$, process $r$ becomes "reachable": any subsequent message exchange that involves $r$ corresponds to a vertex of the conflict graph that is reachable from $v_{\mathsf{start}}$. While sending $\mathbf{v}_2$, process $s$ becomes "reachable", because process $r$ will be reachable when it will receive message $\mathbf{v}_2$. Similary, $q$ becomes reachable after receiving $\mathbf{v}_3$ because $r$ was reachable when it sent $\mathbf{v}_3$, and $p$ becomes reachable after receiving $\mathbf{v}_4$ because $q$ was reachable when it sent $\mathbf{v}_4$. Co-reachability works similarly, but reasoning backwards on the timelines. For instance, process $s$ stops being "co-reachable" while it receives $\mathbf{v}_0$, process $r$ stops being co-reachable after it receives $\mathbf{v}_2$, and process $p$ stops being co-reachable by sending $\mathbf{v}_1$. The only message that is sent by a process being both reachable and co-reachable at the instant of the sending is $\mathbf{v}_2$, therefore it is the only message that will be counted as contributing to the SCC.

More formally, let $e$ be sequence of actions, $\mathsf{CG}(e)$ its conflict graph and $P, Q$ two sets of processes, $\mathsf{Post}_e(P) = \mathsf{Post}^*\Big(\{v \mid \mathsf{procs}(v) \cap P \neq \emptyset\}\Big)$ and $\mathsf{Pre}_e(Q) = \mathsf{Pre}^*\Big(\{v \mid \mathsf{procs}(v) \cap Q \neq \emptyset\}\Big)$ are introduced to represent the local view through $k$-exchanges of $\mathsf{Post}^*(v_{\mathsf{start}})$ and $\mathsf{Pre}^*(v_{\mathsf{stop}})$. For instance, for $e$ as in Example 7, we get $\mathsf{Post}_e(\{\pi\}) = \{(s, \mathbf{v}_0), \mathbf{v}_2, \mathbf{v}_3, \mathbf{v}_4, \mathbf{v}_0\}$ and $\mathsf{Pre}_e(\{\pi\}) = \{\mathbf{v}_0, \mathbf{v}_2, \mathbf{v}_1, (s, \mathbf{v}_0)\}$. In each $k$-exchange $e_i$ the size of the intersection between $\mathsf{Post}_{e_i}(P)$ and $\mathsf{Pre}_{e_i}(Q)$ will give the local contribution of the current $k$-exchange to the calculation of the size of the global SCC. In the transition relation $\xRightarrow[\mathsf{bad}]{e,k}$ this value is stored in variable $\texttt{cnt}$. The last ingredient to consider is to recognise if an edge RS belongs to the SCC. To this aim, we use a function $\texttt{lastisRec} : \mathbb{P} \to \{\mathsf{True}, \mathsf{False}\}$ that for each process stores the information whether the last action in the previous $k$-exchange was a reception or not. Then depending on the value of this variable and if a node is in the current SCC or not the value of $\texttt{sawRS}$ is set accordingly.

The transition relation $\xRightarrow[\mathsf{bad}]{e,k}$ defined in Fig. 7 deals with abstract configurations of the form $(P, Q, \texttt{cnt}, \texttt{sawRS}, \texttt{lastisRec}')$ where $P, Q \subseteq \mathbb{P}$, $\texttt{sawRS}$ is a boolean value, and $\texttt{cnt}$ is a counter bounded by $k+2$. We denote by $\texttt{lastisRec}_0$ the function where all $\texttt{lastisRec}(p) = \mathsf{False}$ for all $p \in \mathbb{P}$.

**Lemma 6.** *Let $e'$ be a feasible $k$-synchronizable execution of $\mathfrak{S}'$. Then $e'$ is a bad execution iff there are $e'' = e_1 \cdots e_n \cdot send(\pi, q, \mathbf{v}) \cdot rec(\pi, q, \mathbf{v})$ with $e_1, \ldots, e_n \in S^{\leq k} R^{\leq k}$ and $msc(e') = msc(e'')$, $P', Q \subseteq \mathbb{P}$, $\texttt{sawRS} \in \{\mathsf{True}, \mathsf{False}\}$, $\texttt{cnt} \in \{0, \ldots, k+2\}$, such that*

$$(\{\pi\}, Q, 0, \mathsf{False}, \texttt{lastisRec}_0) \xRightarrow[\mathsf{bad}]{e_1,k} \cdots \xRightarrow[\mathsf{bad}]{e_n,k} (P', \{\pi\}, \texttt{cnt}, \texttt{sawRS}, \texttt{lastisRec})$$

$$\frac{\begin{gathered} P' = \mathsf{procs}(\mathsf{Post}_e(P)) \qquad Q = \mathsf{procs}(\mathsf{Pre}_e(Q')) \\ SCC_e = \mathsf{Post}_e(P) \cap \mathsf{Pre}_e(Q') \\ \mathtt{cnt}' = \mathsf{min}(k+2, \mathtt{cnt} + n) \quad \text{where } n = |SCC_e| \\ \mathtt{lastisRec}'(q) \Leftrightarrow (\exists v \in SCC_e.\mathsf{proc}_R(v) = q \wedge v \cap R \neq \emptyset) \vee \\ (\mathtt{lastisRec}(q) \wedge \nexists v \in V.\mathsf{proc}_S(v) = q) \\ \mathtt{sawRS}' = \mathtt{sawRS} \vee \\ (\exists v \in SCC_e)(\exists p \in \mathbb{P} \setminus \{\pi\})\ \mathsf{proc}_S(v) = p \wedge \mathtt{lastisRec}(p) \wedge p \in P \cap Q \end{gathered}}{(P, Q, \mathtt{cnt}, \mathtt{sawRS}, \mathtt{lastisRec}) \xrightarrow[\mathsf{bad}]{e,k} (P', Q', \mathtt{cnt}', \mathtt{sawRS}', \mathtt{lastisRec}')}$$

Fig. 7: Definition of the relation $\xrightarrow[\mathsf{bad}]{e,k}$

*and at least one of the two holds: either* $\mathtt{sawRS} = \mathsf{True}$, *or* $\mathtt{cnt} = k + 2$.

*Comparison with [4].* As for the notion of feasibility, to determine if an execution is bad, in [4] the authors use a monitor that builds a path between the send to process $\pi$ and the send from $\pi$. In addition to the problems related to the wrong characterisation of $k$-synchronizability, this monitor not only can detect an $RS$ edge when there should be none, but also it can miss them when they exist. In general, the problem arises because the path is constructed by considering only an endpoint at the time.

We can finally conclude that:

**Theorem 4.** *The $k$-synchronizability of a system $\mathfrak{S}$ is decidable for $k \geq 1$.*

## 6 $k$-synchronizability for Peer-to-Peer Systems

In this section, we will apply $k$-synchronizability to peer-to-peer systems. A peer-to-peer system is a composition of communicating automata where each pair of machines exchange messages via two private FIFO buffers, one per direction of communication. Here we only give an insight on what changes with respect to the mailbox setting.

Causal delivery reveals the order imposed by FIFO buffers. Definition 4 must then be adapted to account for peer-to-peer communication. For instance, two messages that are sent to a same process $p$ by two different processes can be received by $p$ in any order, regardless of any causal dependency between the two sends. Thus, checking causal delivery in peer-to-peer systems is easier than in the mailbox setting, as we do not have to carry information on causal dependencies.

Within a peer-to-peer architecture, MSCs and conflict graphs are defined as within a mailbox communication. Indeed, they represents dependencies over machines, i.e., the order in which the actions can be done on a given machine, and over the send and the reception of a same message, and they do not depend on the type of communication. The notion of $k$-exchange remains also unchanged.

**Decidability of Reachability for $k$-synchronizable Peer-to-Peer Systems.** To establish the decidability of reachability for $k$-synchronizable peer-to-peer systems, we define a transition relation $\xrightarrow[\mathsf{cd}]{e,k}^{\mathsf{p2p}}$ for a sequence of action $e$ describing a $k$-exchange. As for mailbox systems, if a send action is unmatched in the current $k$-exchange, it will stay orphan forever. Moreover, after a process $p$ sent an orphan message to a process $q$, $p$ is forbidden to send any matched message to $q$. Nonetheless, as a consequence of the simpler definition of causal delivery, , we no longer need to work on the conflict graph. Summary nodes and extended edges are not needed and all the necessary information is in function $B$ that solely contains all the forbidden senders for process $p$.

The characterisation of a $k$-synchronizable execution is the same as for mailbox systems as the type of communication is not relevant. We can thus conclude, as within mailbox communication, that reachability is decidable.

**Theorem 5.** *Let $\mathfrak{S}$ be a $k$-synchronizable system and $\vec{l}$ a global control state of $\mathfrak{S}$. The problem whether there exists $e \in asEx(\mathfrak{S})$ and $\mathtt{Buf}$ such that $(\vec{l_0}, \mathtt{Buf}_0) \overset{e}{\Rightarrow} (\vec{l}, \mathtt{Buf})$ is decidable.*

**Decidability of $k$-synchronizability for Peer-to-Peer Systems.** As in mailbox system, the detection of a borderline execution determines whether a system is $k$-synchronizable.

The relation transition $\xrightarrow[\mathsf{feas}]{e,k}^{\mathsf{p2p}}$ allows to obtain feasible executions. Differently from the mailbox setting, we need to save not only the recipient $\mathtt{dest}_\pi$ but also the sender of the delayed message (information stored in variable $\mathtt{exp}_\pi$). The transition rule then checks that there is no message that is violating causal delivery, i.e., there is no message sent by $\mathtt{exp}_\pi$ to $\mathtt{dest}_\pi$ after the deviation. Finally the recognition of bad execution, works in the same way as for mailbox systems. The characterisation of a bad execution and the definition of $\xrightarrow[\mathsf{bad}]{e,k}^{\mathsf{p2p}}$ are, therefore, the same.

As for mailbox systems, we can, thus, conclude that for a given $k$, $k$-synchronizability is decidable.

**Theorem 6.** *The $k$-synchronizability of a system $\mathfrak{S}$ is decidable for $k \geq 1$.*

# 7 Concluding Remarks and Related works

In this paper we have studied $k$-synchronizability for mailbox and peer-to-peer systems. We have corrected the reachability and decidability proofs given in [4]. The flaws in [4] concern fundamental points and we had to propose a considerably different approach. The extended edges of the conflict graph, and the graph-theoretic characterisation of causal delivery as well as summary nodes, have no equivalent in [4]. Transition relations $\xrightarrow[\mathsf{feas}]{e,k}$ and $\xrightarrow[\mathsf{bad}]{e,k}$ building on the graph-theoretic characterisations of causal delivery and $k$-synchronizability, depart considerably from the proposal in [4].

We conclude by commenting on some other related works. The idea of "communication layers" is present in the early works of Elrad and Francez [8] or Chou and Gafni [7]. More recently, Chaouch-Saad *et al.* [6] verified some consensus algorithms using the Heard-Of Model that proceeds by "communication-closed rounds". The concept that an asynchronous system may have an "equivalent" synchronous counterpart has also been widely studied. Lipton's reduction [14] reschedules an execution so as to move the receive actions as close as possible from their corresponding send. Reduction recently received an increasing interest for verification purpose, e.g. by Kragl *et al.* [12], or Gleissenthal *et al.* [11].

Existentially bounded communication systems have been studied by Genest *et al.* [10,15]: a system is existentially $k$-bounded if any execution can be rescheduled in order to become $k$-bounded. This approach targets a broader class of systems than $k$-synchronizability, because it does not require that the execution can be chopped in communication-closed rounds. In the perspective of the current work, an interesting result is the decidability of existential $k$-boundedness for deadlock-free systems of communicating machines with peer-to-peer channels. Despite the more general definition, these older results are incomparable with the present ones, that deal with systems communicating with mailboxes, and not peer-to-peer channels.

Basu and Bultan studied a notion they also called synchronizability, but it differs from the notion studied in the present work; synchronizability and $k$-synchronizability define incomparable classes of communicating systems. The proofs of the decidability of synchronizability [3,2] were shown to have flaws by Finkel and Lozes [9]. A question left open in their paper is whether synchronizability is decidable for mailbox communications, as originally claimed by Basu and Bultan. Akroun and Salaün defined also a property they called stability [1] and that shares many similarities with the synchronizability notion in [2].

Context-bounded model-checking is yet another approach for the automatic verification of concurrent systems. La Torre *et al.* studied systems of communicating machines extended with a calling stack, and showed that under some conditions on the interplay between stack actions and communications, context-bounded reachability was decidable [13]. A context-switch is found in an execution each time two consecutive actions are performed by a different participant. Thus, while $k$-synchronizability limits the number of consecutive sendings, bounded context-switch analysis limits the number of times two consecutive actions are performed by two different processes.

As for future work, it would be interesting to explore how both context-boundedness and communication-closed rounds could be composed. Moreover refinements of the definition of $k$-synchronizability can also be considered. For instance, we conjecture that the current development can be greatly simplified if we forbid linearisation that do not correspond to actual executions.

## References


1. Akroun, L., Salaün, G.: Automated verification of automata communicating via FIFO and bag buffers. Formal Methods in System Design **52**(3), 260–276 (2018). https://doi.org/10.1007/s10703-017-0285-8
2. Basu, S., Bultan, T.: On deciding synchronizability for asynchronously communicating systems. Theor. Comput. Sci. **656**, 60–75 (2016). https://doi.org/10.1016/j.tcs.2016.09.023
3. Basu, S., Bultan, T., Ouederni, M.: Synchronizability for verification of asynchronously communicating systems. In: Kuncak, V., Rybalchenko, A. (eds.) Verification, Model Checking, and Abstract Interpretation - 13th International Conference, VMCAI 2012, Philadelphia, PA, USA, January 22-24, 2012. Proceedings. Lecture Notes in Computer Science, vol. 7148, pp. 56–71. Springer (2012). https://doi.org/10.1007/978-3-642-27940-9_5
4. Bouajjani, A., Enea, C., Ji, K., Qadeer, S.: On the completeness of verifying message passing programs under bounded asynchrony. In: Chockler, H., Weissenbacher, G. (eds.) Computer Aided Verification - 30th International Conference, CAV 2018, Held as Part of the Federated Logic Conference, FloC 2018, Oxford, UK, July 14-17, 2018, Proceedings, Part II. Lecture Notes in Computer Science, vol. 10982, pp. 372–391. Springer (2018). https://doi.org/10.1007/978-3-319-96142-2_23
5. Bouajjani, A., Habermehl, P., Vojnar, T.: Abstract regular model checking. In: Alur, R., Peled, D.A. (eds.) Computer Aided Verification, 16th International Conference, CAV 2004, Boston, MA, USA, July 13-17, 2004, Proceedings. Lecture Notes in Computer Science, vol. 3114, pp. 372–386. Springer (2004). https://doi.org/10.1007/978-3-540-27813-9_29
6. Chaouch-Saad, M., Charron-Bost, B., Merz, S.: A reduction theorem for the verification of round-based distributed algorithms. In: Bournez, O., Potapov, I. (eds.) Reachability Problems, 3rd International Workshop, RP 2009, Palaiseau, France, September 23-25, 2009. Proceedings. Lecture Notes in Computer Science, vol. 5797, pp. 93–106. Springer (2009). https://doi.org/10.1007/978-3-642-04420-5_10
7. Chou, C., Gafni, E.: Understanding and verifying distributed algorithms using stratified decomposition. In: Dolev, D. (ed.) Proceedings of the Seventh Annual ACM Symposium on Principles of Distributed Computing, Toronto, Ontario, Canada, August 15-17, 1988. pp. 44–65. ACM (1988). https://doi.org/10.1145/62546.62556
8. Elrad, T., Francez, N.: Decomposition of distributed programs into communication-closed layers. Sci. Comput. Program. **2**(3), 155–173 (1982). https://doi.org/10.1016/0167-6423(83)90013-8
9. Finkel, A., Lozes, É.: Synchronizability of communicating finite state machines is not decidable. In: Chatzigiannakis, I., Indyk, P., Kuhn, F., Muscholl, A. (eds.) 44th International Colloquium on Automata, Languages, and Programming, ICALP 2017, July 10-14, 2017, Warsaw, Poland. LIPIcs, vol. 80, pp. 122:1–122:14. Schloss Dagstuhl - Leibniz-Zentrum fuer Informatik (2017). https://doi.org/10.4230/LIPIcs.ICALP.2017.122, http://www.dagstuhl.de/dagpub/978-3-95977-041-5
10. Genest, B., Kuske, D., Muscholl, A.: On communicating automata with bounded channels. Fundam. Inform. **80**(1-3), 147–167 (2007), http://content.iospress.com/articles/fundamenta-informaticae/fi80-1-3-09
11. von Gleissenthall, K., Kici, R.G., Bakst, A., Stefan, D., Jhala, R.: Pretend synchrony: synchronous verification of asynchronous distributed programs. PACMPL **3**(POPL), 59:1–59:30 (2019). https://doi.org/10.1145/3290372

12. Kragl, B., Qadeer, S., Henzinger, T.A.: Synchronizing the asynchronous. In: Schewe, S., Zhang, L. (eds.) 29th International Conference on Concurrency Theory, CONCUR 2018, September 4-7, 2018, Beijing, China. LIPIcs, vol. 118, pp. 21:1–21:17. Schloss Dagstuhl - Leibniz-Zentrum fuer Informatik (2018). https://doi.org/10.4230/LIPIcs.CONCUR.2018.21
13. La Torre, S., Madhusudan, P., Parlato, G.: Context-bounded analysis of concurrent queue systems. In: Ramakrishnan, C.R., Rehof, J. (eds.) Tools and Algorithms for the Construction and Analysis of Systems, 14th International Conference, TACAS 2008, Held as Part of the Joint European Conferences on Theory and Practice of Software, ETAPS 2008, Budapest, Hungary, March 29-April 6, 2008. Proceedings. Lecture Notes in Computer Science, vol. 4963, pp. 299–314. Springer (2008). https://doi.org/10.1007/978-3-540-78800-3_21
14. Lipton, R.J.: Reduction: A method of proving properties of parallel programs. Commun. ACM **18**(12), 717–721 (1975). https://doi.org/10.1145/361227.361234
15. Muscholl, A.: Analysis of communicating automata. In: Dediu, A., Fernau, H., Martín-Vide, C. (eds.) Language and Automata Theory and Applications, 4th International Conference, LATA 2010, Trier, Germany, May 24-28, 2010. Proceedings. Lecture Notes in Computer Science, vol. 6031, pp. 50–57. Springer (2010). https://doi.org/10.1007/978-3-642-13089-2_4

# 11

# Relative Full Completeness for Bicategorical Cartesian Closed Structure

Marcelo Fiore[1] and Philip Saville[(✉)2]

[1] Department of Computer Science and Technology, University of Cambridge, UK
marcelo.fiore@cl.cam.ac.uk
[2] School of Informatics, University of Edinburgh, UK
philip.saville@ed.ac.uk

**Abstract.** The glueing construction, defined as a certain comma category, is an important tool for reasoning about type theories, logics, and programming languages. Here we extend the construction to accommodate '2-dimensional theories' of types, terms between types, and rewrites between terms. Taking bicategories as the semantic framework for such systems, we define the glueing bicategory and establish a bicategorical version of the well-known construction of cartesian closed structure on a glueing category. As an application, we show that free finite-product bicategories are fully complete relative to free cartesian closed bicategories, thereby establishing that the higher-order equational theory of rewriting in the simply-typed lambda calculus is a conservative extension of the algebraic equational theory of rewriting in the fragment with finite products only.

**Keywords:** glueing, bicategories, cartesian closure, relative full completeness, rewriting, type theory, conservative extension

## 1 Introduction

***Relative full completeness for cartesian closed structure.*** Every small category $\mathbb{C}$ can be viewed as an algebraic theory. This has sorts the objects of $\mathbb{C}$ with unary operators for each morphism of $\mathbb{C}$ and equations determined by the equalities in $\mathbb{C}$. Suppose one freely extends $\mathbb{C}$ with finite products. Categorically, one obtains the free cartesian category $\mathbb{F}^{\times}[\mathbb{C}]$ on $\mathbb{C}$. From the well-known construction of $\mathbb{F}^{\times}[\mathbb{C}]$ (see *e.g.* [12] and [46, §8]) it is direct that the universal functor $\mathbb{C} \to \mathbb{F}^{\times}[\mathbb{C}]$ is fully-faithful, a property we will refer to as the *relative full completeness* (*c.f.* [2,16]) of $\mathbb{C}$ in $\mathbb{F}^{\times}[\mathbb{C}]$. Type theoretically, $\mathbb{F}^{\times}[\mathbb{C}]$ corresponds to the Simply-Typed Product Calculus (STPC) over the algebraic theory of $\mathbb{C}$, given by taking the fragment of the Simply-Typed Lambda Calculus (STLC) consisting of just the types, rules, and equational theory for products. Relative full completeness corresponds to the STPC being a *conservative extension*.

Consider now the free cartesian closed category $\mathbb{F}^{\times,\to}[\mathbb{C}]$ on $\mathbb{C}$, type-theoretically corresponding to the STLC over the algebraic theory of $\mathbb{C}$. Does the relative full completeness property, and hence conservativity, still hold for either $\mathbb{C}$ in $\mathbb{F}^{\times,\to}[\mathbb{C}]$

or for $\mathbb{F}^{\times}[\mathbb{C}]$ in $\mathbb{F}^{\times,\rightarrow}[\mathbb{C}]$? Precisely, is either the universal functor $\mathbb{C} \to \mathbb{F}^{\times,\rightarrow}[\mathbb{C}]$ or its universal cartesian extension $\mathbb{F}^{\times}[\mathbb{C}] \to \mathbb{F}^{\times,\rightarrow}[\mathbb{C}]$ full and faithful? The answer is affirmative, but the proof is non-trivial. One must either reason proof-theoretically (*e.g.* in the style of [63, Chapter 8]) or employ semantic techniques such as glueing [39, Annexe C].

In this paper we consider the question of relative full completeness in the bicategorical setting. This corresponds to the question of conservativity for 2-dimensional theories of types, terms between types, and rewrites between terms (see [32,20]). We focus on the particular case of the STLC with invertible rewrites given by $\beta$-reductions and $\eta$-expansions, and its STPC fragment. By identifying these two systems with cartesian closed, resp. finite product, structure 'up to isomorphism' one recovers a conservative extension result for rewrites akin to that for terms.

***2-dimensional categories and rewriting.*** It has been known since the 1980s that one may consider 2-dimensional categories as abstract reduction systems (*e.g.* [54,51]): if sorts are 0-cells (objects) and terms are 1-cells (morphisms), then rewrites between terms ought to be 2-cells. Indeed, every sesquicategory (of which 2-categories are a special class) generates a rewriting relation $\rightsquigarrow$ on its 1-cells defined by $f \rightsquigarrow g$ if and only if there exists a 2-cell $f \Rightarrow g$ (*e.g.* [60,58]). Invertible 2-cells may be then thought of as equality witnesses.

The rewriting rules of the STLC arise naturally in this framework: Seely [56] observed that $\beta$-reduction and $\eta$-expansion may be respectively interpreted as the counit and unit of the adjunctions corresponding to lax (directed) products and exponentials in a 2-category (*c.f.* also [34,27]). This approach was taken up by Hilken [32], who developed a '2-dimensional $\lambda$-calculus' with strict products and lax exponentials to study the proof theory of rewriting in the STLC (*c.f.* also [33]).

Our concern here is with equational theories of rewriting, and we follow Seely in viewing weak categorical structure as a semantic model of rewriting modulo an equational theory. We are not aware of non-syntactic examples of 2-dimensional cartesian closed structure that are lax but not pseudo (*i.e.* up to isomorphism) and so adopt *cartesian closed bicategories* as our semantic framework.

From the perspective of rewriting, a sesquicategory embodies the rewriting of terms modulo the monoid laws for identities and composition, while a bicategory embodies the rewriting of terms modulo the equational theory on rewrites given by the triangle and pentagon laws of a monoidal category. Cartesian closed bicategories further embody the usual $\beta$-reductions and $\eta$-expansions of STLC modulo an equational theory on rewrites; for instance, this identifies the composite rewrite $\langle t_1, t_2\rangle \Rightarrow \langle \pi_1(\langle t_1, t_2\rangle), \pi_2(\langle t_1, t_2\rangle)\rangle \Rightarrow \langle t_1, t_2\rangle$ with the identity rewrite. Indeed, in the free cartesian closed bicategory over a signature of base types and constant terms, the quotient of 1-cells by the isomorphism relation provided by 2-cells is in bijection with $\alpha\beta\eta$-equivalence classes of STLC-terms (*c.f.* [55, Chapter 5]).

***Bicategorical relative full completeness.*** The bicategorical notion of relative full completeness arises by generalising from functors that are fully-faithful to pseudofunctors $F : \mathcal{B} \to \mathcal{C}$ that are *locally an equivalence*, that is, for which every hom-functor $F_{X,Y} : \mathcal{B}(X,Y) \to \mathcal{C}(FX,FY)$ is an equivalence of categories. Interpreted in the context of rewriting, this amounts to the *conservativity of rewriting theories*. First, the equational theory of rewriting in $\mathcal{C}$ is conservative over that in $\mathcal{B}$: the hom-functors do not identify distinct rewrites. Second, the reduction relation in $\mathcal{C}(FX,FY)$ is conservative over that in $\mathcal{B}(X,Y)$: whenever $Ff \rightsquigarrow Fg$ in $\mathcal{C}$ then already $f \rightsquigarrow g$ in $\mathcal{B}$. Third, the term structure in $\mathcal{B}$ gets copied by $F$ in $\mathcal{C}$: modulo the equational theory of rewrites, there are no new terms between types in the image of $F$.

***Contributions.*** This paper makes two main contributions.

Our first contribution, in Section 3, is to introduce the *bicategorical glueing* construction and, in Section 4, to initiate the development of its theory. As well as providing an assurance that our notion is the right one, this establishes the basic framework for applications. Importantly, we bicategorify the fundamental folklore result (*e.g.* [40,12,62]) establishing mild conditions under which a glued bicategory is cartesian closed.

Our second contribution, in Section 5, is to employ bicategorical glueing to show that for a bicategory $\mathcal{B}$ with finite-product completion $\mathcal{F}^{\times}[\mathcal{B}]$ and cartesian-closed completion $\mathcal{F}^{\times,\to}[\mathcal{B}]$, the universal pseudofunctor $\mathcal{B} \to \mathcal{F}^{\times,\to}[\mathcal{B}]$ and its universal finite-product-preserving extension $\mathcal{F}^{\times}[\mathcal{B}] \to \mathcal{F}^{\times,\to}[\mathcal{B}]$ are both locally an equivalence. Since one may directly observe that the universal pseudofunctor $\mathcal{B} \to \mathcal{F}^{\times}[\mathcal{B}]$ is locally an equivalence, we obtain *relative full completeness results for bicategorical cartesian closed structure* mirroring those of the categorical setting. Establishing this proof-theoretically would require the development of a 2-dimensional proof theory. Given the complexities already present at the categorical level this seems a serious and interesting undertaking. Here, once the basic bicategorical theory has been established, the proof is relatively compact. This highlights the effectiveness of our approach for the application.

The result may also be expressed type-theoretically. For instance, in terms of the type theories of [20], the type theory $\Lambda_{\text{ps}}^{\times,\to}$ for cartesian closed bicategories is a conservative extension of the type theory $\Lambda_{\text{ps}}^{\times}$ for finite-product bicategories. It follows that, modulo the equational theory of bicategorical products and exponentials, any rewrite between STPC-terms constructed using the $\beta\eta$-rewrites for both products and exponentials may be equally presented as constructed from just the $\beta\eta$-rewrites for products (see [21,55]).

***Further work.*** We view the foundational theory presented here as the starting point for future work. For instance, we plan to incorporate further type structure into the development, such as coproducts (*c.f.* [22,16,4]) and monoidal structure (*c.f.* [31]).

On the other hand, the importance of glueing in the categorical setting suggests that its bicategorical counterpart will find a range of applications. A case in point, which has already been developed, is the proof of a 2-dimensional normalisation property for the type theory $\Lambda_{\text{ps}}^{\times,\to}$ for cartesian closed bicategories of [20] that entails a corresponding bicategorical coherence theorem [21,55]. There are also a variety of syntactic constructions in programming languages and type theory that naturally come with a 2-dimensional semantics (see *e.g.* the use of 2-categorical constructions in [23,14,6,61,35]). In such scenarios, bicategorical glueing may prove useful for establishing properties corresponding to the notions of adequacy and/or canonicity, or for proving further conservativity properties.

## 2 Cartesian closed bicategories

We begin by briefly recapitulating the basic theory of bicategories, including the definition of cartesian closure. A summary of the key definitions is in [41]; for a more extensive introduction see *e.g.* [5,7].

### 2.1 Bicategories

Bicategories axiomatise structures in which the associativity and unit laws of composition only hold up to coherent isomorphism, for instance when composition is defined by a universal property. They are rife in mathematics and theoretical computer science, appearing in the semantics of computation [29,11,49], datatype models [1,13], categorical logic [26], and categorical algebra [19,25,18].

**Definition 1 ([5]).** *A* bicategory $\mathcal{B}$ *consists of*

1. *A class of objects* $ob(\mathcal{B})$*,*
2. *For every* $X, Y \in ob(\mathcal{B})$ *a* hom-category $(\mathcal{B}(X, Y), \bullet, \mathrm{id})$ *with objects* 1-cells $f : X \to Y$ *and morphisms* 2-cells $\alpha : f \Rightarrow f' : X \to Y$*; composition of 2-cells is called* vertical composition*,*
3. *For every* $X, Y, Z \in ob(\mathcal{B})$ *an* identity *functor* $\mathrm{Id}_X : \mathbf{1} \to \mathcal{B}(X, X)$ *(for* $\mathbf{1}$ *the terminal category) and a* horizontal composition *functor* $\circ_{X,Y,Z} : \mathcal{B}(Y, Z) \times \mathcal{B}(X, Y) \to \mathcal{B}(X, Z)$*,*
4. *Invertible 2-cells*

$$\mathbf{a}_{h,g,f} : (h \circ g) \circ f \Rightarrow h \circ (g \circ f) : W \to Z$$
$$\mathbf{l}_f : \mathrm{Id}_X \circ f \Rightarrow f : W \to X$$
$$\mathbf{r}_g : g \circ \mathrm{Id}_X \Rightarrow g : X \to Y$$

*for every* $f : W \to X$*,* $g : X \to Y$ *and* $h : Y \to Z$*, natural in each of their parameters and satisfying a* triangle law *and a* pentagon law *analogous to those for monoidal categories.*

*A bicategory is said to be* locally small *if every hom-category is small.*

*Example 1.* 1. Every 2-category is a bicategory in which the structural isomorphisms are all the identity.
2. For any category $\mathbb{C}$ with pullbacks there exists a *bicategory of spans* over $\mathbb{C}$ [5]. The objects are those of $\mathbb{C}$, 1-cells $A \rightsquigarrow B$ are spans $(A \leftarrow X \to B)$, and 2-cells $(A \leftarrow X \to B) \to (A \leftarrow X' \to B)$ are morphisms $X \to X'$ making the expected diagram commute. Composition is defined using chosen pullbacks.

A bicategory has three notions of 'opposite', depending on whether one reverses 1-cells, 2-cells, or both (see *e.g.* [37, §1.6]). We shall only require the following.

**Definition 2.** *The* opposite *of a bicategory $\mathcal{B}$, denoted $\mathcal{B}^{\mathrm{op}}$, is obtained by setting $\mathcal{B}^{\mathrm{op}}(X,Y) := \mathcal{B}(Y,X)$ for all $X,Y \in \mathcal{B}$.*

A morphism of bicategories is called a *pseudofunctor* (or *homomorphism*) [5]. It is a mapping on objects, 1-cells and 2-cells that preserves horizontal composition up to isomorphism. Vertical composition is preserved strictly.

**Definition 3.** *A* pseudofunctor $(F,\phi,\psi) : \mathcal{B} \to \mathcal{C}$ *between bicategories $\mathcal{B}$ and $\mathcal{C}$ consists of*

1. *A mapping $F : ob(\mathcal{B}) \to ob(\mathcal{C})$,*
2. *A functor $F_{X,Y} : \mathcal{B}(X,Y) \to \mathcal{C}(FX,FY)$ for every $X,Y \in ob(\mathcal{B})$,*
3. *An invertible 2-cell $\psi_X : \mathrm{Id}_{FX} \Rightarrow F(\mathrm{Id}_X)$ for every $X \in ob(\mathcal{B})$,*
4. *An invertible 2-cell $\phi_{f,g} : F(f) \circ F(g) \Rightarrow F(f \circ g)$ for every $g : X \to Y$ and $f : Y \to Z$, natural in $f$ and $g$,*

*subject to two unit laws and an associativity law. A pseudofunctor for which $\phi$ and $\psi$ are both the identity is called* strict*. A pseudofunctor is called* locally $P$ *if every functor $F_{X,Y}$ satisfies the property $P$.*

*Example 2.* A monoidal category is equivalently a one-object bicategory; a monoidal functor is equivalently a pseudofunctor between one-object bicategories.

Pseudofunctors $F,G : \mathcal{B} \to \mathcal{C}$ are related by *pseudonatural transformations*. A pseudonatural transformation $(\mathsf{k},\overline{\mathsf{k}}) : F \Rightarrow G$ consists of a family of 1-cells $(\mathsf{k}_X : FX \to GX)_{X\in\mathcal{B}}$ and, for every $f : X \to Y$, an invertible 2-cell $\overline{\mathsf{k}}_f : \mathsf{k}_Y \circ Ff \Rightarrow Gf \circ \mathsf{k}_X$ witnessing naturality. The 2-cells $\overline{\mathsf{k}}_f$ are required to be natural in $f$ and satisfy two coherence axioms. A morphism of pseudonatural transformations is called a *modification*, and may be thought of as a coherent family of 2-cells.

*Notation 1.* For bicategories $\mathcal{B}$ and $\mathcal{C}$ we write $\mathbf{Bicat}(\mathcal{B},\mathcal{C})$ for the (possibly large) bicategory of pseudofunctors, pseudonatural transformations, and modifications (see *e.g.* [41]). If $\mathcal{C}$ is a 2-category, then so is $\mathbf{Bicat}(\mathcal{B},\mathcal{C})$. We write $\mathbf{Cat}$ for the 2-category of small categories and think of the 2-category $\mathbf{Bicat}(\mathcal{B}^{\mathrm{op}},\mathbf{Cat})$ as a bicategorical version of the presheaf category $\mathrm{Set}^{\mathbb{C}^{\mathrm{op}}}$. As for presheaf categories, one must take care to avoid size issues. We therefore adopt the convention that when considering $\mathbf{Bicat}(\mathcal{B}^{\mathrm{op}},\mathbf{Cat})$ the bicategory $\mathcal{B}$ is small or locally small as appropriate.

*Example 3.* For every bicategory $\mathcal{B}$ and $X \in \mathcal{B}$ there exists the *representable pseudofunctor* $\mathrm{Y}X : \mathcal{B}^{\mathrm{op}} \to \mathbf{Cat}$, defined by $\mathrm{Y}X := \mathcal{B}(-,X)$. The 2-cells $\phi$ and $\psi$ are structural isomorphisms.

The notion of equivalence between bicategories is called biequivalence. A *biequivalence* $\mathcal{B} \simeq \mathcal{C}$ consists of a pair of pseudofunctors $F : \mathcal{B} \leftrightarrows G : \mathcal{C}$ together with equivalences $FG \simeq \mathrm{id}_{\mathcal{C}}$ and $GF \simeq \mathrm{id}_{\mathcal{B}}$ in $\mathbf{Bicat}(\mathcal{C}, \mathcal{C})$ and $\mathbf{Bicat}(\mathcal{B}, \mathcal{B})$ respectively. Equivalences in an arbitrary bicategory are defined by analogy with equivalences of categories, see *e.g.* [42, pp. 28].

*Remark 1.* The coherence theorem for monoidal categories [44, Chapter VII] generalises to bicategories: any bicategory is biequivalent to a 2-category [45] (see [42] for a readable summary of the argument). We are therefore justified in writing simply $\cong$ for composites of $\mathbf{a}, \mathbf{l}$ and $\mathbf{r}$.

As a rule of thumb, a category-theoretic proposition lifts to a bicategorical proposition so long as one takes care to weaken isomorphisms to equivalences and sprinkle the prefixes 'pseudo' and 'bi' in appropriate places. For instance, bicategorical adjoints are called *biadjoints* and bicategorical limits are called *bilimits* [59]. The latter may be thought of as limits in which every cone is filled by a coherent choice of invertible 2-cell. Bilimits are preserved by representable pseudofunctors and by right biadjoints. The *bicategorical Yoneda lemma* [59, §1.9] says that for any pseudofunctor $P : \mathcal{B}^{\mathrm{op}} \to \mathbf{Cat}$, evaluation at the identity determines a pseudonatural family of equivalences $\mathbf{Bicat}(\mathcal{B}^{\mathrm{op}}, \mathbf{Cat})(\mathrm{Y}X, P) \simeq PX$. One may then deduce that the *Yoneda pseudofunctor* $\mathrm{Y} : \mathcal{B} \to \mathbf{Bicat}(\mathcal{B}^{\mathrm{op}}, \mathbf{Cat}) : X \mapsto \mathrm{Y}X$ is locally an equivalence. Another 'bicategorified' lemma is the following, which we shall employ in Section 5.

**Lemma 1.** *1. For pseudofunctors $F, G : \mathcal{B} \to \mathcal{C}$, if $F \simeq G$ and $G$ is locally an equivalence, then so is $F$.*
*2. For pseudofunctors $F : \mathcal{A} \to \mathcal{B}$, $G : \mathcal{B} \to \mathcal{C}$, $H : \mathcal{C} \to \mathcal{D}$, if $G \circ F$ and $H \circ G$ are local equivalences, then so is $F$.*

### 2.2 fp-Bicategories

It is convenient to directly consider all finite products, as this reduces the need to deal with the equivalent objects given by re-bracketing binary products. To avoid confusion with the 'cartesian bicategories' of Carboni and Walters [10,8], we call a bicategory with all finite products an *fp-bicategory*.

**Definition 4.** *An* fp-bicategory $(\mathcal{B}, \Pi_n(-))$ *is a bicategory $\mathcal{B}$ equipped with the following data for every $A_1, \ldots, A_n \in \mathcal{B}$ ($n \in \mathbb{N}$):*

1. *A chosen object $\prod_n(A_1, \ldots, A_n)$,*
2. *Chosen arrows $\pi_k : \prod_n(A_1, \ldots, A_n) \to A_k$ ($k = 1, \ldots, n$), called* projections,
3. *For every $X \in \mathcal{B}$ an adjoint equivalence*

$$\mathcal{B}(X, \textstyle\prod_n(A_1, \ldots, A_n)) \underset{\langle -, \ldots, = \rangle}{\overset{(\pi_1 \circ -, \ldots, \pi_n \circ -)}{\rightleftarrows}} \perp\simeq \textstyle\prod_{i=1}^n \mathcal{B}(X, A_i) \tag{1}$$

*specified by choosing a family of universal arrows (see* e.g. *[44, Theorem IV.2]) with components $\varpi^{(i)}_{f_1, \ldots, f_n} : \pi_i \circ \langle f_1, \ldots, f_n \rangle \Rightarrow f_i$ for $i = 1, \ldots, n$.*

*We call the right adjoint* $\langle -, \ldots, = \rangle$ *the* $n$-ary tupling.

Explicitly, the universal property of $\varpi = (\varpi^{(1)}, \ldots, \varpi^{(n)})$ is the following. For any finite family of 2-cells $(\alpha_i : \pi_i \circ g \Rightarrow f_i : X \to A_i)_{i=1,\ldots,n}$, there exists a 2-cell $\mathsf{p}^\dagger(\alpha_1, \ldots, \alpha_n) : g \Rightarrow \langle f_1, \ldots, f_n \rangle : X \to \prod_n(A_1, \ldots, A_n)$, unique such that

$$\varpi^{(k)}_{f_1,\ldots,f_n} \bullet \left(\pi_k \circ \mathsf{p}^\dagger(\alpha_1, \ldots, \alpha_n)\right) = \alpha_k : \pi_k \circ g \Rightarrow f_k$$

for $k = 1, \ldots, n$. One thereby obtains a functor $\langle -, \ldots, = \rangle$ and an adjunction as in (1) with counit $\varpi = (\varpi^{(1)}, \ldots, \varpi^{(n)})$ and unit $\varsigma_g := \mathsf{p}^\dagger(\mathrm{id}_{\pi_1 \circ g}, \ldots, \mathrm{id}_{\pi_n \circ g}) : g \Rightarrow \langle \pi_1 \circ g, \ldots, \pi_n \circ g \rangle$. This defines a *lax* $n$-ary product structure: one merely obtains an adjunction in (1). One turns it into a bicategorical (*pseudo*) product by further requiring the unit and counit to be invertible. The *terminal object* **1** arises as $\prod_0()$. We adopt the same notation as for categorical products, for example by writing $\prod_{i=1}^n A_i$ for $\prod_n(A_1, \ldots, A_n)$ and $\prod_{i=1}^n f_i$ for $\langle f_1 \circ \pi_1, \ldots, f_n \circ \pi_n \rangle$.

*Example 4.* The bicategory of spans over a *lextensive category* [9] has finite products; such a bicategory is biequivalent to its opposite, so these are in fact biproducts [38, Theorem 6.2]. Biproduct structure arises using the coproduct structure of the underlying category (*c.f.* the biproduct structure of the category of relations).

*Remark 2* (c.f. *Remark 1*). fp-Bicategories satisfy the following coherence theorem: every fp-bicategory is biequivalent to a 2-category with 2-categorical products [52, Theorem 4.1]. Thus, we shall sometimes simply write $\cong$ in diagrams for composites of 2-cells arising from either the bicategorical or product structure. In pasting diagrams we shall omit such 2-cells completely (*c.f.* [30, Remark 3.1.16]; for a detailed exposition, see [64, Appendix A]).

One may think of bicategorical product structure as an intensional version of the familiar categorical structure, except the usual equations (*e.g.* [28]) are now witnessed by natural families of invertible 2-cells. It is useful to introduce explicit names for these 2-cells.

*Notation 2.* In the following, and throughout, we write $A_\bullet$ for a finite sequence $\langle A_1, \ldots, A_n \rangle$.

**Lemma 2.** *For any fp-bicategory* $(\mathcal{B}, \Pi_n(-))$ *there exist canonical choices for the following natural families of invertible 2-cells:*

1. *For every* $(h_i : Y \to A_i)_{i=1,\ldots,n}$ *and* $g : X \to Y$*, a 2-cell* $\mathsf{post}(h_\bullet; g) : \langle h_1, \ldots, h_n \rangle \circ g \Rightarrow \langle h_1 \circ g, \ldots, h_n \circ g \rangle$,
2. *For every* $(h_i : A_i \to B_i)_{i=1,\ldots,n}$ *and* $(g_i : X \to A_i)_{i=1,\ldots,n}$*, a 2-cell* $\mathsf{fuse}(h_\bullet; g_\bullet) : (\prod_{i=1}^n h_i) \circ \langle g_1, \ldots, g_n \rangle \Rightarrow \langle h_1 \circ g_1, \ldots, h_n \circ g_n \rangle$.

In particular, it follows from Lemma 2(2) that there exists a canonical natural family of invertible 2-cells $\Phi_{h_\bullet, g_\bullet} : (\prod_{i=1}^n h_i) \circ (\prod_{i=1}^n g_i) \Rightarrow \prod_{i=1}^n (h_i \circ g_i)$ for any $(h_i : A_i \to B_i)_{i=1,\ldots,n}$ and $(g_j : X_j \to A_j)_{j=1,\ldots,n}$.

In the categorical setting, a cartesian functor preserves products up to isomorphism. An fp-pseudofunctor preserves bicategorical products up to equivalence.

**Definition 5.** *An* fp-pseudofunctor $(F, \mathrm{q}^{\times})$ *between fp-bicategories* $(\mathcal{B}, \Pi_n(-))$ *and* $(\mathcal{C}, \Pi_n(-))$ *is a pseudofunctor* $F : \mathcal{B} \to \mathcal{C}$ *equipped with specified equivalences*

$$\langle F\pi_1, \ldots, F\pi_n \rangle : F(\textstyle\prod_{i=1}^{n} A_i) \leftrightarrows \prod_{i=1}^{n}(FA_i) : \mathrm{q}^{\times}_{A_\bullet}$$

*for every* $A_1, \ldots, A_n \in \mathcal{B}$ $(n \in \mathbb{N})$. *We denote the 2-cells witnessing these equivalences by* $\mathsf{u}^{\times}_{A_\bullet} : \mathrm{Id}_{(\prod_i FA_i)} \Rightarrow \langle F\pi_1, \ldots, F\pi_n \rangle \circ \mathrm{q}^{\times}_{A_\bullet}$ *and* $\mathsf{c}^{\times}_{A_\bullet} : \mathrm{q}^{\times}_{A_\bullet} \circ \langle F\pi_1, \ldots, F\pi_n \rangle \Rightarrow \mathrm{Id}_{(F\Pi_i A_i)}$. *We call* $(F, \mathrm{q}^{\times})$ strict *if* $F$ *is strict and satisfies*

$$F(\textstyle\prod_n (A_1, \ldots, A_n)) = \prod_n (FA_1, \ldots, FA_n)$$

$$F(\pi_i^{A_1, \ldots, A_n}) = \pi_i^{FA_1, \ldots, FA_n} \qquad F\varpi^{(i)}_{t_1, \ldots, t_n} = \varpi^{(i)}_{Ft_1, \ldots, Ft_n}$$

$$F\langle t_1, \ldots, t_n \rangle = \langle Ft_1, \ldots, Ft_n \rangle \qquad \mathrm{q}^{\times}_{A_1, \ldots, A_n} = \mathrm{Id}_{\Pi_n(FA_1, \ldots, FA_n)}$$

*with equivalences given by the 2-cells* $\mathsf{p}^{\dagger}(\mathbf{r}_{\pi_1}, \ldots, \mathbf{r}_{\pi_n}) : \mathrm{Id} \overset{\cong}{\Rightarrow} \langle \pi_1, \ldots, \pi_n \rangle$.

*Notation 3.* For fp-bicategories $\mathcal{B}$ and $\mathcal{C}$ we write **fp-Bicat**$(\mathcal{B}, \mathcal{C})$ for the bicategory of fp-pseudofunctors, pseudonatural transformations and modifications.[3]

We define two further families of 2-cells to witness standard properties of cartesian functors. The first witnesses the fact that any fp-pseudofunctor commutes with the $\prod_n(-, \ldots, =)$ operation. The second witnesses the equality $\langle F\pi_1, \ldots, F\pi_n \rangle \circ F\langle f_1, \ldots, f_n \rangle = \langle Ff_1, \ldots, Ff_n \rangle$ 'unpacking' an $n$-ary tupling from inside $F$.

**Lemma 3.** *Let* $(F, \mathrm{q}^{\times}) : (\mathcal{B}, \Pi_n(-)) \to (\mathcal{C}, \Pi_n(-))$ *be an fp-pseudofunctor.*

1. *For any finite family of 1-cells* $(f_i : A_i \to A_i')_{i=1,\ldots,n}$ *in* $\mathcal{B}$, *there exists an invertible 2-cell* $\mathsf{nat}_{f_\bullet} : \mathrm{q}^{\times}_{A'_\bullet} \circ \prod_{i=1}^{n} Ff_i \Rightarrow F(\prod_{i=1}^{n} f_i) \circ \mathrm{q}^{\times}_{A_\bullet}$ *such that the pair* $(\mathrm{q}^{\times}, \mathsf{nat})$ *forms a a pseudonatural transformation*

$$\textstyle\prod_{i=1}^{n} (F(-), \ldots, F(=)) \Rightarrow (F \circ \prod_{i=1}^{n})(-, \ldots, =)$$

2. *For any finite family of 1-cells* $(f_i : X \to B_i)_{i=1,\ldots,n}$ *in* $\mathcal{B}$, *there exists a canonical choice of naturally invertible 2-cell* $\mathsf{unpack}_{f_\bullet} : \langle F\pi_1, \ldots, F\pi_n \rangle \circ F\langle f_1, \ldots, f_n \rangle \Rightarrow \langle Ff_1, \ldots, Ff_n \rangle : FX \to \prod_{i=1}^{n} FB_i$.

### 2.3 Cartesian closed bicategories

A cartesian closed bicategory is an fp-bicategory $(\mathcal{B}, \Pi_n(-))$ equipped with a biadjunction $(-)\times A \dashv (A \Rightarrow -)$ for every $A \in \mathcal{B}$. Examples include the bicategory of generalised species [17], bicategories of concurrent games [49], and bicategories of operads [26].

---

[3] In the categorical setting, every natural transformation between cartesian functors is monoidal with respect to the cartesian structure and a similar fact is true bicategorically: every pseudonatural transformation is canonically compatible with the product structure, see [55, § 4.1.1].

**Definition 6.** *A* cartesian closed bicategory *or* cc-bicategory *is an fp-bicategory* $(\mathcal{B}, \Pi_n(-))$ *equipped with the following data for every* $A, B \in \mathcal{B}$:

1. *A chosen object* $(A \Rightarrow B)$,
2. *A specified 1-cell* $\mathrm{eval}_{A,B} : (A \Rightarrow B) \times A \to B$,
3. *For every* $X \in \mathcal{B}$, *an adjoint equivalence*

$$\mathcal{B}(X, A \Rightarrow B) \underset{\lambda}{\overset{\mathrm{eval}_{A,B} \circ (- \times A)}{\rightleftarrows}} \mathcal{B}(X \times A, B) \quad \bot\simeq$$

*specified by a choice of universal arrow* $\varepsilon_f : \mathrm{eval}_{A,B} \circ (\lambda f \times A) \overset{\cong}{\Rightarrow} f$.

*We call the functor* $\lambda(-)$ currying *and refer to* $\lambda f$ *as the* currying of $f$.

Explicitly, the counit $\varepsilon$ satisfies the following universal property. For every 1-cell $g : X \to (A \Rightarrow B)$ and 2-cell $\alpha : \mathrm{eval}_{A,B} \circ (g \times A) \Rightarrow f$ there exists a unique 2-cell $\mathsf{e}^{\dagger}(\alpha) : g \Rightarrow \lambda f$ such that $\varepsilon_f \bullet \big(\mathrm{eval}_{A,B} \circ (\mathsf{e}^{\dagger}(\alpha) \times A)\big) = \alpha$. This defines a *lax* exponential structure. One obtains a *pseudo* (bicategorical) exponential structure by further requiring that $\varepsilon$ and the unit $\eta_t := \mathsf{e}^{\dagger}(\mathrm{id}_{\mathrm{eval}_{A,B} \circ (t \times A)})$ are invertible.

*Example 5.* Every 'presheaf' 2-category $\mathbf{Bicat}(\mathcal{B}^{\mathrm{op}}, \mathbf{Cat})$ has all bicategorical limits [52, Proposition 3.6], given pointwise, and is cartesian closed with $(P \Rightarrow Q)X := \mathbf{Bicat}(\mathcal{B}^{\mathrm{op}}, \mathbf{Cat})(\mathrm{Y}X \times P, Q)$ [55, Chapter 6].

As for products, we adopt the notational conventions that are standard in the categorical setting, for example by writing $(f \Rightarrow g) : (A \Rightarrow B) \to (A' \Rightarrow B')$ for the currying of $(g \circ \mathrm{eval}_{A,B}) \circ (\mathrm{Id}_{A \Rightarrow B} \times f)$.

Just as fp-pseudofunctors preserve products up to equivalence, cartesian closed pseudofunctors preserve products and exponentials up to equivalence.

**Definition 7.** *A* cartesian closed pseudofunctor *or* cc-pseudofunctor *between cc-bicategories* $(\mathcal{B}, \Pi_n(-), \Rightarrow)$ *and* $(\mathcal{C}, \Pi_n(-), \Rightarrow)$ *is an fp-pseudofunctor* $(F, \mathrm{q}^{\times})$ *equipped with specified equivalences* $m_{A,B} : F(A \Rightarrow B) \leftrightarrows (FA \Rightarrow FB) : \mathrm{q}^{\Rightarrow}_{A,B}$ *for every* $A, B \in \mathcal{B}$, *where* $m_{A,B} : F(A \Rightarrow B) \to (FA \Rightarrow FB)$ *is the currying of* $F(\mathrm{eval}_{A,B}) \circ \mathrm{q}^{\times}_{A \Rightarrow B, A}$. *A cc-pseudofunctor* $(F, \mathrm{q}^{\times}, \mathrm{q}^{\Rightarrow})$ *is* strict *if* $(F, \mathrm{q}^{\times})$ *is a strict fp-pseudofunctor such that*

$$F(A \Rightarrow B) = (FA \Rightarrow FB)$$
$$F(\mathrm{eval}_{A,B}) = \mathrm{eval}_{FA,FB} \qquad F(\varepsilon_t) = \varepsilon_{Ft}$$
$$F(\lambda t) = \lambda(Ft) \qquad \mathrm{q}^{\Rightarrow}_{A,B} = \mathrm{Id}_{FA \Rightarrow FB}$$

*with equivalences given by the 2-cells*

$$\mathsf{e}^{\dagger}(\mathrm{eval}_{FA,FB} \circ \kappa) : \mathrm{Id}_{(FA \Rightarrow FB)} \overset{\cong}{\Rightarrow} \lambda(\mathrm{eval}_{FA,FB} \circ \mathrm{Id}_{(FA \Rightarrow FB) \times FA})$$

*where* $\kappa$ *is the canonical isomorphism* $\mathrm{Id}_{FA \Rightarrow FB} \times FA \cong \mathrm{Id}_{(FA \Rightarrow FB) \times FA}$.

*Remark 3.* As is well-known in the case of **Cat** (*e.g.* [44, IV.2]), every equivalence $X \simeq Y$ in a bicategory gives rise to an *adjoint equivalence* between $X$ and $Y$ with the same 1-cells (see *e.g.* [42, pp. 28–29]). Thus, one may assume without loss of generality that all the equivalences in the preceding definition are adjoint equivalences. The same observation applies to the definition of fp-pseudofunctors.

*Notation 4.* For cc-bicategories $\mathcal{B}$ and $\mathcal{C}$ we write **cc-Bicat**$(\mathcal{B}, \mathcal{C})$ for the bicategory of cc-pseudofunctors, pseudonatural transformations and modifications (*c.f.* Notation 3).

## 3 Bicategorical glueing

The glueing construction has been discovered in various forms, with correspondingly various names: the notions of logical relation [50,57], sconing [24], Freyd covers, and glueing (*e.g.* [40]) are all closely related (see *e.g.* [47] for an overview of the connections). Originally presented set-theoretically, the technique was quickly given categorical expression [43,47] and is now a standard component of the armoury for studying type theories (*e.g.* [40,12]).

The *glueing* gl$(F)$ of categories $\mathbb{C}$ and $\mathbb{D}$ along a functor $F : \mathbb{C} \to \mathbb{D}$ may be defined as the comma category $(\mathrm{id}_{\mathbb{D}} \downarrow F)$. We define bicategorical glueing analogously.

**Definition 8.**

1. *Let* $F : \mathcal{A} \to \mathcal{C}$ *and* $G : \mathcal{B} \to \mathcal{C}$ *be pseudofunctors of bicategories. The* comma bicategory $(F \downarrow G)$ *has objects triples* $(A \in \mathcal{A}, f : FA \to GB, B \in \mathcal{B})$. *The 1-cells* $(A, f, B) \to (A', f', B')$ *are triples* $(p, \alpha, q)$, *where* $p : A \to A'$ *and* $q : B \to B'$ *are 1-cells and* $\alpha$ *is an invertible 2-cell* $\alpha : f' \circ Fp \Rightarrow Gq \circ f$. *The 2-cells* $(p, \alpha, q) \Rightarrow (p', \alpha', q')$ *are pairs of 2-cells* $(\sigma : p \Rightarrow p', \tau : q \Rightarrow q')$ *such that the following diagram commutes:*

$$\begin{array}{ccc} f' \circ F(p) & \xrightarrow{f' \circ F(\sigma)} & f' \circ F(p') \\ {\scriptstyle \alpha}\big\downarrow & & \big\downarrow{\scriptstyle \alpha'} \\ G(q) \circ f & \xrightarrow[G(\tau) \circ f]{} & G(q') \circ f \end{array} \tag{2}$$

*Identities and horizontal composition are given by the following pasting diagrams.*

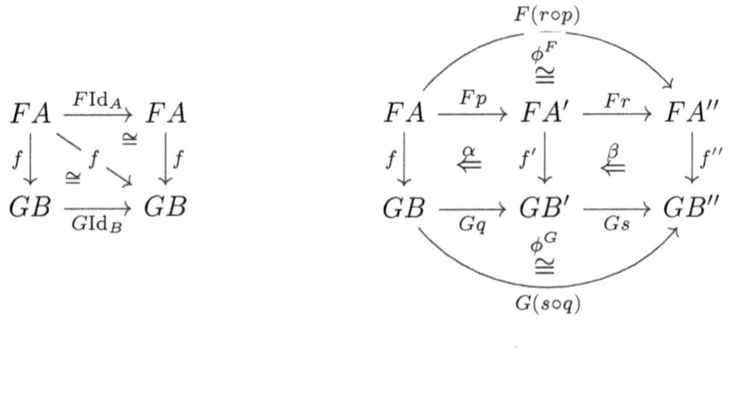

*Vertical composition, the identity 2-cell, and the structural isomorphisms are given component-wise.*

2. *The* glueing bicategory $\mathrm{gl}(\mathfrak{J})$ *of bicategories* $\mathcal{B}$ *and* $\mathcal{C}$ *along a pseudofunctor* $\mathfrak{J} : \mathcal{B} \to \mathcal{C}$ *is the comma bicategory* $(\mathrm{id}_{\mathcal{C}} \downarrow \mathfrak{J})$.

We call axiom (2) the *cylinder condition* due to its shape when viewed as a (3-dimensional) pasting diagram. Note that one directly obtains projection pseudofunctors $\mathcal{B} \xleftarrow{\pi_{\mathrm{dom}}} \mathrm{gl}(\mathfrak{J}) \xrightarrow{\pi_{\mathrm{cod}}} \mathcal{C}$.

We develop some basic theory of glueing bicategories, which we shall put to use in Section 5. We follow the terminology of [15].

**Definition 9.** *Let* $\mathfrak{J} : \mathcal{B} \to \mathcal{X}$ *be a pseudofunctor. The* relative hom-pseudofunctor $\langle\mathfrak{J}\rangle : \mathcal{X} \to \mathbf{Bicat}(\mathcal{B}^{\mathrm{op}}, \mathbf{Cat})$ *is defined by* $\langle\mathfrak{J}\rangle X := \mathcal{X}(\mathfrak{J}(-), X)$.

Following [15], one might call the glueing bicategory $\mathrm{gl}(\langle\mathfrak{J}\rangle)$ associated to a relative hom-pseudofunctor the bicategory of *$\mathcal{B}$-intensional Kripke relations of arity $\mathfrak{J}$*, and view it as an intensional, bicategorical, version of the category of Kripke relations.

The relative hom-pseudofunctor preserves all bilimits that exist in its domain. For products, this may be described explicitly.

**Lemma 4.** *For any fp-bicategory* $(\mathcal{X}, \Pi_n(-))$ *and pseudofunctor* $\mathfrak{J} : \mathcal{B} \to \mathcal{X}$*, the relative hom-pseudofunctor* $\langle\mathfrak{J}\rangle$ *extends canonically to an fp-pseudofunctor.*

*Proof. Take* $\mathrm{q}^{\times}_{X_\bullet}$ *to be the n-ary tupling* $\prod_{i=1}^{n} \mathcal{X}(\mathfrak{J}(-), X_i) \xrightarrow{\simeq} \mathcal{X}(\mathfrak{J}(-), \prod_{i=1}^{n} X_i)$. *This forms a pseudonatural transformation with naturality witnessed by* post.

For any pseudofunctor $\mathfrak{J} : \mathcal{B} \to \mathcal{X}$ there exists a pseudonatural transformation $(l, \bar{l}) : \mathrm{Y} \Rightarrow \langle\mathfrak{J}\rangle \circ \mathfrak{J} : \mathcal{B} \to \mathbf{Bicat}(\mathcal{B}^{\mathrm{op}}, \mathbf{Cat})$ given by the functorial action of $\mathfrak{J}$ on hom-categories. One may therefore define the following.

**Definition 10.** *For any pseudofunctor* $\mathfrak{J} : \mathcal{B} \to \mathcal{X}$*, define the* extended Yoneda pseudofunctor $\underline{\mathrm{Y}} : \mathcal{B} \to \mathrm{gl}(\langle\mathfrak{J}\rangle)$ *by setting* $\underline{\mathrm{Y}}B := \big(\mathrm{Y}B, (l, \bar{l})_{(-,B)}, \mathfrak{J}B\big)$, $\underline{\mathrm{Y}}f := (\mathrm{Y}f, (\phi^{\mathfrak{J}}_{-,f})^{-1}, \mathfrak{J}f)$, *and* $\underline{\mathrm{Y}}(\tau : f \Rightarrow f' : B \to B') := (\mathrm{Y}\tau, \mathfrak{J}\tau)$. *The cylinder condition holds by the naturality of* $\phi^{\mathfrak{J}}$*, and the 2-cells* $\phi^{\underline{\mathrm{Y}}}$ *and* $\psi^{\underline{\mathrm{Y}}}$ *are* $(\phi^{\mathrm{Y}}, \phi^{\mathfrak{J}})$ *and* $(\psi^{\mathrm{Y}}, \psi^{\mathfrak{J}})$*, respectively.*

The extended Yoneda pseudofunctor satisfies a corresponding 'extended Yoneda lemma' (*c.f.* [15, pp. 33]).

**Lemma 5.** *For any pseudofunctor* $\mathfrak{J} : \mathcal{B} \to \mathcal{X}$ *and* $\underline{P} = (P, (\mathsf{k}, \bar{\mathsf{k}}), X) \in \mathrm{gl}(\langle\mathfrak{J}\rangle)$ *there exists an equivalence of pseudofunctors* $\mathrm{gl}(\langle\mathfrak{J}\rangle)(\underline{\mathrm{Y}}(-), \underline{P}) \simeq P$ *and an invertible modification as in the diagram below. Hence* $\underline{\mathrm{Y}}$ *is locally an equivalence.*

$$\begin{array}{ccc} \mathrm{gl}(\langle\mathfrak{J}\rangle)(\underline{\mathrm{Y}}(-), \underline{P}) & \xrightarrow{\quad\simeq\quad} & P \\ & {\scriptstyle \pi_{\mathrm{dom}}} \searrow \quad \Leftarrow\!\cong \quad \swarrow {\scriptstyle (\mathsf{k}, \bar{\mathsf{k}})} & \\ & \mathcal{X}(\mathfrak{J}(-), X) & \end{array}$$

*Proof.* *The arrow marked* $\simeq$ *is the composite of a projection and the equivalence arising from the Yoneda lemma. Its pseudo-inverse is the composite*

$$P \xrightarrow{\simeq} \mathbf{Bicat}(\mathcal{B}^{op}, \mathbf{Cat})(\mathrm{Y}(-), P) \to \mathrm{gl}(\langle\mathfrak{J}\rangle)(\underline{\mathrm{Y}}(-), \underline{P}) \tag{3}$$

*in which the equivalence arises from the Yoneda lemma and the unlabelled pseudofunctor takes a pseudonatural transformation* $(\mathsf{j}, \bar{\mathsf{j}}) : \mathrm{Y}B \Rightarrow P$ *to the triple with first component* $(\mathsf{j}, \bar{\mathsf{j}})$, *third component* $\mathsf{j}_B(\mathsf{k}_B(\mathrm{Id}_B)) : \mathfrak{J}B \to X$ *and second component defined using* $\bar{\mathsf{k}}$ *and* $\bar{\mathsf{j}}$. *Chasing the definitions through and evaluating at* $A, B \in \mathcal{B}$, *one sees that when* $\underline{P} := \underline{\mathrm{Y}}B$ *the composite (3) is equivalent to* $\underline{\mathrm{Y}}_{A,B}$. *Since (3) is locally an equivalence, Lemma 1(1) completes the proof.*

## 4 Cartesian closed structure on the glueing bicategory

It is well-known that, if $\mathbb{C}$ and $\mathbb{D}$ are cartesian closed categories, $\mathbb{D}$ has pullbacks, and $F : \mathbb{C} \to \mathbb{D}$ is cartesian, then $\mathrm{gl}(F)$ is cartesian closed (*e.g.* [40,12]). In this section we prove a corresponding result for the glueing bicategory. We shall be guided by the categorical proof, for which see *e.g.* [43, Proposition 2].

### 4.1 Finite products in gl($\mathfrak{J}$)

**Proposition 1.** *Let* $(\mathcal{B}, \Pi_n(-))$ *and* $(\mathcal{C}, \Pi_n(-))$ *be fp-bicategories and* $(\mathfrak{J}, \mathrm{q}^\times) : \mathcal{B} \to \mathcal{C}$ *be an fp-pseudofunctor. Then* $\mathrm{gl}(\mathfrak{J})$ *is an fp-bicategory with both projection pseudofunctors* $\pi_{\mathrm{dom}}$ *and* $\pi_{\mathrm{cod}}$ *strictly preserving products.*

For a family of objects $(C_i, c_i, B_i)_{i=1,\ldots,n}$, the $n$-ary product $\prod_{i=1}^n (C_i, c_i, B_i)$ is defined to be the tuple $\left(\prod_{i=1}^n C_i, \mathrm{q}^\times_{B_\bullet} \circ \prod_{i=1}^n c_i, \prod_{i=1}^n B_i\right)$. The $k$th projection $\underline{\pi_k}$ is $(\pi_k, \mu_k, \pi_k)$, where $\mu_k$ is defined by commutativity of the following diagram:

$$\begin{array}{ccc}
c_k \circ \pi_k & \xrightarrow{\quad \mu_k \quad} & \mathfrak{J}(\pi_k) \circ (\mathrm{q}^\times_{B_\bullet} \circ \textstyle\prod_i c_i) \\
\downarrow{\scriptstyle (\varpi^{(k)})^{-1}} & & \uparrow{\scriptstyle \cong} \\
\pi_k \circ \textstyle\prod_i c_i & & (\mathfrak{J}\pi_k \circ \mathrm{q}^\times_{B_\bullet}) \circ \textstyle\prod_i c_i \\
\downarrow{\scriptstyle \cong} & & \uparrow{\scriptstyle (\varpi^{(k)} \circ \mathrm{q}^\times_{B_\bullet}) \circ \prod_i c_i} \\
(\pi_k \circ \mathrm{Id}_{(\prod_i \mathfrak{J}B_i)}) \circ \textstyle\prod_i c_i & & ((\pi_k \circ \langle \mathfrak{J}\pi_1, \ldots, \mathfrak{J}\pi_n \rangle) \circ \mathrm{q}^\times_{B_\bullet}) \circ \textstyle\prod_i c_i \\
 & \searrow{\scriptstyle (\pi_k \circ \mathrm{u}^\times_{B_\bullet}) \circ \prod_i c_i} & \uparrow{\scriptstyle \cong} \\
 & & (\pi_k \circ (\langle \mathfrak{J}\pi_1, \ldots, \mathfrak{J}\pi_n \rangle \circ \mathrm{q}^\times_{B_\bullet})) \circ \textstyle\prod_i c_i
\end{array}$$

For an $n$-ary family of 1-cells $(g_i, \alpha_i, f_i) : (Y, y, X) \to (C_i, c_i, B_i)\,(i = 1, \ldots, n)$, the $n$-ary tupling is $(\langle g_1, \ldots, g_n \rangle, \{\alpha_1, \ldots, \alpha_n\}, \langle f_1, \ldots, f_n \rangle)$, where $\{\alpha_1, \ldots, \alpha_n\}$

is the composite

$$
\begin{array}{ccc}
(q_{B_\bullet}^\times \circ \prod_i c_i) \circ \langle g_1, \ldots, g_n \rangle & \xrightarrow{\ \{\alpha_1, \ldots, \alpha_n\}\ } & \mathfrak{J}(\langle f_1, \ldots, f_n \rangle) \circ y \\
\cong \downarrow & & \uparrow \cong \\
q_{B_\bullet}^\times \circ (\prod_i c_i \circ \langle g_1, \ldots, g_n \rangle) & & \mathrm{Id}_{\mathfrak{J}(\prod B_i)} \circ (\mathfrak{J}\langle f_1, \ldots, f_n \rangle \circ y) \\
q_{B_\bullet}^\times \circ \mathrm{fuse} \downarrow & & \uparrow (c_{B_\bullet}^\times \circ \mathfrak{J}\langle f_1, \ldots, f_n \rangle) \circ y \\
q_{B_\bullet}^\times \circ \langle c_1 \circ g_1, \ldots, c_n \circ g_n \rangle & & (q_{B_\bullet}^\times \circ \langle \mathfrak{J}\pi_1, \ldots, \mathfrak{J}\pi_n \rangle) \circ (\mathfrak{J}\langle f_1, \ldots, f_n \rangle \circ y) \\
q_{B_\bullet}^\times \circ \langle \alpha_1, \ldots, \alpha_n \rangle \downarrow & & \uparrow \cong \\
q_{B_\bullet}^\times \circ \langle \mathfrak{J} f_1 \circ y, \ldots, \mathfrak{J} f_n \circ y \rangle & & q_{B_\bullet}^\times \circ ((\langle \mathfrak{J}\pi_1, \ldots, \mathfrak{J}\pi_n \rangle \circ \mathfrak{J}\langle f_1, \ldots, f_n \rangle) \circ y) \\
 & & \uparrow q_{B_\bullet}^\times \circ (\mathrm{unpack}_{f_\bullet}^{-1} \circ y) \\
 & \xrightarrow[\ q_{B_\bullet}^\times \circ \mathrm{post}^{-1}\ ]{} & q_{B_\bullet}^\times \circ (\langle \mathfrak{J} f_1, \ldots, \mathfrak{J} f_n \rangle \circ y)
\end{array}
$$

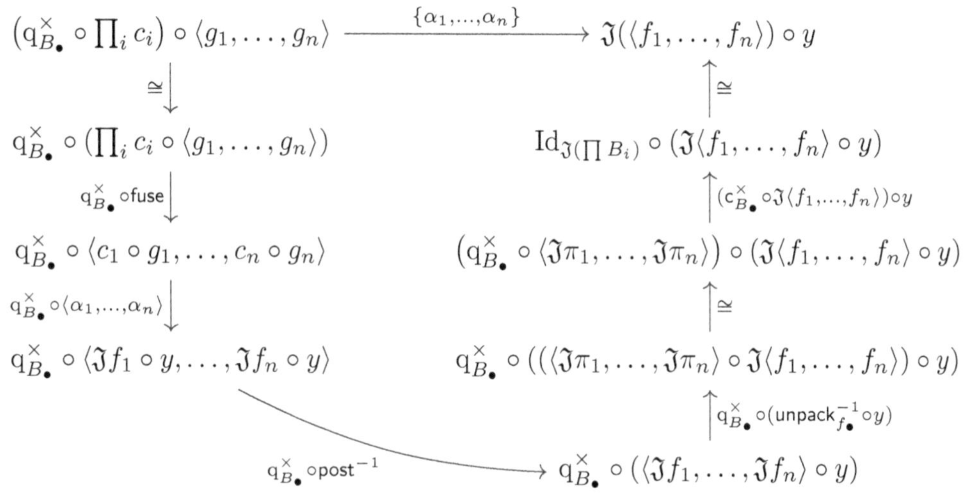

Finally, for every family of 1-cells $(g_i, \alpha_i, f_i) : (Y, y, X) \to (C_i, c_i, B_i)$ $(i = 1, \ldots, n)$ we require a glued 2-cell $\pi_k \circ (\langle g_1, \ldots, g_n \rangle, \{\alpha_1, \ldots, \alpha_n\}, \langle f_1, \ldots, f_n \rangle) \Rightarrow (g_k, \alpha_k, f_k)$ to act as the counit. We take simply $(\varpi_{g_\bullet}^{(k)}, \varpi_{f_\bullet}^{(k)})$. This pair forms a 2-cell in $\mathrm{gl}(\mathfrak{J})$, and the required universal property holds pointwise.

*Remark 4.* If $(\mathfrak{J}, q^\times) : \mathcal{B} \to \mathcal{X}$ is an fp-pseudofunctor, then $\underline{Y} : \mathcal{B} \to \mathrm{gl}(\langle \mathfrak{J} \rangle)$ canonically extends to an fp-pseudofunctor. The pseudoinverse to $\langle \underline{Y}\pi_1, \ldots, \underline{Y}\pi_n \rangle$ is $(\langle -, \ldots, = \rangle, \cong, q^\times)$, where the component of the isomorphism at $(f_i : X \to B_i)_{i=1,\ldots,n}$ is $F\langle f_\bullet \rangle \overset{\cong}{\Rightarrow} \mathrm{Id}_{F(\Pi_i B_i)} \circ F\langle f_\bullet \rangle \xRightarrow{\ (c_{B_\bullet}^\times)^{-1} \circ F\langle f_\bullet \rangle\ } q_{B_\bullet}^\times \circ \langle F\pi_\bullet \rangle \circ F\langle f_\bullet \rangle \xRightarrow{\ q_{B_\bullet}^\times \circ \mathrm{unpack}\ } q_{B_\bullet}^\times \circ \langle F f_\bullet \rangle$.

## 4.2   Exponentials in $\mathrm{gl}(\mathfrak{J})$

As in the 1-categorical case, the definition of currying in $\mathrm{gl}(\mathfrak{J})$ employs pullbacks. A *pullback* of the cospan $(X_1 \to X_0 \leftarrow X_2)$ in a bicategory $\mathcal{B}$ is a bilimit for the strict pseudofunctor $X : (1 \to 0 \leftarrow 2) \to \mathcal{B}$ determined by the cospan. We state the universal property in the form that will be most useful for our applications.

**Lemma 6.** *The pullback of a cospan $(X_1 \xrightarrow{f_1} X_0 \xleftarrow{f_2} X_2)$ in a bicategory $\mathcal{B}$ is determined, up to equivalence, by the following data and properties: a span $(X_1 \xleftarrow{\gamma_1} P \xrightarrow{\gamma_2} X_2)$ in $\mathcal{B}$ and an invertible 2-cell filling the diagram on the left below*

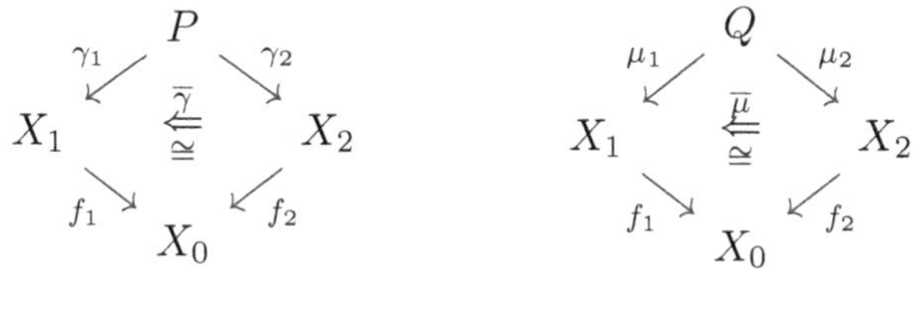

*such that*

1. *for any other diagram as on the right above there exists a* fill-in $(u, \Xi_1, \Xi_2)$, *namely a 1-cell* $u : Q \to P$ *and invertible 2-cells* $\Xi_i : \gamma_i \circ u \Rightarrow \mu_i$ $(i = 1, 2)$ *satisfying*

$$
\begin{array}{ccccc}
(f_2 \circ \gamma_2) \circ u & \xrightarrow{\cong} & f_2 \circ (\gamma_2 \circ u) & \xrightarrow{f_2 \circ \Xi_2} & f_2 \circ \mu_2 \\
{\scriptstyle \overline{\gamma} \circ u}\downarrow & & & & \downarrow{\scriptstyle \overline{\mu}} \\
(f_1 \circ \gamma_1) \circ u & \xrightarrow[\cong]{} & f_1 \circ (\gamma_1 \circ u) & \xrightarrow[f_1 \circ \Xi_1]{} & f_1 \circ \mu_1
\end{array}
$$

2. *for any 1-cells* $v, w : Q \to P$ *and 2-cells* $\Psi_i : \gamma_i \circ v \Rightarrow \gamma_i \circ w$ $(i = 1, 2)$ *satisfying*

$$
\begin{array}{ccccccc}
(f_2 \circ \gamma_2) \circ v & \xrightarrow{\cong} & f_2 \circ (\gamma_2 \circ v) & \xrightarrow{f_2 \circ \Psi_2} & f_2 \circ (\gamma_2 \circ w) & \xrightarrow{\cong} & (f_2 \circ \gamma_2) \circ w \\
{\scriptstyle \overline{\gamma} \circ v}\downarrow & & & & & & \downarrow{\scriptstyle \overline{\gamma} \circ w} \\
(f_1 \circ \gamma_1) \circ v & \xrightarrow[\cong]{} & f_1 \circ (\gamma_1 \circ v) & \xrightarrow[f_1 \circ \Psi_1]{} & f_1 \circ (\gamma_1 \circ w) & \xrightarrow{\cong} & (f_1 \circ \gamma_1) \circ w
\end{array}
$$

*there exists a unique 2-cell* $\Psi : v \Rightarrow w$ *such that* $\Psi_i = \gamma_i \circ \Psi$ $(i = 1, 2)$.

*Example 6.* 1. In **Cat**, the pullback of a cospan $(\mathcal{B} \xrightarrow{F} \mathcal{X} \xleftarrow{G} \mathcal{C})$ is the full subcategory of the comma category $(F \downarrow G)$ consisting of objects of the form $(B, f, C)$ for which $f : FB \to GC$ is an isomorphism. Note that this differs from the strict (2-)categorical pullback in **Cat**, in which every $f$ is required to be an identity (*c.f.* [65, Example 2.1]).
2. Like any bilimit, pullbacks in the bicategory $\mathbf{Bicat}(\mathcal{B}^{\mathrm{op}}, \mathbf{Cat})$ are computed pointwise (see [53, Proposition 3.6]).

We now define exponentials in the glueing bicategory. Precisely, we extend Proposition 1 to the following.

**Theorem 5.** *Let* $(\mathcal{B}, \Pi_n(-), \Rightarrow)$ *and* $(\mathcal{C}, \Pi_n(-), \Rightarrow)$ *be cc-bicategories such that* $\mathcal{C}$ *has pullbacks. For any fp-pseudofunctor* $(\mathfrak{J}, \mathrm{q}^\times) : (\mathcal{B}, \Pi_n(-)) \to (\mathcal{C}, \Pi_n(-))$, *the glueing bicategory* $\mathrm{gl}(\mathfrak{J})$ *has a cartesian closed structure with forgetful pseudofunctor* $\pi_{\mathrm{dom}} : \mathrm{gl}(\mathfrak{J}) \to \mathcal{B}$ *strictly preserving products and exponentials.*

*The evaluation map.* We begin by defining the mapping $(-) \Rightarrow (=)$ and the evaluation 1-cell $\underline{\mathrm{eval}}$. For $\underline{C} := (C, c, B), \underline{C'} := (C', c', B') \in \mathrm{gl}(\mathfrak{J})$ we set $\underline{C} \Rightarrow \underline{C'}$ to be the left-hand vertical leg of the following pullback diagram, in which we write $m_{B,B'} := \lambda(\mathfrak{J}(\mathrm{eval}_{B,B'}) \circ \mathrm{q}^\times_{B \Rightarrow B', B})$.

$$
\begin{array}{ccccc}
C \supset C' & & \xrightarrow{q_{c,c'}} & & (C \Rightarrow C') \\
{\scriptstyle p_{c,c'}}\downarrow & & \overset{\omega_{c,c'}}{\Leftarrow} & & \downarrow{\scriptstyle \lambda(c' \circ \mathrm{eval}_{C,C'})} \\
\mathfrak{J}(B \Rightarrow B') & \xrightarrow[m_{B,B'}]{} & (\mathfrak{J}B \Rightarrow \mathfrak{J}B') & \xrightarrow[\lambda(\mathrm{eval}_{\mathfrak{J}B,\mathfrak{J}B'} \circ ((\mathfrak{J}B \Rightarrow \mathfrak{J}B') \times c))]{} & (C \Rightarrow \mathfrak{J}B')
\end{array}
$$

with the outer composite $\lambda(\mathrm{eval}_{\mathfrak{J}B,\mathfrak{J}B'} \circ ((\mathfrak{J}B \Rightarrow \mathfrak{J}B') \times c)) \circ m_{B,B'}$ from $\mathfrak{J}(B \Rightarrow B')$ to $(C \Rightarrow \mathfrak{J}B')$.

(4)

*Example 7.* The pullback (4) generalises the well-known definition of a *logical relation of varying arity* [36]. Indeed, where $\mathfrak{J} := \langle \mathfrak{K} \rangle$ is the relative hom-pseudofunctor for an fp-pseudofunctor $(\mathfrak{K}, q^{\times}) : \mathcal{B} \to \mathcal{X}$ between cc-bicategories, $A \in \mathcal{B}$ and $X, X' \in \mathcal{X}$, the functor $m_{X,X'}(A)$ takes a 1-cell $f : \mathfrak{K}A \to (X \Rightarrow X')$ in $\mathcal{X}$ to the pseudonatural transformation $\mathrm{Y}A \times \mathcal{X}(\mathfrak{K}(-), X) \Rightarrow \mathcal{X}(\mathfrak{K}(-), X')$ with components $\lambda B \,.\, \lambda(\rho : B \to A, u : \mathfrak{K}B \to X) \,.\, \mathrm{eval}_{X,X'} \circ \langle f \circ \mathfrak{K}(\rho), u \rangle$. Intuitively, therefore, the pullback enforces the usual closure condition defining a logical relation at exponential type, while also tracking the isomorphism witnessing that this condition holds (*c.f.* [36,3,15]).

*Notation 6.* For reasons of space—particularly in pasting diagrams—we will sometimes write $\widetilde{c} := \mathrm{eval}_{\mathfrak{J}B,\mathfrak{J}B'} \circ ((\mathfrak{J}B \Rightarrow \mathfrak{J}B') \times c) : (\mathfrak{J}B \Rightarrow \mathfrak{J}B') \times C \to \mathfrak{J}B'$ when $c : C \to \mathfrak{J}B$ in $\mathcal{C}$.

The evaluation map $\underline{\mathrm{eval}}_{\underline{C},\underline{C'}}$ is defined to be $(\mathrm{eval}_{C,C'} \circ (q_{c,c'} \times C), \mathrm{E}_{\underline{C},\underline{C'}}, \mathrm{eval}_{B,B'})$, where the witnessing 2-cell $\mathrm{E}_{\underline{C},\underline{C'}}$ is given by the pasting diagram below, in which the unlabelled arrow is $q^{\times}_{(B \Rightarrow B', B)} \circ (p_{c,c'} \times c)$.

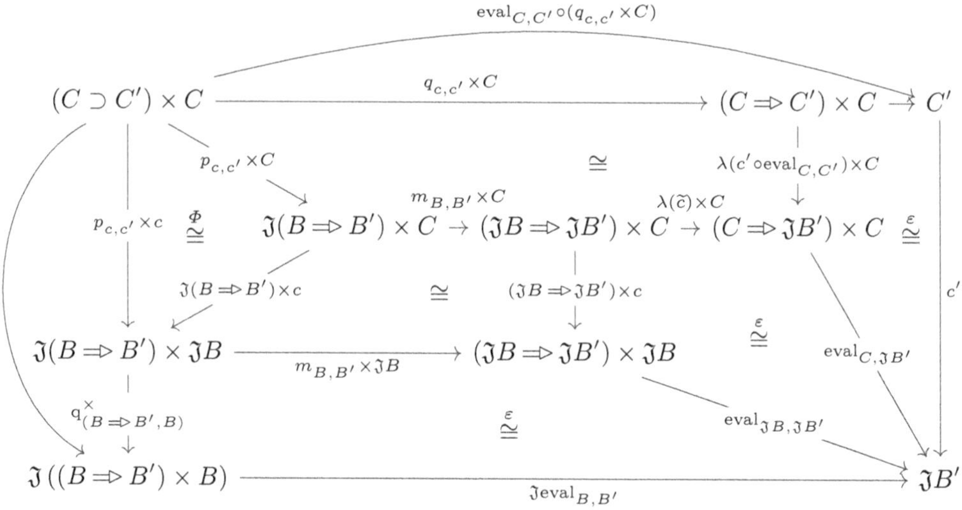


Here the bottom $\cong$ denotes a composite of $\Phi$, structural isomorphisms and $\Phi^{-1}$, and the top $\cong$ denotes a composite of $\omega_{c,c'} \times C$ with instances of $\Phi$, $\Phi^{-1}$, and the structural isomorphisms.

*The currying operation.* Let $\underline{R} := (R, r, Q)$, $\underline{C} := (C, c, B)$ and $\underline{C'} := (C', c', B')$ and suppose given a 1-cell $(t, \alpha, s) : \underline{R} \times \underline{C} \to \underline{C'}$. We construct $\underline{\lambda}(t, \alpha, s)$ using the universal property (4) of the pullback. To this end, we define invertible composites $\mathrm{U}_\alpha$ and $\mathrm{T}_\alpha$ as in the following two diagrams and set $\mathrm{L}_\alpha := \eta^{-1} \bullet \mathsf{e}^{\dagger}(\mathrm{U}_\alpha^{-1} \circ \alpha \circ \mathrm{T}_\alpha) : \lambda(c' \circ \mathrm{eval}_{C,C'}) \circ \lambda t \Rightarrow (\lambda(\widetilde{c}) \circ m_{B,B'}) \circ (\mathfrak{J}(\lambda s) \circ r)$.

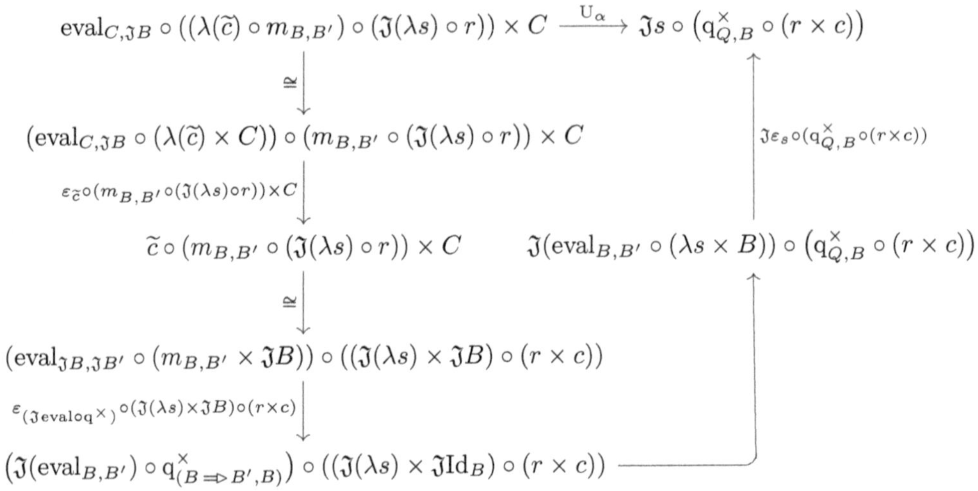
$\mathrm{eval}_{C,\mathfrak{J}B} \circ ((\lambda(\widetilde{c}) \circ m_{B,B'}) \circ (\mathfrak{J}(\lambda s) \circ r)) \times C$
$\mathrm{U}_\alpha$
$\mathfrak{J}s \circ (\mathrm{q}^{\times}_{Q,B} \circ (r \times c))$
$\cong$
$(\mathrm{eval}_{C,\mathfrak{J}B} \circ (\lambda(\widetilde{c}) \times C)) \circ (m_{B,B'} \circ (\mathfrak{J}(\lambda s) \circ r)) \times C$
$\mathfrak{J}\varepsilon_s \circ (\mathrm{q}^{\times}_{Q,B} \circ (r \times c))$
$\varepsilon_{\widetilde{c}} \circ (m_{B,B'} \circ (\mathfrak{J}(\lambda s) \circ r)) \times C$
$\widetilde{c} \circ (m_{B,B'} \circ (\mathfrak{J}(\lambda s) \circ r)) \times C$
$\mathfrak{J}(\mathrm{eval}_{B,B'} \circ (\lambda s \times B)) \circ (\mathrm{q}^{\times}_{Q,B} \circ (r \times c))$
$\cong$
$(\mathrm{eval}_{\mathfrak{J}B,\mathfrak{J}B'} \circ (m_{B,B'} \times \mathfrak{J}B)) \circ ((\mathfrak{J}(\lambda s) \times \mathfrak{J}B) \circ (r \times c))$
$\varepsilon_{(\mathfrak{J}\mathrm{eval} \circ \mathrm{q}^{\times})} \circ (\mathfrak{J}(\lambda s) \times \mathfrak{J}B) \circ (r \times c)$
$(\mathfrak{J}(\mathrm{eval}_{B,B'}) \circ \mathrm{q}^{\times}_{(B \Rightarrow B',B)}) \circ ((\mathfrak{J}(\lambda s) \times \mathfrak{J}\mathrm{Id}_B) \circ (r \times c))$

The unlabelled arrow is the canonical composite of $\mathsf{nat}_{\lambda s,\mathrm{id}_B}$ with $\phi^{\mathfrak{J}}_{\mathrm{eval},\lambda(s)\times B}$ and structural isomorphisms. $\mathrm{T}_\alpha$ is then defined using $\mathrm{U}_\alpha$:

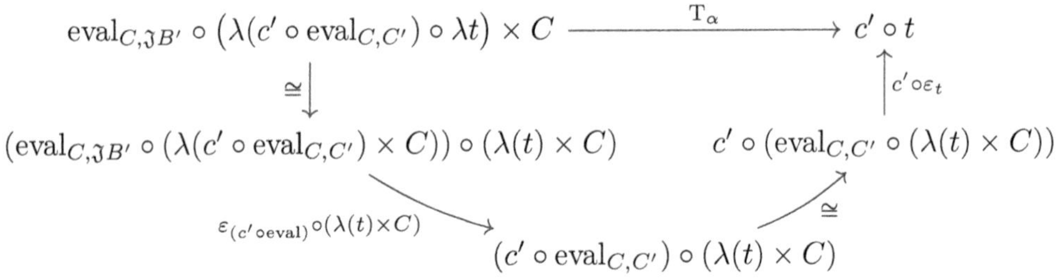
$\mathrm{eval}_{C,\mathfrak{J}B'} \circ (\lambda(c' \circ \mathrm{eval}_{C,C'}) \circ \lambda t) \times C$
$\mathrm{T}_\alpha$
$c' \circ t$
$\cong$
$c' \circ \varepsilon_t$
$(\mathrm{eval}_{C,\mathfrak{J}B'} \circ (\lambda(c' \circ \mathrm{eval}_{C,C'}) \times C)) \circ (\lambda(t) \times C)$
$c' \circ (\mathrm{eval}_{C,C'} \circ (\lambda(t) \times C))$
$\varepsilon_{(c' \circ \mathrm{eval})} \circ (\lambda(t) \times C)$
$\cong$
$(c' \circ \mathrm{eval}_{C,C'}) \circ (\lambda(t) \times C)$

Applying the universal property of the pullback (4) to $\mathrm{L}_\alpha$, one obtains a 1-cell $\underline{\mathsf{lam}}(t)$ and a pair of invertible 2-cells $\Gamma_{c,c'}$ and $\Delta_{c,c'}$ filling the diagram

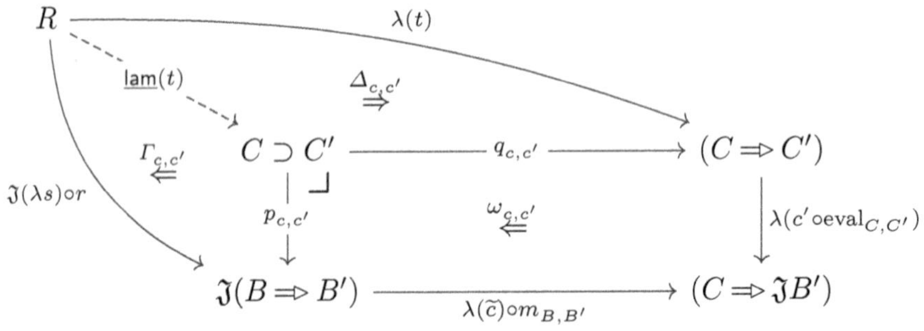
$R$
$\lambda(t)$
$\underline{\mathsf{lam}}(t)$
$\Delta_{c,c'}$
$\Gamma_{c,c'}$
$C \supset C'$
$q_{c,c'}$
$(C \Rightarrow C')$
$\mathfrak{J}(\lambda s) \circ r$
$p_{c,c'}$
$\omega_{c,c'}$
$\lambda(c' \circ \mathrm{eval}_{C,C'})$
$\mathfrak{J}(B \Rightarrow B')$
$(C \Rightarrow \mathfrak{J}B')$
$\lambda(\widetilde{c}) \circ m_{B,B'}$

We define $\underline{\lambda}(t, \alpha, s) := \left(\underline{\mathsf{lam}}(t), \Gamma_{c,c'}, \lambda s\right)$.

*The counit 2-cell.* Finally we come to the counit. For a 1-cell $\underline{t} := (t, \alpha, s) : (R, r, Q) \times (C, c, B) \to (C', c', B')$ the 1-cell $\underline{\mathrm{eval}} \circ \left(\underline{\lambda}(t, \alpha, s) \times (C, c, B)\right)$ unwinds to the pasting diagram below, in which the unlabelled arrow is $\mathrm{q}^{\times}_{Q,B} \circ (r \times c)$:

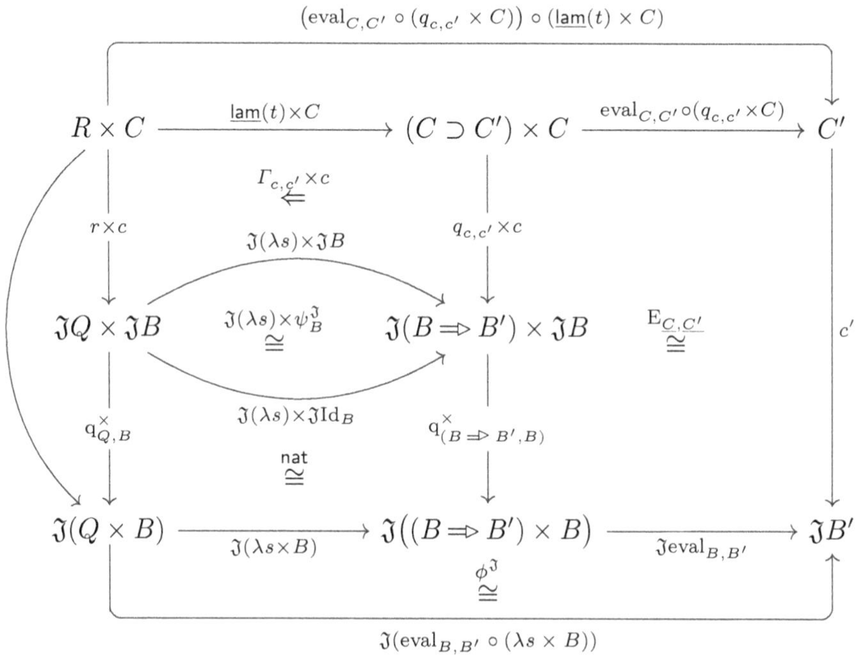


For the counit $\underline{\varepsilon_t}$ we take the 2-cell with first component $\underline{\mathsf{e}}_t$ defined by

$$\begin{array}{ccc}
(\mathrm{eval}_{C,C'} \circ (q_{c,c'} \times C)) \circ (\underline{\mathsf{lam}}(t) \times C) & \xrightarrow{\quad \underline{\mathsf{e}}_t \quad} & t \\
\cong \big\downarrow & & \big\uparrow \varepsilon_t \\
\mathrm{eval}_{C,C'} \circ ((q_{c,c'} \circ \underline{\mathsf{lam}}(t)) \times C) & \xrightarrow[\mathrm{eval}_{C,C'} \circ (\Delta_{c,c'} \times C)]{} & \mathrm{eval}_{C,C'} \circ (\lambda(t) \times C)
\end{array}$$

and second component simply $\varepsilon_s : \mathrm{eval}_{B,B'} \circ (\lambda(s) \times B) \Rightarrow s$. This pair forms an invertible 2-cell in $\mathrm{gl}(\mathfrak{J})$. One checks this satisfies the required universal property in a manner analogous to the 1-categorical case (see [55] for the full details). This completes the proof of Theorem 5.

## 5 Relative full completeness

We apply the theory developed in the preceding two sections to prove the relative full completeness result. As outlined in the introduction, this corresponds to a proof of *conservativity of the theory of rewriting* for the higher-order equational theory of rewriting in STLC over the algebraic equational theory of rewriting in STPC. We adapt 'Lafont's argument' [39, Annexe C] from the form presented in [16], for which we require bicategorical versions of the free cartesian category $\mathbb{F}^{\times}[\mathbb{C}]$ and free cartesian closed category $\mathbb{F}^{\times,\rightarrow}[\mathbb{C}]$ over a category $\mathbb{C}$. In line with the strategy for the STLC (*c.f.* [12, pp. 173–4]), we deal with the contravariance of the pseudofunctor $(- \Rightarrow =)$ by restricting to a bicategory of cc-pseudofunctors, pseudonatural equivalences (that is, pseudonatural transformations for which each component is a given equivalence), and invertible modifications. We denote this with the subscript $\simeq, \cong$.

**Lemma 7.** *For any bicategory $\mathcal{B}$, fp-bicategory $(\mathcal{C}, \Pi_n(-))$ and cc-bicategory $(\mathcal{D}, \Pi_n(-), \Rightarrow)$:*

1. *There exists an fp-bicategory $\mathcal{F}^{\times}[\mathcal{B}]$ and a pseudofunctor $\eta^{\times} : \mathcal{B} \to \mathcal{F}^{\times}[\mathcal{B}]$ such that composition with $\eta^{\times}$ induces a biequivalence*
$$\textbf{fp-Bicat}(\mathcal{F}^{\times}[\mathcal{B}], \mathcal{C}) \xrightarrow{\simeq} \textbf{Bicat}(\mathcal{B}, \mathcal{C})$$
2. *There exists a cc-bicategory $\mathcal{F}^{\times,\to}[\mathcal{B}]$ and a pseudofunctor $\eta^{\Rightarrow} : \mathcal{B} \to \mathcal{F}^{\times,\to}[\mathcal{B}]$ such that composition with $\eta^{\Rightarrow}$ induces a biequivalence*
$$\textbf{cc-Bicat}_{\simeq,\cong}(\mathcal{F}^{\times,\to}[\mathcal{B}], \mathcal{D}) \xrightarrow{\simeq} \textbf{Bicat}(\mathcal{B}, \mathcal{D})$$

*Proof (sketch). A syntactic construction suffices: one defines formal products and exponentials and then quotients by the axioms (see [48, p. 79] or [55]).*

Thus, for any bicategory $\mathcal{B}$, fp-bicategory $(\mathcal{C}, \Pi_n(-))$, and pseudofunctor $F : \mathcal{B} \to \mathcal{C}$ there exists an fp-pseudofunctor $F^{\#} : \mathcal{F}^{\times}[\mathcal{B}] \to \mathcal{C}$ and an equivalence $F^{\#} \circ \eta^{\times} \simeq F$. Moreover, for any fp-pseudofunctor $G : \mathcal{F}^{\times}[\mathcal{B}] \to \mathcal{C}$ such that $G \circ \eta^{\times} \simeq F$ one has $G \simeq F^{\#}$. A corresponding result holds for cc-bicategories and cc-pseudofunctors.

**Theorem 7.** *For any bicategory $\mathcal{B}$ the universal fp-pseudofunctor $\iota : \mathcal{F}^{\times}[\mathcal{B}] \to \mathcal{F}^{\times,\to}[\mathcal{B}]$ extending $\eta^{\Rightarrow}$ is locally an equivalence. Hence $\eta^{\Rightarrow} : \mathcal{B} \to \mathcal{F}^{\times,\to}[\mathcal{B}]$ is locally an equivalence.*

*Proof. Since $\iota$ preserves finite products, the bicategory $\mathrm{gl}(\langle\iota\rangle)$ is cartesian closed (Theorem 5). The composite $\mathrm{K} := \underline{\mathrm{Y}} \circ \eta^{\times} : \mathcal{B} \to \mathrm{gl}(\langle\iota\rangle)$ therefore induces a cc-pseudofunctor $\mathrm{K}^{\#} : \mathcal{F}^{\times,\to}[\mathcal{B}] \to \mathrm{gl}(\langle\iota\rangle)$.*

*First observe that $(\mathrm{K}^{\#} \circ \iota) \circ \eta^{\times} \simeq \mathrm{K}^{\#} \circ \eta^{\Rightarrow} \simeq \mathrm{K} = \underline{\mathrm{Y}} \circ \eta^{\times}$. Since $\underline{\mathrm{Y}}$ is canonically an fp-pseudofunctor (Remark 4), it follows that $\mathrm{K}^{\#} \circ \iota \simeq \underline{\mathrm{Y}}$. Since $\underline{\mathrm{Y}}$ is locally an equivalence (Lemma 5), Lemma 1(1) entails that $\mathrm{K}^{\#} \circ \iota$ is locally an equivalence.*

*Next, examining the definition of $\underline{\mathrm{Y}}$ one sees that $\pi_{\mathrm{dom}} \circ \underline{\mathrm{Y}} = \iota$, and so*
$$(\pi_{\mathrm{dom}} \circ \mathrm{K}^{\#}) \circ \eta^{\Rightarrow} \simeq (\pi_{\mathrm{dom}} \circ \underline{\mathrm{Y}}) \circ \eta^{\times} \simeq \iota \circ \eta^{\times} \simeq \eta^{\Rightarrow}$$
*It follows that $\pi_{\mathrm{dom}} \circ \mathrm{K}^{\#} \simeq \mathrm{id}_{\mathcal{F}^{\times,\to}[\mathcal{B}]}$, and hence that $\pi_{\mathrm{dom}} \circ \mathrm{K}^{\#}$ is also locally an equivalence.*

*Now consider the composite $\mathcal{F}^{\times}[\mathcal{B}] \xrightarrow{\iota} \mathcal{F}^{\times,\to}[\mathcal{B}] \xrightarrow{\mathrm{K}^{\#}} \mathrm{gl}(\langle\iota\rangle) \xrightarrow{\pi_{\mathrm{dom}}} \mathcal{F}^{\times,\to}[\mathcal{B}]$. By Lemma 1(2) and the preceding, $\iota$ is locally an equivalence. Finally, it is direct from the construction of $\mathcal{F}^{\times}[\mathcal{B}]$ that $\eta^{\times}$ is locally an equivalence; thus, so are $\iota \circ \eta^{\times} \simeq \eta^{\Rightarrow}$.*

*Acknowledgements.* We thank all the anonymous reviewers for their comments: these improved the paper substantially. We are especially grateful to the reviewer who pointed out an oversight in the original formulation of Lemma 1(2), which consequently affected the argument in Theorem 7, and provided the elegant fix therein.

The second author was supported by a Royal Society University Research Fellow Enhancement Award.

## References

1. Abbott, M.G.: Categories of containers. Ph.D. thesis, University of Leicester (2003)
2. Abramsky, S., Jagadeesan, R.: Games and full completeness for multiplicative linear logic. Journal of Symbolic Logic **59**(2), 543–574 (1994). https://doi.org/10.2307/2275407
3. Alimohamed, M.: A characterization of lambda definability in categorical models of implicit polymorphism. Theoretical Computer Science **146**(1-2), 5–23 (1995). https://doi.org/10.1016/0304-3975(94)00283-O
4. Balat, V., Di Cosmo, R., Fiore, M.: Extensional normalisation and typed-directed partial evaluation for typed lambda calculus with sums. In: Proceedings of the 31st Annual ACM SIGPLAN-SIGACT Symposium on Principles of Programming Languages. pp. 64–76 (2004)
5. Bénabou, J.: Introduction to bicategories. In: Reports of the Midwest Category Seminar. pp. 1–77. Springer Berlin Heidelberg, Berlin, Heidelberg (1967)
6. Bloom, S.L., Ésik, Z., Labella, A., Manes, E.G.: Iteration 2-theories. Applied Categorical Structures **9**(2), 173–216 (2001). https://doi.org/10.1023/a:1008708924144
7. Borceux, F.: Bicategories and distributors, Encyclopedia of Mathematics and its Applications, vol. 1, pp. 281–324. Cambridge University Press (1994). https://doi.org/10.1017/CBO9780511525858.009
8. Carboni, A., Kelly, G.M., Walters, R.F.C., Wood, R.J.: Cartesian bicategories II. Theory and Applications of Categories **19**(6), 93–124 (2008), http://www.tac.mta.ca/tac/volumes/19/6/19-06abs.html
9. Carboni, A., Lack, S., Walters, R.F.C.: Introduction to extensive and distributive categories. Journal of Pure and Applied Algebra **84**(2), 145–158 (1993). https://doi.org/10.1016/0022-4049(93)90035-r
10. Carboni, A., Walters, R.F.C.: Cartesian bicategories I. Journal of Pure and Applied Algebra **49**(1), 11–32 (1987). https://doi.org/10.1016/0022-4049(87)90121-6
11. Castellan, S., Clairambault, P., Rideau, S., Winskel, G.: Games and strategies as event structures. Logical Methods in Computer Science **13** (2017)
12. Crole, R.L.: Categories for Types. Cambridge University Press (1994). https://doi.org/10.1017/CBO9781139172707
13. Dagand, P.E., McBride, C.: A categorical treatment of ornaments. In: Proceedings of the 28th Annual ACM/IEEE Symposium on Logic in Computer Science. pp. 530–539. IEEE Computer Society, Washington, DC, USA (2013). https://doi.org/10.1109/LICS.2013.60
14. Fiore, M.: Axiomatic Domain Theory in Categories of Partial Maps. Distinguished Dissertations in Computer Science, Cambridge University Press (1996)
15. Fiore, M.: Semantic analysis of normalisation by evaluation for typed lambda calculus. In: Proceedings of the 4th ACM SIGPLAN International Conference on Principles and Practice of Declarative Programming. pp. 26–37. ACM, New York, NY, USA (2002). https://doi.org/10.1145/571157.571161
16. Fiore, M., Di Cosmo, R., Balat, V.: Remarks on isomorphisms in typed lambda calculi with empty and sum types. In: Proceedings of the 28th Annual IEEE Symposium on Logic in Computer Science. pp. 147–156. IEEE Computer Society Press (2002). https://doi.org/10.1109/LICS.2002.1029824
17. Fiore, M., Gambino, N., Hyland, M., Winskel, G.: The cartesian closed bicategory of generalised species of structures. Journal of the London Mathematical Society **77**(1), 203–220 (2007). https://doi.org/10.1112/jlms/jdm096

18. Fiore, M., Gambino, N., Hyland, M., Winskel, G.: Relative pseudomonads, Kleisli bicategories, and substitution monoidal structures. Selecta Mathematica New Series (2017)
19. Fiore, M., Joyal, A.: Theory of para-toposes. Talk at the Category Theory 2015 Conference. Departamento de Matematica, Universidade de Aveiro (Portugal)
20. Fiore, M., Saville, P.: A type theory for cartesian closed bicategories. In: Proceedings of the 34th Annual ACM/IEEE Symposium on Logic in Computer Science (2019). https://doi.org/10.1109/LICS.2019.8785708
21. Fiore, M., Saville, P.: Coherence and normalisation-by-evaluation for bicategorical cartesian closed structure. Preprint (2020)
22. Fiore, M., Simpson, A.: Lambda definability with sums via Grothendieck logical relations. In: Girard, J.Y. (ed.) Typed lambda calculi and applications: 4th international conference. pp. 147–161. Springer Berlin Heidelberg, Berlin, Heidelberg (1999)
23. Freyd, P.: Algebraically complete categories. In: Lecture Notes in Mathematics, pp. 95–104. Springer Berlin Heidelberg (1991). https://doi.org/10.1007/bfb0084215
24. Freyd, P.J., Scedrov, A.: Categories, Allegories. Elsevier North Holland (1990)
25. Gambino, N., Joyal, A.: On operads, bimodules and analytic functors. Memoirs of the American Mathematical Society **249**(1184), 153–192 (2017)
26. Gambino, N., Kock, J.: Polynomial functors and polynomial monads. Mathematical Proceedings of the Cambridge Philosophical Society **154**(1), 153–192 (2013). https://doi.org/10.1017/S0305004112000394
27. Ghani, N.: Adjoint rewriting. Ph.D. thesis, University of Edinburgh (1995)
28. Gibbons, J.: Conditionals in distributive categories. Tech. rep., University of Oxford (1997)
29. G.L. Cattani, Fiore, M., Winskel, G.: A theory of recursive domains with applications to concurrency. In: Proceedings of the 13th Annual IEEE Symposium on Logic in Computer Science. pp. 214–225. IEEE Computer Society (1998)
30. Gurski, N.: An Algebraic Theory of Tricategories. University of Chicago, Department of Mathematics (2006)
31. Hasegawa, M.: Logical predicates for intuitionistic linear type theories. In: Girard, J.Y. (ed.) Typed lambda calculi and applications: 4th international conference. pp. 198–213. Springer Berlin Heidelberg, Berlin, Heidelberg (1999)
32. Hilken, B.: Towards a proof theory of rewriting: the simply typed 2$\lambda$-calculus. Theoretical Computer Science **170**(1), 407–444 (1996). https://doi.org/10.1016/S0304-3975(96)80713-4
33. Hirschowitz, T.: Cartesian closed 2-categories and permutation equivalence in higher-order rewriting. Logical Methods in Computer Science **9**, 1–22 (2013)
34. Jay, C.B., Ghani, N.: The virtues of eta-expansion. Journal of Functional Programming **5**(2), 135–154 (1995). https://doi.org/10.1017/S0956796800001301
35. Johann, P., Polonsky, P.: Higher-kinded data types: Syntax and semantics. In: 34th Annual ACM/IEEE Symposium on Logic in Computer Science. IEEE (2019). https://doi.org/10.1109/lics.2019.8785657
36. Jung, A., Tiuryn, J.: A new characterization of lambda definability. In: Bezem, M., Groote, J.F. (eds.) Typed Lambda Calculi and Applications. pp. 245–257. Springer Berlin Heidelberg, Berlin, Heidelberg (1993)
37. Lack, S.: A 2-Categories Companion, pp. 105–191. Springer New York, New York, NY (2010)
38. Lack, S., Walters, R.F.C., Wood, R.J.: Bicategories of spans as cartesian bicategories. Theory and Applications of Categories **24**(1), 1–24 (2010)

39. Lafont, Y.: Logiques, catégories et machines. Ph.D. thesis, Université Paris VII (1987)
40. Lambek, J., Scott, P.J.: Introduction to Higher Order Categorical Logic. Cambridge University Press, New York, NY, USA (1986)
41. Leinster, T.: Basic bicategories (May 1998), https://arxiv.org/pdf/math/9810017.pdf
42. Leinster, T.: Higher operads, higher categories. No. 298 in London Mathematical Society Lecture Note Series, Cambridge University Press (2004)
43. Ma, Q.M., Reynolds, J.C.: Types, abstraction, and parametric polymorphism, part 2. In: Brookes, S., Main, M., Melton, A., Mislove, M., Schmidt, D. (eds.) Mathematical Foundations of Programming Semantics. pp. 1–40. Springer Berlin Heidelberg, Berlin, Heidelberg (1992)
44. Mac Lane, S.: Categories for the Working Mathematician, Graduate Texts in Mathematics, vol. 5. Springer-Verlag New York, second edn. (1998). https://doi.org/10.1007/978-1-4757-4721-8
45. Mac Lane, S., Paré, R.: Coherence for bicategories and indexed categories. Journal of Pure and Applied Algebra **37**, 59–80 (1985). https://doi.org/10.1016/0022-4049(85)90087-8
46. Marmolejo, F., Wood, R.J.: Kan extensions and lax idempotent pseudomonads. Theory and Applications of Categories **26**(1), 1–29 (2012)
47. Mitchell, J.C., Scedrov, A.: Notes on sconing and relators. In: Börger, E., J., G., Kleine Büning, H., Martini, S., Richter, M.M. (eds.) Computer Science Logic. pp. 352–378. Springer Berlin Heidelberg, Berlin, Heidelberg (1993)
48. Ouaknine, J.: A two-dimensional extension of Lambek's categorical proof theory. Master's thesis, McGill University (1997)
49. Paquet, H.: Probabilistic concurrent game semantics. Ph.D. thesis, University of Cambridge (2020)
50. Plotkin, G.D.: Lambda-definability and logical relations. Tech. rep., University of Edinburgh School of Artificial Intelligence (1973), memorandum SAI-RM-4
51. Power, A.J.: An abstract formulation for rewrite systems. In: Pitt, D.H., Rydeheard, D.E., Dybjer, P., Pitts, A.M., Poigné, A. (eds.) Category Theory and Computer Science. pp. 300–312. Springer Berlin Heidelberg, Berlin, Heidelberg (1989)
52. Power, A.J.: Coherence for bicategories with finite bilimits I. In: Gray, J.W., Scedrov, A. (eds.) Categories in Computer Science and Logic: Proceedings of the AMS-IMS-SIAM Joint Summer Research Conference, vol. 92, pp. 341–349. AMS (1989)
53. Power, A.J.: A general coherence result. Journal of Pure and Applied Algebra **57**(2), 165–173 (1989). https://doi.org/https://doi.org/10.1016/0022-4049(89)90113-8
54. Rydeheard, D.E., Stell, J.G.: Foundations of equational deduction: A categorical treatment of equational proofs and unification algorithms. In: Pitt, D.H., Poigné, A., Rydeheard, D.E. (eds.) Category Theory and Computer Science. pp. 114–139. Springer Berlin Heidelberg, Berlin, Heidelberg (1987)
55. Saville, P.: Cartesian closed bicategories: type theory and coherence. Ph.D. thesis, University of Cambridge (Submitted)
56. Seely, R.A.G.: Modelling computations: A 2-categorical framework. In: Gries, D. (ed.) Proceedings of the 2nd Annual IEEE Symposium on Logic in Computer Science. pp. 65–71. IEEE Computer Society Press (June 1987)
57. Statman, R.: Logical relations and the typed $\lambda$-calculus. Information and Control **65**, 85–97 (1985)
58. Stell, J.: Modelling term rewriting systems by sesqui-categories. In: Proc. Catégories, Algèbres, Esquisses et Néo-Esquisses (1994)

59. Street, R.: Fibrations in bicategories. Cahiers de Topologie et Géométrie Différentielle Catégoriques **21**(2), 111–160 (1980), https://eudml.org/doc/91227
60. Street, R.: Categorical structures. In: Hazewinkel, M. (ed.) Handbook of Algebra, vol. 1, chap. 15, pp. 529–577. Elsevier (1995)
61. Tabareau, N.: Aspect oriented programming: A language for 2-categories. In: Proceedings of the 10th International Workshop on Foundations of Aspect-oriented Languages. pp. 13–17. ACM, New York, NY, USA (2011). https://doi.org/10.1145/1960510.1960514
62. Taylor, P.: Practical Foundations of Mathematics, Cambridge Studies in Advanced Mathematics, vol. 59. Cambridge University Press (1999)
63. Troelstra, A.S., Schwichtenberg, H.: Basic proof theory. No. 43 in Cambridge Tracts in Theoretical Computer Science, Cambridge University Press, second edn. (2000)
64. Verity, D.: Enriched categories, internal categories and change of base. Ph.D. thesis, University of Cambridge (1992), TAC reprint available at http://www.tac.mta.ca/tac/reprints/articles/20/tr20abs.html
65. Weber, M.: Yoneda structures from 2-toposes. Applied Categorical Structures **15**(3), 259–323 (2007). https://doi.org/10.1007/s10485-007-9079-2

# 12

# Cartesian Difference Categories

Mario Alvarez-Picallo[1] and Jean-Simon Pacaud Lemay (✉)[2*]

[1] Department of Computer Science, University of Oxford, Oxford, UK
mario.alvarez-picallo@cs.ox.ac.uk
[2] Department of Computer Science, University of Oxford, Oxford, UK
jean-simon.lemay@kellogg.ox.ac.uk

**Abstract.** Cartesian differential categories are categories equipped with a differential combinator which axiomatizes the directional derivative. Important models of Cartesian differential categories include classical differential calculus of smooth functions and categorical models of the differential $\lambda$-calculus. However, Cartesian differential categories cannot account for other interesting notions of differentiation such as the calculus of finite differences or the Boolean differential calculus. On the other hand, change action models have been shown to capture these examples as well as more "exotic" examples of differentiation. However, change action models are very general and do not share the nice properties of a Cartesian differential category. In this paper, we introduce Cartesian difference categories as a bridge between Cartesian differential categories and change action models. We show that every Cartesian differential category is a Cartesian difference category, and how certain well-behaved change action models are Cartesian difference categories. In particular, Cartesian difference categories model both the differential calculus of smooth functions and the calculus of finite differences. Furthermore, every Cartesian difference category comes equipped with a tangent bundle monad whose Kleisli category is again a Cartesian difference category.

**Keywords:** Cartesian Difference Categories · Cartesian Differential Categories · Change Actions · Calculus Of Finite Differences · Stream Calculus.

## 1 Introduction

In the early 2000s, Ehrhard and Regnier introduced the differential $\lambda$-calculus [10], an extension of the $\lambda$-calculus equipped with a differential combinator capable of taking the derivative of arbitrary higher-order functions. This development, based on models of linear logic equipped with a natural notion of "derivative" [11], sparked a wave of research into categorical models of differentiation.

One of the most notable developments in the area is the introduction of Cartesian differential categories [4] by Blute, Cockett and Seely, which provide an abstract categorical axiomatization of the directional derivative from differential calculus. The relevance of Cartesian differential categories lies in their ability to model both "classical" differential calculus (with the canonical example being the category of Euclidean spaces and smooth functions between) and the differential $\lambda$-calculus (as every categorical model for it gives rise to a Cartesian differential category [14]). However, while Cartesian differential categories have proven to be an immensely successful formalism, they have, by design, some limitations. Firstly, they cannot account for certain "exotic" notions of derivative, such as the difference operator from the calculus of finite differences [16] or the Boolean differential calculus [19]. This is because the axioms of a Cartesian differential category stipulate that derivatives should be linear in their second argument (in the same way that the directional derivative is), whereas these aforementioned discrete sorts of derivative need not be. Additionally, every Cartesian differential category is equipped with a tangent bundle monad [7, 15] whose Kleisli category can be intuitively understood as a category of generalized vector fields. This Kleisli category has an obvious differentiation operator which comes close to making it a Cartesian differential category, but again fails the requirement of being linear in its second argument.

More recently, discrete derivatives have been suggested as a semantic framework for understanding incremental computation. This led to the development of change structures [6] and change actions [2]. Change action models have been successfully used to provide a model for incrementalizing Datalog programs [1], but have also been shown to model the calculus of finite differences as well as the Kleisli category of the tangent bundle monad of a Cartesian differential category. Change action models, however, are very general, lacking many of the nice properties of Cartesian differential categories (for example, addition in a change action model is not required to be commutative), even though they are verified in most change action models. As a consequence of this generality, the tangent bundle endofunctor in a change action model can fail to be a monad.

In this work, we introduce Cartesian difference categories (Section 4.2), whose key ingredients are an infinitesimal extension operator and a difference combinator, whose axioms are a generalization of the differential combinator axioms of a Cartesian differential category. In Section 4.3, we show that every Cartesian differential category is, in fact, a Cartesian difference category whose infinitesimal extension operator is zero, and conversely how every Cartesian difference category admits a full subcategory which is a Cartesian differential category. In Section 4.4, we show that every Cartesian difference category is a change action model, and conversely how a full subcategory of suitably well-behaved objects of a change action model is a Cartesian difference category. In Section 6, we show that every Cartesian difference category comes equipped with a monad whose Kleisli category again a Cartesian difference category. Finally, in Section 5 we provide some examples of Cartesian difference categories; notably, the calculus of finite differences and the stream calculus.

# 2 Cartesian Differential Categories

In this section, we briefly review Cartesian differential categories, so that the reader may compare Cartesian differential categories with the new notion of Cartesian *difference* categories which we introduce in the next section. For a full detailed introduction on Cartesian differential categories, we refer the reader to the original paper [4].

## 2.1 Cartesian Left Additive Categories

Here we recall the definition of Cartesian left additive categories [4] – where "additive" is meant being skew enriched over commutative monoids, which in particular means that we do not assume the existence of additive inverses, i.e., "negative elements". By a Cartesian category we mean a category $\mathbb{X}$ with chosen finite products where we denote the binary product of objects $A$ and $B$ by $A \times B$ with projection maps $\pi_0 : A \times B \to A$ and $\pi_1 : A \times B \to B$ and pairing operation $\langle -, - \rangle$, and the chosen terminal object as $\top$ with unique terminal maps $!_A : A \to \top$.

**Definition 1.** *A* ***left additive category*** *[4] is a category $\mathbb{X}$ such that each hom-set $\mathbb{X}(A, B)$ is a commutative monoid with addition operation $+ : \mathbb{X}(A, B) \times \mathbb{X}(A, B) \to \mathbb{X}(A, B)$ and zero element (called the zero map) $0 \in \mathbb{X}(A, B)$, such that pre-composition preserves the additive structure: $(f + g) \circ h = f \circ h + g \circ h$ and $0 \circ f = 0$. A map $k$ in a left additive category is* ***additive*** *if post-composition by $k$ preserves the additive structure: $k \circ (f + g) = k \circ f + k \circ g$ and $k \circ 0 = 0$. A* ***Cartesian left additive category*** *[4] is a Cartesian category $\mathbb{X}$ which is also a left additive category such all projection maps $\pi_0 : A \times B \to A$ and $\pi_1 : A \times B \to B$ are additive.*

We note that the definition given here of a Cartesian left additive category is slightly different from the one found in [4], but it is indeed equivalent. By [4, Proposition 1.2.2], an equivalent axiomatization is of a Cartesian left additive category is that of a Cartesian category where every object comes equipped with a commutative monoid structure such that the projection maps are monoid morphisms. This will be important later in Section 4.2.

## 2.2 Cartesian Differential Categories

**Definition 2.** *A* ***Cartesian differential category*** *[4] is a Cartesian left additive category equipped with a* ***differential combinator*** *$\mathsf{D}$ of the form*

$$\frac{f : A \to B}{\mathsf{D}[f] : A \times A \to B}$$

*verifying the following coherence conditions:*

**[CD.1]** $\mathsf{D}[f + g] = \mathsf{D}[f] + \mathsf{D}[g]$ *and* $\mathsf{D}[0] = 0$

**[CD.2]** $\mathsf{D}[f] \circ \langle x, y+z \rangle = \mathsf{D}[f] \circ \langle x, y \rangle + \mathsf{D}[f] \circ \langle x, z \rangle$ *and* $\mathsf{D}[f] \circ \langle x, 0 \rangle = 0$
**[CD.3]** $\mathsf{D}[1_A] = \pi_1$ *and* $\mathsf{D}[\pi_0] = \pi_0 \circ \pi_1$ *and* $\mathsf{D}[\pi_1] = \pi_1 \circ \pi_1$
**[CD.4]** $\mathsf{D}[\langle f, g \rangle] = \langle \mathsf{D}[f], \mathsf{D}[g] \rangle$ *and* $\mathsf{D}[!_A] = !_{A \times A}$
**[CD.5]** $\mathsf{D}[g \circ f] = \mathsf{D}[g] \circ \langle f \circ \pi_0, \mathsf{D}[f] \rangle$
**[CD.6]** $\mathsf{D}\left[\mathsf{D}[f]\right] \circ \langle \langle x, y \rangle, \langle 0, z \rangle \rangle = \mathsf{D}[f] \circ \langle x, z \rangle$
**[CD.7]** $\mathsf{D}\left[\mathsf{D}[f]\right] \circ \langle \langle x, y \rangle, \langle z, 0 \rangle \rangle = \mathsf{D}\left[\mathsf{D}[f]\right] \circ \langle \langle x, z \rangle, \langle y, 0 \rangle \rangle$

Note that here, following the more recent work on Cartesian differential categories, we've flipped the convention found in [4], so that the linear argument is in the second argument rather than in the first argument.

We highlight that by [7, Proposition 4.2], the last two axioms **[CD.6]** and **[CD.7]** have an equivalent alternative expression.

**Lemma 1.** *In the presence of the other axioms,* **[CD.6]** *and* **[CD.7]** *are equivalent to:*

**[CD.6.a]** $\mathsf{D}\left[\mathsf{D}[f]\right] \circ \langle \langle x, 0 \rangle, \langle 0, y \rangle \rangle = \mathsf{D}[f] \circ \langle x, y \rangle$
**[CD.7.a]** $\mathsf{D}\left[\mathsf{D}[f]\right] \circ \langle \langle x, y \rangle, \langle z, w \rangle \rangle = \mathsf{D}\left[\mathsf{D}[f]\right] \circ \langle \langle x, z \rangle, \langle y, w \rangle \rangle$

As a Cartesian difference category is a generalization of a Cartesian differential category, we leave the discussion of the intuition of these axioms for later in Section 4.2 below. We also refer to [4, Section 4] for a term calculus which may help better understand the axioms of a Cartesian differential category. The canonical example of a Cartesian differential category is the category of real smooth functions, which we will discuss in Section 5.1. Other interesting examples of can be found throughout the literature such as categorical models of the differential $\lambda$-calculus [10, 14], the subcategory of differential objects of a tangent category [7], and the coKleisli category of a differential category [3, 4].

## 3 Change Action Models

Change actions [1, 2] have recently been proposed as a setting for reasoning about higher-order incremental computation, based on a discrete notion of differentiation. Together with Cartesian differential categories, they provide the core ideas behind Cartesian difference categories. In this section, we quickly review change actions and change action models, in particular, to highlight where some of the axioms of a Cartesian difference category come from. For more details on change actions, we invite readers to see the original paper [2].

### 3.1 Change Actions

**Definition 3.** *A **change action** $\overline{A}$ in a Cartesian category $\mathbb{X}$ is a quintuple $\overline{A} \equiv (A, \Delta A, \oplus_A, +_A, 0_A)$ consisting of two objects $A$ and $\Delta A$, and three maps:*

$$\oplus_A : A \times \Delta A \to A \qquad +_A : \Delta A \times \Delta A \to \Delta A \qquad 0_A : \top \to \Delta A$$

*such that $(\Delta A, +_A, 0_A)$ is a monoid and $\oplus_A : A \times \Delta A \to A$ is an action of $\Delta A$ on $A$, that is, the following equalities hold:*

$$\oplus_A \circ \langle 1_A, 0_A \circ !_A \rangle = 1_A \qquad \oplus_A \circ (1_A \times +_A) = \oplus_A \circ (\oplus_A \times 1_{\Delta A})$$

For a change action $\overline{A}$ and given a pair of maps $f : C \to A$ and $g : C \to \Delta A$, we define $f \oplus_{\overline{A}} g : C \to A$ as $f \oplus_{\overline{A}} g = \oplus_A \circ \langle f, g \rangle$. Similarly, for maps $h : C \to \Delta A$ and $k : C \to \Delta A$, define $h +_{\overline{A}} k = +_A \circ \langle h, k \rangle$. Therefore, that $\oplus_A$ is an action of $\Delta A$ on $A$ can be rewritten as:

$$1_A \oplus_{\overline{A}} 0_A = 1_A \qquad 1_A \oplus_{\overline{A}} (1_{\Delta A} +_{\overline{A}} 1_{\Delta A}) = (1_A \oplus_{\overline{A}} 1_{\Delta A}) \oplus_{\overline{A}} 1_{\Delta A}$$

The intuition behind the above definition is that the monoid $\Delta A$ is a type of possible "changes" or "updates" that might be applied to $A$, with the monoid structure on $\Delta A$ representing the capability to compose updates.

Change actions give rise to a notion of derivative, with a distinctly "discrete" flavour. Given change actions on objects $A$ and $B$, a map $f : A \to B$ can be said to be differentiable when changes to the input (in the sense of elements of $\Delta A$) are mapped to changes to the output (that is, elements of $\Delta B$). In the setting of incremental computation, this is precisely what it means for $f$ to be incrementalizable, with the derivative of $f$ corresponding to an incremental version of $f$.

**Definition 4.** *Let $\overline{A} \equiv (A, \Delta A, \oplus_A, +_A, 0_A)$ and $\overline{B} \equiv (B, \Delta B, \oplus_B, +_B, 0_B)$ be change actions. For a map $f : A \to B$, a map $\boldsymbol{\partial}[f] : A \times \Delta A \to \Delta B$ is a* ***derivative*** *of $f$ whenever the following equalities hold:*

**[CAD.1]** $f \circ (x \oplus_{\overline{A}} y) = f \circ x \oplus_{\overline{B}} (\boldsymbol{\partial}[f] \circ \langle x, y \rangle)$
**[CAD.2]** $\boldsymbol{\partial}[f] \circ \langle x, y +_{\overline{A}} z \rangle = (\boldsymbol{\partial}[f] \circ \langle x, y \rangle) +_{\overline{B}} (\boldsymbol{\partial}[f] \circ \langle x \oplus_{\overline{A}} y, z \rangle)$ *and* $\boldsymbol{\partial}[f] \circ \langle x, 0_B \circ !_B \rangle = 0_B \circ !_{A \times \Delta A}$

The intuition for these axioms will be explained in more detail in Section 4.2 when we explain the axioms of a Cartesian difference category. Note that although there is nothing in the above definition guaranteeing that any given map has at most a single derivative, the chain rule does hold. As a corollary, differentiation is compositional and therefore the change actions in $\mathbb{X}$ form a category.

**Lemma 2.** *Whenever $\boldsymbol{\partial}[f]$ and $\boldsymbol{\partial}[g]$ are derivatives for composable maps $f$ and $g$ respectively, then $\boldsymbol{\partial}[g] \circ \langle f \circ \pi_0, \boldsymbol{\partial}[f] \rangle$ is a derivative for $g \circ f$.*

### 3.2 Change Action Models

**Definition 5.** *Given a Cartesian category $\mathbb{X}$, define its change actions category $\mathsf{CAct}(\mathbb{X})$ as the category whose objects are change actions in $\mathbb{X}$ and whose arrows $\overline{f} : \overline{A} \to \overline{B}$ are the pairs $(f, \boldsymbol{\partial}[f])$, where $f : A \to B$ is an arrow in $\mathbb{X}$ and $\boldsymbol{\partial}[f] : A \times \Delta A \to \Delta B$ is a derivative for $f$. The identity is $(1_A, \pi_1)$, while composition of $(f, \boldsymbol{\partial}[f])$ and $(g, \boldsymbol{\partial}[g])$ is $(g \circ f, \boldsymbol{\partial}[g] \circ \langle f \circ \pi_0, \boldsymbol{\partial}[f] \rangle)$.*

There is an obvious product-preserving forgetful functor $\mathcal{E} : \mathsf{CAct}(\mathbb{X}) \to \mathbb{X}$ sending every change action $(A, \Delta A, \oplus, +, 0)$ to its base object $A$ and every map $(f, \boldsymbol{\partial}[f])$ to the underlying map $f$. As a setting for studying differentiation, the category $\mathsf{CAct}(\mathbb{X})$ is rather lacklustre, since there is no notion of higher derivatives, so we will instead work with change action models. Informally, a change action model consists of a rule which for every object $A$ of $\mathbb{X}$ associates a change action over it, and for every map a choice of a derivative.

**Definition 6.** *A **change action model** is a Cartesian category $\mathbb{X}$ is a product-preserving functor $\alpha : \mathbb{X} \to \mathsf{CAct}(\mathbb{X})$ that is a section of the forgetful functor $\mathcal{E}$.*

For brevity, when $A$ is an object of a change action model, we will write $\Delta A$, $\oplus_A$, $+_A$, and $0_A$ to refer to the components of the corresponding change action $\alpha(A)$. Examples of change action models can be found in [2]. In particular, we highlight that a Cartesian differential category always provides a change model action. We will generalize this result, and show in Section 4.4 that a Cartesian difference category also always provides a change action model.

## 4 Cartesian Difference Categories

In this section, we introduce *Cartesian difference categories*, which are generalizations of Cartesian differential categories. Examples of Cartesian difference categories can be found in Section 5.

### 4.1 Infinitesimal Extensions in Left Additive Categories

We first introduce infinitesimal extensions, which is an operator that turns a map into an "infinitesimal" version of itself – in the sense that every map coincides with its Taylor approximation on infinitesimal elements.

**Definition 7.** *A Cartesian left additive category $\mathbb{X}$ is said to have an **infinitesimal extension** $\varepsilon$ if every homset $\mathbb{X}(A, B)$ comes equipped with a monoid morphism $\varepsilon : \mathbb{X}(A, B) \to \mathbb{X}(A, B)$, that is, $\varepsilon(f + g) = \varepsilon(f) + \varepsilon(g)$ and $\varepsilon(0) = 0$, and such that $\varepsilon(g \circ f) = \varepsilon(g) \circ f$ and $\varepsilon(\pi_0) = \pi_0 \circ \varepsilon(1_{A \times B})$ and $\varepsilon(\pi_1) = \pi_1 \circ \varepsilon(1_{A \times B})$.*

Note that since $\varepsilon(g \circ f) = \varepsilon(g) \circ f$, it follows that $\varepsilon(f) = \varepsilon(1_B) \circ f$ and $\varepsilon(1_A) : A \to A$ is an additive map (Definition 1). In light of this, it turns out that infinitesimal extensions can equivalently be described as a class of additive maps $\varepsilon_A : A \to A$ such that $\varepsilon_{A \times B} = \varepsilon_A \times \varepsilon_B$. The equivalence is given by setting $\varepsilon(f) = \varepsilon_B \circ f$ and $\varepsilon_A = \varepsilon(1_A)$. Furthermore, infinitesimal extensions equipped each object with a canonical change action structure:

**Lemma 3.** *Let $\mathbb{X}$ be a Cartesian left additive category with infinitesimal extension $\varepsilon$. For every object $A$, define the maps $\oplus_A : A \times A \to A$ as $\oplus_A = \pi_0 + \varepsilon(\pi_1)$, $+_A : A \times A \to A$ as $\pi_0 + \pi_1$, and $0_A : \top \to A$ as $0_A = 0$. Then $(A, A, \oplus_A, +_A, 0_A)$ is a change action in $\mathbb{X}$.*

*Proof.* As mentioned earlier, that $(A, +_A, 0_A)$ is a commutative monoid was shown in [4]. On the other hand, that $\oplus_A$ is a change action follows from the fact that $\varepsilon$ preserves the addition. ∎

Setting $\overline{A} \equiv (A, A, \oplus_A, +_A, 0_A)$, we note that $f \oplus_{\overline{A}} g = f + \varepsilon(g)$ and $f +_{\overline{A}} g = f + g$, and so in particular $+_{\overline{A}} = +$. Therefore, from now on we will omit the subscripts and simply write $\oplus$ and $+$.

For every Cartesian left additive category, there are always at least two possible infinitesimal extensions:

**Lemma 4.** *For any Cartesian left additive category $\mathbb{X}$,*

1. *Setting $\varepsilon(f) = 0$ defines an infinitesimal extension on $\mathbb{X}$ and therefore in this case, $\oplus_A = \pi_0$ and $f \oplus g = f$.*
2. *Setting $\varepsilon(f) = f$ defines an infinitesimal extension on $\mathbb{X}$ and therefore in this case, $\oplus_A = +_A$ and $f \oplus g = f + g$.*

We note that while these examples of infinitesimal extensions may seem trivial, they are both very important as they will give rise to key examples of Cartesian difference categories.

## 4.2 Cartesian Difference Categories

**Definition 8.** *A* ***Cartesian difference category*** *is a Cartesian left additive category with an infinitesimal extension $\varepsilon$ which is equipped with a* ***difference combinator*** $\boldsymbol{\partial}$ *of the form:*

$$\frac{f : A \to B}{\boldsymbol{\partial}[f] : A \times A \to B}$$

*verifying the following coherence conditions:*

**[C∂.0]** $f \circ (x + \varepsilon(y)) = f \circ x + \varepsilon\left(\boldsymbol{\partial}[f] \circ \langle x, y\rangle\right)$
**[C∂.1]** $\boldsymbol{\partial}[f + g] = \boldsymbol{\partial}[f] + \boldsymbol{\partial}[g]$, $\boldsymbol{\partial}[0] = 0$, *and* $\boldsymbol{\partial}[\varepsilon(f)] = \varepsilon(\boldsymbol{\partial}[f])$
**[C∂.2]** $\boldsymbol{\partial}[f] \circ \langle x, y + z\rangle = \boldsymbol{\partial}[f] \circ \langle x, y\rangle + \boldsymbol{\partial}[f] \circ \langle x + \varepsilon(y), z\rangle$ *and* $\boldsymbol{\partial}[f] \circ \langle x, 0\rangle = 0$
**[C∂.3]** $\boldsymbol{\partial}[1_A] = \pi_1$ *and* $\boldsymbol{\partial}[\pi_0] = \pi_1; \pi_0$ *and* $\boldsymbol{\partial}[\pi_1] = \pi_1; \pi_0$
**[C∂.4]** $\boldsymbol{\partial}[\langle f, g\rangle] = \langle \boldsymbol{\partial}[f], \boldsymbol{\partial}[g]\rangle$ *and* $\boldsymbol{\partial}[!_A] = !_{A \times A}$
**[C∂.5]** $\boldsymbol{\partial}[g \circ f] = \boldsymbol{\partial}[g] \circ \langle f \circ \pi_0, \boldsymbol{\partial}[f]\rangle$
**[C∂.6]** $\boldsymbol{\partial}\left[\boldsymbol{\partial}[f]\right] \circ \langle\langle x, y\rangle, \langle 0, z\rangle\rangle = \boldsymbol{\partial}[f] \circ \langle x + \varepsilon(y), z\rangle$
**[C∂.7]** $\boldsymbol{\partial}\left[\boldsymbol{\partial}[f]\right] \circ \langle\langle x, y\rangle, \langle z, 0\rangle\rangle = \boldsymbol{\partial}\left[\boldsymbol{\partial}[f]\right] \circ \langle\langle x, z\rangle, \langle y, 0\rangle\rangle$

Before giving some intuition on the axioms **[C∂.0]** to **[C∂.7]**, we first observe that one could have used change action notation to express **[C∂.0]**, **[C∂.2]**, and **[C∂.6]** which would then be written as:

**[C∂.0]** $f \circ (x \oplus y) = (f \circ x) \oplus (\boldsymbol{\partial}[f] \circ \langle x, y\rangle)$
**[C∂.2]** $\boldsymbol{\partial}[f] \circ \langle x, y + z\rangle = \boldsymbol{\partial}[f] \circ \langle x, y\rangle + \boldsymbol{\partial}[f] \circ \langle x \oplus y, z\rangle$ and $\boldsymbol{\partial}[f] \circ \langle x, 0\rangle = 0$
**[C∂.6]** $\boldsymbol{\partial}\left[\boldsymbol{\partial}[f]\right] \circ \langle\langle x, y\rangle, \langle 0, z\rangle\rangle = \boldsymbol{\partial}[f] \circ \langle x \oplus y, z\rangle$

And also, just like Cartesian differential categories, **[C∂.6]** and **[C∂.7]** have alternative equivalent expressions.

**Lemma 5.** *In the presence of the other axioms,* **[C∂.6]** *and* **[C∂.7]** *are equivalent to:*

[**C∂.6.a**] $\partial\left[\partial[f]\right] \circ \langle\langle x, 0\rangle, \langle 0, y\rangle\rangle = \partial[f] \circ \langle x, y\rangle$
[**C∂.7.a**] $\partial\left[\partial[f]\right] \circ \langle\langle x, y\rangle, \langle z, w\rangle\rangle = \partial\left[\partial[f]\right] \circ \langle\langle x, z\rangle, \langle y, w\rangle\rangle$

*Proof.* The proof is essentially the same as [7, Proposition 4.2]. ■

The keen eyed reader will notice that the axioms of a Cartesian difference category are very similar to the axioms of a Cartesian differential category. Indeed, [**C∂.1**], [**C∂.3**], [**C∂.4**], [**C∂.5**], and [**C∂.7**] are the same as their Cartesian differential category counterpart. The axioms which are different are [**C∂.2**] and [**C∂.6**] where the infinitesimal extension $\varepsilon$ is now included, and also there is the new extra axiom [**C∂.0**]. On the other hand, interestingly enough, [**C∂.6.a**] is the same as [**CD.6.a**]. We also point out that writing out [**C∂.0**] and [**C∂.2**] using change action notion, we see that these axioms are precisely [**CAD.1**] and [**CAD.2**] respectively. To better understand [**C∂.0**] to [**C∂.7**] it may be useful to write them out using element-like notation. In element-like notation, [**C∂.0**] is written as:

$$f(x + \varepsilon(y)) = f(x) + \varepsilon\left(\partial[f](x, y)\right)$$

This condition can be read as a generalization of the Kock-Lawvere axiom that characterizes the derivative in from synthetic differential geometry [13]. Broadly speaking, the Kock-Lawvere axiom states that, for any map $f : \mathcal{R} \to \mathcal{R}$ and any $x \in \mathcal{R}$ and $d \in \mathcal{D}$, there exists a unique $f'(x) \in \mathcal{R}$ verifying

$$f(x + d) = f(x) + d \cdot f'(x)$$

where $\mathcal{D}$ is the subset of $\mathcal{R}$ consisting of infinitesimal elements. It is by analogy with the Kock-Lawvere axiom that we refer to $\varepsilon$ as an "infinitesimal extension" as it can be thought of as embedding the space $A$ into a subspace $\varepsilon(A)$ of infinitesimal elements.

[**C∂.1**] states that the differential of a sum of maps is the sum of differentials, and similarly for zero maps and the infinitesimal extension of a map. [**C∂.2**] is the first crucial difference between a Cartesian difference category and a Cartesian differential category. In a Cartesian differential category, the differential of a map is assumed to be additive in its second argument. In a Cartesian difference category, just as derivatives for change actions, while the differential is still required to preserve zeros in its second argument, it is only additive "up to a small perturbation", that is:

$$\partial[f](x, y + z) = \partial[f](x, y) + \partial[f](x + \varepsilon(y), z)$$

[**C∂.3**] tells us what the differential of the identity and projection maps are, while [**C∂.4**] says that the differential of a pairing of maps is the pairing of their differentials. [**C∂.5**] is the chain rule which expresses what the differential of a composition of maps is:

$$\partial[g \circ f](x, y) = \partial[g](f(x), \partial[f](x, y))$$

[**C∂.6**] and [**C∂.7**] tell us how to work with second order differentials. [**C∂.6**] is expressed as follows:

$$\partial\left[\partial[f]\right](x, y, 0, z) = \partial[f](x + \varepsilon(y), z)$$

and finally [**C∂.7**] is expressed as:

$$\partial\left[\partial[f]\right](x, y, z, 0) = \partial\left[\partial[f]\right](x, z, y, 0)$$

It is interesting to note that while [**C∂.6**] is different from [**CD.6**], its alternative version [**C∂.6.a**] is the same as [**CD.6.a**].

$$\partial\left[\partial[f]\right]((x, 0), (0, y)) = \partial[f](x, z)$$

### 4.3 Another look at Cartesian Differential Categories

Here we explain how a Cartesian differential category is a Cartesian difference category where the infinitesimal extension is given by zero.

**Proposition 1.** *Every Cartesian differential category $\mathbb{X}$ with differential combinator $\mathsf{D}$ is a Cartesian difference category where the infinitesimal extension is defined as $\varepsilon(f) = 0$ and the difference combinator is defined to be the differential combinator, $\partial = \mathsf{D}$.*

*Proof.* As noted before, the first two parts of the [**C∂.1**], the second part of [**C∂.2**], [**C∂.3**], [**C∂.4**], [**C∂.5**], and [**C∂.7**] are precisely the same as their Cartesian differential axiom counterparts. On the other hand, since $\varepsilon(f) = 0$, [**C∂.0**] and the third part of [**C∂.1**] trivial state that $0 = 0$, while the first part of [**C∂.2**] and [**C∂.6**] end up being precisely the first part of [**CD.2**] and [**CD.6**]. Therefore, the differential combinator satisfies the Cartesian difference axioms and we conclude that a Cartesian differential category is a Cartesian difference category. ■

Conversely, one can always build a Cartesian differential category from a Cartesian difference category by considering the objects for which the infinitesimal extension is the zero map.

**Proposition 2.** *For a Cartesian difference category $\mathbb{X}$ with infinitesimal extension $\varepsilon$ and difference combinator $\partial$, then $\mathbb{X}_0$, the full subcategory of objects $A$ such that $\varepsilon(1_A) = 0$, is a Cartesian differential category where the differential combinator is defined to be the difference combinator, $\mathsf{D} = \partial$.*

*Proof.* First note that if $\varepsilon(1_A) = 0$ and $\varepsilon(1_B) = 0$, then by definition it also follows that $\varepsilon(1_{A\times B}) = 0$, and also that for the terminal object $\varepsilon(1_\top) = 0$ by uniqueness of maps into the terminal object. Thus $\mathbb{X}_0$ is closed under finite products and is therefore a Cartesian left additive category. Furthermore, we again note that since $\varepsilon(f) = 0$, this implies that for maps between such objects the Cartesian difference axioms are precisely the Cartesian differential axioms. Therefore, the difference combinator is a differential combinator for this subcategory, and so $\mathbb{X}_0$ is a Cartesian differential category. ■

In any Cartesian difference category $\mathbb{X}$, the terminal object $\top$ always satisfies that $\varepsilon(1_\top) = 0$, and so therefore, $\mathbb{X}_0$ is never empty. On the other hand, applying Proposition 2 to a Cartesian differential category results in the entire category. It is also important to note that the above two propositions do not imply that if a difference combinator is a differential combinator then the infinitesimal extension must be zero. In Section 5.3, we provide such an example of a Cartesian differential category that comes equipped with a non-zero infinitesimal extension such that the differential combinator is a difference combinator with respect to this non-zero infinitesimal extension.

### 4.4 Cartesian Difference Categories as Change Action Models

In this section, we show how every Cartesian difference category is a particularly well-behaved change action model, and conversely how every change action model contains a Cartesian difference category.

**Proposition 3.** *Let $\mathbb{X}$ be a Cartesian difference category with infinitesimal extension $\varepsilon$ and difference combinator $\boldsymbol{\partial}$. Define the functor $\alpha : \mathbb{X} \to \mathsf{CAct}(\mathbb{X})$ as $\alpha(A) = (A, A, \oplus_A, +_A, 0_A)$ (as defined in Lemma 3) and $\alpha(f) = (f, \boldsymbol{\partial}[f])$. Then $(\mathbb{X}, \alpha : \mathbb{X} \to \mathsf{CAct}(\mathbb{X}))$ is a change action model.*

*Proof.* By Lemma 3, $(A, A, \oplus_A, +_A, 0_A)$ is a change action and so $\alpha$ is well-defined on objects. While for a map $f$, $\boldsymbol{\partial}[f]$ is a derivative of $f$ in the change action sense since [**C∂.0**] and [**C∂.2**] are precisely [**CAD.1**] and [**CAD.2**], and so $\alpha$ is well-defined on maps. That $\alpha$ preserves identities and composition follows from [**C∂.3**] and [**C∂.5**] respectively, and so $\alpha$ is a functor. That $\alpha$ preserves finite products will follow from [**C∂.3**] and [**C∂.4**]. Lastly, it is clear that $\alpha$ section of the forgetful functor, and therefore we conclude that $(\mathbb{X}, \alpha)$ is a change action model. ■

It is clear that not every change action model is a Cartesian difference category. For example, change action models do not require the addition to be commutative. On the other hand, it can be shown that every change action model contains a Cartesian difference category as a full subcategory.

**Definition 9.** *Let $(\mathbb{X}, \alpha : \mathbb{X} \to \mathsf{CAct}(\mathbb{X}))$ be a change action model. An object $A$ is **flat** whenever the following hold:*

[**F.1**] $\Delta A = A$
[**F.2**] $\alpha(\oplus_A) = (\oplus_A, \oplus_A \circ \pi_1)$
[**F.3**] $0 \oplus_A (0 \oplus_A f) = 0 \oplus_A f$ *for any* $f : U \to A$.
[**F.4**] $\oplus_A$ *is right-injective, that is, if* $\oplus_A \circ \langle f, g\rangle = \oplus_A \circ \langle f, h\rangle$ *then* $g = h$.

We would like to show that for any change action model $(\mathbb{X}, \alpha)$, its full subcategory of flat objects, $\mathsf{Flat}_\alpha$ is a Cartesian difference category. Starting with the finite product structure, since $\alpha$ preserves finite products, it is straightforward to see that $\top$ is Euclidean and if $A$ and $B$ are flat then so is $A \times B$. The sum of maps $f : A \to B$ and $g : A \to B$ in $\mathsf{Flat}_\alpha$ is defined using the change action structure $f +_B g$, while the zero map $0 : A \to B$ is $0 = 0_B \circ !_A$. And so we obtain that:

**Lemma 6.** $\mathsf{Flat}_\alpha$ *is a Cartesian left additive category.*

*Proof.* Most of the Cartesian left additive structure is straightforward. However, since the addition is not required to be commutative for arbitrary change actions, we will show that the addition is commutative for Euclidean objects. Using that $\oplus_B$ is an action, that by [**F.2**] we have that $\oplus_B \circ \pi_1$ is a derivative for $\oplus_B$, and [**CAD.1**], we obtain that:

$$0_B \oplus_B (f +_B g) = (0_B \oplus_B f) \oplus_B g = (0_B \oplus_B g) \oplus_B f = 0_B \oplus_B (g +_B f)$$

By [**F.4**], $\oplus_B$ is right-injective and we conclude that $f + g = g + f$. ∎

As an immediate consequence We note that for any change action model $(\mathbb{X}, \alpha)$, since the terminal object is always flat, $\mathsf{Flat}_\alpha$ is never empty.

We use the action of the change action structure to define the infinitesimal extension. So for a map $f : A \to B$ in $\mathsf{Flat}_\alpha$, define $\varepsilon(f) : A \to B$ as follows:

$$\varepsilon(f) = \oplus_B \circ \langle 0_B \circ !_A, f \rangle = 0 \oplus_B f$$

**Lemma 7.** $\varepsilon$ *is an infinitesimal extension for* $\mathsf{Flat}_\alpha$.

*Proof.* We show that $\varepsilon$ preserve the addition. Following the same idea as in the proof of Lemma 6, we obtain the following:

$$\begin{aligned} &0_B \oplus_B \varepsilon(f +_B g) = 0_B \oplus_B (0_B \oplus_B (f +_B g)) \\ &= (0_B \oplus_B 0_B) \oplus_B ((0_B \oplus_B f) \oplus_B g) = (0_B \oplus_B (0_B \oplus_B f)) \oplus_B (0_B \oplus_B g) \\ &= (0_B \oplus_B \varepsilon(f)) \oplus_B \varepsilon(g) = 0_B \oplus_B (\varepsilon(f) +_B \varepsilon(g)) \end{aligned}$$

Then by [**F.3**], it follows that $\varepsilon(f+g) = \varepsilon(f) + \varepsilon(g)$. The remaining infinitesimal extension axioms are proven in a similar fashion. ∎

Lastly, the difference combinator for $\mathsf{Flat}_\alpha$ is defined in the obvious way, that is, $\boldsymbol{\partial}[f]$ is defined as the second component of $\alpha(f)$.

**Proposition 4.** *Let* $(\mathbb{X}, \alpha : \mathbb{X} \to \mathsf{CAct}(\mathbb{X}))$ *be a change action model. Then* $\mathsf{Flat}_\alpha$ *is a Cartesian difference category.*

*Proof (Sketch).* The full calculations will appear in an upcoming extended journal version of this paper, but we give an informal explanation. [**C∂.0**] and [**C∂.2**] are a straightforward consequences of [**CAD.1**] and [**CAD.2**]. [**C∂.3**] and [**C∂.4**] follow trivially from the fact that $\alpha$ preserves finite products and from the structure of products in $\mathsf{CAct}(\mathbb{X})$, while [**C∂.5**] follows from composition in $\mathsf{CAct}(\mathbb{X})$. [**C∂.1**], [**C∂.6**] and [**C∂.7**] are obtained by mechanical calculation in the spirit of Lemma 6. Note that every axiom except for [**C∂.6**] can be proven without using [**F.3**] ∎

### 4.5 Linear Maps and $\varepsilon$-Linear Maps

An important subclass of maps in a Cartesian differential category is the subclass of *linear maps* [4, Definition 2.2.1]. One can also define linear maps in a Cartesian difference category by using the same definition.

**Definition 10.** *In a Cartesian difference category, a map $f$ is **linear** if the following equality holds: $\partial[f] = f \circ \pi_1$.*

Using element-like notation, a map $f$ is linear if $\partial[f](x, y) = f(y)$. Linear maps in a Cartesian difference category satisfy many of the same properties found in [4, Lemma 2.2.2].

**Lemma 8.** *In a Cartesian difference category,*

1. *If $f : A \to B$ is linear then $\varepsilon(f) = f \circ \varepsilon(1_A)$;*
2. *If $f : A \to B$ is linear, then $f$ is additive (Definition 1);*
3. *Identity maps, projection maps, and zero maps are linear;*
4. *The composite, sum, and pairing of linear maps is linear;*
5. *If $f : A \to B$ and $k : C \to D$ are linear, then for any map $g : B \to C$, the following equality holds: $\partial[k \circ g \circ f] = k \circ \partial[g] \circ (f \times f)$;*
6. *If an isomorphism is linear, then its inverse is linear;*
7. *For any object $A$, $\oplus_A$ and $+_A$ are linear.*

Using element-like notation, the first point of the above lemma says that if $f$ is linear then $f(\varepsilon(x)) = \varepsilon(f(x))$. And while all linear maps are additive, the converse is not necessarily true, see [4, Corollary 2.3.4]. However, an immediate consequence of the above lemma is that the subcategory of linear maps of a Cartesian difference category has finite biproducts.

Another interesting subclass of maps is the subclass of $\varepsilon$-linear maps, which are maps whose infinitesimal extension is linear.

**Definition 11.** *In a Cartesian difference category, a map $f$ is **$\varepsilon$-linear** if $\varepsilon(f)$ is linear.*

**Lemma 9.** *In a Cartesian difference category,*

1. *If $f : A \to B$ is $\varepsilon$-linear then $f \circ (x + \varepsilon(y)) = f \circ x + \varepsilon(f) \circ y$;*
2. *Every linear map is $\varepsilon$-linear;*
3. *The composite, sum, and pairing of $\varepsilon$-linear maps is $\varepsilon$-linear;*
4. *If an isomorphism is $\varepsilon$-linear, then its inverse is again $\varepsilon$-linear.*

Using element-like notation, the first point of the above lemma says that if $f$ is $\varepsilon$-linear then $f(x + \varepsilon(y)) = f(x) + \varepsilon(f(y))$. So $\varepsilon$-linear maps are additive on "infinitesimal" elements (i.e. those of the form $\varepsilon(y)$).

For a Cartesian differential category, linear maps in the Cartesian difference category sense are precisely the same as the Cartesian differential category sense [4, Definition 2.2.1], while every map is $\varepsilon$-linear since $\varepsilon = 0$.

# 5 Examples of Cartesian Difference Categories

## 5.1 Smooth Functions

Every Cartesian differential category is a Cartesian difference category where the infinitesimal extension is zero. As a particular example, we consider the category of real smooth functions, which as mentioned above, can be considered to be the canonical (and motivating) example of a Cartesian differential category.

Let $\mathbb{R}$ be the set of real numbers and let $\mathsf{SMOOTH}$ be the category whose objects are Euclidean spaces $\mathbb{R}^n$ (including the point $\mathbb{R}^0 = \{*\}$), and whose maps are smooth functions $F : \mathbb{R}^n \to \mathbb{R}^m$. $\mathsf{SMOOTH}$ is a Cartesian left additive category where the product structure is given by the standard Cartesian product of Euclidean spaces and where the additive structure is defined by point-wise addition, $(F + G)(\boldsymbol{x}) = F(\boldsymbol{x}) + G(\boldsymbol{x})$ and $0(\boldsymbol{x}) = (0, \ldots, 0)$, where $\boldsymbol{x} \in \mathbb{R}^n$. $\mathsf{SMOOTH}$ is a Cartesian differential category where the differential combinator is defined by the directional derivative of smooth functions. Explicitly, for a smooth function $F : \mathbb{R}^n \to \mathbb{R}^m$, which is in fact a tuple of smooth functions $F = (f_1, \ldots, f_n)$ where $f_i : \mathbb{R}^n \to \mathbb{R}$, $\mathsf{D}[F] : \mathbb{R}^n \times \mathbb{R}^n \to \mathbb{R}^m$ is defined as follows:

$$\mathsf{D}[F](\boldsymbol{x}, \boldsymbol{y}) := \left( \sum_{i=1}^{n} \frac{\partial f_1}{\partial u_i}(\boldsymbol{x}) y_i, \ldots, \sum_{i=1}^{n} \frac{\partial f_n}{\partial u_i}(\boldsymbol{x}) y_i \right)$$

where $\boldsymbol{x} = (x_1, \ldots, x_n), \boldsymbol{y} = (y_1, \ldots, y_n) \in \mathbb{R}^n$. Alternatively, $\mathsf{D}[F]$ can also be defined in terms of the Jacobian matrix of $F$. Therefore $\mathsf{SMOOTH}$ is a Cartesian difference category with infinitesimal extesion $\varepsilon = 0$ and with difference combinator $\mathsf{D}$. Since $\varepsilon = 0$, the induced action is simply $\boldsymbol{x} \oplus_{\mathbb{R}^n} \boldsymbol{y} = \boldsymbol{x}$. Also a smooth function is linear in the Cartesian difference category sense precisely if it is $\mathbb{R}$-linear in the classical sense, and every smooth function is $\varepsilon$-linear.

## 5.2 Calculus of Finite Differences

Here we explain how the difference operator from the calculus of finite differences gives an example of a Cartesian difference category but *not* a Cartesian differential category. This example was the main motivating example for developing Cartesian difference categories. The calculus of finite differences is captured by the category of abelian groups and arbitrary set functions between them.

Let $\overline{\mathsf{Ab}}$ be the category whose objects are abelian groups $G$ (where we use additive notation for group structure) and where a map $f : G \to H$ is simply an arbitrary function between them (and therefore does not necessarily preserve the group structure). $\overline{\mathsf{Ab}}$ is a Cartesian left additive category where the product structure is given by the standard Cartesian product of sets and where the additive structure is again given by point-wise addition, $(f + g)(x) = f(x) + g(x)$ and $0(x) = 0$. $\overline{\mathsf{Ab}}$ is a Cartesian difference category where the infinitesimal extension is simply given by the identity, that is, $\varepsilon(f) = f$, and and where the difference combinator $\boldsymbol{\partial}$ is defined as follows for a map $f : G \to H$:

$$\boldsymbol{\partial}[f](x, y) = f(x + y) - f(x)$$

On the other hand, $\boldsymbol{\partial}$ is not a differential combinator for $\overline{\mathsf{Ab}}$ since it does not satisfy **[CD.6]** and part of **[CD.2]**. Thanks to the addition of the infinitesimal extension, $\boldsymbol{\partial}$ does satisfy **[C∂.2]** and **[C∂.6]**, as well as **[C∂.0]**. However, as noted in [5], it is interesting to note that this $\boldsymbol{\partial}$ does satisfy **[CD.1]**, the second part of **[CD.2]**, **[CD.3]**, **[CD.4]**, **[CD.5]**, **[CD.7]**, and **[CD.6.a]**. It is worth noting that in [5], the goal was to drop the addition and develop a "non-additive" version of Cartesian differential categories.

In $\overline{\mathsf{Ab}}$, since the infinitesimal operator is given by the identity, the induced action is simply the addition, $x \oplus_G y = x + y$. On the other hand, the linear maps in $\overline{\mathsf{Ab}}$ are precisely the group homomorphisms. Indeed, $f$ is linear if $\boldsymbol{\partial}[f](x, y) = f(y)$. But by **[C∂.0]** and **[C∂.2]**, we get that:

$$f(x + y) = f(x) + \boldsymbol{\partial}[f](x, y) = f(x) + f(y) \qquad\qquad f(0) = \boldsymbol{\partial}[f](x, 0) = 0$$

So $f$ is a group homomorphism. Conversely, if $f$ is a group homomorphism:

$$\boldsymbol{\partial}[f](x, y) = f(x + y) - f(x) = f(x) + f(y) - f(x) = f(y)$$

So $f$ is linear. Since $\varepsilon(f) = f$, the $\varepsilon$-linear maps are precisely the linear maps.

## 5.3 Module Morphisms

Here we provide a simple example of a Cartesian difference category whose difference combinator is also a differential combinator, but where the infinitesimal extension is neither zero nor the identity.

Let $R$ be a commutative semiring and let $\mathsf{MOD}_R$ be the category of $R$-modules and $R$-linear maps between them. $\mathsf{MOD}_R$ has finite biproducts and is therefore a Cartesian left additive category where every map is additive. Every $r \in R$ induces an infinitesimal extension $\varepsilon^r$ defined by scalar multiplication, $\varepsilon^r(f)(m) = rf(m)$. Then $\mathsf{MOD}_R$ is a Cartesian difference category with the infinitesimal extension $\varepsilon^r$ for any $r \in R$ and difference combinator $\boldsymbol{\partial}$ defined as:

$$\boldsymbol{\partial}[f](m, n) = f(n)$$

$R$-linearity of $f$ assures that **[C∂.0]** holds, while the remaining Cartesian difference axioms hold trivially. In fact, $\boldsymbol{\partial}$ is also a differential combinator and therefore $\mathsf{MOD}_R$ is also a Cartesian differential category. The induced action is given by $m \oplus_M n = m + rn$. By definition of $\boldsymbol{\partial}$, every map in $\mathsf{MOD}_R$ is linear, and by definition of $\varepsilon^r$ and $R$-linearity, every map is also $\varepsilon$-linear.

## 5.4 Stream calculus

Here we show how one can extend the calculus of finite differences example to stream calculus. The differential calculus of causal functions and interesting applications have recently been studying in [17, 18].

For a set $A$, let $A^\omega$ denote the set of infinite sequences of elements of $A$, where we write $[a_i]$ for the infinite sequence $[a_i] = (a_1, a_2, a_3, \ldots)$ and $a_{i:j}$ for the (finite) subsequence $(a_i, a_{i+1}, \dots, a_j)$. A function $f : A^\omega \to B^\omega$ is **causal** whenever the $n$-th element $f([a_i])_n$ of the output sequence only depends on the first $n$ elements of $[a_i]$, that is, $f$ is causal if and only if whenever $a_{0:n} = b_{0:n}$ then $f([a_i])_{0:n} = f([b_i])_{0:n}$. We now consider streams over abelian groups, so let $\overline{\mathsf{Ab}}^\omega$ be the category whose objects are all the Abelian groups and whose morphisms are causal maps from $G^\omega$ to $H^\omega$. $\overline{\mathsf{Ab}}^\omega$ is a Cartesian left-additive category, where the product is given by the standard product of abelian groups and where the additive structure is lifted point-wise from the structure of $\overline{\mathsf{Ab}}$, that is, $(f+g)([a_i])_n = f([a_i])_n + g([a_i])_n$ and $0([a_i])_n = 0$. In order to define the infinitesimal extension, we first need to define the truncation operator $\mathbf{z}$. So let $G$ be an abelian group and $[a_i] \in G^\omega$, then define the sequence $\mathbf{z}([a_i])$ as:

$$\mathbf{z}([a_i])_0 = 0 \qquad\qquad \mathbf{z}([a_i])_{n+1} = a_{n+1}$$

The category $\overline{\mathsf{Ab}}^\omega$ is a Cartesian difference category where the infinitesimal extension is given by the truncation operator, $\varepsilon(f)([a_i]) = \mathbf{z}(f([a_i]))$,
and where the difference combinator $\boldsymbol{\partial}$ is defined as follows:

$$\begin{aligned} \boldsymbol{\partial}[f]([a_i], [b_i])_0 &= f([a_i] + [b_i])_0 - f([a_i])_0 \\ \boldsymbol{\partial}[f]([a_i], [b_i])_{n+1} &= f([a_i] + \mathbf{z}([b_i]))_{n+1} - f([a_i])_{n+1} \end{aligned}$$

Note the similarities between the difference combinator on $\overline{\mathsf{Ab}}$ and that on $\overline{\mathsf{Ab}}^\omega$. The induced action is computed out to be:

$$([a_i] \oplus [b_i])_0 = a_0 \qquad\qquad ([a_i] \oplus [b_i])_{n+1} = a_{n+1} + b_{n+1}$$

A causal map is linear (in the Cartesian difference category sense) if and only if it is a group homomorphism. While a causal map $f$ is $\varepsilon$-linear if and only if it is a group homomorphism which does not the depend on the 0-th term of its input, that is, $f([a_i]) = f(\mathbf{z}([a_i]))$.

## 6 Tangent Bundles in Cartesian Difference Categories

In this section, we show that the difference combinator of a Cartesian difference category induces a monad, called the *tangent monad*, whose Kleisli category is again a Cartesian difference category. This construction is a generalization of the tangent monad for Cartesian differential categories [7, 15]. However, the Kleisli category of the tangent monad of a Cartesian differential category is *not* a Cartesian differential category, but rather a Cartesian difference category.

### 6.1 The Tangent Bundle Monad

Let $\mathbb{X}$ be a Cartesian difference category with infinitesimal extension $\varepsilon$ and difference combinator $\boldsymbol{\partial}$. Define the functor $\mathsf{T} : \mathbb{X} \to \mathbb{X}$ as follows:

$$\mathsf{T}(A) = A \times A \qquad\qquad \mathsf{T}(f) = \langle f \circ \pi_0, \boldsymbol{\partial}[f] \rangle$$

and define the natural transformations $\eta : 1_{\mathbb{X}} \Rightarrow \mathsf{T}$ and $\mu : \mathsf{T}^2 \Rightarrow \mathsf{T}$ as follows:

$$\eta_A := \langle 1_A, 0 \rangle \qquad \mu_A := \langle \pi_0 \circ \pi_0, \pi_1 \circ \pi_0 + \pi_0 \circ \pi_1 + \varepsilon(\pi_1 \circ \pi_1) \rangle$$

**Proposition 5.** $(\mathsf{T}, \mu, \eta)$ *is a monad.*

*Proof.* Functoriality of $\mathsf{T}$ will follow from **[C∂.3]** and the chain rule **[C∂.5]**. Naturality of $\eta$ and $\mu$ and the monad identities will follow from the remaining difference combinator axioms. The full lengthy brute force calculations will appear in an upcoming extended journal version of this paper. ■

When $\mathbb{X}$ is a Cartesian differential category with the difference structure arising from setting $\varepsilon = 0$, this tangent bundle monad coincides with the standard tangent monad corresponding to its tangent category structure [7, 15].

### 6.2 The Kleisli Category of T

Recall that the Kleisli category of the monad $(\mathsf{T}, \mu, \eta)$ is defined as the category $\mathbb{X}_\mathsf{T}$ whose objects are the objects of $\mathbb{X}$, and where a map $A \to B$ in $\mathbb{X}_\mathsf{T}$ is a map $f : A \to \mathsf{T}(B)$ in $\mathbb{X}$, which would be a pair $f = \langle f_0, f_1 \rangle$ where $f_j : A \to B$. The identity map in $\mathbb{X}_\mathsf{T}$ is the monad unit $\eta_A : A \to \mathsf{T}(A)$, while composition of Kleisli maps $f : A \to \mathsf{T}(B)$ and $g : B \to \mathsf{T}(C)$ is defined as the composite $\mu_C \circ \mathsf{T}(g) \circ f$. To distinguish between composition in $\mathbb{X}$ and $\mathbb{X}_\mathsf{T}$, we denote Kleisli composition as $g \circ^\mathsf{T} f = \mu_C \circ \mathsf{T}(g) \circ f$. If $f = \langle f_0, f_1 \rangle$ and $g = \langle g_0, g_1 \rangle$, then their Kleisli composition can be explicitly computed out to be:

$$g \circ^\mathsf{T} f = \langle g_0, g_1 \rangle \circ^\mathsf{T} \langle f_0, f_1 \rangle = \langle g_0 \circ f_0, \partial[g_0] \circ \langle f_0, f_1 \rangle + g_1 \circ (f_0 + \varepsilon(f_1)) \rangle$$

Kleisli maps can be understood as "generalized" vector fields. Indeed, $\mathsf{T}(A)$ should be thought of as the tangent bundle over $A$, and therefore a vector field would be a map $\langle 1, f \rangle : A \to \mathsf{T}(A)$, which is of course also a Kleisli map. For more details on the intuition behind this Kleisli category see [7]. We now wish to explain how the Kleisli category is again a Cartesian difference category.

We begin by exhibiting the Cartesian left additive structure of the Kleisli category. The product of objects in $\mathbb{X}_\mathsf{T}$ is defined as $A \times B$ with projections $\pi_0^\mathsf{T} : A \times B \to \mathsf{T}(A)$ and $\pi_1^\mathsf{T} : A \times B \to \mathsf{T}(B)$ defined respectively as $\pi_0^\mathsf{T} = \langle \pi_0, 0 \rangle$ and $\pi_1^\mathsf{T} = \langle \pi_1, 0 \rangle$. The pairing of Kleisli maps $f = \langle f_0, f_1 \rangle$ and $g = \langle, g_0, g_1 \rangle$ is defined as $\langle f, g \rangle^\mathsf{T} = \langle \langle f_0, g_0 \rangle, \langle f_1, g_1 \rangle \rangle$. The terminal object is again $\top$ and where the unique map to the terminal object is $!_A^\mathsf{T} = 0$. The sum of Kleisli maps f Kleisli maps $f = \langle f_0, f_1 \rangle$ and $g = \langle, g_0, g_1 \rangle$ is defined as $f +^\mathsf{T} g = f + g = \langle f_0 + g_0, f_1 + g_1 \rangle$, and the zero Kleisli maps is simply $0^\mathsf{T} = 0 = \langle 0, 0 \rangle$. Therefore we conclude that the Kleisli category of the tangent monad is a Cartesian left additive category.

**Lemma 10.** $\mathbb{X}_\mathsf{T}$ *is a Cartesian left additive category.*

The infinitesimal extension $\varepsilon^\mathsf{T}$ for the Kleisli category is defined as follows for a Kleisli map $f = \langle f_0, f_1 \rangle$:

$$\varepsilon^\mathsf{T}(f) = \langle 0, f_0 + \varepsilon(f_1) \rangle$$

**Lemma 11.** *$\varepsilon^{\mathsf{T}}$ is an infinitesimal extension on $\mathbb{X}_{\mathsf{T}}$.*

It is interesting to point out that for an object $A$ the induced action $\oplus_A^{\mathsf{T}}$ can be computed out to be:

$$\oplus_A^{\mathsf{T}} = \pi_0^{\mathsf{T}} +^{\mathsf{T}} \varepsilon^{\mathsf{T}}(\pi_1) = \langle \pi_0, 0\rangle + \langle 0, \pi_1\rangle = \langle \pi_0, \pi_1\rangle = 1_{\mathsf{T}(A)}$$

and we stress that this is the identity of $\mathsf{T}(A)$ in the base category $\mathbb{X}$ (but not in the Kleisli category).

To define the difference combinator for the Kleisli category, first note that difference combinators by definition do not change the codomain. That is, if $f : A \to \mathsf{T}(B)$ is a Kleisli arrow, then the type of its derivative *qua* Kleisli arrow should be $A \times A \to \mathsf{T}(B) \times \mathsf{T}(B)$, which coincides with the type of its derivative in $\mathbb{X}$. Therefore, the difference combinator $\boldsymbol{\partial}^{\mathsf{T}}$ for the Kleisli category can be defined to be the difference combinator of the base category, that is, for a Kleisli map $f = \langle f_0, f_1\rangle$:

$$\boldsymbol{\partial}^{\mathsf{T}}[f] = \boldsymbol{\partial}[f] = \langle \boldsymbol{\partial}[f_0], \boldsymbol{\partial}[f_1]\rangle$$

**Proposition 6.** *For a Cartesian difference category $\mathbb{X}$, the Kleisli category $\mathbb{X}_{\mathsf{T}}$ is a Cartesian difference category with infinitesimal extension $\varepsilon^{\mathsf{T}}$ and difference combinator $\boldsymbol{\partial}^{\mathsf{T}}$.*

*Proof.* The full lengthy brute force calculations will appear in an upcoming extended journal version of this paper. We do note that a crucial identity for this proof is that for any map $f$ in $\mathbb{X}$, the following equality holds:

$$\mathsf{T}(\boldsymbol{\partial}[f]) = \boldsymbol{\partial}\left[\mathsf{T}(f)\right] \circ \langle \pi_0 \times \pi_0, \pi_1 \times \pi_1\rangle$$

This helps simplify many of the calculations for the difference combinator axioms since $\mathsf{T}(\boldsymbol{\partial}[f])$ appears everywhere due to the definition of Kleisli composition. ■

As a result, the Kleisli category of a Cartesian difference category is again a Cartesian difference category, whose infinitesimal extension is neither the identity or the zero map. This allows one to build numerous examples of interesting and exotic Cartesian difference categories, such as the Kleisli category of Cartesian differential categories (or iterating this process, taking the Kleisli category of the Kleisli category). We highlight the importance of this construction in the Cartesian differential case as it does not in general result in a Cartesian differential category. Indeed, even if $\varepsilon = 0$, it is always the case that $\varepsilon^{\mathsf{T}} \neq 0$. We conclude this section by taking a look at the linear maps and the $\varepsilon^{\mathsf{T}}$-linear maps in the Kleisli category. A Kleisli map $f = \langle f_0, f_1\rangle$ is linear in the Kleisli category if $\boldsymbol{\partial}^{\mathsf{T}}[f] = f \circ^{\mathsf{T}} \pi_1^{\mathsf{T}}$, which amounts to requiring that:

$$\langle \boldsymbol{\partial}[f_0], \boldsymbol{\partial}[f_1]\rangle = \langle f_0 \circ \pi_1, f_1 \circ \pi_1\rangle$$

Therefore a Kleisli map is linear in the Kleisli category if and only if it is the pairing of maps which are linear in the base category. On the other hand, $f$ is $\varepsilon^{\mathsf{T}}$-linear if $\varepsilon^{T}(f) = \langle 0, f_0 + \varepsilon(f_1)\rangle$ is linear in the Kleisli category, which in this case amounts to requiring that $f_0 + \varepsilon(f_1)$ is linear. Therefore, if $f_0$ is linear and $f_1$ is $\varepsilon$-linear, then $f$ is $\varepsilon^{\mathsf{T}}$-linear.

## 7 Conclusions and Future Work

We have presented Cartesian difference categories, which generalize Cartesian differential categories to account for more discrete definitions of derivatives while providing an additional structure that is absent in change action models. We have also exhibited important examples and shown that Cartesian difference categories arise quite naturally from considering tangent bundles in any Cartesian differential category. We claim that Cartesian difference categories can facilitate the exploration of differentiation in discrete spaces, by generalizing techniques and ideas from the study of their differential counterparts. For example, Cartesian differential categories can be extended to allow objects whose tangent space is not necessarily isomorphic to the object itself [9]. The same generalization could be applied to Cartesian difference categories – with some caveats: for example, the equation defining a linear map (Definition 10) becomes ill-typed, but the notion of $\varepsilon$-linear map remains meaningful.

Another relevant path to consider is developing the analogue of the "tensor" story for Cartesian difference categories. Indeed, an important source of examples of Cartesian differential categories are the coKleisli categories of a tensor differential category [3, 4]. A similar result likely holds for a hypothetical "tensor difference category", but it is not clear how these should be defined: [$\mathbf{C\partial.2}$] implies that derivatives in the difference sense are non-linear and therefore their interplay with the tensor structure will be much different.

A further generalization of Cartesian differential categories, categories with tangent structure [7] are defined directly in terms of a tangent bundle functor rather than requiring that every tangent bundle be trivial (that is, in a tangent category it may not be the case that $\mathsf{T}A = A \times A$). Some preliminary research on change actions has already shown that, when generalized in this way, change actions are precisely internal categories, but the consequences of this for change action models (and, *a fortiori*, Cartesian difference categories) are not understood. More recently, some work has emerged about differential equations using the language of tangent categories [8]. We believe similar techniques can be applied in a straightforward way to Cartesian difference categories, where they might be of use to give an abstract formalization of discrete dynamical systems and difference equations.

An important open question is whether Cartesian difference categories (or a similar notion) admit an internal language. It is well-known that the differential $\lambda$-calculus can be interpreted in Cartesian closed differential categories [14]. Given their similarities, we believe there will be a very similar "difference $\lambda$-calculus" which could potentially have applications to automatic differentiation (change structures, a notion similar to change actions, have already been proposed as models of forward-mode automatic differentiation [12], although work on the area seems to have stagnated).

Lastly, we should mention that there are adjunctions between the categories of Cartesian difference categories, change action models, and Cartesian differential categories given by Proposition 1, 2, 3, and 4. These adjunctions will be explored in detail in the upcoming journal version of this paper.

## References


1. Alvarez-Picallo, M., Eyers-Taylor, A., Jones, M.P., Ong, C.H.L.: Fixing incremental computation. In: European Symposium on Programming. pp. 525–552. Springer (2019)
2. Alvarez-Picallo, M., Ong, C.H.L.: Change actions: models of generalised differentiation. In: International Conference on Foundations of Software Science and Computation Structures. pp. 45–61. Springer (2019)
3. Blute, R.F., Cockett, J.R.B., Seely, R.A.G.: Differential categories. Mathematical structures in computer science **16**(06), 1049–1083 (2006)
4. Blute, R.F., Cockett, J.R.B., Seely, R.A.G.: Cartesian differential categories. Theory and Applications of Categories **22**(23), 622–672 (2009)
5. Bradet-Legris, J., Reid, H.: Differential forms in non-linear cartesian differential categories (2018), Foundational Methods in Computer Science
6. Cai, Y., Giarrusso, P.G., Rendel, T., Ostermann, K.: A theory of changes for higher-order languages: Incrementalizing $\lambda$-calculi by static differentiation. In: ACM SIGPLAN Notices. vol. 49, pp. 145–155. ACM (2014)
7. Cockett, J.R.B., Cruttwell, G.S.H.: Differential structure, tangent structure, and sdg. Applied Categorical Structures **22**(2), 331–417 (2014)
8. Cockett, J., Cruttwell, G.: Connections in tangent categories. Theory and Applications of Categories **32**(26), 835–888 (2017)
9. Cruttwell, G.S.: Cartesian differential categories revisited. Mathematical Structures in Computer Science **27**(1), 70–91 (2017)
10. Ehrhard, T., Regnier, L.: The differential lambda-calculus. Theoretical Computer Science **309**(1), 1–41 (2003)
11. Ehrhard, T.: An introduction to differential linear logic: proof-nets, models and antiderivatives. Mathematical Structures in Computer Science **28**(7), 995–1060 (2018)
12. Kelly, R., Pearlmutter, B.A., Siskind, J.M.: Evolving the incremental {\lambda} calculus into a model of forward automatic differentiation (ad). arXiv preprint arXiv:1611.03429 (2016)
13. Kock, A.: Synthetic differential geometry, vol. 333. Cambridge University Press (2006)
14. Manzonetto, G.: What is a categorical model of the differential and the resource $\lambda$-calculi? Mathematical Structures in Computer Science **22**(3), 451–520 (2012)
15. Manzyuk, O.: Tangent bundles in differential lambda-categories. arXiv preprint arXiv:1202.0411 (2012)
16. Richardson, C.H.: An introduction to the calculus of finite differences. Van Nostrand (1954)
17. Sprunger, D., Jacobs, B.: The differential calculus of causal functions. arXiv preprint arXiv:1904.10611 (2019)
18. Sprunger, D., Katsumata, S.y.: Differentiable causal computations via delayed trace. In: 2019 34th Annual ACM/IEEE Symposium on Logic in Computer Science (LICS). pp. 1–12. IEEE (2019)
19. Steinbach, B., Posthoff, C.: Boolean differential calculus. In: Logic Functions and Equations, pp. 75–103. Springer (2009)

# Permissions

All chapters in this book were first published by Springer; hereby published with permission under the Creative Commons Attribution License or equivalent. Every chapter published in this book has been scrutinized by our experts. Their significance has been extensively debated. The topics covered herein carry significant findings which will fuel the growth of the discipline. They may even be implemented as practical applications or may be referred to as a beginning point for another development.

The contributors of this book come from diverse backgrounds, making this book a truly international effort. This book will bring forth new frontiers with its revolutionizing research information and detailed analysis of the nascent developments around the world.

We would like to thank all the contributing authors for lending their expertise to make the book truly unique. They have played a crucial role in the development of this book. Without their invaluable contributions this book wouldn't have been possible. They have made vital efforts to compile up to date information on the varied aspects of this subject to make this book a valuable addition to the collection of many professionals and students.

This book was conceptualized with the vision of imparting up-to-date information and advanced data in this field. To ensure the same, a matchless editorial board was set up. Every individual on the board went through rigorous rounds of assessment to prove their worth. After which they invested a large part of their time researching and compiling the most relevant data for our readers.

The editorial board has been involved in producing this book since its inception. They have spent rigorous hours researching and exploring the diverse topics which have resulted in the successful publishing of this book. They have passed on their knowledge of decades through this book. To expedite this challenging task, the publisher supported the team at every step. A small team of assistant editors was also appointed to further simplify the editing procedure and attain best results for the readers.

Apart from the editorial board, the designing team has also invested a significant amount of their time in understanding the subject and creating the most relevant covers. They scrutinized every image to scout for the most suitable representation of the subject and create an appropriate cover for the book.

The publishing team has been an ardent support to the editorial, designing and production team. Their endless efforts to recruit the best for this project, has resulted in the accomplishment of this book. They are a veteran in the field of academics and their pool of knowledge is as vast as their experience in printing. Their expertise and guidance has proved useful at every step. Their uncompromising quality standards have made this book an exceptional effort. Their encouragement from time to time has been an inspiration for everyone.

The publisher and the editorial board hope that this book will prove to be a valuable piece of knowledge for researchers, students, practitioners and scholars across the globe.

# List of Contributors

**Ugo Dal Lago**
Dipartimento di Informatica - Scienza e Ingegneria Università di Bologna, Bologna, Italy

**Giulio Guerrieri and Willem Heijltjes**
Department of Computer Science University of Bath, Bath, UK

**Zinovy Diskin**
McMaster University, Hamilton, Canada

**Cinzia Di Giusto, Laetitia Laversa and Etienne Lozes**
Université Côte d'Azur, CNRS, I3S, Sophia Antipolis, France

**Thomas Ehrhard**
Université de Paris, IRIF, CNRS, F-75013 Paris, France

**Alain Finkel**
LSV, ENS Paris-Saclay, CNRS, Université Paris-Saclay, Cachan, France
Institut Universitaire de France, France

**Serge Haddad and Igor Khmelnitsky**
LSV, ENS Paris-Saclay, CNRS, Université Paris-Saclay, Cachan, France
Inria, France

**Léo Exibard**
Université Libre de Bruxelles, Brussels, Belgium
Aix Marseille Univ, Université de Toulon, CNRS, LIS, Marseille, France

**Emmanuel Filiot**
Université Libre de Bruxelles, Brussels, Belgium

**Pierre-Alain Reynier**
Aix Marseille Univ, Université de Toulon, CNRS, LIS, Marseille, France

**Marcelo P. Fiore, Andrew M. Pitts and S. C. Steenkamp**
Department of Computer Science and Technology University of Cambridge, Cambridge CB3 0FD, UK

**Mai Gehrke**
CNRS and Université Côte d'Azur, Nice, France

**Tomáš Jakl**
CNRS and Université Côte d'Azur, Nice, France

**Luca Reggio**
Institute of Computer Science of the Czech Academy of Sciences, Prague, Czech Republic and Mathematical Institute, University of Bern, Switzerland

**Marcelo Fiore**
Department of Computer Science and Technology, University of Cambridge, UK

**Philip Saville**
School of Informatics, University of Edinburgh, UK

**Filippo Bonchi**
Università di Pisa, Italy

**Robin Piedeleu**
University College London, UK

**Pawel Sobociński**
Tallinn University of Technology, Estonia

**Fabio Zanasi**
University College London, UK

**Béatrice Bérard**
Sorbonne Université, CNRS, LIP6, F-75005 Paris, France

**Benedikt Bollig**
CNRS, LSV & ENS Paris-Saclay, Université Paris-Saclay, Cachan, France

**Mathieu Lehaut**
Sorbonne Université, CNRS, LIP6, F-75005 Paris, France

**Nathalie Sznajder**
Sorbonne Université, CNRS, LIP6, F-75005 Paris, France

**Mario Alvarez-Picallo and Jean-Simon Pacaud Lemay**
Department of Computer Science, University of Oxford, Oxford, UK

# Index